THE FIRST ZIONIST CONGRESS

The First Zionist Congress

An Annotated Translation of the Proceedings

Michael J. Reimer

Cover image: The Zionist Congress in session, 1897 or 1898. Wikimedia Commons/National Photo Collection of Israel.

Published by State University of New York Press, Albany

© 2019 State University of New York

All rights reserved

No part of this book may be used or reproduced in any manner whatsoever without written permission. No part of this book may be stored in a retrieval system or transmitted in any form or by any means including electronic, electrostatic, magnetic tape, mechanical, photocopying, recording, or otherwise without the prior permission in writing of the publisher.

For information, contact State University of New York Press, Albany, NY
www.sunypress.edu

Library of Congress Cataloging-in-Publication Data

Names: Reimer, Michael J., translator.
Title: The first Zionist Congress : an annotated translation of the proceedings / translated and with an introduction by Michael J. Reimer.
Description: Albany, New York : State University of New York, [2019] | Includes bibliographical references and index.
Identifiers: LCCN 2018015533 | ISBN 9781438473130 (hardcover) | ISBN 9781438473147 (e-book) | ISBN 9781438473123 (paperback)
Subjects: LCSH: Zionist Congress (1st : 1897 : Basel, Switzerland)
Classification: LCC DS149 .F4955 2019 | DDC 320.54095694—dc23 LC record available at https://lccn.loc.gov/2018015533

10 9 8 7 6 5 4 3 2 1

CONTENTS

List of Figures and Tables — vii
Acknowledgments — ix

Introduction

    The First Zionist Congress and Jewish History — 1
    A Critical Summary of the Proceedings — 49
    The Need for an English Translation of the Proceedings — 77

The Proceedings

    Day One of the Proceedings, August 29, 1897

        Morning Session — 89
        Afternoon Session — 137

    Day Two of the Proceedings, August 30, 1897

        Morning Session — 203
        Afternoon Session — 227

    Day Three of the Proceedings, August 31, 1897

        Morning Session — 253
        Afternoon Session — 271
        Evening Session — 303

    Appendix — 307

Notes — 321
Glossary — 375
Bibliography — 423
Index — 433

LIST OF FIGURES AND TABLES

FIGURES

I.1.	"Unser Jahrhundert," *Allgemeine Zeitung des Judenthums*, September 13, 1870.	5
I.2.	Jaffa, port of entry for most European immigrants to Palestine, 1890s.	7
I.3.	Jewish farmers in Palestine, 1890s.	8
I.4.	Baron Edmond de Rothschild, ca. 1905.	11
I.5.	Inaugural issue of the Zionist organ, *Die Welt*.	15
I.6.	Herzl on balcony at Hotel Drei Könige during the Zionist Congress.	18
I.7.	The Zionist Congress in session, 1897 or 1898.	19
I.8.	Herzl and delegates on the floor of the Congress, in Basel's Stadtcasino.	39
I.9.	Max Nordau, keynote speaker at the Zionist Congress.	41
I.10.	Title page of the Congress's published proceedings, Vienna, 1898.	81
I.11.	Contents of the Congress's published proceedings, Vienna, 1898.	82

TABLES

I.1.	Provenance of participants at the First Zionist Congress, Basel, 1897.	20
1.1.	Estimates of the Jewish population, Britain and Ireland, 1897.	118
1.2.	Provenance of Jews in Great Britain, ca. 1897.	119
1.3.	Enrollments and revenues of Jewish schools in the UK, ca. 1897.	121
2.1.	M. Moses's scheme to fund colonization through cooperative banks.	250
3.1.	Area and population of Jewish agricultural colonies in Palestine, ca. 1897.	282
3.2.	Major exports and imports of Jaffa, 1895.	284

ACKNOWLEDGMENTS

I have worked on this translation for eight years and have accumulated debts of gratitude to many persons. I extend my appreciation to them all, with sincere apologies to those not mentioned here by name.

I am thankful to God that I have had the health and resources necessary to bring this project to completion.

When I began my work, Yoav Alon supplied me with a copy of the proceedings, as well as giving encouragement and counsel in my teaching and research on Zionism. A summer grant from the Research Grants program of the American University in Cairo (AUC) allowed me to launch this work by employing Heba Khalil as a research assistant. By working on preliminary translations of some important speeches, and by her enthusiasm, she contributed substantively and inspirationally to the present work. Malak Makar reviewed several sections of the translation, alerting me to mistakes in verb tenses. Nareman Amin compiled data vital to making the glossary. I am grateful to all of them for their dedicated labors.

The aforenamed students took a course titled "Zionism and Modern Judaism." The course was designed by my colleague, Mark Sedgwick; I inherited it from him when he left AUC. Teaching the course led to the discovery that the 1897 Congress proceedings had never been translated into English. I register here my respect and appreciation for Mark and for the many students who have taken the course, whose questions and comments have made me a better scholar and also made me believe that this work was worth doing. Also, abundant thanks go to all my department colleagues, but most of all to our marvelous staff, Sherine Emad and Nevien Samir, for their help with a variety of special tasks related to this work, which they have carried out cheerfully, in addition to their normal duties.

I also wish to thank AUC's Faculty Grants Program for additional support of this project, through the approval of a sabbatical leave in 2012 and a grant in 2018 to help with the cost of indexing.

Another group of persons I can acknowledge only by listing their online names (even this list is partial): dude, noli, Hecuba-UK, Werner, igm, Kai,

Reinhard W., CD (DE), MiMo, Philipp, Raudona, Braunbärin, Gibson, no me bré, Selima, manni3, Bob C., wor, HappyWarrior, stonehenge, SD3, Dave7, Erste_Schicht, erasmus, captain flint, Teddy-Toe, her man, AndreasS, Qual der Wal, cassandra, Martin--cal, mad, Nicki (DE), wupperwolf, codero, penguin, Claus, Yora Unfug, Rodos, mikefm, hm--us, Todd, macpet, wienergriessler, mbshu, hereami, Himalia, ludicrous, H.B., Spinatwachtel, California81, Woody 1, Mercury3, Mr Chekov (DE), tigger, isabelll, judex, Andreas_10, Helmi (U.S.), C3PO. They are registered users of the German-English translation forum maintained by LEO (www.leo.org, an online service of LEO GmbH). I submitted hundreds of translation problems to LEO, and I received thoughtful responses from these and other contributors: I express here my sincere appreciation for their guidance. I could not have done this work without the cadre of competent translators regularly answering questions within the LEO forums. Scholars wishing to engage the original text and controversies over the best way to translate certain passages, are advised to consult the archived queries.

Ashby Locke, Assistant University Archivist at George Washington University Library, supplied me with a copy of an early English translation of selected speeches given at the Congress, published by *The Jewish Chronicle* of London and then by Philip Cowen of New York. While this work could not form the basis of the present translation on account of its many deficiencies, access to this text was essential as a point of departure. Of course, its rendering of the German was taken into account where appropriate.

Michael Berkowitz, of University College London, gave encouragement to the present project, answered questions by correspondence, and affirmed the value of this project on several occasions. I thank him for his reassurance that the work was moving on the right track. Mark Muelhauesler, a gifted member of AUC's superb library staff, was helpful in answering questions, as one who moves effortlessly between German and English, among many other languages. He assisted me by obtaining obscure materials and, in particular, overseeing the OCRing of the existing online text, to make it searchable; thanks go to AUC's computer services unit, UACT, for its help in this labor as well. German-speaking colleagues at AUC helped in discussions of the connotations of various expressions; these included Mate Tokić, Julia Seibert, Nicholas Hopkins, and Steffen Stelzer. Thanks to Natalia Suit for help with the Polish and Russian. Thanks also to Dr. Lyumir Georgiev, the head of the Manuscript, Documentary, and Heritage Division, Bulgarian National Library, for help with several Bulgarian expressions and newspaper titles. David Speicher, my colleague in AUC's History Department, assisted by formatting the tables and suggesting changes while proofing and editing several parts of this work. Donald Reid and Steven Glazer commented critically on the introduction; I have benefitted from Professor Glazer's insights in other ways as well, indicated in the Notes; and I am thankful for our longstanding friendship.

A section of a work that appeared previously has been reused: " 'The good Dr Lippe' and Herzl in Basel, 1897: A translation and analysis of the Zionist Congress's opening speech," *Journal of Israeli History* 34 (2015):1, 1–21. Reuse is by permission of Taylor & Francis (the journal website is http://www.tandfonline.com/loi/fjih20). I wish also to express my appreciation to: the Katz Center for Advanced Judaic Studies, University of Pennsylvania, for several photographs from the Lenkin Family Collection, with permission for their reproduction herein; and the Trustees of the Rothschild Archive, London, for a photograph of Baron Edmond de Rothschild, with permission for its reproduction.

My wife Marty's occasional outbursts in pseudo-German kept me in good humor while absorbed in translation. I owe to her my sanity, among many other blessings! Our grown children, Luke, Rachel, and Marie, and their wonderful spouses, listened patiently to answers to the obligatory question, "How is your translation going?" Their interest and encouragement have sustained me. My interest in German was kindled by my parents, John and Margaret Reimer, who grew up speaking Plautdietsch. But their lifelong affirmation has counted for far more than any linguistic heritage. My debt to my parents is beyond measure; they made countless sacrifices so that I could receive an excellent education and have advantages not available to them when they were young.

Rafael Chaiken of SUNY Press has been prompt and professional in handling the manuscript, and I thank him and several others at SUNY Press for their labors on this project and their patience with my queries.

The foregoing acknowledgements show that the merits of the present work are owed, for the most part, to those who have helped me complete it. The errors, misinterpretations, and infelicities are my own.

I was first exposed to the history of Zionism in Dr. John Ruedy's course on the Arab-Israeli conflict at Georgetown University. I took many courses with Dr. Ruedy, who later became my dissertation advisor. I owe an incalculable debt to Dr. Ruedy, in both academic and personal terms. I dedicate the present volume to his memory, and I hope that my career reflects in some measure the scholarly rigor, love for students, burden for justice, and human compassion, which he modeled.

INTRODUCTION

The First Zionist Congress and Jewish History

HOBBES, HERZL, AND THE PREHISTORY OF ZIONISM

The creation of the state of Israel in 1948 culminated the campaign for a Jewish polity that had begun at the First Zionist Congress in Basel in 1897. In comparing Zionism with other nationalist movements, the inauspiciousness of its circumstances stands out, since Jews did not have the usual foundations (i.e., a common land and common language) upon which to erect a nation-state.[1] The absence of these elements is thrown into sharp relief by observing that the drive to establish a Jewish state in Palestine, the principal language of which would be Hebrew, was inaugurated at a conference held in Switzerland, where the debates were conducted in German. Perhaps because of the enormous distance Zionism had to traverse to reach its goal, its history evokes, much more than other modern ventures in state-making, the conditions posited by Thomas Hobbes in his philosophical treatise, *Leviathan*.

Hobbes argued that the origins of the state are to be found in human fear and desire. Fear is primary: "Fear of oppression, disposeth a man to anticipate, or to seek aid by society: for there is no other way by which a man can secure his life and liberty." But this "seeking aid by society," which multiplies exponentially the power of the individual and gives rise to the relative security of the commonwealth, is grounded in positive human desires as well. Among them are the desires for "ease and sensual delight," but also and more significantly for honor and dignity. Desire for the latter constitutes the key to explaining the peculiar behavior of human beings, since they, unlike other social animals, "are continually in competition for honour and dignity... and consequently amongst men there ariseth on that ground, envy and hatred, and finally war." Honor in such a world is derived from a reputation for power, without respect to the justness of the actions producing this reputation: thus, "honour consisteth only in the opinion of power." And because "the greatest of human powers, is that compounded of the powers of most men, united by consent," the sovereignty embodied in the state is worthy of supreme honor. "And as the power, so also the honour of the sovereign, ought to be greater, than that of any, or all the subjects. For in the sovereignty is the fountain of honour."[2]

Hobbes supplies a theoretical entree into Zionism as the product of Jews' justifiable fear and actual experience of oppression, as well as the historically conditioned desire to recover Jewish honor through the establishment of a nation-state. And if we accept Hobbes's declaration that honor consists in "the opinion of power," it becomes clear why Theodor Herzl is esteemed the founder of Zionism.[3] For Herzl it was who established Zionism as an overtly political movement in search of a Jewish sovereignty, proposing, organizing, and presiding over the First Zionist Congress in 1897, in Basel, Switzerland; and who then exercised a Caesar-like dominance over the growing movement for the remainder of his short life. For the 1897 Congress was no isolated event. On the contrary, its participants elected an executive tasked to carry on propaganda, recruitment, fundraising, data-gathering, etc., after the Congress adjourned; it set in train a series of Congresses, which met twenty-two times prior to Israel's independence in 1948, and continued to meet thereafter (the thirty-seventh Zionist Congress took place in October 2015); and it inspired the proliferation of groups affiliated to the Zionist Organization, whereby the whole movement exerted increasing influence on Jews, especially in Europe and North America.[4] Moreover, a proper historical treatment of Herzl's movement must also recognize that "Congress-Zionism" folded into its agenda, besides (1) the quest for autonomy or statehood, both (2) the development of a modern Hebrew culture, and (3) the support of ongoing Jewish immigration to and settlement in Palestine—even if Herzl regarded the latter two endeavors as peripheral to, even subversive of, his political project.[5] Nevertheless, these other, non-Hobbesian strands of Zionism existed before Herzl, and to appreciate the innovation represented by his Congress-Zionism, one must see it against the background of its antecedents.

Hope for the restoration of the Jews to Palestine is a motif in the preaching of the biblical prophets, and synagogue liturgy has included prayers for the ingathering of the exiles and the rebuilding of Jerusalem since ancient times. The pronounced secularism of most Zionists notwithstanding, it would be absurd to suggest that this religious aspiration did not influence the formation of the Zionist program. Nevertheless, Jews praying for a "return" to the Holy Land were not *eo ipso* Zionists, and there was dogmatic opposition from among Orthodox Jews to the three strands of Zionism identified above. The settlement of Jews in

Palestine for the sake of economic productivity and social transformation clashed with traditions, which made that land the destination of pilgrims and scholars of Torah who lived on the charity of their Diaspora brethren; the de-consecration of Hebrew, making it a quotidian means of communication, and the creation of a secular Hebrew culture, were controversial; and the inherently humanistic and dialectical character of political Zionism stood in seemingly irreconcilable conflict with an eschatology in which God would, unilaterally and miraculously, through the agency of his Messiah, restore the Jews to the land, or, to use the biblical idiom, accomplish the Redemption of Israel.

There had been agitation prior to the rise of Zionism for a revision of this traditional eschatology, a movement sometimes termed "active messianism" because it assigned to human agency a pivotal role in producing conditions necessary for the Redemption to occur. This agitation seems to have generated a modest increase in Jews moving to Palestine in the 1700s and 1800s. A leading figure in this school of thought was Rabbi Zvi Hirsch Kalischer of Toruń (Thorn), in German-ruled Poland, who stood firmly within the received tradition as a scholar of the Talmud, yet interpreted the prophecies of Israel's restoration to imply that there would be "a natural beginning of the Redemption," (i.e., a gradual ingathering of Jews into Palestine), supported by philanthropy and secured by diplomacy. In a work published in Hebrew in 1862, *Derishat Zion* ("Seeking Zion"), Kalischer answered Orthodox critics of this scheme by propounding the harmony of charitable support for Torah scholars with the projected establishment of new agricultural settlements by Jews. He argued that contributions from such enterprises would augment the meager income of Torah scholars, allowing them to continue to serve God through their exclusive devotion to worship and study; meanwhile, Jewish farmers would gain merit by fulfilling the Torah's commandments pertaining to agriculture.[6] Kalischer's ideas helped to convince some of Europe's most influential Orthodox rabbis (e.g., Hirsch Hildesheimer of Berlin) to support immediate Jewish settlement in Palestine. Kalischer also helped establish a society for Jewish colonization and obtained funding for an agricultural institute, which the Alliance Israélite Universelle, a non-Zionist aid and advocacy association, set up in Jaffa.[7] Fusing Orthodox Judaism and a kind of proto-Zionism, it is perhaps not surprising that Kalischer's work adumbrates themes that reappear in the hybrid ideology of religious Zionism: the Torah as the basis of the national renaissance; the acquisition and cultivation of land in Palestine in order to fulfill commands of the Torah; the compatibility of charity to support Torah study with creative labor as the basis for national regeneration; settlement and statehood as steps toward the full and final Redemption; the unique and essentially religious nationhood of Israel and its divinely determined connection to the land.[8]

But, from a wider perspective, the circumstances and worldviews within which "mainstream" Zionism took its rise were profoundly different from those which shaped this "active" yet still essentially traditional messianism. David Engel helpfully differentiates the two movements on the basis of several criteria, but above all by characterizing the chronologically earlier one as eschatological and therefore consistent with Jewish doctrines of election and covenant, while the later movement was non- or even anti-eschatological, since it implied, and sometimes openly declared, a repudiation of divine election, proclaiming as its goal the "normalization" of Jewish life, whether economically by turning the Jews into farmers and laborers, or politically by organizing them into a nation-state like other nation-states.[9] Arthur Hertzberg gives a lucid statement of the distinction: "What marks modern Zionism as a fresh beginning in Jewish history is that its ultimate values derive from the general milieu. The Messiah is now identified with the dream of an age of individual liberty, national freedom, and economic and social justice—i.e., with the progressive faith of the nineteenth century."[10]

Since most European states really did see progress in terms of their protection of individual liberties and the establishment of legal equality, proto-Zionist schemes had little purchase among most Jews for most of the nineteenth century. An 1870 editorial in the influential Jewish journal *Allgemeine Zeitung des Judenthums* reflects this sanguine temper, predominant among *Westjuden* (Jews of Western Europe), but widespread among *Ostjuden* (Jews of Eastern Europe) as well.[11]

The author of this article, titled "Unser Jahrhundert" [Our Century], acknowledges the reversals suffered by movements favoring liberal and egalitarian political change, noting that the French Revolution gave way to Napoleonic despotism and that the revolutions of 1848 were defeated by the forces of political reaction. In the religious sphere, the re-establishment of the Jesuits, the assertion of papal infallibility, and the muzzling of Reform Judaism by an ossified Jewish Orthodoxy are cited as victories for bigotry and obscurantism. Yet the author has an unshakeable confidence in the future. He concludes by declaring that the real spirit of the times is expressed in the tendency toward a new moral earnestness, the expansion of citizens' rights and freedoms, international treaties and agreements, and associations for peace, and not in governments' manipulation of the populace by means of an "artificially awakened national identity." The problems of the century are to be regarded as a vast process of fermentation, in which elements of the past are being fused with the ideas of the present. But progress has been substantial and is seen in the normalizing of political and social values that were once unimaginable: the equality of rights of citizens throughout western Europe, without respect to religion; the recent abolition of serfdom in Russia and slavery in the United States; and a newfound legal equality even among different "races." It is easy in retrospect to deride the author's facile faith in the future, but his argument

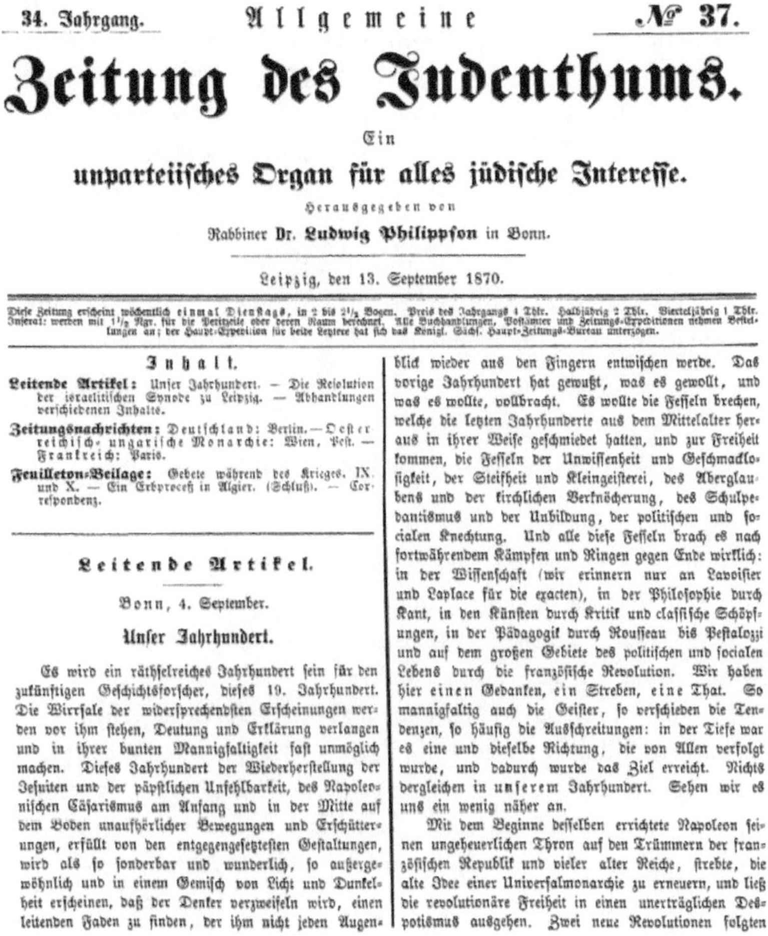

34. Jahrgang. Allgemeine № 37.

Zeitung des Judenthums.

Ein

unparteiisches Organ für alles jüdische Interesse.

Herausgegeben von

Rabbiner Dr. **Ludwig Philippson** in Bonn.

Leipzig, den 13. September 1870.

Diese Zeitung erscheint wöchentlich einmal Dienstags, in 2 bis 2½ Bogen. Preis des Jahrgangs 4 Thlr. Halbjährig 2 Thlr. Vierteljährig 1 Thlr. Inserat: werden mit 1½ Ngr. für die Petitzeile oder deren Raum berechnet. Alle Buchhandlungen, Postämter und Zeitungs-Expeditionen nehmen Bestellungen an; der Haupt-Expedition für beide Letztere hat sich das Königl. Sächs. Haupt-Zeitungs-Bureau unterzogen.

Inhalt.

Leitende Artikel: Unser Jahrhundert. — Die Resolution der israelitischen Synode zu Leipzig. — Abhandlungen verschiedenen Inhalts.

Zeitungsnachrichten: Deutschland: Berlin. — Oesterreichisch-ungarische Monarchie: Wien, Pest. — Frankreich: Paris.

Feuilleton-Beilage: Gebete während des Krieges. IX. und X. — Ein Erbproceß in Algier. (Schluß). — Correspondenz.

Leitende Artikel.

Bonn, 4. September.

Unser Jahrhundert.

Es wird ein räthselreiches Jahrhundert sein für den zukünftigen Geschichtsforscher, dieses 19. Jahrhundert. Die Wirrsale der widersprechendsten Erscheinungen werden vor ihm stehen, Deutung und Erklärung verlangen und in ihrer bunten Mannigfaltigkeit fast unmöglich machen. Dieses Jahrhundert der Wiederherstellung der Jesuiten und der päpstlichen Unfehlbarkeit, des Napoleonischen Cäsarismus am Anfang und in der Mitte auf dem Boden unaufhörlicher Bewegungen und Erschütterungen, erfüllt von den entgegengesetztesten Gestaltungen, wird als so sonderbar und wunderlich, so außergewöhnlich und in einem Gemisch von Licht und Dunkelheit erscheinen, daß der Denker verzweifeln wird, einen leitenden Faden zu finden, der ihm nicht jeden Augenblick wieder aus den Fingern entwischen werde. Das vorige Jahrhundert hat gewußt, was es gewollt, und was es wollte, vollbracht. Es wollte die Fesseln brechen, welche die letzten Jahrhunderte aus dem Mittelalter heraus in ihrer Weise geschmiedet hatten, und zur Freiheit kommen, die Fesseln der Unwissenheit und Geschmacklosigkeit, der Steifheit und Kleingeisterei, des Aberglaubens und der kirchlichen Verknöcherung, des Schulpedantismus und der Unbildung, der politischen und socialen Knechtung. Und alle diese Fesseln brach es nach fortwährendem Kämpfen und Ringen gegen Ende wirklich: in der Wissenschaft (wir erinnern nur an Lavoisier und Laplace für die exacten), in der Philosophie durch Kant, in den Künsten durch Kritik und classische Schöpfungen, in der Pädagogik durch Rousseau bis Pestalozzi und auf dem großen Gebiete des politischen und socialen Lebens durch die französische Revolution. Wir haben hier einen Gedanken, ein Streben, eine That. So mannigfaltig auch die Geister, so verschieden die Tendenzen, so häufig die Ausschreitungen: in der Tiefe war es eine und dieselbe Richtung, die von Allen verfolgt wurde, und dadurch wurde das Ziel erreicht. Nichts dergleichen in unserem Jahrhundert. Sehen wir es uns ein wenig näher an.

Mit dem Beginne desselben errichtete Napoleon seinen ungeheuerlichen Thron auf den Trümmern der französischen Republik und vieler alter Reiche, strebte, die alte Idee einer Universalmonarchie zu erneuern, und ließ die revolutionäre Freiheit in einen unerträglichen Despotismus ausgehen. Zwei neue Revolutionen folgten

FIGURE I.1. "Unser Jahrhundert," leader in *Allgemeine Zeitung des Judenthums*, September 13, 1870. DigitaleSammlungen/Compact Memory, Goethe University, Frankfurt.

was plausible in its context and represents very neatly the historical optimism to which most European Jews subscribed.¹²

For this reason, surveys of events supposedly antecedent to Zionism tend to overestimate the importance of the many stillborn projects for conveying Jews to Palestine, concocted by both Jews and non-Jews prior to the 1880s. Richard Gottheil's diffuse essay on Zionism in the *Jewish Encyclopaedia* of 1906 catalogues a multitude of these schemes, featuring such famous personalities as Napoleon Bonaparte, Lord Shaftesbury, Henry Dunant, Laurence Oliphant, Benjamin Disraeli, and George Eliot, alongside lesser lights such as Mordecai Noah, Abraham Pétavel, Moritz Steinschneider, Joseph Salvador, and Benedetto Musolino. It was perhaps Gottheil's attempt to demonstrate that such plans were an element of the zeitgeist, that the idea was in the air and awaiting realization. Nevertheless, as late as the 1870s, despite a plethora of proposals, general Jewish interest in the subject was almost nil. A Jewish reviewer of Eliot's *Daniel Deronda* suggests that "an imponderable mass of indefinite feelings and vague impulses" might one day motivate Jews to seek to re-establish themselves in Palestine, but there is scant evidence for any nationalist ferment in response to these plans. It was going to take more than "indefinite feelings and vague impulses" to set the Jewish masses in motion.¹³

LEON PINSKER AND THE JEWS UNDER THE TSARS

The first important communal manifestation of Hertzberg's "fresh beginning in Jewish history" occurred rather in the 1880s, when, as a result of persecution and want—in particular the unusually widespread and tacitly tolerated pogroms of 1881 in Russia—Russian and Romanian Jews began to settle in Palestine in small but appreciable numbers.

This spurt of immigration is known as the First Aliya, "Aliya" meaning an "ascent" (recalling the ascent of pilgrims who went "up to Jerusalem" in biblical times), and "First" because the settlers arriving during this time were retrospectively assimilated to later, ordinally designated immigration flows in Israeli historiography (hence, Second Aliya, Third Aliya, etc.). The immigrants of the 1880s and 90s were themselves distinct from traditional Jewish immigrants to Palestine—the pilgrims and Torah scholars—not because they were irreligious (most were observant Jews) but rather because, ostensibly, many were seeking to become economically independent (e.g., by acquiring land and forming agricultural colonies.)¹⁴ Frequently deprived of access to the

FIGURE I.2. Jaffa, port of entry for most European immigrants to Palestine, 1890s. Lenkin Family Collection, Katz Center for Advanced Judaic Studies Library, University of Pennsylvania.

productive, especially the agricultural, sectors of the economy in countries of their birth, immigrants of the First Aliya aimed to set up farms and other enterprises, which would make them basic producers, believing this would break patterns of Jewish "parasitism," regenerate their moral character, and lead to a national revival. Thus, Ahad Ha'am, the Russian-Jewish essayist, described Eretz Israel as answering

> the need to create a fixed center for ourselves by settling a large mass of our brethren in one place on the basis of working the land, so that both Israel and its enemies will know that there is one place under the heavens... where a Jew can raise his head like any other person, earning his bread from the land, by the sweat of his brow, and creating his own national spirit—if this need has any hope of being fulfilled, it is only in Eretz Israel.[15]

The immigrants' goal was a radical break with the existing habitus among Jews: "[T]heir intent is to change their entire way of life, to transform themselves from merchants into workers of the soil...."[16]

FIGURE I.3. Jewish farmers in Palestine, 1890s. Lenkin Family Collection, Katz Center for Advanced Judaic Studies Library, University of Pennsylvania.

It should be added that the First Aliya coincides with a massive outflow of Jews from Russia, Russian Poland, and Romania, mainly directed toward Western Europe and North America, not Palestine. For these Jews, it was economic hardship, not a vision to transform Jewish character, that impelled their emigration.[17]

If emigration from the East was the major practical response to the pogroms in Russia, the principal theoretical response came in the form of a pamphlet titled *Autoemancipation* by Leon Pinsker. It was a landmark in the development of Zionist thought, not only because of its content but because of the position of its author. Pinsker was a proudly Russified Jew, a respected physician, educated in Russian universities and with a record of distinguished service to the Tsarist regime. Prior to the appearance of his booklet, he shared the widespread belief, attested in the 1870 article cited above, that Russia would follow the path of Western European states and ultimately emancipate (i.e., grant legal equality to) its Jews. Based on this optimistic assessment of Russia's future, he had campaigned for Jewish assimilation in Russia. But the pogroms convinced him, as it did vast numbers of other Jews, including especially many middle-class and semi-assimilated Jews, that the hope of winning equality with other Russians was illusory.[18] Given the events of 1881, in which even the Russian intelligentsia had taken a hand, such disillusionment was only natural. However, Pinsker's "manifesto," as Shlomo Avineri terms it, presented a bolder thesis, i.e., that anti-Semitism was an "ethnological" or even pathological condition affecting all peoples and not just Russians. Avineri rightly judges Pinsker's quasi-medical diagnosis of the cause of anti-Semitism to be reductionist and unconvincing. Yet its very reductionism is a sign that Pinsker felt he was dealing with something elemental in human nature. The apparent universality, persistence, and irrationality of Jew-hatred suggested to him that anti-Semitism was a phenomenon not dependent on the existence of a particular set of material or social conditions.[19] And if this were so, then a purely legal remedy such as emancipation could never abolish it; in fact, emancipation bestowed from without was an operative admission that the Jew was not accepted as a social equal.[20] And although Pinsker was wrong in asserting that anti-Semitism could be explained as a species of hereditary pathology,[21] he was right in perceiving that it was generated by powerful, contradictory impulses that were not readily amenable to legislated reforms or rational persuasion.

> This fundamentally similar aversion exists everywhere and always, regardless of whether it is manifested in deeds of violence or vicious jealousy, or masked as tolerance and protection. To be plundered as a Jew or to need protection as a Jew is equally humiliating, equally offensive to the Jews' sense of human dignity.... For the living, the Jew is a dead man, for the natives a foreigner, for the locals a vagrant, for the propertied elements a beggar, for the poor an exploiter and millionaire, for patriots a man without a country, for all classes a hated competitor.[22]

While Pinsker dismissed the fallacious accusations of the anti-Semites, he did not ascribe Gentile hostility toward the Jews solely to ignorance and prejudice. The Jews were held in contempt also because they *were* contemptible, behaving like herd animals, without dignity or solidarity, absorbed only with the need to escape from immediate danger. For Pinsker, this deficiency of character could be remedied only by a radical change in Jewish consciousness and conditions. Jews had first to give up the chimera of seeking equal rights as individuals in the states where they lived: in a world of ethno-national states, individual rights could be secured only by citizenship in an ethno-national state possessing sovereignty. So Jews had to recognize that communal solidarity took precedence over an egoistical quest for individual safety; they had to be transformed from a "scattered herd" into a national community.[23] To fully realize that goal, they would have to relocate and concentrate themselves in a single territory where they would eventually acquire sovereignty. For Pinsker himself, alienated as he was from Jewish religious tradition, that territory did not have to be Palestine; the only criteria that mattered were the land's accessibility, security, and productivity.[24]

The First Aliya began in 1881; Pinsker's pamphlet appeared in 1882. To a great extent, both were effects of the same cause; i.e., the pogroms in Russia triggered by the assassination of Tsar Alexander II.[25] Interestingly, Pinsker hoped his *Mahnruf*, or "cry of warning" (as he subtitled his pamphlet), would provoke a response not only among Jews in Russia, but even more among Western Jews, whom he thought had the talent, freedom, and resources to realize his program—which explains why he wrote in German. He was to be disappointed. Most Western Jews rejected his arguments, regarding *Autoemancipation* as myopic and reactionary. It ignored the astonishing progress made by Jews outside Russia, a progress taken to be irreversible since it was based on "objective" forces; and, for religious liberals, the summons to establish a Jewish nation-state threatened to destroy modern Judaism's sublime spirituality for the sake of an obsolete political identity.[26] As was to be the case with Herzl, Pinsker found his most receptive audience among his fellow *Ostjuden*, especially in Russia, especially those already coalescing into proto-Zionist colonization societies, which went under various names but which are lumped together under the Hebrew rubric *Hovevei Zion* ("Lovers of Zion"). Pinsker was prevailed upon to assume the presidency of a committee to coordinate the activities of these societies, to raise funds to help the existing colonists, as well as to promote further settlement in Palestine. The founding conference of Hovevei Zion took place under his leadership, at Kattowitz (Katowice) in German-ruled Poland, in 1884; there were about thirty delegates in attendance.[27]

The relationship between the First Aliya and Hovevei Zion was loose; as happened later with Congress-Zionism, European campaigning and fundraising were often separate and distinct from the actual immigration and settlement taking place in Palestine. On the whole, Zionist agitation in Europe tended to support and enhance colonization that was occurring spontaneously, or at least independently of any central directorate. But in the case of Hovevei Zion, such support was so slender that many of the colonies established by First Aliya immigrants were saved from collapse only by the intervention of Baron Edmond de Rothschild, a French Jew and scion of the greatest banking dynasty in Europe.[28]

FIGURE I.4. Baron Edmond de Rothschild, ca. 1905. Reproduced with the permission of the Trustees of The Rothschild Archive.

But the lack of external assistance was not the only or even the main problem. Ahad Ha'am's report on his visit to Palestine in 1891 reveals serious misconceptions and moral failings endemic to the new *Yishuv*, as the recently established settler colony was known, that had created the crisis to which the Baron responded. Among these were false notions about the ready availability of fertile land and false characterizations of the Arabs as lazy, inefficient, and naïve.[29] The new immigrants had fantasies of easy riches in what was imagined to be "a new California," and a concomitant aversion to hard physical labor. A deplorable disunity and lack of discretion characterized the various Jewish associations seeking to buy land and plant colonies in Palestine.[30] Finally, there was the hostility of the Ottoman government. Although that hostility was never insuperable, it did complicate efforts to purchase land and put up buildings, since subterfuges and bribery were necessary to circumvent Ottoman regulations.[31]

So, on the one hand, Pinsker had argued that the Jewish problem could be solved only by Jews establishing their own state. On the other hand, most settlers of the First Aliya did not have statehood in view; and Pinsker himself soon recognized that such an aspiration—given the pathetic resources of his constituency, combined with Ottoman resistance to any such scheme—was completely implausible.[32] In the end, this financial incapacity, coupled with the political timidity and organizational incohesiveness of Hovevei Zion, convinced many of its followers to join the new Congress-Zionism of Herzl.[33] Nevertheless, Hovevei Zion paved the way for Herzl by creating a network of activists, particularly among the *Ostjuden*, committed to finding a national solution to the Jewish question. By means of its propaganda, Hovevei Zion contributed to the creation of a self-consciously Jewish public which believed in the viability and legitimacy of the new Jewish settlement in Palestine, even if most members of that public never emigrated there themselves.[34]

THEODOR HERZL'S MOMENT

Herzl deserves credit for reinventing Zionism, but not by means of new arguments. Herzl acknowledged that he had said nothing new in his famous booklet *Der Judenstaat* (*The Jewish State*), which appeared in 1896 and was composed *before* he read Pinsker's pamphlet or made any detailed assessment of the ongoing work of colonization.[35] But if there was little difference between Herzl's booklet and Pinsker's in terms of content, the difference in context was large. The years 1882–1896 witnessed a resurgence of anti-Semitic politics in Western and Central Europe. The movement had begun to gain strength prior to the 1880s, the term "anti-Semitism" having been popularized by a pamphlet published in 1879 alleging that Jews, representing "Semitism," were triumphing over "Germanism."[36] While a pseudo-scientific racialism underlay this argument, the advance of anti-Semitism in the 1880s and 1890s was a result not only of the popularization of racialist ideology but even more of its utility in mobilizing electorates to vote for political groupings opposed to secular-liberal policies and, especially, against social-democratic parties adhering to Marxian principles, since Jews were at the forefront of both these political tendencies. Confusingly, some reactionary, anti-Semitic parties also designated themselves as "socialist," albeit always with a qualifier ("Christian," "German," "National," etc.).[37] The political-economic logic of uniting anti-Semitism with so-called socialism derived from a belief that, because Jews controlled much industrial and financial capital, anti-Semitic measures, by curtailing their influence, would ease the plight of independent tradespeople, factory workers, shopkeepers, and peasants, who were hit hardest by the advance of large-scale production and commerce. Hence the denigration of anti-Semitism as the "socialism of the stupid," especially among Germany's Social Democrats.[38]

Organized anti-Semitism in Germany was manifested in the holding of an anti-Semitic Congress in 1886 in Cassel; in 1892 there were anti-Semitic outbreaks as a consequence of inflammatory pamphlets authored by the proto-Hitlerian demagogue Hermann Ahlwardt, whose wild allegations were often seconded by the Catholic press. German Conservatives saw in Ahlwardt's demagoguery the means of defeating Liberals and Social Democrats, and they therefore formulated a platform in which they pledged themselves to "combat the oppressive and disintegrating Jewish influence on our national life." German anti-Semitism was exported to Austria, and two anti-Semitic leagues were founded there as early as 1882. In the 1890s, a coalition of Christian Socialists and anti-Semites gained the ascendancy in Austrian politics; in 1895, Karl Lueger, an outspoken anti-Semite, was elected mayor of Vienna by the municipal council. In France, Édouard Drumont founded an anti-Semitic league in 1889, and the formal degradation of Captain Alfred Dreyfus on the basis of forged documents proved that Jews were not secure even where they had first been emancipated. Herzl covered the Dreyfus case as a journalist and was no doubt affected by it, although it appears that the deteriorating political situation in his native Austria-Hungary, especially in Vienna, was a more powerful impulse in turning him toward "Zionism."[39]

Actually, Herzl did not coin the "ism" with which his life and thought have become so completely identified. Surprisingly, *Judenstaat* never uses the term. It refers to "Zionists" once and uses the adjective "Zionist" twice, but the terms are employed to disparage projects to colonize Palestine, which Herzl regarded as regressive due to their dependence on philanthropy, their focus on agriculture, and their lack of an overarching plan and political goal. How then did he come to adopt this term as the name for his movement? The Vienna context is again crucial. Around 1882, Jewish students organized a fraternity they called "Kadimah"; the Hebrew word means both "eastward" and "forward," thus suggesting both the students' pride in their ethno-national origins *and* their commitment to secular-progressive values.[40] Seeking to uphold the honor of Jews at the university in Vienna, the society was made up mostly of immigrants from Russia, many of whom had ties to Pinsker and Hovevei Zion. But the leader of the society was the Vienna-born Nathan Birnbaum, who published a journal with a title cribbed from Pinsker, *Selbst-Emancipation*. In 1890, Birnbaum published an article in which he used *Zionismus* as a neologism for Jewish nationalism, the term implying an acceptance of the Palestine orientation of Hovevei Zion ("Zion" synecdochic for Palestine) but demanding that priority be given to political action, as Pinsker's pamphlet had suggested. Birnbaum's group responded enthusiastically to *Judenstaat* when it was published in 1896, inviting Herzl to meet with them; Herzl soon appropriated *Zionismus* to designate his own ideology, because the term had already gained this new political connotation and because the "Zionists" were his most eager proselytizers.[41] Although personal frictions soon developed between Herzl and Birnbaum—Birnbaum resented Herzl's taking over as leader—they were alike in seeking to draw Jews into a Jewish political-national movement, as the only truly effective response to the new anti-Semitism.[42]

If this new anti-Semitism was important in magnifying Herzl's impact, so was his personality and leadership. Herzl differed from Pinsker in the energy he devoted to the cause; it should be remembered that Pinsker was sixty-three at the time of the Kattowitz Conference; Herzl organized the Basel Congress when he was just thirty-seven.[43] In taking over the Zionist movement, Herzl transformed it into a self-avowedly pan-Jewish, institutionally ramified, quasi-parliamentarian movement, under the direction of an elected executive. Before Herzl, Zionism had meant, mostly, resisting assimilation, encouraging small-scale settlement in Palestine, and reviving the use of Hebrew as a vernacular.[44] While it is erroneous to suggest that Herzl was the first to propose a nation-state for Jews—as we have seen, he was preceded by Pinsker, as well as several others[45]—Herzl's iteration of Zionism imparted to it a new status and momentum. The 1897 Congress and its successors gained for Jewish nationalism an international stature, and at the Congresses delegates envisioned grand financial and diplomatic initiatives that would open the way to statehood. These initiatives involved mobilizing vast quantities of capital from Jews all over the world in order to build proto-state institutions, as well as winning legal protection for ongoing settlement with a view to the ultimate attainment of sovereignty.[46] Under Herzl's leadership, the Zionist Organization began to publish its official weekly organ, *Die Welt*, to disseminate its views to the Jewish public; it established the Jewish Colonial Trust (1899), the Zionist bank; and it launched the Jewish National Fund (1901), to finance the acquisition of lands in Palestine that were to remain the common possession of the Jewish people in perpetuity.[47]

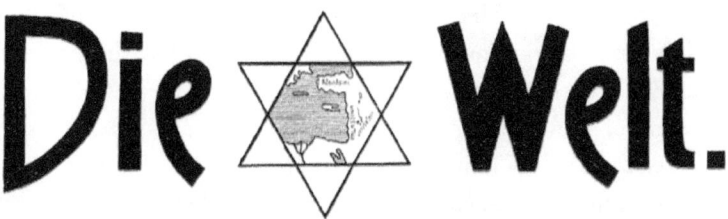

Figure I.5. Inaugural issue of the Zionist organ, *Die Welt*. Digitale Sammlungen/Compact Memory, Goethe University, Frankfurt.

Herzl himself remained committed to the priority of gaining international legitimacy for the cause. Hence his quixotic journeys in search of a "charter," a definitive concession to open Ottoman Palestine to Jewish settlement and guarantee the security of Jewish property holdings there.

Therefore, in evaluating Herzl's place in history, his intellectual contributions are of secondary importance. Rather, it was his charisma, ardor, and determination that set him apart from Pinsker, Birnbaum, and all other forerunners. He assumed a gigantic role within Zionism, acquiring within a short time the aura of a messiah.[48] Chaim Weizmann, looking back on the history of Zionism in 1949, contrasted Herzl's ideas, on the one hand, with his deeds and character, on the other:

> We were right in our instinctive appreciation that what had emerged from the *Judenstaat* was less a concept than a historic personality. The *Judenstaat* by itself would have been nothing more than a nine days' wonder. If Herzl had contented himself with the mere publication of the booklet—as he originally intended to do, before it became clear to him that he was no longer his own master, but the servant of the idea—his name would be remembered today as one of the oddities of Jewish history. What has given greatness to his name is Herzl's role as a man of action, as the founder of the Zionist Congress, and as an example of daring and devotion.[49]

Weizmann was absent from the First Congress, but his reflections are vividly confirmed by the experiences of those present. Joseph Klausner, a twenty-three-year-old student at the University of Heidelberg when he attended the First Congress, and later a distinguished scholar of Jewish history and literature, recalled:

> It is not that Herzl came along and turned us into a nation. For Smolenskin had come before him and stated that we were not a religious grouping but a people. It is not that Herzl gave us a brand-new idea of a Jewish State. Pinsker's "Auto-Emancipation," which had appeared before he came on the scene, stated the idea in a most emphatic manner. But Herzl created something that can be hardly expressed in words. A different atmosphere prevailed, something totally new had come into being. The very same words that had been uttered by Smolenskin and Pinsker acquired a new quality, a new meaning, at the first Zionist Congress. I do not know how to put it. One Hebrew writer was so bold as to apply to Herzl the Biblical verse, "And he was king in Jeshurun."

> Dr. Ehrenpreis, in an appreciation of Herzl in the Hebrew journal, "Hashiloach," called him "an uncrowned king." It can be said that the whole of Zionism acquired something regal, a new quality became apparent in it.... It is not that the ideas were any greater, but that they were charged with a new spirit.... We had youth in those days—the Biluites and students. Some of them will occupy places in the forefront of Zionist history. But can the spirit that prevailed among them be compared to what happened after the first Zionist Congress? Hundreds of thousands of young people who would otherwise have been lost to Jewry, who would have joined other parties and worked for other nations, returned to Judaism, to Zion and to Palestine. What was the reason? It was the great watchword, the great spirit, and also the little things, the imponderabilia, that Herzl understood so well: our flag, the *shekel*, the Actions Committee, the Zionist Organization. All these things effected a radical transformation. I recall the discussions that took place before and after the first Congress. The whole of Jewry had altered, and was no longer recognisable.... Because of the great spirit that had been breathed everything soared to a new plane.[50]

While Klausner's remarks, made for the Congress's jubilee, might be impugned as the gilding of youthful memories, he mentions some of the tangible expressions of the new and "great spirit" that came to pervade the Zionist movement under Herzl; and there is other, corroborating data. Thus, in Russia in 1896, after more than a decade of organized existence, Hovevei Zion had just twenty-three branches; the newly founded Russian Zionist organization had 356 by the end of 1897.[51] Moreover, in contrast to the small, intermittent gatherings of Hovevei Zion, the almost annual Zionist Congresses attracted a large and growing numbers of delegates, from some two hundred in 1897 to 571 in 1903 (Herzl's last Congress).[52] There was also a vast increase over time in "shekel-payers," who joined the Zionist Organization by means of a small financial contribution. This number grew from a little under one hundred thousand in 1900, to over two hundred thousand by 1913, and then to over eight hundred thousand in 1923.[53]

So it was not unreasonable for Klausner, and myriad others, to feel that Herzl's decisive contribution was somehow his organizing of the 1897 Congress. He and many others were powerfully moved by the feeling that there in Basel a new era was beginning. So *Die Welt* was doing no more than giving expression to a widely held feeling when it titled its lead article about the Congress, "Ein geschichtlicher Augenblick" [An Historic Moment].[54]

Figure I.6. Herzl on balcony at Hotel Drei Könige during the Zionist Congress. Wikimedia Commons/National Photo Collection of Israel.

WHY BASEL?—CONTEMPORARY JEWISH OBJECTIONS TO ZIONISM

The formal opening of that Congress took place in the concert hall of Basel's Stadtcasino, on Sunday morning, August 29, 1897. It is salient to note that no rabbi was asked to pray; rather, two Galician Jews with medical degrees conducted the ceremonial opening. At half past nine, Isidor Schalit, a dentist who had helped Herzl to organize the Congress, brought the gavel down thrice to call the meeting to order. Then the first speaker, Dr. Karpel Lippe, mounted the rostrum, covered his head, and recited a prayer before a hushed assembly: "Blessed are you, Lord our God, King of the Universe, who has given us life, sustained us, and allowed us to reach this day."[55] Lippe held a medical degree from a German university but had been long resident in Romania. He had been chosen as the Congress's honorary president because he represented continuity with the past: he had been at the Kattowitz Conference where Pinsker presided and was an outstanding figure among Romania's Hovevei Zion. In his speech to an excited crowd of delegates, he hailed the Congress as "a public assembly of the nation, to protest against 1800 years of persecution." But Lippe also declared that the purpose of the meeting was much greater than that of mere protest: "The object which is set before us for deliberation, is nothing less than the return of the Jews to the land of their fathers, the holy land, which our God, the one true God, promised our patriarch Abraham to be for us his descendants." His address was repeatedly interrupted by cheers; some delegates were moved to tears by the long-awaited realization of their hopes.[56]

FIGURE I.7. The Zionist Congress in session, 1897 or 1898. Wikimedia Commons/ National Photo Collection of Israel.

Lippe's assertion of the Congress's authority to represent world Jewry was given a measure of plausibility by the size and diversity of the gathering. The more than two hundred participants at the Congress came from twenty countries and/or distinct regions. Haiyam Orlan's study of the distribution of the participants by state and region yields the following data[57]:

TABLE I.1. Provenance of participants at First Zionist Congress, Basel, 1897.

Algeria	1	Austria	27
Belgium	1	Bukovina (Romania)	3
Bulgaria	6	Bohemia & Slavonia (Austria)	5
England	11	France	12
Galicia (Austria)	19	Germany	42
Hungary	7	Italy	3
Netherlands	2	Palestine	4
Romania	8	Russia (with Poland, Lithuania, Latvia)	63
Serbia	2	Sweden	1
Switzerland	23	United States	5

An analysis of Orlan's list shows that about half of the participants (121 of 245 known participants) came from regions within the empires of Russia and Austria-Hungary. This is actually proportionately less than the total demographic weight of Jews living in these lands. It is estimated that around 1900 the population of European Jewry was approaching nine million (representing about 80 percent of Jews worldwide). At that time, there were more than five million Jews in the Russian Empire and more than two million in the Austro-Hungarian Empire; i.e., these two empires taken together accounted for more than 75 percent of all Jews in Europe and more than 60 percent worldwide.[58] But since a great many of the Jews ostensibly "representing" other regions had roots in the East, the percentage of *Ostjuden* at the Congress was perhaps not too different from their actual proportion in world Jewry.[59] (This would be even more the case if one excludes Swiss Jews, who were present in disproportionate numbers because of the conference's location. Many Swiss Jews were really observers rather than participants.)

But there were also major Jewish communities that were almost without representation in Basel. The most obvious were the Sephardim and Mizrachim from Morocco to Iran, including in particular the Jewish subjects of the Ottoman Empire. According to Ottoman census data, they numbered well over two hundred thousand at the time of the Congress.[60] It is also worth emphasizing that Orlan's statistics must not be interpreted to mean that delegations at Basel represented all or even most Jews of the lands from which they came. Vital suggests that about a third of the delegates were elected by a local community or association; many others were simply invited or came on their own initiative. Herzl wanted a big assembly for reasons of public relations, and he was not too fussy about the capacity in which participants came.[61] Above all, it must be remembered that the Congress was attended by Jews and Jewish associations sympathetic to Zionism. Obviously, it did not represent millions of individual Jews who were either indifferent or hostile to Zionism, or a vast network of non-Zionist congregations and organizations.

Anecdotal evidence of the problematic "representativeness" of the Congress is found in how it came to be held in Basel, Switzerland—not a self-evident venue for a pan-Jewish conference. Herzl and the committee that convened the Congress had initially wanted to hold it in Munich, a geographically convenient location for Jews travelling from the East, and, because of its numerically significant Jewish community (about ten thousand at the time), possessing the requisite supply of kosher restaurants.[62] The problem was that Munich's leading Jews opposed Zionism and, when they heard through the press about the projected conference, immediately voiced their objections. There were several reasons for their resistance to Zionism and the Zionist Congress. For one thing, Herzl's committee had decided on Munich, and had even begun to publicize the conference, before consulting the local Jewish leadership. For another, Germany's leading Orthodox rabbi, Hirsch Hildesheimer, withdrew his support for the conference. While he wished to encourage assistance for Jews in Palestine, especially those involved in colonization, he had become convinced that Herzl's politically oriented Congress would create difficulties for such work. Piqued at the rabbi's criticism of plans for a more wide-ranging discussion of Zionism's theory and goals, Herzl confided to his diary an allegation that the rabbi was acting from crass pecuniary motives.[63]

Be that as it may, the main reason for local opposition in Munich was rooted in an evolving politics of identity. Jews across most of Western and Central Europe had already been granted legal equality in the nineteenth century, and many had gained unprecedented access to education, distinguished themselves in a variety of professional fields, and even attained high government office. The Jews of Munich, like Jews in many other places, were reacting against the thesis, implicit in political Zionism, that in spite of their apparently full acceptance as compatriots, they possessed an ineffaceable national identity qua Jews, distinct and different from that of their non-Jewish neighbors. In Germany in particular, this position appeared to be completely at variance with the progress Jews had made and continued to make. In spite of the disturbing anti-Semitism noted above, the fact remains that "the history of the Jews in Germany from 1870 to 1930 represented the most spectacular advance any branch [of Jewry] had ever achieved."[64] Given this context, it is easy to understand why Munich's Jewish council wrote a letter to Herzl, stating that "there is not the least bit of sympathy for the movement you lead among members of the faith in our city, and that we regard the holding of the Congress in Munich or Bavaria as a genuine danger to members of our faith." They went on to warn that the anti-Semitic Bavarian press would interpret such a meeting as "supplying proof that Jews had no love or attachment to their fatherland." The hostility of Munich's Jewish leaders toward Zionism also partook of the common Western European condescension toward Eastern Europe, in this case toward the *Ostjuden*, who quickly became a majority among Herzl's supporters. A report to the Munich council, while evincing some sympathy for Herzl's aims, ascribed much of the enthusiasm for Zionism to the emotionalism of Polish Jews, with their perennial attraction to pseudo-messianic movements.[65]

Munich's Jews were not exceptional in their suspicious and negative attitude toward Zionism. Their opposition is additional evidence that the Zionists had to fight on multiple fronts simultaneously, their most implacable opponents being fellow Jews. Walter Laqueur gives a concise statement of the peculiarly Jewish critiques the Zionists had to confront:

> The case against Zionism was, very briefly, that as a secularist movement it was incompatible with the religious character of Judaism; as a political movement it was inconsistent with the spiritual emphasis in Judaism; as a nationalist movement it was out of keeping with the universalist character of Judaism; and it was a threat to the welfare of Jews as it confused gentiles in their thinking about Jews and thus imperilled their status.[66]

Given the dubious position of Zionism vis-a-vis so many sections of Jewry, finding an appropriate venue for the Congress was complicated. Basel was definitely a second, or even third, choice. Interestingly, Basel's Jewish community was very small and generally apathetic toward Zionism, and it remained so for a long time.[67] Herzl did manage to persuade Basel's Orthodox rabbi, Dr. Arthur Cohn, to speak to the Congress just before it adjourned. Even so, Dr. Cohn made it clear that his attitude toward Zionism was ambivalent. He reminded delegates that many Orthodox rabbis were, like himself, distrustful of Zionism, because they feared that it would make its adherents violate Jewish law (though he also admitted that he had been impressed by what he had heard).

But the important thing from the Zionist point of view was that, unlike the Jewish community of Munich, the Jewish community of Basel was not overtly hostile to the movement. As for the city itself, it had several things in its favor. It had the requisite facilities for holding an international conference. The cantonal government was well-disposed toward the Congress, received Herzl warmly, and put several apartments at his disposal for use during the Congress. And the city's population also showed themselves hospitable, in part because of curiosity about the exotic new movement on the part of townspeople and students, in part because of the presence of Protestant Christians— "Christian Zionists," although they did not term themselves as such—whose eschatology predisposed them to support the Jews' return to Palestine. The role of Switzerland as home or host to international organizations and conferences may have influenced Herzl's thinking as well.[68] Whatever the weight of these different factors, the result was that five of the six Congresses before Herzl's death in 1904 were held in Basel. But there was one disadvantage to Basel or any Swiss venue: meeting Jewish dietary requirements was difficult. A Swiss law, passed by referendum in 1893 and representing an undercurrent of popular anti-Semitism, prohibited slaughter according to Jewish ritual requirements. Ironically, given the fact that the Congress had been relocated *from* Germany, the issue was resolved by importing meat across the nearby German border.[69]

WHY JERUSALEM?—ZIONISM QUA NATIONALISM *AND* COLONIALISM

As for Dr. Karpel Lippe's invoking a divine promise as the basis of the Jews' right to Palestine in his opening speech, it contradicted the secular Zionist view, predominant from then until now, which construed the Jews' connection to Palestine in historical and cultural, rather than religious, terms. Given Herzl's original ambivalence toward Zionism's territorial goal, it is perhaps fitting that the key figure in making the secular argument for Palestine at the 1897 Congress was his ideological predecessor and rival, Nathan Birnbaum. Recall that Birnbaum had originated and propagated an expressly political "Zionism." On the first day of the Congress, he gave a major address on the cultural significance of Palestine, presenting that land not primarily as a refuge from anti-Semitism but as the necessary venue for revitalizing a decadent Jewish culture and reuniting a fractured Jewish nation.

According to Birnbaum, the Jews' need for Palestine was not based on a supernatural covenant but rested rather on an entirely pragmatic and popular basis. The fact was that only the land of Palestine, because of its mythic centrality, had both *Anziehungskraft*, "power of attraction," as well as *Festhaltungskraft*, "power of adhesion," over the Jewish masses. Although still committed to the need for Jewish sovereignty over Palestine in 1897, Birnbaum had already begun to shift toward advocacy of a cultural nationalism that did not require statehood. But in his address to the 1897 Congress, he delineates a scenario in which the emotional attachment of Jews to Palestine offers a *Garantieleistung*, a kind of guarantee, that they will not return to the Diaspora, but will remain, despite many a hardship, until they forge a unified and progressive national culture within a newly established Jewish nation-state.[70]

Birnbaum renounced Zionism some years later, but his cultural justification of it at the First Congress is theoretically significant. On the one hand, it shows, as we have just seen, that one could argue for the choice of Palestine on secular grounds, by an appeal to popular feeling and pragmatic necessity. On the other hand, his speech—the first to confront the question of Palestine's centrality to Zionism—says nothing of substance about Palestine's indigenous Arab population. Indeed, in the entire Congress, Arabs are referred to by name just four times, without any exposition of their socio-historical position in Palestine or the contemporary expansion of their population and economy. What can explain this incredible omission? In Birnbaum's case, the reason is clear: his view of both the *Ostjuden* and the Arabs is colored by a dogmatic orientalism. In Birnbaum's vision of the future, the success of Zionism (i.e., the re-establishment of Jews in their own land), gives a revitalizing impulse to the totally stagnant culture of the *Ostjuden*, and restores a cultural and moral authenticity to *Westjuden* as well. But the superiority of *Westjuden* with respect to "civilization," which is equated with economic and technological progress, makes their cultural dominance of the new community sociologically inevitable. So together, *Westjuden* and *Ostjuden* will establish themselves in Palestine. Even though he repeatedly rejects a role for the Jews as missionaries of European culture, he equivocates by asserting that the Jewish people, once established politically in Palestine, will be uniquely qualified to become the intermediary between Orient and Occident. But they will become so only because, in addition to their unique ethical heritage, they will have adopted the modern, progressive values of European civilization. This is what qualifies them for, as he terms it, "a mighty work of civilization."[71]

And how can he be so certain that this *Landnahme*, the seizure of this country so crucial to the future of Jewry, is actually possible? Birnbaum tackles the question of feasibility directly, revealing in the process his stratified conception of culture and power. As he puts it, if one were to propose the establishment of a Jewish state on the moon, or at the North Pole, this would be impossible, because of the natural constraints on the location of human communities.[72] But there are also socio-historical constraints on the establishment of, in particular, a new polity. It cannot be founded in older, culturally advanced, densely populated countries—which allows him to exclude the founding of a new state in China, or a state whose capital would be Berlin, Paris, London, or Rome. But, according to Birnbaum, no such socio-historical obstacle obtains in the case of Ottoman Palestine. Birnbaum's remarks imply that the conquest of Palestine will be easy, based again on his assessment of the balance of cultural power. Whereas a newly emergent culture cannot thrust an older, stronger culture out of its long-established geographical position, on the contrary, a young, ambitious, and aspiring culture (i.e., that of the reawakened Jewish nation) can indeed enter and dominate what he describes as thinly populated zone belonging to an older, moribund culture.[73]

A colonialist-orientalist outlook pervades Birnbaum's address to the Congress, and its symbolic weight gains in significance when we recall that he had been the most influential intellectual exponent of Jewish nationalism in Central Europe before the advent of Herzl. Indeed, he continued to have a devoted following even after Herzl assumed the leadership (thereby provoking Birnbaum's friends and allies). But in spite of the personal quarrel between Herzl and Birnbaum, there is no question that Herzl shared Birnbaum's orientalist devaluation of non-Western cultures. It was not because he had read Birnbaum, but because such a devaluation was integral to the European worldview, especially during this, the high tide of imperialism in Africa and Asia.[74] But what is even more historiographically provocative is Birnbaum's subsequent intellectual evolution. As we have noted, he was soon to break with Zionism. His antipathy toward Herzl was a factor, but more significant in the long run was his change of heart toward the *Ostjuden*. Birnbaum came to believe "that the only authentic Judaism was the Judaism of Eastern Europe." Eventually, this conviction would lead him to embrace Orthodox Judaism, but in the meantime he became an advocate of Yiddish, which was "an autonomous, valuable linguistic vehicle for the expression of unique Jewish cultural values."[75] And in renouncing his orientalism, he also renounced Zionism. Not that Birnbaum was conscience-stricken about the Arabs. Rather, in recognizing that the *Ostjuden* already possessed a creative culture worthy of respect and preservation, he concluded that there was no need to transplant them en masse to Palestine in order to produce a new national-cultural synthesis, as he had argued at the First

Congress.⁷⁶ Stephen Aschheim summarizes Birnbaum's later anti-Zionist position: "[H]e took issue with the Zionists who sought to create a mythical culture of the future on the basis of destroying a vibrant national life of the present."⁷⁷

The focus on Palestine was also a problem for the socialist wing of the Zionist movement, which grew in influence at succeeding congresses. Indeed, many of Israel's founding fathers were self-styled socialists. Yet the Marxian ideal of a progressive, international social revolution appeared to be in total opposition to the revival of an ancient, parochial, national identity in Palestine. Indeed, for precisely this reason, some socialist Zionists were drawn to the Territorialist ideal; i.e., the need for Jews to possess autonomy within a clearly defined territory yes, but somewhere other than Palestine.⁷⁸ Yet there were also socialist Zionists who centered their hopes for the creation of a new Jewish society on Palestine. Most notable among them was Ber Borochov, the principal ideologue of the most rigidly Marxian of Zionist groupings, Poalei Zion (Workers of Zion). Borochov attempted to justify this strange secularist fixation on Palestine by means of several arguments, all of them unconvincing.⁷⁹ The one argument that made sense, at least within a Marxist framework, was that, until the national question had been resolved for oppressed peoples such as the Jews, "normal" (i.e., antagonistic) class relations could not develop. For Jews, "the establishment of the nation under normal conditions of production" was a sine qua non for "a sound class-structure and a sound class-struggle."⁸⁰ The national liberation of the Jews through their re-establishment in a new territory with new "conditions of production" was thus a dialectical advance toward a socialist revolution.

We have therefore two fundamentally different answers to the question, "Why Jerusalem?" one scriptural and essentialist, the other pragmatic and dynamic. The first was that of Lippe and the traditionalist Jews who became Zionists: Jerusalem because of the divine promise. The second was that of Birnbaum, Borochov, and most of the modernists: Jerusalem because of its power to transform the Jews. For Birnbaum, it is the only country where a cultural transformation uniting *Westjuden* and *Ostjuden* can take place. For Borochov and his socialist disciples, it is the only land where the Jewish class structure can be normalized, where Jews will "be integrated into the universal revolutionary process."⁸¹

But whatever the theoretical justification, the determination to make Palestine the national home of the Jewish people required in practice the mass relocation of Europe's Jews from countries they had dwelt in for centuries, to a new land inhabited by another people and possessing a radically different culture and environment. To reiterate a point made at the outset, Zionism did not and could not conform to the pattern of most other nationalist movements, because it had to acquire and settle the land where Jewish sovereignty would be realized. Gershon Shafir has effectively summarized the intertwined difficulties in Zionism's mission, drawing attention to the obstacles it faced not only in obtaining land but also in mobilizing the necessary constituency: "Zionism, then, was a colonization movement which simultaneously had to secure land for its settlers and settlers for its land."[82]

Shafir's sophisticated work is based on a comparative study of Zionism, and he demonstrates the analytical utility of juxtaposing it to other forms of settler colonialism. But, given its exceptional features, does such a juxtaposition, with its implied classification, do justice to Zionism? This question, though historical in nature, has implications for Israel's legitimacy; and it is therefore disputed by many defenders of the Jewish state, largely on account of the stigma attaching today to the designations "colonial" and "colonialist."

There can be no dispute that orientalist motifs were pervasive in Zionist discourse from the movement's inception; the evidence is simply overwhelming, a point to which we will return in a moment. But it is also important to note differences between Zionism and most other colonial projects of the same era. Among these are the Jews' mytho-historical connection to the land the Zionists sought to colonize; the settlers' commitment to the secular modernization of an ancient language and culture; the absence of a metropole or colonizing state (at least until the advent of the Mandate); and the fact that Zionist colonization, unlike so many other encroachments and conquests of this period, was not driven by a quest for resources, markets, or opportunities for capital investment.[83]

Nonetheless, it strains language and logic to absurdity to deny the settler-colonial character of Zionism. While there has been some stimulating debate over this issue, at least three major sets of arguments can be marshalled for the objective validity of this classification.[84] First, there are the structural similarities between Zionism and other colonizing ventures, whether of the same or previous eras of European expansion. Most obviously, the planned, large-scale transplantation of a population into a new territory, especially one inhabited by people of a different language and culture, is the very essence of settler colonialism. But even more, Zionist settlement and labor policies in Palestine borrowed consciously from institutions created to facilitate other colonial projects, such as Prussian land acquisition in Poland and the white South African campaign to maintain segregation with respect to employment.[85] Second, leading Zionists compared Zionism to settler colonialism in other times and places, in order to draw conclusions about its future. Thus Vladimir Jabotinsky urged his readers to recall all known instances of settler colonialism, especially in the Americas, in order to prove that a compromise with the Arabs over Jewish immigration was impossible.[86] Likewise, the congruence of Zionism with white settler-colonial projects elsewhere, especially in Canada and South Africa, was cited by Zionists seeking British endorsement of their program, in discussions leading up to the issuing of the Balfour Declaration.[87] Indeed, Zionism's quest for an alliance with British imperialism was not merely tactical, it was held to be racial and cultural in nature.[88] Third, and perhaps most importantly, the situation in Palestine cannot be analyzed solely or even primarily on the basis of how the Zionists interpreted it (still less how they construe it today) but must reckon with the viewpoint of the land's indigenous people.[89] Prior to 1917, the indigenous response was plainly one of anger and anxiety, produced by fear of a future subordination to an immigrant Jewish population, in addition to protests against Zionist land purchases, and protracted battles over land already purchased but long cultivated by Arabs—even though the amount of land acquired by the Zionists up to that point was small.[90] After World War I, the Arabs saw themselves as forced to accept the imposition of a European population by a European power on account of agreements made between European states, acting under the pressure of the European-based Zionist Organization.[91]

While each of these points could be expanded, even a brief consideration of Zionism's program and institutions, of its polemical and persuasive discourse, and of the indigenous perception of Zionist actions and alliances, compel its classification alongside other European settler-colonial undertakings. And, as was true of all such confrontations, the core conflict between settlers and natives was over land; at the discursive level, the issue was the status of the land.[92] In the latter conflict, the colonialist-orientalist nexus was most conspicuous; as the case of Birnbaum suggests, this nexus was integral to Zionism and could not be repudiated without subverting its ideological coherence.[93] This was true of every tendency within the movement, crucially because every grouping had to assert the Jews' claim to the land in a way that would disparage or discredit the ostensibly stronger Palestinian Arab claim. For those tendencies that emerged before 1914, we may take as evidence the political Zionism of Theodor Herzl; the cultural Zionism of Ahad Ha'am, Nathan Birnbaum, and Martin Buber; the mystical Labor Zionism of Aaron David Gordon; and the socialist Labor Zionism of Ber Borochov and Berl Locker. We will also consider briefly the

Revisionist Zionism of Jabotinsky, important as the ideological parent of the dominant force in current Israeli politics; i.e., the Likud Party.

That colonialist-orientalist values underlay the political Zionism of Herzl is obvious, and even scholars who insist on Herzl's humane intentions admit this fact.[94] *Judenstaat* offers a plan to make a Jewish Palestine into an outpost of European "civilization" amid the "barbarism" of the Orient, and recognizes that such a colony would remain dependent on Europe to guarantee its security. Herzl argues that Europeans should help the Zionists achieve their goals because a Jewish state outside Europe was the solution to the Jewish problem inside Europe, but would also function as a pan-European colony. As Gideon Shimoni has observed, Herzl seldom referred to the historical basis of the Jewish claim: "Rather, his formulations reflected his fin-de-siècle, European-centered world outlook, one for which the right of the European powers to reorder and colonize the rest of the world was axiomatic."[95] But this colonialist worldview was implicit in cultural Zionism as well, despite its many differences with Herzl. Cultural Zionists attacked both traditional Orthodoxy and vernacular Yiddish culture; meanwhile, they resorted to derogatory descriptions of the Arabs and their relationship to Palestine. Thus Ahad Ha'am can wonder at the fertility of Palestine despite the "indolence" of the Arabs; at other times, contradictorily, he indulges the trope of Palestine's aching desolation. As we have seen, Nathan Birnbaum, while still a Zionist, envisioned the Jews' seizure of Palestine as economically and culturally progressive, since the land is currently home to a handful of people with a dying civilization. Martin Buber, one of Ahad Ha'am's disciples and later a proponent of binationalism, nonetheless made the superior material productivity of the Jews in Palestine a key element in his arguments for a Jewish right to Palestine, as though "productivity" were a simple and self-evident measure for determining rights of possession. It is telling that Buber can defend this position only by a bizarre logical leap, rejecting as it were all claims to land anywhere based on genealogically grounded and legally documented rights.[96] A similar sort of claim (which Buber made as well), basing itself on the Jews' allegedly superior spiritual productivity, appears in the works of Aaron David Gordon. Gordon argued that the Jews' title deed is the Bible; not a text *in* the Bible but rather the Bible itself, an expression of Jewish spiritual creativity while living and working in the land.[97] And even though socialists were generally suspicious of so-called historical rights when invoked in international disputes, since they were often pretexts for imperialism, socialist Zionists asserted the Jews' historical connection to Palestine as well, and advanced cultural claims that sound much like those of Buber and Gordon. Thus, Borochov's formulations of the Jews' need for Palestine clearly incorporate the notion of a territorial claim based on history. This idea was expanded by Berl Locker, another socialist Zionist in the interwar era. Locker argues that the Jews' historic right to Palestine was *sui generis*, since it was not a pretext for exploiting the resources of the country for the benefit of a metropole but involved working the land to build it up and make it the home of a homeless nation. Locker admits that this will necessitate abrogation of the Arab right of self-determination, which he says must yield before the (undefined) "higher interests of humanity."[98] As for culture, Borochov the socialist asserted, in complete ignorance of Palestine's realities and in terms recalling the facile judgments of Birnbaum when he was still a Zionist, that the indigenous population had "no independent economic or cultural character" and could therefore "easily and quickly adapt themselves to every cultural model higher than theirs brought from abroad; they are unable to unite in an organized act of resistance to external influences."[99] The higher cultural model is obviously the one to be introduced by European Jews.

As is evident from the foregoing, the ideas of Zionist activists and intellectuals about the Arabs were predetermined by a retrospectively patent orientalism. In some cases, their prejudices went so far as to reject the existence of a distinct Arab culture or feeling of attachment to the land.[100] By contrast, Revisionist Zionism had the merit of recognizing that Palestine's Arabs constituted an authentic nation with patriotic feelings for its land. It was precisely the inevitable resistance of this indigenous nation to Zionist settler-colonialism that necessitated the use of force against it, argued Jabotinsky. Nevertheless, this concession to the Arabs' national identity and the genuineness of their bond with the land, was effectively negated by an orientalism that was, if anything, more crass and categorical than anything produced by Zionism's other tendencies. Of particular relevance is the Revisionist indictment of Arab-Islamic rule over Palestine, which led to "the systematic destruction of the country and a complete absence of any development initiative, as a result of which Eretz Israel was turned into a wretched and exploited provincial backwater, devoid of any cultural or spiritual life."[101]

Ironically, only the religious Zionists did not need to resort to orientalist insinuations or invectives in order to justify the Jewish claim to Palestine, although they too were not averse to slurs against the Arabs. But, in principle, no denigration of the Arabs was implied by the appeal to a divine covenant. The Jews' right to the land was inscribed in the Torah, so all claims to the contrary were ruled out *tout à fait*. The Arab claim was disqualified not because they lacked national solidarity or produced less efficiently or had an inferior culture, but simply because they were not Jews. Secular Zionists could not make such an appeal, hence their resort to the invidious cultural and economic comparisons cited above.[102]

THE GOAL OF ZIONISM: RESTORING THE HISTORICAL AGENCY OF THE JEWS

Of course, any assertion of a European claim to Palestine in 1897 challenged not only the Arab position but, more immediately, existing Ottoman sovereignty over that land. This raises the question of the Zionists' final goal, an issue that exercised delegates to the Congress, as it did Zionists in later years. Did the Zionists need a state? Should they demand it? The answers varied. The first speaker, Dr. Lippe, had answered twice in the negative: first, because the Ottomans would never countenance anything beyond a limited autonomy and, second, because observant Jews would never accept the violations of religious law inherent in the operations of a modern state.[103] Meanwhile, Herzl equivocated. Had he not published a booklet whose title proclaimed the goal of statehood for the Jews? But he had then been forced to give up the explicit demand for a state in his sporadic and ultimately failed attempts to get the Ottomans to agree to a charter for colonization. As for the Basel Program—drafted by Hermann Schapira and Max Bodenheimer, reworked by a committee of jurists, presented to the Congress by Max Nordau, and adopted by the Congress after being slightly amended—the Basel Program made no mention of a state, instead making the goal of Zionism the establishment of a legally secured *Heimstätte* (homeland) in Palestine. Already in June 1897, with the launching of *Die Welt*, Herzl had dropped the use of "Staat" (state) and begun to talk about a "Heimstätte" instead, to mollify the Ottomans; Nordau called this term a "masterpiece of circumlocution."[104] Meanwhile, the statement of what Zionism's final goal should be and how it should be formulated, was the occasion for one of the Congress's most fiery debates. What is missed out in analysis of the debate, however, is the fact that Heimstätte, a vague term in German but generally associated with the acquisition of land for agricultural colonization, was subsequently translated into the various other languages spoken by the delegates. The most important of these was French, the language of international diplomacy at that time and the one the Zionists used in negotiating with the Ottomans. In French, Heimstätte became "patrie," the connotation being that Palestine was to become the "fatherland" of the Jews. For francophone

Ottoman statesmen, the implication that this would mean statehood, sooner or later, was unmistakable.[105]

Although some ambiguity lingered, most committed Zionists regarded a state as an imperative need, no matter which German term the Basel Program used. As Birnbaum said in his address on Jewish national culture, the only way to generate progress among Eastern Jews and restore existential authenticity to Western Jews, was "by once again elevating the Jewish nation to be a people possessing a state."[106] The symbols and forms utilized by the Congress conveyed this message as well. Max Bodenheimer had designed an azure shield worn by every participant, which declared: "The formation of a Jewish state is the only possible solution to the Jewish question."[107] The subject of the Zionist flag sparked earnest discussions in which Herzl took part. Patriotic songs became part of the Zionist repertoire, and the spatial configuration, formal dress, and rules of procedure of the Congress evoked the ethos of a national parliament.[108] It has long been known that Herzl confided to his diary a line seized upon by subsequent biographers as evidence of his political acumen, if not prophet-like status: "At Basel I founded the Jewish state."[109] Yet Herzl's diary is hardly the only place in which he expressed his desires and goals. Thus, off the record but during the conference, Herzl breezily expressed his objective to the committee on organization by declaring that, with the completion of the Zionist movement's constitution, the Jewish state had already come into existence.[110]

If the Zionists' ambiguity concerning their ultimate objective was intended to placate or deceive the Ottoman government, they were wasting their time. The Ottomans cared little about how the Zionists parsed their aims. Not long after the Congress, an Ottoman diplomat warned that the Zionists would not content themselves with becoming Ottoman subjects, but would seek international-legal recognition of their position in Palestine—as the debate over the Basel Program had revealed.[111] Obviously, the Ottomans feared that Jewish activism in and towards Palestine augured another secessionist movement that would undermine the territorial integrity of their empire. For this reason, the Ottoman authorities had sought to prevent Jews from settling in Palestine as early as 1881, with the influx that followed that year's pogroms in Russia; Hovevei Zion had thus encountered Ottoman resistance from the outset. Obviously, this resistance began long before the Basel Congress. Indeed, both the Ottoman and Russian governments were suspicious of Jewish efforts to organize politically and were monitoring the discussions of the Congress, as Lippe, Herzl, and many other delegates knew.[112] The discourse of the Zionist

Congress is thus, in certain respects, shaped by the "absent presence" of both the Russian and Ottoman authorities.

By contrast, Herzl and the Congress showed no respect for the rights or feelings of the indigenous Palestinian Arab population. Indeed, Herzl's zeal to enlist the support of European states at the historical zenith of imperialism, and Zionism's dependence on British tutelage after the issuing of the Balfour Declaration, reinforced the perception of the entire movement as a tool of imperialism and weakened its claim to be an agent of national liberation.[113] As we have already suggested, the Zionists conceived their plan and attempted to sell it as part of the much wider white-European expansion into the non-white non-European world. Rodinson offers a finely balanced assessment of their actions:

> This was perfectly natural given the atmosphere of the period. There is no need to moralize by applying to the Zionist leaders or masses of that time criteria that have become common today. But neither do we have the right to deny that their attitude was what it was, nor to disrgard its objective consequences.[114]

As adumbrated above, Arab anxiety about Jewish immigration to Palestine, which had appeared on occasion during the First Aliya, was now stoked by the overt politicization of that immigration, an inevitable outcome of the regular convening of the Congress and the ongoing activity of the Zionist Executive. While a clearly articulated Arab anti-Zionism would take some time to develop, there was a discernible deterioration in Jewish-Arab relations within Palestine in the wake of the first several Congresses.[115]

While it is natural, in the light of current events, to dwell on how the progress of Zionism affected the Palestinian Arabs, it should not be forgotten that it was also a problem for the long-established Sephardic Jews of Palestine. Ashkenazic Zionists were generally heedless of the impact their actions had on the Sephardim. Indeed, no matter how the Sephardim responded, they were subject to attack. If they embraced Zionism, they were disloyal to the Ottoman state; if they opposed it, they were betraying their own ethno-national community. A prominent Ottoman Jew summarized this dilemma when he declared that

> the central leadership of Zionism is committing a huge crime in its desire to drag the Ottoman Jews after their crazy movement.... Ottoman Jews cannot participate in this movement without being traitors in the eyes of their friends who belong to the other peoples....

They send emissaries to Turkey to spread their ideas among Ottoman Jews and acquire members for their movement, without thinking for a second of the great damage they could cause them, because they will be considered traitors to their homeland.[116]

But in spite of the troubling ramifications for Ottoman Sephardim, Palestine remained the territorial object of the vast majority of Zionists. As we have seen, there were traditional and sentimental bonds to Palestine, common to all Jews; but secular Ashkenazic Zionists saw it as the crucible wherein the Jews would coalesce into a bona fide nation, a nation reentering history. Indeed, it was an article of faith among these nonobservant Jews that only Palestine could supply the conditions necessary for changing the obsequious attitudes and effete lifeways Jews had developed in the Diaspora. No less a figure than David Ben Gurion, head of the Jewish Agency and the first and long-serving prime minister of the new state of Israel, paid tribute to the first First Zionist Congress for inaugurating a new epoch in Jewish history for just this reason. Addressing a gathering of Zionists in Jerusalem at the jubilee of the First Congress, he remarked:

> Since we went into exile we have had many dates in our calendar which will not be expunged from our memory for decades, and maybe centuries, to come. But the anniversary of the event to commemorate which we have assembled here today does not resemble them. The other anniversaries mark things that happened to us. They are a record of persecution, decrees, expulsions, massacres and destruction. Today's date, however, is the greatest in our history since the destruction of our political independence following the defeat of Bar-Kochba.... That day, fifty years ago, made us; and on that day we turned ourselves into a nation in reality. The First Zionist Congress, in 1897, saw the regeneration of a Jewish people conscious of its nationhood and proclaiming its aspiration to become again a people like other peoples, and to lead an independent existence in its own country.[117]

Ben Gurion's emphasis here is similar to that noted by Arthur Hertzberg, on the rupture that Zionism, which took shape as an organized political force at the First Zionist Congress, marked in the long history of the Jews. The question for Ben Gurion is not whether that Congress represented, empirically, world Jewry at the time of its convening. Rather, it is whether it represented the vanguard of a new Jewry, guided not by the traditional quietism of the

Diaspora but inspired by the ancient militancy of the Jews of Palestine. Thus, unlike the massacres and migrations of previous centuries, in which the Jews were objects, Congress-Zionism gave to Jews once again the dignity of subjects, historical agents, a people overcoming its degradation, demanding international recognition and asserting its right to self-determination. Here is more than an echo of Pinsker's pained demand for Jews to recover their communal self-respect. Herzl likewise saw the Jewish state as offering the path toward "the attainment of Jewish pride and self-respect; making Jews independent, masters of their fate; finally, gaining honor in the eyes of Gentiles."[118]

There are subtle differences as well as contiguities of thought between both Pinsker and Herzl on the one hand and Ben Gurion on the other, which are important to an understanding of the subsequent history of Zionism and Israeli society. Whereas Pinsker and Herzl contended, optimistically, that the success of Zionism in creating a Jewish state would make Jews who remained in the Diaspora more secure—either by supplying Jews with a nationality respected by other nations (Pinsker) or by causing anti-Semitism to fade away (Herzl)—Ben Gurion saw the Diaspora as an inherently dangerous and degrading condition. It was dangerous because of "the eternal and ubiquitous nature of anti-Semitism," but it was also degrading, since it affected the character of Diaspora Jews. The two phenomena were joined into a degenerating cycle of cause and effect: Diaspora Jews were "'objectively detestable'; their obnoxious characters, deformed by their powerless and precarious existence among Gentiles, are the reason they have been hated—indeed the reason they have so often hated other Jews and even themselves."[119] Ben Gurion's enormous odium toward the Diaspora was intensified by his generation's encounter with atrocities inconceivable to the liberal-bourgeois founders of Zionism.[120] Yet Pinsker and Herzl could also use shocking pejoratives when speaking of Diaspora Jewry, which suggests that this point of view was not an anomaly in political Zionism. We have already noted Pinsker's comparing the disgraceful behavior of Jews to that of herd animals; Herzl too was not above resorting to anti-Semitic tropes and vulgarities to further his cause. He posited that Jews had been habituated to the pursuit of profit and the neglect of civic virtue, and that only a state could restore their sense of honor and "manliness." Anti-Zionist Jews who refused to accept his program of self-transformation were labelled *Schädlinge* and *Mauschel*, epithets employed by anti-Semites to capture the allegedly vermin-like, parasitic, and money-grubbing character of the Jewish race.[121]

In any event, Ben Gurion's vilification of Diaspora Jewry explains an often-overlooked phenomenon; i.e., that the Holocaust was a source of shame in the new state of Israel, an event better forgotten than remembered. True, the genocide had happened because there had been no Jewish state to rescue the victims; this contribution to the new state's raison d'être has been termed Israel's "perverse" political debt to the Holocaust. But, far more significantly, the general absence of Jewish resistance to oppression, deportation, and mass murder, was viewed by Israel's political and cultural elite as demonstrating only too well the syndrome displayed by the Diaspora Jew. Characterized by his passivity, self-negation, and "feminine" submissiveness, the Diaspora Jew was set in contrast to the Zionist Jew, who was heroic, virile, and self-reliant, regenerated by the experience of living and laboring as part of the new community in Palestine.[122] This viewpoint was not limited to Israel's secular establishment; it affected even the religious leadership, as is demonstrated by an analysis of the wording of the prayer for the state of Israel composed by the Ashkenazic chief rabbi, Isaac Herzog, in 1948. Despite the Orthodox predilection for hewing to tradition, Herzog refused to echo the wording of centuries-old prayers for political authorities "because he saw them as symbolizing Jewish powerlessness and submissiveness to the foreign ruler. He made it a point to compose a completely new prayer, which would stress Jewish sovereignty and independence."[123]

THE CHARACTER OF THE CONGRESS: ETHNICITY AND CLASS, RESPECTABILITY AND EMOTION

Of course, Herzl himself had no prevision of the magnitude of the disaster awaiting European Jewry some four decades after his death, and he retained a basic optimism regarding the future of European "civilization." Nevertheless, his speech to the First Congress asserts, like Pinsker before him and Ben Gurion after him, that the Jews must learn to rely on themselves: "A people can only be helped by itself; and if it cannot do so, then it is quite beyond help."[124] At the same time, Herzl himself had only slowly and somewhat reluctantly come to the conclusion that the Jewish populace should form a body politic in order to undertake its own salvation. His first instinct was rather to conduct a one-man diplomatic campaign to solicit the support of European statesmen for Jewish nationalism, a charter for settlement in Palestine from the Ottoman Sultan, and the financial help of a handful of Jewish aristocrats. Alex Bein, historian and archivist of the Zionist movement, characterized Herzl as a believer in politics from above, who "intended to get the influential circles interested in the new idea of creating a Jewish state and to prepare with their assistance the political conditions, and only later on, he thought, the masses should be organized for emigration."[125] With this conception of politics, it is no surprise that he went first, as Amos Elon puts it, to "princes, pashas, and millionaires."[126]

But the response of the "money Jews" (*Geldjuden*, Herzl's term)[127] was disappointing, so he resolved on appealing to a wider audience by writing *Judenstaat*. Even then, he continued to hope that rich Jews would underwrite his project. But experiences in the summer of 1896 reoriented Herzl's thinking about Jewish politics. First, during a visit to London in the summer of that same year, he realized that Jews with superior wealth and influence were not going to finance this leap into the unknown. Then, on July 12, 1896, he gave an impassioned speech to the Jewish Workingmen's Club in London's East End, to a crowd composed principally of immigrant *Ostjuden*. He was energized by the rapport he had, or perhaps only imagined he had, with these working-class men, as he spoke to them about the Jews' need for their own national state and their capacity to build one. And, certainly, their response was enthusiastic. As he reflected on the event, he remarked, "Now it really only depends on myself whether I shall become the leader of the masses." Following hard on this event was another that laid to rest any remaining hope of enlisting wealthy Jewish benefactors for the cause. On July 18, 1896, Herzl had a rancorous interview with Edmond de Rothschild at the latter's office in Paris. The Baron wanted nothing to do with what he saw as an impractical and dangerous project, which would irritate the Ottoman government, endanger the colonies in Palestine which he had taken under his wing, and encourage anti-Semites in Europe. Even if external political conditions were favorable, the Baron told Herzl that "the Jewish masses cannot be organized." Whereupon Herzl decided that his response would be to "organize our masses right now." He would begin with a "mass agitation," out of which came, among other things, the Basel Congress.[128]

Still, the ethnic, or subethnic, character of the Congress was very different from what Herzl had expected. Herzl had not anticipated that his demotic turn would mean that *Ostjuden*, in particular the Jews of Russia and Russian Poland, would actually become the mainstay of the Zionist movement, as seems obvious in retrospect. In fact, the response of Munich's Jews to Zionism, for the reasons cited above, was characteristic of most Western Jews, the result being that the viability of the Congress depended on the willingness of Russian Jews to attend. After prolonged debates about the merits of participation, a substantial Russian delegation, representing more than a quarter of the delegates, travelled to Basel. And from among them came the most important "faction" within the Congress, consisting of members of Hovevei Zion.[129] They were crucial to the credibility of the Congress, but their presence in large numbers was also a source of tension. They regarded Herzl as a parvenu having insufficient appreciation for the work of his forerunners and, in particular, insufficient solicitude for the well-being of the recently established colonies in Palestine. Herzl, for his part, was determined to prevent an insistence on traditional religious observances from obstructing the establishment of a modern, secular nation-state. The *Kulturfrage* was to provoke clashes within the ranks of the movement itself, and between the Orthodox and the Zionists, since many *Ostjuden* regarded Zionism as a form of sacrilegious modernism.[130]

More in keeping with Herzl's predilections was the class character of the Congress. If Herzl's decision to call the Congress had been driven by a calling to reach "the masses," this did not negate his own desire to endow the movement with international respectability, and the Basel Congress was a thoroughly middle-class affair. Herzl kept a tight rein on the proceedings; the rules of procedure included a provision that limited discussion to items placed on the agenda by the preparatory committee.[131] Herzl did everything in his power to disprove allegations that his following comprised fools and fanatics (*Schwärmer*).[132] His own address to the Congress rejected in advance any appeal to emotion while recounting the injustices Jews had suffered: "We can talk about this today without emotion, without anyone suspecting that we are seeking tears of pity from our enemies. We have come to terms with our situation."[133] On the contrary, this convocation of Jews from many lands was a "solemn occasion," and the repetition of the Jews' solemn confession was only fitting.[134] Whereas Zionism had been treated as a misanthropic, even chiliastic specter, said Herzl, the world will now find out what it actually is: rational, moral, law-respecting, and humane.[135] As a consequence, the tenor of the sessions was generally sober and restrained, at least in Herzl's assessment. Just before adjourning on the last day, he sought to preempt criticism of the Congress by insisting on its restraint and resolution: "We have not hidden our devotion to our cause, yet we were not guilty of a damaging excess of emotion."[136]

At the same time, there *was* a vibrantly emotional side to the Congress, something easily missed if one approaches the Congress solely on the basis of its published proceedings. But other sources help to trace this aspect of participants' experience. While these reports overstate Zionist unity and the extent of worldwide Jewish support for the Congress, they do permit mediated access to both the feelings of individuals and the general mood before and during the conference. We have, for example, Berthold Feiwel, a Moravian lawyer

Figure I.8. Herzl and delegates on the floor of the Congress, in Basel's Stadtcasino. Wikimedia Commons/National Photo Collection of Israel.

and one of Herzl's collaborators, recording his rapturous anticipation as he made his way to Basel by train; the search for fellow Zionists as he travelled; the bright pleasure of finding them, the exchange of heartfelt brotherly greetings; and earnest discussions about "the cause" along the way. Upon arriving in Switzerland, Feiwel waxes lyrical about the glory of the Congress's setting: the solemnity of an Alpine sunset, a solemnity infusing itself into the delegates' very souls. Another, anonymous testimony speaks of the warm hospitality of the townspeople guiding delegates to the Zionist Congress's office, to No. 17 Freie Straße; the anticipation of meeting brother Zionists; the warm embraces, kisses of greeting, and the happy acquaintance-making—a comradeship centered around the Zionist idea being "like an electrical spark leaping from heart to heart and igniting them." In spite of the babel of languages, a mutual comprehension arising from a single proud cry of identity: *Ivri anochi!* [I am a Hebrew!] And on the morning of the first day, an impatient, joyous anticipation, encompassing delegates and audience, as they fill the hall to overflowing and wait for the Congress to begin.[137]

Thus also Samuel Lublinski, writing at the end of the first day, expressing a triumphant satisfaction in how the Congress has already confuted the gloomy and scornful detractors who predicted its failure for want of delegates, proving on the contrary that it is the Zionists and not their critics who understand most truly the hopes and feelings of the Jewish people. Lublinski mocks the fainthearted who urged the leadership to conduct a clandestine diplomacy, presuming that the Jewish masses would shrink in fear from an open declaration of their commitment to Zionism. On the contrary, the *Ostjuden* at the conference, representing those same Jewish masses, are imbued with a "visceral drive, venting itself in an impetuous expression" of support for the cause, which is reined in only by Herzl's counsels of moderation. While restraining their emotions in accord with the president's instructions, they refuse to yield to pleas for "discretion" made on the floor of the Congress by so-called practical men, whose proposals are a denial of "the power of enthusiasm and youth" and who themselves cannot help being carried along by "the general torrent of enthusiasm."[138]

Even within the text of the proceedings, enthusiasm obtrudes from time to time, where "cheers," "applause," "passionate applause," "thunderous applause," and other paraverbal irruptions are noted. Contemporary reports and memoirs of participants augment our emotional history of the Congress. Herzl's first ascent to the rostrum was the occasion for such prolonged and forceful clapping, cheering, foot-stomping, and cane-pounding, the *Jewish Chronicle* could describe it only apophatically: "To say he received an ovation is to use too mild an expression."[139] It was apparently during this prolonged uproar that a Russian Jew, Mordechai Rabinowitz, shouted, "Long live the king," and others took up the messianic acclamation. When he finished speaking, there was a moment of suspenseful silence; then another paroxysm of emotion: peals of applause, wild cheers, men clambering over one another in order to shake his hand, chairs and tables overturned, a woman in the gallery fainting.[140] Herzl was followed by Max Nordau, who was given a similarly clamorous reception. The delegates were swept along by his masterful survey of the Jewish situation throughout the world. Despite his detachment from Zionism, Dr. Arthur Cohn testified that Nordau's address, in particular, had made an indelible impression upon him. The *Jewish Chronicle* commented on the "fever heat of enthusiasm" among the delegates; they repeatedly interrupted to give their loud assent, or wept in response to Nordau's picture of the awful suffering of their Jewish brothers.[141] Herzl declared it the *tour de force* of the conference, emphasizing his approbation to assuage Nordau's apparently bruised ego (Herzl had been elected Congress president despite Nordau's seniority).[142]

It is perhaps surprising that Nordau, an atheist, should have had so powerful an impact on this audience. But by all accounts he did, and on more than one occasion. First, at the conclusion of his speech, Oscar Marmorek of Vienna gave voice to the surging emotions of the assembly:

Dear Brothers! Today is an extraordinary day, extraordinary for a people that has not spoken out for eighteen centuries and that has now sent representatives from all over the world to this place to deliberate concerning itself. Had this Congress been comprised of nothing but these two speeches, which have been received with such great applause, it would have been well worth holding it. Dear brothers! The words we have heard here will never be lost to the history of human civilization nor the history of Jewry. We will never be able to forget what we have heard as long as we live, nor should we. But we should not be the only ones to have heard it.

Whereupon he entered a motion, approved immediately and unanimously, to produce a special, separate publication containing just the speeches of Herzl and Nordau.[143]

FIGURE I.9. Max Nordau, keynote speaker at the Zionist Congress. Wikimedia Commons/National Photo Collection of Israel.

But Nordau was remembered at this Congress for another startling intervention as well, at a Commers, an evening of festivity held just before the Congress began. When Nordau was asked to speak, he first expressed his special sympathy with the Russian Zionists, then went on to cite an *aggadah* based on a text of the prophet Jeremiah: "A voice is heard in Ramah, lamentation and bitter weeping, Rachel weeping for her children."[144] According to the Talmudic story, as the Israelites traveled into exile, they heard a voice from Rachel's tomb telling of a vision of their return, for the mother had asked and received from God a promise of mercy for her children. As Jacob de Haas describes the scene:

> That a radical Parisian writer, debonair, square shouldered, with an imperial beard, one of the most modern of the intellectuals, who a year before was not even known to be a Jew, should in throbbing accents repeat these sentences of the mother's inexpressible woe, was an omen; "deep was calling to deep" across the world in time and space. No cheers but the sound of several hundred men gasping in uncontrolled emotion could be heard as Nordau ended his brief address.[145]

Not all emotion expressed at the Congress arose out of Jewish fellow-feeling; there was considerable bitterness, impatience, and acrimony as well.

Some of the ill will was directed at Jews absent from the Congress because of their disagreement with Zionism. In his opening address, Lippe remarked sarcastically on the passivity of the Hasidim, although he saved his severest sarcasm for Jews who continued to believe in assimilation.[146] Herzl attacked the tellers of tales (*Märchen*) about the danger the Congress would pose to existing settlements in Palestine; he probably had in mind both Baron Edmond de Rothschild and Rabbi Hirsch Hildesheimer, who had refused to participate for this very reason. And Rabbi Mohilewer's letter, read out early on the second day of the Congress, declared as heretical the claims of Reform Jews, and even certain Orthodox rabbis, that the Jewish mission was to remain in Diaspora as "a light to the nations," and that a renewed ethno-national consciousness among Jews would contradict belief in the Messiah—again, reformulated by the modernists as the attainment of social justice, political liberty, and international comity.

The proceedings also make it clear that some participants thought the Congress was being badly managed and neglecting important business. Solomon Rubinstein, a London businessman, complained at the end of the morning session of the first day that the reports being read out were much too long and detailed. His complaint was echoed in the *Jewish Chronicle*, which judged that the day was "wasted by the reading of papers, most of them not even bearing indirectly on the movement."¹⁴⁷ On the second day, Solomon Mandelkern, a Russian Jew resident in Leipzig and an early member of Hovevei Zion, commented that the Congress had been remiss in failing to make public its appreciation for Edmond de Rothschild's support for the colonization of Palestine. Given his strained relations with the Baron, Herzl bristled at this suggestion, replying sharply that Mandelkern was putting the Congress into an awkward dilemma, to wit, either of appearing ungrateful by its silence or of tacitly conceding "principles" which remained to be discussed—an obvious reference to Herzl's criticisms of how precarious and ineffective colonization had been up to that point due to the absence of a charter.

But a far more divisive issue arose shortly after the tense exchange between Mandelkern and Herzl, over the wording of the draft program presented by Max Nordau, in particular the preamble stating the overarching goal of Zionism: *Der Zionismus erstrebt für das jüdische Volk Schaffung einer rechtlich gesicherten Heimstätte in Palästina* (Zionism strives to create a homeland in Palestine for the Jewish people, secured by law). As we have commented, the German term used in the program avoided an explicit demand for statehood, even if the translation of the term into the French "patrie" gave a different impression; and many comments, symbols, and acts of the Zionists belied this intentionally vague formulation of their goal. Nevertheless, having swallowed the circumlocution *Heimstätte*, many Zionists remained unreconciled to the absence in the program of another term they deemed essential to the protection and progress of the new Yishuv. That term was *völkerrechtlich* (international-legal), which they insisted should stand in place of the allegedly less robust *rechtlich* (legal). The man who put the case for the former term was the young Fabius Schach, just twenty-nine at the time of the Congress and a colleague of two of Herzl's most trusted aides, Max Bodenheimer and David Wolffsohn. The proceedings mention the eruption of much noise as Schach began, his first words revealing an overheated atmosphere in which he feels he must assert his *rechtlich* right to criticize the term *rechtlich* in the program! He goes on to challenge the competence of prudentially minded legal scholars—Nordau had just defended the draft program as worthy of acceptance because it represented the intense labors of a committee composed almost entirely of jurists—to define what the Zionists truly needed if they were ever to move beyond the meager results so far achieved, which was above all an international guarantee of their position in Palestine to be given by the European powers.

Schach's demand for a bolder formulation of Zionism's goal was argued yet more forcefully by Leo Motzkin. Motzkin recalled that Pinsker's prophetic cry for Jewish sovereignty in *Autoemancipation*, published fifteen years before the

Basel Congress, had produced only desultory activity on behalf of settlement in Palestine, a few new colonies, and the occasional collection of charitable contributions. Popular enthusiasm had faded as the breadth of Pinsker's original vision had been lost. Motzkin insisted that, even if a frank public announcement of Zionism's final goals were to cause harm to the current work of colonization, this was no reason for subterfuge; the old methods were leading nowhere anyway, as Herzl himself had said, and the notion that concealment of Zionist aims would make the Ottomans more amenable was a delusion. Motzkin, following Schach, insisted on inserting *völkerrechtlich* into the Basel Program, as a sign of the movement's integrity and vision. As Motzkin pointed out, the term *völkerrechtlich* was derived directly from *Judenstaat*. Herzl had used the term *völkerrechtlich* four times in his pamphlet, making it an attribute of: (1) his proposed "Society of Jews," recognized as a state-forming agency; (2) the extraterritorial status of Christian holy places in a Jewish state; (3) the assurance given to the Society of Jews concerning the country it was granted; and (4) the sovereignty held by the Jews over a land sufficient for their needs. This last and most decisive usage occurs in a place where Herzl identifies this kind of sovereignty as his movement's premier goal. The grand irony of this debate was that Herzl was forced to align himself against those who were insisting on a legal position he himself had advocated only a year and a half before as indispensable to the future of Zionism. He tried to bridge the gap between the Congress's two factions by proposing a compromise formula, *öffentlich-rechtlich* (public-legal). Nordau's committee ultimately endorsed Herzl's emendation, while describing it as meaningless! But the majority of the delegates were now satisfied, or perhaps just eager to restore a semblance of unity, and the revised program was adopted by acclamation. Before this happened, the quarrel between Herzl and Schach turned ugly; Schach objected to Herzl's premature closure of debate and stormed out of the hall. A final irony is found in the sequel to this clash, since Schach—an early propagandist for Zionism in Germany, and one for whom the Basel Program had been too meek—turned against the movement and became the editor of anti-Zionist newspapers and journals.[148]

ZIONISM AND THE STATE OF ISRAEL: SOVEREIGNTY AND SURVIVAL

In spite of the rejection of Schach's motion at the First Congress, the means he envisioned for attaining security and sovereignty in Palestine, which was also Herzl's; i.e., through the giving of a guarantee by a European state or states, has actually been an integral element of Zionist policy throughout its history, including the period from the creation of Israel until the present. Such a guarantee was given in the form of the League of Nations Mandate, approved in 1922, confirming the commitment Britain had made in the Balfour Declaration of 1917, the text of that declaration being incorporated verbatim into the Mandate document. Similarly, the admission of the state of Israel to the United Nations in 1949 confirmed prior acceptance of the legitimacy of a Jewish state in the partition resolution of 1947.[149]

As for the situation after 1948, the state of Israel faced serious obstacles in breaking out of its diplomatic and economic isolation. The new state's struggle signalizes the fact that sovereignty, which *Leviathan* treats in its internal or generative aspect, has also an external or relational dimension. That is to say, recognition by preexisting sovereignties is a sine qua non for the establishment and maintenance of a new one.[150] This dialectical component of sovereignty is crucial not only to establish a discursive legitimacy in diplomacy, but—as the case of Israel demonstrates—to afford the newly formed sovereignty access to money and munitions. But the historical development of Israel's dependent relationship on France, Germany, and the United States, in order to maintain itself against the surrounding Arab states, also puts a disturbing question mark against the apparent success of Zionism in securing the Jews' position in the world through the creation of a sovereign nation-state. Did the realization of statehood simply transpose the need of Jews for patronage and protection as individuals—the Zionists despised such *Schutzjuden*, "protected Jews," a reference to the privileges extended by monarchs to a few wealthy Jews in the era before emancipation—to the need of Jews for patronage and protection as a state? Did Jews leave the small and scattered ghettoes of Europe in order to establish one big ghetto in the Middle East?[151]

To many Jews, inside and outside Israel, these questions will seem an impertinence, because the history of Zionism and Israel is understood teleologically, through the lens of the Shoah.[152] After all, Zionism addressed the danger posed by anti-Semitism, and only the Zionists, as alarmist as they sounded at the time, saw the imminence and gravity of that danger.[153] If only the Zionist goal of statehood had been attained sooner, multitudes that were destined to perish in the gas chambers might have been rescued—or so it has been claimed.[154] Indeed, it was the extremist wing of Zionism, the Revisionists, who appear in retrospect the most clear-eyed in this regard. It is impossible now to read Jabotinsky's testimony to the Royal Commission in 1937 without feeling the force of his argument:

I assure you that you face here today, in the Jewish people with its demands [for a state], an Oliver Twist who has, unfortunately, no concessions to make. What can be the concessions? We have got to save millions, many *millions*. I do not know whether it is a question of rehousing one-third of the Jewish race, half of the Jewish race, or a quarter of the Jewish race; I do not know; but it is a question of millions.[155]

Though no Revisionist, Amos Elon makes the same point retrospectively by focusing on the empowerment afforded by state sovereignty. As Elon says, Israelis believe "that the singling out of Jews for extermination was possible only because, of all peoples, only the Jews had no country of their own and thus lacked the minimum means of resistance." He elaborates:

> This does not mean that sovereignty alone automatically guarantees security and survival.... Sovereignty is meaningless without the will power and capability to fight for it. But sovereignty, and that alone, permits a people to foster such will power as is necessary for survival and to prepare the physical means for its realization in practice.
>
> Six million perished not because of a cataclysm of nature, as is evoked by use of that inadequate term "holocaust"; they died not because they lacked courage, but because they lacked the minimum prerequisites for putting such courage to practice.... The holocaust has thus come to confirm one of the basic tenets of classical, nineteenth-century Zionism: without a country of your own you are the scum of the earth, the inevitable prey of beasts.[156]

I have referred above to Richard Gottheil's essay on Zionism, prepared for the *Jewish Encyclopedia* of 1906. Gottheil was a Zionist, and he defines it as a movement "initiated by Theodor Herzl in 1896, and since then dominating Jewish history."[157] In so saying, Gottheil was prospectively accurate concerning the hegemonic position Zionism was to gain over the history, and the historiography, of the Jews. In Elon's terms, this was the case precisely because the Zionist thesis had been vindicated by the events of the Shoah.

However, the survival of a nation must be understood as more than the mere continued existence of a particular ethnic stock; the preservation of a distinctive way of life is an essential element in a nation's raison d'être. While one might assume that for Jews that raison d'être was given in Judaism itself, such an assumption ignores the effects of acculturation. As Ahad Ha'am put it, it was not only the Jews who came out of the ghetto; Judaism had come out too.[158] Zionism, as a form of Jewish modernism, attained its dominance by displacing rival ideologies and orientations, including the Orthodox understanding of Judaism, becoming in effect a surrogate or supplementary religious commitment for vast numbers of Jews. As Israeli historian Mordechai Bar-On once observed, in an assessment that builds on the apperception of Ahad Ha'am:

> Zionism, in its essence, was a revolution that attempted to revive the nationhood of the Jewish people out of the assessment that the religious framework of Judaism was disintegrating and could never again serve as a unifying principle.[159]

And certainly, it cannot be denied that, for a great many individual Jews as well as Jewish congregations, the state of Israel has replaced God and the Torah as the key element in building communal solidarity and organizing communal activity. Lavinia and Dan Cohn-Sherbok state this baldly in their discussion of how non-Orthodox Jews interpret Judaism:

> If keeping the commandments is no longer seen as a preparation for eternity, then what is the point of the continued existence of Judaism? This problem does exercise the non-Orthodox community. For many, the answer lies in the state of Israel. The founding of the Jewish state has become the central focus of their religious and cultural identity. Throughout the world, Jews have a deep admiration for the astonishing achievements of the Israelis in reclaiming the desert and in building a new society. They follow Middle Eastern affairs closely; they give lavishly to Israeli causes and they think seriously of emigrating themselves. For such people, *Judaism has become Zionism* and Jewishness is a national rather than a religious identity.[160]

The Cohn-Sherboks' description of the Judaism of non-Orthodox Jews dovetails with Professor Emil Fackenheim's influential formulation; i.e., that the survival of the Jewish people has become the supreme divine imperative, the 614th commandment. This idea was an element of what has been termed "Holocaust theology."[161] Fackenheim was proposing that a commandment must be added to the traditional reckoning of 613 commandments in the Torah, in order to deal with an unprecedented historical situation in which the survival of the Jewish people hung in the balance. It was a thoroughly un-Orthodox initiative, but one that Fackenheim hoped would unite both secular and religious Jews as an authentic response to Auschwitz. For him, "a commitment to the autonomy and security of the state of Israel" was necessary as an expression of the Jewish people's determination to survive, which somehow had universal spiritual implications. Indeed, the survival and enrichment of Israel was the decisive means of denying Hitler a posthumous victory and fulfilling a transcendental obligation.[162] But even for those Jews who would not legitimize Israel's creation by reference to a divine promise or an addendum to the Torah, the appeal to survival has been persuasive. Thus, the Israeli novelist A.B. Yehoshua sought to predicate the Jews' right to statehood in Palestine upon a "right of survival."[163] A more historically informed and critically nuanced version of this kind of argument is found in the final chapter of Gideon Shimoni's *The Zionist Ideology*, in which he demolishes religious, cultural, and historical arguments for a Jewish right to Palestine, proffering instead greater relative "existential need" and the "line of least injustice" as the most compelling arguments for a state of Israel in Palestine.[164]

In surveying the present situation, it is clear that the mere survival of the Jewish people is no longer at issue. The original three aspirations of Zionism have been triumphantly realized in the state of Israel, in its political-military assertiveness, its linguistic-cultural vitality, and its multifaceted economic development. But most fundamental, and consistent with the impetus Herzl imparted to the movement, has been the attainment of national sovereignty. As Hobbes would have it, Jewish sovereignty in Israel has provided Jews with a new kind of security against oppression and established conditions for the realization of Jewish dignity, since sovereignty is "the fountain of honour." And there is no doubt that the Israelis' achievements, as suggested by the Cohn-Sherboks, have rekindled Jewish pride in many Jews with little prior consciousness of their heritage. As troubling as it is for critics of Zionism, the movement's position as the Jews' new "unifying principle," as the perceived bulwark against annihilation in a Hobbesian world and a profound source of communal self-esteem, explain why anti-Zionism is equated with anti-Semitism by so many Jews. That equation may change, is perhaps already changing, as a generation passes whose experiences and memories cause them to view the existence of Israel as a kind of insurance policy against the revival of anti-Semitism in the West, or to view Israel's conflict with the Arabs as the sequel to the Shoah.[165] It does not mean that Diaspora Jews, any more than Israelis themselves, will automatically endorse the policies of Israel's government. However, there is abundant evidence, both quantitative and qualitative, for a generalized internalization of Zionism, inasmuch as an emotional attachment to Israel remains a defining feature of Jewish identity among most Jews outside Israel.[166]

A Critical Summary of the Proceedings

The public proceedings of the First Zionist Congress extended over a period of three days. A summary of its contents is most conveniently organized with reference to the events of each day.

DAY ONE: AN OUTLINE OF THE CONGRESS'S ACTIVITIES
(ORIGINAL PAGINATION INDICATED IN BRACKETS AS A FINDING AID)

1. Karpel Lippe, inaugural speech [1–4]
2. Theodor Herzl, speech of welcome [4–9]
3. Election of officers [9]
4. Max Nordau, "The General Condition of Jewry" [9–20]
5. Abraham Salz, report on Galician Jewry [20–28]
6. Jacob de Haas, report on British Jewry [28–38]
7. Jacques Bahar, report on Algerian Jewry [39–41]
8. Samuel Pineles, report on Romanian Jewry [39–45]
9. Alexander Mintz, report on Austrian Jewry [46–56]
10. Mayer Ebner, report on Bukovinan Jewry [56–61]
11. Rudolf Schauer, report on German Jewry [61]
12. Gregor Belkovsky, report on Bulgarian Jewry [61–78]
13. János Rónay, report on Hungarian Jewry [78–80]
14. Adam Rosenberg, report on American Jewry [80–81]
15. Nathan Birnbaum, "Justification of the Zionist Program" [82–94]
16. David Farbstein, "Justification of the Zionist Program" [94–108]

Although there may be a few omissions, probably inadvertent, the record of the day's proceedings appears to be reasonably complete, since it runs to 108 pages. There are a few places where there was a bit more discussion than was transcribed; but there were also complaints from the floor that the reports were long and tedious; it seems that the texts of these reports were later inserted directly into the official record (including footnotes).

As the outline shows, day one saw the presentation of reports on the situation of Jews in a variety of countries, but these reports were preceded by speeches of welcome made by Karpel Lippe and Theodor Herzl. It seems that Herzl was irritated by the passion, polemics, and prolixity of Lippe's address; but, if one discounts the very different rhetorical genres they employ, the speeches actually had much in common. Both magnified the Congress as a historic moment for world Jewry; both highlighted the unprecedented unity of Jews of differing tendencies and ideologies taking part in the Congress; both urged the Jews' need of an *Erlösung*, "Redemption"; both envisioned a political agreement with the Ottoman state, guaranteed by the European powers, that would create a self-governing Jewish polity in Palestine. There was, however, a substantive contrast between the two speeches. On the one hand, Lippe supplies a self-referential and more or less synchronic reading of Jewish history, built upon the paradigmatic recurrences laid down in Scripture and tradition; Zionism is interpreted within that matrix. On the other hand, for Herzl, history is contingent, pluralistic, and diachronic, which leads him to propose a uniquely "modern solution" to the paradox posed by the resurgence of anti-Semitism in an age of advancing "civilization."[167]

Surveying the consequences of the anti-Semitic resurgence was the task of the rapporteurs who followed. The series of reports they delivered was inaugurated by Max Nordau's address, which supplied a coup d'oeil of world Jewry in 1897. His overview was epitomized in a compound coinage, *Judennoth*,[168] "Jewish distress"; i.e., a distress peculiar to Jews qua Jews. For Nordau, this distress manifested itself in two forms, material and moral, the former pertaining to the situation of *Ostjuden* and the latter to *Westjuden*.[169] Cataloguing the eastern lands in which Jewish misery was most poignantly tangible at that time—above all, Russia, Romania, and Galicia—Nordau delineated, with a few deft strokes, the other rapporteurs' accounts of the heartbreaking material want affecting a majority of the seven million Jews of the East, over 60 percent of the world's Jews. His address is also notable for being one of just a few to deal directly, if briefly, with the condition of Jews in the Russian Empire; the Empire's delegates and Herzl agreed that the Congress would refrain from public criticism of the Russian government so as to avoid complicating their return home. So the Congress heard no report specifically on Russian Jewry. Nonetheless, Nordau could scarcely offer a survey of world Jewry and ignore entirely the lands where more than five of Europe's nine million Jews dwelt. Nordau noted that, since Russian Jews had not yet been emancipated, they remained subject to old restrictions on their geographical mobility, educational opportunity, and occupational choice. Apart from a small number of affluent and privileged Jews, they were *zusammengepfercht*, "penned up together" in the provinces constituting the Pale of Settlement, deprived of *Luft und Licht*, "air and light," which they were therefore compelled to seek in foreign lands—an obvious reference to the ongoing emigration of Russian Jews, about two million of whom left the Russian Empire between 1881 and 1914.[170] But even in lands where Jews had a theoretical legal equality with non-Jews, such as Austrian Galicia and Bulgaria, popular bigotry and the flouting of the law by officials were turning Jewish life into a daily struggle for existence. And while Western Jews were materially better off, Nordau subjected the history of their emancipation to a devastating critique, arguing that legal equality even in Western lands had been, in nearly all cases—England being the outstanding exception—enacted in defiance of a general antipathy toward the Jews. Nordau makes use here of a contrastive alliteration, setting *Gesetz* (law) over against *Gefühl* (feeling) and asserting the inefficacy of the former if not built firmly upon the latter. The consequence was that the social equality implied by assimilation was at best precarious and at worst, and more commonly, illusory. Nordau's grand conclusion was that European Jewry was in the midst of a comprehensive crisis, with widespread destitution and despair in the East, existential isolation and anomie in the West.

Nordau's comments concerning the ineradicably persistent anti-Semitism of the East, the seemingly sudden reemergence of anti-Semitism in the West, and its destructive and demoralizing impact upon Jews of both regions, clearly resonated with his audience. But his observations raise a critical question concerning the forces that gave to anti-Semitism such dynamism in fin-de-siècle Europe.[171] Nordau himself does not elucidate the causes of anti-Semitism country by country; rather, he is concerned with its overall effects. And he emphasizes repeatedly that Jew-hatred is justified post facto by fabricated allegations. But he does allude to increasingly race-conscious nationalisms, which made even religious conversion futile for Jews seeking to escape discrimination and exclusion. Nordau thereby acknowledges the power that imagined racial hierarchies were exerting on the stratification of nineteenth-century European societies. He also acknowledges that the recent rise to prominence of a handful of super-rich Jews has given a pretext to anti-Semites for their persecution of all Jews, even though most of them are barely able to keep body and soul together.[172]

The other rapporteurs offer their own insights into this question. The empirical evidence they supply, while not without its problems, is broadly plausible and provides both a geography as well as a political economy of anti-Semitism during this period. Western Austria, in particular the city of Vienna, offers perhaps the most provocative and complex case study of anti-Semitism, which reveals both its dissemination in religious and racialist forms, but also its evident utility as an electoral platform. Thus, while the report on Austria foregrounds the racialist strand within the anti-Semitism appearing in Vienna, Bohemia, Moravia, and the Alpine districts, it also argues that anti-Semitism has proven its value to the imperial authorities by diverting the attention of a potentially revolutionary proletariat away from the collusion of the government with the big capitalists and, instead, toward the alleged commercial ruthlessness of the Jews. The Christian Socialism of Karl Lueger exploited this popular notion to win elections in the 1890s, in part by convincing Catholic businessmen and artisans that the success of big Jewish merchants and industrialists was the chief cause of their economic insecurity and decline.[173] And while Lueger's allegations were dubious, it is still plausible to suggest that the dislocating effects of the ongoing capitalist transformation and middle-class fears of economic ruin, first delineated by Marx and affecting Eastern Europe toward the end of the nineteenth century, were potent impulses driving the upsurge in populist anti-Semitic politics. It is also true that many Jews took advantage of new opportunities for profit-making in the European economy, and in some places helped to precipitate those changes.[174] Nevertheless, David Farbstein's argument in the closing speech of the first day, in which he analyzed the economic history and social status of the Jews in the industrial age, supplies a very different perspective on Jewish agency in the rise of capitalism. As Farbstein states:

> The Jews were delighted during the new era of so-called freedom as long as they were needed, as long as there existed no "national" merchant class of tolerable competence.... Now that the Jews are no longer needed, they are hated everywhere, and all the evils rooted in modern economic development are charged to their account.[175]

While Farbstein oversimplifies the origins of modern anti-Semitism, he reminds us that Jews could suffer as well as succeed as a result of the operations of the market.

Even more importantly, the addresses by Nordau and Farbstein enframe the presentations given on day one and function as key elements in a constitutive rhetoric, the discursive genre predominating throughout this founding Congress. Consistent with the operations of this genre, Nordau and Farbstein accomplish their task by assuming and elaborating upon Jewish communal identity: Nordau addresses the Jews as a single community across space, while Farbstein treats them as a single community across time. But as with all constitutive discourse, its use attests to the actual heterogeneity and fissiparousness of the community it attempts to conjure through speech.[176] And the reports of the first day disclose various kinds of divisions among Jews. These divisions reflected differences arising from (1) geography, (2) subethnic identities, (3) political-ideological orientation, (4) religio-intellectual community, and (5) social class.

Geography is the most obvious of the divisions, since the rapporteurs described conditions by country and region, and *pace* Nordau, these conditions varied widely and could not be simply subsumed in generalizations about East and West. To take but one example: Nordau himself remarks, and Jacob de Haas documents, that Jews in England had achieved genuine equality (i.e., that assimilation has succeeded in England). It is the one counterexample Nordau allows to his argument that assimilation has failed and left Western Jews in social and existential limbo. But in fact, assimilation was also succeeding in the United States, with its fast-expanding Jewish population; and in the old lands of Europe, Hungary stands out as another counterexample where conditions for Jews were definitely improving (which Nordau acknowledges, yet discounts as recent, temporary, and perhaps unreal). And the Congress heard almost nothing about Jews in Germany, where, in spite of anti-Semitic campaigns, Jews continued to register unprecedented gains in education, wealth, and status. Indeed, the cursory comments of Rudolf Schauer about German Jews point to the problematic success of assimilation by noting that the children of Berlin's Jews display a shocking ignorance of Jewish history, religion, and culture.

This is not to suggest that the East-West dichotomy had no legitimacy, and virtually all of the Congress's rapporteurs refer to the broad disparity in the economic and cultural levels of *Ostjuden* and *Westjuden*. Nordau transcends this division rhetorically by classifying the afflictions of Jews in both regions as differing forms of *Judennoth*, the one affecting the body and the other the spirit. But even in the act of constituting the Jews' solidarity in suffering, Nordau's regional prejudice intrudes, since he classifies the moral distress of *Westjuden* as "bitterer" than the physical suffering of *Ostjuden*, affecting persons who are "more sophisticated, prouder, and more sensitive." Nathan Birnbaum, whose speech about the cultural basis of Zionism echoes Nordau at many points, is even more brazenly orientalist in his characterization of *Ostjuden*. He denies categorically that any progress or development has occurred within Eastern Jewish culture for two thousand years. Even creative linguistic-cultural movements of the recent past are, according to Birnbaum, merely imitations of and transitions into "Europeanism" and cannot lead on to the creation of a distinctly Jewish form of modernity. Birnbaum argues that *Ostjuden* have a defective culture because it is unmodern, while *Westjuden* have a defective modernity because they have no authentic culture. Zionism, by uniting the two divisions of Jewry in their own land, offers to Jews the only way of fusing authenticity and modernity. But when this occurs, prophesies Birnbaum, the "higher level of civilization" will "conquer the lower," the implication being that *Westjuden* will command the newly united Jewish national community. It was prophecy *ex eventu*, as it were, seeing as the first Zionist Congress was convened and controlled by *Westjuden*.

Further straining relations between the two sections of Ashkenazic Jewry was the large-scale migration of *Ostjuden* to the West, which brought the groups into direct confrontation with one another.[177] Both the records of the Congress and other historical sources attest to friction between indigenous and immigrant Jews in precisely those countries where Jews had advanced the furthest in terms of legal equality and social acceptance. In the 1880s and 90s, as desperate Russian Jews migrated toward Germany to escape pogroms and persecution, they found the attitude of German Jews hardening against them; while contributing money to their support, German Jews tended to avoid personal contact with the immigrants because, as one contemporary observer acerbically commented, they did not wish to be reminded of their distinct identity as Jews.[178] Many Jews of long residence in the United Kingdom kept their distance from recent immigrants from the Russian Empire as well. Citing Jewish periodicals of the period, one historian has summarized the attitude of British Jews toward their Russian coreligionists in this period: "The immigrants reminded British Jews of their lowly and foreign origins; worse still, they reminded the Gentiles. British Jewry wished to be thought of as modern; the immigrants gave, it was argued, the impression of primitivism, or at least of medievalism."[179] Adam Rosenberg, the only rapporteur from the United States at the Congress, noted the intensification of anti-immigrant feeling there, not specific to immigrant Jews but certainly affecting their reception. Other sources attest to the anxiety of long-established American Jews about the impact Russian Jews might have on their own position, "the danger of fanning into a flame any smoldering fires of prejudice."[180] And János Rónay of Hungary, also speaking to the plenary Congress, suggested that, while Hungarian Jews themselves had no interest in Zionism, they could be persuaded to support it as a way of diverting the flow of Jews entering from the East.[181]

Constitutive rhetoric works not only by means of transcendence but also by marginalization and exclusion. Perhaps the most telling marginalization in the Congress's survey of the Jewish condition had to do with subethnic identity, in its treatment of non-Ashkenazic (i.e., Sephardic and Mizrachic [or "Oriental"] Jewry). To be sure, they are mentioned: Nordau makes fleeting reference to the situation of Jews in Morocco and Persia; Jacob de Haas notes the presence of an old Sephardic community in England; Jacques Bahar presents a report on Algeria's Jews; and Gregor Belkovsky's report notes the rift between Sephardic and Ashkenazic Jews in Bulgaria. But their overall marginalization is shown by the almost total discursive invisibility of the Sephardim of most Balkan states and territories (Serbia, Romania, Bosnia, Greece, Macedonia, Thrace) and of the Ottoman Empire. Strikingly, this was true even of the Sephardic Jews of Ottoman Palestine.[182]

A third cause of division among the Jews was political-ideological. The differences here were multiple, some spotlighted at the Congress and others left in shadows. The most important of the anti-Zionist political currents were assimilationism and social radicalism.

Many orators were quick to identify their main nemesis in assimilationism, probably since the Jews who adhered to it were closest to the Zionists in terms of social class and cultural values. Moreover, in spite of the pogroms of 1881, faith in emancipation and assimilation did not disappear even from among the *Ostjuden*. The persistence of this faith explains the intensity of Zionist invective; speakers at the first day of the Congress make repeated attacks on assimilated Jews as cowardly and deluded, but above all as naïve. A particularly stinging rebuke was Farbstein's labelling of assimilated Jews as the ultimate *Schutzjuden*. Farbstein was implying that contemporary Jews were simply imagining that they were full citizens where they had been granted legal equality, when in reality, like the *Schutzjuden* of premodern Europe, they were merely tolerated on account of economic benefits the European states derived from their business activity.[183] A similar kind of political naiveté was emphasized by other rapporteurs on the first day as well. Jacques Bahar ascribes it to Algerian Jews who failed to recognize that their attainment of citizenship was a ploy to keep the republicans in power in Paris; Mayer Ebner discerns it among the Jews of Bukovina, who, having acted as agents of Germanization in the region, awakened to find themselves reviled by racialist German political parties; and Gregor Belkovsky bemoans the fatuity of Bulgarian Jews supporting politicians who promise civic equality, only to find every promise broken.

But naiveté was not a monopoly of Jews believing in liberalism, emancipation, and assimilation, according to the Zionists. They ascribed a similar sort of folly to Jews who put their faith in the radical ideologies proliferating in the 1890s. But this was a socio-political phenomenon of enormous potential influence that was almost entirely ignored by the Zionists at the 1897 Congress. Yet the small founding meeting of the Bund, the General Jewish Labor Union of Russia and Poland, took place just a few weeks after the Basel Congress. And the Bund, which married Jewish cultural nationalism to revolutionary socialism, grew with such rapidity that by 1905 it had become the leading political force among the *Ostjuden* and was, for a brief period, more attractive to Russian Jews than Zionism.[184] The fact that the surging power of these radical ideas among the young and impoverished scarcely registered among the Zionists in 1897 is yet more evidence of the bourgeois character of the Congress. Of course, anti-Semitic propaganda from the nineteenth century until the present has exaggerated the power of the Jews in radical socialist movements, to the point of identifying such movements as elements in a Jewish conspiracy of world domination. At the same time, there can be no doubt that Jews were "overrepresented" in the leadership of such movements.[185]

If assimilationism and revolutionary socialism were the secular panaceas Zionists had to compete with during the first decade of its existence, there were also powerful religio-intellectual currents which had preceded Zionism by decades, if not centuries, which continued to claim the allegiance of millions of Jews and which were implicitly or explicitly opposed to the new movement. We have mentioned Rabbi Mohilewer's denunciation of those who reject Orthodox eschatology and the concept of a Jewish nationality (i.e., Reform Jews). But Mohilewer nowhere refers to Reform Judaism by name, and apart from a few derogatory allusions, the Zionist Congress said nothing about Reform Jews, perhaps because their stronghold was and is in the United States. Oddly, even Adam Rosenberg, who reported on American Jewry in a short address on day one, says nothing about Reform Judaism, even though it was unquestionably the most influential branch of Judaism in the United States at the time.

But far more important, both numerically and organizationally, was traditional Orthodoxy itself, especially in the form of Hasidism, a mystical revivalism which arose in the eighteenth century and spread to Jewish communities all over Eastern Europe.[186] There was a profound gulf between these communities and the Zionists. The leaders of Zionism made no effort to conceal their secularism, and most of the members were products, in one way or another, of the Haskalah, an intellectual movement of the eighteenth and nineteenth centuries that sought to adapt Judaism and Jewish lifeways to the values of modern culture.[187] Meanwhile, the most powerful bastion of opposition to the modernism inherent in the Haskalah, Hovevei Zion, and Congress-Zionism, was Hasidism. That Hasidism was hardly mentioned is perhaps the most revealing exclusion in the studies of the Jewish condition at the Zionist Congress.[188] In fact, while there were exceptions to the rule, most Hasidim maintained their antipathy to Zionism, even religious Zionism, right up until their emigration from Eastern Europe or their destruction in the Shoah.[189]

The fifth cause of division among Jews arose out of differences in social class. Now it is not surprising that most of the speakers on the first day of the Congress sought to downplay the financial power of the Jews, since this was a leitmotif of anti-Semitic propaganda. Rather, they emphasized the prevalence of Jewish poverty, in order to smash the myth, as Nordau phrases it, "that the Jews have all power and authority, that the Jews possess all the wealth of the earth."[190] Nordau acknowledges that there were hundreds of *überreiche Juden* ("super-rich Jews"), but he hastened to label them a "vulgar stratum," occupying the "lowest rung in the esteem of the nation," the dregs of the Jewish "race." The regional rapporteurs also mention the existence of such wealthy Jews, usually in passing, but nonetheless conveying the impression that, within each region, the differences in social status and income level were enormous, that opulent wealth cohabited with utter destitution in the Jewish community. Farbstein had declared that "the Zionists were the poor and oppressed in Israel," whereas their opponents were the complacent rich, but the evidence does not bear out his claim. Farbstein himself admitted that the Zionists had neglected the Jews' need for socio-economic transformation. In fact, the segregation of classes and the weak sense of shared responsibility for the Jewish poor were to remain vexing issues. For example, a 1918 report on Zionism in Poland indicts the Jewish bourgeoisie for its pathetic response to the wretchedness of the Jewish masses. While the report acknowledges that various Jewish political groups, including the Zionists, had done some admirable social work, it also expresses disappointment in how few participated in that work, and notes that even the dedicated few had only a tenuous personal connection with the masses.[191]

While the content of the speeches on day one can thus be analyzed to expose the disunities existing among the Jews, such analysis must not dilute the total impact of the Congress on the subsequent history of Zionism. After all, in spite of predictions to the contrary, the Congress had begun, it was a congress of Jews proudly identifying themselves as Jews, and was therefore much more than the sum of its speeches. There were many different speakers on that first day representing many different regions and holding different points of view. What they said was revealing both in its emphases and in its exclusions. But it must not be overlooked that they spoke from the same rostrum, under the same provisional authority, and understood themselves to be acting in the same cause.

DAY TWO: AN OUTLINE OF THE CONGRESS'S ACTIVITIES (PAGINATION INDICATED IN BRACKETS AS A FINDING AID)

1. Theodor Herzl, summary of incoming communications [109–10]
2. Rabbi Samuel Mohilewer, Hebrew letter translated and read to Congress by Rabbi Armand Kaminka [110–12]
3. Grand Rabbi Zadok Kahn, letter read to Congress [113]
4. Max Nordau, presentation of draft Zionist Program [113–14]
5. Debate and adoption of the amended draft Program [114–19]
6. Max Bodenheimer, "The Zionist Organization" [119–30]
7. Debate on organization, referral to Ad Hoc Committee [130–38]
8. Jacob Bernstein-Kohan, address concerning Zionist priorities and methods [139–46]
9. Moses Moritz, address concerning funding of colonization, by Moses Moritz [147–50]

Our record of proceedings of the second day is incomplete. This is clear from the fact that the text for day two runs to just forty-one pages. Even if the Zionists were late in beginning deliberations,[192] an entire day's speeches and discussions could not be transcribed in so few pages. There are explicit statements in the record that certain texts were read or speeches given, which were not transcribed. Finally, there was much noisy acrimony on day two, as suggested by paraverbal indicators ("much noise," "commotion," "general tumult," etc.) and some of what was spoken or shouted was obviously not taken down.

If on day one the Zionists sought to demonstrate comprehensive knowledge of the distressed condition of world Jewry, on day two they set forth the proposed remedy, since the day witnessed the presentation of the draft Zionist program, what came to be known as the Basel Program, and a tentative plan for a Zionist Organization. Both the draft program and the constitution of the organization were subjects of intense debate that exposed divisions within the ranks of the Zionists. In particular, there was disagreement over the value of a previous generation's labors in colonizing Palestine and over the strategy and tactics that should guide future Zionist action.

Disagreements were to be expected of course, but whenever possible Herzl acted to prevent, contain, or curtail them. For the most part, these interventions were accepted. As one journalist observed: "His thorough command over the varied elements composing the Congress is one of the features of this gathering and is a high tribute to the confidence he has gained."[193] But if the Congress needed Herzl, the converse was also true. In particular, Herzl needed the Congress as a demonstration that there existed a powerful, unified, and international Jewish constituency for the proposals he had made in *Judenstaat*, which would allow him to negotiate with interested statesmen and potential benefactors from a position of quasi-official authority.[194] It was therefore essential to convey an image of consensus among Jews both outside and inside the Congress.

As proof of Jewish unity in support of Zionism from beyond the Congress, Herzl could marshal two forms of evidence. First, Herzl began the day with a report on the immense number of communications received, consisting of telegrams, letters, and petitions in support of the Congress, sent from all over the world and signed by tens of thousands of persons. Second, Herzl emphasized the number and prominence of the rabbis who had endorsed Zionism. He mentions that many declarations of support had been received from Orthodox rabbis, including some "crown rabbis" in Russia.[195] Special notice was taken of the fact that Dr. Isaak Rülf, who had established his reputation as a campaigner for aid to Russian Jewry through numerous journal articles reporting on conditions in the East, had signed the telegram sent from Memel (Prussia). Herzl also had a Hebrew letter of Rabbi Samuel Mohilewer of Bialystok (Russia), a leader of Hovevei Zion, read out to the entire assembly, then translated into German; after this, yet another letter was read, from the Grand Rabbi of France, Zadok Kahn.[196] Given Herzl's desire to expedite business, and the fact that the meeting was substantially behind schedule by the second day, the time devoted to the communications of these three famous rabbis is significant. Their messages of support showed that Zionism was not anti-religious, nor did it undermine the authority of the rabbinate. On the contrary, Herzl hoped the rabbis would use their influence over the masses to promote adhesion to Zionism. Ironically, honoring the rabbis to preserve Jewish unity provoked discord from another direction. For young Zionists of a secular scientific education, Herzl's deference to religious authority was hypocritical and reactionary. Thus, Chaim Weizmann accused Herzl of a confused sort of "clericalism," saying he had "excessive respect for the Jewish clergy, born not of intimacy but of distance."[197]

Of course, Herzl had to maintain unity and cooperation within the Congress itself as well, and the two major items on the agenda of the second day, the proposed program and organization, made this task difficult. The problems were both procedural and substantive, and the debates disclose conflicting attitudes on a range of subjects.

The first procedural problem was getting the draft program accepted. Nordau, who presented the text of the program that had been agreed to by an ad hoc committee, pleaded from the outset for the assembly to adopt it by acclamation. But it was immediately apparent that there were objections to the wording of the program and to circumventing protocol to secure its approval, which ought to have taken place by ballot. Since most of the wrangling about the program came down to differences over a single term, *rechtlich* versus *völkerrechtlich* (see above, "The Character of the Congress"), it was agreed that a speaker should be elected to represent each side of the debate, in order to abridge the increasingly rancorous debate. After these speakers concluded their remarks, Herzl rejected an appeal to continue debate, and, in spite of obvious, ongoing dissent against the program, had it adopted by a transparently manipulated acclamation, in accord with Nordau's initial request.[198]

It is worth reflecting on the substance of what was agreed upon in the program and why the disagreement over a single term became so strident. It has been observed many times that the program does not mention a "state." But there were also other terms omitted from the program—terms that were prominent in discussions at this and subsequent Congresses, including some that are found in Zionist discourse to the present day. For example, there is nothing about the Jews' "return" to Palestine, the "restoration" of the Jewish nation in Palestine, or the colonization of Palestine being a movement toward "redemption."[199] In the absence of these terms, the program offers no justification for demanding Palestine at all, another sign that the Zionist leadership was secularist and futurist, and that the reference to Palestine was more a concession to Jewish sentiment than an a priori religio-ideological commitment. But if the absence of these mytho-historical terms caused no apparent consternation, the absence of *"völkerrechtlich"* did. Strangely, no one objected to omitting from the program any reference to the Jews' ancient history. Meanwhile, partisans of *völkerrechtlich* protested vehemently against the omission of this term, for it signified a decisive break Zionists were making vis-à-vis the Jews' recent history, vis-à-vis organizations antecedent to Congress-Zionism. Thus, Leo Motzkin, who was elected spokesperson for the advocates of *völkerrechtlich*, gave an impassioned address in which he argued that *völkerrechtlich* epitomized the difference between Pinsker and Herzl, Hovevei Zion and Zionism, the futility of a previous generation's labors in colonization and the dynamism of the present generation's drive for political independence. As Motzkin declared, the world must know, Turkey must know, and the new generation of Jewish youth needs to know, how the Zionists are to be distinguished from their forebears. The new Zionists' unabashedly political orientation supplied the basis for solidarity at the Congress, and only a continuing commitment to this orientation would inspire a youthful vanguard to lead the Jewish people toward the national ideal.[200]

The debate on this point is revealing in yet another way, especially when compared to Rabbi Mohilewer's letter, which preceded it. Mohilewer asserted that the foundation of Hibbat Zion had been received Jewish doctrine. Hence, the Torah must be the basis of the Jewish nation's rebirth in its ancestral land. In fact, another significant omission from the Basel Program is silence concerning the Torah and Judaism. However, the focus of debate over the program *was* about what category of law the Zionists should appeal to; and "Torah" means, among other things, law. In brief, the divergent theories of law evoked by the terms *Torah* and *Recht* symbolize the polarized worldviews of Mohilewer and his secularist colleagues within Zionism, however much the latter group clashed over the diction to be inserted into the program. For Mohilewer, law is a revealed way of life, Israel's vocation is to fulfill the law, and the law applies to the individual Jew in every aspect of his behavior, and to the Jews as a community in their relationship to one another, the land, non-Jews, and God. Moreover, the Torah presumes qualitative distinctions among Jews and between Jewish society and other societies. Meanwhile, to Herzl, Nordau, Schach, Motzkin, Mintz, and other secular Zionists, law is determined by consensus rather than revelation, governs social relations in the public sphere, and presumes an equality of status, both among citizens of any given state and among a plurality of sovereign states. Hence the programmatic demand, in its final formulation, for a Jewish homeland to be secured by "public law." But was this enough? Even many of those who accepted the need for a legal guarantee to pursue colonization in Palestine and balked at the strict application of the Torah in a revived Jewish polity, were moved to ask what was specifically Jewish about the *Heimstätte* the Zionists were seeking.[201] Indeed, Max Bodenheimer of Cologne, who spoke after debate on the program was terminated and a slightly amended text approved, broaches the cultural question as a part of his plan for a Zionist organization.

Bodenheimer begins his address by suggesting that the convening of the Congress was itself the foundation of a permanent Zionist organization, because it had awakened the Jewish people to resist their enemies and identify themselves with the Congress. While another speaker impugned the Congress's right to speak for world Jewry, Bodenheimer makes the most forceful assertion of precisely that claim. He posits an organic development of the nation toward statehood; since the Congress is the *jüdische Nationalversammlung* (Jewish national assembly), it is the first tangible expression of Jewish *Machtwille*, the will to political power and, ultimately, state sovereignty.[202] He then turns to his general plan for a Zionist organization, in effect the "Society of Jews" Herzl had proposed in *Judenstaat*.[203] Although he was later criticized for not presenting a more detailed draft, he seems to have thought it sufficient that the Congress approve a few basic principles: (1) that the Congress, which should be held annually in different locations, be recognized as the supreme governing body of Zionism; (2) that participation in the Congress be both direct and representative, with decisions made by voting; (3) that a central executive be elected—an executive that would handle business between meetings of the Congress, including details of how the Zionist organization should be constituted; (4) that regional organizations be established conforming to local laws and conditions and having authorized correspondents to interact with the central executive.

Bodenheimer's draft of a Zionist organization, which, like the draft program, was presented in the morning session of the second day, provoked much discussion and debate. There were appeals for more special committees, an enlarged executive, the collection of more economic data, funding for the production of literature for youth, etc. There was contention over procedure. Apparently, proposals for the organization had already been submitted, which conflicted with Bodenheimer's. Herzl wanted to deal with all the proposals in plenary session, thinking thus to quickly resolve the entire issue, but resistance to this manner of proceeding forced him to accept the formation of an ad hoc committee to review the relevant submissions. Moreover, since the plan for an organization had to take into account conditions in the various countries where Jews lived, the ad hoc committee members were chosen on the basis of nationality.

Like Max Bodenheimer, Jacob Bernstein-Kohan of Kishinev, who gave the major address in the afternoon of the second day, emphasized the urgent need to educate Jews in their own language and history. Bernstein-Kohan was a physician, a veteran of Hovevei Zion, in sympathy with the ideas of Ahad Ha'am, and had the distinction of being the only Russian to deliver a set speech to the Congress.[204] In his view, the essential elements of a Jewish education were the learning of Hebrew and the knowledge of Palestine. He believed the earnest, affectionate study of Palestine, in particular, would prepare those who would later emigrate, and also be the most effective means of inculcating the Zionist ideal into the souls of Jewish youth.[205] Echoing Ahad Ha'am, he argues that a carefully structured cultural and political education should precede the establishment of new colonies, so that the new Yishuv will be built up from a moral and spiritual elite. Again, like Ahad Ha'am, he deplores the lack of any system in the purchasing and settling the land, and calls for the subordination of all such work to a committee to be formed by the Congress.

If Bernstein-Kohan believed that only the Congress could reform the presently disorganized and erratic work of colonization, he also recognized the inherent tension within the Congress between partisans of immediate colonization and those who prioritized the new Yishuv's need for legal protection.[206] Thus, his speech offers an early analysis of the conflict between Herzlian or "political" Zionists, with other Zionists, many of them Hovevei Zion, who favored ongoing colonization, the "practical" Zionists. He attempts to synthesize the two trajectories by positing a sequence wherein the political Zionists obtain Ottoman approval for the further Jewish colonization, the Jewish population and economy expands, and the impressive growth of both prepares the way for an international guarantee of Jewish autonomy in Palestine.[207]

But, regardless of their differing priorities, every faction within Zionism knew that money was required to attain its goals. Political Zionists hoped millions of francs would induce the Sultan to give Herzl a charter for Palestine; practical Zionists wanted millions to purchase land and effect the transfer of tens of thousands of poor *Ostjuden* to Palestine; and money was needed for the propaganda, literature, and classes the Zionists planned to use to recruit many more Jews to the cause—this, besides the outlays required to keep the organization afloat. Indeed, Zionism wanted to prove its superiority to antecedent movements on the basis of its political realism, true, but also on account of its supposed capacity to find funding for its projects. So schemes for raising vast sums of money were addressed by all of the scheduled speeches of the second day, Max Bodenheimer, Jacob Bernstein-Kohan, and finally, Moritz Moses.

Without entering into the details, we note one theme which unites the three set speeches of day two. All refer, explicitly or implicitly, to a national fund to acquire land in Palestine, to be raised among Jewish communities worldwide. This topic was to be treated in greater detail on day three by Hermann Schapira. Shafir has argued that the multiple formulations of such a proposal were the consequence of financial problems in acquiring land in Palestine in the 1880s and 90s, but also the circulation of radical land-reform schemes by European social reformers during this same period.²⁰⁸

If day one described the unity-in-misery of the Jews, then day two sought to set forth their unity-in-aspiration, attested to by their approval of a common program and attempts to forge a common, representative organization. But Zionist unity was not attained solely by means of representation. Herzl had abrogated democratic procedure to get the program approved, even if most of his opponents gave in to his highhandedness. More significantly, the three major speeches of the day simply presume that the Zionists have assembled on behalf of the Jews, are the true guardians of Jewish interests, and therefore have a right to call on the resources of Jews worldwide. To justify this right, Bodenheimer contrasts the Zionist Organization to other Jewish institutions; i.e., international associations such as the Alliance Israélite Universelle and B'nai B'rith, and the multiple thousands of individual Jewish congregations. The first set is apolitical, philanthropic, and assimilationist, while the second cannot produce a national solidarity due to their parochial autonomy. Therefore, the Zionists alone represent Jewish *Machtwille*, the will to empower themselves through the creation of a sovereign nation-state.

We conclude this section by noticing some symmetries and connections between the earlier and later messages of day two. The earlier portion of the day was taken up with communications from three distinguished rabbis, the latter with speeches by three distinguished representatives of the secular Jewish elite—a lawyer, a physician, and a merchant. There was a geographical balance in both groups, since Rabbi Mohilewer and Rabbi Rülf resided in the East and were in close contact with the *Ostjuden*, as were Dr. Bernstein-Kohan and M. Moses; but both Rabbi Kahn and Dr. Bodenheimer, though sympathetic to the plight of the *Ostjuden*, were products of a western Jewish formation. But, whether from East or West, they all shared the previous experience of being active as Hovevei Zion. It has already been observed that prior commitment to Hibbat Zion was the "leading common attribute of the delegates" at the Congress; and this intricately networked aggregation bears out that generalization.²⁰⁹

It has been suggested that Herzl convened the Congress because the question had been raised: for whom did he speak? But the convening of the Congress merely transposed the question to a higher level: for whom did the Zionists speak? The sharpness of their polemics against Jewish detractors shows that, their assumption of a pan-Jewish authority notwithstanding, that question remained unanswered.

DAY THREE: AN OUTLINE OF THE CONGRESS'S ACTIVITIES

1. Theodor Herzl, notice of incoming communications and attendance [151]
2. Dir. Steiner, presenting Draft Constitution of the Zionist Organization [151–52]
3. Debate and Adoption of the Amended Draft Constitution [152–63]
4. Nomination and Election of Members of the Vienna Executive (*Engeres Actionscomité*) and the Zionist General Council (*Grosses Actionscomité*) [163–66]
5. Hermann Schapira, draft proposal for establishing a national fund [166–67]
6. Discussion of national fund [167–68]
7. Moritz Schnirer, recommendations concerning the colonization of Palestine [168–70]
8. Armand Kaminka, report on conditions of the Jewish colonies in Palestine [170–75]
9. Adam Rosenberg, report on economic and social conditions in the Jewish colonies in Palestine [175–80]
10. Willy Bambus and Heinrich Löwe, criticism of reports and recommendations concerning conditions in Palestine [180–83]
11. Marcus Ehrenpreis, report on Hebrew language and literature [183–87]
12. Solomon Rosenheck, intervention concerning the legal status of Yiddish in Galicia [187]
13. Hermann Schapira, intervention concerning the establishment of a Hebrew college in Palestine [187–89]
14. Elections to ad hoc committees on literature and colonization [189]
15. Arthur Cohn, Orthodox Rabbi of Basel: remarks [190]
16. Theodor Herzl, concluding remarks, expressions of thanks, acknowledgements, etc. [190–91]
17. Max Mandelstamm, expression of thanks to and acclamation of Theodor Herzl [191–92]
18. Theodor Herzl, adjournment of Congress [192]

As with day two, there are gaps in the record of day three, since the transcript runs to just forty-one pages. At several points, especially during the zigzagging discussion about the Zionist constitution, the stenographer jotted a summary of what was said instead of taking it down verbatim. In the afternoon, an unseemly clash erupted when Nathan Birnbaum, who had been nominated for the Vienna Executive and elected by acclamation, withdrew, allegedly under pressure. There are multiple paraverbal indicators of the tumult and noise generated by this event, and the record is manifestly incomplete at this point. At least three times on the third day, a delegate injected a comment in a language other than German—in Russian, Hebrew, and English—of which we have no precise record. These non-German digressions were generally brief. The one important exception was a denunciation made in Hebrew by a Russian delegate, of the German and Austrian Jews who, in organizing and leading the Congress, had insisted on German rather than Hebrew as the principal medium of communication. A report of this diatribe is found in London's *Jewish Chronicle*, but no hint of it appears in the published proceedings.[210]

However, there are other reasons for the relative brevity of the transcript. The morning session began an hour late, and much time was absorbed by meetings and activities outside the plenary Congress. Thus, at the end of the morning session, there was a break of indeterminate length, to allow the ad hoc committee on organization to decide on nominations to the Vienna Executive, and the various territorial organizations on their nominations to the Zionist General Council. Another ninety-minute break took place in the evening, between half past seven and nine, before the Congress reconvened for its concluding session.

The unfinished business of day two (i.e., agreeing on the constitution and electing officers) consumed the morning of day three. But the afternoon session saw the introduction of two subjects, which, though alluded to on previous days, had not yet been brought under scrutiny. These were the present condition of the Palestine colonies, along with prospects for further economic development; and the revival of Hebrew language and culture, especially through education. The first of these topics was, according to the Congress's published agenda, to have been handled on the day two. The compression that resulted abridged the time available to discuss both subjects, but the discussion of language and education suffered most. It will be recalled that Palestine colonization and Hebrew culture were the two quasi-nationalist endeavors that had preceded Herzl and were accepted as responsibilities of the new Congress-Zionism, but that Herzl regarded them as marginal and diversionary at best, counterproductive and divisive at worst. Relegating them now to the last working session of the Congress seemed to be a sign of their devaluation, at least to some participants. But it may rather have been because of Herzl's consciousness of their extremely sensitive nature that he delayed their presentation.[211] Be that as it may, even the postponed and abridged treatment of these subjects exposed sharp differences of opinion among the Zionists, particularly over how to assess the present condition of the Palestine colonies.

Day three began like day two, with Herzl remarking on the massive volume of incoming communications. We noted previously the high value Herzl placed on declarations of support from rabbis, as well as criticism of his "clericalism." Day three supplies more grist for this mill, since it was framed by communications from two rabbis, one English and the other Swiss. The only written communication Herzl highlights in opening day three was that of Dr. M. Gaster, whom he misnames "Glaser" and mistitles "the chief rabbi of the synagogues congregations of England" (he was head of the small Sephardic community only).[212] Likewise at the end of the day, "the sensation of the evening" came when Herzl called upon Basel's Orthodox rabbi, Dr. Arthur Cohn, to address the Congress just before it adjourned.[213] Dr. Cohn expressed his reservations toward Zionism, because he and other Orthodox rabbis feared that the Zionist leadership, if successful in establishing a state, would attack the Orthodox and make Jews violate the holy law. At the same time, he confessed that he had learned much, especially about the *Ostjuden*, and had been moved by the brilliant speeches and the delegates' enthusiasm. He concluded by appealing to Herzl to reassure him concerning Zionism's respect for the convictions of the Orthodox. Herzl replied with a guarded affirmative.

Nonetheless, Herzl had no intention of ceding any substantive authority to the rabbis, such as had occurred among Hovevei Zion, and the next subject of discussion, regarding the constitution of the Zionist Organization, was informed entirely by secular democratic values.[214] Thus, rabbis did not vote as a class separate from other Jews, and although two rabbis—Isaak Rülf and Samuel Mohilewer— were members of the Zionist General Council, for Germany and Russia respectively, they held no power of veto over Zionist policy-making. To ensure that Congress-Zionism was demarcated from Hibbat Zion in this and other respects, the Congress was given supreme authority over the movement.[215]

The proposal for organization had been referred to an ad hoc committee on day two, and the recommendation of that committee was presented by Heinrich York-Steiner ("Dir. Steiner" in the proceedings), a Viennese journalist who had helped Herzl launch the Zionist weekly, *Die Welt*. Steiner read out the committee's draft, consisting of nine articles, after which there was a motion to approve it by acclamation. This motion was either ignored or rejected; instead, the draft was voted article by article, but, in the case of several articles, only after the consideration of amendments and an allowance of time for questions and debate.[216] Perhaps because there was so much debate, which veered abruptly from topic to topic, often without any explanatory transition—probably another sign of lacunae in our transcript—this section of the proceedings makes for tedious and confusing reading. The delegates had a somewhat similar response to this session, since the *Jewish Chronicle* reported that there were "evident symptoms of weariness." Nonetheless, the session also featured issues of long-term importance, which included (1) defining membership and relations of authority, (2) setting rules of representation and political process, and (3) clarifying the Zionists' relations with other Jewish political groupings. Not surprisingly, divisions appearing during this session augured the emergence of factions based on divergent ideological tendencies.

Defining membership and establishing lines of authority are fundamental to any organization. There was general agreement that the contribution of a small sum of money to the Zionist cause should confer membership, meaning the right to vote; the sum varied in amount from country to country but was everywhere called "the shekel." There was also general agreement that supreme authority belonged to the Congress, but it met for brief periods only and also infrequently (annually at first, less frequently later). Hence the need for the aforementioned bipartite Executive to implement decisions of one Congress and organize the next. In theory, this Executive was elected by and subordinate to the Congress. What was not so clear was the Executive's relationship to the territorial organizations, which was a question of some delicacy. Austria and Russia had laws prohibiting the establishment of international organizations, so defining the territorial organizations as directly subject to the Executive would have led to the suppression of Zionist associations in these empires, where the vast majority of Jews lived.[217] As a result, the Zionist Organization was not, legally, an international body, since constituent territorial organizations remained autonomous, the Vienna Executive having no binding authority over them (a political structure that Hobbes would have found terminally deficient). In fact, even if the draft constitution had made them subject to the Executive, the situation would have been much the same, since the Zionist Organization lacked means of enforcement vis-à-vis constituent groups. Thus, relative to most political parties, where power is concentrated in the leadership regardless of ideology, the Zionist Organization was quite decentralized. This reflected the fact that, like it or not, it had to be built on the foundations of preexisting associations, in particular, of Hovevei Zion. But these centrifugal tendencies were powerfully offset by Herzl's charismatic authority and the inefficient mechanisms by which the General Council related to the Vienna Executive.[218] Moreover, since Herzl usually presided over both the Executive and the Congress, there was a definite conflict of interest that compromised the Congress's supremacy; after his death, these positions were, more properly, separated from one another.[219]

The means of determining representation and authorizing participation in future Congresses were other thorny issues. Participants in the First Congress had come by virtue of Herzl's invitation. But now that an interterritorial organization was being set up that was supposed to be democratic, it was necessary to decide who had the right to vote, how and how many representatives would be elected, and who would be permitted to attend and speak at the Congress. As we have just seen, voting rights were dependent on payment of a shekel, presumably to a local Zionist association. Electing representatives was problematic because Jews could not conduct a public poll like other electorates, and because the Zionist associations were geographically and organizationally disparate. In the end, there was tacit agreement not to scrutinize too closely the means by which delegates were elected. Finally, there was an altercation over the rights of non-representatives to take part in the Congress. The issue here was, according to David Farbstein, of democracy versus plutocracy. Farbstein and other leftist delegates contended that permitting persons without an electoral mandate to vote (perhaps even to speak?) at the Congress, would violate democratic principle, since only well-to-do Zionists could afford to attend without the authorization and funding of territorial associations. Others, notably Max Bodenheimer, urged that the Congress not be "degraded" into a mere assembly of delegates.[220]

The difference between Bodenheimer and Farbstein reflected a difference between, as the *Jewish Chronicle* put it, conservatives and radicals at the Congress. In terms of organization, the conservatives were willing to leave matters of membership and voting vague and trust decisions of the Executive, which was equivalent to conferring a wide-ranging authority on Herzl. Meanwhile, the radicals wanted a strict interpretation of internal democracy written into the articles of organization. Moreover, as proof that the Zionists were not a bourgeois party made up of wealthy gentleman for whom politics was merely a leisure-time activity, they insisted on both a reasonable salary and recognized seat for the secretary-general of the Vienna Executive. Although the differences between the two groups were ultimately bridged, the prospect of the Congress disintegrating into an ideological melee was not to be taken lightly. Indeed, when one speaker declared, "Every Jew who holds to his religion must be a Social Democrat!" Herzl promptly ruled the speaker out of order.[221] It should be recalled here that Germany's Social Democrats, whose party had been illegal until 1890, were still stigmatized by the authorities as dangerous, unpatriotic radicals. Herzl, who consistently sought to induce the German elite to embrace Zionism and who was to meet Kaiser Wilhelm II a little over a year later in Palestine, certainly did not want Zionism identified with such a movement.[222] Moreover, he had acted to preserve unity among the delegates, who adhered to various and conflicting political orientations. At any rate, soon after this intervention, a speaker challenged the Congress's self-conception as a movement of the entire Jewish people—he suggested that the Zionists should recognize that they themselves were really nothing more than another party—and this time it was the delegates who shouted him down.[223] In reality, the Zionist Organization was both: an umbrella movement embracing Jews of many different political and religio-ideological affiliations, but also only one of many activist associations canvassing for support within Jewish communities.

Actually, the controversy over the position of secretary-general cannot be explained solely, or even primarily, as a function of ideology. The deeper implications of that particular argument were laid bare in perhaps the Congress's most heated exchange, one in which "passions were let loose," which posed the most serious threat to Herzl's authority as president.[224] The occasion for this fracas was the election of the five-man Vienna Executive by the plenary Congress, which took place during the afternoon session. The committee on organization, evidently acting as a nominating committee, put forward the names of both Theodor Herzl and Nathan Birnbaum for the Executive, among others; but after the approval of the entire slate by acclamation, Birnbaum declined the position, which triggered an outburst of anger.[225] In Birnbaum's mind, Herzl was an interloper. Herzl detected and reciprocated Birnbaum's hostility from the beginning; and his disdain for Birnbaum was redoubled by the latter's self-pitying letters begging Herzl's financial assistance. Intriguingly, in April 1896, Herzl had actually suggested a secretaryship as a temporary solution to Birnbaum's money problems. Now it appears that Birnbaum's allies at the Congress were pushing Herzl into fulfilling that commitment.[226] In this context, the discussion about the imposition of a secretary-general on the Executive and the necessity of paying him a salary must be read as ill-concealed attempts to reward Birnbaum for his service to the movement and to weaken Herzl's dominance. Thus, when Birnbaum declined a position on the committee because of "pressure"—the implication being that the pressure came from Herzl or his henchmen—it sparked a revolt of the Birnbaum faction against Herzl. The situation was fraught with emotion, and, to their credit, the principals did what they could to avoid a direct clash. Birnbaum did not join in the dispute on the floor of the Congress, and later disavowed the intervention of his partisans in a letter to Herzl; Herzl quite properly recused himself from presiding at this point.[227]

What was the overall significance of this dispute? Externally, there were few differences between Herzl and Birnbaum, at least in 1897. Both were secular Jewish intellectuals, graduates of the University of Vienna, believers in the superiority of the *Westjuden*, advocates of giving priority to political action; apparently they even looked alike.[228] Yet inner differences of experience, personality, and social class outweighed these similarities, and their struggle for supremacy within Zionism foreshadowed larger and longer struggles in the history of the movement. Birnbaum and his friends were examples of the residual resentment of veteran activists toward Herzl's appropriation of "their" movement and his devaluation of their labors. The struggle with Birnbaum revealed the arrogant, irascible, and autocratic side of Herzl's personality. Perhaps most importantly, the clash disclosed a structural bias within the Zionist movement, derived from both its bourgeois values and lack of institutionalized finances. Birnbaum was in a weak position to contend for leadership of the new movement because of his penury, while Herzl was a man of wealth—no Rothschild, to be sure, but still able to draw on a considerable fortune in order to provide for urgent needs and to offer patronage.[229] Recall that Herzl had been reluctant to mobilize "the people," preferring a scheme launched and superintended by Jewish plutocrats; and even the Congress was not really representative of the range of class divisions among Europe's Jews. Yet, as we have also seen, a vocal grouping within the new movement took as their organizational template Germany's Social Democratic Party (SPD). By 1897, the SPD had been in existence for over two decades and was on its way to becoming, both practically and theoretically, the prototype of the modern mass political party. In spite of enormous differences in ideology and social composition, there were some structural similarities between the two movements.[230]

Regional prejudices were also in evidence in the discussion about representation on the Zionist General Council, although a substantial rectification, in favor of the *Ostjuden*, took place as a result of the debate on the floor. Of course, the principle of territorial identity was itself an admission that the Jews were, at best, a nation *within* other nations, and could not be treated as a single constituency. The shift toward greater representation for the *Ostjuden* can be seen by comparing the draft constitution's allocation of seats on this committee with the results of the election to that same committee after it had been enlarged from fifteen to twenty-three.[231] It was perhaps an indication of the leadership's willingness to accord the *Ostjuden* a greater measure of influence in future decision-making, although it should be recalled that the Zionist General Council, like the Vienna Executive, was often ignored by Herzl.[232]

As we noted in our discussion of day two, the organization of a national fund had been mooted by Max Bodenheimer, Jacob Bernstein-Kohan, and Moritz Moses. The organization of this institution was to be the theme of Hermann Schapira's address on day three. The Keren Kayemeth Le-Israel (KKL), or Jewish National Fund (JNF), was founded in 1901, after being approved at the Fifth Zionist Congress; it became the premier institution of Zionist-directed land acquisition and colonization, especially during the Mandate era.[233] But its basic principles—the assumption of a pan-Jewish mandate to collect funds worldwide, ownership vested in the people as a whole, inalienability of properties acquired, and a policy of ethnic exclusivity—were all adumbrated on days two and three of the First Congress.[234] And the second chairman of KKL/JNF, who served in that capacity 1907–1914, was Max Bodenheimer. It was another evidence of the seminal nature of that First Congress, in terms of its ideas, institutions, and personalities. It was also proof of a persistent and troubling exclusion; i.e., the absence of any discussion of *whose* land was to be acquired in the process of making a *Heimstätte* in Palestine.[235]

Schapira's projected national fund was an apt transition to the next set of presentations, which concerned Palestine colonization. The original agenda mentions a report on this subject by Dr. M.T. Schnirer, a former member of the Birnbaum-led fraternity in Vienna (Kadima), now a physician and friend of Herzl, who had helped him organize the Basel Congress. In fact, there were three reports on Palestine: the scheduled one by Schnirer; another by Armand Kaminka, a rabbi and litterateur working in Prague; and another long report, this one by Adam Rosenberg, a German-American lawyer and settlement-activist, who had arrived in Switzerland from Palestine, where he had been living, 1895–1897. There was considerable redundancy in the reports, perhaps important because the data supplied justified a ban on further colonization without legal sanction, which confirmed Herzl's position. Rosenberg's report was especially critical of the past and present management of colonization. His report was promptly challenged by comments from the floor made by Willy Bambus and Heinrich Löwe of Berlin. Löwe, like Rosenberg, had been living in Palestine until quite recently and claimed he had been authorized to represent Palestine's Jews in Basel.

Schnirer, Kaminka, and Rosenberg inveigh in particular against Rothschild's overbearing administration, as it undermines the immigrants' initiative and reproduces the same pattern of dependence found in the older

Halukka system. It should be noted that the problems cited here correspond to those identified by Ahad Ha'am in his 1891 essay, "Truth from Eretz Israel." In brief, the colonies are afflicted by corruption, dependency, and paternalism. The precision of this correspondence adds credence to the accusations; and another report from 1890 confirms them as well.[236] And what of the solutions? Again, our rapporteurs are in overall agreement. First, the imperative need for a legal sanction to continue colonization. Second, a change of values within the colonies, toward the ideal of the yeoman farmer. Ahad Ha'am had taken this point even further, arguing for colonization to be carried out by a spiritual elite, carefully prepared for their task of founding a new Jewish nation; but in either case, there was an acknowledgement that the Palestine community as presently constituted was morally deficient. Third, a structural change that would transfer the management of the colonies away from foreign patrons, whether the Paris Committee of Hovevei Zion established in 1894 or the Rothschild administrations, and the reconstitution of their governance as free, cooperative enterprises. In his final comments to the Congress, Herzl returns to this theme, remarking obliquely on a stream of complaints he has been receiving from colonists and insinuating that reforms are urgent. But Kaminka and Rosenberg go further, advocating large-scale investment in order to expand opportunities for employment, including employment in nonagricultural sectors, for both present colonists and prospective immigrants.

As noted, these reports did not pass without ripostes, made by Willy Bambus and Heinrich Löwe. Bambus was a veteran activist in various Jewish causes; Löwe, like Rosenberg, had been living in Palestine until recently. Bambus and Löwe were close friends; they had led the Hovevei Zion of Berlin and collaborated in the establishment of a Jewish-nationalist society, Jung Israel. They saw Schnirer, Kaminka, and Rosenberg as representing Herzl's essentially negative position toward the present state of the colonies. Bambus and Löwe on the other hand represented a segment of activists that rejected Herzl's dismissive treatment of its labors and continued to lobby for practical efforts to advance Jewish settlement in Palestine. The substance of their protest was that judgments against the agricultural colonies set up in the 1880s and 90s were unfair and premature. While acknowledging mistakes and difficulties, they assert that such schemes require many years to become self-sustaining. Moreover, both men took umbrage at assertions that Hibbat Zion and its Palestine projects were being run inefficiently, undemocratically, and without proper accountability. Bambus rejects Rosenberg's accusation that the Paris Committee, set up in 1894 to coordinate Hovevei Zion in Western Europe, was an oligarchic and unaccountable body; he is angry at what he regards as slander against the character of a committee he had helped set up. Löwe is more subtle but no less scathing in his attack on the rapporteurs and Herzl. His extemporaneous address recalls the Congress's inaugural address by praising "old warriors" (*alte Kämpfer*) without whose efforts "we" would not be in Palestine, thanking Karpel Lippe by name—Lippe, who had preceded Herzl at the rostrum on the first day and delayed his appearance, to Herzl's chagrin. Meanwhile, Löwe pointedly omits Herzl's name when he says that "outsiders" allege that our work is badly managed and that colonization will take hundreds of years if we hold to our current modus operandi.

Even though there were bitter personal and policy differences between Herzl, Schnirer, Kaminka, and Rosenberg on one side, and Bambus and Löwe on the other, there was also common ground. Three areas of agreement stand out. First, they all had a naïve faith that professions of respect for the Sultan and his government would open the way for the issuance of a charter, or permission for immediate further colonization, or both. Second, there was tacit agreement on the need for subsidies to provide employment for Palestine's Jews. The employment crisis in Palestine was already acute, according to Rosenberg and Löwe; it was a problem that would face the immigrants of the Second Aliya a few years hence and would call forth solutions that defied the logic of the local market for labor.[237] Third, in Bambus's rejoinder to Rosenberg, he presumes a prejudice on which all were again tacitly agreed; i.e., that colonization by Ashkenazic Jews was necessary because of the cultural and economic inferiority of the native Jewish population.

Culture—more specifically, language, literature, and education—was the focus of the last set of speeches on the last day of the Congress. As already noted, this subject was last on the agenda not only because of Herzl's lack of interest in it but also because he knew it was potentially explosive. Herzl had noted in his speech of welcome to the delegates that one of Zionism's strengths, especially compared to rival ideological groupings, was its inclusion of both secular and religious Jews. An insistence on secular definitions of culture and education would cause the disaffection of the religious Zionists. So Herzl was probably not at all displeased that, in the evening of August 31, there was time for just one truncated address on Hebrew language and literature, given by Marcus Ehrenpreis, a rabbi working in Croatia but born in Galicia and educated in Germany.

Ehrenpreis's address begins by overstating the unanimity of participants regarding the importance of his subject. It is true that interest in the revival of Hebrew preceded both practical and political Zionism, a phenomenon he interprets as "latent Zionism." However that may be, Zionism is now reciprocating by kindling love of the Hebrew language and its literature in many new places. But Hebrew came first. In his memorable words: "The Jewish people got homesick and began to speak Hebrew." He offers no explanation of this fanciful idea, but the redeployment of a sacred and scholarly language for vernacular uses was certainly significant, perhaps a manifestation of the yearning for an anchor of authenticity amid the dizzying winds of assimilation. As such, the speech was an appropriate conclusion to the Congress, since it echoes and enlarges upon Nordau's diagnosis of the soul-sick *Westjuden*, and resonates with the summons of Ahad Ha'am and Nathan Birnbaum to reengage the classical sources of Judaism in the context of modern culture. Like Ahad Ha'am and Birnbaum, Ehrenpreis couples the revival of Jewish culture with the revival of Jewish nationhood in Palestine. Both are described in terms of a mythic "return"; both represent the struggle for an authentic identity so characteristic of modern nationalisms. Although Ehrenpreis does not take so strong an ideological position himself—he later distanced himself from both the Hebrew revival and Zionism—for many Zionist colonists, speaking Hebrew was integral to their recovery from the "diseased" condition of Diaspora. This antipathy to the traditions of Jewish life in Europe, including Yiddish, is what explains the inseparability of Hebrew and Palestine in the minds of, in particular, the immigrants of the Second Aliya.

Many of these immigrants, seeking to break with the allegedly effete culture of the Diaspora, even rejected the label "Jew" in favor of "Hebrew." For the same reason, they loathed Yiddish, since it was viewed as "weak, exilic, adaptable, compromising," in contrast to the conquering power of the Hebrew tongue. Moreover, unlike Hebrew, Yiddish lacked a historical connection to Eretz Israel. Instead, it was rootless, like the Diaspora Jews who spoke it: "It belonged to no territory, since it was spoken by a parasitic population on territory belonging to other languages."[238]

Ehrenpreis does not engage these explosive issues, although he was obviously aware of them. He regrets that he must address the Congress in German rather than Hebrew, and proposes a system of Hebrew schools to counteract French influence over the Yishuv. Having grown up in Galicia, he certainly knew Yiddish and its importance for the *Ostjuden*. But his interest is not in popular culture; a poet and scholar himself, he is rather concerned about written culture, which is why his proposals have to do with scholarship, newspapers, literature, translation, schools, and a potential university. And, like the orators who inaugurated the Congress—Lippe, Herzl, and Nordau—for the most part he employs a rhetoric of transcendence, which often simply presumes the unity it seeks to establish.

And it was the image of Zionism's unity and gentility that Herzl sought to reinforce in his last substantive comments to the Congress, just before it adjourned late on Tuesday evening. He does so in a variety of ways. As we have seen, he reassures Arthur Cohn and his Orthodox audience that Zionism will respect their religious convictions. In a spirit of tolerance for the partisans of colonization, he registers the existence of grievances among the colonists but, in view of their controversial character, tables them for later discussion by the Zionist Executive. He thanks the people and municipality of Basel for their hospitality, naming the mayor who attended part of the proceedings. He also names and thanks a group he calls "Christian Zionists," for their presence and support. The last group to whom he offers thanks are the Zionists who preceded him, who go unnamed; the clashes on the floor over Birnbaum's position and Bambus's eruption were perhaps too fresh in his mind to say more.

Herzl was too busy to write much about the Congress while it was going on, but he wrote a long entry in his diary a few days later, on September 3, 1897. This entry contains his oft-quoted comment about the Congress, where he asserts that at Basel he "founded the Jewish state." The statement has often been taken as a kind of prophecy, since he also adds, with what seems astonishing prescience, that the state will arise in no less than fifty years; and Israel was indeed established almost exactly fifty years later. But to focus on the interval of time misses the deeper significance of this entry, for Herzl makes here an astute observation about the volitional, forensic, and performative aspects of state-making:

> The essence of a State lies in the will of the people for a State.... A territory is merely the concrete basis; the State itself, when it possesses a territory, still remains something abstract.... At Basel, accordingly, I have created the abstraction.... I gradually worked the people up into the atmosphere of a State and made them feel that they were its National Assembly.[239]

Even though Herzl was not thinking of Hobbes, his conception of the state as the product of collective desire, will, and imagination, was one Hobbes would have recognized. The 1897 Basel Congress was the critical first move toward the making of the Jewish Leviathan.

The Need for an English Translation of the Proceedings

Astonishingly, in the 120 years since the Congress, only two translations of its proceedings have appeared, into Hebrew in 1997 and into French in 2013.[240] Why the century-long delay in translating this seminal text? What accounts for the continuing absence of an English translation until now? While explaining a lacuna is always somewhat speculative, the answers seem to be related to the politics of language, and unwarranted assumptions about the accessibility of this text.

First, it should be remembered that, as the Zionist bridgehead in Palestine expanded, it was Hebrew rather than German which, according to Zionist ideology, mediated the transformation of Jewish character as well as the establishment of a new form of Jewish community. By contrast, from the 1930s onward, German was the primary language through which the alleged racial inferiority of the Jews was enunciated, while the revelation of the Holocaust produced a revulsion amongst many Jews against all things German. These changes may have led to a reluctance to confront the Germanic aspects of the early Zionist movement.[241] Michael Berkowitz remarks on the irony of this development: "It was nearly forgotten that it was the German language that had expressed the Jews' greatest hopes for national liberation even within the fold of Zionism."[242]

A second factor would appear to be a certain scholarly complacency about the accessibility and value of this foundational text.[243] The tacit consensus was perhaps something like this: the most important speeches had been rendered into English; the events of the Congress had been analyzed in the existing historiography, much of it also in English; scholars wishing to know more could consult the German text; what need then of a translation? Ignored was the fact that the speeches previously translated, as just indicated, represent a small proportion of the acts of the Congress; that historians had neglected to analyze, or had treated prejudicially, major speeches and controversies at the Congress—often because of a tendency to adopt Herzl's condescending view of his subordinates and rivals, as expressed in his letters and diaries; that the text contains vast amounts of valuable empirical data, seldom used by scholars, about Jewish communities inside and outside Europe; and that the proceedings bristle with obscure words, phrases, and allusions, which make deciphering their meaning difficult even for scholars with the requisite competencies in language.[244]

In addition, prior to the present work, there was one purportedly complete translation of the proceedings for readers of English, published by Philip Cowen of New York, in 1897.[245] Cowen's text compiles reports previously published in London's *Jewish Chronicle (JC)* [hereinafter *JC/Cowen*]. But despite the subtitle's claim ("The Proceedings in Full"), the book is not a full translation of the proceedings; rather, it is severely abridged. *JC/Cowen* is sixty pages in length, while the German original is two hundred pages. And while *JC/Cowen* supplies illuminating details about the atmosphere at the Congress, it has full translations of only a few speeches, and even these are seriously flawed.[246] Most of what was said is either treated in an extremely cursory fashion or omitted; for example, the theoretically significant addresses of Nathan Birnbaum and David Farbstein are given short shrift.[247] *JC/Cowen* abounds with other problems, and no scholar would judge it to be a full or dependable translation of the proceedings.

One example of the neglect of the rich potential the proceedings hold is the general neglect of the role of Dr. Karpel Lippe in early Zionism. Lippe preceded Herzl on the rostrum as the honorary president and first speaker at the 1897 Congress. (I have offered a translation and commentary on his speech in a previously published article, "'The good Dr. Lippe' and Herzl in Basel, 1897: A translation and analysis of the Zionist Congress's opening speech," which appeared in *The Journal of Israeli History* 34:1 (2015): 1–21. I have amended the translation and notes from that article in the present work, but wish to acknowledge its reuse with permission from *JIH*.)

THE PRESENT TRANSLATION: METHODOLOGICAL AND PRACTICAL CONSIDERATIONS

I have benefited from several books in translation studies that theorize the various aspects of translation; i.e., by drawing attention to the need to (1) identify precisely the genre of a text, (2) examine the background and position of the author(s), (3) remark the sociolinguistic registers present in the text, (4) evaluate the extralinguistic circumstances, and (5) understand the impact of the text on the original audience, in assessing the accuracy and adequacy of potential translations.[248] As this set of criteria indicates, any large-scale project of translation is dauntingly complex, but the issues highlighted here supply an agenda for theorizing a translation of the text at hand.

First, with respect to genre, the proceedings of the Zionist Congress originated as an oral text. But, unlike oral texts of a ritual or imaginative nature, this one has no ongoing performative function.[249] Rather, it is a "frozen" record of plenary addresses, committee reports, general discussions, the reading out of telegrams, etc., produced by many different persons, all of an occasional nature, the whole being unified and structured by parliamentary modalities—hence the employment of parliamentary-procedural jargon in the translation. Also, as is true of most stenographic records, there are errors in transcribing speeches. It has therefore been necessary, for the sake of coherence, to correct apparent errors and inconsistencies; the annotations usually indicate where such corrections have been made, although some are so obvious and minor they have not been considered worthy of a note.

Second, the genre implies that "authorship" of the text is inherently multiple. Indeed, the text gives us mediated access to the voices and views of individuals from various lands, since the Congress assembled Zionists from many parts of Europe and beyond. Yet the multiplicity and diversity of authorship is also mitigated: in its oral expression, by the tacit subordination of the speakers to the antecedent authority of the organizers of the Congress; in its written form, by the presentation of the text as a unified, printed work, in which speeches are distinguished from one another only by date, time, and attribution. Thus, the obvious and cacophonous multivocality of the text does not abrogate its intended underlying unity.

Third, this unity is reinforced by the fact that most speakers addressed the Congress in German. Given the importance of formality to Herzl, as a means of demonstrating the gravity of the Zionist cause, speakers addressing specific themes and rapporteurs presenting the situation of Jews in various countries, were nearly all men with an excellent command of standard German. To be sure, for many participants, German was not their native tongue. Chaim Weizmann, who attended subsequent Congresses, distinguished between the "proper" German spoken by men who had been raised and educated in German-speaking environments, and what he termed *Kongressdeutsch*, a German strongly influenced by Yiddish pronunciations and spoken by, in particular, the Russian delegates.[250] Indeed, as noted in the critical summary, a few speeches and commentary were given in another language entirely. In these cases, the remarks were sometimes rendered into German on the spot, sometimes translated into

German later for the published stenographic record, or, in some cases, never recorded or translated at all.[251] We are dealing here with a linguistic unity both intrinsic to the Congress's organization, but also one that has been imposed, to a certain extent, post facto. The issue is worth noting, but it has only rarely influenced the present translation, since accents of the speakers are seldom accessible in such a printed text. However, the fact that this was only the first in a series of congresses, and that many participants spoke German as a second or third language, should be borne in mind. The terminology in use was not always precise; and many important concepts that were later crucial to Zionist ideology possessed considerable fluidity at this stage.

Fourth, the process of defining terms and settling differences was also conditioned by Jewish history and culture, which introduces extra-Germanic and extralinguistic variables into the text, when for example Hebrew terms are simply transcribed rather than translated. The annotations are intended to alert readers to the nuances evoked in such passages.

Fifth, assessing the verbal impact of these speeches and trying to reproduce it is difficult at this distance in time. Moreover, standard German has undergone considerable semantic and syntactical change in the past century, and the German of the Congress already featured numerous archaisms in diction and orthography. The same changes have occurred in the target language, English. I have tried nonetheless to capture the highflown and convoluted German of the Congress through a somewhat stiff and exalted English. This style, now regarded as stilted, has gone out of fashion in both languages, but there seemed no other way to represent the original German. Of course, the impact these speeches made was to a considerable extent also a result of extra-linguistic factors, and there can be no doubt that the event of the Congress was emotionally powerful, so this style must have seemed to the participants, especially at the time, entirely appropriate.

The plan of the original text divides the proceedings according to time, the days of the conference, and named speakers. The individual sessions thereof form the relevant units; we thus have divisions titled "I. Verhandlungstag. 29. August 1897. Vormittags-Sitzung." And so on. This formatting has been retained in the translation, since recognition of the original sequence in which the speeches and debates took place is essential to understanding them in their internal context. The content of the various days has been studied in detail above ("Critical Summary of the Congress Proceedings"). The original text is also supplied with an eight-page appendix, in which are recorded the names and cities of origin of the associations and individuals who had conveyed petitions or salutations to the Congress.

Zionisten-Congress in Basel
(29., 30. und 31. August 1897)

Offizielles Protokoll

Wien. 1898.
Verlag des Vereines "Erez-Israel"

FIGURE I.10. Title page of the Congress's published proceedings, Vienna, 1898.

In all, I have sought to produce a translation that is both semantically nuanced and historically sensitive. While readily acknowledging my fallibility as both scholar and translator, I offer here a few final observations on methods of interpretation, as well as some specific principles that guide the present translation.

An inherent tension exists in contemporary hermeneutics between "close reading" and "intertextuality."[252] It seems to me that both approaches have value and I have tried to balance them against one another. Thus, my point of departure has been to read each speech inductively (i.e., to allow it to define

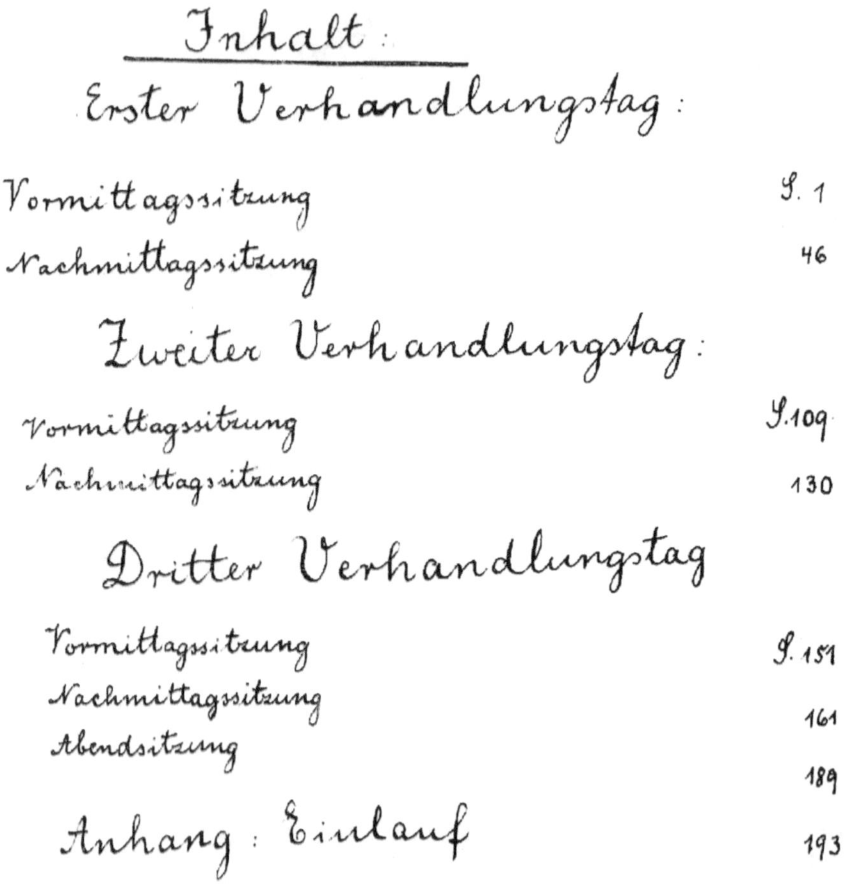

Inhalt:

Erster Verhandlungstag:

Vormittagssitzung — S. 1
Nachmittagssitzung — 46

Zweiter Verhandlungstag:

Vormittagssitzung — S. 109
Nachmittagssitzung — 130

Dritter Verhandlungstag

Vormittagssitzung — S. 151
Nachmittagssitzung — 161
Abendsitzung — 189

Anhang: Einlauf — 193

FIGURE I.11. Contents of the Congress's published proceedings, Vienna, 1898.

its terms, interpret its concepts, and evoke its contexts, by itself). It seems to me that in dealing with any large, intellectually sophisticated, and self-consciously argued source text, an appreciation of intra-textual integrity is foundational. At the most elementary level, this means taking intelligibility and coherence as given. For the purposes of translation, it means comparing keywords, phraseology, idiomatic usages, etc., within a single self-contained unit of text, to establish their connotations, in order to determine the most appropriate equivalents in the target language. So saying, I am aware that in intimating that one should, or even can, determine authorial intention, or that a text is self-contained or fully coherent, I am swimming against the current of rhetorical studies. The theory of intertextuality has heightened our awareness of the thoroughgoing allusiveness of every text. Certainly, I affirm the legitimacy of searching out the conscious and unconscious external dependencies of texts; i.e., how a text emerges "under the jurisdiction of other discourses which impose a universe upon it."[253] One way to apply this insight has been by reading behind and beyond the text. This has meant, among other things, delving into works of Herzl's predecessors; analyzing relevant sections of Herzl's letters and diaries; and exploring articles in the contemporary periodical press, especially journals produced for a Jewish readership. Fortunately, vast quantities of this material are now digitized.[254] To be sure, scholars exploring literature antecedent to or contemporary with the Congress have discovered and will continue to discover a great many connections I have missed.

Nearly all the speeches and comments recorded at the Congress were made by named individuals. While the theory of intertextuality is sometimes enlisted to reduce the salience of authorship, I would argue for the opposite conclusion, especially in a multivocal text like this one. It is precisely because the speaker within the text is an orchestrator of preexisting texts that it is imperative to attend to his specific socio-historical circumstances. In practical terms, this reinforces the need for biographical and bibliographical data; some of these data are compiled in a glossary appended to the translation.[255] An asterisk is used to indicate people and terms included in the glossary.

Dictionaries, both German-German and German-English, have been indispensable.[256] But of far greater utility than any dictionary has been the community of translators active at LEO, the online translation forum sponsored by the University of Munich, to which my debt is enormous.

As for the relationship between the source- and target-texts specific to this work, I have adopted the following as guidelines:

1. Respect for the diction, and the sentence and paragraph divisions, of the source-text, to the greatest extent possible. A conscious effort has been made to avoid an inappropriate modernizing and simplifying of formal spoken nineteenth-century German. The momentousness of the occasion was in the minds of all the participants; a colloquializing translation would misrepresent the self-conscious sobriety pervading the Congress's deliberations. In practice, this has dictated a sentence-by-sentence translation. *Every sentence in the original has its equivalent in the translation.* Comparison of the original with the translation is facilitated by the insertion of a bracketed number (e.g., [24]), indicating the original pagination throughout the translated text. However, because of the unusual length of many German sentences, the page number of the original has been inserted *before* the beginning of the first sentence whose words appear on the page indicated; in some cases, that sentence will have begun on the previous page in the original.

    The reader is alerted to the fact that the original text had footnotes in several places; these have been retained as footnotes, although their numbering (given here in Roman numerals) has been altered. My own annotations to the text appear separately, as endnotes (given here in Arabic numerals). Normal parentheses, ( ), are used when these appear in the original text; in general, the insertions I have made appear rather in square brackets, [ ]. The one important exception to this rule has to do with page numbers, where square brackets are also used, as indicated above.

    In addition, I freely admit that I have found it impossible to maintain consistency with respect to names, especially place names. In general, except for names that have entered into widespread English usage, I have used the Germanic form of names, including personal and place names now perhaps more commonly known in their Slavic forms. But the Congress was held in German, so German forms have been given preference. At the same time, there are multiple exceptions even to this "rule."

    Also, it should be noted that, in order to conform to the stylistic standards of United States publishing with respect to translated works, and SUNY Press house style, some liberties have been taken in deviating from the formatting of the original text.

2. Moreover, at the cost of some awkwardness, I have tried to preserve the text's historical and linguistic distance from present-day anglophone audiences, since the oratory of the Congress reflects the assumptions, values, and consciousness, of fin-de-siècle Europe, in particular of fin-de-siècle German-speaking Central Europe. If this is sometimes a source of confusion, the reader is urged to consult the annotations and glossary. These may help to clarify the host of allusions within the text to European and Ottoman history.

3. At the same time, the German text must be put into a readily intelligible English. An unduly literal translation would also mislead, since it would produce the impression that our speakers were not only pretentious but inarticulate. Hoping that the text will be used not only by scholars but also by students in a variety of fields, I have sought to balance accessibility against authenticity. I leave it to them to judge the measure of my success.

Zionists' Congress in Basel

August 29, 30, and 31, 1897

Official Record of Proceedings

Vienna 1898.
Erez-Israel Society Press.

[1]Day One of the Proceedings
August 29, 1897

Morning Session

Honorary President, Dr. Karl Lippe* (Jassy): About seventeen years ago I received a letter from a Hebrew litterateur by the name of Akiwa Chashmal,* in which he indicated to me that a certain Lazar Rokeah* had come to Romania from Safed in Palestine, in order to agitate for the formation of Jewish colonies in Palestine. Soon thereafter, in a humble room in a suburb in Jassy, I was commissioned to canvass for the same, orally and in writing. There soon arose twenty-seven committees in twenty-seven cities in the country and a central committee in Galata, to whose membership Herr Samuel Pineles* and I belonged. The first two colonies from Romania were the result of this propaganda, Zikhron Ya'akov* and Rosh Pina.* As these colonies were transferred into better hands, our committee ceased to exist. But Herr Pineles and I did not cease to be active in the cause. I was at the conference in Kattowitz,* among whose participants present here today were also, besides myself, Herr Jasinowski* and Herr Moses.*

While that assembly was foundational for Zionist efforts, it represented a mere fraction of Jewry. This Congress represents, on the contrary, the whole of Jewry.

What a mighty leap from that humble room in a Jassy suburb to this hall in Basel, what unanticipated progress from Chashmal and Rokeah to Herzl* and Nordau*!

This assembly of envoys of Jewish societies and of Jews filled with enthusiasm for the cause, is the first of its kind in the eighteen hundred years of the third exile. It is the expression of an international movement taking hold in all ranks of Israel, to bring to fruition a national idea which, during the long period of the exile, the *Golus Edom*,* has been locked up in the bosom of Jewry and struggled in vain toward realization. O what a great and beautiful day this day is in the history of Israel, truly!

[2] The object which is set before us for deliberation is nothing less than the return of the Jews to the land of their fathers, the Holy Land, which our God, the one true God, promised our forefather Abraham to be for us his descendants.[1]

For centuries we have been waiting in vain for a redemption from the hard *Golus* by means of divine, supernatural miracles, and now, tired of the long wait, pressed on all sides by enemies, we want to attempt our redemption in a natural way, in order to return to our ancient fatherland, like our forefathers in Mitzrayim* and Babylon.[2] They also regained possession of the fatherland in the natural way of historical development. After the exodus from Egypt our fathers conquered the land of the patriarchs in the natural way of warfare under Moses, Joshua, the judges and kings. The exiles in Babylon returned on the basis of diplomatic negotiations with Cyrus,* king of the Persians, and an international treaty that is preserved verbatim in our holy scriptures.[3] The prophet Zechariah did promise them a supernatural redemption, when he consoled them with these words: "Your king (the Messiah) will come to you, humbly riding on an ass."[4] But our ancestors did not bide their time waiting for the fulfillment of this promise, but used the first opportunity that offered itself and returned home. The prophet Isaiah did not find it unseemly to bestow the title of Messiah on the Persian king, a pagan Gentile.[5]

We too, like these our ancestors 2509 years ago, want no more to await the ass-rider of Babylon, the Messiah, but want likewise to return on the basis of an international treaty to Eretz Yisrael [the land of Israel].

Our Hasidim, who still await the ass-riding king, may wish to remain in *Golus* and wait for his arrival; but if they permit beggars, idlers, and doddering old men to settle down in the Holy Land and support them with alms, then we cannot be forbidden to dispatch vigorous young people eager to work, who through work and diligence will transform the desolate land into an Eden.[6] And should the humble king really make an appearance in the end, our workers will prepare him a reception more dignified than those spongers.

But we are not at all concealing from ourselves that our position is far more difficult than that of the exiles of Babylon. At the time of the Babylonian exile, both Babylon and Palestine were provinces of the Persian Empire. Zerubbabel, Ezra, and Nehemiah[7] had only to secure the permission of the Persian government for the Jews to remove from one province of their state into another. The task of our immigrants is more difficult. [3] The latter come as foreign nationals requesting admission to a province within the Turkish domains. But in the well-known grace of the reigning Sultan,* convinced of the loyalty of his

Jewish subjects, convinced that Jews bring blessings everywhere they settle, His Majesty the Sultan will not fail to incorporate into his empire a greater number of such diligent civilizing elements.

To the assimilated[8] among us, who do not want to accompany us, who in perverse self-denial renounce the honorable title of "nation" for themselves, and who perceive in the Zionist movement a threat to their citizenship, and who see their salvation entirely in terms of their complete absorption into other nations, we address the words which the Jewish commander used to direct to his soldiers before battle: "Let everyone who is fearful or fainthearted remain at home."[9]

A nation like Israel, which, for three thousand years, even without any compulsory education, tolerated no illiterates in its midst; a nation which even all the powers of hell over the course of millennia could not rob of its national consciousness, still possesses vigor enough to lead an independent national existence and cannot give up on itself.

As a nation, we have a history rich in great deeds and wide of influence; and the first struggle for freedom that world history can point to is the exodus of our fathers from Egypt, with which the history of nations really begins. But the history of Israel is the history of the world-conquering idea. The first well-ordered, humane code of law is the Jewish one.

Our ancient classical literature, known as the Bible, is translated into all civilized and semicivilized languages; it serves hundreds of millions of families as their household devotional book. The priests of all confessions make use of our songs (the Psalms). The Jewish nation lacks only its fatherland to be complete. It is precisely about this that we wish to deliberate. To us, the fear of the assimilated with regard to the colonization of Palestine is unintelligible. How can this colonization be injurious to those fellow tribesmen who remain behind in other nations? Hitherto there are thirty-two Jewish settlements in the Holy Land, and we have not been affected at all by these; the Palestine exhibition in Berlin, Cologne, and Breslau has caused just as little damage. The numerous other energetic and industrious Jewish immigrants to Jerusalem and other cities have done us just as little harm.

But the Congress, yea, the Congress! [4] This Congress is, apart from the specific object to which it addresses itself, nothing other than a public assembly of the nation, to protest against eighteen hundred years of persecution, oppression, and violence, like every minority whose rights have been impaired and injured. While our human rights are curtailed on all sides, shall we give up even that one right that remains to us, the right of complaint? In spite of unspeakable and never-ending injustice we have had to suffer, we Jews have not despaired of humanity, and in the hope that neither anti-Semitism nor misconceived and perversely practiced Christian love has extinguished the public conscience of Europe, we intend to appeal to this conscience. We must lodge our complaint against governments, peoples, and clergy.

For a long time we have believed that we would find our salvation in the Aryan civilization to which we have become attached. But it has betrayed us. As Jeremiah once lamented: "I called my familiar friends and they have betrayed me."[10]

As our ancestors travelled from Egypt, many assimilated persons joined them. But they had not the courage to struggle against a hostile destiny and cried out at the first adversity that confronted them: "Let us appoint for ourselves a leader and return to Mitzrayim."[11] But we cry: "Let us appoint for ourselves a leader and return to Jerusalem."[12] We must escape the brutal and superior forces we face and return to our old homeland, and if our mission among the nations has not yet been fulfilled, we will retrieve whatever is lacking from there.[13]

"For from Zion* alone the teaching will go forth, and the word of God only from Jerusalem."[14] (Loud applause.)

The proposal of Dr. Lippe to dispatch a profession of loyalty and gratitude to the Sultan is accepted without debate by acclamation.[15]

HONORARY PRESIDENT: I yield the floor to Dr. Theodor Herzl for his speech of welcome.

DR. THEODOR HERZL (VIENNA): Honored members of the Congress! As one of the conveners of this Congress, the honor has fallen to me to offer you greetings. I will do it with just a few words, since each one of us should economize with the precious minutes of the Congress if we want to serve the cause. In three days we have much important business to transact. We wish to lay the cornerstone of the house in which the Jewish nation will one day find shelter. What we are about is something so great that we may speak of it only in the simplest terms. So far as can be judged at present, in these three days an overview of the present state of the Jewish question will be provided. A vast amount of material has been divided up amongst our rapporteurs.

We will listen to reports about the situation of Jews in various countries. [5] You all know, if perhaps only in a vague sort of way, that this situation is, with few exceptions, not encouraging. We would scarcely have come together were it otherwise. There has been a long hiatus in our sharing of a common destiny, although the scattered sections of Jewry have had everywhere to endure similar trials. But only in our day, through the miracles of modern communication, has there existed the possibility of understanding and association among those long separated. And in this era, which is otherwise so sublime, we see and feel ourselves everywhere surrounded by the old hatred. Anti-Semitism is the modern name of this movement, which is only too well known to you. The first reaction the Jews of today had to this movement was surprise, which then changed to pain and anger. Our enemies do not perhaps realize how deeply—touching our very souls—they wounded those among us, whom they quite possibly were not primarily seeking to harm. It was precisely modern, educated Jewry, which had outgrown the ghetto and lost the old habits of haggling, that was thrust through to the heart. We can talk about this today without emotion, without anyone suspecting that we are seeking tears of pity from our enemies. We have come to terms with our situation.

For ages, outsiders have been misinformed about us. The feeling of group solidarity, for which we have been so frequently and fiercely reproached, was in the process of complete dissolution when we were attacked by anti-Semitism. The latter has caused it to regain its strength. We have, so to speak, come home. Zionism means a returning home to Jewish identity before the return to the country of the Jews. We sons who have returned find many things in the ancestral home that cry out for improvement; in particular, we have brothers steeped in misery. Yet we have been welcomed in the ancient house because, as is known to all, we do not presume the right to subvert cherished institutions. This will become plain with the development of the Zionist program.

Zionism has already set in train something remarkable, which was thought to be impossible: the close association of the ultramodern and ultraconservative elements of Jewry. That this has occurred without undignified concessions being made, or a sacrifice of intellect being offered by either one or the other party, is further proof, if more proof were required, of the nationhood of the Jews. A union of this kind is possible only upon the basis of a real nationhood.

Disputes are sure to take place about an organization that everyone realizes is a necessity. The way things are organized is the proof of any movement's rationality. But here is a point that cannot be made too clearly or energetically. We Zionists desire, for the solution of the Jewish question, not an international association but merely an international discussion. [6] This distinction is for us of the utmost importance, as I certainly need not explain to you. This fact has also lent legitimacy to the convening of our Congress. We will have nothing to do with intrigues, secret maneuvers, underhanded dealings; ours is a free discussion under the constant and rational scrutiny of public opinion. One of the first positive results of our movement, already discernible in broad outlines, is the conversion of the Jewish question into the Zion question.

A great popular national movement such as this has to be approached from every angle. The Congress will therefore concern itself as well with the intellectual means for the revival and cultivation of Jewish national self-consciousness. Even on this point we have to combat misconceptions. We are not contemplating the surrender of any gains made by modern civilization; rather, we contemplate the further advance of civilization implied by the advance of knowledge.

At any rate, the intellectual vitality of the Jews has always been less of an issue than their physical condition, as you well know. The very practical forerunners of today's Zionist movement realized this when they commenced with the setting-up of a specifically Jewish agriculture. With respect to the experiments in colonization in Palestine and Argentina, we should and shall speak, all of us, with nothing but sincere gratitude. But they are just the first and not the last word of the Zionist movement. The latter must grow if it is to exist at all. A people can only be helped by itself; and if it cannot do that, then it is quite beyond help. We Zionists want to arouse our people to self-help. But premature and unhealthy expectations must not be aroused in the process. Again, for this reason, the public nature of the discussion our Congress aims to have is of great value. Anyone who considers the matter without emotion will have to admit that Zionism can attain its goal in no other way, than by an unconstrained discussion with the relevant political actors. As you know, the difficulties pertaining to the licensing of colonization were not created by Zionism in its present form. One must ask oneself what interest these storytellers really have in such fables. The confidence of the government, with which negotiations over the settlement of the Jewish popular masses on a large scale are desired, can be gained by speaking candidly and acting in good faith. The benefits our people are able to offer as a quid pro quo are so significant that the negotiations from the outset will be endowed with a satisfactory level of seriousness. It would be an idle business to spend much time talking about what sort of legal form the agreement will ultimately take. But one thing ought to be maintained as an inviolable principle: its basis must be a condition of legal right and not tolerance. We have had by now quite enough of the experience of tolerance and living as Jews under the [revocable] "protection" of the state.[16]

[7] Therefore, our movement is just being reasonable when it aims at publicly acknowledged legal guarantees. The colonization conducted thus far has attained everything it could attain given its limitations. It has confirmed the aptitude, so much disputed, of Jews for agricultural work. It has furnished

proof thereof for all time, as one would put it in the language of jurisprudence. But it is not and cannot be in its hitherto existing form, the solution to the Jewish question. In addition, let us admit frankly that it has not met with a very significant response. Why? Because Jews are able to calculate, indeed one might say that they can calculate only too well. If we assume that there are nine million Jews and that colonization were to succeed in settling ten thousand of them annually in Palestine, the solution to the Jewish question would require nine hundred years. It appears unfeasible.

Now you know that the number of ten thousand settlers annually is already unrealistic—that is, under present conditions. With such a number, the Turkish government would immediately revive the former prohibitions on immigration—which would be all right by us.[17] For whoever thinks that the Jews can as it were smuggle themselves into the land of their forefathers, deceives himself or is deceiving others. Nowhere else would the appearance of Jews be so quickly taken notice of as in the historic homeland of the nation, precisely because it is the historic homeland. And it would not be at all in our interest to go there prematurely. The immigration of Jews means an influx of energies of extraordinary intensity for this land that is now so poor, indeed for the entire Ottoman Empire. In addition, His Majesty the Sultan has had only the best experiences with his Jewish subjects, even as he has been to them a kindly sovereign. Thus, conditions exist in which the prudent and positive handling of matters may get us to our goal. The financial assistance the Jews can offer Turkey is not inconsiderable and would serve to remove many internal maladies from which this country suffers.[18] If part of the Eastern question could be solved at the same time as the Jewish question, it would be in the interest of all civilized nations. The settlement of Jews would probably also lead to improved conditions for the Christians in the East.

But not only from this perspective can Zionism count on the sympathy of the nations. They know that controversy about the Jews in many countries has had catastrophic effects on the government. Taking sides for the Jews means having the agitated masses against you. Taking sides against the Jews entails, on account of the Jews' peculiar influence on international commerce, severe economic consequences. Examples of this can be found in Russia. [8] If, finally, the government behaves with neutrality, the Jews will perceive themselves to be without protection in the existing order and hasten to join the radicals. Zionism, the self-help of the Jews, opens a way out of these perplexing difficulties. Zionism is quite simply the peacemaker. And it happens to Zionism as is common to peacemakers: it must do the most fighting. But if, among the more or less honorable arguments against our movement, we are also charged with a defect of patriotism, the judgment against this dubious accusation is self-evident. For what better service can one perform for one's country, than to help in securing the internal peace of its citizens?[19] To be sure, we are not envisioning a complete exodus of Jews from any one place. Those who can or want to be assimilated will remain behind and be absorbed. When, after a proper agreement with the relevant political agents Jewish migration begins in an orderly fashion, for every country the migration will last only as long as that country wants to dispose of its Jews. How is this outflow of Jews going to end? Simply through the ebbing and finally the cessation of anti-Semitism. Thus do we understand and anticipate the solving of the Jewish question.

My colleagues and I have said all of this before. We will spare no pains in repeating it, again and again, until we are understood. On this solemn occasion, on which Jews from so many countries have come together in response to a summons, the ancient summons of the nation, today let our profession of faith be solemnly recited.[20] Do we not have a fleeting presentiment of great events when we realize that the hopes and expectations of many hundreds of thousands of our people are focused at this moment upon our assembly? The news of our deliberations and decisions will race forth in the next hour to distant lands, nay even across the oceans. Therefore, this Congress must emanate reasoned discourse and reassurance. Everyone everywhere is going to learn what Zionism, which has been treated as though it were some kind of chiliastic specter, really is: a morally upright, law-abiding, and humane movement, in pursuit of the goal for which our people yearn. It has been possible and even proper to ignore what individuals among us have written or said—but what the Congress proclaims cannot be thus ignored. Let the Congress therefore, which is henceforth the master of its public debates, manage these debates like a wise master.

Finally, the Congress shall provide for its own continuance, so that we do not take our leave of one another without impact or effect. In this Congress we are creating for the Jewish people an agency they have not hitherto possessed, but which it has needed most urgently for its survival. Our cause is too great to be subject to the ambition and caprice of individual persons. If it is to succeed, it must be elevated to an institutional level. [9] And our Congress will live on eternally, not just until the redemption out of our longstanding misery has been accomplished, but indeed afterwards as well. Today we stand upon the hospitable soil of this free city—but who knows where we will be a year from now?

But wherever we are and no matter how long it takes to complete our work, let our Congress be earnest and sublime, offering blessing to the unfortunate, causing offense to no one, restoring to all Jews their dignity, and making them worthy of a history whose glory, if perhaps now faded, is nonetheless imperishable! (Passionate applause.)

Herr Sam. Pineles was commissioned by the preparatory committee to make the following proposal for the election of officers:

President: Dr. Theodor Herzl
First Vice President: Dr. Max Nordau
Second Vice President: Dr. Abraham Salz*
Third Vice President: Samuel Pineles
Secretaries: Hebrew, Eng. M. Ussishkin;* German, Dr. Schauer;* Russian, V. Temkin;* English, J. de Haas.*
Assessors: Rabb. Dr. M. Ehrenpreis,* Dr. Alexander Mintz,* Dr. M.T. Schnirer,* David Wolffsohn.*

The preceding are hereupon elected by acclamation.
Dr. Herzl assumes the presidency.

PRESIDENT: The influx of communications arriving from every part of the world has been so enormous that the leadership has not yet been able to put them in order. We would like therefore to postpone temporarily this item on the agenda, until a semblance of order has been achieved; therefore we will proceed to the next item: "The general condition of the Jews"; I give the floor to our rapporteur, Herr Dr. Max Nordau.[21]

DR. MAX NORDAU (PARIS): Those presenting specialized reports on individual countries will describe for you in detail the condition of our brothers in these different states. I have been able to consult some of these reports but not others. But even with regard to the countries about which I have received no data from my colleagues, I have some knowledge based partly on my own observation and partly on other sources, enough at any rate to permit me, without presumption, to sketch a general picture of the condition of Jewry at the close of the nineteenth century.

Overall, this picture can be painted in a single hue. Wherever Jews are settled in relatively large numbers among the Gentile peoples, we find the

Jews in distress. It is not the common kind of distress, which is perhaps the unalterable temporal fate of our species. It is a peculiar kind of distress, which the Jews experience not because they are men but because they are Jews, and of which they would be free if they were not Jews.

Jewish distress takes two forms, one material and one moral. In Eastern Europe, North Africa, and Western Asia—that is, in those regions where the overwhelming majority dwells, probably nine-tenths of all Jews—Jewish distress is to be understood quite literally. [10] It is a daily affliction of the body; anxiety about the next day; an agonizing struggle to maintain a bare existence. In Western Europe, the Jews' struggle for existence has become somewhat easier, although recently a tendency has appeared making this struggle once again more difficult even here. But they are tormented less by issues of food, shelter, and physical security. Here, it is a distress of the spirit. It consists in daily offenses against one's self-esteem and sense of dignity. It consists in the harsh repression of their pursuit of higher satisfactions, the striving toward which no Gentile ever need deny himself.

In Russia, whose Jewish population amounts to more than five million and which is home to more than half of all Jews, our brothers are subject to many legal restrictions. Only a numerically insignificant Jewish sect, the Karaites,* enjoy the same rights as the Christian subjects of the Tsar. To the rest of the Jews, residence in much of the country is forbidden.[22] Only certain categories of Jews enjoy freedom of movement (e.g., first-guild merchants, holders of academic titles, etc.).[23] But to belong to the first-guild merchants one has to be rich, which only a few Russian Jews are; likewise, not many Jews in Russia are able to acquire academic titles since government secondary schools and colleges admit Jews only in very limited numbers, and foreign diplomas grant no legal rights. It is forbidden to Jews to enter certain occupations that are open to Russian Christians. These unfortunates are penned up together in a few provincial governorates where there is no opportunity for them to exercise their capabilities and good will.[24] The educational resources of the state are hardly available to them, and they cannot develop their own because they are too poor. Whoever is able to emigrate does so, in order to find in a foreign land the light and air that is denied to him in his homeland. But those who are not young enough or brave enough remain in their misery and deteriorate mentally, morally, and physically.

We hear from Romania, with its quarter-million Jews, that our brothers there also have no legal rights. They are permitted to reside only in the cities, subject to every caprice of the authorities and even of lower officials, exposed from time to time to the bloody violence of the rabble, and are in the worst of economic conditions. Our Romanian rapporteur estimates that half of all Romanian Jews are completely destitute.

The conditions our Galician rapporteur discloses to us are dreadful. According to the information supplied by Herr Dr. Salz, of the 772,000 Jews of Galicia, seventy percent are beggars in the literal sense, beggars by trade, asking charity but of course not receiving it in most cases. I do not wish to anticipate the other details of his report. You should not have to feel twice the revulsion this report will arouse in you.

[11] As for the conditions in Western Austria with its approximately four hundred thousand Jews, the declaration of Herr Dr. Mintz is most telling, that out of twenty-five thousand Jewish households in Vienna, fifteen thousand are completely unable to pay their rates to the autonomous Jewish community on account of poverty. Of the ten thousand ratepayers, ninety percent are assessed at the lowest rate. But even out of this category of lowest ratepayers, three-fourths are incapable of discharging their fiscal obligation. The written law in Austria, unlike that of Russia and Romania, does not recognize a distinction between Jews and Christians. But the public authorities treat the law with a cool indifference, as though it were a dead letter, and popular custom has reestablished the interdiction of Jews that the legislator had suppressed. Social ostracism makes earning a living more difficult for the Jews and will make it quite impossible in the near future in many cases.

From Bulgaria we hear the same plaintive cry: a hypocritical law that recognizes no legal distinction between different confessions, which the authorities however ignore; hostility in all social groups which frightens the Jews away; distress and misery without hope of improvement for the overwhelming majority of Jews.

In Hungary the Jews do not complain. They are in full possession of all the rights of citizens; they are able to work, earn a living, and their economic position is improving. Of course, this happy condition has not yet lasted long enough to make it possible for the majority of Jews to work their way up from deepest poverty, and thus most Jews in Hungary as well have not yet even begun to experience prosperity. Moreover, those familiar with conditions there assure us that even in Hungary Jew-hatred smolders below the surface and will break out with devastating effect at the first opportunity.

I must leave aside the one hundred and fifty thousand Jews of Morocco, and the Jews of Persia, whose numbers are unknown to me. The poorest no longer have strength enough to rise up against their misery. They endure it all in dull resignation without complaining, crying out for our attention only when the rabble invades their ghetto to plunder, rape, and murder them.

The lands I have referred to determine the fate of well over seven million Jews. All of them, with the exception of Hungary, have, by means of restrictions on their legal rights and official or social discrimination, degraded the Jews to the rank of proletarians or professional beggars, without giving them even the hope of raising themselves above this economic position by means of a mighty exertion of individual or collective effort.[25]

[12] Certain "practical" people, who refuse to entertain any "futile dreaming" but direct their efforts to what is readily accessible and achievable,[26] are of the opinion that the lifting of the legally enforced restrictions on civil rights would assuage the misery of Jews in Eastern Europe. Galicia can be summoned as a witness to refute this view. But not just Galicia. The medicine of legal emancipation* has been tried in all states at the highest stage of civilization. Let us consider what the experiment teaches.

The Jews of Western Europe are not subject to any restriction on their rights. They can move about and develop themselves in freedom, just like their Christian compatriots. The economic consequences of this freedom of movement have been, without doubt, most favorable. The racial characteristics of Jews—diligence, perseverance, sobriety, thrift—have brought about a rapid shrinking of the Jewish proletariat, which would have disappeared entirely in some lands had it not been replenished by Jewish immigration from the East. The emancipated Jews of the West are attaining relatively quickly a modicum of prosperity. At any rate, the struggle for daily bread does not assume the dreadful forms that are described to us in reports about Russia, Romania, and Galicia. But among these Jews another kind of Jewish distress arises, of a moral kind.

The Jew of the West has bread, but one does not live by bread alone.[27] The Jew of the West is scarcely ever put in jeopardy of life and limb by mob hatred, but wounds of the flesh are not the only ones that cause pain and from which one may bleed to death. The Jew of the West has interpreted emancipation as real liberation and has hastened to draw the ultimate conclusions that flow from this. But the nations advise him that he errs in being so ingenuously logical. The law is magnanimous in establishing a theory of equal rights. But the praxis of government and society makes a mockery of this theory, like the nomination of Sancho Panza to the splendid position of viceroy of the island of Barataria.[28] The Jew says naïvely: "I am a human being and I deem nothing human as alien to me." The answer comes back to him: "Not so fast! Your humanity must be made use of carefully; you lack the proper conception of honor, sense of duty, morality, love of country, and idealism, and we must therefore exclude you from functions that require these qualities of character."

No one has ever attempted to substantiate these terrible accusations on the basis of facts. At most, now and again the example of an individual Jew, the dregs of his tribe and of humanity, is triumphantly cited, and, against all principles of correct thought and inference, audaciously generalized. However, this generalizing is strongly substantiated from a psychological point of view. It is the habit of human consciousness to invent post facto justifications that sound reasonable, for the prejudices which emotion has evoked. Folk wisdom recognized this psychological law long ago and captured it in its own perceptive way through vivid formulations. [13] "Whoever wants to drown a dog," says the proverb, "first declares him mad."[29] People ascribe every vice to the Jews in order to prove to themselves that they are right to detest them. But what takes precedence in reality is that people detest the Jews.

I must make a grievous declaration: the peoples that emancipated the Jews indulged in self-deception with regard to their feelings. In order for it to produce its full effect, the emancipation should have been accomplished in feeling before being enacted in law. But that was not the case. The opposite was the case. The history of Jewish emancipation is one of the most remarkable chapters in the history of European thought. Jewish emancipation is not the result of a realization that a tribe of people had been severely mistreated, that horrors had been inflicted on them and that it was high time to atone for the injustice of a thousand years; rather, it is solely the result of the rectilinear, geometrical mode of thought of French rationalism in the eighteenth century. Without regard for the emotional life, this rationalism used pure logic to posit principles having the certainty of a mathematical axiom, and then insisted on bringing this structure of pure reason into the world of realities. "Perish the colonies rather than one principle!" as the well-known cry goes, which represents the application of the rationalist method to politics.[30] Jewish emancipation represents another, as it were, automatic application of rationalist method. The philosophy of Rousseau and the Encyclopedists had led to the Declaration of the Rights of Man. From the Declaration of the Rights of Man, the rigid logic of the men of the Great Revolution deduced the notion of Jewish emancipation. They laid out a perfectly proper syllogism: every human being has certain rights by nature; the Jews are human beings; consequently, the Jews have by nature the rights of human beings. And so equality of rights for Jews was proclaimed in France not out of brotherly sentiment toward the Jews but because logic demanded it. Popular emotion may have resisted it, but the philosophy of the revolution commanded that principles be put before feelings. Pardon me the expression, which contains no ingratitude: the men of 1792 emancipated us because of a doctrinaire adherence to principles.

The rest of Western Europe imitated the example of France, likewise not under the pressure of sentiment but rather because civilized peoples felt themselves to be under a kind of moral compulsion to adopt the advances of the Great Revolution. Just as the France of the revolution gave to the world the metric system of weights and measures, so also it created a sort of metric of morality that other countries, whether reluctantly or eagerly, adopted as the standard measure of their position in the scale of civilization. [14] A country that claimed to have an advanced civilization had to possess certain institutions created, endorsed, or developed by the Great Revolution (e.g., popular representation, freedom of the press, trial by jury, division of powers, etc). Now Jewish emancipation was also one of the indispensable institutional furnishings of a highly civilized political household, rather in the way that a piano should not be missing from a proper salon, even if no one in the family could play it. Thus were Jews in Western Europe emancipated, not because of an impulse of the soul but in imitation of a political fashion, not because peoples had decided in their hearts to extend the hand of brotherhood to the Jews, but rather because the leading minds had accepted a certain European ideal of civilization that required among other things that Jewish emancipation should be inscribed in the code of law. There is only one country to which all of the foregoing does not apply. It is England. The progress made by the English people is not imposed from the outside. It is a development from within. In England, Jewish emancipation is a reality. It is not merely something written, it is something lived. It had been accomplished in sentiment long before it was explicitly confirmed by the legislature. Out of respect for tradition, there was in England a certain reluctance to formally abolish legal restrictions on the rights of nonconformists, while the English had already for a full generation made no social distinction between Christians and Jews. Naturally, a great people with an intensely active intellectual life is not unaffected by intellectual currents of the age, including intellectual aberrations, and thus even in England isolated instances of anti-Semitism are to be observed. But anti-Semitism in England is only the aping of a Continental fashion, a costume put on by silly fools out of foppery and conceit, the latest thing from abroad and something to show off with. Overall, you will find the facts and statistics so richly compiled in the report of Mr. de Haas about the situation of Jews in England, to be the most consoling of all the reports submitted to you.

Emancipation has altered completely the character of the Jew and made him into a new creature. The Jew without legal rights in the period before emancipation was a stranger among the peoples, yet he did not think even for a moment about rebelling against this condition. He felt himself to be a member of a special tribe that had nothing in common with the country's other inhabitants. He did not like the yellow patch Jews were compelled to wear on their cloak, because it was an official invitation for the mob to commit brutalities approved in advance by the authorities; yet he freely insisted upon his peculiarity more strongly than any yellow patch could have done. Wherever the authorities did not wall him into a ghetto, he erected one for himself. He wanted to dwell with his own people and to have nothing other than business relations with his Christian neighbors. [15] In the word "ghetto" there are now connotations of disgrace and degradation. The racial psychologist and historian of culture recognize however that the ghetto, whatever the peoples might have intended it to be, was felt by the Jews of the past to be not a prison but a place of refuge. Through an irony of history, it was only the ghetto that made it possible for the Jews to survive the appalling persecutions of the Middle Ages. In the ghetto the Jew had his own world; it was a secure homeland for him, the intellectual and moral equivalent of a fatherland; here were the companions by whom one wished to be and could be valued; here there existed a public whose favorable opinion was the goal of those ambitious for honor, and whose deprecation and displeasure was the punishment for disgraceful conduct; here all qualities that were distinctively Jewish were esteemed, and by their specific development one could gain that admiration which is such a powerful spur to action for the human soul. What did it matter if those things that were prized in the ghetto were scorned by the outside world? The opinion of outsiders did not matter, since it was the opinion of ignorant enemies. He strove to oblige his brothers in religion, and the obliging of these brothers gave a genuine meaning to his life. Thus, from a moral standpoint, ghetto Jews lived a holistic life. Their outward situation was insecure and often in grave danger, but inwardly they achieved an integrated development peculiarly their own, and their lives were not at all fragmented. They were persons of inward harmony, to whom none of the elements of a normal social existence was lacking. They understood intuitively the crucial importance of the ghetto for their inner life, and they had but one concern, to protect its existence by erecting an invisible wall around it that was thicker and higher than the actual stone walls that enclosed it. All Jewish usages and customs were directed unconsciously toward the single purpose of preserving Jewry in a separate existence from the Gentile peoples, to nourish

Jewish communal solidarity, to make the individual Jew feel at all times that he was lost and would perish if he surrendered his peculiar existence. This tendency toward communal separatism was the origin of most of the ritual laws which, for the average Jew, became identical with his understanding of his faith itself; and similarly, other purely external and often adventitious marks of distinctiveness in dress and conduct, once they had become thoroughly established among the Jews, received religious sanction,[31] in order that they be all the more certainly preserved. Caftans, ringlets, fur caps, and Yiddish, obviously have nothing to do with religion. But Jews of the East look askance at the fellow tribesman who dresses in European clothing and speaks any European language properly, as though it were the first step toward apostasy from the faith. [16] For he has cut the bonds between himself and his fellow tribesmen, and these latter feel that these bonds alone guarantee that connection to a community without which the individual is unable to sustain himself in the long run, morally, spiritually, and in the final analysis even materially.

This was the psychology of the ghetto Jew. Then came legal emancipation. The law assured Jews that they were full citizens of the countries in which they were born. The law also exercised a certain influence on those who enacted it, and occasioned, during a honeymoon period, heartfelt expressions by Christians, who interpreted the law in a most encouraging way. Delirious with joy, the Jew hurried at once to burn all his bridges behind him. He now had another homeland, he did not need the ghetto anymore; he had another kind of social connection, so he no longer needed to associate only with his coreligionists. His instinct of self-preservation adapted itself immediately and completely to his new condition. Previously this instinct had been directed toward the strictest separation; now it was striving toward the closest possible association and assimilation. An expedient mimicry took the place of an identity-saving contrariety. Depending on the country, this situation lasted for one or two generations, with surprising success. The Jew could believe that he was really just another German, Frenchman, Italian, etc., like all his other countrymen, and was drawing like them from the same deep spring of national community, in a measure essential to the full development of the individual soul.

Then, after a dormancy of thirty to sixty years, about two decades ago, anti-Semitism in Western Europe broke out afresh, issuing from the depths of the national soul, and disclosed to the eyes of the horrified Jew his real situation, which he had not understood. He could still participate like others in voting for deputies representing the Commons, but he witnessed his own exclusion, whether in polite or crude ways, from the associations and assemblies of his

Christian compatriots. He still had the right to move about freely, but everywhere he ran into signs enjoining him: "No admittance to Jews." He still had the right to carry out the duties of a citizen of the state, but rights that went beyond the basic right to vote, the nobler rights granted to talent and ability, these rights were brusquely denied him.

Such is the current situation of the emancipated Jew in Western Europe. He has given up his specifically Jewish ethos, but the Gentile peoples declare to him that he has not acquired their ethos. He shuns his fellow tribesmen since anti-Semitism has made them odious even to him, but his countrymen reject him when he seeks their company. He has lost his home in the ghetto, and he is denied a home in his native land. He has no ground beneath his feet and no connection with a greater community of which he is an accepted and legitimate member. [17] He cannot depend on a fair, let alone charitable, judgment of his character and achievements from his Christian countrymen, and with his Jewish countrymen he has lost his connection; he has the sense that the world is hostile toward him, and while seeking and yearning for emotional warmth, he sees no place in which to find it.

This is the moral deprivation of Jews, which is more bitter than the physical, because it afflicts persons who are more sophisticated, prouder, and more sensitive. The emancipated Jew is rootless, insecure in his relationship to his neighbors, fearful in his contact with strangers, distrustful of the secret feelings even of his friends. He dissipates his highest powers in the suppressing and annihilating, or at least in the wearisome concealing, of his true self, since he worries that this self might be recognized as Jewish, and he never experiences the satisfaction of acknowledging himself to be what he is, to simply be himself in all his thoughts and feelings, in every sound of his voice, blinking of his eyelids, and play of his fingers. He is inwardly crippled and outwardly artificial; he is thus ever an object of ridicule, repugnant to persons of a nobler, aesthetic temperament, as are all things counterfeit.

All the better Jews of Western Europe groan under this distressing burden and seek rescue and relief. They no longer have that faith which gives the patience to endure sorrows, because they are acknowledged as the providence of a chastening but nonetheless loving God. They no longer have the hope that Messiah is coming and will raise them to glory on a day of miracles. Some seek to save themselves by a flight from Judaism. Of course, racial anti-Semitism, which denies baptism's transforming power, is leaving little prospect for this scheme of redemption. Nor is it a course that commends itself to those we have been discussing, those who are mostly without religious faith—I am of course not talking about the minority of sincere believers—that they should enter the Christian community by means of a blasphemous lie. In any case, this way out produces a new breed of Marranos,* which is far worse than the old one. The medieval Marranos had an idealistic streak, a secret yearning for authenticity consisting in heartbreaking pangs of conscience and regret, and often enough they sought atonement and purification in premeditated, intentional martyrdom. The new Marranos take leave of Judaism with anger and bitterness, but in their heart of hearts, even if unacknowledged by themselves, they also resent Christendom for their own degradation and dishonesty, and the hatred which has forced them to live a lie. I shudder for the future development of this new race of Marranos, who are without the moral moorings of any tradition, whose spirits are poisoned with enmity toward their own people as well as foreigners, whose self-respect has been destroyed by the ever-present consciousness of a fundamental lie. [18] Others expect salvation from Zionism, which to them is not the fulfillment of a mythical promise of scripture but rather the path to an existence in which the Jew will finally find himself in possession of the most basic and primordial conditions for living, which every Gentile, in both worlds, takes for granted—namely, a secure social position, a sympathetic community, the possibility of using all his creative energies in the development of his true self, instead of abusing these powers in a self-destructive suppressing or falsifying or disguising of his identity. Finally, there are others who rebel against the deception of being a Marrano, but who are so intimately bonded to their fatherland that they feel the renunciation inevitably contained in Zionism to be too harsh and cruel—they give themselves over to the most extreme revolutionary activity, with a vague ulterior notion that, with the destruction of the status quo and the construction of a new world, Jew-hatred may perhaps not be among the artifacts salvaged from the ruins of the old system and brought over into the new.

    Such is the portrait of Israel at the close of the nineteenth century. To put it in a word: the Jews are, in their majority, a tribe of ostracized beggars. More industrious and resourceful than the average European, to say nothing of indolent Asiatics and Africans, the Jew is condemned to the worst misery of the proletarian, because he is not permitted to make free use of his energies. [His poverty grinds down his character and destroys his body.][32] Animated by an overmastering hunger, nay a ravenous appetite for education, he sees himself repulsed from those places where knowledge is to be had—a man like the mythological Tantalus with respect to education, in this unmythological age of ours. Endowed with a tremendous impulse whose force propels him again and again up from the miry depths into which those around him have sunk him and sought to bury him, he smashes his skull against the thick ice sheet of hatred and contempt that has been spread out over his head. A social being unlike almost any other, a social being whose faith even commends to him as actions most meritorious and pleasing to God, for three to be gathered together in order to eat and ten in order to pray—he is excluded from the normal social existence of his countrymen and condemned to a tragic solitude. He is accused of aggressive self-promotion, but he strives for superiority only because people deny him equality. He is reproached for his emotional solidarity with Jews throughout the world, but his real misfortune is that he uprooted the last trace of Jewish solidarity from his heart at the first positive word about emancipation, to make room for an exclusive love of his compatriots. [19] Stunned by the hail of anti-Semitic accusations, he begins to doubt himself and almost comes round to thinking of himself as the physical and spiritual monster that his mortal enemies make him out to be. He can often be heard muttering, that he must learn from his enemies and try to cure himself of the deficiencies he is upbraided for, not taking into consideration that these anti-Semitic accusations are utterly useless and worthless to him, since they are not the criticism of deficiencies actually observed but rather the effects of a psychological law, according to which children, savages, and malicious fools make certain creatures and things responsible for their troubles and then feel antipathy toward them. At the time of the Black Death, Jews were accused of well-poisoning; today, farmers accuse them of lowering the price of grain; craftsmen accuse them of wiping out small businesses; conservatives charge them with being anarchists. Where there are no Jews, other commonly despised groups within the population are designated as the source of these grievances— usually foreigners, but sometimes indigenous minorities, sects, or societies. The anthropomorphizing of aversions proves nothing against those who are accused, it proves only that their accusers already hated them when they [the accusers] began to suffer and looked around for a scapegoat.

This picture would not be complete without my adding one more feature. A myth in which even serious and educated persons believe, who need not even be anti-Semites, alleges that the Jews have all power and authority, that the Jews possess all the wealth of the earth. These Jews, these sinister manipulators of authority, who do not even have the power to protect their fellow tribesmen against the bloodlust of miserable mobs of Arabs, Moroccans, and Persians! These Jews, the incarnation of Mammon, of whom well above half do not own a stone on which to lay their heads, or rags with which to cover the nakedness of their bodies! This is the scorn that enters in and drips poison into wounds already inflicted by hatred. To be sure, there are several hundred super-rich Jews, whose clamorous millions are noticed far and wide. But what do these people have in common with Israel? Most of them—I readily make exception for a minority—belong to the most vulgar stratum within Jewry, and a process of natural selection has fitted them for occupations in which one can quickly earn millions and sometimes billions—but don't ask me how! In a normal and fully integrated Jewish society such persons would, on account of their inborn character, occupy the very lowest rung in the esteem of the nation, and certainly would never receive the titles of nobility and high honors which Christian society bestows on them. The Judaism of the prophets and Tannaim,* the Judaism of Hillel,* Philo,* Ibn Gabirol,* Judah Halevi,*[33] Maimonides,* Spinoza,* Heine,* knows nothing of these men, who like to flaunt their money, who devalue what we revere and cherish what we disdain. [20] These people are the main pretext for the new Jew-hatred, which has more of an economic than a religious basis. For Jewry, which suffers on their account, they have never done anything besides throw to it some charity, which is no sacrifice for them, and they have nourished the continuance of a chronic condition peculiar to the Jews: parasitism. For idealistic causes their assistance has never been available and probably never will be. Many of these types actually leave Judaism behind, so we wish them well on their journey and only lament the fact that they are after all of Jewish blood, albeit of its dregs.

No one can be indifferent to Jewish distress, the Christian nations no less than we Jews. It is a great sin to allow a tribe, whose talents even their worst enemies have not denied, to descend to spiritual and physical distress; it is a sin against the tribe and a sin against the building-up of civilization, in which the Jewish tribe wishes to be, and is able to be, a not insignificant collaborator. And it may turn out to be a great danger to the nations to embitter strong-willed persons by unjust treatment, whose capacity for good as well as evil is above the average, thus making them enemies of the established order. Microbiology teaches us that tiny life-forms that are harmless as long as they live in the open air, turn into frightful agents of disease when deprived of oxygen, when they are, to put it in scientific terms, changed into their anaerobic forms. Governments and peoples should think twice before making the Jew an anaerobic life-form! There might be severe repercussions for themselves and others, no matter what actions they then took in order to eradicate the noxious creature the Jew shall have become by their own fault.[34]

That Jewish distress cries out for remedy we have seen. To find the remedy will be the great task of this Congress. I yield the floor now to my fellow rapporteurs, who will amplify and complete the picture I have sketched in broad outlines, and you will have the feeling, as you hear their presentations, that you are listening to Kinnot.* (Passionate, enthusiastic assent.)

PRESIDENT: Herr Architect Oscar Marmorek* has the floor.

OSCAR MARMOREK: Dear brothers! Today is an extraordinary day, extraordinary for a people that has not spoken out for eighteen centuries and that has now sent representatives from all over the world to this place to deliberate concerning itself. Had this Congress been comprised of nothing but these two speeches, which have been received with such great applause, it would have been well worth holding it.

Dear brothers! The words we have heard here will never be lost to the history of human civilization nor the history of Jewry. We will never be able to forget what we have heard as long as we live, nor should we. But we should not be the only ones to have heard it. It should also be read. All should know what we are, what we want, and what we want to do. [21] We will hear yet other reports, besides that of Herr Dr. Nordau, which will delineate for us the dismal situation of the Jews. But I think I speak for everyone when I propose that the two addresses heard thus far be made into a special publication. And before we proceed any further with our business, we will be fulfilling an important obligation when we express our heartfelt thanks to Herr Dr. Herzl and Herr Dr. Nordau for what they have offered to us thus far. (Tremendous applause.)

PRESIDENT: It has already been decided to publish the complete stenographic proceedings. I do not think issuing a special publication of the two speeches is at all advisable, since we would thereby be slighting the other speakers whose reports we have not yet listened to; nevertheless, I will bring Marmorek's motion to a vote. I am not inclined to permit further discussion. Those gentlemen who are in favor of the proposed publication will raise their hands. (The motion is adopted unanimously.)

Pause.

PRESIDENT: Some amendments to Marmorek's motion have been indicated; however, since they have to do with purely technical issues of putting the decision into effect, I think you will accept to leave the definitive handling of this matter to the Congress's committee; I would like to ask you from now on to put into writing all motions which are made, to be delivered to me or another elected officer.

I now give the floor to the rapporteur on the situation of the Jews in Galicia, Herr Dr. Salz:

DR. A. SALZ (TARNÓW): The first section of my report will concern itself with the intellectual, moral, and political aspects of the situation of the Jews of Galicia:

Galicia, inhabited in its western parts by Poles and in its eastern parts by Ruthenians, and whose inhabitants are culturally and economically backward vis-à-vis the Western lands of Europe for historical reasons that will not be discussed here, is similar to other lands in Eastern Europe in which the Jews have sojourned for centuries, in that there is a specifically Jewish-Galician identity, an identity that has been the cause of much lively discussion, but which has also far too often been used quite unjustifiably as the object of the most severe attacks. His unusual dress, his distinctive Jewish-German dialect, which was brought with him from his sojourn in southern Germany and tenaciously retained on account of an oft-misunderstood conservatism—these things have erected a wall of division between him and his Western tribal brothers, which makes mutual understanding significantly more difficult. Yet, beneath these externals, the Galician Jews have retained a warm Jewish heart, which requires only the slightest stimulus to cause it to blaze up and burn once again for the welfare of Jewry. [22] I said "once again" because Galician Jews have not been at their present stage of civilization and in their present state of apathy for very long. As late as the first half of our century, Galicia was the center of Jewish learning and Jewish communal life. Erter,* Krochmal,* and Rapoport,* were writing and working at that time in Galicia.[35]

But the onset of assimilation, which began to work its mischief in the second half of our century, unfortunately caused a change of direction, since, as a result of it, a section of Galician Jews became estranged from the Jewish way of life without being inducted into a better culture, whereas the other, overwhelmingly greater section of the population, the Orthodox-Hasidic, stringently isolated themselves and became ossified into a sanctimonious formalism.

Until recently, these two camps, the assimilated Jews with their indifference to all things Jewish and the Hasidim with their exclusivity, have stood harshly opposed to one another—however, the ever increasing anti-Semitism on the one hand and the unifying bond of the Zion idea on the other, are gradually beginning to bring the discerning men from both camps nearer to one another and to mitigate their harshly contradictory positions.

The general level of education of Galician Jews differs but little from that of the rest of the Jews of Eastern Europe, even though it must also be admitted that, given the legally guaranteed freedom enjoyed by the Jews of Austria, the Galician Jews have neglected to do many things they could and should have done to raise their level of education.

Nevertheless, the Galician Jews have, in relation to the indigenous population, a significantly lower number of illiterates, and, when we consider that every progressive Jew now sends his child to public school and every conservative has his children acquire the skills of reading and writing in the Heder (i.e., the Hebrew school), one cannot really speak at all about truly illiterate persons among the Galician Jewish youth. I take the opportunity now to cite some statistical data about the attendance of Galician Jews at public schools at the secondary level. Unfortunately, we do not have data about the number of Jewish children in *Volksschulen*.[36]

In the Galician *Gymnasien*,[37] the Jewish pupils amounted to: in 1877, 15½ percent of the total number of pupils; in 1890, 18½ percent. In the *Realschulen*,[38] they amounted to: in 1877, 19 percent of the total number of pupils; in 1890, 14½ percent.

[23] In the teacher training institutes, they amounted to: in 1875, 0.24 percent (1 Jew); in 1880, 6 percent of the male students (fifty-eight students); and 13 percent of the females (ninety-four students); in 1890, 3 percent of the males (twenty-seven students) and 8 percent of the females (forty-five students).

The decrease may be explained by the fact that Jews are now not permitted to hold public teaching positions at all, except to offer instruction in the Jewish religion.

In the trade schools there were, in 1882, thirty-nine Jews studying among 1,325 Christians, and in 1886, 294 Jews among 2,015 Christians. At Lemberg University, in 1871, 7.2 percent of all students were Jews; in 1880, 9.4 percent; and in 1890, 20 percent. At the technical college in Lemberg, in 1894, there were twenty-five Jews studying among 254 Christians; in 1895, twenty-one Jews among 248 Christians; and in 1896, thirty-one Jews among 324 Christians.

In order to pass judgment against the much-maligned moral character of the Galician Jews, their foes cleverly omit to put this issue in its proper light.

I do not wish to conceal the fact that crime statistics concerning Galician Jews show that they account for a more substantial proportion of offenses arising from greed, than the indigenous population. It cannot be overemphasized, however, that due to the utterly negligible proportion of Jews committing other kinds of offenses, any "surplus" in the former category is entirely offset, and that the Jews' exclusive concern with commerce is what fosters this kind of offense.

With regard to politics, the Jews of Galicia play a quite deplorable role, inasmuch as they act as stooges for the Polish *szlachta*,[39] who oppress the other classes of society; they obtain thereby the "right" to be efficiently plundered by Masovian railway and mine laborers, who are thus incited against them.

Events in Chodorow, Schodnica, and the atrocities committed by soldiers in Tarnów, were the well-earned "reward" for the subservience which the Jews of Galicia practiced toward the government and the Polish *szlachta* in the last elections, with astonishing disregard for their own basic interests.

[24] However, the most detestable corruption and the worst despotism are fostered in the Jewish communities of Galicia, and if some political good sense and nobility of character are to be awakened among the Jews of Galicia, of which there are some hopeful signs, the struggle for reform will have to begin in the individual community, the key to the Galician general elections.[40]

I come now to the second section of my report, to the discussion of the economic situation of the Jews of Galicia. In this, I am beholden to the following sources: A. Korkis: *Statistische Daten* [Statistical Data] (manuscripts); Rutowski: *Jahrbücher für die Statistik Galiziens* [Statistical Annual of Galicia], Lemberg, 1887, 1893, 1894; *Rundfrage an die Bezirksausschüsse, israelitischen Cultusgemeindevorstände und Privatpersonen über die wirtschaftliche Lage der Juden Galiziens von Seiten des Hilfscomités für die nothleidende galizische Judenschaft* [A survey of district committees, Jewish community councils, and private individuals, concerning the economic situation of the Jews of Galicia, done by the Committee to Aid Impoverished Galician Jews], (President, Dr. Arnold de Porada Rappaport; Secretary, Hermann Feldstein, 1895); Pilat: *Statistische Mittheilungen des statistischen Landesbureaus* [Statistical Reports of the Provincial Office of Statistics], 1895; *Jahresberichte der k.k. Lemberger Universität* [Annual Reports of the Imperial Austrian University of Lemberg]; *Jahresberichte der technischen Hochschule in Lemberg* [Annual Reports of the Technical College in Lemberg]; E. Kietz: *Statistische Monatschrift* [Statistical Monthly], 1883; Dr. Alfred Nossig: "Socialhygiene der Juden" ["Social hygiene of the Jews"] (page 134), and also "Materialen zur Statistik des jüdischen Stammes" [Sources for Statistics of the Jewish Tribe] and "Versuch einer Lösung der jüdischen Frage" [An Attempt at Solving the Jewish Question].

Galicia belongs to those lands of Eastern Europe where the Jews are most densely distributed.

Upon a surface area of 78,497 km² and among an overall population of 6,529,626 souls—but with the vast majority of them packed into the cities and towns—there live in Galicia, according to the 1890 census, 772,213 Jews. While we have in Galicia no Pale of Settlement* as in Russia, and Jews in Galicia are permitted by Austrian law to settle anywhere, actual conditions have had the effect of assigning the Jews to the cities and towns as their places of residence. Around 71 percent of the total Jewish population of Galicia live in the cities and towns of Galicia, reaching a figure of 60 percent or more of the total population in several of these cities, whereas they constitute on average 38.4 percent of the total urban population of Galicia.

The remaining section of the Jewish population consists of scattered individual families or clusters of families in the rural areas, they constitute scarcely 3.28 percent of the total rural population.

Among the rural Jewish population there are 630 registered Jewish landowners, a very small fraction of small independent cultivators, tenant farmers, and mill owners, the rest of the rural inhabitants being, notwithstanding their residing in the country, haberdashers, innkeepers, employees, and laborers.

Thus, the core of the Jewish population of Galicia is found in the cities.

[25] The disinclination of the Jewish population to become landowners is a logical consequence of actual conditions and exists despite the fact that since 1867 the law in Austria has permitted freedom of movement.

On the one hand, while the Jews themselves acquired a sort of aversion to the practice of agriculture and became habituated to commerce and shopkeeping during the many centuries when there were legal constraints on their ownership of land, they are now, after the removal of legal constraints, still deterred from settling in the countryside by the animus of the indigenous rural population and by the chicanery of the autonomous communities and district administrations.

The consistent rejection of Jewish students applying to the two existing Galician agricultural schools and to the horticultural schools, which are nonetheless maintained by Jewish tax revenues, is not atypical.

The Poles and Ruthenians covet every foot of soil, and a storm of indignation is raised by the newspapers whenever they are made aware of the fact that a Jew has acquired a sizeable tract of land.

When the Podhajce property was purchased by a Lemberg Jew some years ago, such agitation seized both the provincial press and a wide swath of the population, that the Jew revoked the purchase as quickly as possible.

Under such conditions, the bulk of Galician Jews have of necessity taken up residence in the cities and market towns. The 70 percent of all Galician Jews who, crammed into the cities, manage to eke out a living, are thereby forced to apply themselves to handicrafts and commerce, due to their lack of access to other lines of work.

Since Austria does not keep occupational statistics, we lack precise data about the distribution of the urban occupations among the Jews and the ratio of Jews to Christians working in the same occupation; from the following summary it may, however, be possible to form an approximate idea of the situation of this, the main component of the Galician Jewish population.

Of the so-called free professions, only the professions of attorney and physician are open to the Jews of Galicia, while the other free professions, above all civil service, are for now almost entirely out of reach. [26] Until several years ago, when the number of positions open in the railway, postal, and telegraph services was greater than the number of Christian candidates, the Jews were able, at least in this branch of government administration, to find acceptance and promotion into at least the lowest ranks of the service; however, since for some time now this shortage in qualified Christians for positions in public service has ceased, a rollback of the Jewish element even in this sector has become quite noticeable.

The situation has come to the point where applicants competing for even a lowly position in the state or provincial administrations are quite often frankly advised that their application is being rejected solely on account of their religious affiliation.

As far as big business is concerned, Jews are in fact looking to be active in this sector, but since this province is capital-poor and lacks an ethos of entrepreneurship, big industry has not really advanced at all and is still very much in its infancy; therefore, the proportion of Jewish capitalists in this sector is also very low.

The majority of Jewish city-dwellers are therefore divided into craftsmen, merchants, shopkeepers, agents, brokers, tavern-keepers, casual laborers, and beggars.

On the basis of a survey of the economic circumstances of the Jews, which was conducted several years ago by the Hilfscomité für die nothleidende galizische Judenschaft [Committee to Aid Impoverished Galician Jews], an organization set up by a representative in the Austrian parliament, Dr. Rappaport, we are able to gain an approximate idea of the situation and the distribution of the individual occupational groups.

This survey obtained statistical data from only 126 localities.

In this region of just 126 localities live forty-five thousand Jewish merchants, shopkeepers, and agents, fourteen thousand craftsmen,[41] twelve thousand Jewish tavern-keepers, thirty-six thousand Jews who are casual laborers, and thirty-eight thousand Jews who depend on public charity.

Since the thirty-six thousand Jews who are casual laborers are rather to be counted among the unemployed than to be considered as those classified as having a certain occupation, the distressing picture emerges that, among 145,000 Jews, seventy-four thousand are found to be either unemployed or are outright beggars.

[27] And if one considers that, in the answers to the survey mentioned above, all of the fourteen thousand craftsmen, twelve thousand innkeepers, and forty-five thousand merchants are registered euphemistically under these rubrics, whereas anyone who has stayed in a small town in Galicia will certainly realize after only a brief observation that nearly half of these so-called craftsmen are wretched jobbers, half of the tavern-keepers are utterly destitute persons, and nearly half of the so-called merchants are essentially impoverished peddlers and degenerate village hawkers, then we do not err but are fully warranted in our asserting that, of the 145,000 Jews residing in the 126 named Galician localities, scarcely thirty-five to forty thousand find themselves in more or less decent material circumstances and are capable of attaining or surpassing the basic Galician "Standard of life,"[42] whereas the remaining Jews, numbering circa one hundred thousand are either already beggars or are well on the way to beggary.

The situation of the Jews in all the other localities in Galicia is similar to that of these 126 localities.

This is the material condition, rather the condition of material distress, of the Jewish city-dwellers of Galicia.

And there is no prospect for improvement at the moment and for the near future, on the contrary there are several signs which give us every reason to believe that the Jews of Galicia are facing a very severe and unrelenting competitive struggle, a struggle in which the Jews, as the weaker party, will of necessity succumb.

The indigenous population, which until now has stood aloof from commerce and has competed with the Jews only in the handicraft sector, has in recent decades not only given up its aversion to the vocation of commerce but has also begun an organized struggle to dispossess the Jewish commercial class.

This movement is being underwritten in the most energetic way, materially, by the provincial government and the most noteworthy provincial credit institutions, and morally, by means of anti-Jewish agitation by the clergy.

With the aid of Jewish tax revenues, societies are everywhere being founded, so-called Kólka rolnizce [agrarian centers], whose goal is to open "Christian retail stores" (sklepiki chrzescianskie) in the cities and villages of Galicia, in order to steal customers from Jewish merchants and even to force them into beggary or emigration.

Until now, around 2,600 Christian retail stores have been set up in this manner, with their number constantly on the increase; they have already destroyed thousands of Jewish livelihoods.

The Ruthenians too have taken the same path, even if they are not being underwritten by the provincial authorities and depend solely on their national societies for financing.

This systematically organized struggle to displace the Jewish commercial class finds its most powerful support in the currently predominant trend of Austrian legislation.

This legislation, with its laws concerning the observance of Sunday, laws concerning peddling, tax rates, and many other laws—bear the indisputable stamp of Christian-Socialist reforms and are aimed, directly or indirectly, consciously or unconsciously, against small Jewish merchants and shopkeepers.

However, those who suffer most under these laws are the Jewish middlemen of Galicia, who are hit worst by the restrictions of these Christian-Socialist reforms and who are slowly but steadily approaching material ruin.

[28] Thus the Jews of Galicia are now being deprived even of the vocation of trade, which until several centuries ago they held almost exclusively, and from which they were able to draw an income that was, if not luxurious, at least halfway tolerable.

No one should be surprised, therefore, that under such circumstances, where it is impossible for them to practice agriculture, they are forbidden to enter the civil service, and applying themselves to commerce is becoming difficult, the proletarianization and degeneration of the Jewish masses of Galicia is proceeding apace, and the emigration of the Jews is assuming ever-greater dimensions.

We have no precise statistical data concerning the full extent of Jewish emigration from Galicia, however it has been established on the basis of an approximate calculation that in the decade 1880–1890 forty-four thousand Jews took leave of Galicia.

This stream of emigration is flowing mainly towards Lower Austria (Vienna), England, America, Germany, Hungary, etc., where it jeopardizes the already weakened economic position of the Jews living there, and also nourishes the preexisting or nascent anti-Semitism in those same places.

The great and acute Jewish problem of Galicia, with its unfathomable mass misery, with its bleakness and despair—this problem has a significance not to be underestimated, not only for the Galician Jews but also for the entirety of Western Jewry.

The precarious position of the 772,000 Jews of Galicia, which cries out for immediate remedy, has an intimate and at present inescapably interdependent relationship with the position of Jews in Western countries; and if the latter, without regard for their momentarily better and more fortunate situation, seek a constructive and radical solution to the Jewish question in general, and extend a helping hand to the specifically Galician Jewish problem in particular, they will be acting not only in the interest of the entire Jewish nation but also, to no inconsiderable extent, in their own most fundamental interest as well. (Loud applause.)

PRESIDENT: The editor, Herr J. de Haas, has the floor for a report on the situation of the Jews in England.

JACOB DE HAAS (LONDON, SPEAKING IN ENGLISH): A variety of factors combine to make it impossible to offer a thoroughly precise survey of the situation of Jews in Great Britain and Ireland. First, no confessional census takes place, which permits only conjectures about numbers; second, the Jewish community has no central bureau where numbers could be collected and collated. Third, the majority of Jewish charities publish no reports or statistical tables on the basis of which a survey could be drawn up. [29] The majority of the statistics offered in this summary (except for references to commercial companies and so-called mutual profit associations[43]) are drawn from Josef Jacob's 1896/7 annual, emended or amplified by my personal knowledge of the conditions of the English Jewish community.

The English Jewish community was established in London when Sephardic Jews were granted readmission to the country. At that time,

Menasseh Ben Israel* and Antonio Carvajal* stood at the head of the community, the latter having acquired residency in the previous, Cromwellian period. The Sephardic element did not, however, grow numerically. Rather, it was German and Dutch merchants who strengthened the Jewish community in the seventeenth century. But it was only the political unrest on the Continent, which began at the end of the eighteenth century and continued into the first half of our century, that brought a great mass of Jews to English shores; these gradually settled in the commercial centers of the English provinces and the capital cities of Scotland and Ireland. Finally, the Russian persecutions of the year 1880 resulted in a wave of immigration that, without doubt, doubled the Jewish population of the British Isles in one decade.

Because the author of the aforementioned annual bases his figures on the theory that Jewish weddings number ten per thousand while deaths are twenty-five per thousand, he infers the following:

Table 1.1. **Estimates of the Jewish population, Britain and Ireland, 1897.**

London	64,280
Wales and the English provinces	33,070
Scotland	2,060
Ireland	1,779
Total	101,189 Jews

On the basis of the compilation of the lists of members of synagogues, various companies, commercial associations, etc., it is possible to make a certain correction to these figures; at any rate, I for myself will avoid all theorizing and say simply that 150,000 might be the correct estimate.

According their country of origin, there are the following groups of Jews in Great Britain:

TABLE 1.2. **Provenance of Jews in Great Britain, ca. 1897.**

Natives	approximately 20%
German	approximately 7%
Dutch	approximately 5%
Russo-Polish	approximately 58%
Other foreigners	approximately 10%
Total	100 %

Religious conditions: the English Jewish community is divided into three sections: a) Orthodox Ashkenazim; b) Sephardim; c) Reform.

[30] a) There exists a distinction between the Orthodoxy of the indigenous and the foreign Jews. In theory, all Jewish congregations of the "United Kingdoms" (categories b and c excepted) as well as those in every part of the British Empire, are under the spiritual authority of the Chief Rabbi of the United [Hebrew] Congregations.[44]

There is no consistory or rabbinical council, although a conference of religious functionaries may be convened by the Chief Rabbi to discuss issues of ritual law, but the decision of the conference is again reserved solely to the Chief Rabbi, who must be Orthodox.

Unity within Great Britain is maintained by means of the establishment of local chaplaincies, yet it must be emphasized: 1. that the stipend of the Chief Rabbi is defrayed almost entirely by the "United Synagogue"; 2. that in London as well as in the provinces, individual congregations are under the jurisdiction of their rabbis.

Religious administration is being displaced to a large extent by a financial superintendancy. In London, the thirteen largest synagogues constitute, from a financial standpoint, the "United Synagogue."[45] On account of the mutual advantages to be gained, the smaller synagogues have united similarly into a "Federation of Smaller Synagogues."[46] No such organization exists in the provinces and every congregation must take care of its own needs.

The English-speaking religious functionaries of the congregations (only a few are actual rabbis) have been trained in Jewish and Aryan colleges. The cantors and slaughterers are foreigners. Not every congregation is able to employ so many officeholders, therefore it often happens that one and the same person fills all of these offices. Matters such as Shechita* are managed by a financial committee of laymen while religious problems are handled by Dr. Adler,* Dayan Spiers,* and Dr. Gaster.*

The Sephardic community has three synagogues in London and one in Manchester, and maintains independent communal institutions out of its own means.

There are three Reform synagogues in England, in London, Manchester, and Bradford, which are connected only by the ideas they hold in common.

The government subsidizes neither the synagogues nor the functionaries.

The religious education of children is provided for in six ways: 1. by means of parochial schools; 2. religious education classes in association with boarding schools; 3. religious education classes in association with synagogues; 4. Talmud-Torah schools, founded and maintained by foreign Jews; 5. Hedorim, or private, traditional Hebrew schools in the densely populated districts; 6. private instruction.

[31] Education: some data about education has just been given, but the following must also be added: according to English law, every child must receive education free of charge, and a new parliamentary bill would even confer a subsidy upon the parochial schools.

Parochial schools are institutions that, while under the oversight of the government and subsidized by the latter, are nonetheless not public schools and whose occasional deficits have to be covered through collections, gifts, etc.

The majority of Jewish children receive instruction in boarding schools—that is, in secular subjects only—but the Jewish community provides for extra-curricular religious instruction after regular school hours and on Sabbath or Sunday. The pedagogy is quite defective; in many of the smallest congregations the local functionary gives the children private instruction, and the same happens now and again even in London.

There are, to be sure, private Jewish boarding schools, but at the two great universities, there is no Jewish house[i] as is found at one of the better public schools.[47]

---

i   "Jewish house" is a building dedicated to the religious needs of the colleges.

London University attracts many Jewish students, but on the whole it cannot be said that there is a drive to enter academic vocations in England such as one finds among the Jews of the Continent.

There is no teachers' training college for Jews, although in the theological college known as "Jews' College" classical Jewish literature is taught; the students here belong mostly to the poorer classes.[48]

As for the following figures to do with education, it should be noted that, as a result of the predilection for high-sounding names, it was often difficult to distinguish between an actual school and a mere class.

Most provincial bodies do not publish reports, so their balance sheets usually ought to be qualified with the word "approximate"; nevertheless, the real figures will not differ greatly from the actual budget.[49]

TABLE 1.3. **Enrollments and revenues of Jewish schools in UK, ca. 1897.**

	Number	Revenue
Colleges	25	5,478
London schools	7,906	31,452
London classes in religion	9,000	2,500
London Talmud-Torah schools	1,200	2,000
London Hedorim	6,000	6,250
General education outside London	5,601	9,075
Total	29,732	56,755

[32] Charity: It may be inferred from the records of charitable activity that large sums are devoted to this purpose. English Jews say with pride "that not one Jew is left to depend upon public rations or allocations," in other words, that no Jew makes use of relief to the urban poor, to which the Jews themselves also naturally contribute.

This is quite true in general; however, a large percentage of the East London Jews receive medical assistance in the city's hospitals for the poor.

As elsewhere, so in England, the principle is adhered to that the Kehilla* must support its own poor. The idea of *Rachmanut*, of distributing alms without conditions, has just about disappeared, and even synagogue poor relief is managed by means of rigorous institutions. A major institution of this kind is the "London Jewish Board of Guardians for the Relief of the Jewish Poor." The latter serves as a model for all the provincial aid committees and has earned for itself a fine reputation through its competent administration of poor relief.

Resources for relief consist of funds from invested capital, from collections, and, chiefly, from donations.

The guiding principle of all these benevolent institutions is that they not encourage begging as a way of life, and for this reason loans are granted. It is gratifying to be able to say that the honesty of poor Jews is so great, that the loss due to bad debts is miniscule, even though loans are given without any collateral.

Poor relief may be divided into the following categories:

a. Assistance in the form of providing food, or money for food.
b. Assistance in the form of loans.
c. Assistance in the form of supplying employment.
d. Assistance in the form of having boys and girls learn a certain trade.
e. By means of paying for transportation.
f. By means of providing for ritual necessities, such as *matzo* and burial.
g. Lifelong or annual pensions.
h. Lodgings for the elderly.
i. Contributions to hospitals having Jewish wards.
j. Lodgings and education for orphans, deaf-mutes, and the chronically disabled.

Regarding a. Aid committees and other charitable organizations supply money or money-orders for food and clothing.

Regarding b. Requires very large sums; loans run from one to twenty-five pounds sterling.

Regarding c. The aid committee in London (Board of Guardians) employs seamstresses, and the bureau of the Russian Jewish committee supplies work and gives training in manual trades.

[33] Regarding d. Is being successfully implemented. The relevant institutions train boys and girls in manual trades, while they are advanced the

premiums, or cost of instruction, which the apprentices have to pay back. In addition, loans for tools are given and apprentices receive specialized technical instruction in technical classes set up for this purpose. All children have Sabbath and holy days off.

Regarding e. Transportation devours vast sums, a large part of which is consumed in the provinces, since the aid committees pay for the conveyance of the transient poor from one city to another, and thereby the sponger is turned into a vagabond.

Regarding f. Matzo is dispensed by the congregation which, along with other local charitable institutions, defrays the costs of burial for poor Jews.

Regarding g. Widows, the chronically disabled, and the blind, receive lifelong or regular week-to-week aid from various organizations.

Regarding h. The elderly who are feeble are housed in so-called "homes" which are paid for by voluntary contributions of the community. In some poor houses, the residents are granted allowances.

Regarding i. There is no Jewish hospital in Great Britain, however a dispensary for the poor is in the process of being set up in London. English Jews underwrite the public hospitals staffed by volunteers, in which several Jewish wards are maintained.

Regarding j. Only one Jewish orphanage exists in Great Britain, one deaf-mute institute, and one home for the chronically ill. In addition to two convalescent homes that already exist, a hospital for consumptive patients is also to be built, through the kindness of Baroness Hirsch.*

There are yet three major institutions that must be mentioned: the Board of Deputies,[50] charged with safeguarding Jewish interests affected by parliamentary enactments; this board upholds those privileges which make it possible for Jews to observe Sabbaths and holy days.

The Board of Delegates,[51] for all inhabitants of greater London as well as several provincial communities; it has altogether an annual income of three hundred pounds sterling. Like the Anglo-Jewish Association,* it also has a foreign affairs committee, which represents the interests of foreign Jews to the British Foreign Office.

The Anglo-Jewish Association works in conjunction with the Alliance Israélite Universelle* by supporting schools in the Orient. Their revenue comes to about two thousand pounds sterling annually. [34] This association owns shares in the Jewish Colonization Association* and, in 1880, turned over Russian-Jewish affairs to the Russian-Jewish Committee; the latter raised altogether two hundred thousand pounds sterling, of which thirty-five thousand pounds sterling are still available.

The Russian-Jewish Committee has authority over matters pertaining to Russian Jews, in the London and provincial "Board of Guardians" or aid committees; furthermore, it maintains night schools at its own cost, and pays for the education of Russian-Jewish students at Swiss universities.

Political situation. In political terms, English Jews are fully emancipated and are able to hold any government office, except for the position of Lord Chancellor, who, because he is at the same time the father confessor to the queen, must belong to the English state church.

Facts and figures, which attest to the dignity of Jews as peers and barons as well as the number of Jewish members of parliament, are of personal rather than political interest, since no one can say that any rank is off-limits for religious reasons or that only a Jew is able to stand for Jewish rights. It is very unlikely that Jews have a disproportionate number of votes and hold the same views in political matters.

Formerly, a sense of obligation existed that, since the Liberals were responsible for the emancipation of Jews, the Jews ought to belong to the Liberal Party, but the Jewish parliamentarians are presently, with one exception, all Conservatives and Unionists.

Jews hold offices and positions in all branches of government administration; notwithstanding this fact, it would be incorrect to maintain that the current of anti-Semitism has no force. Lord Salisbury's motion to restrict immigration was directed entirely at the Jewish influx, and although the matter was dropped, it remains a part of the government's program.

A certain nervous fear has recently taken hold of English Jews holding positions of responsibility, but however great the impulse might be to propose a special protection for the Jews through legislation, it is nonetheless always quite scrupulously avoided.

Social. Concerning the social conditions of Jews in England, no direct statistics of any kind can be adduced; but collating all the data given in the following exposition may yield some interesting conclusions.

Social distinctions obviously coincide with political and economic stratification, with only a slight deviation in evidence.

The great center of Jewish life is East London, and here each of three different Jewish communities leads a different life: the Jews born in England, the Russian-Polish Jew, the Dutch Jew.

[35] The antipathy between the two latter groups is as a rule greater that that between the first two; each community leads the life of the land of its birth.

The following few facts characterize the situation:

a. The domestic life of the Jews has not been shattered, although the influence of "clubbing" is making itself felt.
b. The women still preserve the old moral ideals to which the Jews owe so much; this cannot be said of the men.
c. One's way of life with respect to the practice of piety and ritual ceremony, will depend on one's pecuniary status.
d. The great proclivity for literature on the part of Continental Jews is not characteristic of English Jewry.
e. The Jews are big patrons of the opera, music, and the concert hall, as is further confirmed by the fact that an itinerant Yiddish operetta troupe settled for some time in London.
f. Life in the provinces is cheaper than in London, and the Jews there usually have more in the way of common ideals, which are naturally affected by the defects of life in small towns.
g. Among the English Jews, a preference for betting on horse-races prevails, whereas foreign Jews indulge in card-playing and games of dice.

In England, very few Jewish children are born out of wedlock, a fact surely to be ascribed to religious and moral principles. Another related reality is the desire to marry.

A very long and interesting report could be written on this theme; since however Jewish ideals in this area vary but little, it is superfluous to present anything more than the following observations: the frequency of marriage is higher among the poor than among the rich or any other class. Various funds support young couples, so that they are able to establish their own households, while the fees for ritual aspects of the wedding ceremonial are reduced or in many cases even waived entirely, in order to prevent the practice of "stille Chaznoth,"[52] which is permitted by Jewish law, though not by English law. Marriages with large age disparities occur relatively more often among the poor than among other classes. The foreign element is resolutely against having bachelors and spinsters, and the Schadchen* still plays a role, albeit not to the same extent as in the past.

The middle classes are the least inclined toward marriage, and the following observations with respect to this point may be of interest:

[36] The average number of Jewish marriages contracted annually in England is around twelve hundred, of which there are:

50 percent among the poor,
25 percent among the lower-middle class,
10 percent among the middle class,
15 percent among the wealthy.

Men as well as women adhere to their marriage vows. Cases of divorce are rare, and cases of "abandonment" among the poor are in reality nothing more than the men, with the consent of their wives, seeking their fortune abroad.

The wages of the working classes amount to between one pound five shillings and two pounds per week, and the lists of the so-called mutual profit associations show that the Jews are diligent. In the same vein, a fact to be noted is that many Jews make use of the government's savings banks.

Since the issue of usury touches on the social life, it may also be observed that although there are undoubtedly Jews who lend money, the number of those who borrow it is even greater.

It is well known that Jews are sober and industrious, and the loans they contract serve to some extent a religio-social purpose. It is customary to make special provision in the household for holy days, for children and women to get new clothes; indeed, in these matters the Jews are somewhat profligate.

Delinquent Jewish children are taken to be housed in a state reform institution; they number on average about fifteen annually, up to a maximum of fifty.

There are few Jewish prisoners. Their crimes consist mostly of petty offenses and robberies, only very rarely acts of violence. The average number in all English prisons runs to about four hundred, but no more than 130 are in custody at any one time.

The good understanding between Jewish masters and servants that existed previously has disappeared in recent years. The struggle carried on by the workers has alienated the two parties: the worker has become aggressive, and this has caused a division, which has not been without its influence on social life.

Economic. Owing to the lack of absolutely reliable data, this section of my report has turned out to be the most difficult.

Four classes are considered here: 1. The poor. 2. The middle class. 3. The affluent. 4. The opulently rich.

Obviously, these can be divided further into subclasses, with reference to which the following perceptions stand out:

[37] 1. The poor are comprised of "spongers," the class of casual laborers, and a working class, which has been so reduced in circumstances by the

downturn in business that they are also making claims on charity, albeit more subtly. 2. The middle class is the most dynamic body, experiencing constant augmentation from the lower classes. 3. The affluent constitute a goodly percentage; this denotes the upper-middle class. 4. The opulent comprises persons who have an annual income of at least one thousand pounds sterling, up to millionaires.

A different and more precise classification of the Jewish people can be formulated:

1. The working classes,
2. The employers,
3. The professional classes,
4. The commercial class.

Regarding 1. Men and women, boys and girls, all work. Three-quarters of the Jewish population engage in crafts such as: tailoring, the making of slippers, boot- and shoemaking, cloak-making, and, above all, cigarette and cigar manufacture.—A second group of occupations pursued by Jews are: book printing, the making of clothing from furs, and carpentry.—The third group: barbers, clock-makers, gold- and silversmiths, jewelers.—The fourth group: house-painters, tinsmiths, installers of gas lighting, blacksmiths, wainwrights, and plumbers.

The average wages are fair. Trade unions exist among men and women, but they wax and wane.

At present there is a battle going on about the eight-hour workday, but this is not so serious an issue to workers as that of achieving higher wages and healthy workplaces.

Trade union statistics are of interest insofar as they prove that the Jews are workers, in the broadest sense of the word.

The problem of the laborer until now is that he has followed too blindly certain leaders, which has, to his disadvantage, produced a stronger opposing force. However, this no longer applies to the tailoring business, where masters and journeymen have united for their mutual benefit; the journeymen may well have to work very hard, but not like their Gentile counterparts.

Regarding 2. In some types of business, the masters have united with the purpose of not only opposing their assistants but also, by means of mutual support, protecting themselves against a stringent prosecution on the part of the government officials who seek to enforce a strict supervision of factories. It may be said with certainty that the stringent enforcement of the regulatory laws will drive the small manufacturers out of business, because the cost of building the legally prescribed sanitary workplaces stands in disproportion to the invested capital.

[38] In the tailoring business, the employers are mostly men who have risen from the working classes. The natural tendency to become employers on a small scale is characteristically Jewish, but one may well ask if this aspect of character is not to blame for many economic problems.

Regarding 3. To the Jewish professional classes belong: attorneys, a few art critics and artists, novelists and journalists. There are few Jewish professors at the universities (except for the Rabbinics chair and Hebrew librarian); at the same time, there are a great many teachers of mathematics and the empirical sciences.

The defense attorney is the modern vocation of the very wealthy, while the majority of those members of the middle class who do not practice a trade are employed in various branches of the civil service.

There are also some well-known Jewish military officers, but as a rule military service is not popular among Jews.

Regarding 4. The commercial class is undoubtedly the strongest among the Jews. The poorest merchants are the peddlers, although this occupation is dying out; the richest merchants represent the big firms in the City of London. Every sector having to do with trade has its Jewish retailers, merchants, commission agents, and brokers, but this is above all true of the trade in colonial products.

The other center of Jewish business activity is the stock market and its auxiliaries, such as banks, financial offices, all the way down to simple currency exchange counters.

Whether the number of Jews speculating on the stock market is proportionate to their numbers or not, one thing is beyond question, viz., that they cannot be charged with doing anything at all disreputable in their way of doing business.

Zionism. Concerning this movement, I may say simply that it was organized in 1890 within the already existing Hovevei Zion* and that it presently counts about thirty individual associations with about three thousand members; their annual revenue is about 250 pounds sterling.

In recent days, nationalist agitation has not been pursued with the same zeal by the organization's officers as in the beginning, with the result that a slackening of interest in colonizing work, the main activity the society has been engaged in, has begun to manifest itself among the members. (Loud applause.)

PRESIDENT: I think we can refrain from a verbatim translation of what we have just heard. The report of Herr de Haas will in any case be published, and it is not appropriate, in view of its exemplary presentation of facts, to reduce it to an abstract. Herr Bahar* has the floor to speak concerning the situation of Jews in Algeria:

[39] JACQUES BAHAR (PARIS): Highly honored Assembly! Just a few hours ago I was entrusted with the unanticipated task of reporting concerning our Algerian brethren, and I did not think I should evade this duty, all the more since I have lived among them, and suffered and struggled with them, for the past nearly five years. At the same time I must ask your indulgence with respect to the imperfect documentation of this report and on account of my mixed and unliterary German, since even though my command of German makes it like a second mother tongue to me, still it is only an acquired language.

As we know, our Algerian Jews derive mostly from slaves sold by the Spanish to the Algerian Beys, who, after their expulsion by the Catholic Isabella, were supposed to be shipped off to Turkey. What kind of free men can be made out of former slaves we know unfortunately only too well, and thus it was that the emancipation that took place after 1870, with its freedom and equality, fell upon many unprepared shoulders, shoulders bowed down by centuries of servitude and contempt.

And although this observation is an honest acknowledgement of the truth, it also serves to highlight the tremendous progress which the present generation has realized with respect to trade and commerce.

The history of this emancipation, which is being exploited as a pretext for the most atrocious persecution, may require a short discussion here, and all the more so since even in France it is little known.

When in the middle of the 1870 war the National Assembly was elected, Gambetta* and Crémieux* acted with impunity as members of the Government of National Defense.[53] Gambetta had a well-grounded fear of the advent of a hostile, monarchist majority and made known his worries to Crémieux. The latter found only one solution; i.e., to increase the number of voters in some districts, which, in conformity with the electoral law, would result in an increase in the number of delegates. He suggested to him therefore to make all Algerian Jews French citizens and arranged matters, which was quite easy, so that they voted for their Republican liberators to a man.[54] The Arabs had nothing against this scheme, and had even expressed themselves decisively in favor of it in a prior inquiry. — Signed documents concerning this matter are still extant.

[40] The Christians, or the French residing there, were delighted with this, for the fall of the Empire relieved them at the same time of the detested "Sabre Regiments" of the military governor, and they found in the unexpected republican collaboration of the Jews a guarantee against the return of the Empire.[55]

So for many years Jews and Christians walked together, which unfortunately in all lands and at all times can be regarded as the most infallible harbinger of strife. For the Republican Party, which had been initially in opposition, finally came to power and its loyal Jews followed after like sheep.

But the Christians had continued to evolve in their politics and had joined the radical opposition party that appeared in the meantime. Now we must not forget that all French possessions outside Europe are nothing more than colonies run by high-ranking officials, and that only those who are in good standing with the government will be appointed as officials and receive advancement in the service; and since the Jews had become, on account of the deputies they elected, the darlings of the government, it occurred that they ultimately came to control these offices, and consequently to rule over the immigrant and native-born French themselves.

He who has risen to power without virtue, may indeed abuse and finally lose it.

At first the Jews had been taunted, then detested. They were reproached for greed. The younger generation felt themselves humiliated and turned their backs on business: if we want to be respected by the Christians, we must become like them. And the Christians being civil officials, what did our politically naïve brethren do? They used their influence to become civil officials. They poured oil on the fire, which leaped up all the higher, since the Christians were no longer able to stand the competition. The Arab, being pressed for his last pence by all officials, ran straight to the Jew, who knew his language wonderfully well and with whom he could at least deal, and from whom he could at times even receive justice.

Until 1890, the governorship of Algeria was in the gift of the deputies, who themselves were dependent on the Jews. But at that time, the present governor, Cambon,* was seeking autocratic power. He had first to remove the deputies and replace them with his own men, although those who were now his enemies supported the same government to which Cambon owed his office. He was therefore unable to injure them in a direct political attack without compromising both the government and himself. He got round this difficulty by inaugurating a campaign of the most despicable slander, not against the deputies but against their most powerful supporters, and without any basis in fact. By paying for false accusations, he had them arrested and convicted. At the same time the Jews were attacked and, since the elections occurred in the meantime, Cambon acquired the autocratic power he sought, which he enjoys until today.

[41] This then is the still unwritten political history of what might be called the "teething problems" of the Algerian Jews.

Now new elections are due, and the recent riots in Algeria were planned with the aim of demoralizing the Jews, in order to give Cambon the victory.[56]

Things have actually become much worse over the past four years, the addition of the fanaticism of the Spanish Christians and their priests making an easing of the situation very unlikely. The hostility of the Arab is not to be taken too seriously. The Arab is not jealous of the Jews, since he does not want to become a Frenchman and despises his own brethren who have been naturalized.[57] That will be evident to anyone who knows that among the Mohammedans religious, civil, and penal laws form a unity and that the renunciation of any part thereof is equivalent to a complete conversion. They think that this is also the case with us and therefore they pay little attention to the Jews. If it is easy to incite the Arabs against the Jews, that is the case only because they regard it as the beginning of the massacre of Christians they have long thirsted for. We owe the quick suppression of the latest riots to this only recently acknowledged fact.

Algeria has forty-five thousand Jews, of which more than thirty thousand live in the deepest misery.

The race is extremely intelligent, very responsive to education, and affords examples of charming women of vivacity and beauty. The men are of powerful build and picturesque stature. Especially among the common people, one Jew is more than a match for three strong Christians. The latter know this also, which is why they would rather incite, as they tried to do in Tlemcen,[58] two thousand Arabs against one hundred Jews. The Jews possess great wealth. As elsewhere, they pay out readily and generously, but they have no real means of defense in the face of danger, either beforehand or afterward. The older generation is disappearing. The younger generation has at times already shown its capacity to act nobly and with political skill.

Craft schools for boys and girls have been established but are helping only a little against the frightful misery. Besides, bands of poor Jews are continuously coming in from Morocco.

I believe that the Zionist movement will find a joyous reception there and will signify a redemption for these my beloved brethren. Until now they have not the least notion about it. (Loud applause).

PRESIDENT: HERR Samuel Pineles will make a report to us about the situation of Jews in Romania.

SAMUEL PINELES (GALATZ): Most honorable attendees! [42] I convey to the Congress the warm greetings of two hundred fifty thousand Jews, about 20 percent of whom are asking; i.e., more than fifty thousand persons, in more than nine thousand petitions, that the Congress take the initiative to approach His Majesty the Sultan, and engage the support of public opinion in Europe to create a homeland in Palestine, secured by law.[59] They want to leave a land, and the sooner the better, in which people regard them with distrust, as though they were intruders, and reproach them for taking bread out of the mouths of the indigenous population.

The situation of Jews in Romania is completely different from that in other lands. Settled for centuries in Moldavia and Wallachia, the Jews have had their lay officers, rabbis, charitable institutions, taxes, etc., recognized by the authorities and have enjoyed relative prosperity.

In the second quarter of this century Tsar Nicholas I* appeared. Then things changed. The Tsar, fearing that Jews in Russia would evade military service, snatched Jewish children at a tender age away from their parents and sent them off to the Don Cossacks, where they were reared to become cannon fodder in the wars with the Turks. This policy induced great numbers of our Jewish coreligionists to cross over the Pruth to begin a new life on Moldavian soil, mostly under altered names. Precisely because they were not members of well-to-do families, they came to these inhospitable regions, as they were at that time, devoid of almost any financial means or education—putting their faith in the God of Israel.

Sometimes a father together with his child made it across; often it was just one or the other of them arriving at the first good place to lodge on this side of the Pruth, where their companions in misfortune were already present, who received the refugees. For the young people, it was out of the frying pan into the fire. But they could remain Jews; they did not have to profane the Sabbath or partake of unkosher foods—and that was the essential goal their parents had in view!!

These children were assigned according to their age: the youngest to the Heder, where they learned to read Hebrew and pray; the older and more mature, according to their physical and mental capacities, to the Jews of the villages to serve as temporary help in the taverns, etc.; in the cities in various sectors of service, as domestic servants, store clerks, and craftsmen (mostly as cobblers, tailors, carpenters, tinsmiths, house painters, goldsmiths, clockmakers, and a few as locksmiths, blacksmiths, and turners).

Even from Galicia and Bukovina there came many poor Jews, and some of higher status, teachers of Hebrew and German, who were everywhere happily received, sought after, and highly regarded. Nearly all the elderly, who had not attended public schools, owed the little knowledge they had to these men. Even bookkeepers and correspondents found good positions in the larger business firms.

[43] The Peace of Paris brought to the Danubian principalities a great increase in trade and commerce.[60] Now even well-to-do Jewish families arrived from Galicia, at first the men with proper passports, then after some years their wives and children; the wives were for the most part not supplied with passports and had obtained by a change of name documents as protégés of various consulates, in particular those of Austria, Prussia, Holland, France, Turkey, and even Greece!

Under Prince Cuza* the Jews attained a modicum of prosperity by means of commerce, in the villages as well as the cities, without however their acquiring great wealth, as one has often been led to believe.

While the Jews migrated southward, the Greeks and Bulgarians advanced from the opposite direction, and in so doing they occupied first the cities and towns along the Danube, then all of Wallachia. No reproach therefore attaches to our coreligionists in this respect. On the other hand, while the resident Jews formed a constant element of peace and compliance with regard to the authorities, the Greeks succeeded in making themselves masters of the country and viewed with displeasure the commercial progress of the Jews. In 1859, they even took the lead in the terrible Jew-baiting in Galatz, in following the popular formula of a blood libel before Easter. The Romanians, who otherwise had lived on the best of terms with the Jews, ultimately became devout disciples of the Greeks, and only a handful of instigators was needed to provoke, on a piddling pretext, brawls that soon degenerated into pillaging and rape, which ruined many families and made life bitter for others, as proved by the well-known scenes of disorder in Berlad, Bacau, Bucharest, Darabani, Galatz (for the second time), Cahul, and Ismail (which was at that time Romanian).

Since then some Romanians have taken pleasure in these agitations, and it soon became the custom to regard the Jews as useful scapegoats. The old Talmudic saying is once again confirmed: "Kol hametzar leYisrael na'aseh rosh"; i.e., "Whoever oppresses Israel will lead the party!" and thus have many a Romanian statesman attained to office and honors; but more than that, the Jewish question was really surging, and, coming along now in its wake, the period of sufferings began. Since then laws and restrictions were and are being devised, in order to make dwelling in the country repugnant to us. Whether and to what extent the Romanians had reason to act in this way is not in question. Everyone is master in his own house! Anyhow, since the Berlin Treaty, people no longer speak of Jews but rather "aliens."

[44] The Romanians fear that their national identity would be in jeopardy within the course of a few generations, were they to make the Jews, whom they all regard as aliens, legally equal to other citizens en masse—and the reasons for this fear are economic! Therefore, they leave the Jews free to practice their faith and to worship, but impede them in procuring a living in accord with their abilities. The Romanians want to make sure that the Berlin Treaty will not be applied to them, as e.g. was done in Serbia and Bulgaria, precisely because Romania maintains that the Jews in this country are aliens![61] And after these conflicts, the Romanian Minister Sturdza* was right, from his own point of view, that the "Jewish state" is the only real solution to the Jewish question, especially for Romania.

The nation is not, in the main, against the Jews, neither the high nor low clergy, nor the peasants (making allowance for exceptions)—but the ten-thousand-strong elite are afraid that the Jews, through their intelligence, their commerce, and their industry, would seize everything for themselves. Even the educated youth are against legal equality, as well as the cadres of officials, for reasons that are easy to guess.

The Armenians and the Gypsies, who have been emancipated en masse, have all been merged into the Romanian nation by being entirely assimilated, which will never be the case with the Jews!

Let us say that at most half of the Jews are well off and have a livelihood. What will happen to the other half, whose livelihoods are uncertain or who are at risk from day to day and truly do not know how to provide their families with their daily bread? Every occupation is represented in this latter group, workers, merchants, craftsmen, scholars.

Many families that had earned an honest living have, in recent decades, been reduced to begging; many that had lived in the villages have been driven out of house and home. The most bitter poverty has entered in, where prosperity once ruled.

All this has occurred in the name of the law—just as is said in Talmudic legend, that the pious do not die; rather, the angel of death takes their souls away with a kiss!

Thus, no Jew can be a peddler, he cannot sell either tobacco or matches, he cannot be an attorney, druggist, or military officer, cannot exercise the duties of public office; i.e., a Jew can be neither judge nor local official, neither police nor customs officer, neither postal nor telegraph nor telephone employee, neither railway official nor bank clerk, nor an engineer for national or municipal government, neither professor nor instructor in any public school at the national or local level, neither physician in a public hospital, nor grain merchant or shipbroker—indeed, not even a street sweeper!

[45] The public hospitals are closed to Jews who are ill (except if he has a referral); primary schools are closed to Jewish children, even if a fee is paid ("unless there is room"); no Jew is admitted at all into the craft or military schools, a Jewish child is never granted a scholarship, etc.

What then are all these hundreds, or indeed thousands, of families to do? What are their young people to do, who have completed their studies successfully but who cannot become attorneys, engineers, druggists, teachers, civil officials, or military officers? What is to become of the erstwhile inhabitants of the villages, who wander from place to place—a burden to Jewish communities and themselves!

There is only one answer: the Jews must leave Romania!

Naturally not all and not all at once, but slowly, steadily, little by little! And just as the main body of the Jews coming from Galicia and Russia settled the country over a period of about seventy years, it will take several decades until they have left the country.

One only has to lay out the channel for drainage; the floods, once in motion, will quickly find their way.

The illusions of getting legal equality, held by some of the privileged Jews, will burst like soap bubbles; the same thing will happen to the younger generation, who have fulfilled their required military service and indulge in the same delusion.

Our situation is therefore more pitiable than elsewhere; it is nevertheless ignored by our fellow tribesmen in other lands. No support or aid of any kind has thus far come to them as to the Jews of other countries, who are not regarded by their governments as aliens. But the Romanian Jews are better than their reputation and deserve a better destiny. (Loud applause).

PRESIDENT: Mr. Rubinstein has the floor.

RUBINSTEIN: (London, speaks in English).

PRESIDENT: Mr. Rubinstein suggests that the reports not be read out at such length, so that more time can be given to the discussion of individual points. I think rather that it would be an encroachment on the other gentlemen, were we to act on this suggestion. A solution may be found by asking the gentlemen to address as briefly as possible the most important points. We are hoping we can complete a great deal of work today. The rapporteurs shall use the noon recess to abridge their reports. I am suspending the proceedings until 3:00 p.m.

[46] Day One, Afternoon Session

PRESIDENT: Herr Dr. Mintz has the floor, to deliver the report on the situation of Jews in Austria.

DR. ALEXANDER MINTZ (VIENNA): Highly honored assembly! The task has fallen to me to report concerning the situation of Jews in Austria—a task grievous in itself but doubly painful for an Austrian, since the subject I must deal with embraces all the woes of my fatherland.

I stand here on foreign soil, and I will therefore take care to refrain from any statement that could be construed as an accusation against my fatherland.

Indeed, going beyond this, I will refrain from speaking even where I might be in a position to speak, mindful of the biblical command: "You shall not uncover the nakedness of your father!"[1]

But what I cannot and will not conceal is the injustice and humiliation that we Jews of Austria have to endure.

Hatred never tires of censuring us in Austria as elsewhere, and for many years now it has inflicted on us the deepest wounds. And the oppression is growing—for anti-Semitism has been victorious. The triumph of anti-Semitism is putting its distinctive stamp on our position—indeed, on the position of my fatherland.

And so I will speak also, first and foremost, about this victory. Without question, it signifies the victory of the people over the government.

My respected colleagues, you all know the events that warrant my making this judgment: the dissolving of the Vienna municipal council in November 1895, the results of the new elections in February and March 1896, the unfortunate outcome of elections to the Lower Austrian provincial assembly in August 1896, the nonconfirmation of Dr. Lueger,* and finally his present, undisputed position of dominance.

This triumph of anti-Semitism was a victory of the masses over state power, indeed over the supremacy of the crown. Its own strength can be measured against the strength of the state's power, whose means were employed to bring about its downfall; it proved itself invincible in the constitutional electoral contest.

And these things show the peculiarity of the Jewish distress in Austria: our rights are being throttled by means of the law.

But permit me to ask the question: what is the basis of our rights?

In answering this question we are led to a self-evident conclusion. We must differentiate conceptually between the general sphere of rights, of Jewry as a legally recognized religious community, and the individual sphere of rights, of individual Jewish coreligionists.

[47] As a legally recognized religious community, Jews are distinguished by prerogatives that do not belong to other, unrecognized confessions: in essence, through the privilege of communal, public exercise of their religion and through the privilege of autonomous communal governance. *Pro persona*, however, each individual of the community has a claim to equality with other citizens guaranteed by the state constitution.

It goes without saying that, according to the law, we are nothing other than a confession: the law disregards our national character.

This is the nature of the legal position that has been ascribed to us Jews of Austria by the letter of the law.

But anti-Semitism, which thirsts for our disenfranchisement, has begun by undermining the foundation of the rights conceded to us—namely, the proposition established in law that we are solely a confession. Schönerer* and his followers have spread the rallying cry coming from Germany and determining ever since the entire direction taken by anti-Semitism: the faith of the Jews is irrelevant, the one and only thing that is relevant is their ethnic stock, and for this reason they deserve to be stripped of their rights.

It is well known that anti-Semitism in Austria has become "Old Catholic"[2] over the years—thus the anti-Semites have incorporated into their program of agitation also the denigration of our faith; but these calumnies are and were just one more weapon to annihilate our rights as citizens and ultimately our very existence.

But this suffices to explain why anti-Semitism preserves just those rights that we enjoy as a confession, because what it truly detests, what it battles against so passionately, is not our God but us, ourselves! And while it seems to take aim against the books of our faith and the religious works of our forefathers, in truth it takes aim at the hearts of Jews and their children! For this is also the doctrine of Austrian anti-Semitism. That is, that the Jews are an inferior race, dangerous to the public and deserving of annihilation; therefore anti-Semitism passes down its hatred from generation to generation, in the conviction that even the waters of baptism do not have the power to purge the "wickedness of our nature." Hence, Austrian anti-Semitism takes no cognizance not only of statutory law, on the strength of which the Jew is to be regarded as a German, Slav, or Hungarian; it also disregards the Christian dogma of the purifying power of baptism, and scorns it in spite of anti-Semitism's undoubted religious zeal—so intense and overmastering is this Jew-hatred.

[48] By the central thesis of its theory, in declaring Jewry as an alien, incorrigibly wicked race, anti-Semitism defies the norms of both state and church, and it does not hesitate to uphold the independence of its interpretation over against the highest authorities.

In spite of all that, anti-Semitism has continued to hold the field; but while noting once again its extraordinary triumph, I wish to mention at the same time the impulse by which the government of Austria was induced to capitulate.

The anti-Semitism of my fatherland is not only nationalist but also socialist.

It has had in mind not only to isolate the Jews by malicious stereotyping of their ethnic stock, it has also sought to demonstrate that they are exploiters par excellence, the epitome of all corruption and the source of all misery.

Thereby a lightning rod had been fashioned, well suited to divert the threat of Marxian socialism away from the ruling authorities and direct it onto the heads of the Jews.

The Church had already made up its mind, in this and other matters, about the utility of anti-Semitism—thus it was already in alliance with anti-Semitism when Count Badeni* went to battle against it. But even for His Excellency, the moment of enlightenment arrived. Dr. Lueger took office as mayor and his performance made him worthy of his hire: in the last election to the Imperial Council, he defeated the Social Democratic Party in Vienna decisively.

In this manner, anti-Semitism has found official access to the royal court. Its cause was compromised by Schönerer vis-à-vis the authorities, but with Lueger it gained favor and honor at the very highest level.

But in this way the situation of the Jews has taken a serious turn for the worse.

For ultimately, it is a short step from the sanctioning of anti-Semitism to the sanctioning of laws against the Jews.

But, passing over this rather fine point—what is certain is that the tendency toward parliamentary motions hostile to Jews has intensified from year to year. These are mostly draft laws concerning the protection of industry, but advocacy for industry is sometimes just a parliamentary euphemism for hostility to Jews.

I stated that anti-Semitism is a popular movement, and I have shown how it has won over to itself church and state.

I conclude this portion of my report by observing: anti-Semitism is already at the moment the common property of every national grouping in Austria. No matter how intense the struggle between them, no matter how deeply the conflict between Germans, Czechs, and Poles makes itself felt, in this one point, the point about the Jews, they all come together.

And up to the present, they have all also manifested their anti-Semitism in the most thoroughly practical ways. With your kind permission, we will take a little time to visit Jew-hatred in the midst of its work.

[49] In one respect, we have been treated the same in every province of the Austrian Empire; everywhere we have been reviled, mocked, and defamed—we have been spared no insult, anywhere.

Not a day passes, nay nary an hour, without an offense against our honor.

In the sessions of the parliament and in public meetings, from the pulpit and in the lecture hall, in shops and streets, in every place and on every occasion, the hatred of our enemies assails us.

The Jews are not human beings, according to Gregorig,* a member of the parliament; they are a rabble accursed by God that must be eradicated, according to Schneider,* another member of parliament; "It doesn't matter if they are hanged or beheaded," according to the mayor of Vienna, Dr. Lueger; they make use of Christian blood, according to Father Deckert*; thus speak the leaders, and the populace repeat these falsehoods.

The Jews are usurers and swindlers, without exception, libertines and pimps, the epitome of all wickedness. This is the derisive refrain that is repeated without ceasing; this is the reigning conception of us, as it is expressed in taverns and salons, in the army, and even in the courts of law. This blind hatred goes to such extremes, that one poor Jew who was making his way down the streets of Vienna with a blond albeit non-Aryan child was assaulted by a mob of fanatical women and detained on the allegation that he had kidnapped the child in order to slaughter it for ritual purposes. This hatred generates incidents, such as happened recently in the city of Baden near Vienna, where a young child feigned that a family presumed to be Jewish was going to assault him for ritual purposes, or, to take a second and likewise recent case, a thirteen-year-old boy shouting "Jew! Jew!" felled one of his peers by throwing a stone at him, injuring him critically.

I could multiply instances of the same: but what need of examples in view of the fact that expressions of this fierce hatred fill the columns of our newspapers and have attained the most distressing notoriety?

And truly, the speaker of the assembly of Lower Austria, Baron Gudenus,* was correct in what he said about the strength of anti-Semitism: the blood and tears of its victims attest to its strength!

Are its victims to be counted? Is this a question of statistics? It is quite enough to know how Jew-hatred in Austria operates and the points at which it chooses to attack us.

[50] It is our character that this hatred is dragging into the gutter, and it is our inmost, inborn nature that it is trampling upon.

It holds our emotions in suspicion, misconstrues our words, imputes to us crimes, divests us of our merits, murders our good name, and slanders the honor of our women!

These are the tactics of Jew-hatred, tactics whose dreadful character may be judged by the depressing depth of ruin to which anti-Semitism has plunged us.

I speak here of the irretrievable loss to us of *joie de vivre*, boldness of spirit, and physical energy. But if this were not enough, there is yet another effect: the capacity of anti-Semitism is much, much greater, since it sets us apart and alone in the midst of party politics, erects walls around us in the marketplace, and banishes us to a spiritual ghetto!

The isolating of Jewry, that is anti-Semitism's next goal, and it has almost achieved it, by isolating us in the political, social, and economic spheres.

With respect to politics, anti-Semitism has had an effect that is actually disintegrating. The water of baptism has turned into a corrosive acid, which has dissolved the German Liberal Party into its constituent elements, giving rise to the German Nationalists, the German People's Party, the German Progressives, the Social-Politicals, etc.; which has been able to generate an anti-Semitic group from the Young Czech Party; and which has begun to erode even the powerful organization of a class-conscious proletariat.

The Jewish issue has become a node of crystallization, around which ever new political factions and splinter groups have taken shape. But the Jews themselves have remained excluded from all such groupings.

This holds true for Western Austria, which is my particular subject to discuss; in Galicia, whose conditions have been treated in detail as the subject of a special report and which I will therefore refer to scarcely at all—in Galicia, I say, there is no possibility of a coalition being formed that would include the Jews, because in public affairs the Jew is regarded by the Poles only as an "agent," in the commonly pejorative sense of that word.

In Western Austria, the political parties have either thrown us out or are giving us to understand—and this holds true even for the Social Democrats—that they are perfectly capable of doing without our cooperation. To be sure, we are sometimes permitted to participate in politics for a while; thus it was, for example, that the German Nationalist deputy, Hoffmann von Wellenhof,* made us aware of the fact that, for the present and as long as the struggle over a language law was raging, we might lend our support to the Germans; but as soon as this struggle was decided, the moratorium would come to an end and we could then expect further persecutions.[3]

[51] Naturally, the decline of our influence in representative bodies is bound up with our political isolation. The percentage of Jewish deputies and other Jewish officials had not corresponded to the numerical strength of Jewry even before now; but at present the disparity stands out even more obviously. In addition, the traditions by virtue of which we are excluded from higher ranks of public service in judicial and administrative affairs, continue in full force. But even more than this, the custom of having to produce a baptismal certificate in order to even gain entry to public service and to secure even inferior positions, is not only practiced, it is openly admitted to.

Thus, an advisor to an Austrian provincial committee declared that, to fill a position of district physician, no Jew could be nominated; in order to matriculate at the military institutes, the producing of a baptismal certificate is required *nudis verbis*; just recently it has become quite clear that Jewish applicants for positions as trainees at the law courts have been deliberately passed over by the higher authorities. In this respect as well, it appears as though the government wishes to anticipate anti-Semitism. And so it is certainly no surprise that the government unhesitatingly gives it a free hand when it expresses itself in autonomous institutions, notwithstanding the government's right of surveillance; and, under these circumstances, who is going to take special notice of the fact that the city of Vienna is rejecting without exception every Jew petitioning for the right of domicile?

But the isolating of the Jews is expressed also and no less intensely in the social arena, and here too all the provinces exhibit approximately the same features. Dealings with Jews in Western Austria are defined perhaps more by hatred, while in Galicia it is contempt; but here as well as there, we can be described as virtually proscribed in a social sense. Familiar relations between Christian and Jewish families are a rarity; Christian and Jewish students, even in primary and trade schools, are hostile toward one another; in the German student clubs, anti-Semitism has produced an unprecedented savagery through the awakening of the most brutal instincts. And, regrettably, it must be observed that it is the faculty that have brought the seed of Jew-hatred to full development, and anything parents might have omitted in this regard the educators are making up for with utmost zeal. Indeed, anti-Semitism has infiltrated even into the elite among the faculty; the professors at the German universities of Bohemia participate enthusiastically in the events of the anti-Semitic societies.

Under these circumstances it is only natural that anti-Semitism is expelling us from societies, clubs, and other associations.

[52] Everywhere and in all places, social activities and sport are organized on a nationalistic basis—that is to say, on the basis of being *judenrein*.[4]

Gymnastics, cycling, and choral arts are being Christianized with a pedantic thoroughness. The unconstrained, genial, interconfessional social interaction in various types of associations, which used to prevail in Vienna, Reichenberg, Troppau, and Graz, has ceased, possibly forever. The Bund der Deutschen in Böhmen [League of Germans in Bohemia] offers perhaps an example of just how rapidly an exclusivism rooted in hostility to Jews is gaining ground. In just two years, this anti-Semitic association has succeeded in creating over 150 local groups, counting thousands of members.

Incidentally, the money for creating such nationalist groups is raised not infrequently from the Jews; this is what happened, *ad exemplum*, with the founding of the German House in Prague. In effect, we are being "allowed" to pay for the rods by which we are being chastised! Everywhere and in all places, we are driven out with scourging, and to the marks which distinguish us from others are added the welts we are receiving.

But, as you know, the anti-Semites speak of our wealth, which compensates us for the loss of official positions and honors.

Well, we all know that tales of our superior economic position are a singularly big lie. Here again it is a matter of percentages, and you have heard today about the unspeakable misery in which the bulk of the Jewish population languishes, the Jews of Galicia.

And even in Lower Austria, Bohemia, and Moravia, where the Jews stand in a stronger position financially than in other provinces, about two-thirds have been proletarianized.

Thus for example, fifteen thousand out of twenty thousand households—of course, I am just using round figures—labor under such distress, that they cannot be called upon at all to pay the Jewish communal rates. Of the ten thousand rate payers, 90 percent are assessed at the lowest rate out of regard for their precarious situation, and barely a quarter of these are able to pay the prescribed contribution.

The decline of trade done through middlemen, which in Western Austria is indeed mainly controlled by Jews, has made itself felt among them with such a truly frightful intensity, that the Jews are now producing a vast host of the unemployed. And the desperation among Jewish merchants, physicians, attorneys in finding appropriate work, is on average greater than that found among their Christian counterparts of the same class.

[53] Nevertheless, anti-Semitism, with its fierce animosity toward our "affluence," can hardly contain its bitter anger; in every locality, in every household, there is propaganda about the need to break our alleged predominance, with boycotting recommended as the most effective means: "Don't buy anything from Jews!" This cry has been transmitted from Vienna to all of Austria, and thousands of the poorest Jewish shopkeepers can testify to its effect. And Galicia in particular is striving with systematic calculation to isolate Jewry economically.

How, by establishing so-called Christian firms, founding peasant consumer cooperatives, and forming exclusive credit unions—how, by means of all these initiatives, to which the provincial assembly of Galicia devotes thousands of gulden annually, and which, in a calculated fashion, deprive the Jews of their livelihood, and by which, in a premeditated fashion, their terrible misery is further augmented—it is not possible for me to describe these things within the framework of my report. I limit myself to the observation that Galicia disposes of a veritable arsenal of practices hostile to Jews.

The Jew-hatred of Galicia can probably be best characterized as a commercial anti-Semitism; on the other hand a racialist anti-Semitism is proliferating chiefly in Lower Austria, Bohemia, Moravia, and the Alpine provinces. But everywhere, far and near, the religious chord resonates with the expressions of this hatred, which is, so to speak, native-born and raised.

I emphasized that our disenfranchisement is taking place by legal means; the ballot paper and the press are the principal means employed in the struggle against us—without question, we are being defeated by weapons entirely legal and constitutional.

But, from time to time, all the boundaries of the law are breached by instincts whipped to a frenzy. Race hatred and greed pass over from propaganda of the word to propaganda of the deed, from petitions and resolutions to plunder and murder. And who is going to deny—I speak of Galicia—that in recent times, the outrages have become more frequent? And who should think this strange? The tension is too great, and the explosion is only natural and can be averted only by an escape valve. Indeed! By the escape valve of colonization.

The imminent dangers our brother tribesmen are exposed to in Galicia would already be quite enough to give justification for Zionism. Still, although the limits of my subject compel me to keep to the delineation of actual conditions and to avoid drawing conclusions as much as possible, and although I should therefore refrain from arguing for Zionism in Austria specifically on the basis of our situation in Austria, nevertheless, I wish to emphasize, in order to avoid misunderstanding, that it is absolutely not the case that Zionism finds exclusive justification for itself in the bloody demonstrations of Jew-hatred. [54] These are simply the visible evidence of the fact that in Austria too, assimilation is compatible neither with our own higher feelings nor with the baser emotions of other people. The injustice which is inflicted upon us in the name of the law, is not less, indeed it is perhaps far more effective, in awakening a Zionist consciousness, than anti-Semitic acts of violence or the massacres of Jews in Tarnów, Schodnica, or Chodorow.

The fact is that the legitimacy of Zionism is recognized by thousands upon thousands in Austria too.

The masses, in particular the Jewish proletarians of Galicia, are hurrying on ahead of the bourgeoisie in this regard. Distress has sharpened their vision. And the youth are accompanying them; the momentum of feeling has lifted them above the quotidian. Our students have flocked to the Zionist banner by the hundreds. In Vienna alone, five hundred have sworn their commitment to the idea of Zionism. But even the well-established citizens among us are beginning to sense the significance of colonization in Palestine and the great importance of Zionist endeavors. They are joining company with the poor and the students.

Zionism is growing also in my fatherland.

There is a budding and sprouting filled with promise, and the astounding development of its power fills us with the proudest memories and makes us dream of extraordinary things in a great future.

Even in the present Zionism has had a beneficial impact, for it has raised us up and we have shaken off spurious friendship; it has made us strong and we have found our true selves.

How the Jews of Austria have striven, with self-sacrifice and self-denial all through the years, to save and secure the national patrimony of others!

From 1848 on, they have been pillars of Germanism in Bohemia, Moravia, and Bukovina. They sacrificed their property, their freedom, and their Jewish identity, for the glory of Poland. They are sacrificing even now their Jewish identity for the glory of Hungary.

Again and again, they are enthralled by alien national ideologies, although the inevitable disillusionment is something terrible.

And how has their willingness to sacrifice been rewarded; who among their "Christian brothers" even remembers their acts of nationalist devotion? In Galicia in particular, how do people there honor the memory of those men who kindled in their Jewish compatriots an unparalleled self-renunciation for the cause of Polonism, at a time when this ardor had been buried under a mass of corpses?[5] These educated young people and these old Orthodox firebrands—who mentions them today? Does anyone today still sing the praise of Chief Rabbi Meisels,* who stood at the head of the movement and then languished in the Warsaw dungeons?

[55] Well, the Jews of Austria are in no need of thanks for their self-sacrifice, and this redounds entirely to their credit.

But they are imposing their services, they are competing for the favor of their tormentors, they are wasting themselves for the sake of their worst enemies—and there, just there, is where their ignominy begins.

That the Jews of Western Austria after all these things are, at this moment, flirting with the German nationalists—we can only be ashamed of such a spectacle.

But it is said to be a calculated political move; well, then it is something that is not without its humorous side. A sheep that wants to howl with the wolves—a sheep in wolf's clothing—thus do Austria's "Mosaic Germans" offer themselves, and this ludicrous masquerade is the consequence of their cleverness. But enough. I ask: is it possible for anyone to exert himself more zealously to divest himself of his inborn character on behalf of alien peoples, than the Jews of my fatherland?

But the scourgings of anti-Semitism have awakened our pride and *amour propre*, and the yearning for the happiness of a home.

Our blood rose in anger, and we discovered that it was the blood of our forefathers, our heart cried out and we recognized that it spoke the language of our ancestors.

But there are still, apart from the German nationalists, groups within our Jewry who are not open to this realization, who deny our unique identity, who keep on desiring and expecting the elimination of all barriers, and their favorite argument is Hungary, that paradise beyond the Leitha.[6]

Well, I have till now scarcely touched on conditions in Hungary, and I think there would be little profit in adducing much descriptive detail in order to set them in their proper light.

For, were I to speak of the terrible poverty of the Jewish masses in Hungary—which is in fact indisputable—or were I to speak of the never-ending outbreaks of the blood libel—I would be countered by those who rhapsodize about laws limiting the role of the church, the full legal recognition of the Jewish faith, the liberal pronouncements of various prelates, the professional advancement of Jewish judges, the celebrations of brotherhood in the press, and they would go on about the prosperity of individuals, the comfort enjoyed by many, and the patriotic enthusiasm of all Jews.[7]

And then, on the other hand, it would probably be my duty to demonstrate that something is nonetheless rotten in the land of Hungary,[8] and to tell of the miasma which penetrates this seemingly so healthy air.

And could I actually do this, could I speak of the victims the pestilential air or, ultimately, a raging storm will carry off?

[56] Pronouncing a gloomy prophecy is a disagreeable and dubious task, and my heart's feeling is naturally inclined toward those who look to the future with complete confidence.

So I will just note the fact that the number of pessimists is increasing; and they are saying that the serpent of anti-Semitism is slithering into the paradise beyond the Leitha as well; and they claim to see already the glint of the flaming sword, and they believe that even the Jews of Hungary will eat of the tree of knowledge—the knowledge which is called Zion.[9]

These apprehensions are, however, of a kind that contain within them a hope, compensating for the distress of the present day and inspiring in its sublime grandeur—a hope called Zion.

And so hanging over the general picture of our situation I have sketched out with a few quick strokes, is a turbid, dusky mood: the much-vaunted sun of brotherhood has been extinguished in Austria as well.

But from the East there blazes up a brightness, which points our way through the night and the wilderness, to a place we love, love with all the passion of our tormented hearts—to the place that is called Zion! (Loud applause.)

PRESIDENT: Dr. Mayer Ebner* has the floor for his report about the situation of Jews in Bukovina.

Dr. Mayer Ebner (Czernowitz): Bukovina is usually mentioned in the same breath as Galicia. Long welded together politically with the latter territory, Bukovina was nothing more than an appendage to Galicia and was treated as thus by empire and government. Galicia and Bukovina are regarded as semi-Asiatic by educated West Europeans. It is where civilization fades away, where the winds of the Asiatic steppes begin to blow. It is said of Bukovina that the people there go about in tunics and spend their lives tussling about with growly bears.

This is about all that is known about Bukovina in the West. That which makes the region truly interesting from a cultural and ethnographic point of view is entirely unknown to people in the West. This small territory containing five hundred thousand persons, is inhabited by an array of ethnic groups. Bukovina affords a picture of Austria in miniature. The main ethnic groups are the Romanians and the Ruthenians. But we find also, in not inconsiderable numbers, Poles, Germans, Armenians, Hungarians, Lipovans, and Jews.

The number of Jews in Bukovina amounts to over sixty thousand, and it is therefore more than 10 percent of the total population of the territory. Bukovina is thus home to perhaps more Jews than the whole of France. Bukovina, like Galicia, belongs to a class of countries—as our enemies say—that is "saturated" with Jews. [57] After the Ruthenians, they are the single largest ethnic group in Bukovina. As such, they are in a position, luckily or unluckily, where they cannot avoid playing a political role.

At one time Bukovina was called the "El Dorado"[10] of the Jews. But the time is past when such a description had some justification in fact. Dratted politics has been largely responsible for this reversal of fortunes. The Jews form a compact mass in the provincial capital and in the other larger and smaller towns, a mass which, by virtue of numbers and astuteness, is often decisive, especially in elections to various representative bodies, that follow Austria's old and antiquated system of voting by socio-economic groups.[11] The Jews in the cities supply the major contingent of the educated classes. As shareholders in the biggest credit institutions, they have a decisive influence on the political convictions of their own people.

The Jews in Bukovina have accomplished something remarkable. They have Germanized the Romanian and Ruthenian areas. The language in all offices is German; the provincial diet holds its proceedings in German; the provincial school council is in German; German is the language of instruction in colleges and secondary schools; in town councils it is German that is spoken for the most part; German newspapers are the ones most widely read; street signs and public notices are in German; even in the primary schools in the countryside, German is taught. At first sight one would take Bukovina to be a German province.

It is a plain fact that the Jews in the cities were and are the German pioneers of the territory. The Jews have felt themselves—I use the past tense advisedly—to be Germans, have been loyal to the Germans, and were the most outstanding "voting cattle"[12] supporting the German Liberal Party. Hence, German representatives were elected in the cities of the territory. Even at a time when the foundations of the German Liberal Party in Austria had been shaken, the Jews in my homeland persisted in sending a German Liberal delegate to parliament.

What the Jews in Bukovina have experienced is nothing new to those familiar with Jewish history. The Liberal Party's fragmenting came as a revelation to the Germans. Apostles of the racialist views of Schönerer were not wanting. Immediately a new association arose, "Christian Germans of Bukovina." This was the kick from behind; this was the reward for the Jews' foolish, decades-long devotion to German culture. "This is what you get," said the Romanians, while the Ruthenians jeered. "Kicked from behind!" said the Jews to themselves, mortified. This was the thanks we get for cherishing German ideas, for being pioneers of Germanism in regions where that famous German ordnance has not yet penetrated, in regions not yet fertilized by the bones of a Pomeranian musketeer.[13]

[58] The Jews in Bukovina are now about to make a second mistake. They are going to jump out of the frying pan into the fire. They are seeking to attach themselves to the Romanians.

A terrible hatred exists in the province against the Jew. This Jew-hatred is latent; it is only quite seldom expressed openly among us. Some years ago a quite lively movement was to be seen, which was orchestrated by some Gentile ecstatics[14] known locally as "poroks," against the Jews in the countryside. The provincial newspaper had stories about violent incidents against Jews, pillagings, attacks, and the like.

The Jew in Bukovina is hated: first, because he is a Jew; second because he appears to be well off— I will return to this subject—and third, because of his irrational involvement in German Liberal politics, but mostly for every other reason. The Jew is almost below contempt. The Aryan, as he pronounces "Zyd"[15] through his teeth, does so as though he wanted to spit. Incidentally, he does not even face the Jew while doing it.

In vain do Jewish grandees and those Jews who consider themselves "society," exert themselves in adapting to Aryan ways. They are rewarded with outright rejection. The social walls of the ghetto have not ceased to exist.

In this struggle to be recognized as social equals, we have disgraced ourselves. The Jew has in many ways lost the moral backbone of the man who will not prostrate himself even before the highest human authority. Rather, he is cringing and sycophantic. To have a Christian at one's table is regarded as a high honor, to be admitted to a Christian's table is regarded as temporal bliss.

The economic life of the Jews in Bukovina is very depressing. Truth to tell, the living standard of the Jews in Bukovina is getting worse from day to day. Of course, there are also some people who are quite rich. This wealth makes itself felt in the extension of the cities: "The houses in the city belong to the Jews," says the Aryan. It is true; but does the fact that there are a thousand rich men abolish the reality that fifty thousand eke out a wretched existence?

The Jewish population in the province earns its living in part from trade, in part from tavernkeeping, in part from craft production, and only here and there from agriculture.

Trade and craft production are no longer very profitable. One finds even honest old businessmen going bankrupt at the end of their lives and winding up as poor people, burdens upon the charitable societies. On all sides, Jews are constrained in the possibility of earning a living. [59] The peasants in the countryside get together—the preacher instructs them what to do in order to set up a retail cooperative; meanwhile the Jewish retailer is forced, with his wife and children in tow, into a life of beggary. A large segment of Jewry earns its living from tavernkeeping; then suddenly concessions are withdrawn and the Jew is left penniless.

I speak candidly when I say that it is often not anti-Semitism that motivates the ruling elite to implement such measures; it is often consideration for the condition of the rural population, who are frequently addicted to alcohol. But for us these measures mean increasing the number of Jewish beggars.

The sight of this endless throng of professional beggars is a positively shameful sight. They move from city to city, from province to province. Here they are chased away by dogs; there they are pushed across the border by gendarmes; here someone tosses a penny into their hand. What is to become of these people?

If one goes into the lower sections of the city of Czernowitz, the immensity of the cumulative misery is a powerful shock. Entire families, consisting of ten or more members, are confined to a squalid cellar. There are families that are literally dying a slow death by starvation. Fortunate is the man who gets twelve to fifteen gulden per month. It is not necessary for me to delineate the misery here. It suffices for me to say that the overwhelming majority of Jews in Bukovina are desperately poor.

The Jewish class of craftsmen suffers on account of a prejudice held by both Aryans and Jews. The erroneous belief that the Christian is the superior workman is widespread. The Jewish cobbler, carpenter, tailor, is quite often exposed to a tacit boycott by his fellow tribesmen.

We are witnessing the emergence of a new threat. In this country the Jews' need of education is very great. Although they make up only 10 percentof the total population, they make up 40 percent of those attending school, especially at the secondary and college level. The *Gymnasien* are 50 percent Jewish, as are the *Realschulen*, and the universities are no different, where the bulk of the law students are Jews. Year after year, a certain number of the latter complete their degrees and avidly start searching for official positions. But then they are brought to an abrupt halt. The financial administration is closing its doors, the government civil service does not accept Jews on principle, and the other departments follow suit. The same principle is observed even in the judiciary. Let the Jewish legal trainees be ever so competent, their diligence impresses no one and their proficiency is unwelcome because it provokes comparisons. With the introduction of a new law affecting civil litigation in Austria, there is a palpable dearth of judicial officials. The material out of which competent and fair judges could be had is available in abundance, but it has one defect—it is Jewish. [60] Any Aryan who has six weeks of experience will have priority in receiving appointment over colleagues who have waited twenty times as long for an appointment and who, in hopeful folly, will continue to wait for a long time.

The *pro tempore* authorities make no attempt to conceal it. They do not want Jews; they do not want to have their departments "inundated," as they put it, with Jews. But they do not even admit Jews in numbers that would correspond to "the Jews' proportion in the population" (a popular phrase). When all is said and done, they simply don't want us.

Here are qualified people, standing with doctoral degrees in hand. What is to be done?

The Christian state gives them to understand that they must perform only a trivial act in order to put an end to all their distress. They are to submit to baptism. There are instances of applicants being appointed immediately after baptism.

The authorities competent to appoint also underwrite the missionary labors of the Catholic Church. Young people are given the choice: hunger or baptism, and the numbers are increasing of those who renounce Judaism in order to obtain their daily bread. A time will come when our entire intelligentsia will enter the Church's fold, partly under duress and partly due to a weariness caused by long-lasting pressure and palpable hatred.

This prospect is, for those who desire the preservation of Judaism, quite sad and depressing.

Our overproduction of middle-class intelligentsias—as Dr. Herzl has so aptly termed it[16]—is producing an intellectual proletariat, and if our surplus intelligentsia flee to the camp of the radical revolutionaries, that is interpreted as meaning that the Jews are undermining the edifice of the state, the Jews are our misfortune, etc.

A thousand causes, one effect. Why are we hated? The reality is simply that we are hated, that we live under a condition of constraint. We are indeed an unfortunate people.

It only remains for me to say something about the Zionist movement in Bukovina. I think the most advisable course for us is to avoid overstatements and to speak the truth.

Over a period of five years, the Jewish-nationalist academic association "Hasmonaea"* has done battle with unusual zeal for the good cause of Zionism, but the Jews have been deaf to their fervent speeches because they have not yet witnessed a big massacre of Jews. Faced with hostility on every side, the Hasmonaea held out for five years, until there were simply no more recruits.

But the old guard of Hasmonaea has kept on. They have set up a Zionist society in Czernowitz, which has seen unusual growth within a short period of time. Zionist groups have arisen in Radanz and Suczawa, in Frumosa and Seret. While it is true that the movement's influence is widening, it is still far from being a popular movement. [61] Confidence in the movement is still lacking; the masses want to see results. If we succeed in implementing Zionism on a larger scale, the people will certainly be cheering us on.

In the name of the Zionist society I represent, I am here to give expression to the hope that, with our eyes fixed on the goal, with courage and without trepidation, we will enter upon that path that leads to victory, to the redemption of our people from shame and servitude. (Lively applause.)

PRESIDENT: Herr Dr. Schauer has the floor for his report concerning the situation of Jews in Germany.

Dr. Schauer (Bingen): As the rapporteur concerning the situation of Jews in Germany, I declare that the portrayal of the emotional suffering of West European Jews made known to you by Dr. Nordau is the picture of the suffering of the German Jew. The Gentile population and the powers that be—with the exception of a quite small section of men of high standing, intellectually and morally—relate to the Jews precisely the way Dr. Nordau has so eloquently delineated. I think that adding anything would detract from the powerful impact of his address.

But I would like to refer to just one issue, which Dr. Nordau did not touch on. It is one of the causes for the absence of Jewish self-consciousness, and it is the inadequacy of instruction in Jewish history and culture in Germany. Thus, investigation by the Prussian Ministry of Public Instruction has shown that more than fourteen hundred Jewish children in Berlin are growing up without receiving religious instruction. This is a shockingly large number, made even more shocking when we consider that this generation, which has been growing up and continues to grow up without genuine knowledge of Judaism, has recourse only to the propaganda of our enemies as the source of its "knowledge."

We German Zionists want to see to it that this situation is changed. We want to see to it that the German Jew learns of his glorious past, understands that he must have a future worthy of this glorious past, and remembers the dying words of the old Maccabean, which he called out to his heroic sons long ago: "Call to mind the deeds performed by your fathers in their generations, then will you attain high fame and an immortal name."[17] (Lively applause.)

President: Herr Professor Belkovsky* has the floor to report on the situation of the Jews in Bulgaria.[18]

Professor Gregor Belkovsky (Sofia): Highly honored assembly! Bulgaria—the newest state in Europe and child of the Berlin Congress—has, during its nineteen-year existence, attracted a great deal of attention from the European public, for reasons that are well known. It has already found itself a historian.[19] [62] But notwithstanding this fact, it may be fairly asserted that there exists in Europe no very clear idea about this state. Why this is the case it is not our business here. But this assertion is even more true with respect to the Jewish population of this state, whose destiny, way of life, and present situation remain obscure because they have not attracted the attention of anyone with the ability to delineate them. This is unjust, because even though the number of our fellow tribesmen in Bulgaria is very small, and even though the situation of world Jewry does not hang upon the weal and woe of Bulgarian Jews, still, the situation of the Jewish population of this land is certainly no less deserving of attention in and of itself, than that of our brothers in other lands.

In Bulgaria we are dealing with a population that, hived off from the Turkish polity, has formed a polity which pretends to hegemony over the Balkan peninsula. We are dealing with the population of a state that owes its origins to ideas of freedom belonging to a century proud of its great ideas.

Taking the foregoing as our standpoint and acknowledging the significance of our task, we deemed it necessary to undertake an inquiry particularly into the economic area, in order in this way to secure the relevant data. As was to be expected, such an inquiry, depending entirely upon private initiative and lacking the resources required for the undertaking, was unable to yield satisfactory results. Moreover, the conduct of the inquiry, as *res nova*, ran up against the distrust of certain groups—indeed was even subject to opposition.

Although we were able to record the necessary data through personal observation in Sofia by visiting the relevant quarter, the leaders of the local Zionist committees outside the capital were not always able to do the same, even though we commissioned them to do so and supplied them with specific instructions and questionnaires.

Thus, this report cannot pretend to be based on all of the data that would be necessary to fully illuminate the situation of the Jews in Bulgaria. Nonetheless, I would hope that the honorable members of the Congress will give their attention to what has been included.

The Political Situation. Over a period of several decades in this century in particular, it has been asserted as axiomatic that the political situation of the Jews depends upon the form of government in the state. This dogma constitutes the cornerstone of the worldview of an enormous number of our fellow tribesmen, serving for a great number of these same Jews as a foundational principle in thinking about how to improve their status in the world.

[63] Now the honor falls to this small state of proving that the treatment of Jews in a constitutional state furnished with liberal institutions can be such as to destroy at least a significant part of the foundation on which the incurable optimist takes his stand. Inasmuch as other much older states have been competing with Romania in the nineteenth century, in asserting a primordial right to systematically persecute the Jews, it is hardly surprising that this tendency has found much support in Bulgaria as well, and, let us go further to say, was bound to do so. It should be emphasized first and foremost that a great number of Bulgarian political leaders took refuge in Romania before the

reestablishment of their state, which offered them abundant opportunity to ingest generous quantities of contagious Jew-hatred. Since Western Europe was still relatively unknown to the Bulgarians, they formed their conception about Western cultural tendencies according to what they saw in Romania, which is called—whether rightly or wrongly may be left undecided—"Soeur cadette de la France [France's younger sister]." But let us not be unfair to Romania. Whoever, like us, has had opportunity to come to know Bulgarian conditions as an eyewitness, will surely have to admit that the Bulgarians were in no need of Romanian schooling to be able to not only assert but also emphatically put into practice "Bulgaria for the Bulgarians" as an all-encompassing principle of their lives at every moment.

It has been imagined that the Bulgarians are intellectually backward and inefficient as a people but that morally they are good-hearted. This is not at all the case. Egoistic, vindictive, greedy for money and gain, stingy and crafty, the Bulgarian is also ambitious, capable of intellectual labor, resolute, methodical, energetic, diligent, and intent on profiting from every situation. Thanks to all of these character traits, the Bulgarian cannot look on calmly when an alien—and even the indigenous Jew is forever regarded as the most alien of aliens—finds a way of making a living in his country. No matter what the Jew might achieve and however virtuous he may be, the Bulgarian holds to the view that the Jew is eating *his* bread ("jade bulgarsky Gab").

This is not the place for going into minute detail. But if we want to find the key to answering the question about how the political situation of the Jews in Bulgaria may develop and what awaits them there, at least a brief overview of the stance taken by the various political parties toward the Jews is absolutely necessary.

Naturally, even Bulgaria has its liberal and conservative parties, which display a variety factions and shades of opinion. [64] But it would be a mistake to think that there is any difference in principle between the parties with respect to their doctrines toward the Jews.[20] The Jew is not at all Bulgarian, and that is quite enough to determine the conduct of the humblest political actor toward the Jews at all times. If one still wishes to make a distinction between the parties in their doctrine concerning the Jews, it is almost certainly not going to be found in their beliefs about the Jews but in the manner in which they put these beliefs into practice. From this standpoint, there is a clear distinction to be made between the Karavelovists, Tsankovists, and Unionists on the one hand, and the Conservative, Stambolovist, and Radoslavist parties on the other.[21]

Karavelov's disciples think that may be counted as genuine democrats when they never miss an opportunity to inveigh against the Jews in their party newspaper, *Zname*.[22] This conduct has its positive side, for the Jews see clearly and know what the Karavelovists might be aiming to do as the governing party.

Karavelov already inaugurated a practical anti-Semitism as minister at the time when the battlefield was still smelling of Jewish blood.[23] He was the one who shifted the weekly market day to Saturday, the one who already in 1882, in the Chamber of Deputies, accused the Jews of exploiting the Bulgarian population, the one who sought to snatch away the last means of livelihood from small Jewish merchants, the one who publicly branded the Jews as morally depraved persons on account of their importation of silver rubles from Romania, which were circulated and exchanged at that time.

The Jews are not so happy with the other parties. It is actually hard to say whether or not the Karavelovists are worse anti-Semites than the Tsankovists. But one thing is clear: the current organ of the Tsankovists, *Svetlina*, like the earlier one, *Suglasie*,[24] has not been so violent in its attacks. No less than the Karavelovists, they want to tear everything away from the Jews, but they want to do it with fine-sounding words. It is true that the Unionists, who owe their name to the hoped-for union of Bulgaria with East Rumelia, were, as an opposition party, quite radical and liberal, rhapsodizing about noble ideals in their party organ, *Pregoso*.[25] But a comparison of what *Pregoso* used to preach and what it is saying now that its patrons are in power, is a striking manifestation of duplicity. It deserves to be emphasized that the supporters of the Unionist party are exploiting almost every opportunity to translate their feelings toward our fellow tribesmen into action.

We have evidence of this from the very recent past. [65] The government was authorized to take out a ten million gulden loan for the benefit of the Bulgarian agricultural credit union. Around this time, the government learned that conditions of the loan would be much more favorable if it amounted to at least thirty million. Since the Bulgarian population already owed, on very harsh terms, at least one hundred million francs to private parties, the government presented to the legislature a draft law concerning the contracting of a loan with Banque de Paris et des Pays Bas, Banque internationale de Paris, and Banque J. et R. Priviléguée des Pays Autrichiens. One would think that in such cases the delegates would perceive their task and duty to lie in protecting the interests of the people and therefore to take into consideration factors pertaining only directly to the issue at hand. That might even have happened, if the Austrian Länderbank had not participated in the consortium. For several reasons, having to do with details we will not go into here, the Bulgarian hates Austria with every fiber of his being and calls it "Jew-land" or, as he puts it in Bulgarian, "Chifutska Avstriya." So the following declarations were to be heard in the legislature during debate over this issue: "We want nothing to do with the Länderbank. It should never receive our support. Let us hold to our honor by taking money from banks in which Jewish capital and speculation have almost no share, such as Crédit Lyonnais." Unfortunately, we do not know if the napoleons stored in the vaults of the Länderbank differ from those of the Crédit Lyonnais, and we are still laboring under the delusion that Jewish napoleons, even if they are in the Länderbank, are worth no less than those of the Crédit Lyonnais. However that may be, the fact is that the honorable deputies were opposed to concluding a loan with a consortium in which the Länderbank was participating because some Jewish shareholders stood to gain a few francs in the transaction. But it must also be emphasized here that the conditions for a Bulgarian loan had never been more favorable than in the case of the loan in question. (A full 1 percent reduction in the rate of interest was agreed to in exchange for only a slight decrease, of around two francs, in the issuing price of the bond.) Even the president of the Chamber had to acknowledge these advantages. "Although the government," he said, "has contracted the loan, not with Crédit Lyonnais, but with people we find obnoxious, nevertheless it must be admitted that the conditions are favorable to us." (Proceedings of the National Assembly, 9th Legislature, vol. 4, no. 11).

Anyone who follows the politics of the Balkan states knows very well that the current government consists not only of Unionists but of Conservatives as well. And it is precisely the latter party that has been thwarting the plans of the former, to take steps against the Jews in one field of activity or another.

[66] If there has been a Bulgarian man entirely free of various prejudices against the Jews, it was Stambolov. Recognizing the capabilities and intellectual prowess of the Jews, this statesman sought to put them to use for the benefit of his fatherland. In the two decades of the Bulgarian state's existence, Jews never had it so good as during his period in power. Everyone in the capital knows that Stambolov's government was even inclined to make available a goodly amount of land out of the state domains for the founding of several colonies of immigrant Jews. We do not know exactly what influenced the Bulgarian government to distance itself from this scheme. Popular opinion would like to shift the blame onto the shoulders of our fellow tribesmen. But it should be borne in mind that Stambolov's followers had an entirely different view of the

Jews from that of their chief, and sought on repeated occasions to effectively undo what Stambolov had done for the Jews.

To conclude our discussion of the position the various parties take toward the Jews, mention should be made of the Radoslavist party, and what should be said concerning it in this regard is just that its adherents on the whole share the views of the Stambolovist party.

As an issue closely connected with the issue of the position of the parties toward the Jews, it may be worth considering the actual participation of the Jews in the political life of the new state as well.

It is fair to assert that, in general, the Bulgarian Jews involve themselves very little in politics, their guiding principle in this regard being always to go along with the government. If any government on one or another occasion needs the Jews, or rather the Jews' votes, it will flirt with them and perhaps even make them some promises. And whoever is familiar with the way Bulgarian ministers operate will not bother asking if any one of them has ever kept his promises. Perhaps it cannot be otherwise. He who is for everyone is for no one at all.

But it would be wrong were we not to add to the foregoing the observation that there are a number of Bulgarian Jews who have quite openly attached themselves to a political party, campaign for this party alone, expose themselves to various attacks on the part of the governing party, and, whenever the party they support wins, garner a few old bones to chew on. There are Jewish party members of this type in both the Stambolovist and the Radoslavist camps.

[67] Since the Jews are not active in politics on a national or local level, it is no surprise that, although more than twenty-seven thousand Jews live in Bulgaria, with more than sixty-five hundred in Sofia alone, our fellow tribesmen have not a single representative in the Chamber. However, three years ago something extraordinary happened. In the electoral district of Dobrich, which has a very small Jewish population, a Jew was elected as deputy. When the elections for deputies were called in 1894, our fellow tribesman Peter Gabe was nominated as a candidate alongside Prime Minister Stoilov,[26] in the small eastern city of Balchik-Dobrich. He received a majority of the votes and was declared representative by the electoral commission in accordance with the law. But his election was annulled by his fellow members of the Chamber. And who is this man, who, going head to head with the prime minister, defeated him by 208 votes but was then turned away empty-handed? Peter Gabe is a Russian Jew who leased land in the vicinity of Yelisavetgrad during the years 1875–1882, in order to farm it with his own hands. As Gabe tells it: "In 1881, I saw with my own eyes how mobs razed the houses of peaceful inhabitants

and molested the Jews. Then came the law of 1882, which took from the Jews the possibility of leasing land. These circumstances caused me to leave Russia." (Proceedings of the Session of the 8th Volkov, 1.S., I.B., 487–503). In 1884, Gabe settled in Bulgaria and devoted himself once again to agriculture, but not just agriculture. He also wrote a great deal and was active in charitable causes. He did research on the national economy and financial system. He earned much credit with the Bulgarian government when, thanks to his literary and political activity, a special law for two districts was adopted by the Chamber, to put a stop to usury. Usury was a cancer that had rooted itself deeply into the society of eastern Bulgaria. Gabe had the courage to broach this complex issue and to prove the necessity of radical surgery. That won him the affection of those oppressed by usury, but, naturally, also incurred the hatred of the usurers.

His activity in the field of economics also led, after the fall of Stambolov, to his being named as a member of a tax commission set up to tackle various financial issues, which contributed greatly to his popularity. And in spite of all this, there was the annulment of his election![i] In the commission charged with reviewing the election results, there was talk of Gabe's lack of national credentials. A member of the commission passed this on to us, and it agrees with the arguments in the contestation that was filed.[ii]

[68] To keep such cases from arising in the future, a law was passed in the same session of the Chamber, upon the initiative of the current mayor of Sofia, according to which "a naturalized Bulgarian acquires the right to stand for office only after the passage of 15 years."

Working hand in hand with this semiofficial and official anti-Semitism is the anti-Semitism fostered by the press. Until recently we have had in Bulgaria a paper titled "Bulgaria without Jews" (*Bulgaria bez Evrei*), published by a certain Mitakov.[27] The Bulgarian dictionary contains no terms of abuse, the penal code no crimes, which this paper would not hurl at the Jews or impute

---

i   Proceedings of the National Assembly, 8th Legislature, 493.

ii "Even if we admit in the end to something we do not believe is correct, i.e., that this election was legal and that the elected representative for Baldich is Peter Gabe, the question would arise as to what kind of person he is. For this person, who wishes to be recognized as Peter Gabe, and whom the electoral commission officially declared to be elected, is not Peter Gabe but rather a Russian Jew known to us by the name of Eliezer, a nihilist (sic!!) from Russia, who escaped with a foreign passport, adopted the pseudonym Peter Gabe, and was accepted as a Bulgarian subject under this name." (Ibid., 487–88) to them. Featured first and foremost is that hobbyhorse of Western European anti-Semitism—the blood libel. There are no rights Herr Mitakov would not wish to deprive the Jews of.

Besides the paper, Herr Mitakov published several pamphlets with the same content, in the composing of which he evidently had Rohling's* works in front of him. After Mitakov was put in prison for insulting the prince and had to discontinue his paper, his work was carried on by a fine fellow who calls himself Major Osman Bey.* It is also worth emphasizing that the Bulgarian monthly *Vera i Razun* ("Faith and Reason"), edited by a preacher named Mina G. Minkov, publishes quite violent anti-Semitic articles, specifically to prove the Jews' use of Christian blood. Various pamphlets are being issued to combat anti-Semitism in Bulgaria. It need not be specially emphasized that they have not eliminated superstitions. Rarely do the Easter holidays pass without the Jews being overcome by fear, if anywhere a child goes missing from a Christian.

It is thus true to say, with regard to Bulgaria, that various social groupings are working for the de facto annulment of the legal equality of Jews, turning it into something that exists only on paper in accord with the European pattern, with the Jews' political rights recognized only insofar as one or another of the parties in government is able to profit from them.

The Economic Situation. [69] The political strength of every state is dependent on its economic condition; but one can imagine another kind of connection between these two factors. That is, the political rebirth of a people can act as a powerful means of revitalizing its economic conditions and opening up a new era in its economic life. This is brilliantly confirmed by the course of economic development in Bulgaria, awakened anew to political life. Even though the natural resources are still mostly unexploited, and existing economic institutions are still very primitive, the economic historian can nonetheless already register great progress.

Although Bulgaria, from the point of view of Western Europe, must still be considered a capital-poor country, it has nevertheless multiplied its national assets. In 1884 the national bank had only 2.4 million francs in deposits, as that term is used in modern banking; now it has more than forty-seven million. Likewise the agricultural credit unions, which previously represented balances of only a few hundred thousands, are now valued at more than five million.

The annual total savings should be estimated as much higher, though, since the last five years of Bulgarian economic life can be described as a period that has seen the creation of all kinds of stockholding companies in various lines of production, which have put enormous demands on capital for a country such as Bulgaria. Foreign capital has not had much to do with this, since the loans contracted by the state have been used for building railways and equipping the army. And in the private sector, foreign capitalists were able neither to obtain concessions nor to collaborate with the Bulgarian. Some Bulgarian professors have even made it their business, in the monthly publication "Proceedings of the Bulgarian Economics Society," to prove the harmfulness of foreign capital, which is said to belong totally to the Jews.

The population's greatly increased ability to pay taxes will weigh heavily in determining the growth of the nation's wealth. At the beginning of the 1880s Bulgaria operated with a budget for expenditures of around twenty million francs; a decade later it was already one hundred million. It should also be borne in mind that the amount of not only movable but also immovable property owned by the Bulgarian population has been greatly augmented. Bulgaria's rural population, which after all represents 5/6 of the total, has augmented its landholdings very markedly thanks to the emigration of the Turks. Numerous building projects, indeed the transformation of entire cities, also testify to the fact of increasing wealth. [70] Even the number of inhabitants has seen a relatively strong increase. In 1871, northern Bulgaria had 2,007,919 souls; in 1885, south Bulgaria had 975,030; in 1888, united Bulgaria already had 3,154,375; in 1893, 3,310,713; and now 3.5 million inhabitants.

Before concluding these general observations, I would like to add that Bulgaria has no rural proletariat and certainly no poverty in the Western European sense of that term. There is a dearth of manpower, but not of possibilities for employment and jobs, which can amply supply the material needs of life. It is a country richly blessed awaiting only the activity of men, in order for it to yield to them its treasures.

We can now pass on to the question impelled by these preliminary general observations: to what extent precisely have the Jews also participated in this increase of national wealth, and how indeed are they employed?

It is perhaps not superfluous to emphasize here that among the indigenous Sephardic Jews there is not a single cultivator of the soil. The reasons why our fellow tribesmen in various lands were unable to devote themselves to agriculture are well known to us. But the revolution in the conditions of land tenure in Bulgaria, owing to the emigration of the Turks; the absurdly low cost of land; and the state's free grant of various landed estates even to foreigners (e.g., most recently to Slavonians)—compel us to ask why, after all, there is no one even among the indigenous Jews for whom the cultivation of the soil is a source for earning a living.

From the statements made by Jews who live in the villages as merchants and are familiar with rural conditions, we have been able to ascertain that the Bulgarian populace uses every possible means to prevent Jews from purchasing land. My informants tell me that they dare not take their women and children with them into the villages, that they themselves must stay away from the village at certain times, indeed that their sojourning in the countryside exposes them to various kinds of rancor and persecution from the Bulgarian populace.

And so we see why our fellow tribesmen in Bulgaria are shopkeepers, craftsmen, and porters.

The Sephardic Jew has a big competitor in retailing, specifically in the person of the Macedonian-Bulgarian. The latter, often starting off his business with a few francs and peddling his wares on the streets, knows how to raise himself up within a short time, so that in just a few years he is making sales worth several thousands. [71] The Macedonian is displacing the Sephardic Jew by virtue of his vast energy, great shrewdness and long-term vision, great circumspection, stolid nature, and quick decisiveness. Therefore, it is not unusual to find that the marketing of various products that previously, under Turkish rule, belonged exclusively to Jews, is now in the hands of the Macedonians. We are watching the process by which the wholesale trade is becoming concentrated in their hands.

To be perfectly accurate, we should add that there are also Jews who have made big profits since the reestablishment of the Bulgarian state, but their number is so small that the Bulgarians themselves almost never assert that the Sephardim are capitalists.

The other social class among the Jews comprises various craftsmen–cobblers, tailors, tinsmiths, glaziers, house painters, cabinetmakers, turners, hatmakers, goldsmiths, upholsterers, umbrella-makers, clockmakers, etc. An impressive number of our fellow tribesmen are porters and many of them are engaged in what is called "loketoya"; i.e., they have no fixed occupation—rather, as the folk idiom has it, they live "on air," on whatever falls into their hands. Today the "loketoyer" gets some money from selling chickens, tomorrow he hires a carriage to transport various items for someone, and the next day he sits in the road all day, waiting for whatever else the good Lord will bring his way.

What we have seen on many occasions with our own eyes and what we know from the letters of friends reaching us from the countryside, permit us to assert that there is already mass misery among Jews in Bulgaria.

Anyone who needs persuading about this can go to the capital of Bulgaria, where the Jews inhabit special quarters, called Iuch-Bunar and Dor-Bunar. In these low-lying parts of the city, full of bogs, the nurseries of Sofia's epidemic diseases, and surrounded by various other stinking ponds, eight out of every ten of our coreligionists in Sofia live in such unspeakable poverty and misery that visiting the homes they inhabit will cause one to positively shudder.

The houses, built out of brick, clay, or packed earth, are so cramped that you have to double over in order to slip into a room. We have ourselves seen some residents crawl like Eskimos. Everything is caked with mud: the old people, the children, and the house. And everywhere a hideous odor. If there is not an open pit outside that passes for a latrine, then it will usually form a section of the kitchen itself, abutting the wall where the bread is baked. The clay floors, entirely without covering, are muddy and often even inundated by water. The air is noxious, stifling. [72] We have taken measurements in nearly one hundred dwellings, and it turns out that the average room has a surface area of sixteen to twenty square meters. If one takes into consideration that the height of the rooms seldom exceeds 1.8 meters and that several individuals are present in one room, we may permitted to infer that the inhabitants of such rooms never get enough of even the contaminated air around them. There is almost no furniture in the rooms. Along the walls are low Turkish benches (called "minderluks"), and we have to hold our notebook on our knees. Everyone always sleeps on the floor, and for this purpose bolsters are brought out from a storage closet. Under these circumstances it is no surprise that the hearth becomes a hotbed of depravity.

We hasten to note that, almost without exception, the occupants of these houses are their owners. Thus, someone seeking to apply directly a European criterion of class, would have to say that a Jewish proletariat does not exist in Bulgaria.

Let us now make an effort to see how these people live. Annual income fluctuates between five hundred and one thousand francs, of which eighteen to twenty-five francs per month are spent on bread, eight to twelve on vegetables, eight to twelve on meat, and five to ten on drinks. The people drink mostly schnapps.

This circumstance alone; i.e., that the main item of expenditure is bread and that meat, though cheap, is consumed only in very small quantities supplies proof that Jewish homeowners are eking out a kind of existence, which the propertyless Western European worker, at least in many countries, would certainly not envy.

Thus you have, in its general features, the economic situation of the Jewish population in Bulgaria, whose wretched existence does not attract attention simply because its numbers are relatively small. It often happens that parents put their very small children to work, girls six or seven years of age, in order to improve their economic position by their weekly earnings of, hard as it is to believe, ten centimes. No wonder, under such conditions, that the main pillars of morality are collapsing, nor is it surprising, given the lack of an appropriate training of the intellectual and moral powers—as we will see a bit later—mainly attributable to the bitter economic situation, if even among the Sephardim, who hold so stubbornly to the traditions of Judaism, there are cases of young girls who submit to baptism in order to obtain, through marriage to a Bulgarian man, the secure "enjoyment" of his beatings and a crust of bread.

In making this report about the economic situation, we cannot banish from our minds the impression made upon us by the Jewish quarter in Sofia after a heavy downpour of rain.

[73] We visited the homes in Iuch-Bunar and Dor-Bunar on a spring day after a heavy rain. What a wretched and deplorable scene! To get from one house to the next, the people had to walk barefoot up to the knees in water. And inside the rooms! The low benches, the household furnishings, perhaps in some places a table or cradle—all swimming in water. And the heartbreaking stories of the inhabitants. When a heavy rain begins at night, the people must leave their sleeping place—the floor—and stand guard to wait and see if the enemy—the water—will appear. If it does, they leave their homes and consign their furnishings to fate, until a company of firemen or soldiers have made channels to remove the water from the streets or else pumped it out of the rooms. Such is the El Dorado of the Jews in the youngest state of Europe.

Intellectual development. Significant as the economic factor may be in the present social order and in its influence on the social position of the individual, yet it cannot be denied that much also depends on intellectual development; therefore, we would like now to delve more deeply into the question of the cultural condition of the Jews in Bulgaria.

Here we are obliged to affirm, with astonishment, that the Bulgarians have made colossal strides forward in the path of their intellectual development, during the nineteen-year existence of their state. During a short period of time, they have sought with unceasing energy to retrieve what they neglected during a servitude lasting five centuries. All of Bulgaria is covered by a great network of schools; a multitude of young Bulgarians go abroad at state expense in order to train in every possible field of specialization. Unfortunately, owing to the reactionary politics now everywhere dominant, and to the current, ethically unhealthy conditions of Bulgaria, the Bulgarian is completely unable to mitigate the qualities of his moral character during his sojourn even in the civilized countries, even when he has finished his university studies. But if the moral development among the Bulgarians has not at all kept pace with their intellectual development, the Jews by comparison have not advanced at all in the latter respect. There are several factors at work here, as we will see in a moment. At any rate, the fact remains that, of the indigenous Jewish population, very few have received a modern European education until now. The number of Jewish illiterates is, incidentally, no greater than those of other nationalities living in Bulgaria.

[74] According to the scanty statistical data of 1863, which were derived from records of marriages, illiteracy among men was 23.24 percent and among women 40.31 percent. Of Jews qualifying for military service, illiterates were: in 1888, 29.22 percent; in 1889, 39.61 percent; in 1890, 54.06 percent; in 1891, 25.68 percent; in 1892, 22.35 percent; in 1893, 51.49 percent (*Review of Students*, No. 1). But it should not be overlooked that Jews registered as literate include persons who can read only a prayerbook. Naturally, such persons are not equipped with the necessary means to be able to carry on the current struggle to earn a living, nor are they capable of judging what kind of position they could or should take towards any of the issues of the day.

The existing Jewish schools can scarcely claim that they are equal to their important tasks. First and foremost, it should be borne in mind that in the schools of the Alliance Israélite Universelle it is almost exclusively Sephardic children who can be accepted. Either French or Ladino is spoken in these schools. Since our Ashkenazic brothers are not able to speak either of these languages, it is as a rule impossible for their children to attend Sephardic schools. Since the number of Ashkenazim in every city is too small to defray the costs of a school out of their own resources, their children would have to remain in a very neglected state, were there not various mission schools present everywhere. It hardly needs to be emphasized that our children are pulled away from a Jewish way of life in these schools, even if it is not their formally declared purpose. But even in the specifically Jewish schools, the knowledge of Judaism and its history is not cultivated. Graduates of these schools were unable to answer our questions about the most important moments in our history. Who were Ezra and Nehemiah, and what did they achieve; by whom and when did Judea become an imperial province? To all of these questions we received no answer.

In order to fulfill our promise, we wish to also examine briefly the causes to which this degenerate intellectual condition of the Bulgarian Jews is to be ascribed.

We must admit that the thirst for knowledge is not particularly strong among the Sephardic Jews. Of course, their atrocious economic circumstances contribute to this. But there are also objective factors that stand as obstacles in their way. The Bulgarian government, which shrinks from no material sacrifice to support every Bulgarian striving for education, has adapted the schools specifically for the Orthodox Christian population to such an extent that one would think there was no one belonging to another confession among the Bulgarian citizenry. Attending school on the Jewish Sabbath is very difficult for the Sephardic population, who still observe the day. [75] One would think that this young state which boasts so often of its religious tolerance would after all concede to the Jews at least as much as was done previously by Russia; i.e., not to have to write on the Sabbath.

The Bulgarian government will not even provide for the religious instruction of the Jewish population by means of special Jewish teachers. The government sees no contradiction between the constitutionally recognized principle of legal equality and the fact that, whereas Orthodox Christian secondary school students receive instruction in their religion, the Jews do not. Not even in the history curriculum will the government afford opportunity to make known to the students the most outstanding moments in our history. Just recently it published a curriculum for the schools where we find the following passage: "Oriental peoples. A historical and cultural survey of Egyptians, Assyrians, Babylonians, Persians, Phoenicians, Carthaginians, and Indians." The history curriculum thus totally ignores the Jews. Their history possesses nothing of interest—or perhaps there are other factors at work.

And what the history curriculum has left out, instructors try to compensate for at other opportune moments. Last year a geography teacher in a secondary school, in the presence of Jewish pupils, made the following observation in his lecture about Greece: "Truly, it is hard to say whether the Jews are worse scoundrels than the Greeks, but when it comes to deceit, it appears that they may be entitled to pre-eminence." Such pronouncements by the teachers, reinforced by a similar training in the family, are the reason why Jewish pupils are exposed to various kinds of derision and abuse as "Chifuti" on the part of their Bulgarian schoolmates.

The social status of the Jews. In determining the social status of Jews in a given country, it is common practice to pay particular attention to how many

Jews are found in state service. The census of officials done in Bulgaria last year puts us in a position to begin by applying this criterion. Out of 20,509 officials, forty-seven are of "Mosaic confession" and of those thirty-three are listed as "Jews"; i.e., those who had the courage to state that they were Jews by nationality. The remainder was attached to other nationalities. When we bear in mind that the population of Bulgaria comprises 3,300,000, and that Jews form 1/132 of the population, they would properly be represented by 154 with the status of an official.

Unfortunately, reports of the statistical bureau do not state how officials are distributed by rank according to their religion or nationality. [76] But we can safely assume we are correct in reporting here, that the Jews are assigned the lowest positions and that they have no prospect of advancing. The greatest number of Jewish officials is in the Ministry of War. Among the fifteen holding official positions therein, not more than three, to our knowledge, hold officer rank, the rest being subalterns. The Ministry of Interior comes next in line, where we have some physicians, who are gradually being driven out of service by devious means and replaced by Bulgarians. Some of our fellow tribesmen are also attached to this ministry as policemen. The Ministry of Communications has the same number of Jewish officials, who are currently employed as engineers and architects on big Bulgarian construction projects. There are very few Jews in other ministries. Two ministries—namely Finance and Commerce—are *judenrein* or, more precisely, have become *judenrein*.[28] And other ministries are competing to follow their example.

An incident that occurred just recently can cast light on the social relations between Jews and Bulgarians.

Since a church was unable or unwilling to pay off a heavy burden of debt, its creditors—thank God there were no Jews among them—put under distraint property of the church not required for conducting mass. The church also owned a certain piece of land not contiguous with the churchyard and located on another street. Since a Jew bid more than others when it was sold at auction, he had a clear legal right to be recognized as the owner. But when it was learned that a Jew had acquired the plot, the party organs of Tsankov and Karavelov wrote quite violent articles, the church vestry lodged a protest with the government, the parishioners organized a meeting in the churchyard where they declared that they could not allow under any circumstance a Jew to come into possession of church property. Some threatened the purchaser if he did not renounce his claim. Since the new owner was well acquainted with the Bulgarian character, which proceeds very quickly from words to deeds when something of material value is at stake, he could not in fact exercise his valid right. At the outset he sought to cool tempers by making a large donation to the church and by instigating some newspapers to write some lines in his favor and defending his right as a citizen of the state to take part in the auction like any other full-blooded Bulgarian. To make himself feel a little more secure, he left Sofia to await in another locality the final decision of the church vestry. When the vestry and the parishioners persisted in their decision, our citizen realized that he had no alternative but to abandon his valid right and revoke the purchase.

This is an example of what legal equality means in Bulgaria. [77] Perhaps more pertinent is the trouble the Jewish congregation of Sofia got itself into last year. Until about a year ago, a synagogue built in the Moorish style could be seen beside a church, on a street just off the main boulevard. Now the synagogue's council took the decision to erect an extension on a piece of land owned by the synagogue, in order to meet their expanding needs. Construction began. Meanwhile, it was learned that the church vestry, acting through the bishop, was taking steps to lodge a protest with the government against the work undertaken by the Jewish congregation. It didn't seem at all proper to the vestry that, first, a synagogue should be located in the same neighborhood, and second, that the open land should belong to the synagogue rather than the church. Members of the synagogue council went immediately with documents in hand when summoned by the government minister. The government appointed a special commission tasked with deciding the question of who was, according to the documents and surveys, the owner of the disputed property. Even this commission had to acknowledge the valid right of the Jewish congregation. And what happened? The newspapers began to inveigh against the Jews. This malicious mouthpiece of public opinion, which of course was also artificially stirred up, supplied the government with the chance to remonstrate in a "friendly" way with the synagogue council, that it was in the Jews' own interest to renounce ownership of the disputed land and to carry on with building the synagogue elsewhere. Indeed, the minister observed, your Western European Jewish brothers do not build synagogues on major streets, but on various out-of-the-way sidestreets, away from the areas with the busiest traffic. So the Jewish congregation had not only to hand over the open land to the church, but also discontinue building of the synagogue. And it is acutely painful now to see, instead of the new extension, shops for used goods that have turned the area beside the synagogue into a flea market. But it is not only the possession of material goods that is insecure. Often things of much higher value of a different character are being exposed to the "good will" of the Bulgarians. And in particular, various legal judgments of late are such as to diminish the Jews' feeling of security. Jewish persons and houses are pelted with stones. Women and girls dare not venture far from their homes as soon as it gets dark. When a Bulgarian invites his comrades "Hayde na koina," it means that they will go in pursuit of a Jewish girl to rape her. It is telling that one of these Bulgarians, when called to account, maintained that he had something like *jus primae noctis*.[29]

There is an absolute gulf between the Jews and the Bulgarians. [78] Imbued with arrogance and suspicion, the latter avoid dealings with the former and in the capital seek company in a club exclusively for gentlemen ("Slavoyanskaye Besseda"); exceptionally, certain Jews are invited to this society's balls, if they have attractive daughters. And as in Sofia, so also in the provinces. One of our confidants from south Bulgaria writes to us:

> When speaking of our fellow tribesmen, it should be known that we do not enjoy the same rights as our fellow citizens. A majority of the Jews comprises merchants and artisans, and these are the ones who are first of all subject to the physical abuse of non-Jewish colleagues in the same line of work. Proof of this fact is to be found in the circumstance that the number of artisans and merchants is declining day by day, and that the Jews are being forced to go into the big cities in order to eke out a living. In our region, where there is in fact no government authority, a Jew cannot go about freely without being maltreated and without epithets which are well known to you.... A Jew cannot raise his voice at all, for the surrounding society, which will not tolerate the equality of Jews, forces him immediately into silence. If a Jew has a legal case, it will be put on the docket only after a very long time, the excuse being that the court is occupied with other cases.
>
> We are unable, with few exceptions, to send our children to Bulgarian schools, because of the insults they will be exposed to from their fellow students, who go unpunished.

All of the factors emphasized in this report suffice to explain why even the Bulgarian Jew yearns for a new redemption in our beloved historic homeland, why every Jewish ear in Bulgaria, where the idea of the Congress met with a great positive response, is listening to everything said in this assembly, why even Bulgarian Jewry is awaiting with excitement the results of the Congress's labors. May the results be truly crowned with success and lead to the realization of our sublime goal! (Lively applause.)

PRESIDENT: Herr Dr. Rónay* has the floor for a report on the situation of Jews in Hungary.

DR. JÁNOS RÓNAY (BLAZSFALVA): Highly honored assembly! The judgment on my fatherland you have heard[30] has thrust me through to the heart.[31] Unfortunately, I have to admit that some of it is indeed valid. Without having prepared a speech, I will say briefly what still needs to be said. In Hungary, which is an autonomous and powerful state, freedom and justice stand forth like a rock in the sea. But anyone who thinks historically will have to ask himself: is there absolutely no possibility that sooner or later the floods of reaction and barbarism shall rise so high as to inundate the rock and cause it to crumble away? [79] Hungary has not only a free constitution but also an honest, liberal, benevolent, and energetic government. But the other elements in the state are not all animated by this noble spirit. In terms of demographics, Hungary consists of two halves: "Hungarian" Hungary, within which the Jews are to be reckoned, accounts for less than half; the so-called nationalities form the other half. Those belonging to the latter group are quite honorable people as private individuals; but the private individual is entirely different, and the human being turns into something entirely different, when overcome by any kind of political passion.[32] We have gotten along tolerably well with the nationalities that make up more than half the state. But presently a myth has been invented by the Hungarians and anti-Semites, that the Hungarians would have gone bankrupt without the Jews. It is not true but it is believed. Men hoping to realize particularistic demands believe that the Jews stand in their way. Thus, hatred toward the Jews has developed within the greater half of the state. But even among the Magyars,[33] the clerics would rather join the enemies of the state than have to make concessions to liberalism. A few weeks ago the so-called People's Party, which could actually be termed a Christian-Socialist party, declared publicly in the Hungarian parliament, in alluding to the trial of Jews in Tisza-Eszlár, that there was no real anti-Semitism in Hungary yet, but that there certainly would be soon!![34] But it is not just this fraction of the Hungarians but also the others, who are offended by the impertinent idea that they cannot exist without the Jews. The result is that, while one group of chauvinists screams that we have still not been sufficiently Magyarized, the other Hungarians call us "fifty kreuzer Magyars," because the application for changing one's name requires only a fifty kreuzer stamp. A confessional newspaper, which has fulminated against Zionism, recently had to admit that the situation in Hungary is darkening. Nevertheless, we hope that liberalism will prevail.

As of yet, active Zionism finds no fertile soil in Hungary; nonetheless, there is a need to distribute explanatory literature. Jews and Christians have an ongoing fear of the immigration of Polish Jews driven out of Russia. If just to divert these poor people from Hungary, the Hungarians ought to support Zionism. Moreover, explanation is needed in order to show that Zionism does not clash with patriotism. I declare in the name of all Hungarians that, as long as we are not marching into Palestine, we will remain good Hungarian patriots. If we do go marching into Palestine, we will be just as good patriots there as we are Hungarian patriots today. Gentlemen! My vision is this: I believe that if the Hungarian Jew emigrates to Palestine, he will carry with him a feeling of gratitude toward his former fatherland. [80] I wish for all Jews of all countries, that they cherish the same feelings for their fatherland that I do for mine. Then will it come to pass that the most concentrated and condensed form of patriotism, along with a truly heartfelt sympathy for all the peoples on earth, takes shape in one small people. Then Jewry will become the heart of all peoples. (Lively applause.)

PRESIDENT: I give the floor to the honorable Adam Rosenberg,* attorney at law, to make his report on the situation of Jews in America.

ADAM ROSENBERG (NEW YORK): Gentlemen! I had no time to prepare a report about America; I had to limit myself to making a few observations. I will be brief. In America, Jewry has reached the last stage of its journey. The result is that, out of one million Jews who now live in America, there are at least 25 percent whose yearning, whose weariness of Europe, which drove them to America, the new promised land—has metamorphosed into the old yearning for the old promised homeland. And if we keep up our work, the other 75 percent in every part of the country will be added to this 25 percent.

The internal political conditions in America, insofar as these have to do with the treatment of Jews by the American authorities, are very much the same as in England. As everyone knows, America may be viewed as a daughter country of England and owes its traditions to the motherland. The American Jew has nothing to complain about in this respect, but in another respect he may. America is the great refuge of persecuted Jews from the great European countries, and this circumstance has created conditions in America which are different from those prevailing in England. We have about 60 percent East European Jews, the majority of these being Russian and Polish. America is the most developed land in capitalist terms. The pressure that weighs upon the masses is more pronounced there than elsewhere, and since, as we all know, the persecuted Jews from East Europe did not take a pleasure cruise to America, this pressure hits them harder than others.

With respect to immigration to America, we can distinguish two periods. In the beginning, twenty years ago, people went to America to make their fortune, and many who went there seeking their fortune also found it. Immigrating later were those who, at a minimum, were seeking a place to settle,[35] who wanted to improve their economic condition, and who did not and will not succeed. We have arrived at a point where, just as the proletariat has attained such prominence in the life of the European peoples, so also here, it has been continually swelling in numbers. [81] Public opinion has now risen up to oppose further immigration, which would bring in social elements that burden public institutions. It has been necessary to take account of public opinion and issue new immigration laws. All these immigration laws are not anti-Semitic but are rather a political-economic self-defense.

Among the American Jews we have a solidarity based on a special kind of mutual aid, a well-known religious organization that has legal recognition in Europe. There has been much misunderstanding about it, as I have had occasion to observe. This religious organization has a material basis, in that it constitutes a kind of life insurance, a kind of fund to cover expenses related to death, or the like.

To be sure, there is in America also a kind of anti-Semitism. But it is only a fashion imported by foreign immigrant elements. Until now it has not become an epidemic, but it is possible that it will spread farther.

However, we American Jews are favored by the fact that there exist no "nations" in America but rather just a conglomeration of different races.

People have tried to pursue a colonization policy in America; even in the United States, Jewish colonies have been formed. Until now, they have not proven very successful. Instead of the colonists practicing agriculture alone, they have a mix of occupations; in one season they are farmers, in another factory workers. Colonization has emanated from owners of industry and Jewish businessmen, who have used and exploited the cause. Now and then they have tried horticulture as well.

There is another interesting phenomenon worth mentioning, a certain impulse among Jews previously assimilated, a disposition bringing them back to the old ways of Judaism. It is best expressed in the founding of a so-called National Council of Jewish Women, which is being built up on a national basis, though not consciously.[36] We have a Jewish women's movement. What I can tell you about them is that a young Russian rabbi received a charge from rich Jewish women to hold a cycle of lectures on Jewish history and Jewish literature for well-to-do social groups in various cities. This is an indication that women rather than men may prove to be the vanguard of Zionism. In general, Zionism in America nowadays is spread only among the Russian immigrants who have sought their fortune but have not found it.

In closing, I want only to express a wish that the work of our Congress may be successful. May the next Congress take place in Jerusalem. (Hearty assent.)

PRESIDENT: Dr. Max Nordau has the floor.

DR. MAX NORDAU: Models of brevity and objectivity are needed. [82] I will therefore simply implore the honored assembly to take note of the reports they have heard, and perhaps also of the following motion of Herr S. R. Landau* and Herr Dr. S. Werner,* which reads:

> Since precise knowledge of social differentiation and economic situation is necessary for the realization of the Zionist program, the Congress resolves to compile occupational statistics concerning the Jews.
>
> To this end, a labor committee has been set up for every country, consisting of at least three members, with the right of cooptation.
>
> The labor committees are to complete their work within the next year and to submit it to the next Congress.

I can only recommend to you the adoption of this motion.

PRESIDENT: I give the floor to Herr Dr. Kaminka.*

DR. A. KAMINKA (PRAGUE): I would like to observe that this motion belongs under the category of "organization." Therefore, it is recommended to postpone it until we deal with the issue of organization.

PRESIDENT: Herr Marmorek has the floor.

OSCAR MARMOREK: I support the motion of Dr. Kaminka, since I would like to offer some amendments.

PRESIDENT: Herr Dr. Bodenheimer* has the floor.

Dr. Bodenheimer (Cologne): I would like to support Kaminka's motion. Such a motion cannot be voted on before settling the issue of organization. Therefore, I am also for postponing the motion.

President: Herr Dr. Landau has the floor.

Dr. S.R. Landau (Vienna): I have not given reasons for the motion because it speaks for itself and because this also was not done by the rapporteurs. I think the motion finds its best justification in what has been set forth today. What has been set forth today is, for the most part, not sufficiently documented by statistics because we do not have these documents. We can only sketch in a general way the condition of the Jews. The motion has nothing to do with the issue of organization. The organization is to be merely the agency for executing decisions of the Congress. The aim of this motion is to enable us to survey our ranks, to get to know our army. In my view, this has nothing to do with the decision about the issue of organization. If the gentlemen are in agreement, I ask them to adopt the motion; if not, I ask them to reject it.

President: Herewith I bring Kaminka's motion for a postponement to a vote.
    Kaminka's motion is adopted.

Pause

President: I give the floor to Herr Dr. Nathan Birnbaum.*

Dr. Nathan Birnbaum (Berlin): Highly honored assembly! Justifying a movement means demonstrating its historical necessity. In the case of Zionism, this demonstration depends upon two empirical premises: the Jews' distinctive economic life and the Jews' distinctive national life. [83] On the Jews' economic life as a basis for Zionism, my co-rapporteur, Herr Dr. Farbstein,* will address you, while the task has fallen to me to justify Zionism from the standpoint of the Jews' national life. To be sure, on account of the intrinsic unity of these subjects, it will not always be possible to strictly observe this division of labor.

I have spoken of the distinctiveness of the Jews' national life as a fact. I must add that it is a fact that is often disavowed. Those who deny it belong to all kinds of political affiliations at the national level, and the overwhelming number of these are Jews. True, they are becoming fewer day by day, and the weight of their disavowal is also reduced by the fact that they are for the most part motivated not by a deliberate search for truth but by biases. Now and then one may indeed find serious men among them. But their presence in this group is to be explained by a misunderstanding. Because they—in part justifiably and in part unjustifiably—no longer find a sense of Jewish national identity in themselves, they conclude, in an easily understood if totally unjustified way, that the generality of Jews is also devoid of it. If they were able to open themselves up a bit more, Jewish national identity would become a palpable reality for them.

The question of whether or not a nation exists is decided in the affirmative from that moment when even one person acknowledges the nation in question; he may or may not count himself as belonging to it. But the Jewish nation is acknowledged as such not by one person but by hundreds of thousands, nearly all Gentiles being of this view; and I believe that any unbiased person who is not influenced by defensive tendencies will, at the very least, give to the latter's opinions their full weight.

At most, one might have doubts about whether use of the words "nation" and "national identity" was precisely applicable, about whether in choosing these words the fine distinctions were being observed, which scientific study makes and must make, between *Nation*, *Stamm*, and *Volk*.[37] Such doubts can best be met by declaring that, basically, it does not matter to Zionism which of the aforesaid designations is most scientific. Zionism asserts its validity in all these cases. This is true even though Zionism is quite aware that today's Jewish national identity—to stick with that term—does not fit with current typologies, but rather that it presents a mass of anomalies. And Zionism even admits, on top of all that, that it owes its existence to these irregularities.

The Jewish nation of today is divided into two culturally very dissimilar sections—the smaller section existing in Western civilization, and the larger non-European section comprising both the Yiddish-speaking Jewry[38] of Eastern Europe and the truly Oriental Jews.[39] Both of these two main divisions exhibit anomalies in their national character. [84] The Eastern Jews—that is the Yiddish speakers, who make up three-quarters of the Jewish people—have a separate national identity, which expresses itself in appearance and speech, in literature and art, in manners and customs, in religious, social, and legal institutions; in other words they possess their own culture. But this culture is not progressive, for reasons that I will return to. It has not taken part in any kind of development. It has remained the same for two thousand years. Of course, movements have appeared in the ghetto which one might at first glance interpret as the normal progress of a culture—throughout the Middle Ages as well as in the present. And especially today. One need think only of the great surge of Yiddish literature and Yiddish theater. However, if we look more closely we find herein absolutely no self-generated advances having an effect on the culture of Eastern Jewry, rather, one is dealing simply with a rising civilization movement that happens to coincide to a certain extent with a rising class movement within Jewry itself. No steps of cultural progress are occurring, only a stepping out of native culture and into European civilization. Even the new Hebrew literature before the advent of Zionism bore in itself the character of being merely another transition into Europeanism. More and more, new flocks of Jews possessing their own indigenous culture are striving toward Europeanism, swelling the ranks of those who have long since arrived at this goal.

Now the amazing thing is that, even with this "conversion," the national-cultural anomaly of the Jews is in no way eliminated; it only changes its form.

In order to satisfy ourselves of this fact, let us first determine the essence of what is called "European civilization." One commonly speaks of "European culture." This usage leads to various illusions. It accustoms us to believe in a common identity belonging to all modern Western nations; i.e., to fashion for us an internationalism, or to speak of a new, pan-European nation in the process of formation. Both notions are utterly false. European civilization consists of two elements—the precipitates of the past cultural eras of various peoples, and the effects of the common economic conditions of civilized nations. The second element is the most conspicuous, but neither one nor the other abolishes national identity as such. On the contrary, European civilization cannot at all dispense with national identity. Europeanism is a grand interlocking mechanism, into which every people must first breathe the vitalizing breath of its national particularity, its national culture, for it to be set in motion for its (the people's) own purposes.

Thus do we understand why even Europeanized Jews constitute an anomaly in the cultural life of the peoples. [85] In leaving behind ghetto culture they relinquish their distinctive national culture. But they do not adopt the national identity and culture of another people. They lead now an isolated existence, sharply demarcated from others yet without authenticity. Their habitus of body and mind is different from that of the peoples among which they dwell, but unlike them it is not integrated into a way of life. It is like the case of persons who may bring with them an unusual aptitude for an occupation of some kind, which distinguishes them from their fellow citizens, yet who are unable to attain a solid professional position, to a concentrated honing of their skills.

Thus, the situation is that European Jews possess nothing that would enable them to give to European civilization a way of life adapted to their own character. So, while they learn much of civilizing value from it, they do not create new cultural values from the interaction of their own spirit with this civilization. On the contrary. Because they see it differently from other people, because they see it as an abstraction, they are led astray into powerful delusions and misconceptions.

To begin with, true to human nature, most of them think their abnormality to be normal. That is why it so often happens that they imagine Europeanism to be a denationalized internationalism, whereas in reality only in them is Europeanism without national identity. Because of this they bring an injurious element into the socialist movement, to which their creative spirit has otherwise made a beneficial contribution. Persons possessed of a stronger national feeling are unnecessarily repelled thereby and driven directly into embracing chauvinism. But even those more receptive to internationalist propaganda quickly turn away, likewise dissatisfied, from Jewish agitators. Then the old Jew-hatred makes its appearance in modern form, the outspoken or timid anti-Semitism, the instinctive antipathy of everyone, the well-fed as well as the disinherited, against persons who are nationless, indeterminate, suspicious.

It is even worse when Europeanized Jews are not misled by their abstract Europeanism into internationalist fantasies but instead perceive it in a clear-eyed manner. For them it is then reduced to a naked, modern system of profit-making, reposing on some mummies of culture. The result is the appearance of those Jews, poor and rich, whose god is money. Of course, there are ample numbers of these servants of mammon around, and perhaps just as many among other peoples. But they cannot have such a corrupting effect there, because their crude profit-driven perspective is offset by powerful cultural counterweights in the national community. And moreover, they will be at most reckoned alongside others; but not so with us, because it is said of us, as defenseless strangers, that we are cold, heartless men of the counting house. More raw material for anti-Semitism.

[86] A third disastrous effect of this abstract Europeanism—but in contradistinction to the two foregoing cases, arising from a presentiment of its inadequacy—is that movement which has taken a futile path by trying to breathe life into its Europeanism: assimilation. We are not speaking of that assimilation which has the boldness of complete apostasy through baptism or intermarriage. The casualties caused by these are more, one might say, arithmetical, inasmuch as every people endures them, and they therefore pose—even if they are more frequent and more serious among the Jews—no substantive danger. No, the question is not about radical, bona fide assimilation, but rather that

cowardly expedient of a so-called assimilation maintaining a so-called Mosaic confession. As hopeless from the outset as this doctrine is, given its inherent contradiction, its deleterious impact must in no way be underestimated. It has produced within Western Jewry a discordant character that is even worse than the excesses of internationalist fantasy and mammon-driven calculation. It has cheated eminent spirits out of the positive national identity they sought to attain; it has enlisted honest men in a lifelong masquerade and thereby caused their moral disintegration; it has incited base social elements to race for the prize of maximum assimilation; i.e., of the greatest talent in aping others.[40] This disgusting show shares the responsibility, with nebulous internationalism and brazen mammon-idolatry, for the tremendous growth of anti-Semitism.

Thus we are seeing, even in the realm of civilized Jewry, which appears to many naïve souls as a kind of salvation from the rigidity of the ghetto, cultural forces constrained or even transmuted into culture-destroying forces. We are seeing the old, I would almost call it "venerable," Jew-hatred turned into anti-Semitism, into a thoroughly anticivilizational and anticultural current. For that is what it is. It leads the peoples astray with respect to humankind's most important issues; it corrupts national, political, social, and religious movements; and it comes not even one step closer to solving the Jewish question, its raison d'être. It knows of no means of removing the Jews from the life of European peoples, and even if it did, in the final analysis precious little would be achieved for these peoples. Ultimately, the Jewish question is only a detail for them—even if at times a very disturbing one. The Jewish question is truly only the principal issue, the existential question, for those essentially and immediately involved, for ourselves, for us for whom body and soul are at stake in it—in the East and in the West. We must therefore also consider how it is to be solved. It must be our own concern, to restore a progressive impulse to Eastern Jews, to animate the dead Europeanism of Western Jews. [87] These things are only possible on the Zionist path, by once again elevating the Jewish nation to be a people possessing a state.

One very often hears it asserted, with great learned self-assurance, that Zionism has been produced by anti-Semitism as a backlash against the latter.

Now it is certainly not to be denied that the growth of the Zionist movement coincides with the growth of anti-Semitism, and it is natural to draw the conclusion that Zionism lives at the mercy of anti-Semitism. Yet this would be an egregious error of logic. One has only to recall that every movement has its causes and its conjunctures, attracting by means of the former its pioneers, by means of the latter its troops.

However, Zionism can assert proudly concerning itself, that all those who have stood and are standing at its head, either have for a long time already grown beyond being motivated by anti-Semitic conjunctures, or have from the very beginning been moved by the anomalous nature of Jewish national existence—in other words, have been filled with a yearning for a normal, progressive, national cultural life. In this respect they are the disciples of a great series of men of past centuries who had the same yearning. But the Zionist leaders were born under more favorable stars than their predecessors, not because anti-Semitism is coming to their aid, but rather because they have at their disposal what the others did not have, a people prepared for their purposes by European civilization.

Indeed, as long as the ascending movement toward civilization, from the ghetto into the European camp, was only very meager, the Zionist current could have no hope of succeeding. For it lacked a people with strength of will. This is not learned in the ghetto. The ghetto knows only about yearning. Only with the mass ascent of Jews into Europeanism in the West, and as in the East a generation arose which learned the power of the will from Western civilization, with its great dynamic nations, was the way paved for Zionism. Now there was no longer any other way. It was now only a question of time before Zionism gained acceptance and suppressed the short-lived aberration of assimilation. At the same time, the future development of the Jewish people was inseparably connected to European civilization by this process. In this civilization the daughter of Israel came of age and reached maturity for the bridegroom. But the bridegroom, the future husband, who is to awaken her to a new, fertile, life-giving existence, is her own land.

The lack of their own land is the thing that has been the cause of the hitherto anomalous nature of the Jews' national existence. Without its own land, the Europeanism of the Western Jew is barren, and without its own land the national culture of the Eastern Jews has remained in stagnation. [88] Let them have their own land and the Jews of the East will become a progressive cultural element, the Jews of the West will become Europeans with a national character, from the two will be formed a united people with Western civilization and an authentic, progressive national culture.

Let us begin our demonstration of this thesis with the Jews of the East!
Why is their indigenous culture unprogressive?
First of all, because they are without an economic basis of support that is not denied to other national cultures. They possess no national economy; on the contrary they live within an alien national economy and not on an equal

footing with those who properly belong to it. The old Jew-hatred has arranged it thus. The most profitable occupations are entirely closed to them, speculative occupations are in part closed, only criminal occupations are as available to them as to everyone else. This anomalous economic condition engenders on the one side an enormous, fatalistic pauperism, on the other side a reckless mammonism. The former group, those reduced to misery, have absolutely nothing; the others, the money-grubbers, to the extent that they come into money, have no use for Jewish culture, which they despise along with poverty. But this situation will be completely different with their own land and an accompanying political organization of some sort. This political organization—regardless of whether it is a presently existing form or a socialist one of the future—will have as one of its functions, I would even say its main function, to organize its population economically. If such an organization exists—however wretched an economic order it might turn out to be—it will still provide the material means for the support of national culture. For then there could never be such a widespread incapacity of popular strata, never entire social classes lost as far as paying communal rates[41] goes, as is presently the case with the Jews of the East.

But it is not merely qua political organization that a country of their own will guarantee to Eastern Jews a capacity for progress; it will also have this effect directly in and of itself. This is because there is yet a second cause for the stagnation of indigenous Eastern Jewish culture. A stable structure, such as this culture is, must have some kind of foundation on which it rests. This foundation is the law, therefore something spiritual. But only something spiritual can bind the spirit. For an advance to be possible, a law must not be merely the foundation of culture, but has to be something more, much more, it has to move forward with and within the total spiritual development of the people. But the foundation for this can be only the soil of the earthly homeland. For it does not have the power to seize and shackle the people's soul. It merely fills it with its odor—conveyed in particular by the class of peasants, which maintains the closest and most intimate bonds with it.

[89] It is not only the Jews of the East who are in need of this odor of earth, which attends the national culture in all its ways, in its deepening and broadening, in order to transform their ghetto culture into a progressive national culture. Even the Jews of the West are in need of it and it alone, in order to overcome their abstract Europeanism. The process of recovery will take place differently among them than among their Eastern brethren. While the latter will recover directly through the Zionist solution, their transformation occurring in a single act, the former require two acts. The first is already

long behind them. It consisted in putting to death their Jewish ghetto culture by means of Europeanism. Thus they broke free from their stagnation, from an unceasing concern with the past. They participate in the life of the present, but it is not their own life they live. Therefore, the second act has to come, which will change for them their alien life into an authentic one. Therefore, their natural and national qualities of character must receive the territorial foundation, which will confer on them a cultural distinctiveness along with a capacity for cultural progress.

Once this happens, there will be nothing standing between these two redeemed elements of the Jewish people. Or will there? Will there not be trouble, since these live in European civilization and those do not? No, because the error here lies in the question itself. It must not be forgotten that we are not here concerned about those who remain behind in their fatherlands of the *Golus*—the impact of the distant new homeland on this group is still to be dealt with—rather, we are talking about those who, in that one land which they determine to be their common national home, will have gathered in order to live together. But the only possible outcome then is for the higher level of civilization, which means in essence the more developed economy, to conquer the lower. There can be no doubt about this. And if this is certain, then the adjustment of their ways of life—the sole question still to be dealt with—is only a matter of a relatively short period of time. An integrated Jewish nation with a progressive national culture and European civilization is made possible by the land.

Nonetheless, one ought not to think that the cultural gain from the Jews' eventual assumption of control over a country would be all on the Jewish side. We will certainly no longer be the missionaries of culture, but we can find satisfaction in the fact, which should not remain unnoticed by others; i.e., that a general cultural benefit would accompany the redemption we aspire to for our people—in fact a twofold benefit. First of all, the restoration of a Jewish cultural center means the gradual but certain solution of the Jewish question, which surely has adverse effects on the culture of the Gentile nations as well. This question is solved just as soon as the latter feel they are able to dispense with the special legal or social measures they have taken against the Jews. [90] However, this can occur—on the whole and apart from ephemeral political constellations—only when the Jews are no longer attracting notice anywhere by reason of their numbers or professional monopolies, and when they can claim a respect legally recognized by other nations. But both of these prerequisites become possible only by reason of the Jewish homeland. The stronger it becomes, the greater and more occupationally diverse the Jewish influx into it from every country becomes, the less insecure and more honorable will become the national, social, and cultural position of the Jews in exile, and the more it will appear thus even to the Jews.

Far greater than this indirect gain, however, is the direct advantage humankind will derive from a rehabilitation of the Jewish people legally recognized by other nations. By this historic event, the map of European civilization will be enriched by a new cultural hue, a new people will be inducted into a Europeanism that is concrete and alive—a new people and yet an old and well-tested one. It is a people that has contributed so much to the individual national constituents of the common civilization of the West, and that by virtue of its talents and its peculiar development would still seem qualified to take a substantive part in a mighty work of civilization. In fact, Europeanism is to be valued less on account of what it is today than on account of the great possibilities existing within it, on account of the fruits that are certain to develop from its seed. When Europe's economic machine is animated no less by social-ethical than by political-aesthetic cultural principles, or more precisely, once these two principles have been brought into an indissoluble unity, the Europeanism thus ennobled will become the highest blessing to humankind. And who would be better qualified to lead all peoples in this ascent to a future level of civilization than that people which has been, by the course of its destiny, trained up to possess this very capacity—than Israel, which has acquired in four millennia an unparalleled instinct for social justice and has gained from modern European civilization, like a schoolmistress giving lively and thorough instruction, an appreciation of the power of the state and the beauty of life. With this fortunate mixture of spiritual attainments, truly, it does not need to lead a homeless, gypsy-like existence—a burden to itself and a joy to no one.

"Well then; but can one intervene arbitrarily in the course of history?" an anxiety-ridden scholarship objects. Arbitrarily? Does history play itself out, as we perceive it, in any other way, than by persons setting themselves goals, pursuing them, and achieving or failing to achieve them? And is there, or has there ever been, another way to be assured of the historical appropriateness of a step taken, than by putting its congruity with history to the test? [91] If this test has a satisfactory outcome, one may well believe one's impulses and desires to be on the right track. Such indirect proof is justified with regard to political movements, and is the only one possible. Direct proofs *pro futuro* are simply excluded. That would be to engage in historical fortunetelling. That is not our business. On the other hand, the Zionist movement, like every great movement, has something prophetic about it. But one must have the faculties to perceive it.

However, we are far from arriving at the end of our line of argument. For what has thus far been said about Zionism's congruity with history has had to do only with the necessity of assuming control over a land. The Jews need a land, they must have it in the course of their development, and will undoubtedly possess it. That was the conclusion. Bound up with this conclusion, for anyone who does not insist on a written guarantee, is the certainty that some tiny but suitable corner of the earth will be found. But Zionism goes further. Its demand is for Palestine. Therefore, we must also justify this claim, specifically from the cultural-historical standpoint.

Naturally, it is possible to assert this claim from a purely emotional standpoint, and no doubt can exist that a large section of Zionists are really guided only by their feelings in this regard. Now it would be absurd to hold in contempt the romantic and pious feelings of others simply because one is oneself a rationalistic person or has feelings that run in a different direction. Even so, emotions that are to be put at the service of the collective whole have to be put to the test beforehand with respect to their benefit to the same. And the champions of a Jewish polity[42] could justifiably be opposed to Palestine, in spite of the Jewish people's feelings for the land, and perhaps even their own feelings, if there were virtually nothing positive to be done with these feelings. But in fact a great deal can be done with these feelings. For the land the Jews are in need of does not absolutely have to possess a special power of attraction—the prospect of turning misery into comfort in the end makes every country right for the emigrant—but it is absolutely necessary that it possess another power—a power of adhesion. The land must be able to hold onto the Jewish newcomers long enough for the lengthy process to be brought to completion, of converting a rootless, wandering people of commerce into a sedentary people with all manner of occupation, especially however that of agriculture—in other words, converting a nation without culture into a nation with culture.

And only Palestine has this power, through the emotions with which it inspires the masses of the Jewish people. [92] These emotions are the only instruments that promise success, having already been tested in various colonizing experiments, in breaking the chains of *Golus* and ghetto, which will be dragged behind Israel as it goes on toward freedom and which will attempt to drag Israel back. Or to put the case into an admittedly very modern and modified biblical image to make it clearer—the feelings for Zion are alone able to prevent the new settlers, on account of the harsh realities accompanying their newfound freedom and culture, from looking back with longing at the flesh-pots, which were more often empty than full, in the countries of the *Golus*, and from giving in to this yearning.[43]

This kind of guarantee afforded by Palestine possesses such a great advantage, that on this account alone it is really the only land worth considering.

But there is something else Palestine has in its favor. As we saw in the case of Zionism, so also with regard to Palestine, alongside the benefit to the Jews themselves, a benefit for humanity will come. Here it must be emphasized again: we do not desire to be missionaries of civilization or culture anywhere, neither in the West nor in the East. But it would give us a double pleasure that, precisely by the choice of Palestine, we receive once again the opportunity to cooperate in a work of humanity, and once again in the most prominent way. A Jewish people possessing a sovereign state, established in Palestine, will not only be, inwardly, the intermediary between the social-ethical and the political-aesthetic principles in Europeanism, but will also be, outwardly, the long-sought mediator between Orient and Occident. For if any people is qualified for this it is the Jewish people, with their inherited Oriental nature and their European upbringing; and if any country is suited to be the territorial base for the job of intermediary, it is Palestine, with its proximity to Europe, its position on the Suez canal, and as an inevitable way station for the railway route to India.

It is clear then that the choice of Palestine, far from being an arbitrary one, very much to the contrary, strengthens the assurance that acquisition of a land by Israel is historically appropriate.

Nevertheless, objections specifically against Palestine are also raised. In keeping with the more concrete object of this attack, the argument alleging arbitrariness from the standpoint of the philosophy of history, is turned into a claim of practical impossibility.

Impossible! This is a very dangerous word, a word by which every new enterprise, every new political activity, can in effect be paralyzed. This word is the death of all action, if, beyond the limits of acknowledged impossibilities in nature or history, it becomes a vague bogeyman. Were the Zionists resolved, let us say, to set up a Jewish polity on the moon or even on the North Pole—that would be impossible. Or, not to rove so far, if they sought merely to establish it in China or with Berlin, Paris, London, or Rome as its capital, that would also be impossible, and specifically for historical reasons. [93] For it is simply out of the question for a new culture, still weak, to thrust out an old culture, still strong, from its densely populated cities. On the contrary, it is entirely possible for a young, aspiring, and therefore stronger culture to enter a thinly populated country that is home to an old but decadent culture.

Once this has been established, no more may be said about impossibilities but at most about difficulties and obstacles. But he who is bold and patient does not shrink back from these.

From this standpoint, in the face of such mere difficulties, my task of justifying Zionism is done. Therefore, it goes beyond my task when I deal ever so briefly with the principal difficulties.

To this category belongs for example the doubt that we will not be able to endure the competition of other, older, and stronger cultures aspiring to control Palestine. The situation is not as bad as all that. If it were, then many small nation-states would not have arisen in the last several decades.[44] The mutual jealousy of the powers on the one hand, and on the other the fact that, in spite of all materialistic theories, idealistic motives also have their influence on the founding of new states, are factors that ought to dispel such fears. Other difficulties not to be underestimated are that Jews at present form such a small percentage of the Palestine population, or that they are not as popular in Europe as the Greeks were at the beginning of this century,[45] but these disadvantages are again offset by particular advantages, such as the superior intelligence of the Jewish people, their proverbial obstinacy and tenacity, and finally the help that is to be expected from the honest and moderate anti-Semites. Besides these, there will be in addition the out-and-out philo-Zionists—because Zionism promises the realization of many hopes for the civilizing work of European groups. One also hears quite often of hesitation on account of the Holy Sepulchre.[46] All such complications can in fact be prevented by extraterritorializing the Christian holy places.

But enough! I have the feeling that I have already permitted myself to go much too much into details that do not properly belong to the justification of Zionism. We see very well the difficulties we will have to overcome at every step. [94] Indeed, we have convened the Congress with the awareness that we are just at the beginning of a campaign, in the ever-changing course of which we will confront some positions that seem impregnable, sustain some defeats, but at the same time with the resolve not to allow ourselves to be deterred by partial disappointments and temporary setbacks, and with the inward conviction that our ultimate victory is certain. If only we do our duty, formulate our goals, raise our demands, and appeal to the interest and idealism of our fellow Europeans, everything else will fall into place—our Zion will rise again, for tormented and humiliated Israel the place of redemption and comfort, for the noblest European manner of life a new and fertile home. (Loud applause).

PRESIDENT: Dr. David Farbstein has the floor.

DR. DAVID FARBSTEIN (ZÜRICH): Honored attendees! We have assembled here in order to debate the path which the Zionists should pursue. First we have to make it clear: what do the Zionists want and why do they want it?[47] The Zionists want, by means of a systematic emigration of Jews to Palestine, not only to bring into being a Jewish society, but also to bring about a change in the Jews' economic mode of life, to make small Jewish shopkeepers and craftspeople into a people working in agriculture and industry. The Zionists want this because they represent the view that an emancipation of the Jews from their mode of economic life hitherto, just like an emancipation of the Jews in an overall national, religious, and cultural sense, can take place only in a country belonging to the Jews.[iii]

We have heard what the Zionists want and why they want it. Now arises the second question: who are the Zionists? "The Zionists form no party, people from all parties can join them. Zionism embraces all parties of the Jewish people. Zionism is the Jewish people on the march."[iv] Zionism is not a party, nevertheless it will cause a grouping of the Jews into social classes with the certainty and force of a mechanistic natural law[v]; for the Zionists are the poor and oppressed in Israel, while the anti-Zionists (i.e., those Jews standing in hostile opposition to Zionism) are the well-fed and satisfied, who are content to be despised and insulted, and who do not forgive those dissatisfied and impatient Jews who dare to exert themselves, having no regard for the calm, comfortable life of egoists who fear some long-term negative effect on themselves from the Zionist movement.[vi] Obviously, we are not thinking here about those Jews who are neither actively hostile nor actively favorable to Zionism, because they doubt the feasibility of the Zionist project.

[95] The goal and striving of the Zionists is therefore clear, and nevertheless it is continually misrepresented and misunderstood. Some consider us reactionary clerics, others as anti-religious subversives. We are said by our opponents to be a well-fed party of the intelligentsia, our entire aspiration being directed toward making the rabbis amongst us into Jewish bishops, the

---

iii Cf. D. Farbstein, *Die Welt*, no. 5.
iv Th. Herzl, *Die Welt*, no. 7 [quote not closed in original].
v   Max Nordau, *Die Welt*, no. 2.
vi Cf. Nordau, ibid.

physicians into state medical officers, lawyers into public prosecutors, etc., in the Jewish state.

We have to admit that a section of the Zionists is itself responsible for this misinterpretation of Zionism's character and goals. Each and every modern movement has been in its origins a movement of the intelligentsia, of students. Zionism has also undergone this development. However, Zionist students, rabbis, physicians, and lawyers, have put far too little emphasis on the aspect of Zionism which they ought to have strongly underscored. While they have not entirely suppressed it, still, they have done far too little to call attention to the socio-political character of Zionism. Strictly speaking, the old Zionists cannot be reproached on this account. As Zionists, they were aware that Zionism is not merely a national but also a socio-political and an economic-reform movement. The first Zionists, such as Rabbi Hirsch Kalischer* and Moses Hess,* emphasized this explicitly.[vii] Levanda* depicted the entire Zionist movement as "a striving towards physical labor, towards farming and agriculture, towards the producing of bread with one's own hands."[viii] The colonizing experiments in Palestine were and are simply an affirmation of the theoretical expositions of the Zionists. The old Zionists made just this one mistake, that they too often adduced Zionism as a means of defense against anti-Semitism and did not refer as often to Zionism's significance in terms of autonomy and economic reform.

In my present report in justification of Zionism, I wish to lay emphasis, first and foremost, on the socio-political aspect of Zionism. Dr. Birnbaum has already emphasized the national and cultural aspect. Due to a deficiency in works on the cultural history of the Jews, or rather works on economic history and socio-political works, my present report cannot be the last word "on the Jewish question"; rather it must be an attempt, a contribution to explaining the Jewish question. We have to try to apprehend the current Jewish question on the basis of the history of the Jews in exile, and here we should call to mind what Spinoza once said, that one should not laugh or weep over history, rather, one must grasp its meaning.

The Jews are a people congenitally disposed to trade; they have to remain thus and absolutely cannot change. [96] We hear this proverbial wisdom on all sides. We believe that this assertion is incorrect and unhistorical. The extant Talmudic law proves that even in Babylon the Jews were still an agricultural

---

vii   Cf. Moses Hess, *Rom und Jerusalem* [Rome and Jerusalem].
viii Levanda's notebook, *Palestine* (Rus.), 1884, 13.

people. The Talmud is the law of an agrarian people.[ix] Only as a result of certain conditions were the Jews forced to make a living as merchants dispersed among the peoples, and today other conditions are forcing the Jews to seek a home for themselves and give up their former way of life.

To put it briefly, the Jews were a purely agricultural people in their homeland and still later in Babylon; only when they were expelled from their threshold did they have to turn to trade. The causes of this turning are easily explained. The population of the cities in our time is, as we know, growing at the expense of the rural population. The impoverished landowner or the landless peasant can, if he migrates to the city during our capitalist period with its division of labor, find a position as an official, employee in a business, or laborer. In the Middle Ages, in the medieval "era of barter," it was much more difficult for the expropriated nobleman[48] or peasant to find an occupation in the city. Even in the Middle Ages we hear constantly about poor vagrants, poor devils without property or work who were subjected as vagabonds to the most gruesome punishments. And it was even worse in ancient times.

The economic conditions of Jewry were such that there were almost no slaves in the Jewish state.[x] Jewish society comprised peasants, landowners, free agricultural workers, and a few craftsmen and shopkeepers. Jewish society is then blown apart, the Jew is driven from his soil, from his homeland, even out of Babylon, in which he finds his second homeland. The Jew sets out and enters a society where there are, besides slaves, only rich and poor, where "the landless freeman is absolutely unable to earn a living."[xi] The Jew enters a country where there are no productive professions, no peasants, no craftsmen, where no industry exists outside the closed private firm, where *omnia domi nascuntur*.[49] The Jew also wants to make a living. The rich Jew, if he is a Roman citizen, will perhaps become a big landowner, who also "forces the poor out of the possession of land and property." [97] But there are few rich Jews and as a rule Jews,

---

ix   Cf. vol. 2, Babylonian Talmud, Tractate B'rachot [Berakhot] 5a; also Bücher: *Entstehung des Volkswirtschaft* [Origins of the National Economy], 15, 38, 39, "N'sikim" [Nezikin]; i.e., the payment of damages due to the destruction of agricultural goods is obligatory in the Talmud.

x   Cf. D. Farbstein: *Das Recht der unfreien und der freien Arbeiter nach jüdisch-talmudischem Recht* [The Law of Unfree and Free Laborers according to Jewish-Talmudic Law]. Frankfurt-am-Main, 1896.

xi   Cf. Bücher: loc. cit., 24.

as "foreigners," are not permitted Roman citizenship and landownership, for the indigenous lords are not interested in letting go of a part of their dominion.

To the Jew the only thing left is to become a proletarian or a slave. At that time, to be a proletarian means to live "at the expense of society" as a beggar, and who then is going to take up the cause of the poor "foreign" Jew, where is a Gracchus* to be found who will attend to the distribution of bread to the Jewish proletarians? At best, the Jew can become a slave. Indeed, many Jews fell into slavery and over time totally disappeared as Jews. The great multitude will have resisted the decline into slavery; they sought for themselves some livelihood, in order to be "free" and at the same time "capable of earning a living." The great multitude had to disperse, and that the majority of these dispersed Jews should have to live by trade "is a matter almost beyond doubt for the political economists."[xii] The Jew, whether during the time of the shadow-state or after the downfall of the Jewish state, driven out by the Romans and Syrians, has to become a merchant. The Jew becomes a city dweller, forming the beginning of a free bourgeoisie—and this beginning signifies at the same time the beginning of the modern Jewish question.

The Middle Ages come next. The history of the Jews in the Middle Ages is the pattern of the history of the Jewry in the present—and in the future, if the Jews are to continue to live as foreigners and guests in foreign lands.[50] The Jews are favored as long as they are needed; they are persecuted, they are despised, when they are not needed.

In the Middle Ages, the Jew is unable to acquire any land,[xiii] or become a soldier, or perform any military service, so as not compete with the Gentile knights chiefly concerned with predation.[xiv] The Jew, who neither wants to nor can become a serf, applies himself to trade. In the first half of the Middle Ages, the Jews were the merchants[xv] "for the Jews could only eke out a living through trade."[xvi] The foreign Jewish race was forced to "let itself be used to satisfy the

---

xii Cf. Roscher: *Die Stellung der Juden im Mittelalter* [The Position of the Jews in the Middle Ages], in *Tübinger Zeitschrift für die gesammte Staatswissenschaft*, 1875, 508.

xiii Nübling: *Die Judengemeinden des Mittelalters* [Jewish Communities of the Middle Ages], xxxix ad 69; Ashley: *Englische Wirtschaftsgeschichte* [English Economic History], 1:206.

xiv Nübling, loc. cit., xxvi; cf. Lamprecht, loc. cit., 461.

xv Lamprecht, loc. cit., 1452.

xvi Cf. Nübling, loc. cit., 173.

needs of the stronger race."[xvii] [98] "The Jews satisfied a great need at that time, the need for professional commercial activity"[xviii] and that "as a consequence of their business activity, they did not seek to settle in great numbers in any single place but instead to settle in as many places as possible."[xix]

But the Jew is a foreigner, the Jew as foreigner is to be "uprooted and annihilated when he is no longer of service."[xx] The Jew is a foreign commodity, imported only as long as native industry has not developed. Even in the Middle Ages, Jews were permitted to engage in trade only so long as an indigenous national merchant class had not yet begun to prosper.[xxi] The persecutions of the Jews began first in Byzantium, in "the primary commercial center of Christendom during the entire period of the early Middle Ages,"[xxii] then follow in Italy, in "the first fully developed people of the Middle Ages," then in southern France, Germany, England, etc.[xxiii] The Jews are accused of driving workers out of the country,[xxiv] people turn against them for importing foreign goods and suppressing the price of local goods;[xxv] finally, people complain about "these dogs of hell who send Christian money out of the country with their written conjuring."[xxvi] So the Jews were prohibited from trading in commodities. The Jews, it was said, are "foreigners," "speculators," therefore trading in goods and residential properties is prohibited to them, only the trade in "unregulated goods," "the exchange of money and foreign currencies" is permitted.[xxvii]

Therefore, the Jew has to become a moneychanger, since he is also not permitted to belong to a guild, because Jews and persons practicing disreputable

---

xvii   Cf. Gumplowicz: *Der Rassenkampf* [Struggle of the Races], 164.

xviii   Roscher, loc. cit., 506.

xix   Bücher: *Die Bevölkerung von Frankfurt am Main* [The Population of Frankfurt am Main], 527.

xx   Cf. Gumplowicz, loc. cit., 177.

xxi   Roscher, loc. cit., and also Saitschik: *Beiträge zur rechtlichen Stellung der Juden* [Studies in the Legal Position of the Jews], 7–8.

xxii   Roscher, loc. cit., 512f.

xxiii   Nübling, loc. cit., 117.

xxiv   Ibid., 46.

xxv   Cf. Bücher, loc. cit., 64.

xxvi   Geering: *Handel und Industrie der Stadt Basel* [Commerce and Industry of the City of Basel], 274.

xxvii   Nübling, loc. cit., 72.

trades cannot enter guilds.[xxviii] The Jew must become a usurer, not only because he wants to earn a living but rather principally because he is forced into it. The Jew in the Middle Ages is an object, a means of exploitation in the hands of the various dominant classes, a means of exploitation by which the rest of the people are exploited and the pockets of the lords are to be filled. A medieval Jewish commentator on Maimonides offers this quintessential description of the Jewish question in the Middle Ages. In his codification of Talmudic law, Maimonides cites the Talmudic view concerning usury, which was also that of the legal scholars, that taking interest from foreigners was permitted but that usury on the contrary was forbidden. A medieval Jewish commentator observes at this point: "Today we are permitted to practice usury as well, since the interest-money does not remain with us; it flows into the pockets of the lords and grandees."

[99] At first it was the sovereigns who "legally extorted money from the Jews and who seem even to have made the extortion an integral component of their financial policy."[xxix] The Jew was forced to become a usurer; therefore he became odious to everyone; then "it was possible to alternately favor and plunder the Jew, for the Jew after all was regarded as the personal enemy of every debtor."[xxx] The Jews "constituted a kind of royal domain, they were given the opportunity to enrich themselves, in order thereby to profit from them"[xxxi] and "the Jews were obliged for the sake of their own security to make themselves into a tool by which the nation was robbed."[xxxii] Soon the cities arose. In Germany, Jewry was given in pledge to the cities by the Empire.[xxxiii] The small-minded guild masters made quite sure that the Jew not pursue any craft and the "merchant class arising from the class of urban proprietors" that the Jew not carry on any trade in commodities. The Jew is forced to be a pawnbroker and a usurer; he must be a usurer, for it is in the cities' interest that the Jews exploit the nobility and the cities gather the spoils for themselves in the form

---

xxviii   Cf. Geering, loc. cit., 46.

xxix   Lamprecht, loc. cit., 1456.

xxx   Rogers' *Geschichte der englishen Arbeit* [The History of English Labor], 6.

xxxi   Vocke: *Geschichte der Steuern des britischen Reiches* [History of Taxation in the British Empire], 161f.

xxxii   Ashley: *Englische Wirtschaftsgeschichte*, 1:206.

xxxiii   Geering, loc. cit., 214; Bücher: *Die Bevölkerung von Frankfurt am Main*, 527; Saitschik, loc. cit., 35; Lamprecht, loc. cit., 1455.

of taxes.ˣˣˣⁱᵛ And thus also right down to the lesser lords, who mortgaged their "ground-rents" and revenues to the Jews. The Jews alone had the right, but also at the same time "the obligation, to satisfy in full the needs of the sovereign power and its dependents for money, against a sufficient collateral," so the Jews were forced to be "public usurers."ˣˣˣᵛ In the second half of the Middle Ages the Jew sank down to the status of "usury Jew"[51]; he declined not only physically and economically but also intellectually.ˣˣˣᵛⁱ Only from the seventeenth century on do things begin to go better for the Jew, when, on account of the development of modern large-scale industry, the Jew becomes useful again "for the carrying on of trade, commerce, manufacturing, and the like."ˣˣˣᵛⁱⁱ

The blessed Age of Emancipation arrived. True, the emancipation took place partly because of idealistic motives, but principally only because emancipation of the Jews was in the interest of their liberators. [100] There is a need for the Jews in modern times; therefore the Jews are treated with favor. The history of the Jews in modern times is just a mirror image of the Jews' history in the Middle Ages.

The noble Joseph of Austria* was one of the first who wanted to improve the position of the Jews. Nonetheless, it has to be noted that, in the Edict of Tolerance* he issued, what was also very important to him was that the Jews are promoting industry and trade. As late as 1779, the philosopher Frederick the Great* had not yet conferred on Moses Mendelssohn* the privilege of being "a Jew under royal protection,"[52] while the bankers Abraham Markus,* Veitel Ephraim,* and Daniel Itzig*[53] received already in 1761 "the liberty enjoyed by Christian bankers, both before the courts and elsewhere," since "protection was granted to Jews chiefly in order for them to carry on trade, commerce, manufacturing, factory-industry, and the like." The emancipation of the Jews had, right from the outset, the condition that the Jews should remain merchants.

The reason for the emancipation of the Jews in the nineteenth century is to be sought in our capitalist economic development. The modern era needed Jews as merchants. Freedom of trade brought with it the liberation of the Jews,

---

xxxiv Cf. Nübling, 174f. and LXXV f., n.30a, loc. cit., 217f.

xxxv Lamprecht, 1:849, 1449, and 1453.

xxxvi Cf. Chwolson: *Reischit Maasei Hadfus b'Israel* (Heb.), 33 and 45.

xxxvii Cf. Bücher: *Die Bevölkerung von Frankfurt am Main*, 572, 587f.; Geering, loc. cit., 390, 454f.; Nübling, 541f.; Mehring: *Lessing-Legende* [The Lessing Legend], 252f.

of the merchants. In Germany, Austria, Switzerland, etc., the final emancipation of the Jews took place in the years 1860–1867; i.e., the period when the Cobdenite* free-trade era in Europe begins.

As liberated citizens, the Jews were neither better nor worse than the rest of the citizen population. They had "superlative achievements to their credit in nearly all areas of intellectual activity, in science, in literature, etc." With respect to economics, "Germany would perhaps not have risen so quickly to the top vis-à-vis the older economic cultures of England and France, had it not been for the help provided to it around the middle of our century by the special attributes of the Jewish race."[xxxviii]

The Jews were delighted during this new era of so-called freedom as long as they were needed, as long as there existed no "national" merchant class of tolerable competence. The Jews were treated with favor in Germany and Austria, Bulgaria and Serbia.[xxxix] As late as 1882, the Vienna city council, today an intensely anti-Semitic body, sent five thousand gulden to help poor Russian Jews.[xl] Now that the Jews are no longer needed, they are hated everywhere, and all the evils rooted in modern economic development are charged to their account.

So much for the situation of Jews in general. Now for something about the situation of Jews in Eastern Europe. [101] We will truly apprehend the situation of Jews in Eastern Europe only when we have a clear understanding of the history of the Jews in Poland in the Middle Ages. The East European Jews are, after all, the Polish Jews.

Generally speaking, the history of the Jews in Poland was similar to that of the Jews in Western Europe. We will refer to just two peculiarities. In Poland there were large, so-called royal cities, and towns subject to the aristocracy. In the "royal" cities lived the German colonists, who alone possessed the rights of citizens. Serfs, practitioners of disreputable trades, and Jews, could not become citizens of the city[xli] and were therefore not permitted to practice a craft in the big cities[xlii] and could trade in commodities only insofar as they

---

xxxviii Förster, Prof. W.: *Die Ethik des Nationalismus und der Judenfrage* [The Ethics of Nationalism and the Jewish Question], 16.

xxxix Alliance Israélite Universelle, *Bericht für die Periode 1860–1885* [Report for the Period 1860–1885], 17–23.

xl Idem, *Bericht für 1882* [Report for 1882], 1:21.

xli Bandtkie: *Prawo prywatne polskie* [Polish Private Law], 116.

xlii Ibid., 129.

had received permission to do so by the citizenry, in accord with an agreed-upon concession.[xliii] On the other hand, in the towns subject to the aristocracy, they were able to eke out a living as small retailers and craftsmen.[xliv] But in these places they were among those legally and economically dependent on the aristocracy, the *plebs ultimae classis*.[xlv] The aristocrat was the master of the Jews with *ius vitae ac necis*;[xlvi] the aristocrat was the Jew's principal customer and he could use the Jew as his tool, as a usurer or tavernkeeper, to exploit the peasantry.[54]—This brief description suffices to explain to us why there is still today a Jewish population consisting of small craftsmen, small retailers, and the like, living in the towns of the erstwhile Republic of Poland.

We can now to proceed to a description of the present position of the Jews in Eastern Europe. We will limit ourselves mainly to Lithuania and southwest Russia. For these regions we have quite precise statistical figures to guide us, in the splendid work of Professor Subottin of St. Petersburg. At any rate, the conditions in the other lands are no better. We have just heard about the sad situation of the Jews in Galicia and Romania from Herr Dr. Salz and Herr Pineles. But first and foremost, a brief word of warning.

When Voltaire* published his pamphlet against the Jews, some rich Portuguese Jews appeared and asserted: Voltaire was correct in his remarks insofar as he was passing judgment on the German Jews.[55] This craven behavior on the part of great men of the previous century became habitual. Many a comfortable West European Jew thinks he still has the right today to cast stones at his poor Polish and Russian brothers. [102] Herr Alfred Naquet* "even wishes to believe that the Jews in Russia and Romania are a deplorable and vulgar race, just as one so often hears."[xlvii] Against this habit a determined protest must for once be registered. East European Jews are poor but honorable people, a large section of them earning their bread by the sweat of their

---

xliii Ibid., 123; and Kraushaar: *Historja żydów w Polsce* [History of the Jews in Poland], 88.

xliv Kraushaar, loc. cit., 21; and Band[t]kie, loc. cit., 129.

xlv Bandtkie: *Historja prawa polskiego* [The History of Polish Law], 541 ["people of the lowest class"].

xlvi Kraushaar, loc. cit., 16; and Bandtkie, loc. cit., 290 and 637 ["right over life and death"].

xlvii Hermann Bahr: *Der Antisemitismus* [Anti-Semitism], 106.

face, and even the East European Jewish usurer is perhaps morally superior to a West European like Herr Arton.[56]

A large section of the Jews of Eastern Europe are engaged in trade.[xlviii] But in Russia there is also a large number of Jewish craftsmen. In a publication issued in 1891 we read that, according to official statistics, 12 percent of the Jews residing in the Pale of Settlement are said to be craftsmen.[xlix] However, we can assert with certainty that in Lithuania the percentage is much higher. There, Jewry constitutes the greater part, percentagewise, of all craftsmen; e.g., 62 percent in Vilnius,[l] 73 percent in Kovno,[li] 52 percent in Odessa,[lii] etc. Jewish craftsmen comprise one third to one quarter of the Jewish population in many cities.[liii] Besides these, there are many unskilled and factory workers. In the industrial city of Bialystok nearly 90 percent of the Jewish population consists of those doing physical labor.[liv]

At first glance, the issue reduces itself to one of social class alone, and one might readily arrive at the illusory conclusion that the Jews of Eastern Europe will become a factory proletariat in the course of time, that there is therefore not a Jewish question but merely a social one. This conclusion would be entirely wrong.

Neither in Galicia nor in the Pale of Settlement in southwest Russia are there conditions that would make possible the emergence of large- or even medium-scale industry, in the true sense of the word. The Jewish craftsmen are either masters working alone or masters who employ at most a journeyman and an apprentice. For example, in the province of Volhynia there are 47,800 craftsmen, of which 32,100 are masters and 15,700 journeymen and apprentices,[lv] in the province of Kiev twenty-three thousand Jewish craftsmen make

---

xlviii Cf. Moschilrach (Heb.), 1:8, 177f.; Subbotin: *W. Tschertie ossiedlosti* (Rus.) [In the Pale of Settlement], 1:10, 18, 66, 72, 74, 116, 129; 2:2, 16, 23, 45, 143, 171, 212, 214, 215, 217, 218.

xlix *Die Verfolgung der Juden* [The Persecution of the Jews], published by "Jüdische Presse," Berlin, 1891, 21.

l Subottin, 1:72.

li Ibid., 1:127.

lii Ibid., 2:227.

liii Ibid., 1:149, 59f.; 2:225f.

liv Ibid., 1:63.

lv Subottin, 2:150.

up 7 percent of the total Jewish population, among whom eleven thousand are masters and twelve thousand journeymen and apprentices.[lvi] [103] In Minsk, which features a large Jewish population, there are 1,812 journeymen for 3,515 masters.[lvii] Clearly, the number of craftsmen is far in excess of what is needed. Master and journeyman alike are beggars.[lviii] In the vicinity of Minsk, for example, there is one master craftsman for every seven inhabitants of the city.[lix]

Jewish factory workers are employed almost exclusively in Jewish factories which are closed on Saturdays.[lx] The East European Jew remains unwilling to profane the Sabbath. This is also one of the main reasons why the transformation of East European Jewry into a factory proletariat is out of the question. The number of factories closed on Saturdays is very small, because there are few rich Jews there.[lxi]

For example, the city of Zhytomyr, with its Jewish population of twenty-three thousand,[lxii] has altogether "4 Jews owning assets worth 100,000 rubles, several hundred with a relatively secure livelihood, and the rest of the populace consists of beggars."[lxiii] The wealthy Jew, the rich manufacturer, once again cannot employ Jewish workers, since his factory, especially if it has been converted into a shareholding concern, has to operate on Saturdays. Even in the metropolis of Odessa, where in fact more wealthy Jews live, those making a living from physical labor amount to scarcely one third of the total Jewish population, although there are many dockhands and unskilled Jewish workers there.[lxiv]

It may be objected: one should not rule out the hope that, with the passage of time, "the artificial boundaries of the Pale of Settlement for the Jews in Russia will be abolished,"[lxv] and "if the educated Jewish population were able to diffuse itself into the immense Russian Empire, it would begin immediately

---

lvi   Ibid., 179.
lvii Cf. Report of the Alliance Israélite Universelle for August 1896, 103.
lviii Subbotin, loc. cit.
lix   Ibid., 1:31.
lx   Subottin, 1:5, 128, 132; 2:59, 96, 178, 225 *et passim*.
lxi   Subottin, loc. cit., 1:61, 88; 2:6, 7, 55, 99, 103, 105, 151, 202, 205.
lxii Ibid., 2:141.
lxiii Ibid., 2:151.
lxiv Ibid., 2:229. Cf. Alliance Israélite Universelle, Report for 1896, 142.
lxv   Alliance Israélite Universelle, ibid., 1883, 10.

to improve itself and make an increasing contribution to the prospering of the country's industry, commerce, and agriculture."[lxvi] This objection will be made by those unable to grasp the fact that the principal reason for the misery of the Jews of Eastern Europe is not anti-Semitic or Judeophobic activities but simply the overpopulation of the small cities and towns. [104] Anti-Semitism affects first and foremost the Jewish intelligentsia. But the Jewish question is not a question of the small class of Jewish intellectuals but of the bulk of the Jewish people.

We must state frankly that "the abolition of the artificial boundaries of the Pale of Settlement" would be a palliative measure and only for a certain class of Jews. Only the wealthy Jew would be able to migrate into the interior of Russia. Assuming that all were able to migrate, they would certainly continue to pursue commerce. On the one hand, they would still have the obstacle of Saturday work in their new location,[lxvii] and on the other hand, no one elects to become a laborer if he can find an easier way of making a living. In the "immense Russian Empire" they will have quite sufficient opportunity to earn a living as merchants. Owing to the Jews, there would surely "soon take place a visible improvement in the economic condition of the provinces of the interior of Russia."[lxviii] But the reaction, in the form of anti-Semitism, would also set in, as soon as an indigenous "national" merchant class arose.

The misery among the Jews of Eastern Europe is therefore, given the prevailing circumstances, a daunting reality. We have heard that in Galicia 70 percent of the Jews are beggars. In Russia too, half of the Jews are paupers who live, so to speak, "on air." In Vilnius, almost 95 percent of the Jews live in poverty,[lxix] in Berdycev 75 percent have no regular employment,[lxx] and it is the same in Warsaw, Minsk, Kishinev, Lublin, Lodz, etc.[lxxi] It is even worse for the Jews in the small cities and towns. One can easily imagine the situation of these poor Jews, who make up 50 to 80 percent of the total population

---

lxvi Ibid., 1881, 43–44.
lxvii Cf. N. Sokolow in the "Hazefirah" 1897, no. 47.
lxviii Alliance Israélite Universelle, Report for 1881, 44.
lxix Subottin, loc. cit., 96.
lxx Ibid., 2:121.
lxxi Cf. *Die Welt* [The World], no. 9, 10; Report of the Alliance Israélite Universelle, March 1897, 34f; and Subottin, 1:50, 86, 88; 2:79, 120, 121, 124, 180, 181, *et passim*.

in small localities.[lxxii] In Congress Poland,* the Jewish population in towns of not more than ten thousand inhabitants amounts to 40 to 70 percent of the total population.[lxxiii] Poland, which stands so far behind France in terms of its economy, has an urban population nearly as large (and mostly Jewish), as France.[lxxiv] What misery must then prevail among this people which is so economically backward!

[105] Up to this point we have touched only on the economic aspect of the Jewish question. But the Jewish question is also a national question. The Gentile has seen and still sees the Jew as ever the "foreigner." The economic situation of the Jews was and is just the consequence of the fact that Jews have been regarded as "foreigners," as belonging to a foreign nation. The Jewish question has become an economic one because the Jews have constituted and constitute a foreign nation. The Zionists recognize the dual character of the Jewish question, for they know that "with the Jews, far more than with nations oppressed on their own soil, national independence must precede any political progress. A common home territory is the first prerequisite for them to have healthy working conditions."[lxxv]

The Jewish question is also an ethical question. We will not stick our heads in the sand, ostrich-like, as a way of defending ourselves. We know that present conditions among the Jews are causing some classes of the population to decline in intellectual and moral terms as well. After all, in the Jew as pariah, all nobler human impulses are forcibly suppressed. What the emancipation of the Jew has added up to, the only freedom conceded to the Jew, is just the freedom of trade, the freedom of haggling. The danger exists that the Jews in this second half of the modern era will atrophy intellectually, just as was the case in the second half of the Middle Ages, due to the pressure of Judeophobia. Wherever pauperism reigns, as it does in Eastern Europe, it is surely no surprise that for many the morale needed to be economically productive is destroyed.

---

lxxii Subottin, 1:4, 49, 50, 56, 110; 2:9, 73, 78, 94, 102, 131, 157, 181, 182, 185, 187.
lxxiii Dr. Z. Daszynska: Ze statystyki Iudnosciwej Królestwa Polskiego [On the population statistics of Congress Poland], in *Ateneum* 1893, 388.
lxxiv Ibid., 386.
lxxv Moses Hess, *Rom und Jerusalem*, 110. [The reference is clearly intended to emphasize that political independence is necessary for economic improvements to take place, albeit Farbstein's quoting of Hess here is somewhat confusing. More to the point, Farbstein was influenced by the socialist Zionism of Nachman Syrkin, the argument here echoing Syrkin's thesis regarding the relationship of socialism and Jewish nationalism.]

"Human beings as social creatures, like social plants and animals, require for their vitality and progress, a tract of ground that is open and free, without which they descend to become parasites that are able maintain themselves only at the expense of another's productivity."[lxxvi]

> We know that within Jewry the need for healthy working conditions is deeply felt, which has as its basis the human exploitation of nature. We recognize the great exertions being made among us, in order to train our younger Jewish generation to be productive laborers. But we also know that the Jews in exile, at least as regards the majority, are unable to devote themselves to work of this kind, because they lack the first prerequisite for this kind of work, the soil of the fatherland, and because they cannot intermingle with the peoples whom they live dispersed among, without being unfaithful to their national religion.[lxxvii]
>
> We can spare ourselves the enumeration of the sins we are reproached for or we ourselves acknowledge. [106] We want to do away with the cause of all our sins. We want to change our way of life. This is where a change must occur. Certainly, we are not going to endorse everything Schäffle* says about the Jews.[lxxviii] But we must concede to Schäffle that the *causa causarum* of all the problems is that "the Jewish national community lacks territorial unity and fatherland."[lxxix]
>
> We come then to the conclusion and may set forth the following two postulates on the basis of our foregoing remarks:
>
> 1. There were historical causes that turned the Jews, particularly in Western Europe, into merchants. Jews became an urban bourgeois population, with or without their willing it, but without the possibility of freely developing the intellectual and cultural aspects of their existence. The better part of the Western European Jewish bourgeoisie has been compelled by the force of facts to go over to Zionism. For this section of Jewry, Zionism is a rebellion against life in exile, in which their identity is degraded to that of being middlemen and petty traders. Zionism is for them an act of self-help, a striving toward a national, economic, and intellectual renaissance of the Jewish people.

---

lxxvi Hess, ibid., 110.
lxxvii Ibid., 111.
lxxviii Schäffle, *Bau und Leben des socialen Körpers* [Construction and Life of the Social Body]; 1:402; 2:74, 90; 4:460f.
lxxix Ibid., 3:90.

2. The Jews of Eastern Europe, for historical reasons, were turned into small merchants, small shopkeepers, and small craftsmen. The Jews of Eastern Europe[57] cannot develop freely, neither economically nor intellectually, in their places of settlement. All efforts toward creating healthy working conditions for Jews there remain without success or issue in this region, perhaps because they would lead indirectly to the destruction of Jewish religious practice, or for lack of the right economic conditions in their places of settlement. Therefore, the Jews of Eastern Europe find their only escape route in Zionism; i.e., in striving, by means of an orderly emigration to Palestine, not only to bring into being a Jewish society but also to change and improve the economic way of life of the Jews.

We have seen thus far what the Zionists want and why they want it. Let us also listen to the foes of Zionism. The foes of Zionism are the assimilated Jews and the so-called philanthropic practical men.

Assimilated Jews are the ultimate *Schutzjuden*.[58] They tell themselves, great-grandfather was a Jew protected by the Junkers,* his grandson was the same in relation to the free cities, and therefore the great-grandson shall be a Jew protected by the liberal bourgeoisie or some other faction. [107] Assimilated Jews are also the most anarchistic, laissez-aller and laissez-faire politicians with regard to the Jewish question. For them, the Jewish question simply does not exist. But assimilated Jewry is de facto dead. So let us leave the dead to rest in peace and proceed to the so-called philanthropic "practical men."

The practical men designate themselves as the "real" or the "true Zionists." They fall into two groups. To the first group belong those who want no politics or political Zionism, only small-scale experiments in colonization. The practical men talk much about their practical achievements so far. That is untrue, at least until now. The Zionist colonizing movement has been "practically" active for almost seventeen years.

During this period scarcely seven thousand Jewish farmers have been settled in Palestine, while within this same interval more than one million Jews emigrated from Russia[lxxx]; annually, thirty thousand Russian Jews have come into New York alone.[lxxxi] The small achievements hitherto are also not

---

lxxx *Die Welt*, no. 12, 8.
lxxxi Cf. *Allgemeine Zeitung des Judenthums*, 1897, no. 3.

due to the work of these "practical men" but principally of the well-known benefactor[59] and also partly of the Palestine Colonization Society[60] in Russia.

Therefore, the practical men have no right to talk about their "practical" achievements. Actually, they could achieve nothing more. The settlement of farmers in Palestine is more foolish than high-minded anyhow, "if it takes place without an international legal guarantee."[lxxxii] The "political conditions" are the chief difficulty in the colonization of Palestine,[lxxxiii] and lack of security is the chief obstacle to a dedication to the intensive cultivation of the soil, in this rich land so favored by nature.[lxxxiv] A single edict would suffice "to bring to an end all colonization and emigration."[lxxxv]

The second group consist of ambivalent "now on the one hand, now on the other hand" Jews. "We charmed you with our verses, but our prose did not please you."[61] As long as the Zionists constituted a utopian party, these practical men were "also Zionists." But now the Zionists want a Jewish state, something which the "now on the one hand, now on the other hand" Jews cannot tolerate. We Zionists disdain to conceal our views and aims.[62] We declare openly, "obtaining a common national soil, working for legal conditions under the protection of which the work can thrive"—these are the foundations upon which Jewry will rise up once more, by which the whole of Jewry will be revitalized.[lxxxvi] We are well acquainted with the magnitude and difficulty of the task before us. [108] We know we will attain our goal, though, only when the desire for freedom shall have penetrated the mass of the Jewish people. "If our united desires for freedom become so strong that we are able forge them into a mighty hammer—only then will we be able to break apart the chains of misery and degradation by which we are bound." (Loud applause.)

PRESIDENT: The agenda promises a report about incoming messages. The quantity of incoming messages has been so prodigious that such a report cannot be made, for there are over 550 telegrams, letters of endorsement, proposals, and the like. The petitions received have around fifty thousand signatures. Every moment brings more and more new dispatches from all parts of both worlds,

---

lxxxii   Th. Herzl, *Die Welt*, no. 7.
lxxxiii Alliance Israélite Universelle, Report for 1883, 2:25.
lxxxiv   Ibid., 1884, 1:59.
lxxxv   Ibid., 30.
lxxxvi   Moses Hess: *Rom und Jerusalem*.

with both North and South America contributing. The smallest number of dispatches bear individual signatures, the largest number coming from assemblies, societies, etc. This corpus of messages will be sorted by morning, if possible, and information about it will be given in detail.

The session is closed.

Day Two of the Proceedings
August 30, 1897

Morning Session

PRESIDENT: It is still not possible even now to give a complete overview of the incoming messages—only an approximate one—since new ones are being received continuously. Based on a rough estimation of their contents, it is evident that people are offering their affirmation of the Congress from places all over the world. An initial count has indicated that among the 550 telegrams and other declarations of support of every kind are six thousand signatures. It is worthy of remark that many declarations of support have the signatures of associations, as well as some signed by Orthodox rabbis and even Russia's so-called Crown Rabbis.* From other countries, various distinguished members of Jewish organizations are represented in the addresses. Many expressions of support come from popular assemblies and societies. Moreover, petitions are arriving, on which the number of signatures is actually enormous. Yesterday the figure of fifty thousand was mentioned, but this figure is being surpassed by far. At any rate, it will not be possible to work through all of this in these three days. A later publication will give the number of signatures found on the petitions and other more exact information will also be made available. These data will also constitute the raw material for the statistical committee. It may be of interest for me to read out the text of the petitions collected by the Galician society for colonization in particular:

> To the honorable gentlemen-delegates of the 'Ahawath Zion' Society to the Zionists' Congress at Basel. We the undersigned request that you submit in our name to the honorable Congress, the sincere declaration that we are prepared, under constitutional and material guarantees to be made by the Congress, and especially if the colonization of Palestine were under international legal protection, to settle in the land of our fathers.

You shall hereby kindly take note of and clarify as you deem appropriate, that we do not consider ourselves to be in any way bound by this declaration, nor does it impose any obligations on you or the honorable Congress, since we desire our declaration to be seen solely as transmitting information.

[110] More detailed data with respect to our material and family circumstances have been carefully entered in the appropriate sections. Finally, we request that you assure in our name the honorable Zionist Congress of our warmest sympathies; may its decisions redound to the benefit of our poor people; may it be granted to them to lay the foundation-stone for the rebuilding of the Jewish nation![1]

A small contribution was levied from every individual who signed the petition. The collection of these signatures was thus not without cost. The committee will use them for the stated purpose of colonization.

From among the incoming communications, I will first of all have the Hebrew letter of greeting of Rabbi Samuel Mohilewer* of Bialystok read out.[2]

Dr. Armand Kaminka (Prague) reads out the letter of Rabbi Mohilewer and adds the German translation: "My health does not permit me to respond to your invitation in person. I am therefore sending my grandson as witness that my heart is with you. From the depth of my soul, I pray to Heaven that He may be with the envoys of the Jewish people, teaching them what they must say, so that they act in the spirit of the holy Torah and in conformity with the laws of the state. May He support them in executing their plans and obtaining the favor of governments, etc., to which they will propose the solution of the Jewish question.[3] May He imbue our brothers themselves with the spirit of love for our unfortunate people and for their land! Amen.

Now I will permit myself to make some suggestions.

1. Concerning the goals of the Congress, it suffices for me to cite the invitation of the committee: 'The Congress is striving to do only what is feasible and attainable. What is ascribed to it to the contrary is simply untrue. What the Congress will do will take place in public, all its proceedings will conform to the laws of the individual countries as well as to our obligations as citizens. We pledge in particular that the Congress will take into account the Russian Zionists and their

political circumstances.[14] I hope that this promise will be kept and that, even if some be opposed to it, they will remain in the minority.[5] Such is my hope, and I wish to add, that the main purpose of the Congress must be to strive to procure the permission of the Turkish government for settlement. We must strive toward this end with all our might, for the entire work of colonization depends upon it.

2. A central directorate will most likely be elected at the Congress, which is external to Russia: we must take care that it consists of men who are devoted body and soul to our goals.[6]

3. The Congress should enunciate its conviction, that all good Zionists[7] should maintain brotherly unity and love, even if their religious views diverge, even if one regards the other as irreligious. The pious can just imagine what they would do if their house were on fire—they would gladly welcome even an irreligious rescuer. This is precisely our situation. [111] A great fire has broken out around us and threatens to annihilate us. Our enemies multiply from day to day, their numbers already run into the millions, and were they not afraid of the laws, they would swallow us alive.[8] Now brothers have arisen for us, who reach out their hands to us in our distress, who desire to do their utmost to free our people from distress. Can we refuse this help? Take heed, that the bond of brotherhood be not destroyed![9]

4. Moreover, let all Zionists acknowledge and be possessed of the absolute conviction, that "Yishuv Eretz Yisrael"[10] (i.e., the purchase of land, the building of houses, the cultivation of fields and gardens), is one of the most significant commands of our Torah, some of our ancient sages asserting that it is equal to the whole Torah. This is to be explained by the fact that the preservation of our nation depends on it. Whoever believes and knows this is a true Zionist; without this conviction, anyone who joins us is just giving alms as to any other cause.

5. The foundation for "Love of Zion"[11] is the upholding of our received Jewish doctrine.[12] I do not wish to offend anyone, for our sages said: "I doubt if there is anyone in this generation qualified to preach morality." I am simply asserting in a general way that the Torah has got to be the basis of our rebirth in the land of our fathers.

6. Our task consists simply in building and planting, not annihilating and destroying.[13] We must not harm the institution of Halukka,*[14] upon which the life of thousands depends, so long as these have not found another source to maintain themselves.

7. In order to make propaganda for our idea, we need to send out capable spokesmen into all countries where Jews are living. We have come to know from our own experience, the need for and benefits of having such preachers. Likewise written propaganda has to be distributed through the press, in Hebrew, Yiddish, and all other languages. It is imperative to produce a brochure of high quality in form and content, in Russian, German, French, English, and Italian, as a way of presenting the Zionist idea to the decision makers in every country, so that the latter may be informed about our goals.[15] The lack of such documents is keenly felt.

8. With respect to the national fund, we must strive to have the J.C.A. [Jewish Colonization Association] in Paris devote a portion of its funds to the colonization of Palestine. We must also win over still other wealthy Jews to our side. It would also be good to arrange for a portion of the monies collected for colonization always to be raised in support of the national fund.

In my view, the Congress ought to send a letter of thanks to Baron Eduard [Edmond de] Rothschild,* in consideration of his achievements in support of colonization. After all, he is the first Jew since the destruction of our state to commit to so great a work, to have given many millions for the sake of this work, and to be willing to make yet further sacrifices. The first Zionist assembly of Jews[16] from all countries ought to show its gratitude and recognition to such a man.

In conclusion, I would that my brothers take the following to heart: [112]

For two thousand years we have hoped for the Redeemer, who would liberate us from the bitter *Golus* and lead our scattered people from the ends of the earth into our land, where we are to find a peaceful home.[17] This belief lives mightily within us and has been our only consolation in evil times. And despite there having arisen among us in the past century people who deny this faith and banished our hopes from their hearts, yea even from their prayers, all the rest of the people hold fast to this hope; it constitutes their daily prayer and lifts them up in their affliction. Recently even some so-called Orthodox rabbis in the West have risen up against it. One of these stated that all the words of consolation and promises of our prophets are just allegories. The Redeemer will not appear in order that Israel return to its land and end its *Golus*, rather the Redeemer will appear to the entire world, to bring about the acceptance of God's kingdom. Conversely, Israel will continue to wander as a light among the nations, as it has done until now. Others have brusquely declared that the national idea conflicts with the messianic idea of our religion. Now I must openly declare that all this is not true. From time immemorial, our faith and hope has been that the Messiah would appear, gather the outcasts of Israel, and lead them again into the land of our fathers. Instead of wandering in foreign lands as we have until now, we are to become a nation once more in the fullest meaning of the word. Instead of being exposed to the scorn of the nations as we have been until now, we are to be at that time honored and respected by all. This is the faith and hope which issues forth from the words of our prophets and teachers, and to this our people holds fast! We are certainly not bigoted against other peoples and believe no less than they in the promises of our prophets to all humanity. We pray on New Year's Day and the Day of Atonement: "O God, grant that the fear of You may be upon all Your works and the dread of You upon all Your creatures, that all works may fear You and all creatures worship You, that they may all be united in one bond, earnestly to do Your will...." But another prayer follows this one: "Grant, O God, honor to Your people, praise to those who worship You, good hope to those who seek You, access to those who trust in You,[18] joy to Your land and rejoicing to Your city and the increase of power to Your servant David." And truly, the honor of our people, its praise and good hope depend solely upon our land, upon the joy and rejoicing of our city. Only then will unrighteousness shut its mouth, all wickedness vanish like smoke, and the dominion of evil be abolished from the earth.[19]

> May God, the protector of Israel and his Redeemer, cause His word to be fulfilled: "Thus says God, I am helping my people from the east and the west and will bring them to dwell in Jerusalem, to be only one people and I their one God, in truth and righteousness (Zech. 8)."[20]

PRESIDENT: The presidency trusts it has acted in accord with the Congress's wishes, in having sent to Rabbis Samuel Mohilewer and Dr. Ruelf,* who have expressed their support for the Congress, notices of appreciation. (Loud, joyous affirmation.) In regard to Dr. Ruelf's letter, I think it best to refrain from sharing it, since there will be occasion to publish it.

[113] Dr. S. Mandelkern* (Leipzig): I would like to mention something just briefly. Yesterday already I noticed that nothing was said about the great works which Edmund von [Edmond de] Rothschild has accomplished through his colonizing efforts. I believe that it has been only on account of his successes that Jewry as a whole has been encouraged to continue what he has done as an individual. I think it would have been nice, already at the beginning of the session, for this work to have been mentioned, and I think it would be a good thing now for him to receive three cheers.

President: I must draw to your attention here to the fact that with this proposal we are prejudging an important issue: we thus put the Congress in an awkward position. We must choose between either seeming ingratitude or the surrendering of principles which still remain to be debated by us. Therefore, I think it best to be content with the hearing of this comment and to pass over this motion to return to the day's agenda. (Loud agreement.)[21]

President: I would like to read out another communication which is of great interest. While it is not explicitly stated in the letter that it is intended for public consumption, still, since there is no note attached concerning confidentiality, I think it not improper to read out the letter of Grand Rabbi Zadok Kahn.* (Reading of the letter.)[22]

Dr. Nordau: Honored assembly! On Saturday, in your preparatory session, you appointed a five-man committee to prepare a draft of the Zionist program and to present it to you. The committee assumed that it went without saying that, besides the five elected members, the two gentlemen, Professor Schapira* and Dr. Bodenheimer, as authors of the earlier draft of the program, should likewise join the committee. The seven-member committee held three long, laborious sessions. The result of these many hours of strenuous effort is the draft which you should by now have before you. By a cursory reading of it you will not realize what a mass of work lies behind these few lines of intentionally terse prose. Sitting on the committee there were—besides Prof. Schapira, who brought to the work his clear, mathematically trained mind, and a heart filled with genuine Jewish idealism, and myself, who can boast no other qualification than my good will—only intelligent and learned lawyers, who subjected every word to the most astute and analytical criticism, and who let no word pass that could not stand up to this devastating critique. And nevertheless, in the end it was our great pleasure to have the product which emerged from such tremendous pulverizing and hammering, accepted unanimously by the committee. Anyone familiar with lawyers' habits of thought, of whom it is alleged, that every lawyer worth his salt has at least two opinions about every conceivable question; whoever also knows that you can search the world over looking for two lawyers who are of the same opinion on any point; whoever considers further that, to lawyers' customary habits of thought there was added in this case the peculiarly Jewish traits of character—you know that we are accused of being the most obstinate, stiff-necked, uncompromising, stubbornly opinionated people, utterly intolerant of any opinion but our own—whoever considers all this, will be able to appreciate the incredible fact of unanimity as something so astonishing that it borders on the miraculous. [114] I am now imploring you urgently: follow the example of your committee!

The draft takes account of every legitimate sensibility. It is fair to the passionate and the prudent, the militant and the fainthearted. Adopt it without debate, without a vote, by acclamation! Let its adoption be by vocal affirmation! Your unanimity will transform it into a new inscription on Israel's banner, marking out the path for the willing and working of our tribe, for generations to come.

The draft reads:

> Zionism strives to create a homeland in Palestine for the Jewish people, secured by law.
>
> To attain this goal, the Congress envisages the following means:
>
> 1. The effective promotion of settling Palestine with Jewish agriculturalists, craftsmen, and those pursuing other trades and professions.[23]
> 2. The organizing and uniting of all Jewry by means of appropriate regional and general organizations, in accord with the laws of the land.
> 3. The strengthening of Jewish national feeling and consciousness.
> 4. Preliminary steps toward obtaining governmental agreements necessary to attain the goal of Zionism.

SAMUEL PINELES: I am also in favor of adopting the draft by acclamation.

FABIUS SCHACH* (COLOGNE): (Much noise as he begins to speak.) If there is going to be talk about what is "legal," then I am claiming the valid right to be heard first. Gentlemen! I am no lawyer and I have no cause to regret that I do not look at the world through the distorting lens of the *corpus juris*. There are people who think more clearly and naturally than lawyers, and some laymen, by their own sound reasoning, have a better grasp of what is legal, than a lawyer. Gentlemen! We want to convey hereby the foundational ideas of Zionism, and for this it is absolutely necessary that we say clearly in our program what we are striving for. A national Jewish home, that is the goal we are striving for, not a refuge granted for mercy's sake. We want to make the land of our fathers the land of our future. It goes without saying that we will not win it by the sword, but rather by peaceful negotiations with the Sultan mediated by the states of Europe. But without international guarantees our national home can never attain security. No concessions can be made that undermine what is fundamental to our efforts. The term lacking here in this program is the pillar of Zionism that we cannot possibly renounce. It is the innocent term, "by international law."[24] I belong to the militants not the fainthearted. A healthy popular movement has never yet been brought into being by prudent caution and scholarly reservation. Why should we not show our true colors? Why should we not acknowledge: we do not want to be tolerated any longer, we want to have the rights of citizenship on our native soil? Without a national bastion, without international guarantees, the continuing existence of a small people is never secure. Our striving must be directed to winning over the Sultan and the European states to our cause, showing them that we are a peaceable civilized element and that we will benefit ourselves and the world if we are aided in getting a national, legally secured homeland. [115] But this gathering point for a resurrected Jewish people has to be endowed with international legality! If we relinquish this, we will have renounced our main goal, and we will have left the path of a consistent Zionism. (Commotion.)

PRESIDENT: This little break will perhaps have helped to restore some order to the debate. I think Herr Schach from Cologne has made a certain mistake. For the draft, the most conciliatory yet sufficiently clear formula has been sought. I am not the committee's interpreter. I myself used a term in my speech yesterday which might recommend itself for inclusion; i.e., the term, "by public law."[25] We all know what we need, and it is not necessary to enter into a debate about what goes without saying, only to realize later that it was a purely semantic dispute. The difference between our efforts and those made previously consists in our giving clear preference to legal rights over tolerance. Pray do not make the job of the Executive more difficult by a perhaps too precise expression of what you intend. After all, this does not mean that an offer would be accepted that is worth no more than what our fellow tribesmen already have right now over there, where they are now. There is the tacit assumption that only such conditions can be accepted as would fulfill the projected program which inspires us all. I would like to recommend to you once again, not to let the debate become too wide-ranging. Let us not drown in verbosity!

OSKAR MARMOREK: Honored assembly! Since a debate is arising over the draft program, I would like to propose that the report of Dr. Bodenheimer be listened to first, because it is relevant to this point; otherwise we will have this debate again later. I move to listen to the report of Dr. Bodenheimer first.

DR. LANDAU: The draft program was prepared by several lawyers. I myself have had the honor of belonging to this committee. So as not to lose too much time, I propose the selection of representative speakers, with a pause of five minutes for those wishing to speak for or against to be able to agree on a representative speaker.

Marmorek's motion to postpone debate until after the Bodenheimer report is rejected.

Landau's motion to select representative speakers is adopted.

PRESIDENT: So, representative speakers will be chosen. I am interrupting the session for five minutes so that the gentlemen may reach agreement. It goes without saying that only those gentlemen who previously indicated their intention to speak are to take part in the selection of the representative speakers.

Pause.

DR. KORNBLÜH*: I would simply like to ask whether or not the ladies have the right to vote.[26]

PRESIDENT: It goes without saying that the ladies are very honored guests, but do not take part in voting.—Herr Motzkin* has the floor.

[116] MOTZKIN (KIEV): I have just received the honorable task of making a statement with respect to the first point of the program. Even though it is very difficult for me to give, instantly and with complete clarity, the reasons for my judgment with regard to the point under discussion, still, I consider it my duty to do so. We represent the viewpoint, that the term "by international law" has to appear in the program, and in fact with exactly the same meaning

as Dr. Herzl has given it in his pamphlet. When the work *Autoemancipation** appeared fifteen years ago, the idea was openly proclaimed for the first time, that Jewry desired a "homeland secured by international law" and could hope for such only by taking steps in the sense of engaging in public activity.[27] With time the significance of this prophetic admonition attenuated to such an extent that, first, the only thing that remained was a colonization society for Palestine, then the creation of a handful of colonies, and finally nothing but the collecting of funds for charity. It was a great historic ideal, but all that remained was some insignificant work. Of this genuine and pure idea, what was conveyed to the people? The key point—that we are striving, by means of our program, to solve the Jewish question—was almost forgotten.

Great therefore was the enthusiasm with which we received the first step toward the realization of that historic beginning, this Congress, powerful was the resonance which Herzl's very first summons found in our souls. For us, it does not have to do with a word, rather with our entire future way of operating; the word is merely a symbol of this. According to our view, it is of utmost importance that the Congress articulate publicly its solution to the Jewish question. The world is occupied with the Jewish question while the Jews have taken a position in relation to it that is nothing if not humiliating. Our standpoint, our protest, will be different if we declare: We want our own home, in fact a home manifest to the whole world. We do not want to be accused of disguising our goals. Everyone understands that a people must have a home, so we too can approach the world with the demand that we be granted this home. Certainly, our goal will not be attained simply by making this demand. Likewise, we do not think that diplomatic representatives are going to suddenly appear in order to fulfill our wishes. But if we diffuse the idea into society more and more, that the solution to the Jewish question is to be conceived of only in this sense; if we also adapt our operations among the Jews to the same goal; if we agitate for it among the entire Jewish people; if we, if I can put it thus, give our people a thorough going-over, albeit in a genteel way; if we do all this, we can count on inward and outward success. Then we will come, I hope, to be in a position to undertake our operations in the name of the whole Jewish nation, and prepare ourselves for momentous historical events.

Many think that we might cause a great deal of damage to the work of colonization through our excessive youthful zeal, and our "lack of discretion." It is quite possible that coming forward publicly we will cause some problems for the practical work at the present time. But gentlemen! The colonizing activity of recent years, continued in the old-fashioned way, is going to lead nowhere anyway. In fifteen years we have settled several thousands of Jewish farmers, which has aroused but little interest among the Jews. [117] It is a sad fact that so-called "practical" activity has alienated the Zionist movement from the people, from our hearts; we, the youth, are fed up with that petty work going on under the mask of benevolence, without plan, without organization, done in underhanded ways, and without hope. At the beginning of the 1880s, did not the Russian Jewish student body hail the Zionist ideal? When the greatness of Zionism faded, so did the enthusiasm.

What guarantees do we have henceforward that our way of operating will not change, if we do not adopt from the start a fixed program in which it is stated that we are seeking to found in Palestine a "homeland secured by international law"? We need not fear those who draw back because they are too cowardly and lacking in courage to follow us, for they have been of little benefit to us up till now. As for colonizing work, the Jewish nation has been able to raise annually only francs by the tens of thousands and members by the thousands; do we really believe that if it were an existential issue, it would have consciously acted in this way, displaying such a low degree of idealism for it? But the idea that this cause has to do with its salvation, with its rescue, with the solution of the great national question, which cannot be denied—this idea was no longer brought home to the popular Jewish masses, and still they offered sufficient sums for colonists in distant Palestine.

Would that you give to us, the younger generation, real work! Would that you cause us to come before the whole Jewish people with the ideal of the homeland, seeking to awaken the appreciation of our fixed program and organizing the people for a political endeavor, in new ways and with new methods. Dissimulating has led nowhere; if we do not stir up the whole of the press and the general public with plain speaking, our successes will be minimal even with the Jews. Therefore I say: all dissimulations are nothing but the self-deception of those who think the Turkish government does not know that we are establishing ourselves in Palestine and want to begin a national political life. It has got to know it; for it is precisely this government that the great Zionist league has to enter into relations and negotiations with.

And one last thing: how is it possible for us to found a unified league in spite of our divergent worldviews? It is just the ideal of a "homeland secured by international law" which has totally suppressed all divisions among us relative to other issues, divisions of a religious nature or in our conception of the national idea, which would otherwise also be so natural to us. It is therefore important for our solidarity, for the solidarity of the whole Jewish people, that our ideal be articulated clearly.

Dr. Mintz speaks as the representative of the formulation which the commission gave to the program.

Dr. Nordau: I would reproach myself, were I, by rambling on and on, to dilute the impression which the outstanding statements of the foregoing spokesmen have obviously made on you. But nothing has been adduced in this admittedly brief discussion which I take to be reason enough to depart from my first recommendation. [118] On the contrary, the feelings which have been vented in a somewhat confused manner, strengthen me in my desire to see the debate closed, in fact by vocal affirmation. We all want to accentuate what unites us and put in the background what divides us. Factions are certain to appear among us later on; there will be no lack of serious divisions. But let us at least give to our movement at its point of departure the example of an imposing consensus by unanimous adoption of the program by acclamation! (Enthusiastic shouts: Vote!)

Dr. Blumenfeld* (on voting): I will be brief. I think I am not amiss in requesting that voting take place by name, so that the issue is not be decided by lung power or handclapping, so the result is clear and unequivocal; I move therefore that there be a vote by name on this point, for "by international law" or "by law."

President: There are actually three motions: the motion of the committee, then the motion of Herr Motzkin, and third, the motion for "by public law." But many of those in attendance today may have a misapprehension. The gentlemen of the committee, motivated by their desire to produce a unified declaration of the First Congress, have agreed on terms with the widest range of meaning, which would include the narrower range as well; they have thereby not indicated explicitly to what extent they support the narrowest range, if I can define it thus (i.e., the "by international law" position); they have held it in reserve but have not abandoned it. If we are, possibly, nearer to the realization of our ideals than one might imagine, then certain reasons of expediency may justify a more discreet formulation, which however by no means implies an abandoning of this position. I think the one who produces a quicker resolution is the one who is serving the cause. The relative proportions of the votes are already obvious. But we would all like to see the motion for the program adopted unanimously and, with this in mind, I would like to point out that perhaps the choice of the term "by public law" will be agreed to by every lawyer. I take the liberty to recommend this insertion, which does not misrepresent our program, to the committee for discussion, and if they agree to this wording, to put it to a vote.

Dr. Bodenheimer: I move that if a deliberation is still to take place, twelve or fourteen gentlemen be elected to deliberate on the program once again. (General opposition.) I perceive the general mood, and I therefore withdraw my motion.

Fabius Schach: Gentlemen! I have an urgent request: We are not talking just in this hall, we are speaking in public to the world. Every word has public significance. What will other people say, if they hear later that debate was closed on such a motion? I make a motion with regard to the rules of procedure, that the debate be reopened. (The speaker leaves the hall amid a general tumult.)

President: By reason of the selection of representative speakers, the debate is closed. I have moved that the commission withdraw to undertake a revision and to communicate this to the Congress.

Pause

[119] President: Herr Dr. Nordau, chairman of the committee, has the floor.

Dr. Nordau: The program committee has withdrawn for further deliberation; it has satisfied itself that there is actually no reason to alter its position and that the addition of "public" to "legal" would actually express nothing not already contained in the original text. However, to offer the needed example of strenuous self-subordination in the interest of a much-sought-after unity, the committee has decided to concede to the proposal for the insertion of this word. The first section will therefore read:

> Zionism strives to create a homeland in Palestine for the Jewish people, secured by public law.

The committee now recommends this formulation for unanimous approval. (Enthusiastic cheers.)

The motion appears to carry by acclamation.

Dr. Blumenfeld withdraws his motion in the face of the great enthusiasm.

Motzkin: Those gentlemen who asked for the words "by international law" declare themselves satisfied with the change to "by public law" and state that their conviction is thereby frankly and honestly pronounced to the world. (Much applause.)

Dr. Herzl: Herr Dr. Bodenheimer has the floor for his report concerning the Zionist organization.

Dr. M.J. Bodenheimer (Cologne): Worthy members of the Congress! The idea of calling us here, assembling us for a communal consultation—we who are animated by a common conviction, who are imbued with a common will, to give to our people a firm foundation on which to base its future—that was already the beginning of a Zionist organization. The simple fact of the Congress has rendered invaluable services and provided significant benefits to the cause, even if our proceedings were to remain without any direct practical result. Just as an idea often powerfully stimulates both soul and body, spurring us on to energetic action, where we had previously allowed our powers to languish in idle lethargy, even so the idea of the Congress has shaken Jewry everywhere out of a millennium-long slumber and brought it around to recognize its existence. Just as a storm of wind scatters fertile seeds into distant lands, even so has this idea, everywhere where the Zionist movement has found entry, awakened new life and compelled partisans of our cause to organize themselves, in order to stand up to our enemies arising on all sides from among our fellow tribesmen, and to declare their enthusiastic support for the first Jewish national assembly. It will now be our task to justify the hopes our like-minded colleagues have pinned to the development of this seed of an organization by means of our assembly.

[120] The question of whether and why we need an organization at all, is almost certainly not one which any sympathetic colleague will raise; nonetheless, we will give this question brief consideration. Every form of life has organs it brings into the world at birth, by which it sustains and propagates itself, and it develops these organs for activity adapted to said purpose. But the case is different with so-called social and political bodies. The distinguishing feature of such a body, of a spiritual community of multiple persons, is that it needs to create special organs to express its communal commitment to the attainment of its ideals. An ethnically defined people is also such a social and political body; if it organizes itself, creating instruments for sustaining and developing, then

it becomes an organized ethnic body; i.e., a nation. The highest expression and goal of an organization of this kind is its recognition in international law as a state.[28] For this reason, the state is designated in juristic philosophy as the people's legally organized will to power. Not every nation has the capacity to ascend to the highest stage of development. Only peoples of superlative spiritual strength and individual character have attained this goal; but the drive is inherent to every nation, to prove its individual character and strength by forming a state. Accordingly, where several nations coexist within a larger political confederation, each aspires either to subjugate the other nations to its own individual character and suppress them, if it feels itself strong enough to do this, or, in the other case, to separate itself from the state as a whole and to establish itself as an independent state. Therefore, however the organization of an ethnically defined people may be constituted, it must offer the possibility of going on toward forming itself into a state, it must carry within it, at its core, the seed of state formation. The entire misery of the Jewish people since the loss of national independence consists in the fact that it did not possess, and as an insignificant minority could not possess, sufficient power to acquire sovereignty as a state, that it also did not or could not create anywhere an organized life in order to separate from the states in which it lived dispersed, to be able to form an independent commonwealth.

But did the Jewish people really lack such an organization? Has not this people always organized itself into communities? Indeed! But the disunity of these individual communities, among which there existed no unifying connection, definitely did not allow for any national development. Uniting the entire people for common purposes was totally inconceivable with these localized institutions lacking a national center. Now it might be said that there did exist after all associations which embrace all of Jewry without distinction of citizenship, one need only think of the Alliance Israélite Universelle or the American B'nai B'rith.* [121] But these associations really cannot be termed a "national" organization, inasmuch as they have divested themselves on principle of any political character and seek to support their fellow tribesmen from a purely philanthropic standpoint.

Besides, these associations are based to some extent upon the principle of assimilation; thus, were they to move beyond it into dealing with political affairs, they would represent not a national but an international organization. That these associations are made up of Jews alone is not seen by the associations themselves as an end in itself, but rather an accidental, extrinsic circumstance which, in the view of their founders and directors, will cease as soon as the principles of philanthropy have attained general acceptance through the elimination of religious prejudices. Evidently these people expect this idyllic condition in the very near future: in this, the wish seems to be father to the thought. An otherwise intelligent and educated gentleman, a distinguished merchant, promised me that this paradisal age will certainly come within five or, at the latest, twenty years. And then they talk to us about utopias![29]

Therefore, all these organizations offer no possibility whatever of further evolution toward the idea of a state, toward the legal conceptualization of the national will-to-power.

Indeed, if it is our view that the Jewish people are in need of a separate polity for their self-preservation and cultural development, and this conviction has been expressed—if we are in need of a homeland where the unique Jewish character can develop itself freely, where Jewish talent and capability can undergo a comprehensive test of its worth in every area of life, unhindered by the pressure and restriction to which every minority is subject—then we must create special organs and a new national organization for this purpose. But this means that our organization is not only a Zionist one, rather, the entire Jewish people forms its object and basis.

We are convinced that the assimilationist organizations existing hitherto have not been an expression of the Jewish people and its will-to-power; they are rather solely that of a clique of financiers, who anyway are internationalists only too happy to cloak their materialistic, mammonistic tendencies behind an overlay of disingenuous patriotism. In the mouth of such people the word "patriotism" is being abused, and their whole behavior is a farce.

We do not need a mandate in order to create a national Jewish organization, as the protesting rabbis would have it.[30] [122] Those men, animated by the desire to help their people to be liberated from oppression and injustice, at any time and in any country, who have summoned their brothers to the work of national unification and pledged their lives to this sacred cause—have they ever waited for the mandate of servile apostates and cowardly hypocrites? When the desire to help their oppressed people lives in the bosom of hundreds of ardent men, then the conviction of the necessity of the liberating act is the only mandate that can stir them to collective action.[31]

Therefore, since at present we alone represent the Jewish people, it falls to us, as the Jewish national assembly, based on a constituency of a substantial part of the Jewish people, to prepare the fundamental institutions regarded as prerequisites for the making of a state—namely:

a. Organizing those among the people who feel their Jewish national identity.
b. Connecting the culture of the latter with a specific country.

Whether then, under these preparatory conditions, a state will actually develop, whether this summit point of a national culture for the Jewish people can once again be reached—the solution to this question can be confidently left to the future; we have to leave it to divine providence.

Now that we have discussed the fact that we need an organization, and why we need it, we will now go on to investigate how the organization should be constituted in order to serve our cause.

The foundation of this organization must be a clear, brief program which establishes the essential principles that unite us as a party and separate us from other intellectual tendencies within Jewry. As the soul and mind determine a person's actions, so also must the program always take its place as the reference point of our party's operations. In the nature of things, this program has to be a general one which embraces Zionists of all countries in a common bond and is a specific bond within every country where a separate Zionist group is to be found. The general program can contain only that which unites us all; here I can surely express frankly my personal opinion in favor of "the establishment of a homeland secured by international law for oppressed fellow tribesmen and an indication of the necessary means thereto."

We can pursue this goal without involving ourselves in the domestic political conditions of existing states. None of them should feel disturbed by this program. We are not attacking any nation or confession, nor are we infringing their established rights. On the contrary, we want to do away with a seed of strife and discord for those fellow tribesmen who feel themselves harassed on account of national or confessional frictions, by creating a refuge where they can develop their individual character without thereby clashing with other nations or confessions.

[123] Even the Turkish government will not be threatened by our aspirations. The Jewish people gratefully acknowledges the tolerance which the Turkish Sultans have always practiced toward the Jews, and will never forget that they opened their empire in hospitality to them at the time of the Spanish Inquisition.[32] We too have the earnest intention of reaching, by means of our organization, an international legal agreement on the basis of common interests, without impairing the sovereignty of the Sultan in any way.

Our program constitutes a safety valve both in relation to anti-Semitism and in relation to continually growing Jewish misery, especially in Eastern Europe. Can there be a more humane, a nobler undertaking, than to provide work and peaceful livelihood through the labor of their own hands, to a hungry people yearning for bread, to the Russian-Polish, Galician, and Romanian Jews?

Whereas the general program excludes on principle our involvement in the status of the Jewish population in individual countries and their political or social position vis-à-vis the nations among whom they dwell, each of the individual organizations will take up the matter of adjusting this status according to the circumstances in their individual countries.

What follows are examples of perspectives which have to be considered:

An appalling condition of economic and social distress prevails among the Jewish population in Galicia. For this population to be of benefit for our cause, whether by material support of colonizing work or by contributing the manpower fit for colonizing, this condition of distress must first be eliminated or at least mitigated. In addition, it is not enough merely to awaken the hope of the poor man for a brighter future, who today is close to starvation as a result of anti-Jewish legislation; the just demands of the present are urgent. The foremost duty of our partisans in Galicia, springing from a sense of national solidarity, is interceding with aid for our brothers and working to remedy the abuses that have given rise to their misery. Investigating and fighting against the source of this condition of distress on its own, is therefore a principal object of the Galician organization.

An essentially different task will arise for the Zionists of the European West. Here a sense of belonging to a nation has almost completely disappeared among the Jews, on account of the appearance of civic equality. Indeed, the Jew feels his community with other Jews forced upon him by birth not only, as Heinrich Heine says, as a misfortune, but almost as a disgrace which he seeks to conceal as much as possible on account of hostile currents. [124] The result is an existential equivocation and bewilderment which virtually precludes manly pride, self-awareness, and a pure sense of happiness, and which also makes it impossible for the Jews to offer a systematic defense of their common interests.[33] It is necessary, by giving attention to our history, to awaken the awareness that we have always been regarded as a national unit, in spite of our dispersion among the peoples, and that in this respect even the so-called emancipation did not change anything. While this solidarity has hitherto manifested itself, unfortunately, almost entirely in the commonality of suffering and oppression, now, through Zionism, a common striving toward a better and realizable future is taking its place as its focus and goal. Who can deny this community of interests where a history written with blood and tears, where the strong voice of shared distress, speak more eloquently to our empathetic hearts than the empty noise of words?

Consequently, for the Zionists of the West, the cultivation of Jewish history will be the main object of their activity.

But the principal task of the individual organizations in all countries will be to disseminate our ideas to the mass of the Jewish people, to recruit new partisans to our flag, and in so doing to make it possible to carry out our plans.

Considered from these perspectives, the Congress is to be regarded as the chief organ of Zionists the world over. Every Zionist must be accorded the right to participate in this assembly which will take place each year in a different location, and to exercise his right to vote. It would be advisable to give the Zionists of the location where the Congress takes place, the right to vote only through the agency of their delegates, to prevent their holding disproportionate power in the assembly.

My recommendation also proposes:

The Congress is to elect a Central Committee each time it meets, to prepare for the next World Congress as well as for the dispatch of day-to-day business.

This Central Committee elects three special committees from within its membership:

a. for propaganda
b. for diplomatic-financial business
c. for colonizing-practical activity

Each time it meets, the World Congress will determine the number of members of the Central Committee, as well as its seat. It will also decide how many persons the Central Committee can add to its numbers by way of appointment.

The Central Committee will set up at its seat a central bureau with three departments corresponding to the special committees.

[125] At least nine members of the Central Committee must have their domicile at the location of its seat.

The territorial committees are elected by the territorial assemblies of Zionists in the same manner as the Central Committee; otherwise, they organize themselves independently according to their specific conditions. The territorial committees will also set up bureaus which, under the committees' direction, will handle regular correspondence and make propaganda.

The territorial committees determine who from among their members will be authorized to correspond with the Central Committee.

By "diplomatic-financial business" is intended those activities that have as their object negotiating with the Turkish government in order to secure our colonizing work and the obtaining of governmental or international guarantees for this work, but it also includes directing negotiations with the powers, and with "haute finance," in order to obtain the necessary financial means for colonizing-practical activity.

This last subject is too extensive and depends too much on conditions existing at the moment, to be discussed in further detail here. It may be mentioned that not only does founding agricultural colonies fall under this heading, but also creating and financing industrial establishments, building railways and other means of transportation, investing in ports, and instituting colonial self-government.

For this organization to accomplish anything it will require a fund, it will need money, which is obviously necessary for things besides making war.[34] The question of how this national fund is to be constituted, has occupied the leading minds of our movement to an extraordinary extent, the evidence of which is that I have been sent a great number of detailed proposals on this very point.[35] I will report only briefly concerning them, since the gentlemen in question will presumably be making specific motions and giving their arguments for them.

What all of these proposals have in common is that they are large in scale right from the outset and presuppose that the fund requires an enormous pool of capital.

Herr Professor Dr. Schapira wants to establish a fund through one-time and ongoing collections, which cannot, however, be tapped until it has reached the amount of ten million pounds sterling. Two-thirds of this fund can be applied only to the acquisition of lands, which, however, are not to be alienated again, but are only to be leased for periods of forty-nine years. The expenditure of an amount larger than the annual interest can take place only on the basis of a plebiscite of the Jewish people.

[126] Our venerable champion in Silesia, Herr Moses from Kattowitz, wants to raise the fund by founding cooperative societies. Every member will be obliged to pay ten to fifteen kronen to subscribe and 100 to 150 kronen per annum.[36] For his participation, the member of the society receives landed estates and agricultural equipment, with an obligation to pay the interest on their value at a rate of 4 or 5 percent until the full amount of five thousand

krone has been paid in. Herr Moses hopes in this fashion to obtain access to share capital of about one billion.

Even one of the eldest persons in our young movement, Herr Dr. Bierer* from Sofia, has taken up this question. He and the delegate of the Romanian Grand Lodge belonging to the Order of B'nai B'rith, which constitutes a praiseworthy exception to the drive for assimilation characterizing similar societies in other countries—Herr Dr. Bierer and Herr Brociner* concur in their proposal to levy a regular contribution to the Zionist fund annually on all Jewish *patresfamilias*.

All these proposals offer interesting perspectives and undoubtedly contain something of value; and perhaps the proposal of Bierer and Brociner for Eastern Europe is feasible, I cannot judge. The idea of Dr. Schapira gives rise to serious reservations on two counts. He wants to combine, as the economic basis of the prospective polity, the land tenure reform of Dr. Hertzka* and Flürscheim* with the ancient biblical prescriptions for the year of Jubilee, and at the same time to introduce the plebiscite into questions of administration. It seems to me extremely risky to determine national-economic institutions in the still-to-be-created polity, but especially to make decisions without prior experiments, and to adopt a system whose implementation in the so-called *Freilandcolonieen* has taken place without a single one of these colonies having so far attained to a prosperous state of development.[37] A plebiscite as envisioned by Professor Schapira seems to me practically impossible to implement.

Gentleman, it will scarcely be possible to procure a large pool of capital by means of the cooperative societies projected by Herr Moses, since by far the great bulk of manpower available for colonization does not have the required five thousand kronen, and those who have the necessary capital do not, for the most part, have the desire or capacity for agricultural colonization. Yet, it being the foundation of every national economy, we too must begin our colonizing efforts with agriculture.

However, I can say with some confidence that the solution to the question is much simpler than people think. I scarcely need emphasize that my remarks follow closely what has already been stated, particularly in the work of my friend Dr. Herzl.

[127] Capital resembles, if I may use a somewhat daring image, a well-bred young woman, who bashfully hides herself when a frivolous and foppish suitor goes looking for her; thus does capital seem to disappear when new projects of doubtful security go looking for money in the market. As soon as

a safe venture, a profitable project appears, capital is there in abundance, it practically throws itself at us.

Sums raised by voluntary contributions will suffice for the present, to cover the costs of campaigning and making propaganda for our idea.

Since we cannot count on other banking institutions, the first task of the financial committee to be appointed will be to establish a bank specific to our purposes, in a word, a Jewish bank.[38]

The bank's purpose will be to promote agrarian, industrial, and commercial enterprises of the Jewish colonists in Syria and Palestine. As long as it remains impossible to employ its capital in this way, the bank will be able, like any other financial institution, to employ its disposable capital for the industrial and commercial purposes of its choosing. However, if investment for the aforesaid purposes is adequately secured, whether by the colonists, corporations, or specialized enterprises, then the bank is required to allocate up to at least one-half of its working capital to these purposes.

As for the funds transferred to it by private individuals for purposes of investment or management and irrespective of their being Jews or non-Jews, the bank ought to be obliged by its bylaws to employ them solely for economically productive enterprises.

The national fund to be administered separately from this bank and acquired through collections and donations, may be employed for founding model colonies or the purposes stipulated by the donors. The costs of the bank-initiated attempts to create an industry in the colonies could be paid for out of it as well. If conditions in the Jewish colonies are secure, the bank will be able to transfer its head office there as the Jewish National Bank.

This bank, in association with the Central Committee in Vienna, is likewise the agency best suited to enter into negotiation with the Turkish government with regard to concessions to purchase land, etc.

Determining in detail how to organize the bank or delimit the field of its competence, cannot be either the task of this report or the object of your resolutions.

[128] The third point of my report, concerning "agitation," I should be able to dispose of quickly, since we have in the political parties the best models of this. But I would like to draw attention to a peculiar phenomenon, which is, in my view, particularly noteworthy.

It appears that there is virtually no need in Russia and Romania for a special agitation for our cause. The masses there have already been won over. The funds raised there might be needed at most to promote light Hebrew literature by founding popular libraries, publishing inexpensive Hebrew classics as proposed by our colleague Herr Dr. Ehrenpreis, and subsidizing the Hebrew daily press. The funds left over should serve to win over the Jewish masses in West Europe to the Zionist idea.

Agitation should consist chiefly in the activity of itinerant orators whose task it will be to inform Jewish as well as Gentile populations in Germany, France, England, and America, about the significance and goals of our movement. These itinerant orators may well be, at the same time, the directors of the bureaus in their respective countries. There will surely be no dearth of the requisite talents among us.

The next step will be to create a daily paper or at least a periodical in each country, that will deal with questions relating to our movement, partly in a scholarly and partly in a polemical fashion, and at the same time will keep the Jewish population updated about everything it needs to know. Where this pertains, the preexisting press is to be won over. A proposal worth noting is made by our colleague from Lemberg, Herr Bader,* who thinks there is a need to establish a daily Zionist paper in Yiddish for Galicia. If such a paper comes into existence, I would like to request that, as far as possible, it also promote the Hebrew language by including more serious, belletristic works.

Next, as the third step, would be the bureaus of the territorial organizations publishing and disseminating pamphlets and flyers to make propaganda, in the same way the National-jüdische Vereinigung für Deutschland [Jewish-National Association for Germany] has made a successful start.

Moreover, activism can be substantively promoted through the founding of Jewish athletic clubs, as a colleague from Prague suggests to me in a letter, as well as through such academic associations.[39] Quite apart from the socio-political significance of our movement, it would also be of immeasurable value to the moral development of our Jewish youth, if they could be diverted from the amusements of modern urban life, with their ruinous effect on heart and mind, and directed toward shared and uplifting mental exertions and invigorating physical exercises.

[129] However, to disseminate our idea the principal way will always be through personal agitation. He who is imbued with devotion to the truth of our principles will be the best champion for these same principles within his own social group, by means of a living message. He will dispel with little effort the prejudices against our movement and be able to put suspicions that are raised in their true light. When we stir up the hearts and minds of those personally known to us and with whom we interact as colleagues and friends, "agitation" will become a reality in its true and literal sense. The bonds of friendship, which party strife would threaten to rend apart, will be made firmer

and will be imbued with new meaning through common striving toward a beautiful, sublime goal.

To conclude. In the introduction to my address I compared the organized people to a living body. Unfortunately, the Jewish people is at present a life form whose organs have become debilitated and disabled as a result of centuries of inactivity.

Our task it is to revive these organs, to infuse the body politic once again with the spirit of fresh striving and glad confidence, so that this languishing people may become healthy and strong and able once again to present rich gifts from its free spirit to humankind.

We have no need to prove that we are bleeding from a thousand wounds, and every day inflicts new ones upon us. But we recognize that our condition is critical because we have for the most part lost even the natural capacity to feel the blows landing upon us, to evade or react to them, so little does the instinct of self-preservation still activate our people.

Only thus can it be explained that there are individual tribesmen in our day like the ancient defectors to the Romans or Christians, who go so far as to deny the Jewish misery, which is desperately knocking at our doors from the East. But let us not join issue with these Jewish scoffers, which the impulse of the moment might easily mislead us into doing. History will brush them aside, thereby giving its judgment on the derisive words of those gentlemen, as it has stigmatized forever those who betrayed the people in ancient times, the Hellenistic High Priest, Menelaus,* and the defector to Rome, Flavius Josephus.*

The ship of the Jewish people is wandering aimlessly on a turbulent sea, without captain or helmsman to guide it to a life-saving port. The disaster has been going on now for centuries. Give to the people its leaders, and the skillfully piloted ship will very soon, with the glad rejoicing of its crew, reach the lush shore, a country which promises us the palm of peace and the sun of freedom.

[130] We stand upon the soil of the Swiss, who attained their freedom centuries ago under circumstances much more difficult than those which stand in the way of our cause. But let us be imbued with the spirit of these men, take our hearts in our hands, show ourselves the courageous champions of our commitment, and the victory of our cause is certain.

But the spirit which permeated those men is different from the spirit of discord and disunity which has often been so detrimental to the Jewish people.

So let a spirit of unity, the spirit of the oath taken at the Rütli, waft as well over our assembly of new Swiss confederates.[40] (Lively applause.)

Day Two, Afternoon Session

President: Herr Dr. Blumenfeld has the floor.

Dr. Blumenfeld: As I have taken the liberty of submitting a brief motion, permit me to briefly explain the motion, anticipating a favorable response. Today, Herr Dr. Nordau read out to us the draft of the Congress's program, adding his request that it be accepted *en bloc*, thus avoiding any further discussion. After several queries concerning the draft had been made, Dr. Nordau declared that answers to these queries were already to be found in the draft. So I move to have the draft program and likewise the relevant explanatory materials printed up.[1]

President: I am giving the floor to Herr Dr. Schaffer.*

Dr. Schaffer (Baltimore): Our program has been kept very concise; but the reason that it was composed in this way is so that it would encompass various points of view. If one explanation were given, then various explanations would have to be given—that is, according the interpretation of this one or that one. I beg you not to bring up again the controversy which we have happily settled. Rather, it should be left to every individual delegate to explain the program at home as seems best to him.

President: I give the floor to Herr Dr. Neumark.*

Dr. Neumark: We have restored unity today. It was done with some difficulty. It might perhaps have been done with less abruptness in the exercise of protocol, but at least unity was restored, and if we make yet another statement concerning the program's evolution, we will be forced to go into detail with regard to individual terms.

President: I give the floor to Herr Dr. Blumenfeld.

Dr. Blumenfeld: I am not demanding that any particular issue has to be delineated in more detail; there need be only a clarification of how the committee and the Congress interprets every single substantive term. This will be of great benefit to us in winning over the general public to support our goals.

[131] President: I would like to draw Herr Dr. Blumenfeld's attention to the fact that there cannot be one valid interpretation per se; I think rather that, in a certain sense, such an interpretation is found in the Congress's debate, which anyone can read and is available in the stenographic record. The motion is before us: printing of the program, with the relevant explanatory materials.

Upon being put to a vote, the printing of the program is approved; but the publishing of explanatory materials is rejected by a large majority.

President: We move to a discussion of Point 3 on the day's agenda.[2]

Marmorek: We have arrived at the crucial point of our deliberations. We all know that Jewish distress is real; we are united in wanting to relieve it; but the first thing required to achieve idealistic purposes is organization. As to what constitutes a sound organization the Social Democratic Party can teach us, although we are against this party in principle. What it has attained it has attained only through organization. The organization must not concentrate a load of work on the shoulders of a few, who, even with the best of intentions, are totally unable to accomplish it. I move the following:

The Zionist Congress resolves in favor of an organization with local-, provincial-, and state-level committees, to be set up in accordance with the relevant state laws. Additionally, but separate from these, committees with special assignments have to be created, namely:

1. A committee to study the demography of our people and occupational statistics.
2. A committee for the study of geography and Palestine colonization.
3. A committee for organization and propaganda.
4. A committee for the press, especially the party press, with the latter to be given special attention. It would also have to concern itself, among other things, with the cultural affairs of the Jewish people.
5. A finance committee.

6. A committee to prepare for the next Congress. The arrangements for the present Congress were well done, but we feel that further strides are possible. For this reason a separate committee for the next Congress should be appointed.

DR. KAMINKA: The motions just presented are, on the whole, somewhat premature. We are still without an overview. A motion should be made for appointing a committee to promote practical colonization. The necessity for it will be self-evident after you have heard the report on colonization. Similarly, after you have heard the proceedings having to do with Hebrew literature, you will know to what extent a committee to deal with all forms of Hebrew or Jewish literature is required. We wish therefore to postpone these motions until the proceedings shall have been thus far completed.

DAVID WOLFFSOHN (COLOGNE): I would like to note that this item on the agenda is probably the most important and the most difficult; I would like therefore to move to elect a committee of seven members to assess all of the motions made by members of the Congress having to do with organization. [132] This committee will then prepare the motions today and come back to us tomorrow, which will make dealing with this whole issue much easier. I propose to elect to this commission the following gentlemen: Dr. Herzl, Dr. Nordau, Dr. Bodenheimer, Dr. Schnirer, Dr. Bernstein, Director Steiner,* and Mr. de Haas from London. If necessary, this committee can also coopt others. I think this is the best way for us to move forward.

HEINRICH BIRKENSTEIN* (FRANKFURT AM MAIN): Of all the items and reports, the most interesting to me has been the consideration of political economy. I would like you to take heed that this item not be lost from view and be given attention at least equal to that of the other items mentioned thus far. For example, in Germany, political economy is given very little attention in every political discussion. In the Reichstag and in assemblies, the dearth of knowledge about political economy is absolutely palpable. I call to mind the issue of the silver and gold standard. How many people do we have in Germany who have any clear idea about this question? Even the study of political economy is lacking in Germany. On the other hand, I think that political economy would find fertile soil among our people. It is extremely important that the gentlemen nominate a committee to pursue these endeavors.

DR. SCHAFFER: I must advise strongly against setting up separate committees. Maintaining committees costs money. The money would have to be raised since the funds for it have not yet been raised. I conceive the situation differently. We need only an organization with five or six persons, the idea being that they divide up the work among themselves. Each person will take charge of a certain area, so that various separate committees are not necessary, which might cause confusion.

SCHACH: Gentlemen! We Jews are usually reproached for being too practical. Would that it were so! If we knew how to do practical work for our people, we would not today have assembled the First Zionist Congress, and we would have met somewhere other than Basel. This same impractical attitude is manifesting itself right now. We have heard great, magnificent speeches, but they all show us only what we would like to do, not what we actually should do. That we are a people, that we must be a people if we do not wish to perish, we know well enough, but now we have to be shown the way we are to travel—that is the task of the Congress. Emphasis is being put on lectures and not discussions, on the airing of opinions, and that is a mistake. Again and again we are expected to adopt motions *en bloc*, before different schools of thought have been heard from. If someone announces a report concerning agitation, I would have expected him to submit to us a printed scheme of agitation beforehand. Instead of this, we have heard yet again proof that the Jews constitute a nation. This is the place where we ought to be expressing our opinions about proposals, the place for giving and taking useful suggestions. We have no time here for learned, theoretical expositions! Gentlemen! We represent, formally, half a million fellow tribesmen, but de facto we are here as the legitimate representatives of seven million Jews, for the national spirit of the Jewish people has given us a mandate to do so. [133] Indeed, at this moment the whole Jewish people is directing its gaze at us and awaits from us consolation and practical counsel. I want to draw your attention to one important item, to agitation that is given vitality by belles lettres. Gentlemen! We are not a party in the sense of modern political parties. What unites is not political dogmas but vital interests. We belong to one another, flesh and blood, body and soul, past and future. Therefore, we also cannot agitate the way other parties do. We will make an impression on our brothers and sisters, not by means of flyers and programs, nor by scholarly works, but rather by good popular literature. If we want to win over the people, then we must create a popular literature. We need good stories with the national spirit, to inspire Jewish women with our ideals, for these women are guardians of the souls of children, and they are to raise the future generation as Jewish nationalist. Thus, we need Jewish youth literature like daily bread, to be able to make an impression on the tender mind of the child. People are surprised that the corpus of ghetto literature of recent decades is so shallow, tedious, stale, and lifeless, and they do not realize that only the national spirit can create a national literature. They do not want to be "national" and therefore are only capable of producing commissioned works according to a template. But now, the Jewish people having awakened, we want to portray the soul of the people with all its nuances and give new life to its individual character. To this end we want to write works for the youth and the people, and all Jewry will be grateful to us for doing so. Gentlemen! I do not wish to introduce a formal motion, only to offer the suggestion that the committee direct its attention to this item. It would be well if a special committee of men with experience were to be formed for this purpose. Our spiritual future depends on the creation of a good popular literature!

DR. BODENHEIMER: The suggestions that have been offered are extremely useful and instructive. But it seems to me that we have gotten into a general discussion of the issue of organization. I think all the motions should be referred to a committee that will examine them. Being aware that there are about one hundred motions of the most varied kind with regard to the organization, my view is that they should be submitted to a committee to be examined and evaluated; otherwise, if we go on like this, we will not finish in three days or even ten. We have to arrive at a rational form of organization. Not a single speaker has expressed his opinion about the motion to appoint a committee. It has been observed that the motions regarding organization have not been communicated in printed form. This observation is fair, since every member needs to know something about it. But do not forget that the Congress itself is a mere improvisation! But to remedy the error to some degree, the scheme of organization has been given out for immediate printing and should be available in an hour.

[134] PRESIDENT: As I understand rules of procedure, a vote is first to be taken on Wolffsohn's motion, the additional suggestions come only afterward; I cannot imagine that the motions of the committee would be handled more smoothly than those now coming from the floor of the Congress. This time, to save time, the motion should not be referred to committee—rather, the basic question should first be addressed and then we shall return to the agenda.

SHOUT FROM THE FLOOR: All of the motions should be referred to a committee for sorting, to put them in sequential order.

PRESIDENT: We cannot adhere strictly to the minutiae of parliamentary procedure, because we have only three days at our disposal. If a motion is submitted which contravenes the Congress's bylaws, it will obviously be set aside. The speakers have all the motions which conform to the bylaws. I do not think that we will proceed more quickly by first bringing the principle of appointing a committee to a vote, which would then have to submit the various motions to the appropriate persons in the plenary session.

DR. SCHNIRER: What is going to happen? The committee will select a number of the motions and suggestions; some they will find to be of value, others they will set aside. Do you think that anyone will be dissuaded from presenting his recommendations? If so, you are misjudging human vanity. Therefore, let us not elect a committee but rather take up the motions in order.

WOLFFSOHN: I would like to ask again for my motion to be voted on first. Referring all motions to a committee that will handle them all will greatly facilitate matters; otherwise, we could be sitting here for another three days, or six, without arriving at any goal. The committee should examine the motions. I ask to have a vote on this; then we will see what the Congress thinks!

DR. LANDAU: Honorable assembly! I find it very regrettable and really not comprehensible, that we have no concrete drafts put before us for item two as well as item three, toward which we are to take a position. It is perhaps not easy to do when it comes to the respect to the question of the program, but it is different in the case of the organization. Early this morning we listened to a very interesting speech by Dr. Bodenheimer, with his suggestions; but we have no precise, clear proposal for organization. But this is exactly what is needed. The organization has to be adapted to each country's conditions. If we had a precise draft today, we would be much better off in this respect. Despite my being otherwise opposed to it, I think we have no choice now but to appoint a committee with the same specific purpose the program committee was appointed for. It would then prepare certain drafts worthy of discussion. It is obvious that the question of the program is different from the question of the organization, and that a decision about a comprehensive organization can be reached only on the basis of the draft. What was pointed out by the president is important; it has to do with whether those who have not conveyed motions to the committee shall be prevented from making motions from the floor. If we had a draft, we would be able to say that such and such has been submitted in accord with parliamentary custom; then we would have to take a position on it. I will ask you to keep another thing in mind—namely the question of the composition of the committee. We are in general opposed to giving consideration to the nationality of individual members, for we are all Zionists. [135] But I think on this item we simply must give consideration to nationality, for every country has different conditions; therefore, I must implore you to make your decision along the lines I have indicated.

Dr. Farbstein: The question of the organization is undoubtedly one of the most important. I do not think we will be able to fully deal with it here. It is absolutely necessary for the question of the organization to be submitted to a committee. As Dr. Landau observed, we have to reckon with the various regions. The organization has to treat issues of culture as well as political economy. Therefore, representatives of various professions must be elected to the committee. A committee of seven members, as Herr Wolffsohn proposes, is a halfway measure. I recommend a committee of eleven to submit a draft of the organization on Tuesday. When the committee's draft is available, then it remains only for the plenary Congress to adopt or reject it. A draft from the minority should also be submitted, if one-third of the members are in favor of it.

W. Temkin (Elisabethgrad) speaks in Russian. He draws attention to the fact that an indigenous Zionist organization already exists in Russia, which operates strictly according to the country's laws. The Russian delegates need to consult among themselves at the present moment, in order to agree on their position. He asks for a postponement of the debate.

Marmorek: We did not come before the Congress with a finished draft of the organization. The purpose of the committee is to make suggestions about how the study of the organization question should proceed in the near future. We have, as you know, our press; we have our associations; we cannot do anything except select who is to do the work. I believe that the proposal of Herr Wolffsohn is very much to the point; at the same time I would like to affirm the suggestion that a census of the Jewish people be conducted by means of the Jewish communities themselves. In this way we will finally know who and what we are. I ask for Wolffsohn's motion to be adopted; I give full acknowledgement to the reservations of the Russian delegates; I ask for the motion to be adopted so that we can finally move forward.

Dr. Bodenheimer: It is completely impossible for us to make a binding decision about the organization today; it would also be impossible if the printed draft text were present, because the conditions in the individual countries are too varied to allow us to reconcile them without further ado. Therefore, to create an organization for the future, there is nothing to do but content ourselves with scheduling the next Congress and electing a Central Committee to make preparations. The latter would have the responsibility, and it would be within its power, to receive proposals having to do with organization and examine them thoroughly, and then the next Congress would be able to make a definitive decision. Jurists of all countries should be consulted on this issue. The organization's rules are the constitution of our party, and they ought not to be presented in a large assembly such as today's without preparation; it has to be thoroughly prepared. I am being reproached for not having prepared, as though I were personally responsible. That is a severe reproach. [136] We are meeting one another for the first time, and I, as an individual, was simply unable to tackle such a large assignment; it has been my desire only to make a suggestion, to offer a framework, and I hope that the committee makes use of some of my suggestions. Therefore, it is my hope and desire that we come to an agreement on just these two points! The Congress is the governing body of the Zionists of the entire world, and a Central Committee shall be elected, to which the organization question will be referred. A general secretary of the Zionist Party shall be named; the Central Committee will do this on its own. It is my view that, if this is to be decided upon today, it will simply be decided in principle: the Congress is the governing body of the Zionist Party or Organization. Likewise, a Central Committee is to be elected. If this question is settled, then tomorrow morning the only things are scheduling the next Congress and electing the Central Committee. In this way we will be done with the organization question and will have time today to address both of the other two sections of item three.

President: Item three of the agenda consists of three sections.[3] Most important is the one having to do with centralization of Zionist activity. This item concerns a question of juristic intricacy, whereas the other two sections have to do with things which are not of such complex difficulty. It is perhaps necessary to set aside this item temporarily, until tomorrow, and then put it at the top of the agenda. The other two matters would remain open for discussion.

DR. NEUMARK: Honored assembly! We have been in session now for nearly two days. The work we have done so far has been preparatory; we have not yet gotten down to our real work. Now it appears that we confront an insoluble problem. It is being recommended that we elect a committee to deliberate on this important item. The committee is to make recommendations to us and we are to adopt them *en bloc*. True, we perhaps do not any longer have enough time to be able to deal with all of the motions that have been made, and it appears that, after all, we have to deliver these motions to a committee to classify them under subheadings and bring out new points of view. I would like to recommend giving this committee a directive, and I would like to ask you to respond to this directive. We have come here to listen and to deliberate. The most important thing we are deliberating about is: what should we do, and what is our task? Many have already worked for years, and now we come here and still do not know what we wish to do. What exactly is the new point of view this Congress has supplied? Until now, we have been involved with the aspect of internal policy. But agitation is both internal and external: so we have to concern ourselves with external policy as well. If we want to focus on internal agitation, then we have to bear in mind that those of us here represent only a tiny fraction of Jewry; so we have to take this into account and this is just one aspect of our activity. The second aspect would be the external. If we wish then to give the committee a directive, we should specify these two different orientations.

DR. ROSENHECK*: I would like only to comment on what has been said and abstain from any other additional suggestion. In principle, I am in favor of the motion according to which a commission is to be elected. [137] As far as the second issue is concerned, whether seven or eleven members should be elected, I think all countries should be given consideration. After the adoption of the motion creating a committee, if it takes place, I would like to implore you to interrupt the session so that members from individual countries can come to an agreement with regard to numbers. A definite number of persons on the committee should not be set in advance; rather, the number should be adjusted according to the number of countries. We assume that we are dealing with serious, mature men, who did not come here to fritter away the time; we can depend on the gentlemen in attendance. As for Dr. Neumark's amendment,

I must demur. If we get involved in the giving of directives, we will again be going backward and not toward the goal. Therefore, it would be better for each individual group to give the directive and deliberate on it.

DIRECTOR STEINER (VIENNA): Highly honored assembly! I will be brief and simply indicate how to proceed. The handling of this entire question should be removed from the agenda and a committee elected that will submit one draft out of all the existing drafts to do with organization, which will be read out tomorrow and examined by every region. Those making motions and the regional delegations are to be summoned by the committee to express and defend their view. The text then adopted shall be in effect provisionally for a year, until the next Congress.

PRESIDENT: It has been moved to close debate without hearing any more speakers.

DR. SCHLAPOSCHNIKOV (KHARKOV): The Russian representatives have not yet agreed among themselves about how they might participate in the organization. It would be well to interrupt the session.

PRESIDENT: I am interrupting the session for a quarter-hour so the gentlemen from Russia can confer briefly among themselves.

Pause

MOTZKIN (FOR THE RUSSIAN MEMBERS): We view the election of a central bureau, in which the entire Congress shall take part, as one of the main goals of the Congress. As for other matters of organization, these depend rather on the organization of each country.

PRESIDENT (AFTER CONDUCTING THE VOTE): The motion to appoint a committee to submit a draft of the organization is adopted. We are suspending discussion of the organization question until tomorrow morning. First, we will proceed to the election of the committee. There are various motions concerning the committee's size and composition.

WOLFFSOHN: I have nothing against raising the number of committee members from seven to eleven.

The President asks for the nomination of candidates, which then takes place with participation from Herr Wolffsohn and other members of the Congress.

PRESIDENT: It is not appropriate that the names of candidates be tossed about in this manner. I deem it advisable to take the vote by means of paper ballots; voting will not take too long.

DR. KAMINKA: Perhaps those nominated could be allowed to meet and select eleven members themselves; it would easier and simpler than voting by ballot.

[138] DR. KORNBLÜH: I am in agreement with the motion of Dr. Landau, that eleven members be elected; but I think that all eleven should be elected by the plenary Congress; it is no proper election to say that these members have been recommended and elected. Every member should receive a ballot and write down as many names as the number of committee members to be elected.

PRESIDENT: I too feel that the election can be carried out only by secret ballot.

GOITEIN* (FRANKFURT AM MAIN): I recommend that every country elect its representatives (e.g., Russia three representatives, Austria three representatives, America one representative, etc).

PRESIDENT: I think that, in this case, there will be disputes within the country delegations, if we adopt Goitein's motion.

DR. ROSENHECK: I am obliged to remark that the previous speaker was repeating my motion. There is a motion I submitted, that every country should elect one or two of its delegates to the committee.

WOLFFSOHN: First, I must correct Herr Dr. Kornblüh. I did not intend to impose my recommendation but stated it simply as a recommendation; I draw your attention to the fact that there are more than eleven gentlemen proposed. Now if each person is supposed to select eleven gentlemen and each person writes down a name different from others, it is possible that a second election will be necessary because no one will get a majority, and we might spend our time this way until 11:00 in the evening. This committee cannot decide anything at all without the Congress also agreeing. I ask for the election of eleven members for our work so we can move forward.

PRESIDENT: No one else has asked to speak about procedure. I will first have the motion of Rosenheck and Goitein brought to a vote. The motion carries.

Now we must deal with how many from the individual countries; the following proposal has been made: two Germans from the Reich, three Austrians, two Russians, one Romanian, one Bulgarian, one American, one Englishman.

The motion carries.

The gentlemen are free to vote for whomever they wish; e.g., an Englishman can be elected for Bulgaria, or otherwise; the only condition is that there be a sufficient representation of the individual countries in the composing of the committee.

Five-minute pause

PRESIDENT: We lack a member of the committee for England. The gentlemen from England do not wish to take part in this vote for reasons of principle, specifically because they do not deem proper the allocation of seats by country. The committee consists of the following gentlemen: for Germany, Dr. Birnbaum and Dr. Bodenheimer; for Austria, Dr. Herzl, Dr. Salz, Director Steiner; for Russia, Dr. Bernstein-Kohan,* Professor Mandelstamm*; for Romania, Pineles; for Bulgaria, Professor Belkovsky; for America, Rosenberg. For England, I recommend, let the Congress itself elect Mr. de Haas.

Mr. de Haas is elected by acclamation.

PRESIDENT: I give the floor to Herr Dr. Jacob Bernstein-Kohan, for a report he will deliver on behalf of the Zionist society in Kishinev.

[139] DR. JACOB BERNSTEIN-KOHAN (KISHINEV): During an existence in exile lasting nearly two thousand years, filled with the most frightful persecutions and oppressions committed by nearly all peoples with whom the ever-wandering and harassed Jewish people came into contact, this people not only did not decrease in number but rather has constantly, if slowly, increased. For the most part, the Jews stood on a higher cultural and intellectual level than the peoples among whom they were fated to carry on their miserable existence. Not only is the Jewish people not moving toward its own dissolution, nor has it lost its nationality, but rather on the contrary it contains within itself a powerful and vigorous national strength with which it is indeed capable of realizing its highest national ideals. These national ideals, which were delineated in the dimness

of antiquity by the lawgiving genius of the great Moses and elaborated and enlarged upon by later Jewish philosophers and prophets, and which were, by humanist scholars of recent centuries, including the nineteenth, recognized and expounded upon as the foundation of all human ideals—in the realization of these ideals consists the national rebirth of the Jewish people. The decline of the national ideals of the Jewish people can be traced back solely and exclusively to the calamitous two-thousand year Jewish *Golus*. Indeed, this is what accounts for the depressed material and moral condition of the people, as well as the exhaustion of all its national energies in the unequal struggle with the Gentiles. To put an end to the *Golus* is the sole means by which to terminate this ceaseless, perpetual, and unequal struggle, which hinders the Jewish people in the development of its spiritual and moral endowments and impedes the attaining of its highest national ideals. The Jewish people must seek political independence, it must strive for its own political rebirth.

In the first centuries after the downfall of the Jewish kingdom the striving for political rebirth among the Jews, who were already at that time dispersed and far from the sacred homeland, was intense. But historical conjunctures were always such that the political initiative of isolated Jewish groups—an armed initiative in accord with the spirit of the age—was smothered in its infancy. By and by, Jewry lost faith in its political future and seemed to be paralyzed by a daily struggle for its livelihood among other peoples, whose political power at that time was rooted in the principle of superior armed strength.[4] [140] Only in the last quarter of this century, in which the political life of the peoples has begun to conform to their natural national characteristics, and the principle of superior armed strength has gradually been subordinated to the power of civilization, have isolated groups among the Jews also awakened out of their lethargic condition of political hopelessness and proclaimed the idea of putting an end to the Jewish *Golus* through the return of the Jews to national political independence in the land of their ancestors. This great idea found favor immediately in the hearts of those Jews who had a strong love for their enslaved and downtrodden brothers, and for the Jewish honor that had been trampled upon. They joined hands to form a widespread if loosely organized association, Hovevei Zion.[5] Yet even until quite recently, the ideas and program of Hovevei Zion, whose numbers are increasing enormously day by day and which recruits its members principally from among the intelligentsia of Jewry, have penetrated far too little among our popular masses. For, as a consequence of our long *Golus*, the masses have absolutely no political education and therefore no faith in their political powers and no hope for a political future. The political education of the Jewish popular masses, the development and cultivation of a firm belief in Israel's political future in the reclaimed ancient homeland, is the first and most fundamental task of the Zionists.

For this purpose the Zionists must raise the general level of Jewish knowledge in the popular masses. In each city having a Zionist society, a model Jewish school for the education of Jews growing to adulthood now must be founded and popular lectures and discussions should be arranged. In these schools the people will become familiar with Jewish history as well as the present condition of the Jewish nation, and likewise be instructed about everything that is happening to reclaim the Holy Land and to set up a political establishment there. The international Zionist Congress should choose, from among its membership, an "education committee" consisting of the persons most competent in matters having to do with Jewish popular education. This committee, which must have at its disposal the best scholarly resources in ever increasing number as well as large sums of money, should offer its assistance to local societies in the form of appropriate advice and counsel, as well as with scholarly books, and—if necessary—with the dispatch of teachers and money. Besides the general schools, the local societies will have to provide for a sufficient number of agricultural and technical schools, whose pupils, inculcated with the spirit of Palestine, would be in a position to immigrate to Palestine in the near future, to establish model agricultural colonies there as well as founding technical and industrial establishments. While a special program will be developed for each type of school, the curriculum in all these schools absolutely must include two subjects; i.e., a) Hebrew as a vernacular language, and b) the study of Palestine. The latter subject should cover the total of knowledge of Palestine heretofore acquired and what remains to be known. [141] The precise and thorough study of this subject will be beneficial not only for those intending to immigrate to Palestine, but also will be the best means of agitation for the Zionist idea among our adolescent youth and persons in close relation to them, and will contribute much to elevating our national self-consciousness and political education. For this generation Palestine will cease to be a mere utterance, which speaks neither to soul nor reason, an empty, meaningless word in the daily liturgy. It will become for them rather the goal of the most passionate longing, the dearest ideal, for whose attainment they will exert all their physical and spiritual powers. Indeed, striving for this ideal alone, acting ardently for the idea of Palestine, Jewish youth will find for themselves a rightful satisfaction, they will be elevated morally, they will begin to feel themselves as a nation among nations, equal and equally justified in its existence.[6]

The acquisition of Palestine should be considered the second and more powerful means of bringing rebirth to the Jewish people; and should this prove to be impossible to accomplish at one stroke, then it must take place gradually but as quickly as possible. And if more quickly then more easily. First of all because the fate of Palestine is uncertain and the country may be more easily obtained from Turkey than from another power. Second, because at any moment other nations may seek to colonize the country (something that is already happening now to some extent).[7] Finally, the purchases made of Palestine's soil are facts contributing substantially to strengthening the faith of Jews in the future of the Zionist idea. The founding of the first colonies in Palestine has produced a substantially greater movement and fermentation in all branches of the Jewish people than all of the fiery newspaper articles and speeches, and no sermon of the anti-Zionists has so discredited the cause as the suspension of colonization. Even now, without possessing sufficient faith in the Palestine idea or hope in its political future, the Jewish people takes a lively interest in the Palestine colonies; but it is moved to pain at the dependency of the colonies, distrusting the intentions of the ruling barons.

The question of how we are to obtain Palestine is an issue of keenest interest to all Zionists. One group believes only in gradual and slow colonization, the infiltration of the country. The other party, without declaring itself the foe of colonization, is of the opinion that colonization ought to be suspended and that all activity should be directed toward obtaining Palestine from the Sublime Porte, in order to establish there an autonomous Jewish state under Turkish suzerainty, and toward winning over all the powers of Europe to this plan. This second party therefore proposes to work to put the Zionist question before a European Congress. These two tendencies are caught up in a heated controversy and are threatening to bring about a split in the Zionist camp.[8]

[142] It is to be hoped that the Congress, attended as it is also by Hovevei Zion,[9] who recognize its importance and are inspired by the ideal of the political national rebirth of the Jewish people, will be able to examine the two approaches and choose the more appropriate one. To me it seems that only a union of the two proposals (i.e., pursuing both approaches) can take us to the goal. There can be no doubt that Palestine will not be obtained for the Jews without the consent of Turkey and sanction of the European Concert, and that the political question of Palestine must sooner or later come before a forum of European and Turkish diplomats. But this will take place only in a rather distant future, after the overcoming of the greatest difficulties. We must not deceive ourselves. The struggle, for example, which several peoples of the Balkan

Peninsula have fought to a successful conclusion, was much easier than ours, since the peoples in question lived on their own soil, while in Palestine there are few Jews and little Jewish cultural life. Furthermore, the powers and the peoples subject to them are accustomed to thinking about solving the Jewish question in an entirely different manner, and it may be quite hard for us to guide their thoughts in an unaccustomed direction and to interest them in a cause in which the bulk of Jewry itself shows far too little interest. Therefore, the question of political independence in Palestine seems not to be a question for the immediate future. Perhaps it is even better that way.[10] We have mentioned above that our people lack a Jewish political education. Were Palestine to be turned over to us immediately, the least desirable element of the Jewish people would probably end up there. Thanks to their mental aptitude the Jews would nonetheless establish themselves there, and they would constitute a state like many other modern states, with all the same and probably even worse social deficiencies, and with an unstable political foundation. A state's most important force; i.e., the political patriotism of the people would be lacking. Patriotism can attain a high degree of development in the future Jewish state only if it comprises the best or best prepared elements of the Jewish people. The eighteen-hundred year *Golus* has unfortunately caused far more damage than one might think at first glance. True, there still glimmers in the depths of the Jewish soul the spark of Jewish nationalist and Zionist fire; but a great part of the current Jewish generation has lost all capacity to lead an independent Jewish life with a morality arising from the national community.[11] An independent Jewry can therefore be constituted only out of the minority of its best elements and from future generations. Wherefore patience is necessary. We should not beat our heads against the wall. [143] Based on the principle of "gradualism" that was pursued in the first fifteen years of the Palestine movement, one achieved but little, not because it was the wrong approach but because its representatives acted too feebly, without sufficient energy or willingness to sacrifice. Hovevei Zion and the numerous Palestine societies worked without a system, each group on its own, without a plan and without having behind them the strength of a party. Rather, they experienced the weakness and helplessness of being alone, having formed neither among the Jews nor among other peoples a stable party. The colonization societies acquired their members in quite insufficient quantity and from among a class of the Jewish people that is itself not very numerous, indeed precisely among that section of the people most ill-adapted to become "Palestinized." The Jewish people itself was not at all attracted to these societies. There has been no propaganda for Palestine among the people, the proof of which is that there exists no Palestine journal in Yiddish. Colonization itself has been badly and ineffectively organized, which is why so few colonies have been founded up till now, and even these are far from having a secure future. The indigenous Palestinian Jews have been attracted to join in colonization hardly at all, and nothing has been done to give to the Jewish inhabitants of towns and villages of Palestine an appropriate political direction. The international Congress of Zionists will unite all Hovevei Zion into an organic whole, declare itself a party among Jews and other peoples, and rapidly forward the cause, with forces organized and adapted to the purpose. The aforesaid education center will, by its energetic intellectual and moral propaganda, increase greatly the number of Zionists, principally among the older youth and the popular masses. Considering the great mental capacities of the Jewish people, it can be anticipated that a great many of the next generation will be so conditioned that they will not merely contribute a little money to the general cause of the resurrection of Jewry, but rather will regard this resurrection as their life goal. These our descendants will apply all their powers to settle themselves in Palestine. Thus, the Congress must, in addition to the "education center," also elect a committee for Palestine colonization, to which, in accord with carefully prepared regulations, all the colonization societies of all countries are to be subordinated. This committee must study the country of Palestine precisely and in detail; with the help of the colonization societies, it must purchase large tracts of land suitable for agriculture and establish there, first of all, a number of colonies with the right kind of Jews from among those currently in Europe and Palestine. The greater the number of persons capable of colonizing, the more colonies it will be possible to establish. [144] The colonies are to be organized in such a way that they are property of the colonists and not the property of rich benefactors, no matter how worthy; this, in order that they do not suffer privation, since the material satisfaction of a people binds it to its land and makes it possible for it to develop and flourish mentally and physically. Concurrent with the agricultural colonies, the committee must establish Jewish factories, if at first only on a small scale, in different localities in Palestine, and to promote the building and acquiring of houses and other property in the cities, as well cultivating various branches of industry.

Furthermore, the Congress must elect a "political committee" from among persons in attendance or those absent. Its first task will be to somehow obtain the permission of the Turkish government to found colonies in Palestine having privileges which make them independent of the arbitrary authority of the Turkish administration in Palestine. Furthermore, this committee will concern itself with propaganda for the Zionist idea among all nations where the Jews reside and with all governments, and must prepare the issue of Jewish national political independence for a future congress of the great powers. It is to be expected that after several years—or in the worst case after several decades—if in this way the Jewish population of Palestine shall have increased substantially, if Palestine has a great many, perhaps hundreds, of Jewish colonies, Jewish factories and workshops, and industry and commerce in the hands of a strong Jewish population inculcated with a national political mentality, and the bulk of the Jews in other countries shall form a powerful party gravitating toward their center in Palestine—that then the political committee will be in a position to present the Palestine question to a congress of the great powers in an entirely different light and be fully assured of a favorable outcome of its efforts.

Of course, to accomplish all of these goals very large funds will be necessary, and there arises the difficult question of whence these funds are to come. Of course, they must be donated by the Jews themselves. But the Jewish people, possessing no country of its own, is an extremely poor people. The great accumulations of money found in the hands of a small number of Jews who are profiting continually from their capital, seem to the whole world to be a great national treasury and have given the Jews the reputation of being a wealthy people. In fact they are less so than other peoples. But Jews are hardworking and industrious; in their labor lies their wealth, and this wealth of Jewish labor will have to suffice to supply the means required. [145] We leave it to those persons more competent in financial matters to handle the financial side of the Palestine question not only in the details but also in its principal features, both the question of how these capital funds are to be obtained, as well as how to make use of them in the most effective way; we wish here to touch on only a few main points that have already given rise at the theoretical level to diametrically opposed views among the Zionists. Up till now, there have been basically two ways of buying land and setting up colonies. One way is by establishing colonies whose costs are borne by an individual (Rothschild's colonies), the other in which costs are borne by colonization societies (the Odessa Committee,* the "Esra*" society in Berlin, "Zion*" in Austria, etc.). Many Zionist are against both methods. They are against the first because it can lead to the enserfment of the colonists by individual capitalists. There may thus arise a small class of capitalist landowners and a great mass of landless cultivators and poor workers having no security against dispossession. Against the second it is objected that this is merely charity, not a popular cause. The nation would become dependent on the benevolence of the affluent. Let us examine each of these two ways more closely. There is certainly no doubt that Baron von Rothschild has been instrumental in capitalizing the existing colonization of Palestine, by taking several Jewish colonies under his protection and continually providing them with funds. Nonetheless, it is erroneous to think that this benevolent Jewish baron thereby rescued the colonization of Palestine. Certainly he rescued some Jewish colonies and along with them several hundred Jewish families, but the colonization of Palestine would not have been a lost cause even without the Baron and his great investments; it would have been delayed only a certain number of years. The pioneers of colonization did not depend on von Rothschild when they first sank their bloodied fingers into the soil of the homeland, and their courage and inspiration would yet have lasted long enough to purge away with their own sweat and blood the great evil of neglect and barrenness from the Holy Land. Had we not one but many affluent and benevolent persons with a heart for Palestine, such as Baron von Rothschild has, we might be able to point with pride not to ten or twenty but to hundreds of flourishing colonies in Palestine. Though in that case we would have in Palestine a few dozen rich latifundists and no independent farmers. It would be no different than it is now, where the colonists of the Baron do not know what belongs to them and what to their patron, upon whose will they are all, collectively and individually, absolutely dependent. Indeed, that is why some Zionists warn against every kind of association with the Jewish capitalists, which can cause only harm to the people. [146] For our part, we do not doubt that genuine patriots are to be found among wealthy Jews just as among the populace, without greed or desire to dominate, who will gladly donate funds to the great popular cause. Only with such capitalists can the Zionists enter into relations or the Congress and its Executive Committee do business, only wealthy persons of this sort are in a position to accelerate the cause of acquiring Palestine and reviving the Jewish people.

As for the benevolent colonization societies, they are distinguished by the fact that their funds and the estates acquired by these funds belong not to an individual but to the people as a whole.[12] These societies are indispensable. History and experience show that there is a great number of Jews who, as a consequence of their poverty, will not be capable of subscribing to any undertaking or association, whereas they may become outstanding workmen able to support themselves in the future. Immediate assistance for this large group is needed, in the form of a national fund. Furthermore, resources for the entire propaganda of Zionism, the entire great work of educating and transforming our people, can be drawn only from the coffers of such societies. Many take exception to the idea of charity, since they are accustomed to associate this word with what degrades rather than honors humankind. But the charity of the Zionist societies is not to be identified with that of a rich man contemptuously throwing a bone to his fellow men who have been reduced to begging; nor is it the favor of a heartless aristocrat based on wretched ambition, insolent deception, and duplicity; rather it is a benevolence that issues from the people itself, which seeks neither gratitude nor recognition; it is the self-help of the common people. It is true that the cause has appeared somewhat differently until now, at least to us in the Odessa Committee. The greater part of the sums coming into our treasury has not always been given freely and cheerfully, but rather under the pressure of one or another of the committee's members. God have mercy on these benefactors, from whom contributions have been effectively seized, who think that Zionism takes aim only at their pockets, to whom the size of their money bags is their life's chief concern, constituting their mental and moral horizon. Such are the flowers and fruits of the Jewish *Golus*. From now on the members of the colonization societies ought to be only free men, who contribute from their resources voluntarily and gladly to the cause of the Jewish people, their own cause. This type of member we will find mostly among the populace; but enrollment must be made easier for him. The ordinary man gives away the few pennies he has saved from his wretched labor more readily, than do the rich their wretched hundreds. We want to cease distributing tens of thousands in penny allotments, we want to make out of these pennies millions, in order to demolish the *Golus* and rescue the Jewish people's honor. (Loud applause).

[147] M. Moses (Kattowitz): Honored assembly! "God helps those who help themselves," says the proverb. Among all issues having to do with the national rebirth of our Jewish people, surely the most important is that which concerns the colonization of Palestine. The colonies founded thus far owe their genesis to the activity of various colonization societies and individual benefactors. These generally successful attempts at colonization in Palestine spur us on to pursue this activity on a large scale. But the resources of the various colonization societies and even the resources of very wealthy, individual benefactors do not suffice for this purpose. The settlement of Palestine by Jews is a question of money in the truest sense of the word: it requires many hundreds of millions of francs. To raise sums like this, there are two different approaches: either (1) the founding of a great bank issuing stock, or (2) the founding of cooperatives to acquire landed estates in Palestine. Both approaches are excellently suited to the purpose, since the landholdings to be acquired will increase continuously in value through their

growing productivity and potential for cultivation, and their increasing population and trade, etc., so that there is no danger of losing the invested capital. However, the fact that our Jewish-national aspirations are running up against the opposition of many rich Jews, suggests to us that our adversaries might buy up this stock in order to disrupt and destroy our work. This danger has to be reckoned with, even if the individual shares are divided up and distributed in small certificates worth ten to twenty-five francs. Moreover, in this way the accumulation of great funds (millions) would be made very difficult.

Far more secure and less vulnerable to any disruption is the other approach: the founding of cooperatives for the acquisition of landed estates in Palestine. (The construction of factories and the setting-up of trading houses must be left entirely to the action of private individuals.) The landed estate of a colonist must include: one dwelling, stable, shed, etc., and enough field and garden land so that a family consisting of five persons will have enough to pay the expenses of living a life of modest comfort. These expenses must also include livestock and furnishings and fittings. All of this will probably cost around five thousand to six thousand francs. Every member of a cooperative with limited liability must guarantee this amount. The Jews of Romania, Galicia, and Russia are to be considered first. In these lands, from fifty to one hundred and two hundred and more members will unite in a cooperative society. Several of these cooperative societies in one territory will form a group and these will have in the capital city or in the largest community of that territory their central administration. Every cooperative society will organize for itself a cooperative bank. The revenue of the latter will be formed from (1) the subscription fee and (2) the deposits of members, assets, etc. The savings deposits of the members will bear a moderate rate of interest. The members will receive an annual dividend for their paid-up capital, while the subscription funds, which must not be less than ten francs per member, will form a reserve fund and be applied to defray the cost of administration.

[148] The central administrations (or central banks) of one territory's cooperative banks will stand in the closest relationship with other such central banks in other territories, and these will be responsible to an executive committee—which will be subject to the office of the Congress in Vienna. These would be the basic features of this organization.

This being accomplished, an active propaganda will begin in the individual cooperatives of the various lands. The admission of members and the collection of subscription monies and of members' assets will be continued, and up to one-tenth of the amounts received will be made over to the territory's main bank (the central bank of the cooperatives in a given territory).

Now there are sure to be men in every country who want to settle in Palestine and who also are financially equipped to be able to quickly pay five to six thousand francs for the landed property to be acquired, with all that goes with it. These amounts will immediately be invested at interest and this category of settlers: Class I will receive a dividend until they take full possession of their property. The administration has no more claims in the form of payments or interest, etc., against this class. However, this class of settlers will remain liable to the society for five years, to promote the creditworthiness of all members of this scheme. There will be other members of the cooperative who will be able to deposit only four thousand, three thousand, or only two thousand, or even only one thousand francs. This Class II will receive the same landed property of the same size and quality as Class I, and also will receive according to the amount deposited, until they take possession, a corresponding dividend, but they will supply to the administration a mortgage document for the difference between their deposit of four thousand, three thousand, or two thousand, and the five thousand or six thousand required. To be sure, these mortgage debts will be subject to a still to be determined but modest, quarterly rate of interest. This interest must be paid on time. However, there will be very many who, besides the subscription fee of ten francs, can pay annually from about ten to fifty, up to one hundred, five hundred, and nine hundred francs. They will form Class III. Even these will receive a dividend on their paid-up amounts, minus the fee for subscription. This absolutely must be paid, so that the ordinary man may be convinced that there is no deception involved and will have faith in the program. This accumulation of various amounts, such as subscription fees, members' assets, savings deposits, donations, bequests, etc., as I will discuss in more detail later, will continue until there are one million francs, or its strict equivalent, either in the country's central bank or, collectively, in the provincial banks. Class I and Class II now receive their properties. The latter group submit their mortgage documents, which in the event of a liquidity shortage, will be redeemed for cash by banking institutions that are allied with or well disposed to our cause. From the remainder of the one million francs and the amounts received for the mortgage securities, landed properties will be acquired and transferred by lot to the members belonging to Class III. These latter will owe to the administration an amount equal to the entire value of the property minus their credited deposits as members, and will submit a mortgage document of the corresponding amount. These mortgage borrowers will be able to pay off their debt in installments of one hundred francs. These payments must be entered promptly into the mortgage debt document. Sales of these landed estates to non-Jews will be forbidden. Every colonist will remain liable to the administration for a period of five years after the property he received is paid off in full. As long as the colonist is liable, he can sell all or part of his property, to Jews, only with the approval of the administration. [149] Arrears in interest payments will be registered and borne by the mortgage borrower. Whoever intentionally neglects his landed property, diminishes its value by mismanagement, whoever falls behind more than three years in interest payments, will have his property taken away by the administration, with return of the paid-up amount, and the property will be put into better economic hands.

If one assumes the total number of Jews in the entire world to be ten million and reckons about a fifth to be *patresfamilias*, this yields a number of two million; by an ongoing and untiring agitation, within the foreseeable future, let us say ten to fifteen years, out of these two million *patresfamilias* one tenth, or two hundred thousand independent men, will be won over to register in such limited-liability cooperatives—that yields a figure of two hundred thousand times five thousand francs, a share capital equal to one billion.

A point not to be undervalued is that of appropriating the school savings plan (penny savings) funds at all the Jewish schools in the world. The period of saving extends not only throughout the primary school years, but also into the years of adolescence for young men and women. If these small savings are invested at interest in the cooperative banks, in the course of time some millions of francs will be accumulated. But besides the financial question, a factor important to every Zionist is that the Jewish child, young man, and young woman, learns to save and work for our national cause from an early age, in order to produce and provide for the same in their mature years. In this way we will produce for ourselves a big reserve army, while we Zionists of today are obliged to constantly do battle with all kinds of hostile riffraff.

Not less important is the activity of the free Zionist societies. These must not become static; they have to keep active by moving from city to city. Contributions from these societies should come after paying expenses of agitation, under a special rubric in the funds of the cooperative banks. Annually, two to three times at Simchat Torah, Hannukah, or Purim, or at least once per year, a special event might well be mounted by them in the larger communities. If this is done in the right way, these society events will develop very easily into Jewish popular-national events, which will not only bring into the society's treasury very considerable balances, but will constantly supply a number of new members for these societies, as experience has shown. Through the manifold connections in and with the populace our efforts will have an ever more popular character. The societies, especially the cooperatives, will receive small gifts, large donations, bequests, estates, etc., that will benefit those colonists who are able to deposit little or nothing. This amount might also be applied to the most varied tasks of religious charity; e.g., schools, hospitals, homes for the aged. Over the years these amounts will increase and are not to be undervalued.

Since the opportunity to settle in Palestine as a free man in a dignified way will be greeted with gladness by the poorer Jews and also made use of by them in great numbers, the poor relief programs of every community will be to a great extent unburdened. It is therefore only fair that individual communities be approached on the part of our administration to make certain contributions. [150] No community can evade making these just and justified payments for reasons of conscience.[13] Supposing there to be in the entire world about fifty thousand synagogue congregations and each were to give annually for this purpose a minimum amount of one hundred francs, they would supply thus an annual income of five million francs.

By this comprehensive plan, they will produce in uninterrupted fashion, a steady inflow of great financial resources:

TABLE 2.1. M. Moses's scheme to fund colonization through cooperative banks (in millions of francs).

1. From subscription fees of two hundred thousand members at 10 francs	= 2
2. From annual credit payments of members over about 15 years, from 200,000 members, provisionally at 2,500 francs	= 500
3. Repayable savings deposits over 15 years	= 50
4. Interest received over 15 years at 4 percent	= 20
5. Amounts from school collections over 15 years	= 15
6. Amounts from voluntary societies	= 2
7. Donations, bequests, etc.	= 1
8. From congregations in the first 15 years	= 5
Francs	584 million

cont'd on next page

Table 2.1 (cont'd)

Against this stands the payments to depositors	= 55
And to that is added interest to savers (see above, 3, 4, and 5) at 2½ percent	= 1.375
Dividends on five hundred millions at 2½ percent	= 12.5
Salaries, administration, etc.	= 5
Miscellaneous	= 0.125
Total	74 million
Balance	510 million

According to this calculation based on probable totals, the net income in the first fifteen years will run to 510 million francs. Taking into consideration that the landed estates to be acquired will rise continuously in value due to the increasing population, agriculture, and trade, taking also into consideration the skillfulness, industry, sobriety, and creditworthiness of our Jewish people, and considering further that a corporation which in an unusually short time will have a net income of five hundred million francs—or the equivalent in the ownership of landed properties—without exceeding the limits of its ability to meet its obligations, and considering finally that a corporation obligated for one billion francs without having reached the limit of its ability to pay could very easily borrow another two to three billion, and that is such an enormous amount that it will more than suffice for a provisional national community of 2 ½ to 4 millions— indeed it would suffice to produce for that community nearly ideal conditions. All this can and will be achieved, if only we begin aright and continue with persistence in the right way. Every Jew is called to this task. We will achieve it, if everyone will exert himself conscientiously at his post, to do his duty and his obligation and always act according to the motto: "All for one and one for all!" To this end may the Almighty give us his blessing! Amen. (Loud applause).

PRESIDENT: Herr Wolffsohn will now make public the list of those in attendance. (The total number of delegates present came to 204.)

The session is closed.

[151] Day Three of the Proceedings
August 31, 1897

Morning Session

PRESIDENT: I will have to forego reading out the declarations of support in order not to delay the members of the Congress. We will display the individual declarations in one of the anterooms, where you will have the opportunity to inspect the great mass of incoming texts. Among the declarations received I will mention only that of Reverend Glaser, chief rabbi of the synagogue congregations of England, who expresses his warmest sympathy for the goals of the Congress.[1]

As for the attendance list that was read out yesterday, I will just note that those gentlemen who do not wish to appear in the published list or who want to make a correction, may apply to Herr Wolffsohn concerning this matter.[2]

The floor belongs to Herr Steiner, chairman of the committee for organizational bylaws.

DIR. STEINER: The committee has taken in hand to advise concerning organization, fully aware of the seriousness of its task. What we have to decide about now is, so to speak, the backbone of the Zionist movement. We have had an almost countless number of proposals put forward and have made use of something from very many of them, although we have done so in such a fragmentary way that it will scarcely be noticed. We have had to leave most of what has been proposed to be decided by the territorial organizations. What we have submitted is very concise, every word having been weighed. We have had to keep in view the legal conditions in individual countries, and we have also given consideration to the juristic thinking of our committee members, especially with regard to well-tested organizations, which have spread all over the world and have been active for centuries, which have been taken as models. We ask you to accept that it is the best organizational plan that could be reached for the present. I will read out to you the draft in its entirety and comment briefly, and then submit each individual article once again to a vote, if the president agrees.

1. The governing authority of the Zionists is the Congress.[3]
2. [152] Alinea 1. Every Zionist who wants to have the right to participate in electing delegates to the Congress, will pay an annual and voluntary contribution for Zionist purposes of at least one shekel equivalent to 1 franc = 2 shillings = ½ dollar = ½ gulden = 40 kopeks = 1 mark.—This sum is intended only for the most impoverished brothers, and everyone whose circumstances permit is obligated to pay more.

    Alinea 2. Every one hundred contributors will elect one delegate; every delegate can assume the representation of several groups but may not cast more than ten votes—We adopted ten as the maximum number of votes lest a few individuals represent entire provinces and acquire a great number of votes in order to tyrannize the Congress.
3. By the casting of ballots, the Congress will elect a Zionist Actions Committee[4] to carry out decisions, conduct business, and determine the location of the next Congress.
4. The Actions Committee will have its seat in Vienna and will comprise fifteen members, of whom five must have their permanent domicile in Vienna, while the remainder are distributed among the territorially organized Zionist organizations in the following way:

    Austria, Galicia, and Bukovina two, Germany one, Russia two, Romania one, England, France, and North America one representative each, Serbia and Bulgaria one. The Actions Committee members from outside Vienna will be elected by the Congress, but after their nomination by the territorially organized Zionist groups. The five permanent members from Vienna will be nominated and elected by the plenary Congress.
5. Every member of the Committee not domiciled in Vienna will have the right, after having received previous approval of the Vienna-based Actions Committee, to delegate a Zionist proxy in the Actions Committee.—This, honored assembly, is necessary in order that there occur no interruption in the conduct of business. Every individual member must have his proxy in Vienna who represents him in the

Actions Committee, attends consultations, and who has also been empowered to vote on behalf of his foreign principal.

6. The members of the Actions Committee represent the Executive of the Actions Committee vis-à-vis their territorial committee.—Thereby we engage the issue of territorial administration only insofar as we say that this administration establishes the connection with the territorial organization as a whole, and the individual member forms the link between the Executive Committee[5] and the territorial committee.

7. The Actions Committee will appoint a General Secretary who has his residence in Vienna.

8. The Actions Committee will appoint other committees as needed.

9. The organization and agitation of the Zionists in their individual countries conforms to the requirements and laws of the land in question, and the Actions Committee is to be notified about the form which these take.

Thus the draft of the organization.

PRESIDENT: Herr Dr. Bodenheimer has the floor.

DR. BODENHEIMER: This morning the organizational and financial plans which I had the honor to report on yesterday have been presented to you in printed form. I had already formed the opinion yesterday, and I expressed it, that this unofficial work done by a few persons ought not be made the basis of this Congress, but rather should be only the raw material the committee has to work with. [153] I am also of the view that this work of the committee cannot be the definitive organization of the Zionist Congress; rather it is something that must be put in place so that we do not disperse without having accomplished something, so that an agency exists to prepare the next Congress and examine incoming proposals, so that we are able to enter into our work successfully at the next Congress. I am therefore of the opinion that we accept the proposals as they are submitted by the committee, in fact without much debate. We can leave matters arising to the Actions Committee to be elected, by empowering this Committee, in the event that it proves impossible to carry out some of these decisions, to make such changes itself as are necessary. For this reason, it will be up to the Actions Committee to obtain a legal immunity from the Congress. I am convinced that the Executive will not undertake anything contravening the interests of the Congress. For us to be able to get on with our work, I would press you to accept all the paragraphs as proposed, unless a quite strong reservation against any one of them is to be urged. To be sure, I am not of the view that gentlemen who have put forward definite proposals should not expound them today. On the contrary, it will be of great interest to hear the individual proposals being made. If you want to return home with firm confidence that we have done something permanent, with which we can manage for the future, then accept the proposals of the committee by acclamation.

President: It will not be superfluous to emphasize that what is done right now has only a provisional character. Given the manner in which the Congress has been summoned and constituted, we cannot bind the will of future Congresses; it is instead a matter of ensuring that actions the Congress takes next year will not be subject to dispute and delay. If you will regard the proposed organization as not being definitive and assume the good will of the Committee to improve itself and offer something better to the next Congress, you will rest content with the proposal made.

Sigmund Bromberg* (Tarnów): In relation to the proposals of the rapporteur on organization, I must comment that the wording of the proposals is not entirely appropriate just insofar as they lay down quite specific instructions. Thus, for example: that every one hundred contributing members are able to elect a delegate to the Congress. If we adopt this provision, we will have decided something that binds the hands of the Actions Committee. And that this proposal is impractical and improper is beyond doubt. I propose therefore that the wording of the article in question be kept as general as possible. It cannot be implemented. We cannot make a rule to assemble every one hundred paying members as a voting body; rather, we have Zionist societies dispersed throughout the whole world. These stable organizations ought to dispatch the delegates. This is the most proper way, either the societies or the committees of the corresponding territorial organizations. We must put it in a general way so that everything is included.

President: The issue of the general discussion is whether we actually want to enter into the particulars of the draft. If the Congress goes into the draft, it will become a matter of discussing specifics, dealing with each individual point.—The gentlemen who are recognized to speak are Dr. Bernstein-Kohan, Dr. Schnirer, Professor Schapira, and Schiller.

Dr. Blumenfeld: I move the election of representative speakers.

[154] Motzkin: I think it is quite inappropriate to arrange matters thus, even though we must economize our use of time. There is certainly no question of principle involved; on the contrary everyone just wants to emphasize specific points.

President: We will indeed go into the discussion of specifics later and then everyone can speak about individual points.

Motzkin: I move to reject the election of representative speakers.

President: The gentlemen who are for the election of representative speakers may raise their hands.
    The motion was adopted.

President: Herr Professor Schapira has the floor, on behalf of the previously named speakers.

Professor Schapira: Highly honored assembly! The high responsibility which I have accepted compels me to clarify the situation for myself and others. I would not want under any circumstances to delay the discussion further, and I am most concerned to deal as briefly as possible, and objectively, with the issue of organization. But I cannot help expressing my desire to be informed as to whether the intention exists to bring up for discussion, in particular, the issue of the national fund, after finishing with the question of organization? If this is the case, then those I represent renounce all further debates and are agreed that the special debate be entered into.[6]

President: You will have opportunity to express yourself about this matter.

Schapira: Then we are quite satisfied.

President: We proceed now to paragraph 1: "The principal agency of the Zionists is the Congress."

Dr. Kornblüh: I think a short paragraph stating the rules of procedure should be included.

President: Rules of procedure will indeed be submitted to the next Congress. I would like to move that the paragraph be adopted.

Dr. Ehrenpreis: I would like to propose that it be written: "is the Congress convening annually."

President: From my point of view, even this is a binding of decision making for the future, which is not necessary to make now. If we decide at the close of this Congress that we will convene again in a year, so also next year's Congress will determine when it will convene again.

Paragraph 1 is adopted in its original form.
The president reads out paragraph 2.

Dr. Schnirer: To simplify the discussion I think it preferable to have a separate discussion of each of the two halves of this paragraph, because I think that there will be no disagreement about the first half, whereas there may be divergent points of view about how these funds are to be collected and about the number of Zionists who are to elect a delegate. I think therefore there should be a separate discussion of the two halves.

Steiner: I am in agreement with this proposal.

Dr. Landau: Gentlemen! This proposal seems to me incomplete, since it does not contain a clear statement of who can participate in the Congress: only delegates or also members. [155] Concerning this paragraph I move: "Only delegates may participate in the Congress." Then there is a stylistic correction that would have to be made to the remaining section: "The Congress is comprised of delegates. Each delegate is to be elected by every 100 members." So, I am proposing that this particular sentence be placed at the beginning.

Karl Herbst* (Sofia): Until now the organization of the Zionists has been loose. Now what's going to happen is that everyone who pays in has the right to vote. To whom does he make payment? To the hitherto loose organization, or to whom? It ought to be determined where he is to pay his money. The contributions that are made to the societies are for the most part intended for local uses. I would like to propose it read something to the effect of: "to the territorial treasury, which is to make contributions to the central treasury."

PRESIDENT: It will appear in the course of discussion that a bureau to prepare for the next Congress will be set up, which will be recipient of contributions.

DR. BODENHEIMER: I wish to speak against the Landau motion. I have serious misgivings about such a formulation of the paragraph. The Congress is not a meeting of delegates but rather, if it is to have any long-term significance at all, it must be an assembly of all Zionists, and every Zionist who contributes something to the communal organization should be in a position in this one place where he is permitted to express himself, to do precisely that. I would urge you not to degrade the Congress into a meeting of delegates. I also have serious misgivings about the territorial organization. We can safely leave the determination of voting rights to the Actions Committee, which will work out the particular modalities with the territorial organizations before the next Congress takes place. Trusting its judgment, we should hand over this issue to the Actions Committee to be elected, which will be in a position to evaluate how the provisions concerning voting rights are to be applied.

BAHAR: If the figures are yet provisional, I have no comment; if they were to be definitive, I would ask why one franc is made equivalent to two shillings. It is not at all the correct rate.

STEINER: The amount of the contribution was determined by the delegates of the different countries. Each one said: in our case, so-and-so-much can be gotten even from the poorest. We have fixed the shekel according the ability of Jews of the different countries.

BAHAR: If one is poor, one is poor without respect to currency. One can be poor in a currency measured in the millions, or in francs and dollars. Why is a poor Englishman to pay two shillings and the poor Oriental only one franc?

STEINER: The representatives of different countries have indicated that this is the correct amount; it was for this purpose that we chose representatives of every country.

DR. FARBSTEIN: I would like to make several comments. 1) Whether delegates only or everyone present has the right to vote? I would be for delegates only because that is the democratic system while the other is the plutocratic, since the poor are not able to attend. We would have a Congress of the rich, and the poor would not be represented. 2) It reads: "pays a shekel." But it doesn't say to whom; a notation has to be made, "pays to a local group." I would like to have this added.

[156] PRESIDENT: Herr Herbst proposes the same. You may wish to offer an amendment together.

DR. FARBSTEIN: 3) With respect to the shilling, I would like to comment further: there can be scarcely any doubt that the vast majority of Jews in England are unable to pay two shillings. I would like therefore to propose we say: one shilling, on account of the Russian-Polish proletariat living in Liverpool, London, Manchester, etc.

SCHACH: I will be brief. I find the first paragraph lacking in clarity. First of all, a word is lacking: "Zionist Party." Instead of "everyone who wants to have the right," the wording should be, "every member of the Zionist Party shall pay" so-and-so-much. (Loud opposition.) Come now, gentlemen, who do we really suppose ourselves to be? We certainly cannot yet claim that we are the people. There are many who belong to the Jewish people who have not joined with us. We are a party. We are a party like every other party. Therefore let the text read: "Every member of the Zionist Party, etc." We ought to say in addition: "Everyone will pay a franc," and this amount should then be made the basis of the contributions of other countries.[7]

DR. NEUMARK: I think that even non-delegate members should participate in the Congress. The Central Committee should decide about this, and since the Central Committee cannot be on familiar terms with the members in the individual countries, it would be best to arrange things so that the Central Committee decides together with the different territorial organizations as to whether or not a certain Zionist should be permitted to attend the Congress as a member.

S. LUBLINSKI* (BERLIN): Dr. Bodenheimer has demonstrated in a superlative way that the Congress must by no means be reduced to a convention of delegates. It seems to me that the worst thing would be for us to declare openly that the Congress doesn't care how a delegate is chosen, and I propose therefore that such a draft not be approved; rather that we simply say: anyone designated by the Congress can be a member.

Bromberg: We have had quite enough time over the past two days listening to statements and speeches. Now we want to get down to work! I move therefore to close the debate without hearing any more speakers.

This motion carried.

Dr. Schnirer: In order to avoid misunderstandings, I wish to declare once and for all: closing the list of speakers means that no additional speakers will be admitted. Closing the debate means: nothing more can be said.

Dr. Blumenfeld: I made known previously my desire to speak but was overlooked. (President: I beg pardon.) I do not want to want to submit a motion, only to ask for a clarification. One is entitled to ask for a clarification at any time. I want to ask what will happen if there are more than one hundred members but fewer than two hundred members in a certain location. We do not have a printed draft before us; consequently, we do not know what it contains.

President: We could not find a printer who could print the draft in so short a time.

[157] Steiner: A question of principle, which is quite out of place, has been raised. It is the question of whether only delegates to the Congress may participate. Every Zionist may indeed participate, but only the delegates vote; otherwise the Congress would be wrongly constituted. Putting in an additional clause is pointless because this is self-evident. We are affirming that every Zionist can elect delegates. The question of how electing is to take place has been raised as well. We cannot involve ourselves here in the organization and modality of how votes are to be submitted, for if we were to define the existing societies as agents of the Executive, dissolution of the societies in several countries would immediately ensue. In Austria, for example, this would occur immediately. For this reason a somewhat vague provision is absolutely necessary. Let us say that a country has eight hundred Zionists who furnish contributions and as a consequence are able to elect eight delegates. The latter will be chosen by paper ballot. An election where persons convene and vote and perhaps travel from

Odessa to Warsaw, is completely impossible. A society that has more than one hundred members can also vote independently. But we in the Congress can know only aggregates. Russia, for example, pays so-and-so-much to the Congress and has the right to elect so-and-so-many delegates. The other question is the affair of the territorial organization at home.

Dr. Landau: In view of the fact that only delegates should have the right to vote, I withdraw my motion.

Steiner: I move that Alinea a be adopted without amendment.

Schach: I likewise withdraw my motion.

President (reading the motion of Herbst): "A place will be designated where payments to qualify for voting rights will be made." (To Herbst): I draw your attention to the fact that if this amendment is adopted, we will have to initiate a big debate concerning the authorized location. Is it your intention to initiate this debate right now or to present it only later in connection with the article that deals with the Congress's bureau?

Herbst: I withdraw my motion.

Alinea a of article 2 is adopted by vote.
The President reads out Alinea b.

Dr. Blumenfeld: I would like to take the liberty of making the following motion. I am envisioning what is meant by every one hundred members in any given location. But I cannot envision what the rapporteur has described, that the number of members of an entire country will be calculated and then a quotient arrived at that will yield the number of delegates. It may thus occur that many groups of Zionists will remain without representation. For, it is well known that the biggest concentrations of Zionists are found in the metropolises; but, if the aim is for Zionists of all countries to have a proportionate representation, then it is in my view most proper to construe that every one hundred members in any location would have the right to elect a delegate. If there are groups in a locality that have fewer, I would grant even them the right to elect a delegate, and for the members beyond one hundred I would likewise accord the right to a delegate. Gentlemen! [158] We can certainly lose nothing if the Congress be attended by a great number. I think you will concede that it will be only an advantage for our people if the number of participants is increased as liberally as possible. Every one hundred members in a location will elect a delegate. If the number of members is less than one hundred, they will likewise elect one; over one hundred warrants yet another delegate. I will take the liberty to add something concerning the rights of those attending the Congress not as delegates but as ordinary participants. I would support the right of non-delegates to speak but not vote. I would like to propose supplementary clauses to this effect.

Pause of ten minutes.

PRESIDENT: I draw your attention to the fact that, if we are going to continue the discussion in this fashion, we will never get beyond this point. The Congress will conclude this evening, though. If you wish for us to complete everything, I recommend you strive to be extremely brief.

DR. SCHNIRER: I think that this appeal will not suffice for us to really get somewhere. We are already approaching noon. If we want to debate this question ever so briefly, we will have to keep going all together at least till noon, which will really wear us out. We must decide right now whether we want to drop one or another of the items on the program. We must decide about this right now; otherwise it will soon be 6:00 p.m. and then adieu.

DR. BODENHEIMER: I have greater confidence in the good will of those present, and if they attest their will in the same way that the committee has done, we will come swiftly to the goal. The committee has furnished a different version of Alinea b, which I believe can be adopted immediately by acclamation. I ask the rapporteur to read out Alinea b in the alternative version.

STEINER: The following wording was agreed to by the commission to take into account the interests of all: "Every local Zionist group shall elect a delegate to the Congress. If the number of members exceeds 100, they shall elect for every additional 100 or fraction thereof another delegate. No delegate may hold by himself more than 10 votes." A further amendment was proposed by Professor Schapira which reads: "One delegate similarly empowered to vote shall be elected by every 20 non-delegates in attendance at the Congress."

PRESIDENT: I regret that the commission failed to inform me ahead of time. Obviously, special consideration is being given to persons who have taken a keen interest in Zionism but who have no mandate. I think that consideration can be given in a different way, though. After all, when the next Congress will take place will be known for a long time in advance. So, the committed Zionist will apply to the Committee and inquire of its office, under what conditions may I participate? Then the office will have printed forms with the notice: secure the mandate of so-and-so-many people who are qualified to vote. The office will certainly know where persons seeking delegates are. [159] If the proposal of Schapira is implemented, we would breach the principle of representation. Anyway, with respect to this draft it is only a matter of about a year. It is provisional. If we have been able to bring off this assembly provisionally, the committee to come will be able accomplish still greater things. That 20 people who come together from different directions should elect a representative seems to me unfeasible. Leave the matter open. The suggested text: "Every local Zionist group" is entirely sufficient. If we accept the paragraph suggested by Herr Professor Schapira, many people will still be sitting in the gallery, and among them might be the one who would have had the most to say.

STEINER: I withdraw the amendment.

DR. EHRENPREIS: I move that the text read: "Societies or local groups." Furthermore, I propose the amendment: "Societies and local groups may elect their delegates even from among Zionists outside their group."

The commission's motion is adopted by vote.

PRESIDENT: This Alinea will now be sent back to the commission to give it a certain juristic elegance. The motion made by Dr. Blumenfeld reads: "Paying Zionists who join the Congress as private persons, have only the right to participate in discussions but not to take part in voting." Herr Dr. Blumenfeld has the floor.

DR. BLUMENFELD: As I have just said, the position of non-delegate Zionists at the Congress must be mentioned in the second article. I believe this is covered if we say that they are permitted only the right to take part in the discussions but not in the voting.

PRESIDENT: I draw your attention to the fact that the new text reads: "Paying Zionists." The right to take part in discussions will depend on one's paying. I do not think this is an appropriate formulation. If we had thought so, we would have given consideration at this Congress to paying Zionists. It was my view that Blumenfeld's motion is a barely altered repetition of Neumark's motion.

DR. BODENHEIMER: I think there still exists a misunderstanding. It has been mentioned by our colleague Schauer that the question of the participation of individual Zionists at the Congress is also to be raised, and that it is self-evident that every Zionist may take part.[8] Alinea 2 does not make a determination concerning the voting rights of individual Zionists, and consequently we must leave this determination to the commission to be set up. We are unable to reach agreement about it.

PRESIDENT: It is most regrettable that we are all legal scholars, for they find the clearest things unclear. Since we are already agreed in principle, we can leave this article to the commission. We can set our minds at ease about it, and let us not lose any more time on it, since we need so much to make use of the afternoon. I am asking you to take heed.

DR. BLUMENFELD: I withdraw my motion.

[160] PRESIDENT: Questions settled in the commission cannot of course be binding on the Congress. But within the commission you will have opportunity for an exchange of views which, it is hoped, will set your minds at ease. We have to restrict our exchange of views here, anticipating the shortness of time facing us in the afternoon. Herr Dr. Blumenfeld has a perfectly legitimate reservation. Though we are conducting our discussion in such a summary fashion, it is not of course intended to suggest that the reservation is not entirely justified. We move now to paragraph 3. (He reads out the paragraph.)

SCHACH: In our discussion of paragraph 2 we omitted the stipulation that a person may not hold a combined total of more than ten votes.

PRESIDENT: Separate treatment of this point was certainly not required and consequently this stipulation has been adopted. It has been repeatedly read out. The intention of this section is plainly the protection of the minority.

Paragraph 3 is adopted without debate.
President reads out paragraph 4.

Dr. Ebner: Considering that Bukovina counts sixty thousand Jews, I move that a member for Bukovina be elected to the Executive Committee.[9]

Bromberg: One can discern from the mood, that still other territories will be asking for recognition and wanting a representative. In light of this fact, I move that the Actions Committee comprise a larger number, indeed at least twenty-five members, of which five must reside in Vienna.

Wolffsohn: I will also make a motion that Palestine be represented in the Actions Committee.

Dr. Bodenheimer proposes twenty-one, agreeing with Bromberg with respect to other details.

President: Obviously, it will be the commission which puts this provision as well into definitive form. The commission is also in agreement with twenty-one members to be elected as follows: five, permanently resident in Vienna, are to be chosen by a direct vote of the Congress. The others will be decided upon by their territorial organizations and groups. The results submitted from the territorial organizations will just be ratified by the Congress. Taking into account the several countries, we have the following draft: Vienna five, Austria without Galicia and Bukovina one, Galicia two, Bukovina one, Russia four, France one, England one, America one, Palestine one, Romania two, Bulgaria and Serbia one, Germany two. We have thus a total of twenty-two and will have to eliminate one.

Dr. Farbstein: I would move that twenty-three be chosen.

Dr. Blumenfeld: I would like to see a representative also for the Oriental countries.
    The motion of Dr. Farbstein is adopted.

Isidor Schalit* (Vienna): I make the motion: the General Secretary belongs to the Actions Committee and has a seat and vote on that committee. I base this motion on the fact that we do not wish for the man we honor with such a position to hold a conditional appointment. Therefore he must have a seat and a vote like the rest of the members.[10]

[161] STEINER: Whoever this individual may be, I feel nonetheless compelled to say: our task here is a higher one, than to craft individual paragraphs to fit a single individual. According to my interpretation, the General Secretary is the executive agent. Nothing other than this is to be inferred. We have created the possibility for him to have an advisory role and position in the administration of affairs, since foreign delegates have the right to appoint representatives in Vienna.

PRESIDENT: I would like to point out that Schalit's motion actually anticipates the constitution of the committee. Either this special position is simply allowed for, or the person who is going to be the General Secretary is prescribed for this committee in advance. I do not think that anyone will agree to hold a representative position under such a condition.[11] We cannot appoint a functionary without giving him a task to perform. I do not understand this motion at all.

DR. KORNBLÜH: Will the General Secretary hold a salaried or honorary position? If salaried, then the motion is improper.

PRESIDENT: The motion is, in my view, a legal impossibility. If a colleague of our movement receives an honorary appointment, it will not disqualify him, nor does anyone have this in mind. If we only want to elect someone like this, who has proved his utility.

A motion to close debate without listening to other speakers is adopted.

SCHALIT: I was thinking that precisely because it is to be a salaried position, the man in question who occupies it will not be a dependent and will be equal to the others. After all, it is thus among the Social Democrats. We are not a bourgeois party. We heard this today from Dr. Farbstein. We must keep the democratic principle everywhere at the forefront, and what I proposed corresponds to the democratic principle. Precisely because the Secretary is salaried, he is to have a seat and a vote.

BROMBERG: I concur fully with the statements made by Herr Schalit. However, it is not appropriate to vote on this motion at this time, before discussing the matter as a whole. I move to table the motion until we come to deal with the position of the General Secretary. A new position is being created, General

Secretary, and nothing at all has been mentioned about whether he is supposed to be elected by us here.

STEINER: I concur with Bromberg's proposal. We have to decide first if a General Secretary is to be elected at all.

The tabling of Schalit's motion is adopted.
Paragraph 4 is adopted.
The President reads out paragraph 5.

BIRKENSTEIN: I would just like to insert that a foreign member may also designate a foreigner to represent him in Vienna.

SCHACH: I would like to have it emphasized that it is not permitted for any of the five Vienna-based members to represent a foreign member.

HERBST: I do not think that our goal is met if members are elected who are in Vienna but are not from the country they are to represent. Otherwise it would suffice for the five in Vienna to form the commission.

STEINER: I would like to make the following elucidation. The task of such a representative is conceived of as follows: he holds a seat but not a vote in the advisory committees. As the need arises, he obtains reports from his principal. Consequently, he has to reside in Vienna, so that he can be present at consultations.

[162] HERBST: I would be entirely satisfied if it were stipulated that the persons in question do not have the right to vote.

DR. LANDAU: I would like to ask for a bit of your patience. I have felt a certain misgiving, inasmuch as it would be possible to change one's proxy arbitrarily. Therefore, I move to amend by saying that the proxy is to be appointed for a complete administrative period.

PRESIDENT: I am now bringing the paragraph to a vote.

The paragraph is adopted.
The President reads out paragraph 6.
The latter is adopted without debate.

The President reads out paragraph 7.

DR. SCHNIRER: Gentlemen, please! If you consider how complex the workings of the Actions Committee are, you will realize it makes no sense to have one General Secretary. We need several secretaries. We will certainly not be able to find one General Secretary who speaks German, French, English, Russian, etc. And if he is not able to speak all of these languages, he will not be in a position to sift through and supervise the business to be done. We must therefore have a number of competent staff who are employed and salaried, whom we designate as secretaries. And one from among the Central Committee will be the unsalaried chief secretary, who will supervise the work of the secretaries.

DR. FARBSTEIN: Dr. Schnirer has a quite erroneous conception of the task. He conceives of it more as an office for handling correspondence. The General Secretary is to stand at the head of a general bureau carrying out all kinds of work. In other words, he must be a trusted liaison. Therefore he must be a General Secretary and not merely a correspondent; otherwise we could take on any clerk. We need a trusted liaison, who in this or that situation will stand in for a member of the Actions Committee.

DR. KORNBLÜH: Just a few words. I am an attorney and do not belong to the bourgeois party. Every Jew who holds to his religion must be a Social Democrat.

PRESIDENT: I would like to draw your attention to something. We have not agreed to discuss this issue. I think the most proper way is for us to be for all parties. We have not convened here in a party conference, and we are not going to permit a takeover of the Congress by any one party.

BROMBERG: I move that the General Secretary be elected by the Congress from within the Actions Committee, specifying that he hold a salaried position.

PRESIDENT: Again, two things are being confused. If we elect a General Secretary and at the same time stipulate his salary, we are setting up a new functionary with as yet undefined assignments, and we are granting to the person in question an honorarium. It seems to me more proper to separate the two issues. Honoraria are never made the object of public discussion. This discussion seems to originate with the very gentlemen who would not want to degrade this person in any way. Consequently, it seems proper to me to leave this question to the Committee. If this Committee does not fulfill its duties to the satisfaction of the Congress, it will have the means to make this known. Such things are not to be discussed in advance.

[163] BROMBERG repeats his motion.

DR. SCHNIRER: Bromberg's motion is not clear enough, since he does not say by whom the Secretary is to be elected.

PRESIDENT: I will draw your attention to the fact that the committee is proposing that the Actions Committee elect the Secretary.

Article 7 is adopted in the language of the committee.
The President reads out article 8.
The latter is adopted without debate.
The President reads out article 9.

LANDAU: I move a resolution regarding this point: "The Actions Committee is to publish an index of the Zionist party newspapers." I think we can simply take note of this: surely no objection can be raised against it.

PRESIDENT: With this the entire draft of the commission is finished, and you will perhaps waive examining it all yet again? (Voices: Yes!)

MARMOREK: I think that, to save time, nominations for election to the Committee should be made during lunch.

BIRKENSTEIN: I move that we not take a midday break or only a one-hour break, to complete the agenda. The gentlemen will come to an agreement during the break, and at the same time we will make sure paper ballots are distributed, and in individual groups the gentlemen will come to an agreement as they see fit.

STEINER reads out the individual groups and the numbers of members to be elected.

PRESIDENT: You can agree among yourselves concerning this question, as you wish. Persons who are absent must not be elected,[12] rather let any recommendations come from the territorial groups.

Day Three, Afternoon Session

PRESIDENT: The gentlemen have had long enough now for their deliberation. I am going to proceed to a vote and give the floor to the chairman of the commission, Herr Director Steiner.

STEINER: It has been decided with respect to the method of voting, that the five members of the Actions Committee who must be resident in Vienna are to be elected by the Congress, while the remaining representatives of the individual territorial organizations, after being announced by the latter, are to be confirmed by the Congress. For the election of the five members from Vienna, the committee recommends to you the following gentlemen: Dr. Theodor Herzl, Dr. M. Schnirer, Dr. O. Kokesch,* Dr. N. Birnbaum, Johann Meyer* [Kremenetzky] (applause after the reading of each name).

WOLFFSOHN: I declare in the name of the German Zionists their acceptance of the recommended list.

DR. KAMINKA: I move the election of Stiassny, the government surveyor.

DR. D. MALZ* (LEMBERG) expresses his opposition.
It is decided to conduct the election by acclamation.

[164] DR. BLUMENFELD moves to vote for each name individually by acclamation. (The motion is rejected.)
The five gentlemen nominated are elected by acclamation.

DR. BIRNBAUM: While I am very grateful to be elected, I hereby declare that I am unable to accept.

SCHILLER (LEMBERG) asserts that moral pressure has been exerted on Dr. Birnbaum to decline the office. (Great commotion.)

PRESIDENT: I implore the speaker to express himself more plainly; I implore him to indicate more precisely from which quarter pressure has been exerted on Dr. Birnbaum, whether from the presidency or from any other direction in the assembly. (Wild applause. Shouts: Names! Indecency! Great commotion.)

SCHILLER: I am unable to name names. (Tremendous uproar.)

DR. MALZ: Dr. Birnbaum must take the office. We should not recognize his refusal. (Loud applause.) Without Birnbaum there would be no Herzl, no Zionist movement in Austria. (Cheers and opposition. Shouts of "enough!")

PRESIDENT: You will understand that in this matter I am unable to preside with the firmness required. At the same time I implore the speaker to supply facts, so that he does not give cause for his right to speak to be withdrawn. (Uproarious applause, sharp protests.) But that there be no doubt and not to interfere with Herr Dr. Malz in his remarks, I am ceding the presidency to Dr. Nordau. (Uproarious cheers. Shouts: Cut him off!)

VICE PRESIDENT (DR. NORDAU) comments that Dr. Malz has had opportunity to recognize the general mood and would now perhaps reconsider his words. (Thunderous cheers. Scattered protests.)

DR. MALZ declares he does not want to set the gentlemen against one another. But one is overcome by a feeling of resentment to see a man so deserving being forced out. (Shouts: Enough! Enough! Much noise.) It is the duty of the Congress to Dr. Birnbaum, who has dedicated his entire life to the cause, caring nothing for his own needs ... (Tremendous tumult. The vice president rings the bell for order for several minutes in vain. The speaker yields the floor.)

DR. HEINRICH LOEWE* (JAFFA) makes a declaration in the name of Dr. Birnbaum, who is not present in the hall, that he has declined the election entirely of his own free will, for purely personal reasons. (Applause.)

STEINER points out that this entire business has been unnecessary. Birnbaum may indeed be an Austrian, but he does not reside in Vienna, rather in Berlin. (Thunderous applause. Protest.)

ADOLF STAND* (LEMBERG) emphasizes the merits of Dr. Landau.

THE PRESIDENT interrupts him; he cannot permit these statements, since it would be unfair to the other candidates, whose merits have not been presented as well.

STAND: Perhaps they have none. (Much noise.)
Ballots for the election of a replacement are distributed.
[165] Those elected in accord with the recommendation of their respective territorial organizations are: for Austria, Primarius Dr. Kornfeld* in Brünn (Galicia and Bukovina excepted); for Galicia, Herr Dr. A. Salz in Tarnów and Dr. A. Korkis* in Lemberg; for Bukovina, Dr. Maier Ebner in Czernowitz; for Russia, Rabbi Mohilewer in Bialystok, Professor Mandelstamm in Kiev, Dr. Bernstein-Kohan in Kischinev, and Dr. Jassinowski in Warsaw; for Romania, Dr. K. Lippe in Jassy and Samuel Pineles in Galatz; for Bulgaria and Serbia, Professor Bielkowski [Belkovsky]; for all the other oriental Jews in Africa and Asia, J.B. Bahar from Paris; for France, Bernard Lazare* in Paris; for Germany, Dr. Rülf in Memel and Dr. Bodenheimer in Cologne.

For Palestine, North America, and England, nomination to offices is reserved to the popular assemblies to be organized for this purpose.

PRESIDENT: Now that the business of voting has been completed, we wish to proceed to a discussion of item b of the third article, concerning the national fund, and Dr. Bodenheimer has the floor.

DR. BODENHEIMER: The question of the national fund is certainly one of the most important that might occupy the Congress, but I think the entire assembly will agree that, precisely because of the importance of the issue, no binding decisions concerning specific proposals submitted to the commission can be taken at this late hour. The commission has therefore not begun detailed examination of the proposals. The commission is of the opinion that the elected Central Committee undertake a thorough examination of all motions and recommendations, and that then, in the course of the year, a reasonable and practical solution to this extremely important question will become possible. I have submitted to you a printed financial prospectus, according to which the first task will be to found a Jewish bank. Founding a bank in no way precludes the national fund. However, that we not disperse entirely without results, I would like to have the question settled in principle, that we are in need of a Zionist fund or a national fund. If the assembly is in agreement, then the question of carrying it out, of creating a framework in conjunction with separate organizations, can be set in train. I would like to propose to you the following resolution: "The assembly affirms that it regards as necessary the creation of a fund for Zionist purposes, and that it consigns all proposals received to the Central Committee, to examine them and present a draft proposal to create a national fund at the next Congress."

DAVIDSOHN*: First, I would like to ask the president to read out a resolution that was submitted and has twenty signatures. It is to be found in the bureau and is supplied with a Russian translation. The resolution says: "The Congress resolves to create an organization from among its members pledged to address a summons to the entire nation, for the purpose of creating a national fund in the amount of 10 million pounds sterling."

The results of the outstanding election are announced. Dr. Mintz obtained fifty-two votes, Dr. Landau fifty-five. The remaining votes were split several ways. Since no one attained an absolute majority, a runoff is to be arranged.

[166] PRESIDENT: I think it necessary to ask the Actions Committee to make and present a plan before the next Congress for managing incoming funds. Now to a proposal of Herr Professor Schapira that has been in hand for quite some time.[i]

---

i The proposal of Professor Dr. Schapira reads:

Imagine if our ancestors had, at the time of their going into exile, set aside an ever-so-small sum of money for the future; we would today be able to acquire with this money great tracts of land. What our ancestors did not do, partly from inability, partly from neglect, is what we are obliged to do for ourselves and our descendants.

Legacies for future times are subject to the risk of being used later for purposes other than originally intended. Taking this concern into account as far as possible is the aim of this proposal:

1. From all the Jews in the world, rich and poor without any distinction, as far as permitted by the laws of the respective states to which the Jews in question belong, one-time and periodic contributions are to be collected to establish a general Jewish fund.

2. Two-thirds of the fund thus created shall be considered a territorial fund and may be used only for the acquisition of a Jewish territory, whereas one-third shall be used for the upkeep and cultivation of the acquired territory as well as for general Jewish purposes of equal significance.

Let us show some tolerance in letting the speakers have their say, so long as it does not obstruct the proceedings. Herr Professor Schapira wishes to have the floor.

SCHAPIRA: Honored assembly! I will abuse neither your time nor your patience. In general, I am of the same opinion as Dr. Bodenheimer and the other gentlemen, that at present we should avoid as much as possible adopting any final resolutions with respect to the national fund. If the Congress decides to

---

3. The acquired territory may never be alienated nor even sold to individual Jews; rather it can only be leased, in fact for at most forty-nine years and in accord with principles yet to be elaborated.

4. The aforesaid fund with its principal and interest may not be touched until it has reached an amount of at least ten million pounds sterling.

5. Before any sum is withdrawn from the fund, a guarantee must first be provided that the amount will be replaced in full in at most fifty years.

6. For the expenditure of any amount in excess of the annual interest (i.e., out of the permanent capital of the fund) a majority vote taken in a plebiscite to discern the will of the Jewish people is required insofar as this is at all feasible.

7. If the amount to be spent exceeds one-half of the permanent capital, the expenditure requires at least a two-thirds majority of all ascertainable votes.

8. Expenditure in an amount up to that of the annual interest may occur by a decision of the administration.

9. Insofar as possible, anticipated expenditures shall be proposed to the people or their representatives one year in advance. Only in urgent, exceptional cases is the administration permitted to indemnify the fund retroactively in the course of the following year.

10. The administration is to be appointed provisionally by the present Congress. The next Congress will appoint definitively for the coming ten years. In the course of the next ten years, fixed rules of governance for the future administration are to be set down.

11. Amendments to these articles may be made only upon the basis of a plebiscite with at least a two-thirds majority of the ascertainable votes.

12. An announcement on three separate occasions at intervals of ten years must precede such a plebiscite, which must be circulated every time among all Jews insofar as possible.

leave this question to the Committee, I am in complete agreement. But I would just like to emphasize that, as far as I can discern, a great number of brothers here with me have expressed the wish that, besides the other funds, a territorial fund be set up. Second, to prevent money from the territorial fund being used later for other purposes, that precautions to that effect be incorporated into the bylaws. Third, that the fund should absolutely never be depleted. These are the three basic principles from which I would not wish to deviate. I will insist on proposing these three recommendations to you for their adoption in principle, at the same time informing you that there are gentlemen present here and now who are prepared to designate a considerable sum in support of these principles, and the Congress would actually only have to decide to take this sum into safekeeping under the stated conditions. There is in my proposal a delicate point having to do with the matter of a plebiscite. I would happily let it go; i.e., during consideration in the commission. [167] We want to leave the commission a free hand, but I do want to direct this request to the commission, that it take steps to make sure that the points I have mentioned are taken into account. If it be requested that a resume of these recommendations be turned into a formal motion, I would remark that the first four articles contain the basic principles, and I would be happy if these were adopted in principle only. It is wrong to think that I am demanding ten millions for my fund. The fund should definitely be established and remain as an endowment, and should not be touched until it reaches about one million. These are the basic principles I propose.

DR. BODENHEIMER: I am afraid of provoking a prolonged debate if I enter into the particulars of the statement made by our most esteemed Professor Schapira. But I would like to remark that I too made an intellectual sacrifice by presenting a financial prospectus I had drafted in which the establishment of a Jewish bank took priority, with the explicit declaration that I did not consider it to be a proper object for the Congress's discussions and decisions because I think that it ought to be discussed beforehand by a smaller committee. But in order to bring about a resolution of differences, I permit myself to make the following recommendation: the assembly declares, in principle, that it deems the creation of a national fund and the establishment of a Jewish bank as necessary, that therefore the Actions Committee to be elected submit a thoroughly elaborated plan for the same to the next Congress.

As Professor Schapira has declared, individual members have declared themselves ready to designate contributions for a national fund. Similarly, I am informed that there are men of finance who are ready to take part in establishing the bank. [168] I wish therefore the assembly also to declare itself agreed in principle on establishing a Jewish bank, and that persons interested in the national fund and in the Jewish bank meet together and submit separate drafts to the committee. There is no other way to proceed today, and may I recommend most strongly that these proposals be accepted all around.

PRESIDENT: A well-considered motion for the closure of debate has been presented. I think that we can decide nothing definitively, since we have projects that cannot really be discussed further without being examined by experts. It is therefore perhaps not out of place for us to leave the examination of all these suggestions to the Committee. You will be kept up to date through the labors of the Committee, and it is enough that the suggestion has been made public. I am now bringing the motion for the closure of debate to a vote.

Closing of debate without hearing additional speakers is adopted.

The resolution of Davidsohn is likewise adopted.

MOTZKIN: I would simply like to inquire: Does the creation of a national fund depend on the next Congress, or is it to take place immediately?

PRESIDENT: Whoever wants to give something to the national fund may do so. Later, if the Congress does not adopt it, the money will again be at his disposal.

BODENHEIMER: If the Congress adopts my resolution, it has decided in principle for the national fund.

The resolution of Bodenheimer is adopted.

PRESIDENT: Herr Herbst from Bulgaria wishes to have it noted in the proceedings that the delegate of the Bulgarian central society, "Zion," abstained in the election of the committee member from Serbia and Bulgaria.

SEFF speaks Russian.

PRESIDENT: We are going on to item 4. Herr Dr. Schnirer has the floor for his report on the colonization of Palestine.[1]

DR. SCHNIRER (VIENNA) limits his report, in view of the shortness of time, to a discussion of two general points, the consideration of which is of great significance for the Zionist movement. The first point concerns the issue of whether or not colonizing should continue for the present. According to the program adopted by the Congress, Zionism strives to create a homeland in Palestine for the Jewish people, secured by public law. As among the means of attaining this goal, our program designates "the effective promotion of settling Palestine, etc." From the wording of the program, one might draw the conclusion that all further immigration of Jews into Palestine is to be suspended, as long as the desired public-legal guarantee does not exist. The wording of the program admits however of another interpretation. [169] This second view, shared by many of our associates, is that it is possible to carry on with colonizing, just as before, without regard to the non-existent "public-legal security" that we all hope to obtain. Against this latter view, the rapporteur asserts that colonizing activity has been carried out in a manner that can fill every honest Zionist only with grief. It is an open secret—which the modern Zionist movement, whose motto is candor and truth, has no reason to conceal—that bribery has played a big role in the colonizing work done thus far. But the one who bribes others corrupts not only those who are bribed but also degrades himself. The work of national renaissance that we are beginning must never, ever be advanced by such means. Therefore, let the cry go forth from this Congress: "Away with the baksheesh* economy, which serves only to satisfy the greed of individuals ill-disposed toward their own people, and to inflict severe moral wounds on our fellow tribesmen." (Applause.)

Our colonies in Palestine are, to be sure, of tremendous significance for our movement, not only because they have supplied proof once and for all that the Jews have an aptitude for agriculture, but also because, to a certain extent, they are experimental stations showing the way for the future development of agriculture and industry in Palestine. Therefore, the greatest emphasis must be placed on strengthening the colonies not yet firmly established. On the other hand, new colonies—in view of the factors cited—are to be established only out of manpower already present in Palestine, and of course without resorting to illegal or dishonest methods of any kind.

A second issue addressed by the rapporteur concerns the independence of the Palestinian colonists. It is a well-known fact that in some colonies founded through private benevolence, the good will of the noble, well-intentioned benefactor has not sufficed to turn the colonists into contented, free human beings, but rather, on account of an unhealthy system of subsidies and the not always disinterested management of affairs by the administrators, slaves are being bred who will remain forever in financial bondage, who are fully conscious of their undignified, dependent status, and who suffer much because of it. This mistake must be avoided in any new colonies to be founded, the colonists must not become "second edition" Halukka Jews but rather yeoman farmers and independent men. (Applause.)

The speaker listed the following theses at the conclusion of his report:

1. Further immigration of Jews into Palestine must be refrained from so long as the "public-legal security" for the settlements does not exist.
2. The colonies to be founded using manpower already present in Palestine are to be set up only with a free cooperative organization as their basis.

[170] I am only too aware—Dr. Schnirer concludes—that we are today still not in a position to have these our views generally accepted. But what the Congress can and must do today is to assert its influence so that in all Zionist undertakings the principle be adhered to, that Zionism is not only a social and economic movement but rather first and foremost a national and ethical one. (Loud applause.)

PRESIDENT: Herr Dr. Kaminka has the floor.

DR. KAMINKA (PRAGUE): The flame of longing for the restoration of Zion in the hearts of the Jewish people has never been extinguished since the downfall of the state. Political Zionism, which was not able to venture forth openly, took refuge under the protection of religion and benevolence. But there are countless pronouncements in the Talmud and Midrash, as well as in the later, post-exilic literature, which characterize the colonization of Palestine by Jews as a religious command, as a sacred duty. The most striking is the passage in the Talmud: "He who lives outside of Palestine, it is as though he were serving foreign gods and denying his religion," and likewise the saying in the Midrash: "If Israel speaks of 'rest,' it must have Jerusalem in mind, for only of Jerusalem can it be said, 'It is my abiding place of rest'" (Ps. 135).[2] Throughout the Middle Ages the return to the Holy Land was not only the object of fervent prayers, but also the final word of every lesson and public speech, the "ceterum censeo" of Israel.[3] No preacher, no rabbi, would close an address to the people without adding the words: "And for Zion a redeemer shall come."[4] How then was the redemption imagined? Mostly of course in a miraculous way, through a supernatural intervention of God, according to the generally prevailing mystical conceptions. Yet even in the Middle Ages there was no want of men who did not hesitate to affirm emphatically that the redemption of Israel would take place by natural means. Rabbi David Kimchi,* in his exposition of one of the verses of the Psalms, takes occasion to remark: "Help comes ever truly from God, but it comes by human hands. Thus was the return of the Jews from Babylon effected by the agency of King Cyrus, and so shall the future, final redemption develop in a natural way." Likewise, Maimonides spoke often quite clearly about the messianic age, declaring it to be the time of both the restoration of the Jewish state and the time when the redemption of Israel would take shape by natural means.

Whereas in the Middle Ages it was chiefly religion that directed the Jews' gaze to Palestine, in modern times Jewish benevolence has turned instinctively toward the Holy Land. [171] Numerous humanitarian institutions have been founded there by European Jews, by societies and individuals. Moses Montefiore* travelled there himself repeatedly and sought to improve the living conditions of the indigent Jewish population of Jerusalem—who were to a great extent dependent on charity (Halukka). When the Alliance Israélite Universelle was founded, Charles Netter* effected the establishment of an agricultural school in Jaffa (1869), under the name "Mikveh Israel"* (the Hope of Israel)—in doing so, he unwittingly took the first step in the plan of the modern Zionist program.[5] But some years even before that, in 1861, an esteemed rabbi Zvi Hirsch Kalischer in Thorn [Toruń], published a noteworthy text, *Derishat Zion*,* in which he appealed to his contemporaries in the name of religion to found societies for the colonization of Palestine by Jews, and suggested that the honor of Jewry—on analogy with Italians, Hungarians, Poles, and other peoples who ventured life and property to stand up for their fatherland—demanded that they likewise risk everything in order to regain their ancient Palestinian homeland. David Gordon,* one of the founders of modern Jewish journalism, has for his part warmly advocated for the project, which took on an urgent significance on account of the troubles faced by Jews in Romania and the persecutions in Russia which took place soon thereafter.

The years of horror, 1881 and 1882, gave a special impulse to the colonization of Palestine. A stream of immigrants, plundered and economically ruined families, poured forth toward the western Russian border, and the question arose: whither with these unfortunates? The committees offering help were immediately ready with advice: to America! And millions were spent on transporting numerous families, some of whom, because they were unable to establish themselves financially, had to be conveyed back across the ocean some years later with the help of new donations.[6] But from among the people itself, from the heart of those sensitive not only to the intense, transitory sorrow of those dreadful years, but also to the millennial, historic lamentation of the Jewish people, the outcry issued forth with elemental force: to Palestine, to our own country, where Israel, everywhere harassed through so many centuries, would finally find rest and a dignified existence. In Hebrew and Russian journals this project was proclaimed in glowing terms. The prophetic promises, familiar to every Jew, suddenly took on a current meaning and were enthusiastically received as rays of light illuminating a new era. Dr. L. Pinsker,* a respected physician in Odessa, through his pamphlet, *Autoemancipation*, which caused a justifiable sensation, familiarized even educated Jewish circles with the idea that Israel had to become conscious of its national life and endeavor to obtain its own land.

[172] The first to immigrate to Palestine as a consequence of renewed pressure in 1882, were, in part, families that possessed some resources and thought to settle themselves there independently; and, in part, young men gripped by nationalist fervor, who travelled to the Holy Land without practical goals. Among them were even students under the name "Bilu"* (an acronym of the first letters of "Beth Jacob lechù venelcha"—House of Jacob, let us go!), who united with one another in a Romantic spirit, in order to migrate as colonists to the land of the ancestors. Soon however the first immigrants found themselves in financial distress, and funds had to be sent to them from Russia by Hovevei Zion.⁷ Groups and societies were formed in various cities to support the colonists. To facilitate concerted action,⁸ a delegates' conference was organized in Kattowitz in autumn 1884 and, on the occasion of the centenary of Montefiore's* birth which was celebrated in 1885, a general association of Hovevei Zion groups was founded in Russia as the Montefiore Foundation, under the name "Maskereth Moshe" [Remembrance of Moses]. Dr. Pinsker was elected president, and eighteen prominent men were to be in association with him. This committee was tasked with: 1) obtaining an official permit from the Russian government; 2) effecting the elimination of difficulties with the Turkish government that had already appeared by that time; 3) sending a committee to Palestine to conduct an on-site examination of the things needed by the colonies that had already been set up; 4) assisting new colonists in settling.

Commissioned by the association, K.W. Wissotzky* travelled to Palestine early in 1885 and on the basis of his report the three colonies of Petah Tikva,* Gedera,* and Yesud HaMa`ala* were recommended for assistance. In the year 1890, after many futile efforts, the permission of the Russian government was finally secured for the official organization of the Colonization Company in Odessa, through the late Alexander Zederbaum,* editor of *HaMelitz*.* From that time, it has been known as "The Company for the Assistance of Jews Engaged in Agriculture and Industry in Palestine and Syria." Its membership has fluctuated between twenty-seven hundred and forty-eight hundred, with revenue amounting to approximately thirty thousand to forty-five thousand rubles per annum, but it has to be taken into account that the company is forbidden by provincial law to establish branches or an effective organization beyond that of Odessa's.

In the years 1885–1890, the company was in a position to spend the amount of about 275,181 francs in support of the colonies, and it has spent since the official permission:

> 1890–1893: approximately 215,137 francs
> 1893–1896: approximately 206,069 francs
> In the past year: approximately 179,992 francs.
> The total since 1890 is thus approximately 601,128 francs.

[173] However, even with these subventions little would have been accomplished had not the Baron E. v. R. [Edmond von Rothschild] granted partial subventions to those colonies besides the ones founded and maintained entirely by himself. In recent years many colonies have also been subsidized by large sums given by the Esra* society in Berlin, as well as being supported by Hovevei Zion[9] in Paris and London, and in the past year a contribution from the governing board of the great Baron Hirsch Foundation (Jewish Colonization Association) was also finally granted for colonization in Palestine.

The present position of the colonies is as follows:

TABLE 3.1. Area and population of Jewish agricultural colonies in Palestine, ca. 1897.

	a) in Judea	
	Dunums	Souls
Rishon LeZion* (since 1882)	6,600	400
Petah Tikva (since 1878)	13,850	670
Wadi Chanin*	4,090	670
Gedera (est. 1882 by Bilu Society)	3,000	100
`Ekron* (1882, by Baron v. R.)	4,090	160
Rehovot* (1890 Menuha VeNahala Society in Warsaw)	10,500	170
Be'er Tuvia*/Qastina*	5,600	120
Motza*	400	15
Har-Tuv*	5,000	20

continued on next page

Table 3.1 (cont'd)

	b) in Galilee	
Zikhron Ya'akov including environs (1882, est. by Hovevei Zion of Galatz, then taken over by the Baron)	16,000	650
Hadera,* on the Mediterranean (1891, by a society in Russia)	29,000	170
Rosh Pina (est. 1882, subsidized by the Baron, silk-spinning mill)	6,000	350
Yesud HaMa'alah	2,500	100
Mishmar HaYarden* (guard post on the Jordan, assisted by Esra and Jew. Col. Assn.)	2,600	87
Ein Zeitim*...	3,000	25
Metulla* (Baron R.)...	12,000	180
Approximate totals	118,230	3,372

... of which thirty thousand dunums are devoted to viticulture (about eight million vines have been planted) and about five thousand dunums to fruit production.

As far as life in the colonies is concerned, it is to be deplored that in the larger and better-appointed colonies too much of the French spirit and proclivity for luxury prevail. The parents strive to have their children educated in Paris and still harbor a certain contempt for the simple and healthy life of the farmer. [174] Yet the colonist families are taking root more and more. The younger people speak Hebrew, regard themselves as true natives, and work with diligence and devotion. The Hebrew secondary school in Jaffa is an important venue for the cultivating of the national spirit and also deserves, from the practical point of view, the attention of the supporters of colonization. Furthermore, it is important that, besides agriculture, industry and commerce are being promoted by the recent immigration; various proposals in this regard have been made, the examining of which will be the object of a special committee to be elected by the Congress. The commercial activity of the country is at present relatively insignificant. I will cite here some statistics about the foreign commerce of Jaffa. In 1895 the value of exports through Jaffa amounted to:

TABLE 3.2. Major exports and imports of Jaffa, 1895.

Exports
(Articles of more than one hundred thousand francs in commercial value per annum)

Manufactured articles, items of carved wood, from Jerusalem	375,000
Lupines	100,000
Oranges	1,500,000
Poppies	750,000
Soap	555,000
Fruits and vegetables	225,000
Wine	125,000
Together with various other articles the total export value =	4,472,500 francs

Imports
(Articles of more than one hundred thousand francs in commercial value per annum)

Coal	200,000
Coffee (from Arabia)	525,000
Medicaments	200,000
Flour	300,000
Herring	175,000
Glass and porcelain	150,000
Iron and other metals	450,000
Machinery	100,000
Indigo and other dyes	125,000
Cloth, wool, silk	175,000
Paper	175,000
Potatoes	240,000
Sugar	525,000
Wine and Liquor	150,000
Lumber	450,000
Including articles of lesser value, the total amount of imports =	ca. 7,371,599 francs.

These figures may serve as a guide for many industrial ventures. [175] It will be the task of the Congress though, in expanding the scope of colonization, to ascertain which industries might be successfully transplanted to Palestine.

However, the effective expansion of colonization requires a methodical preparation, but above all certain legal reforms or special privileges such as those the Congress is expecting to receive from the benevolence of His Majesty the Sultan. For it is impossible for colonizing to continue as it has until now. The mass immigration of Jews has been forbidden, as is well known; but the prohibition has been tightened by lower officials to the extent that no Jew is permitted to disembark in Jaffa (with the exception of French, English, and American Jews). The Arabs mock and molest the new arrivals who have secured a permission by indirect means. No landed property is to be entered in the land register under the name of a Jew. The means of acquiring land is in any case frightfully troublesome. A notorious example was reported to me. The colony of Hadera was originally the property of eighteen persons, whose shares however were not demarcated; when the colony was acquired in 1891 by a company consisting of seventy persons, a deed of purchase had to be issued by every one of the previous owners to every single one of the purchasers; thus, no fewer than 1261 court documents were required! And if in this way one is lucky enough to at least get the land registered in a legally valid way, that is just the beginning of the awful woes involved in putting up a building, since not one single house may be built without the direct authorization of Constantinople. Furthermore, one can build only inside a colony if the shares of property have been demarcated; the demarcation must be done by the government and is, again, very expensive. Only by large-scale action launched by the Congress and aimed at attaining a situation secured by public law, can the impediments to a comprehensive colonization be removed.

And if we are in earnest, that action will certainly succeed. (Loud applause.)

PRESIDENT: Herr Adam Rosenberg has the floor, for a report on the conditions in Palestine.

ADAM ROSENBERG: I will not detain you for long but will come immediately to the point.

The natural agricultural production of Palestine may be summarized as follows:

Palestine produces crops belonging to Central European, subtropical, and tropical climates. The first-named type are found in the elevated regions (Lebanon, upper Galilee, and the Judean highlands).

The tropical types flourish in the Ghor or Jordan valley, and in the Bekaa, ancient Coelosyria. [176] All other areas produce subtropical types. Let us now summarize the agricultural potential of the ancient Israelite land:

1. for field crops; e.g., wheat, barley, sesame, maize corn, chick peas, beans, lupines, vetch, etc.—the Hawran in Transjordan, the former breadbasket of Asia Minor, upper Galilee, the plains of Jezreel and Sharon, and southern Judea (between Gaza and Hebron).
2. for viticulture—lower Galilee, Judea, and Lebanon.
3. for olive cultivation—the entire region of Palestine.
4. for citrus fruits (oranges, citrons, etc.)—the environs of Jaffa and Saida (ancient Sidon), Beirut, and Damascus.
5. for raising mulberry trees for manufacturing silk—Lebanon and upper Galilee, in which a silk factory is in operation at the colony of Rosh Pina.
6. for the production of perfumes—the shores of Lake Tiberias and Lake Meron [Huleh]; on the latter is situated the colony of Yesud HaMa'alah, in which large-scale experiments in this direction are being made; similar efforts are being undertaken also in Rishon LeZion. In short, Palestine is even today "a land of wheat and barley, a land of vines, figs, and pomegranates, a land of olive oil and date-honey," "it is a land of mountains and valleys, where springs and aquifers flow forth in the valleys and upon the mountains."[10]

Mineral baths and hot springs are present in abundance around the Dead Sea, near Tiberias and in Gilead.

The chemical industry is capable of extraordinary development and the mineral resources are significant. Colocynths grow in abundance in Judea. They are employed in the manufacture of dyes. The shores of the Dead Sea offer an inexhaustible store for producing asphalt, iodine, bromine, sulphur, and rock salt.

Now we want to confirm a noteworthy fact mentioned by explorers of Palestine, with respect to the possibility of expanding agriculture in Transjordan. Recently, remains of ancient cultivation extending far into the Syrian Desert have been discovered; and large-scale Roman-era aqueducts and reservoirs have also been found in the desert at the supposed biblical site of Beyer or Bozah.[11] If the great quantities of water which swell the streams and small lakes of Transjordan during the rainy season were retained in basins, it would be possible "for cultivation to be pushed out farther and farther into the desert by means of artificial irrigation." Desert and wasteland would be turned into a "place of delight, the steppe would shout for joy and blossom as the rose." The old haggadic passage about the miraculous elasticity of our Holy Land would be literally confirmed.

[177] I endorse completely the principles advanced by Dr. Schnirer in his report concerning the system under which colonization has been carried out thus far, which were indeed things I had previously expressed, verbally and in writing, based on my own observation.

1. Without prejudice to the existing colonies, which obviously should be maintained as is appropriate, the work of colonization as hitherto carried out demands a radical, thoroughgoing reform. Not one step toward new colonizing projects until a secure legal status is provided! Every person with knowledge of the situation cannot but affirm without reservation the sharp but totally justified criticism which Dr. Schnirer has made of the existing "baksheesh system." All those who take part in it, the Turkish officials as well as the Jewish agents, are completely corrupted by this dreadful baksheesh system. It has been suggested to me that the existing Jewish colonies should in no way be undervalued as experimental agricultural stations. But, all the same, the welfare of approximately one thousand families is not be to be experimented with for long; and high-minded, financially strong patrons would in any case be able to serve this current stage in the cause of Zionism much more appropriately and effectively through the establishment of scientifically directed, well-funded estates, than has occurred thus far.

2. In colonization work rightly practiced, no administrative or tutelary structure, rather free cooperative labor under a unified, democratically constituted, central directorate. To this end, regulation and oversight of immigration and settlement on the part of the central directorate.

A word about the "Zion Central Committee"* organized in Paris in January 1894. At the outset the aim was that this committee direct the entire work of colonization. For a reason which it is not appropriate to make public, its total effect was ultimately limited to establishing the workers' colony of Qastina, and supporting or reorganizing Mishmar HaYarden in conjunction with the I.C.A. [J.C.A] An effort is being made at present to settle landed estates previously purchased by another party with compatriots already resident in Palestine, above all with students of Mikveh Israel, but also with Jewish agricultural laborers and with a large section of the urban Jewish youth from Jerusalem, Safed, Tiberias, Damascus, etc., whose dearest wish is to cultivate the land in a productive manner.

It should be emphasized here that among the colonies not under the patronage of the Russian committee of Hovevei Zion, the French spirit has predominated, a spirit that is hardly conducive to the greater good of Zionism.

[178] Even in the settlements whose founding the I.C.A. has recently projected, this un-Jewish spirit is likely to predominate as much as ever. In addition, the relations of dependency that exist at present among most colonists cannot contribute to the formation of a healthy, vigorous, free, and independent class of Jewish farmers.

The inefficacy of the "Zion Central Committee" in playing the guiding role in the movement is due to the following reasons:

1. Since the members of the Committee reside in Paris, London, and Berlin, and the Russian representative must obtain the counsel of Odessa before any important decision, the functioning of the Committee is the most cumbersome imaginable. Besides, every member has his own occupation which absorbs his best time and energy, while he is able to attend to the Committee's work only in his spare time.

2. Notwithstanding that the method of voting requires that two members residing outside of Paris have a seat and vote in the committee, the composition of the committee can only be described as thoroughly arbitrary and undemocratic precisely because the preponderant influence of the Paris representatives does not admit of free and open proceedings fair to all Zionists. Three or four gentlemen in Paris, and the same number in Jaffa, and in the majority of cases only the latter, have the final decision concerning the specific use of funds, while the masses who donate the money are not given any kind of accounting of the use of funds, or at most a very incomplete, general one. In addition, they are given little say with regard to the nature of the projects.

Based on the foregoing, certain inescapable truths must be taken to heart concerning a true and proper Zionist organization:

1. Its Central Committee must be composed of men who devote all their time and energy to the central administration. No leisure-time Zionists!—The Zionist Organization must provide these men, if necessary, with an honorarium.

2. The central directorate must not be oligarchic but rather democratically constituted, and responsible to the Congress in all essential matters.

I leave the description of systems of Halukka and Jewish education to my friend Dr. Heinrich Loewe, who has recently made a detailed examination of these in Palestine. I will remark only that Halukka can by no means be done away with as long as there is nothing better to put in its place. But a reform of Halukka is urgently needed.

In this connection, I wish to cite in passing, some data concerning Jewish labor conditions in Jerusalem, which I owe mainly to my friend, Wilhelm Gross,* commercial agent in Jaffa and Jerusalem. [179] During the last two decades, the number of Jewish laborers and craftsmen has increased significantly due to the recent movement of colonization, so much so that at present the supply of labor there far exceeds the demand. Out of approximately two thousand families to be considered in this context, scarcely four hundred are finding a meager employment. One can vividly imagine the resulting misery. The only possible remedy is obviously the creation of opportunities for work, which would also give significant impetus to the reform of Halukka. Thus, top priority to the diversification of the branches of industry already in existence. Many raw or semifinished goods are exported to Europe instead of being turned into marketable products in-country. Labor is cheap in Palestine and the country offers a wide field for profitable capital investments. The development of industry and trade in Palestine is extraordinarily promising.

The following proposals made by Herr Gross and Herr Bambus* may be presented here in the form of suggestions:

1. Appointing a commission of experts from various countries to examine the existing Halukka system and Palestine's labor conditions, and, on the basis of their report, if possible, reaching agreement with the Palestine societies and the I.C.A. [J.C.A] on implementing the proposed reform.

2. As a step preparatory to attaining the secure legal condition absolutely indispensable for the colonization of Palestine, creating an agency for the protection of legal rights (comprising European Zionists familiar with Turkish law).

Concerning Palestine's exports and imports, the following may be suggested:

1. The founding of commercial companies, wherever appropriate.

2. Establishing a warehouse or permanent bazaar in Jaffa, where products of Jewish diligence and Jewish skill will be kept in stock for retail distribution inside and outside the country.

3. Founding an agricultural and commercial bank.

The distress of workers would be relieved:

1. By promoting cottage industry.

2. By decentralizing; i.e., transferring the surplus craftsmen and laborers in certain cities, especially Jerusalem, to the cities and towns of the interior, where a class of craftsmen is to be found only in small numbers, if at all.

Herr Gross will submit other information concerning the commercial and industrial conditions of Palestine, relevant statistical data, and suggestions for the amelioration of Jewish labor conditions, to a commission to be set up for this purpose.

The bulk of Palestine's Jewish population are devoted heart and soul to their national identity as Jews.[12]

[180] A leader of the Orthodox in Jerusalem, the overseer[13] of a large congregation, recently commented: with the consent of the powers and the self-help of the Jews the *Geulah* [redemption] will come, and we are thus preparing the way for *Moschiach* [Messiah].

Missionary work in Palestine, which has been occupied with the capture of souls, has been almost entirely paralyzed with the beginning of the new era of colonization. (Loud applause.)

VICE PRESIDENT (DR. LIPPE) announces that Dr. Mintz appears to have been elected to the Actions Committee in Vienna, in the place of Dr. Birnbaum who withdrew.

DR. MINTZ: I declare my acceptance of the mandate bestowed on me and offer my heartfelt thanks that you have honored me with your confidence.

Kaminka's motion was adopted without further discussion.

BAMBUS: Honored assembly! It is no pleasant task to contradict, yet I am obliged to do so because I think what the preceding speaker, Rosenberg, has suggested does not correspond to the facts and should not be treated as though it were entirely determinative for future action. It is maintained that the Central Committee in Paris is poorly staffed and that it is oligarchically constituted. It is composed of delegates of the existing West European Palestine societies; i.e., authorized representatives. If for example the German society, with its twenty-five hundred members, elects its delegates to Central Committee in Paris, I cannot see why that should be viewed as oligarchic. If the gentlemen in Paris enjoy the trust of these thousands, I think that their conduct of affairs can hardly be termed oligarchic. If they do not satisfy the demands everyone is making of them, I remind you of the difficulties referred to today. These difficulties are undeniable. No one disputes them, but these gentlemen who have done the work must also not be condemned for not having accomplished more. They would certainly have accomplished more if these difficulties had not existed already for many years. I would like to declare openly and clearly that our colonization in its entirety has been experimental until today, and it will have to remain such for a long time. It is not possible to colonize a country such as this in twenty years, which has not been properly surveyed for agriculture. Colonization on a large scale could not be implemented even if there were no legal obstacles. It will still take many years. An experiment in agriculture takes years. We have made such experiments and should continue to make them. I believe that the first requirement is to continue the experiment. It is a preparation that is absolutely necessary. No one has demanded that we subordinate ourselves to the Central Committee in Paris, but we do demand that everything be handled with the consent of the existing societies. We certainly do not want to attack one other; rather we want to complement one another. Cooperative efforts will profit us more than unilateral ones. I also want to draw attention to an important point—it is the important issue of commerce and industry, which are also necessary. We can at present promote commerce and industry while we have to suspend agriculture. The marketing of Palestine's commercial products in Europe is likewise an issue of cardinal importance for further colonization. [181] Palestine produces a great many agricultural products; whoever is active in the sale of such products is at the same time providing for colonization. Colonization will be productive only if it is profitable. Our task is certainly not to promote commerce and industry in the Holy Land by means of charity; rather, it should be determined which branches of business are most profitable, so as not to paralyze private initiative and put everything under central control. We are counting on awakening the Palestine initiative of the individual, which we can do if we do not proceed according to a rigid model, but rather by stimulating the necessary competition through publicity in the newspapers and by offering aid to private individuals. The establishment of a bank has been contemplated for a long time, and it will probably also exist by the next Congress. True, the Jew in Palestine does not conform in every respect to the European spirit. True, and it is to be explained by the past history of those Jews. They are not acquainted with European cultural life. Therefore, it is of decisive significance that European Jews migrate there in greater numbers. The energy of West European Jews is needed by those who are there and if the commission proceeds in this direction, it will certainly accomplish very great things, and I hope that not everyone's activity will be focused solely on obtaining the permission to continue colonization, but also on making profitable use of it.

KAMINKA: I passed over the activity of the west European societies because I did not want to detain you. The question is certainly not about how much has been accomplished in quantitative terms. If the Congress appoints a committee now, it will in any case, as Herr Bambus intends, act in concert with both the Odessa and Paris committees* in order to remove difficulties, independently of the other goals which the Congress has set.

PRESIDENT: Honored Assembly! One thousand rosters have been printed, so there are more than enough to go around.
    (The rosters are distributed. Pause.)

STEINER: I would like to ask the assembly to return the rosters once again; they are completely wrong.
    (The rosters are gathered up again.)

DR. LÖWE*: I regret having to mount the podium because I want to say only a few words. I do not want to speak about colonization, since I have not yet spent as much time in Palestine as the gentlemen who have spoken today about it in such detail. For this reason I am not taking the liberty to bring before you the kind of statistical data as did the previous speakers. Herr Markus was so kind as to remind me that it is twenty-three years since the present Sultan ascended the throne.[14] I cannot help but affirm that we Jews of Palestine are obliged to this kindly ruler. I think that a representative of Palestine has the duty, while definitely keeping ourselves clear of idolatry, to call to mind those old warriors who struggled for Palestine, and we must admit that we would not be in Palestine if those men had not worked for us. [182] I must remind you, because it has been forgotten, that two Romanian Zionists are present here, who first struggled for our cause: Dr. Lippe and Pineles; I would like to express to them both my heartfelt thanks.

Although I am not officially a delegate, I have nonetheless been given the specific task by our brothers and sympathetic colleagues in Palestine of declaring that we take the same position as Zionists the world over and expressing this clearly here at the Congress. We are not expecting our wishes to be taken into account. If perchance the Congress were to cause the colonists to suffer, we will bear it gladly, as we have hitherto endured suffering for the sake of the restoration of the Jewish people, for the revival of the Jewish spirit. (Loud applause.) But let us not forget that passing judgment on current colonization is not so simple. There may be outsiders who allege that our colonization has been incorrectly managed. We are told that hundreds of years are perhaps needed, if we proceed in the old way of doing things.[15] Nevertheless, we are of the opinion that it is absolutely necessary to clarify our legal rights so we can pursue colonization on the broadest possible basis. We need to realize that colonization consists not only of agriculture; rather, every Jew immigrating to Palestine is a colonist. In this respect, much has already been accomplished. While we may not have succeeded thus far, nevertheless I would like to point out that not only are there six or seven thousand colonists in Palestine, but that we have many more colonists, that every Jew in Palestine is a colonist. We have *inter alia* in Jerusalem, by my calculation, forty thousand; in Hebron fifteen thousand; in Jaffa fifty-five hundred; in Tiberias four thousand; in the colonies seven thousand; in sum about seventy thousand Jews in Palestine. That is, out of a population of four to five hundred thousand inhabitants, 15 percent of the population. The increase in the population working in industry is as you know much more significant than that working in agriculture. We owe this increase above all to the position we occupy. I admit that the implementation of the laws is not the same as in Europe and also cannot be the same, just as there are countries in Europe where the laws are not so precisely implemented either. But it is precisely the government's protection which has led, despite many difficulties, to the vigorous development of our Jewish community. I would be the last one not to concede that there are serious wrongs in Palestine, but I know how to remove the bitter shell and find the sweet kernel within.

Coming to the matter of Halukka, I have to say that I am definitely not an opponent of it, and that it is not our business to do away with it. What is our business is not to give more direct assistance to the population, but rather to raise them up to higher levels by providing employment for the great majority who want to work. But there is a deep-seated evil in German and Austrian Halukka. Everyone receives so much that he can live on it. Distribution has to be made so that the Moroccan Jew and the Russian Jew are assisted in an equitable way. We should try to fund the settlement of poor Moroccan Jews out of those allocations which are benefitting only the well-to-do. We have in Jerusalem alone thirty thousand Jews who want to work and can work and are Turkish citizens. [183] The government even says that we are doing a work of which it is the primary beneficiary. I will cut short my remarks and just emphasize that the colonization of Palestine is at an experimental stage. It has been said by a great authority on agriculture: "We have worked for twenty years and still do not know all the agricultural systems which might be applicable." I would ask the Congress to keep this in mind as it does its work.

PRESIDENT: There is still a long line of speakers registered to speak.

DR. NEUMARK: I move: that, in view of the late hour and the important report about Hebrew literature still to be made, the suggestion of the rapporteur be put to a vote, and thereafter the rapporteur dealing with Hebrew literature be given the floor.

Neumark's motion is carried.

VICE PRESIDENT: The rapporteur concerning Hebrew language and literature has the floor.

DR. MARCUS EHRENPREIS (DIAKOVAR): Highly honored members of the Congress! I regret most deeply that this subject, in which we all have such a serious interest, is being dealt with only at the twelfth hour, as it were. I regret this all the more, since the issue of the national education of our youth deserved to have, within the context of my report, a detailed treatment. But the lateness of the hour makes it impossible for me to go into this issue, and I will also have to forego treating the actual subject of my report with the desired thoroughness I had originally intended. I will limit myself to a general justification of my proposals.

Gentlemen! I am to speak herein about the revival of the Hebrew language and literature; I am to supply evidence that the revival of the Hebrew language is inextricably connected to the rebirth of the Jewish people. The fact that here, at the First World Congress of Zionists, I have to speak to you in German about the Hebrew language, is the strongest proof of this connection. This is not a fantasy some doctrinaires have taken into their heads. The feeling lives within all of us that the Zionist solution to the Jewish question is about more than just bread. Many here have sought to bring to the fore the economic aspect of Zionism. But the Jewish question is certainly not just the question of hungry Jews, but also and to an equal extent that of well-fed Jews. Our Zionism is the consequence of a deep yearning for a purpose in life that is peculiarly ours. We want the schism within our souls to be healed. Our great cultural hunger is our great distress. And because our national spirit will be able to flourish only within its own peculiar forms, for this reason the Hebrew language must come to life once more. [184] We want to return to the Hebrew language just as we want to return to our historic homeland. As we all believe that we can properly celebrate our political resurrection only on the soil of Palestine, so the conviction lives in all of us that our spiritual rebirth is possible only in the context of the Hebrew language.

Our predecessors in the course of the last century had already arrived at this realization. Pre-Zionist Hebrew literature since the beginning of the emancipation of the Jews, is, taken as a whole, the expression of a latent Zionism. The Jewish people got homesick and began to speak Hebrew. I must unfortunately forego tracing this literary development even in its broadest outlines here. We have an indigenous Hebrew literature. Until now, people in Europe have not taken notice of our literary movement. Modern literary criticism occupies itself with the most insignificant amateur belletrists of emerging ethnicities—though for us Europe has neither ear nor eye. Naturally, it has been the cause of deep pain, that Europe has ignored the cry of our souls. We have our poets, scholars, publicists, pioneering spirits, who have shared our sorrows, shared our hopes, and shared the quiet yearning in our hearts. Who knows these great martyrs of the spirit? Just as the world is accustomed to treat all things Jewish with injustice, so people have likewise ignored our national intellectual life. And what pains us even more: even the majority of Jews are unfamiliar with this work. But things are beginning to change. Zionism, by its nature, has reawakened love of the Hebrew language. The augmented literary output proves this. Daily papers and periodical journals appearing in Russia and Palestine prove the astounding vitality and power of expression which the Hebrew language has attained in recent years. Moreover, two publishing houses are flourishing in Warsaw: "Achiassaf"* and "Tuschia." The financial statements of both these companies have been sent to me. Both have exceedingly positive achievements to their credit. To mention just one example, the Achiassaf company has already sold four thousand copies of the Hebrew translation of Lippert's* *History of Civilization*.¹⁶ And it is definitely not a generally accessible book. This also shows how great the demand for education is among our brothers in the East.

All of these efforts have been until now, like all Zionist activity, isolated and unorganized. But change is now on the way. Just as we have assembled here in order to give our entire movement a unified organization, we also want to see the revival of the Hebrew language go forward from now on in a methodical, well-organized way. This work will have to be, first and foremost, pedagogical. [185] It is crucial that instruction in Hebrew become an integral component in the education of our youth. To be sure, there are many parents who would gladly give their children instruction in Hebrew, but they lack the means. There are no teachers, no proper textbooks, no established method of instruction. Only a very few are in a position to surmount these obstacles. This is where our efforts really need to be concentrated. We need to create a central directorate tasked to set up free courses in Hebrew wherever feasible and where demand exists, and to handle the procuring of textbooks and readers. What I have in mind is the founding of a kind of general association of Hebrew schools, patterned after the German and Slavic School Associations.*¹⁷ I believe that establishing such an association of schools would be very easy to implement. Let us suppose that there are fifty thousand Jews in the entire world who are just as committed as we are to seeing the Hebrew language revived among our people; each one will pay a minimum annual contribution of about one franc. My dear gentlemen! With an annual income of fifty thousand francs, the association of Hebrew schools could support an impressive number of courses of instruction, publish textbooks, and promote new pedagogical products through prize competitions set for this purpose.

But even other, greater, and more serious tasks having to do with national education, could be assigned to this association. I have received very valuable suggestions and recommendations by various parties in this regard, which however, to my regret, I am not able to present. We have to content ourselves, in view of the advanced hour, to hand all of these projects over to the Executive Committee for their consideration. However, one proposal which I have to mention originates with Herr Dr. Schapira; Professor Schapira proposes the establishment of a Hebrew university in Jerusalem or Jaffa. (Loud applause.)

Dear gentlemen! I regret being unable to join you in applauding. To be sure, I wish with my whole heart, just as you do, to live to see the moment when we will have our own venue for cultivating scholarship on our own native soil; and certainly, I am also persuaded of the necessity of supplying our young people from all countries who are at university with a scholarly refuge where they can pursue their studies in a dignified way, free of the snubs and incitements of their Aryan colleagues; and finally, I too can certainly appreciate what a brilliant flowering of our entire intellectual life the founding of a Hebrew university would bring about. But gentlemen, where is the human material for this project at this time? [186] After all, we have to imagine students who have a secondary school education and at the same time possess a corresponding level of Hebrew. But such students do not exist, at least not many. It is perfectly obvious to me that we cannot talk about a Hebrew university while we do not have a *Gymnasium* where Hebrew is the language of instruction. That would be the second big assignment of the school association. We should proceed as soon as possible to expand, in stages, the existing four-level primary school in Jaffa into a *Gymnasium*. In this primary school Hebrew is the language of instruction and, from what we hear, the recently closed fourth class, the so-called Wysocki class, is to be reopened again soon. Consider, dear gentlemen, that educational conditions in Palestine make it imperative that we give special attention to the school system that exists there. The schools that have been founded in the Orient by the Parisian "Alliance" are for the most part nurseries of French assimilation. I regret to have to say it here, since we certainly have every reason to pay tribute to the Paris society for its efforts in the Orient. But, in the interest of truth, this reality must not be concealed. I have in hand several reports coming from reliable parties in Palestine, all of which concur in stating that the French spirit, and the cultivation of the French language, predominate in the schools of the Alliance. This fact has been confirmed to me by several persons who are present here, who have precise knowledge about the conditions of schools in Palestine. It is not my task to delve into what other motives might be at work here. But the fact remains. So the fact also remains that our most pressing task must be to provide a remedy. The Hebrew *Gymnasium* in Jaffa will paralyze this French influence. It constitutes the natural beginning of our national cultural work. Then stone upon stone will follow, until the proud building is completed. Along with it and at the same time, Hebrew literary production, with its lofty goals, will expand, and will educate the people for the great future of national independence.

I will conclude. In summarizing what has been said, I make the following two motions:

I. The Congress resolves to found a general association of Hebrew schools with the object of setting up free courses of instruction in the Hebrew language. The Hebrew committee to be elected is entrusted with the necessary preparatory steps.

II. The Congress will elect a Hebrew literature commission as a section of the Executive Committee, with the following tasks:

1. To support and establish Hebrew periodicals and to subsidize Hebrew books.
2. To promote young Hebrew authors and send them on educational missions.
[187] 3. Indeed, to provide for everything conducive to promoting the Hebrew language and its literature.

(A final appeal follows, in Hebrew.) (Loud applause.)

Dr. Rosenheck: Highly esteemed assembly! If I have taken the liberty to follow up on the speech of Herr Dr. Ehrenpreis with a few words, I have not done so intending to enter into a debate, for a debate on such a subject is as foolish as it is futile. I asked to speak in order to implore this noble Congress to adopt several brief resolutions, which we want to bring to the attention of the Actions Committee.

Highly esteemed assembly! As one of the representatives of the compact multitude of Galician Jews, I must state that in Galicia there are seven hundred and fifty thousand Jews who speak no language except Yiddish.[18] Notwithstanding, they have to pretend to use Polish as their colloquial tongue, even if they are not able to speak it. That is perhaps of incidental significance. After all, in the final analysis it is a borrowed language. It is therefore a matter of indifference whether one speaks Polish or Yiddish. However, Yiddish is written in the same characters as our holy language and it is, based on an old decree of Emperor Joseph, forbidden for Jewish script to be used for legal purposes. This prohibition has been upheld as a legal ordinance until the present. Yet another disadvantage arises from this. Because many are fluent in no language other than Yiddish, they often come into conflict with the law for this reason alone. They do not have permission to appear in court speaking their own language, even though they are a nationality recognized by the state, while other tiny minorities, like the Ruthenians in Bukovina, have been able to obtain it.[19] The Jew is therefore put into the awkward position of having to speak Polish or Ruthenian. I move the following:

This honorable Congress wishes to formulate the following resolution and refer it to the Actions Committee: 1. Courses specifically for instruction in Hebrew are to be set up by all Galician Zionist societies. 2. Efforts are to be made to have the Hebrew script legally recognized and to have Yiddish recognized as the language of the seven hundred and fifty thousand Jews so recognized by the state, so that the latter are not forced to use a foreign language but can use their own language to testify in court.

Professor Dr. Schapira: Most honored assembly! I would find myself in a very delicate position if I were to defend the idea I suggested, after the words of the preceding speaker have been received with such enthusiasm, as they have properly deserved to be: and it is quite impossible that I should augment still further the impact already made by those words concerning the Hebrew language. It is however such an important point that I cannot pass over it in silence. I had made a motion for the establishing of a college (not a university)[20] in Palestine:

> The Congress is requested to resolve to energetically implement the following plan:
>
> In the Jewish colonies to be founded in Palestine, a unified center is to be created for all efforts directed toward religious and moral education as well as the intellectual training of Jews. [188] This center is to be produced by establishing a college (beit midrash ha-torah ha-hokhmah ve ha-avodah) for the acquisition of religious, scientific, and practical knowledge, with one general, combined department and three major subdivisions:
>
> a. Theology Department.
> b. Department of Theoretical Sciences.
> c. Department of Technical and Agronomic Studies.

Since I have to accept at present, for the sake of time, that my motion not be taken up for discussion by the plenum, I do not wish to provoke a debate. I am in complete agreement that the motion be referred to the committee for discussion. But, because the point is very important, I would just like to be able to express what I have in mind.

I have been reproached for indulging in utopian fantasy by talking about a postsecondary institution when we still do not have primary schools.

Gentlemen! As a university instructor, would I not realize that a college cannot be opened without having the preparatory school? You are making a twofold error if you suppose this about me. In fact, I have emphatically not taken existing institutions, and the canonical categories of German *Gymnasium* and *Universität* and their programs, as a model. I have a very different idea about this school. I have a very different conception of a college, which is to offer training in independent research and other kinds of scholarly work, and in practical activities. But I would have to go into greater detail about my project to make this clear to you. This I cannot do here, nor do I wish to. However, as was expressed clearly in the bylaws of the Zionist society in Heidelberg, which was founded many years ago, it has to do with

> creating a unified center for all efforts directed at intellectual training in the Palestinian colonies that are to be established. It is to be produced by establishing a college for the acquisition of religious, scientific, and technical knowledge (a. theological; b. theoretical; and c. technical-agronomic departments).

Of course, what I also had in mind was, that if someone wishes to be educated at the beginning level, there also has to be support for this cultural level. But what we are lacking most is a center for our culture; and it is the creation of just such a center for all of the cultural issues faced by Jews in general that we are dealing with. The task is so great and complex, and also requires so much preparation, that I suggested it already twenty years ago, when as yet there existed no trace of colonies, although I knew that such a suggestion would seem utterly incredible at the time. But by and by many have come to understand what it would entail. In the course of years I have read and heard this proposal made repeatedly by various parties. People are beginning to grasp the importance of the matter.

[189] Now, gentlemen, you must realize that, if we really do understand what it entails, it will demand a very substantial work of preparation. To gear up for these labors was the main reason why I made this motion. I hand it over thus to the committee, to consider the task in its various aspects, and among other things also to enlist people in the production of textbooks in Hebrew for all subjects to be taught in this institute. The men who volunteer may wish to coordinate with me; I will gladly share information about it. These are pretty much the main points that I wanted to touch on in a tentative way. I hope to submit a more detailed project in the near future. May the promise be fulfilled for us: *ki mi-Zion tetze torah udvar Adonai mi-Yerushalayim.* (For

from Zion will go forth instruction and the word of God from Jerusalem.)[21] (Thunderous applause.)

BAHAR (speaks out of turn, which the presidency draws to his attention, whereupon he breaks off.)

VICE PRESIDENT: Dr Kaminka moves the closing of debate.
 Adopted.
 The motions made by Dr. Ehrenpreis with regard to founding a general association of Hebrew schools and organizing a standing committee for literature, are put to a vote and unanimously adopted.
 Consequently, the election to the literature commission is undertaken. The following gentlemen are deputized: E. Ben-Yehuda* (Jerusalem), Dr. M. Ehrenpreis (Diakovar), A. Ginzberg* (Odessa), Dr. A. Kaminka (Prague), N. Sokolow* (Warsaw).
 In the commission for practical colonization, the gentlemen elected are: W. Bambus, Dr. Kaminka, Dr. Mintz, Rubenstein,* Dr. Schnirer.
 Adjournment at 7:30 p.m.

Day Three, Evening Session
(beginning at 9:00 p.m.)

President: There are still some proposals pending, which seem to pertain to matters already decided on. I will read them out and then submit them to the commission.

The motion of Dr. Landau and Dr. Werner with regard to appointing a committee to ascertain occupational statistics for the Jews is referred to the Actions Committee.

S. Massel* (speaking in English.)[1]

President (translating): Herr Massel desires the uniting of the existing Hovevei Zion and other colonization societies with our movement. It is a desire we ourselves have. But I do not think it can happen by the Congress's action; rather, it would have to be the other way around.

[190] Dr. Cohn* (Rabbi of Basel) who is given a thunderous welcome as he mounts the podium: Honored assembly! You receive me with thunderous applause I have done nothing so far to deserve. I have not been a friend of Zionism and am still not, until now, inspired by this cause, which fills your heart with enthusiasm, as I can see. I thank you for inviting me to be your guest at your Congress. You have given me some unforgettable moments. When I remember the speeches of Dr. Herzl and Dr. Nordau, my heart swells with deep emotion. Any Orthodox Jew could endorse the speech of Dr. Nordau, word for word and line for line.

Many speeches have been given that I will not forget as long as I live; I am glad that the Congress was able to take place in Basel and I to attend it. I have been much enlightened about the distress of our brothers in the East, which I had no idea about. I have become acquainted with Zionism and seen that it is a movement we have altogether underestimated. (Tremendous applause.) I must once again refuse to accept the applause; I must make it clear that I am a religious Jew. My hope is that national Jewish identity will be the transition to religious Jewish identity.[2] I am coming to that which I was commissioned to present to the honorable presidency of the Congress.

You will find it baffling that in Germany the movement has made until now little progress, so to speak, that Orthodox rabbis in particular, to whom indeed everything related to Zion is treated with reverence, have approached Zionism with coolness. We Orthodox Jews have had so many bitter experiences in the course of these centuries—not because of Zionism but for other reasons—we have been all too often subject to assault. The child who has been burned fears the fire. We are afraid that if the Jewish state were to arise now, that its party leadership, which we know does not honor our views, would attack the Orthodox. Personally, I do not believe it. That is the explanation why the Orthodox have behaved with such coolness until now. In particular, Orthodox rabbis, as much as they are in sympathy with the colonization of Palestine, are afraid that in the settlements to be founded in the Holy Land, Jews might be forced to violate the sanctity of the Sabbath. They are afraid that, given the religious orientation of the majority, those might be favored who share the latter's viewpoint. If we could be satisfied about this point by an explicit declaration, the hesitation would cease, and we would make efforts to bring about, from among our colleagues, a reorientation toward Zionism. I ask the presidency for his opinion as to the position the Zionists propose to take with respect to this religious issue. (Applause.)

PRESIDENT: First of all, I thank His Honor, Herr Dr. Cohn, for his *bona fide* appearance as our erstwhile opponent, and for the frankness of his request, which I will certainly not attempt to respond to in detail. I can assure you, Zionism intends nothing that might violate the religious conviction of any orientation within Jewry. (Thunderous applause.)

As an addendum to one item of the agenda, I must make a brief observation. [191] In the course of the past year I have received many complaints from Palestine concerning grievances in the colonies. I think I am acting according to the wish of the majority of the Congress by not going into detailed treatment of these complaints, but leaving it to the commission to obtain a more detailed clarification. Our Congress has been conducted with such dignity that we do not want to introduce any discord. Difficulties exist everywhere, in all human undertakings, and likewise here. I think these grievances are taken into account by alluding to them.

We are now at the provisional conclusion of our work. We must first of all express our thanks to our host city, which has received us with such good will, to the government, which has given us various proofs of its sympathy, by facilitating preparations for the Congress and by the attendance of the cantonal government's president, Professor Dr. Paul Speiser,* during a portion of the proceedings. Furthermore, we must thank—which is certainly [not] in contradiction to the declaration to Herr Dr. Cohn[3]—the Christian Zionists, and in particular I mention the names of Mr. Dunant,* founder of the Red Cross, Rev. John Mitchell, Rev. Hechler* from Vienna, Baron Manteuffel,* Col. Count Bentinck, who also took part in our proceedings, and many others. Of course, we also want to remember the Jewish Zionists who worked on this project before us. Their names are known to us all, and permit me to embrace them all with our gratitude.

Gentlemen! I will conclude for the present. Permit me a few words more, of a personal nature. In presiding over these proceedings, I have been perhaps sometimes too weak and sometimes too strong, but I had good intentions and we have accomplished something significant. I believe that in many places people with Schadenfreude have been watching with expectation for the appearance of much folly and fanaticism. I believe that Zionism need not be ashamed of its First Congress. The Congress has been moderate but resolute. [We did not hide our devotion to our cause, yet we were not guilty of a damaging excess of emotion.][4] We cannot say how things will turn out in the future. But that we have done something significant for our people, who are suffering directly and indirectly, by assembling ourselves in this way to discuss their destiny—this is something not only we ourselves affirm, but also those outside this hall. If we want to put a plow in the hand of the downtrodden, does anyone dare ask if they would prefer labor to misery and defenselessness? Ask them, indeed! No, on the day when the plow rests once again in the newly strengthened hand of the Jewish farmer, the Jewish question will have been solved. (Applause lasting several minutes.)

Professor Dr. Max Mandelstamm (Kiev): Most esteemed ladies and gentlemen! I believe that I act in accord with countless numbers of my countrymen and all of the members of the Congress, when I hereby express our deeply felt thanks to the men who, with a great readiness to sacrifice and by the exertion of their moral and physical powers, have guided the preparations and proceedings. First, to all the members of the provisional committees. Next, to that "great man in Israel,"[5] who has been able to give profound and heart-stirring expression to our two-thousand-year old sorrow. I mean Herr Dr. Max Nordau.[6] [192] But first and foremost, to the courageous man to whom we principally owe our thanks, that we are assembled here from all over the world to provide for the future of our people. I mean the highly esteemed president of the Congress, Herr Dr. Theodor Herzl. (The assembled rise from their seats and burst forth in cheering.) Likewise, I believe that I speak for the members of the Congress when I ask earnestly of the most esteemed Herr President, that the hard labor which he is performing and which still awaits him, and also the irksome things that have befallen him and are yet to befall him—that these should not keep him from bringing to a victorious conclusion the difficult work that has been initiated, in the same way, with the same spirit, and the same joyous self-sacrifice. Long live the president of the First Congress of Zionists, Herr Dr. Theodor Herzl! (Thunderous applause.)

PRESIDENT: The First Congress of Zionists is over. (Tremendous peals of applause in the entire hall, and in the galleries.)

[193] APPENDIX

Incoming Messages

PETITIONS[i]

2,654 petitioners from Galicia and Bukovina have addressed themselves to the Congress, representing a group totaling 15,459, specifically from the following cities and towns: Bohorodzany, Boryslaw, Brody, Buczacz, Bukaczowce, Czortkow, Drohobycz, Dubiceko, Dynow, Grodek, Halicz, Horodenka, Jablonow, Jagielnica, Jaroslaw, Jaryszow, Jaworno, Jazlowice, Kalusz, Korolowka, Lemberg, Oest.-Novosielitza, Pilzno, Pruchnik, Przemysl, Radautz, Radlow, Radziechow, Ropczyce, Rozniatow, Rymanow, Rzeszow, Sniatyn, Stanislau, Storozynetz, Tarnobrzeg, Tarnów, Tlumacz, Tluste, Tuchow, Ustřyki, Zaleszczyki, Zbaraz, Zurawno.

The text of the Galician-Bukovinan petitions is found on page [109] of these proceedings.

5,258 petitions were received from Romania, corresponding to a group numbering 37,043, specifically from these cities and localities: Adjut, Alexandria, Bacau, Bazesti, Basien, Beresti, Birvola, Botusani, Braila, Bucecea, Bucharest, Burdujan, Buzien, Constanza, Craiova, Dragermaret, Draguseni, Foltischemi, Fokschani, Frumsa, Galatz, Ganesti, Giurgiu, Horlan, Husi, Jassy, Igalie, Isocca, Jvesti, Macui, Maizanesti, Machuriti, Moinesti, Odobesti, Murgeni Karya, Palea Rea, Pancesti, Pancui, Pascani, Piatra, Piatra N., Piteschti, Plojesti, Podu Iloi, Puciosa, Radanti Roma, Radaceni, Roman, Rogdana, Rosnov, Sarat, Sascut, Simonesti, Sitov. Sulitza, Suneni, Staninesti, Stefanesti, Targaviste, Talpa, Takutsch, Tg. Niamtz,

---

i   The petitions from Russia are counted together with the messages of greetings [see #2, "Greetings"].

Tg. Frumos, Tg. Ocna, Turnu Magurel, Tefurnus, Tetschinciu, Tulcea, Vadeni, Vaslui.[ii]

The Romanian petitions have the following text:

"To the honorable Zionists' Congress" in Munich.

I the undersigned ask the honorable Congress to receive me among the number of..., to be settled in Palestine.

I have at my disposal assets... comprising.... I am going at my own expense and risk, or with expenses covered by the "Zionists." My family consists of, as given in detail elsewhere; i.e., the number of persons is.... I am travelling on my own initiative because I and my family do not foresee having either a livelihood or a future in Romania.

I am ready to obey the call of the Zionists, in accord with the decision of the Congress, and will not object to the fixing of a date for me and my family to be transported, holding no one else responsible for this.

I ask only that the honorable Congress receive me among those to be settled in Palestine, under adequate international and constitutional guarantees, and that the Congress take steps with respect to His Majesty the Sultan, to attract the support of the powers and of the public opinion of Europe, and to cause the necessary funds to be raised.

GREETINGS

TELEGRAMS

Argentina

Buenos Aires, Choveve Zion, President, Eng. Son.

[194] *Bulgaria*

Philippopel. Pro-Zionist Colleagues of Philippopel — Eng. Schamlajewski.

---

ii   The above list of place names is given as found in the German text with some exceptions for well-known English place names (e.g., Bucharest [Ger. "Bukarest"]). The reader will recall that German *w* corresponds to English *v* and *j* to *y*, and also that Slavic spellings of these names often differ quite substantially from their traditional spelling in either German or English when searching for their location on contemporary maps.

Rustschuk. Zion. Committee, Mair Covo, Jacob Behdjet, Josef Benisch, Boneo Roschnak, David Benyes, Mayr Sloy, Nissim Naniel, Jacob Maschiath, Jachiel Choew.

Sofia. Chief Rabbi—Eng. Deutsch, Dr. Bierer, Blumenthal, Negler, Löwinger, Donovici, Rath, Ludmir, Friedmann—Central Society, "Zion."—Zionist National Committee of Bulgaria—Ashkenazi Congregation, Eisenberg, Eisenschreiber, Horn, Herschkowitz, Kohn, Kupferwasser, Nathanson, Silberstein, Schutzmann.

Germany

Berlin. Golmann, university student.
Breslau. Dr. Finkl.
Cologne. Jewish Nationalist Union—Saul Chim.
Cottbus. Jewish-nationalist *Gymnasium* Students.
Danzig. Pro-Zionist Colleagues of Danzig.
Darmstadt. "Kadimah" Society.
Eydkuhnen. Dowgoleitzky Albert, Simon Goldberg, Gordon Lehrer.
Königsberg. Pro-Zionist Colleagues of Königsberg.
Magdeburg. Hermann, Max. Ludwig Schiller, Family Geis, Philipp Meier, David Glauber, Louis and Eduard Löwe.
Memel. Scheinhaus—Rubin—Dr. Rülf—Sally Wolffsohn.
Munich. Felix Perles.
Norderney. A. Horodisch—Samuel Rappoport.
Schwirwind. Jecheskiel Friedmann.
Westerland. Leon Horowitz.

Great Britain

Belfast. Belfast Zionist.
Birmingham. Mozzult Birmingham.
Bournemouth. Dr. M. Gaster.
Edinburgh. Jewish in Edinburgh Rev. paterson [sic].
Glasgow. Glasgow Jews.
Leeds. Leeds Zionist—Hebrew Literature Society.
Liverpool. Ancient Order of Maccabaens, Liverpool—Isaak Blacks.
London. Ancient Order of Maccabaens, London—Hebbleth waite—Bnei Zion.
Manchester. Manchester Zionist.

Rochester. Rochester Hebrew School.
Southampton. Robert Bentwich.

Italy

Rome. Marco Baruch—Pro-Zionist Colleagues.

Austria-Hungary (excluding Galicia and Bukovina)

Aussee. Paul Naschauer.
Baden bei Wien. Loebl.
Bielitz. "Emunah."
Brünn. Independent "Zion" Society. Chairman Loewenstein—Academic associations, "Veritas," "Zephirah."
Diakova. Jewish Congregational Council President, Dr. Spitzer, Hermann Kohn, Jul. Mahler, Jacob Fuchs, Chief Cantor Waissmann, Moritz Guttmann, Josef Herzler, Elias Schwarz.
Dux. Dr. Albert Fischl, Otto Taussig.
Falkenau bei Eger. Leopold Kohn.
Franzensbad. L. Reich.
Ischl. Dr. Karl Pollak.
Kanitz. "Astra," Frey.
Karoly Falva. Jacques Gerle, Royal Hungarian Circuit Judge.
Karlsbad. Fassel.
Kattowitz. Meruk.
[195] Kaumberg. "Zion," President Meisels.
Krottoschin. Isidor Dobrzynski.
Mondsee. Prince Friedrich Wrede.
Marienbad. W. Wissocky, M. Eliasberg.
Oderberg. Dr. Beer.
Olmütz. "Zion" branch.
Prague. Prague's Pro-Zionist Colleagues.
Salzburg. Max Kohn, Ernst Heller, Max Schacht.
Teschen. Dr. Adolf Leimdörfer.
Temes-Kubin. Regina Nadasy, Moritz Reiner, Bernh. Hajduschka.
Virovitica. Dr. Kaufmann.
Vienna. Dr. Smollis—Isid Polascek—N. Pineles—Independent "Favorites" Society—Jonas Willheimer—Silberbusch—"Ivria."—Zwischenbrücker Jews—thirty-five jewelers and dealers in manufactured goods—Dr. Kokesch, Dr. S. Werner. Dr. Jul.

and L. Werner, Frau Dr. Kornfeld, Dr. Schwarz, Dr. Goldberg, Dr. Kreysling and Dr. Brod—Leon Weiss, Heinrich Bard, Simon Dresdner—Max Jaffe—Dr. A. Marmorek—"Moria."—Depskin.
Zaymoni. M. Chon.

Austria (Galicia and Bukovina)

Bolechow. Jewish Youth—Tikwath Israel, President Blumenfeld.
Bohorodzany. Esrath Israel.
Boryslaw. "Ahawath Zion," Chaim Friedmann, Aron Wechsel, Chairmen.
Brody. Jewish Youth.
Brzezany. "Bnei Zion," Maiblum, President, Falk, Vice-President.
Czorikow. Bnei Zion.
Drohobycz. Israel Ernst—Zion—J.F. Lauterbach—Selig Spieler—H.O. Hermann—Schreier Bernhard—Feiwel Lauterbach, Michael Zwangheim—Zionist Youth. — M. Feuerstein. A. Schreier.
Dolina. Juda Leib Littwak.
Dubienko. Samuel Philipp, landed proprietor.
Glyniany. Chaim Barall, S. Ungar, Heinrich Mehlmann—Coreligionists of Glyniany.
Horodenko. Zionists.
Jablonow. Abraham Kenner—Salomon Hecht—Salomon Sack.
Jaroslau. Bnei Zion—Dr. Kormany—Academic Association, "Bnei Zion."
Jaremcze. Dr. Sam. Schoor, Isid. Ettinger, J. Lurie, J. Landau, Max Lurie, Herscherr.
Jaworzno. Local committee of Ahawath Zion.
Krakau. Choveve Erez Israel—Sam. Leib Ornstein—Dr. Leopold Bader.
Kolomea. Halle, Merchant—M. Schaffer—Sussmann Fischbach—Jacob Baydoff—Anselm Büschel—Feiwel Wuhl—Löbel Taubes—Osias Fadenhecht—M. Rothfeld—Aron Shuster and Wife—Littmann Soicher. Ch. Drimmer—Dr. Schuster—Dr. Lazar Zipper—Jonas Kiesler—Mendel Friedmann.
Kossow. David Iltis, Jonas Schutzmann, S.A. Häusler, Jacob J. Munk.
Lanout. Leib Glanzer—Eisig Pasternak—Hirsch Tannebaum—H. Ramer—Local committee of Ahawath Zion.
Lemberg. Juda Leo Landau—K. Auerbach—J. Mayer, university student—Josef Sprecher—Carl Stand—Lemberg Zionist Youth—Caroline Lourie, Bronislawa, Grünberg, Nesia Geierberg—Party committee of the Society

of Zionists—Moses Ewinger—Emil Silberstein—Galician Zionist Party Directorate—D. Schreiber, Zion—Dr. Berdyczewski—President of "Ahawath Zion," Jul. Hirtfeld—E. Heiner—Moses Rohatin—Jacob Ehrlich—"Pryslosc" Administration—"Ivria," President, A. Schorr, Secretary, S. Schorr—O. Baseches.

Monasterzyska. Löblich, Halpern, Lilienfeld, Aron Kupfer—Monasterzyska Zionists—Michael Kornblüh, Schaje Safrin, Hillel Hessel, Salomon Safrin, Josef Safrin, Berhard Safrin.

Ozydow. M.L. Tempel.

Pilzno. Dr. Kornhäuser.

[196] Podgorze. Jacob M. Marcus—Sal. Marcus—Pinkas Silberfeld. S. Cohen— Sturzmann—N. Meierstam—M.D. Brafmann—Josef Schenker—H. Silberfeld—Simon Borgenicht—Menasche Sperling.

Przemysl. Feiwel Eisig, H. Brandmark—Aron Mayer, Israel Freiwillig—Isidor Mahler—A newly formed Jewish assembly—Leo Stierer—Avigdor Mermelstein.

Rohatyn. Nagelberg—Ahawath Zion—Bnei Zion—Schalom Melzer.

Rymanow. Jacob Lerner Pelzig, for the congregation.

Rzeszow. Chowewe Zion.

Ropczyce. Moses Stern—J.L. Koretz.

Radauiz. Rabbi Schapira.

Siobodo. Neiger Lippe.

Stanislau. Erez Israel.

Solka. Zion-Committee.

Sanow. N. Segall.

Sniatyn. Zionists.

Slatina. Zionist members of the congregation.

Skole. Dr. E Friedländer—Moses Sterner, university student—Dr. Rosa Feuerstein—Julie Fränkel. "Dorsche Mada" Society, Dr. Friedlander, Dr. Kräuterblüh, Engel, Halpern, Klein—A newly formed assembly—Dr. Hescheles—A Jewish socialist—Jacob Korkis.

Stryj. Jehuda L. Schönfeld—Local committee—Abner Katz—Zionist preparatory school students—Ch. Memeles—Eberhard Brothers—Dr. Nadel.

Tarnów. Dr. Rost—D. Flamm—Lichtblau family—Ahawath Zion.

Tarnopol. Bnei Zion—Rosa Pomeranz—Jewish Youth.

Tlumacz. Society of Zionists.

Tarnobrzeg. A. Plasznik. M. Bander, Hrboni. Bienenstock, M. Leibel—Jechiel Lamm. — "Erez Israel" Society.

Tiuste. Zion.

Ustrzyki dolne. Ch. J. Eis—Moses Ernst.
Zbaracz. Josef Süssermann.
Zloczow. Schwadron, for many Zionists.
Zolynia. Dr. Lancs.

Romania

Bacau. Societate bickur cholim—Choveve Zion—Kraus, Klein.
Berlad. Choveve Zion—Lazar Zisser.
Braila. Braila Zionists.
Bucecea. Michael Grauer.
Bucharest. Choveve Zion—Brociner—Asiel, Editor—Bucharest University students: Stern, Rosenberg, Brillant, Schönberger, Lazarowitsch— Aron Zwiebel—Zionist Society, President, Dr. Lupescu, Vice President, Silberstein— Josef Zwiebel. — Ch. Segall— one hundred enthusiastic Zionists.
Botosani. For the assembly of one thousand coreligionists: Leon Goldschläger, Isr. Mises, Josef Sussmann, Weintraub, Schächter, Isak Ficker, Alter Tauber, Elias Kohn. — Bnei Zion.
Butschesti. Rabbi M. Margulies.
Constanca. Choveve Zion.
Craiova. Choveve Zion, President Jacobsohn.
Dorohoi. Choveve Zion.
Galatz. Jewish Craftsmen Union—House-painters Union—Tailors' Assistants Union—Israel. Apprentice Craftsmen Union—President, Jewish Congregation, J. Goldberg—H.H. Cohen.
Haskovo. Committee of Zionists.
Jassy. Choveve Zion—Committee of Zionists—"Ohole Schem" Society.
Piatra. Marc. Engelberg, Bernhard and Nath. Weinmann—Bnei Zion— Choveve Zion. Samsony—Abr.Itel, Schorr Daniel.
Piatra N. Choveve Zion.
Philibe. Romano, Attorney at Law.
Ploiesti. Union of Zionists—M. Neuman.
Pescau. Pres. Shlechter.
[197] Piteschti. Moritz Neuburger.
Plojeschtl. Rabbi Breizis.
Roman. Choveve Zion.
Tulcea. Goldring, for the Zionists—Sam. Ellmann.
Turn-Severin. Loge Stern.

Russia

From twenty-two localities, thirty-eight telegrams from forty-five private individuals and twenty-five organizations arrived.

Switzerland

Lucerne. Abraham Weil.

Serbia

Belgrade. Belgrade Zionists.

Turkey

Pera. Mayer.

U.S.A.

Baltimore. Chovevei Zion.
Boston. Boston Zionist.
Brooklyn. Brooklyn Zionist—Plenary session of the Choveve Zion—Dr. Singer, Guillof, Roth, Waizner.
San Francisco. Jsidore Wyers—Ephraim Deynard.

WRITTEN COMMUNICATIONS

Bulgaria

Saskovo. "Doresh le Zion" Society, Jehuda Benbassat, N. Geron.
Sophia. B. Tunokemer, L. Reitzer, S. Sternberg, S. Abramowsk, J. Spettey, A. Grünberg, L. Marku, M. Jost, J. Gasch, A. Laxemburg, Jakub Moseef, M. Becus, Pollak, H. Asen, Lupu Ornstein, S. Ornstein, N. Gaster, J. Flaschner, Dr. Ruben Bierer, Ad. Hess, J.W. Löwinger, Levi Friedmann, M. Brunner, M. Düssburg, M. Ratt, M. Feldhendler, Murko Wilzkowsky, M. Ornstein, Wilhelm Leidinger, Juda Steiner, Merland, A. Lieblich, Rubinstein, Boris Goldstein, V. Michelsohn, Josef Löwinger, Simon Gaster, Heinrich Dunowitz, Dietrich Löwy, G. Schwarz, Hermann Löwinger, Sigmund Unger—Don Pessach Ivio.

Germany

Berlin. Friedrich Heinrich Müller.
Memel. Chaim Ferkus, Israel Rabinowitz.

Soden. Noah Finkelstein.

France

Paris. R. Maller—Association des Étudiants Israelites Russes.

Great Britain

London. D.M. Gaster, Chief Rabbi of the Spanish and Portuguese Congregations of Great Britain—David Wolffe—C.B. Halvay.
Montreal (Canada). Lazarus Cohen.

Italy

Bagni di S. Giuliano. M.C. Lewis.
Mondovia. Dr. Felice Momighirno.
Rome. Josef Marco Baruch.

Austria-Hungary

Auspitz. Sigm. Löwy, Josef Knöpfelmacher, S. Redlich, Assistant Engineer, Dr. Riehs M. Knöpfelmacher, Johann Redlich, Josef Hirsch Redlich, Assistant Physician, L. Riehs, Bertha Benedikt, Wilhelm Abeles, Jakob Eisinger, Adolf Fink, L. Kratianer, Adolf Zaitschek, Emanuel Eisinger, Jakob M. Eisinger, Max Drucker, G. Werner, Adolf Redlich.

[198] Alt-Neu-Jóve. Israelite "Daughter" Congregation. Josef Breuer.

Austerlitz. Ig. Krampilcek, Josef Strach, Samuel Kollek, Ed. Korischoner, Jakob Strach, Sigm. Rehuick, Lustig, L. Schönburg, Moriz Huss, Michael Korperl, Arnold Engelsroth, Josef Koller, Moriz Klar, Josef Reifler, Ig. Zack, Ed. Fischer, Julus Fürst, Adolf Jellinek, Jonas Hikl, Jakob Jellinek, Johann Mandl, S. Diamant, Dr. Beer, Sig. Weinstein, Heinr. Flesch, S. Weinstein, H. Kuhner, Leopold Eppstein, Moriz Preiss, Dr. Schimatschek, Arnold Korperl, S. Haulinger.

Boskowitz. H. Spielmann, Hatschek, Moriz Basch, Simon Wolkenstein, Robert Gach, Alfred Basch, Leopold M. Basch, Max Eisler, Daniel Markus, Julius Tichy, Karl Springer, Oskar Basch, Leopold Calmus, Jakob Grüner, S. Fried, Daniel Spielmann, Julius Rischou, Alois Eisenstein, Max Fuchs, Beer, Daniel Kurz, N. Fest, Richard Basch, J. Knöpfelmacher, Moriz Zeid, Heinrich Färber, Adolf Tychof, Josef Schwarz, Josef Mayer, Moriz Mayer, Ignaz Bix.

Brünn. Dr. Löwenstein, Dr. Weiner, Ludwig Strasser, Eng. Teichner Arthur, Berthold Feiwel, H. Wilhelm, N. Jork Steiner, W. Sonderling, Josef Feiwel,

R. Freund, Ernst Feiwel, Adolf Taussig, Jaques Feuereisen, Juda Wiesner, Broth, A. Weinberg, Berth. Tintner, Th. Sommer, J. Bix, Rudolf Deutsch, Rudolf Zeisel, Robert Löwenberg, Max Pick, Oscar Lewith, Eng. Ig. Hajek, Dr. S. Kornfeld, S. Hönigsfeld, M. Kirschner, Emil Afran, Leo Schönbeck, Julius Ponner, J. Kohn, J. Feiwel, M. Huber, J. Jeiteles, D. Taussig, J. Mömel, B. Epstein, D. Engel, L. Rosenzweig, S. Lustig, B. Oberländer, S. Grätzer, F. Politzer, A. Schallinger, R. Steiner, A. Steiner, M. Hickl, O. Hüttner, S. Bock, S. Czeczewiczka, O. Krämer, A. Lustig, R. Nassau, E. Glaser, W. Guber, R. Munk, H. Strasser, Rosa Strasser, A. Taussig, H. Lamez, D. Strasser, J. Ekler, A. Friedmann, L. Schlesinger, Hartmann, O. Neumann, Oppenheim, R. Stricker, A. Munk.

Dees. Dr. Nathan Friedländer.

Eibenschitz. David Sinaiberger, Jewish Congregational Council President, Is. Steiner, Congregational Council, Max Sinaiberger, Ludwig Weiss, Jakob Ehrlich, Ed. Jellinek, Moriz Samek, J. Samek, Schallinger, Gustak Samek, Moriz Goldmann, Jakob Gerstmann, Julius Waldmann, Senior Instructor, Georg Fischer, Moriz Finger, Ignaz Sinaiberger, Dr. Hahndl, Samuel Meier, Mayor, Eduard Sinaiberger, Dr. Weiss, Moriz Jellinek, Wolf Jellinek, Gustav Stein, Moriz Schallinger, G. Schallinger, Leopold Skutetzky, Jenjö Schallinger, Friedrich Siegmund, Alois Graisetzer, Congregational Council, Samuel Feldmann, Simon Hampl, Alex. Stern, Samuel Pretzner, Herm. Wilkowitsch, Cantor, Albert Jellinek, Ed. Wiltschek, Adolf Weinberger, Gerson Friedrich, Leopold Sinaiberger, Alois Pollak, Wilhelm Löwenstein, Senior Cantor, Ignaz Černovsky, Bernhard Freiberger, Moriz Löwensohn, R. Neubauer, Salomon Katz.

Göding. Moriz Ullman, Instructor in Religion, Sam. Wudak, Franz Weiss, Leopold Holzmann, S. Spitz, H. Samstag, Max Seidler, Em. Feuer, Arthur Weinberger, Emanuel Fanto, Marcus Früh, Adolf Morgenstern, Bernh. Körner, Josef Winterstern, Arnold Kornfeld, Adolf Wodak, Alois Schlesinger, E. Müller, Simon Merk, Hermann Fleissig, Bernhard Kohn, Karl Körner, Adolf Jokl, Alois Fischer, Simon Fischer, Ignaz Wasservogl, Cantor Ig. Schmidt, R. Mondschein, Weiss, Arthur Feuer.

Kanitz. Jewish Congregation. Jewish Congregational Council President, Sigm. Haas. — For the Academic-Holiday Fraternity, "Astra," Josef Frey.

Kostel. Josef Eisinger, Headmaster (serving in a private school), Siegfried Eisinger, Hermann Eisinger, Jakob Eisinger, Berthold Eisinger, Bernhard Eisinger, Johann Neumann, Hermann Glasspiegel, Adolf Löwy, Adolf Kohnberger, Josef Hirsch, Josef M. Eisinger, Emanuel Blau, Cantor, Jakob

Löwi, Heinrich Neumann, Emanuel Neumann, Alois Vielgut, Julius Löwy, Salomon Eisinger.

Kremsier. Karl Liebmann, Jewish Congregational Council President, Rudolf Pollak, Vice President of the Jewish Congregation, Magister Pollak, Practicing Physician, Michael Vogel, Instructor, Bernhard Baumgarten, Instructor.

Lomnitz. Josef Steinhauer, Adolf Spitz, Wilhelm Elsner, Josef Deutsch Sr., Leopold Bauer, David Zeisel, Josef Sagher, Moriz Lieber, Josef Deutsch, Leopold Gerstmann, Dr. Simon Wolfsohn, Rabbi.

[199] Märisch-Weisskirchen. In the name of seven hundred Jewish citizens, Alois Riesenheld as chairman, Rudolf Löwy as secretary.

Nachod. Dr. H. Goitein, Rabbi.

Olmütz. In the name of the citizens and students: S. Zweig, Brucker.

Prague. Ben Israel.

Ung.-Hradisch. Schallinger, Physician, Dawid Zweigenthal, Jakob Krenn, Isidor Donnat, Hermann Spiegler, Moriz Schmitz, Alois Grohslicht, Samuel Weiss, Rudolf Winter, Max Kaiser, Alois Zweigenthal, Ed. Weitzmann, Jakob Ehrenfreund, Katharina Ehrenfreund, Josef Lamberg, Eduard Winter, Josef Klinger, Jewish Academic-Holiday Fraternity, "Achiwa."

Vienna. In the name of the Academic Association, "Libanonia": K. Altmann, Th. Müller—Emil Jellinek—Michael Pasto, Rabbi of the Turkish congregation.

Austria (Galicia and Bukovina)

Brzezany. Towarzystwo "Bnei Zion."

Buczacz. Editors, "Sifre schaaschujim."

Czemichowce near Zbaraz. Wolf Goldfisch, Jechiel Schwarz, J. Wahrhaftig, A. Teitelbaum (plus three illegible names.)

Czortków. Berisch Meinhart—Aron Szwarz, Hersch Blank, Berl Hausner Jr., Szachne Bergmann, Alter Knecht, Chaim Israel Kornbluth, Simche Rintel, Moses Szeinhaut, Meschel Glaser, Gerson Leib Weissmann, Chaim Dawid Girnberg, Mechel Hornstein, Hersch Platzmann, Osias Altmann, Ele Winkler, Elias Hersch Timer, Nuchim Bezner, Moses Salzbach, Meyer Hellerbach, Mordchy Skalka, Menachim Altnaj, Josef Buchberg, Chaim Herz Trembowler, Meyer Rath, Aba Hellmann, Salomon Hersch Sonnenschein, Osias Klesmer, Hersch Schwarzbard, Abraham Kornblüth, Menachim Silbermann, Isak Elias Bäcker, Aron Kirschner, Rachmiel

Grünspann, Dawid Bäumer, Ivel Reiss, Chaim Hersch Hellmann, Josel Heller, Mendel Getter, Jacob Kirschner, Samul Winter, Simon Hölzel, Szaja Szlojmy Fischthal, Samuel Altman, Elias Myer Tunys, Dawid Barbar, Isak Reiss, Mendel J. Szweiger, Marcus Glaser, Jona Weingast, Salmen Rosenblum, Szapse Reinstein, Salomon Erberger, Samuel Katz, Israel Getter, Juda Leib Herzog, Wolf Getter, Tobie Szwarz, Nusen Hellerbach, Moses Sonnenschein, Hersch Gründlinger, Meyer Lande, Samuel Leon Szorr, Samuel Korn, Isak Finkelmann, Wolf Bodinger, Rubin Knecht, Jacób Leib Szwarz, Kopel Strudel, Mechel Sane Freimann, Moses Rosenblum, Baruch Hersch Rost, Mechel Platzmann, Leib Rost, Salomon Szön, Rubin Preminger, Benzion Rauch, Mojsche Reiss, Salomon Stadmann, Joel Hausner, Leiser Salzinger, Israel Tafler, Juda Fränkel, Eisig Bodinger, Josef Hellmann, Samuel Kanel, Hersch Winter, Meyer Margulies, Mendel Tischler, Meilach Raucher, Nussen Hellerbach, Mendel Sonnenschein, Abraham Kornbluth, Chaim Sonnenschein, Samuel Leib Bilman, Moses Szlomowicz, Dawid Rothleder, Nachman Hersch Blitz, Isak Wolf Blitz, Samuel Blitz, Isak Fleischmann, Salomon Aszkenas, Mendel Falik, Samuel Falik, Josef Buchberg, Chaim Hersch Hellmann, Jacob Zwieback, Moses Lande, Marcus Glatter, Dawid Hölzel, Isak Hausner, Israel Hausner, Mechel Hausner, Marcus Szwarz, Hersch Axelrad, Josef Rubel, Hersch Goldstein, Nuchim Stöckel, Jonas Rosenzweig, Juda Szächter, Beisach Atman, Chaim Horowitz, Josef Geizer, Hersch Barbar, Eisig Kleinmann, Samuel Nussenbaum, Chaim Mechel Elling, Moses Chane, Jägerndorf, Chanine Gerstner, Samuel Margulies, Mechel Pomeranz, Josef Weinraub, Hersch Leib Fuchs, Hildl Hausner, Osias Kruh, Jacob Ostersetzer, Leon Rosenzweig, Moses Szorr, Dawid Seiden, Dawid Elling, Josef Margulies, Isak Königsberg, Leib Szwebel, Chaim Rost, Hersch Weissmann, Abraham Nussenbaum, Mechel Nussenbaum, Mechel Hornstein, Simson Fischer, Chaim Blitz, Isak Elias Bäcker, Isak Szeukelbach, Josef Szwarz, Hillel Hausner, Gedalie Kohn, Don Rosenzweig, Kalmen, Sommerschein, Israel Sonnenschein, Dawid Sonnenschein, Abraham Harlig, Meyer Szwarz, Mendel Rosenzweig, Jona Zachmann, Jacob Hausner, Berl Hausner, Samuel Axelrad, Israel J. Rosenzweig, Samuel Lande, Elias Gramm, Israel Chaim Meinhard, Leon Kronrad, Isak Rosenblatt, Hermann Tater, Leibisch Diftler, Simon Skalka, [200] Psachie Rosenblatt, Berl Jäger, Dawid Pollak, Hersch Weissmann, S. Jolles, Moses Weissmann, Ch. Mandler, H. Barbar, Jacob Leib Handschuh, Nachmen Chajet, Jacob Dawid Rubin, Abraham

Salzinger, Leiser Bruckner, Moses Berl Lande, Marcus Sternlieb, M. Eder, Chain Osia Neid, Osias Lande.

Drohobycz. Local chapter, "Ahawas Zion."

Gologory. Rabbi Lazar Mischel.

Jaworno. Feiwel Gross, Josef Gross, Aron Jüzger, A. Silberschatz, R. Klein from Pogorze.

Krakau. G.L. Horowitz, Deputy Rabbi—Julius Schönwetter.

Lemberg. Ida Moritz—Žyd ze Lwowa [Jew of Lvov]—Elias Grünberg.

Lubien wielky near Lemerg. In the name of the patients at the spa: Samuel Wassermann.

Radlow. Local chapter of the "Ahawas Zion" Society.

Rohatyn. Chamber of Commerce.

Rozniatow. Local chapter of "Ahawas Zion."

Roznow. Salomon Okner.

Sereth. Pinkus Burstyn, District Rabbi, Kalmann Hecht, Tobias Hecht, Dr. Benkendorf, Samuel Rappaport, Akiba Schreiber, Feiwel Lenzer, Peltz Weinlaub, Israel Zelter, Leib Peretz, David Achselrod, Max Schulbaum, Mendel Rittersporn, Isaak W. Wielach, Eisig Sommer, David Gottesmann, Mendel Gottesmann, Mendel Klein, Atter Schäffer, Marcus Bal, Feibisch Klinger, Julius Auerbach, Abraham Beer, Marcus Wechsler, Jakob Wolf Gabe, Mendel Kaczer, Benj. Horowitz, Wolf Goldschläger, Meier Klein, Alex. Goldschläger, Israel Händler, Jakob Stetter, Moses Meier, Isaak Jamfolsky, Isaak Klein, Benj. Medler, Schulem Hajek, Isaak Rosenkranz, Meilech Gleichner, Abraham Blaufeld, Mechel Weidenfeld, Elias Berler, Abr. Beer, Hersch Weintraub, Juda Dawids, Jakob Weutuch, Moses Goldschläger, Jakob Nadler, Jonas Berger, Elias Fleischer.

Stanislau. J.L. Zweig.

Stryj. A.J. Kreis.

Stryjewka near Zbaratz. Salomo Horowitz, Pinchas Horowitz, Elieser Auerbach, David Schafkopf, S. Friedmann, plus two illegible names.

Ustrzyki dolne. Fifty mostly illegible Hebrew signatures.

Zaleszczyky. Aron L. Lagstein—For the "Zion" Society: Juda Elias Baumann, Elias Glaser, Baruch Koffler, Feiwel, Seidmann, Oskar Glaser, Aron L. Lagstein, Nison Getzler, Josef Glaser, Dawid Harnick, L. Linder.

Zaryczow. "Doresch Lezion" Society.

Zbaraz. Local chapter of "Ahawas Zion" Society—"Hazeionim Hzehirem" Society (Zionist Youth).

Romania.

Bottuschan. "Bnej Zion."
Galatz. Jesajas Wechsler.
Namalosa. Elias Klein.
Piatra. Todros Lehrer—B. Samsony.
Pitest. Moriz Neuberger.
Varna. Ferd. Goldstein, Marcus Cohn, Edmund Jeitner, Jos. Dio, J.L. Drechsler, Paul S. Panitz, B. Chaim Boschanoff, J.S. Braunstein, Hermann Bierten, M. Feldmann, Jakob Hirsch.
Vaslui. Naftali Marcus.

Russia.

Letters of greeting and petitions from sixty-three Russian cities arrived. All together they bore 3,651 signatures.

Turkey.

Jaffa. "Bnej Mosche"—Sixty-one signatures.

U.S.A.

New York. "The Lovers of Zion."—Shovey Zion—The amalgamated Zionist organizations of Greater New York—Rev. Dr. H. Pereira Mendes—Dr. Michael Singer.
New York-Brooklyn. Chowewe Zion.

NOTES

NOTES TO INTRODUCTION

1. As Leon Pinsker observed in 1882. See his *Autoemanzipation*, 6th ed. (Berlin: Jüdischer Verlag, 1933), [6], http://ldn-knigi.lib.ru/JUDAICA/LPinskA.htm. See also Arthur Hertzberg, *The Zionist Idea: A Historical Analysis and Reader* (Philadelphia: Jewish Publication Society, 1997), 15.

2. Thomas Hobbes, *Leviathan*, ed. Michael Oakeshott (New York: Touchstone, 1962), 81–82, 74, 76, 72, 131, 141. On power and honor in Hobbes's thought, see D.D. Raphael, *Hobbes: Morals and Politics* (London: Routledge, 1977), 48–49. Francis Fukuyama argues that Hobbes differed from Hegel in deprecating and undervaluing the thymotic dimension of the human personality, the "desire for recognition." See his *The End of History and the Last Man* (New York: Avon Books, 1992), chs. 14 to 15. I think Fukuyama overstates the difference, but the point is that for both political philosophers, the quest for honor or recognition is understood to be a constant of human psychology and a fundamental factor in the formation of the state.

3. Not to suggest Herzl had read Hobbes—I use Hobbes because of his theoretical relevance, not because his ideas had any demonstrable influence on Zionist thought. At the same time, Herzl's political conceptions are often strikingly Hobbesian. Herzl favored a Prussian-style state possessing sweeping powers over society. Although the state may arise as a product of social consent, "... the state's efficacy required that it be experienced as a power above human artifice and will, evoking obedience and reverence." See Jacques Kornberg, *Theodor Herzl: From Assimilation to Zionism* (Bloomington: Indiana University Press, 1993), 164–69, quoting 166.

4. The precise identity and affiliation of such groups must be examined case by case, as many of the groups existed prior to the First Congress and were only notionally co-opted by the new Zionist Organization. See Ivonne Meybohm, *David Wolffsohn: Aufsteiger, Grenzgänger, Mediator—Eine biographische Annäherung an die Geschichte der frühen Zionistischen Organisation (1897–1914)* (Göttingen: Vandenhoek & Ruprecht, 2013), 122–23. Meybohm also calls into question the historiographical overvaluing of Herzl; her work on Wolffsohn,

which also considers the contributions of other persons and groups, is a corrective to this tendency.

5. David Engel, *Zionism* (Harlow, UK: Pearson-Longman, 2009), 51. On Herzl's opposition to unauthorized colonization, see *Der Judenstaat: Versuch einer moderner Lösung der Judenfrage* (Vienna: M. Breitenstein, 1896), section titled "Allgemeiner Theil: Der Plan," https://www.gutenberg.org/files/28865/28865-h/28865-h.htm; on the "extremism" of Hebrew revivalists, see Hertzberg, *Zionist Idea*, 623 ("Afterword," 1997 ed.).

6. Hertzberg, *Zionist Idea*, 108–14; *Zionisten-Congress in Basel (29, 30, und 31. August 1897): Offizielles Protokoll* (Vienna: Verlag des Vereines "Erez-Israel," 1898) hereafter *ZC 1897*, [171], in the address by R. Armand Kaminka tracing the prehistory of Zionism at the First Zionist Congress (bracketed numbers indicate pagination in the original German text).

7. Richard Gottheil, "Zionism," *Jewish Encyclopedia*, ed. Isidore Singer et al. (New York: Funk and Wagnalls, 1901–06), www.jewishencyclopedia.com. Hereafter *JE 1906*; Hertzberg, *Zionist Idea*, 110.

8. As seen in Hertzberg's gallery of religious nationalists, including Rabbi Samuel Mohilewer, Yehiel Michael Pines, Rabbi Abraham Isaac Kook, and Samuel Hayyim Landau. An important difference should be noted, though. These rabbis and publicists assert their theses against a predominantly secular Zionism; this conflict did not exist in Kalischer's lifetime.

The view that the state of Israel represents the "first fruits" of the Redemption is embodied in a prayer for the state, composed in 1948 and now incorporated in synagogue liturgies throughout the world, including those used in many Orthodox congregations. See Rabbi Dalia Marx, "The Prayer for the State of Israel: Universalism and Particularism," in *All the World: Universalism, Particularism, and the High Holy Days*, ed. Rabbi Lawrence A. Hoffman (Woodstock, VT: Jewish Lights Publishing, 2014), 49–76.

9. The two most important figures in early Zionism, Leon Pinsker and Theodor Herzl, rejected the traditional dogmas of election and eschatology. See Hertzberg, *Zionist Idea*, 191–92 and 230.

10. Hertzberg, *Zionist Idea*, 18.

11. The journal's title is best translated, "General Journal of Jewish Affairs." Founded in 1837, it continued to be published until 1922. As for Jewish geography, no definite boundary separated the Jews of West and East; the division can be challenged and was, especially since there was much East-West migration. An important article in this context is Binyamin W. Segel, "Das Judenvolk und die vier Weltgegenden," *Ost und West*, Heft 8/9, Aug.-Sept. 1916, 319–30,

http://sammlungen.ub.uni-frankfurt.de/cm/periodical/pageview/2608330. However, subjective consciousness of this division is strongly attested, in the Congress and elsewhere. Roughly speaking, *Ostjuden* were those Jews residing in Galicia and Bukovina, Russian Poland, Russia's Pale of Settlement, and Romania, whereas *Westjuden* were the Jews of the German Reich, the western parts of the Austro-Hungarian Empire, France, The Netherlands, and the United Kingdom. (The division appears to apply only to Ashkenazim.) With large-scale migration taking place from the 1880s to the 1920s, these identities were obviously not static.

The article cited above, by B. Segel, explores differentiations within the *Ostjuden* and deplores prejudices they hold against one another. In a personal communication, my friend and colleague, Professor Steve Glazer of Graceland University, observed that the *Ostjuden/Westjuden* distinction is better considered a cultural marker than a geographic one, and that the appearance of subethnic hierarchies is a widespread phenomenon among oppressed minorities, owing to their internalizing of value judgments made against them. I wish to register here my thanks to Professor Glazer for his insights. The latter theme is also explored briefly by Gershon Shafir, *Land, Labor, and the Origins of the Israeli-Palestinian Conflict, 1882–1914* (Cambridge: Cambridge University Press, 1989), 148–49.

12. *Allgemeine Zeitung des Judenthums*, Sept. 13, 1870, No. 34, 717–21.

13. Gottheil, "Zionism." A similar catalogue of stillborn proposals for a restoration of Jewish nationhood can be found in Walter Laqueur, *A History of Zionism* (New York: Schocken Books, 1978), 42–46. Intriguingly, Edward Said, in his essay, "Zionism from the Standpoint of Its Victims," refers to Eliot's novel as evidence of Zionist plans for Palestine. But there is no evidence Eliot's novel had any influence on immigrant-settlers who began to arrive in 1881. See Edward Said, *The Question of Palestine* (New York: Times Books, 1979), chapter 2.

At the same time, in a remarkable instance of life imitating art, Colonel Goldsmid, an English Jew who led his country's Hovevei Zion, introduced himself to Herzl with the declaration, "I am Daniel Deronda." Like Deronda, he had been raised in Christian home, only to discover his Jewish origins, whereupon he reconverted and supported Jewish settlement in Palestine. While Herzl was initially enchanted with Goldsmid, he later castigated him and most of Western Europe's Hovevei Zion as timorous do-nothings, on account of their refusal to back Congress-Zionism. See *Theodor Herzl: Briefe und Tagebücher*, ed. Alex Bein et al., 7 vols. (Berlin: Propyläen Verlag, 1983–1996): 2.284–85 (Nov. 25, 1895); 2.497–99 (Apr. 4, 1897).

14. Eran Kaplan and Derek Penslar, eds., *The Origins of Israel, 1882–1948: A Documentary History* (Madison: University of Wisconsin Press, 2011), 14–15. Kaplan and Penslar note that most First Aliya immigrants settled in the towns; a small but important fraction became pioneers of a Jewish-owned agricultural sector.

15. Alan Dowty, "Much Ado about Little: Ahad Ha'am's 'Truth from Eretz Yisrael,' Zionism, and the Arabs," *Israel Studies* 5:2 (2000): 154–81, esp. 161; hereinafter Dowty-Ahad Ha'am, "Truth."

16. Dowty-Ahad Ha'am, "Truth," 163.

17. David Vital, *The Origins of Zionism*, (Oxford: Clarendon, 1975), 74–100; for Ahad Ha'am, America held the answer to the Jews' urgent economic need (Dowty-Ahad Ha'am, "Truth," 161). David Farbstein, in his address to the First Congress, asserted that the number of Jews exiting the Russian Empire 1881–1897 was in excess of one million. See *ZC 1897*, [107].

18. Vital, *Origins of Zionism*, 59–60.

19. Shlomo Avineri, *The Making of Modern Zionism: The Intellectual Origins of the Jewish State* (New York: Basic Books, 1981), 75–77.

20. Pinsker anticipated, almost verbatim, Nordau's argument at the First Congress, that legal emancipation not based on prior social acceptance was futile.

21. Pinsker's explanation of the the persistence of anti-Semitism "bears the marks of concepts drawn from his medical training in an era of prevalent scientific positivism that attributed much to instinct and heredity." See Gideon Shimoni, *The Zionist Ideology* (Hanover, NH: Brandeis University Press, 1995), 33–34.

22. Pinsker, *Autoemanzipation*, 6th ed., 9–10 and 13 (author's translation); cf. Hertzberg, *Zionist Idea*, 186, 188.

23. As emphasized by Ahad Ha'am's "Ein Stolzer Jude," introduction to Pinsker, *Autoemanzipation*, 6th ed., 3–4.

24. Hertzberg, *Zionist Idea*, 194.

25. The assassination took place on March 13, 1881; the pogroms that followed are analyzed in Vital, *Origins of Zionism*, 49–59.

26. Vital, *Origins of Zionism*, 135–36; Walter Laqueur, "Zionism and its Liberal Critics, 1896–1948," *Journal of Contemporary History* 6:4 (1971): 164.

27. Vital, *Origins of Zionism*, 163–64.

28. Getzel Kressel, "Baron Edmond James de Rothschild," *Encyclopaedia Judaica*, 2nd ed.; hereafter *EJ*, 2nd ed.

29. Dowty-Ahad Ha'am, "Truth," 162, 168–69. Ahad Ha'am's assessment of the Arabs is contradictory. He first declares them to be indolent (160); yet

all other statements about conditions in Palestine belie this assertion (see esp. 161–62, 166, 173–76).

30. Ahad Ha'am complained of the lack of coordination between the various settlement societies in Europe, which led to land speculation and the waste of resources. See Dowty-Ahad Ha'am, "Truth," 160–81. The reference to California is an allusion to the "gold rush" of 1848–1849.

31. Vital, *Origins of Zionism*, 184–86; Neville Mandel, "Ottoman Practice and Restraictions on Jewish Settlement in Palestine: 1881–1908," *Middle Eastern Studies* 11:1 (1975): 33–46; Dowty-Ahad Ha'am, "Truth," 162.

32. His opening address at Kattowitz omitted reference to the political goals of Hovevei Zion. Vital, *Origins of Zionism*, 165–66.

33. On the weaknesses of Hovevei Zion, see Vital, *Origins of Zionism*, 164, 184–85.

34. The involvement in Hovevei Zion was the "leading common attribute" of the participants in the 1897 Congress (Vital, *Origins of Zionism*, 359). The idea of creating a Jewish public sphere comes from Michael Berkowitz, "Die Schaffung einer jüdischen Öffentlichkeit: Theodor Herzl und der Baseler Kongress von 1897," in *Europäische Öffentlichkeit: transnationale Kommunikation seit dem 18. Jahrhundert*, eds. Jörge Requate and Martin Schulze Wessel, (Frankfurt: Campus Verlag, 2002), 79–91. Berkowitz argues plausibly that Congress-Zionism produced such a sphere; I would simply suggest that the groundwork was laid by Hovevei Zion, inasmuch as their labors in agitation and association were crucial to the success of the early Congresses.

35. The translation of the title of Herzl's booklet is problematic. Although the 1896 English translation bore the title *The Jewish State*, and Herzl raised no objection to it, the German is better translated as *The Jews' State*, as argued by Henk Overberg in his new translation of *Der Judenstaat* (first published in 1997). Overberg deals with the translation issue in: Theodor Herzl, *The Jews' State, A Critical English Translation*, intro. and trans. Henk Overberg (Lanham, MD: Rowman and Littlefield, 2012), 3–6.

36. Wilhelm Marr, *Der Sieg des Judenthums über das Germanenthum, vom nicht confessionellen Standpunkt aus betrachtet* (Bern: Rudolph Costenoble, 1879).

37. The point comes from the socialist Zionist, Nahman Syrkin (Hertzberg, *The Zionist Idea*, 344).

38. Or "the socialism of fools." On this phrase's use and origin, see Richard J. Evans, *The Coming of the Third Reich* (New York: Penguin Books, 2005), 173 and 496n31. Syrkin anticipated later analyses of the causes of this popular, "socialist" anti-Semitism, the matrix out of which fascism was born. See Avineri, *Making of Modern Zionism*, 128–29.

39. Lucien Wolf, "Anti-Semitism," in *Encyclopaedia Britannica*, 11th ed.; Henry J. Cohn, "Theodor Herzl's Conversion to Zionism," *Jewish Social Studies* 32:2 (1970): 101–10.

40. Overberg, *Jews' State*, 22.

41. "Disciples awaiting the Master, they were to play a crucial role in spreading the word." See Ernst Pawel, *The Labyrinth of Exile: A Life of Theodor Herzl* (New York: Farrar, Straus, and Giroux, 1989), 272.

42. Vital, *Origins of Zionism*, 222–23, 270; Shimoni, *Zionist Ideology*, 39, 88–89; Overberg, *Jews' State*, 22–25. On conflict between Birnbaum and Herzl, see Jess Olson, "The Late Zionism of Nathan Birnbaum: The Herzl Controversy Reconsidered," *AJS Review* 31:2 (2007): 241–76; and Olson, *Nathan Birnbaum and Jewish Modernity: Architect of Zionism, Yiddishism, and Orthodoxy* (Stanford, CA: Stanford University Press, 2013), chapter 2.

43. Vital, *Origins of Zionism*, 259–60. Vital highlights the contrasts between Pinsker and Herzl. What follows here summarizes his discussion of Herzl in *Origins of Zionism*, chapter 9.

44. It was Herzl's cosmopolitanism, alienation from Jewish tradition, and relative immunity from communal pressures, that enabled him to make this change of emphasis. It was something perhaps impossible for *Ostjuden*; Herzl was, as Chaim Weizmann put it, "unencumbered" by the preconceptions of *Ostjuden*. See his *Trial and Error: The Autobiography of Chaim Weizmann* (London: Hamish Hamilton, 1949), 61; see also Howard M. Sachar, *A History of Israel: From the Rise of Zionism to Our Time* (New York: Knopf, 1979), 41.

45. In addition to Birnbaum, who had tried to revive Pinsker's orientation within Zionism, Meybohm cites R. Isaak Rülf and Max Bodenheimer as publishing works proposing, explicitly or implicitly, Jewish statehood—Rülf in 1883 and Bodenheimer in 1891 (*David Wolffsohn*, 44–46).

46. Herzl envisioned the Jews undertaking to relieve Ottoman financial woes. As a quid pro quo, the Ottomans would charter Jewish settlement in Palestine (*Judenstaat*, section titled "Palästina oder Argentien?").

47. Walter Lehn, "The Jewish National Fund," *Journal of Palestine Studies* 3:4 (1974): 74–96, esp. 89.

48. Vital, *Origins of Zionism*, 260.

49. Weizmann, *Trial and Error*, 62. In *Origins of Zionism*, Vital writes in the same vein:

> His impact on the course of Jewish history cannot be accounted for without overriding attention to Herzl the public figure and the man of

action, rather than the ideologue, to Herzl the brilliant leader, Herzl the organizer of the Jewish national revival, Herzl 'the King of the Jews.' It was there that his distinction and originality lay, rather than his ideas—which were clear enough... but marred by the superficiality of his analysis of the condition of the Jews, and by the *naïveté* of his programme of action, and in no essential respect really new, even if Herzl himself did not at first know this. (237)

50. *The Jubilee of the First Zionist Congress, 1897–1947* (Jerusalem: Executive of the Zionist Organization, 1947), 37–38; hereafter *Jubilee*.

51. Jonathan Frankel, "Parties and Ideologies: Hibat Tsiyon and the Bund," *YIVO Encyclopedia of Jews in Eastern Europe*, ed. Gershon D. Hundert, 2 vols. (New Haven, CT: Yale University Press, 2008). Online ed. http://www.yivoencyclopedia.org; hereafter *YIVO Encyclopedia*.

However, in assessing organizational statistics, Meybohm's caveat applies (*David Wolffsohn*, 122–23).

52. *Jubilee*, 98. Uncertainty attaches to the number at the First Congress since some participants did not officially register; some Russian Jews feared reprisals for taking part (Vital, *Origins*, 356–57). On the conflicting tabulations of participants, see Haiyim Orlan, "The Participants in the First Zionist Congress," *Herzl Year Book (1965)* (New York: Herzl Press, 1965), 133–52.

53. *Jubilee*, 98.

54. *Die Welt*, Sept. 3, 1897, 1. The digitized version is now available at http://sammlungen.ub.uni-frankfurt.de/cm/periodical/titleinfo/3315709. Another contemporary reflection on the Congress emphasizing its visionary qualities is found in Israel Zangwill, *Dreamers of the Ghetto* (1898; repr., New York: Harper and Brothers, 1989); see chapter 11, "Dreamers in Congress," 430–40.

55. Lawrence J. Epstein, *The Dream of Zion: The Story of the First Zionist Congress* (Lanham, MD: Rowman and Littlefield, 2016), 58–59. Epstein's title obviously derives from Zangwill, *Dreamers of the Ghetto* (1898).

56. Vital, *Origins of Zionism*, 356; Laqueur, *History of Zionism*, 104; *The Proceedings of the Zionist Congress held at Basle, Switzerland, August 29, 30, and 31, 1897*, reprinted from *The Jewish Chronicle* of London (New York: Philip Cowen, 1897), 7–8, 10–12; hereafter *JC/Cowen*; *ZC 1897*, [1–4].

57. Orlan, "Participants," 137–44. The total number of participants based on this list comes to 245; but this is based on a broad definition of "participant." For example, of the twenty-three participants from Switzerland, most were present only to observe.

58. Paula E. Hyman, "Jews and Judaism," in *Europe 1789–1914: Encyclopedia of the Age of Industry and Empire*, ed. John Merriman and Jay Winter, 5 vols. (Detroit: Charles Scribner's Sons, 2006), 3:1227–34, esp. 1227. The statistics on the distribution of Jews worldwide are not always reliable, but a useful contemporary source is "Statistics of the Jews," *The American Jewish Yearbook, 5660/1899–1900*, ed. Cyrus Adler (Philadelphia: Jewish Publication Society, 1899), 1:283–85.

59. Vital, *Origins of Zionism*, 359.

60. Kemal Karpat, *Ottoman Population, 1830–1914: Demographic and Social Characteristics* (Madison: University of Wisconsin Press, 1985), 160. Much higher numbers for Jews in Turkey were given by *The American Jewish Yearbook 5660/1899–1900* ("Statistics of the Jews"), where a total of three hundred and fifty thousand is given; and, if one included Bulgaria and Egypt (still under Ottoman suzerainty), the total was close to four hundred thousand (283–85).

61. See his letter to Belkovsky, June 30, 1897, cited in Vital, *Origins of Zionism*, 357–58.

62. To be fair, Herzl had had Switzerland in mind from the beginning, though he favored Zürich, not Basel. See Werner J. Cahnman, "Munich and the First Zionist Congress," *Historia Judaica* 3 (1941): 8; Laqueur, *History of Zionism*, 103.

63. Cahnman, "Munich and the First Zionist Congress," 10; the full entry is in *Theodor Herzl: Briefe und Tagebücher* (May 9, 1897), 2:507–8. Herzl claims he was privy to a confidential communication in which the rabbi admitted he withdrew for fear he would lose his donors.

64. Laqueur, "Zionism and Its Liberal Critics," 168, citing a statement of Nahum Goldmann.

65. Cahnman, "Munich and the First Zionist Congress," 7–23. See in particular appendices 2 and 3; Cahnman transcribed the original documents, including the minutes of a meeting at which *Der Judenstaat* was summarized and the planned Congress was rejected, as well as the Munich council's letters to Herzl and Herzl's letter to the council (translations here by author).

66. Laqueur, "Zionism and Its Liberal Critics," 180.

67. On relations between the people of Basel, Jews and non-Jews, and the Zionists, see Patrick Kury, "Jüdische Lebenswelten in einer Zeit raschen Wandels. Ostjuden, Zionistenkongresse, Überfremdungsängste um 1900," in *Acht Jahrhunderte Juden in Basel: 200 Jahre Israelitische Gemeinde, Basel*, ed. Heiko Haumann (Basel: Schwabe Verlag, 2005), 140–51. The generalizations that follow are also based on Kury's research.

68. As for international organizations, the most famous and enduring was probably the Red Cross, founded in 1863 by Henri Dunant, whose name was mentioned by Herzl as a "Christian Zionist." Among other international organizations holding conferences in Switzerland around the same time was the Second Socialist International; its Third Congress took place in 1893 in Zürich.

69. *JC/Cowen*, 5–6; *Die Welt*, Sept. 3, 1897, 11–12.

70. *ZC 1897*, [82–94]. Shlomo Kaplansky of the Austrian Poalei Zion offered a draft program to the party's 1906 conference which follows Birnbaum's logic precisely; indeed, even much of the language is the same. Kaplansky argues that the Jews required

> a country which has the power of attraction capable of keeping the Jewish masses on the soil.... These prerequisites exist only in the historic fatherland of the Jews... which has... remained for thousands of years in the minds of the Jewish people as the only country of its future and liberty. (Quoted in Shimoni, *Zionist Ideology*, 364.)

71. *ZC 1897*, [90], Ger. "ein gewaltiges Civilisationswerk."

72. By an apparent coincidence, Maxime Rodinson suggested that he would not have objected to Zionism if it had only proposed a Jewish state on the moon! See his *Cult, Ghetto, and State: The Persistence of the Jewish Question*, trans. Jon Rothschild (London: Al Saqi Books, 1983), 155. I thank Professor Steve Glazer for drawing my attention to Rodinson's comment.

73. *ZC 1897*, [92–93]. Again, Rodinson appears to echo Birnbaum. See his *Israel: A Colonial-Settler State?*, trans. David Thorstad (New York: Monad Press, 1973), 39–40.

Olson's *Nathan Birnbaum and Jewish Modernity*, while exploring Birnbaum's intellectual oeuvre in enormous detail, says little of substance about his speech at the First Congress (87). Was Birnbaum's view of the *Ostjuden* changing even before 1897 (as suggested on 102)? Perhaps, but his view of their culture was still extremely negative. Also, there are arguments in the speech that repeat those set out in his essay on race and culture, *Die jüdische Moderne*, published in 1896 (Olson, 109–17), but there are also some seemingly important differences (the subject is too intricate for fuller treatment here).

74. See Derek J. Penslar, "Herzl and the Palestinian Arabs: Myth and Counter-Myth," *Journal of Israeli History* 24:1 (2005): 65–77, esp. 73–75. On the origins of orientalism, see Edward W. Said, *Orientalism* (New York: Vintage Books, 1979). Said traces European discourse about "Orientals," including the peoples of the Middle East, especially in the nineteenth century. As he shows,

this discourse categorized them as "backward, degenerate, uncivilized, and retarded." Said continues:

> The point is that the very designation of something as Oriental involved an already pronounced evaluative judgment, and in the case of the peoples inhabiting the decayed Ottoman Empire, an implicit program of action. Since the Oriental was a member of a subject race, he had to be subjected: it was that simple. (207)

See also Meybohm, *David Wolffsohn*, 279–89. While distinguishing Zionism from other forms of European colonialism, Meybohm documents the pervasive use of colonialist rhetoric within the early Zionist movement.

75. Steven E. Aschheim, *Brothers and Strangers: The East European Jew in German and German-Jewish Consciousness, 1800–1923* (Madison: University of Wisconsin Press, 1999), 114–15. On the totality of Birnbaum's intellectual evolution, the most important study is Olson, *Nathan Birnbaum and Jewish Modernity*; on his embrace of Yiddish culture, see chapter 4.

76. It should be noted that Birnbaum continued to encourage Jewish settlement in Palestine, but without ulterior political motives. See "Birnbaum, Nathan" *Encyclopedia of Zionism and Israel*, ed. Raphael Patai, 2 vols. (New York: Herzl Press, 1971), 1:140–41.

77. Aschheim, *Brothers and Strangers*, 116.

78. Frankel, "Parties and Ideologies: The Parties in Ebb and Flow (1900–1914)," *YIVO Encyclopedia*.

79. See Hertzberg, *Zionist Idea*, 365–66. According to Borochov, Palestine had three advantages over other lands: it was at a stage of economic development suitable for the implantation of Jewish capital and labor; Jewish immigrants would face little competition in settling the country; it was the only land that would remain open to Jews toward which they would therefore gravitate.

80. Borochov, *The National Question and the Class Struggle*, trans. Poale Zion (1903), https://en.wikisource.org/wiki/The_National_Question_and_the_Class_Struggle.

81. Avineri, *Making of Modern Zionism*, 150.

82. *Land, Labor, and Origins*, 155. Concerning this point, Epstein's *Dream of Zion* (68) is completely ahistorical, categorically disavowing the colonialist character of Zionism.

83. Most of these distinctives are alluded to by Derek J. Penslar, "What We Talk About When We Talk About Colonialism: A Response to Joshua Cole and Elizabeth Thompson," in *Colonialism and the Jews*, ed. Ethan B. Katz et al. (Bloomington: Indiana University Press, 2017), 332.

84. See the scholarly dialogue in *Colonialism and the Jews*, ed. Katz et al.; the relevant texts are in Part 3, chapters 12 to 15, titled "Zionism and Colonialism." Chapter 12 reprints Derek J. Penslar's essay, "Is Zionism a colonial movement?" from *Israel in History: The Jewish State in Comparative Perspective* (London: Routledge, 2007). Joshua Cole and Elizabeth Thompson penned critiques of Penslar's essay (chs. 13 and 14); Penslar composed a final response to round off the dialogue (chapter 15). The range of discussion was much wider and deeper than can be compassed here.

85. Gabriel Piterberg, *The Returns of Zion* (London: Verson, 2008), 69–86. Piterberg's study includes a superb review of the historiography of settler colonialism and the congruities of Zionism with other settler-colonial projects, focusing on the documented influence of settler-colonial programs outside Palestine on the thinking of Zionist leaders such as Chaim Arlosoroff and Arthur Ruppin.

86. In his 1923 article, "The Iron Wall." An annotated edition is in Kaplan and Penslar, *Origins of Israel*, 257–63.

87. Jonathan Schneer, *The Balfour Declaration: The Origins of the Arab-Israeli Conflict* (Toronto: Anchor Canada, 2012), 197–99.

88. In addition to the discussions leading to the Balfour Declaration (cited above), these affinities were highlighted by Israel Zangwill, who proposed Jewish colonization in Kenya, Canada, and Australia, to reinforce Britain's power where the white population was sparse ("Mr. Chamberlain and Zionism," *The Times*, July 9, 1914, 4). This self-view of the Jews as modern, white Europeans—and therefore alien to the backward, nonwhite peoples of the colonial periphery—was found among the *Ostjuden* as well. In 1907, Joseph Klausner, editor of *HaShiloah*, spoke for most Zionists when he rejected Yitzhak Epstein's call for an integrative approach to relations with the Arabs: "We Jews, who have lived two thousand years and more among cultured peoples, cannot and must not descend again to the cultural level of the semi-savage peoples." See Alan Dowty, "'A Question That Outweighs All Others': Yitzhak Epstein and Zionist Recognition of the Arab Issue," *Israel Studies* 6:1 (2001): 34–54, quoting 38; hereinafter Dowty-Epstein, "Question."

89. A point made forcefully by Elizabeth F. Thompson, "Moving Zionism to Asia: Texts and Tactics of Colonial Settlement, 1917–1921," in *Colonialism and the Jews*, ed. Katz et al., 317–26. It is the thrust of Said's "Zionism from the Standpoint of Its Victims" (*Question of Palestine*, chapter 2).

90. See Neville Mandel, *The Arabs and Zionism before World War I* (Berkeley: University of California Press, 1976).

91. Thompson, "Moving Zionism to Asia," 322–25; Rodinson, *Israel: A Colonial-Settler State?*, 55–56.

92. The land question was recognized by sensitive observers at an early stage of Zionist colonization. Thus Yitzhak Epstein, addressing the impact of Zionist land purchases on Arab *fellahin* as early as 1905, rebukes his colleagues: "But, if we do not want to deceive ourselves with a conventional lie, we must admit that we have driven impoverished people from their humble abode and taken bread out of their mouths. Where will the dispossessed, with only a little money, turn?" (Dowty-Epstein, "Question," 41). In fact, the displacement of indigenous peoples from collectively held lands, primarily in order for white settlers to exploit its agricultural potential, has been at the heart of settler-colonial projects the world over. See Patrick Wolfe, "Settler colonialism and the elimination of the native," *Journal of Genocide Research* 8:4 (2006): 387–409.

93. As Penslar notes: "From the time of Herzl onward, the Zionist political elite was eager to appeal to the interests of the Great Powers, and the Zionist movement as a whole was shot through with Orientalist conceptions of Arab degeneracy and primitiveness" (*Israel in History*, 91). While Penslar seems to regard this mentality as regrettable but incidental to the Zionist program, I argue rather that Zionist claims were inseparable from an orientalist devaluation of the Arab position.

94. Penslar, "Herzl and the Palestinian Arabs," 72–75.

95. Shimoni, *Zionist Ideology*, 352.

96. Shimoni, *Zionist Ideology*, 345–50; Hertzberg, *Zionist Idea*, 463–65.

97. Shimoni, *Zionist Ideology*, 350–51.

98. Shimoni, *Zionist Ideology*, 364–66.

99. See Zachary Lockman, *Comrades and Enemies: Arab and Jewish Workers in Palestine, 1906–1948* (Berkeley: University of California, 1996), 41 (Lockman's translation of Borochov).

100. Only a few voices were raised in protest against this bigoted view of the Arabs and the supposed superficiality of their bond with the land. The most heartfelt plea to respect the Arabs and their love of the land was again that made by Epstein in 1905 (Dowty-Epstein, "Question,").

101. Jabotinsky once declared that "everything that is oriental, is doomed"; in another context he asserted that "we, the Jews, have nothing in common with the so-called East—thank God." Jabotinsky was in full agreement with the colonialist conception of Herzl and the (Zionist) Birnbaum with respect to the Zionist mission in colonizing Palestine. As Yaacov Shavit summarizes that view: "Thus the Jews were not returning to the East in order to be absorbed by it, but to transplant European culture from geographical Europe to the East— to sow it into the soil of Asia." See Yaacov Shavit, *Jabotinsky and the Revisionist*

Movement, 1925–1948 (Abingdon: Frank Cass, 1988), 244–71; quotations are from 245–47.

102. In the end, such appeals were totally subjective and therefore worthless for establishing a right in international law; on which, see Shimoni, *Zionist Ideology*, 343, 348–49, 359.

103. Lippe made these points in his review of Herzl's book, published in the Berlin journal *Zion* 7:8 (Aug. 30, 1897): 193–96, as noted by Vital, *Origins of Zionism*, 169, 277n36.

104. The most up-to-date study of Zionist terminology is Meybohm, *David Wolffsohn*; on *Heimstätte*, see 266–69. Vital also notes: "In fact Herzl had realized long before the convening of the Congress that there could be no negotiation with the Ottomans on the basis of a plan to establish a Jewish *state* and had ceased to employ the term" (Vital, *Origins of Zionism*, 366). Nordau, in presenting the Basel Program, declared it a veritable miracle because of the achievement of unanimity by the legal scholars who had toiled over it (*ZC 1897*, [113–14]). But Bodenheimer, an advisory member of the committee, was not satisfied; see Vital, *Origins of Zionism*, 366, and the discussion below. "Masterpiece of circumlocution" is from Ludger Heid, "Der schönste Mann," *Zeit Online*, Aug. 29, 1997, www.zeit.de/1997/36/Der_schoenste_Mann.

105. Meybohm, *David Wolffsohn*, 266–69.

106. *ZC 1897*, [86–87]: "durch die Wiedererhebung der jüdischen Nation zu einem Staatsvolke."

107. "Die Bildung eines Judenstaates ist die einzig mögliche Lösung der Judenfrage." The German is in *JC/Cowen* (59), the English in Vital, *Origins of Zionism* (354).

108. Michael Berkowitz, "Die Schaffung einer jüdischen Öffentlichkeit," 85–88.

109. *Theodor Herzl: Briefe und Tagebücher*, 2:538–39 (Sept. 2, 1897): "In Basel habe ich den Judenstaat gegründet." This statement shows plainly that the modification of his vocabulary in dealing with the Ottomans had not changed the ultimate aim enunciated in *Judenstaat*. See also Laqueur, *History of Zionism*, 108, 135. The ascription of prophet-like foresight to Herzl derives from the startling accuracy of his prediction made in his diary, that the Jewish state would arise in fifty years.

110. Jacob de Haas, *Theodor Herzl: A Biographical Study*, 2 vols. (Chicago: Leonard Co., 1927), 1:176.

111. Mim Kemal Öke, "The Ottoman Empire, Zionism, and the Question of Palestine (1880–1908)," *International Journal of Middle East Studies* 14 (1982): 329–41, esp. 331–32; *ZC 1897*, [113–19].

112. *JC/Cowen* (42) asserts that the Basel Program's omission of the term "state" was done to appease Russian delegates who feared the reaction of the Russian, rather than the Ottoman, government.

113. Said, *Question of Palestine*, 68–69.

114. Rodinson, *Israel: A Colonial-Settler State?*, 46. Interestingly, Penslar is not as ready as Rodinson to exculpate Herzl and his supporters, noting the presence of contemporary critics, as well as advocates, of imperialism (see his "Herzl and the Palestinian Arabs," 73–75).

115. Neville J. Mandel, "Ottoman Policy and Restrictions on Jewish Settlement in Palestine: 1881–1908—Part I," *Middle Eastern Studies* 10:3 (1974): 312–32; *Arabs and Zionism before World War I*, chapter 2. Mandel argues that the first Zionist Congress's stated goal of creating a homeland in Palestine for the Jews soon began to disquiet relations between Arabs and Jewish immigrants (40–41).

116. Michelle Campos, "Between 'Beloved Ottomania' and 'The Land of Israel': the Struggle over Ottomanism and Zionism among Palestine's Sephardi Jews, 1908–1913," *International Journal of Middle East Studies* 37 (2005): 461–83, quoting 472–73.

117. *Jubilee*, 25—speech by David Ben-Gurion titled "On the Threshold of the Jewish State," 25–28.

118. Kornberg, *Theodor Herzl*, 160.

119. Albert S. Lindemann, *Esau's Tears: Modern Anti-Semitism and the Rise of the Jews* (Cambridge: Cambridge University Press, 1997), xviii.

120. Zeev Tzahor, "David Ben Gurion's Attitude Toward the Diaspora," *Judaism* 32.1 (1983): 9–22. Ben Gurion's lifelong aversion to the Diaspora was exacerbated by the horrors of Hitlerism: "The bitter lesson of the Holocaust intensified his negative attitude to the Diaspora" (16).

121. Kornberg, *Theodor Herzl*, 161–66.

122. Idith Zertal, *Israel's Holocaust and the Politics of Nationhood*, trans. Chaya Galai (Cambridge: Cambridge University Press, 2005), 59–60; Ronit Lentin, *Israel and the Daughters of the Shoah: Reoccupying the Territories of Silence* (New York: Berghahn Books, 2000), 2, 6, 206–07. See also Tzahor, "David Ben Gurion's Attitude," 9–22, esp. the quotations on 11.

Hannah Arendt argued that one of Ben Gurion's aims for the trial was teaching Diaspora Jews "the difference between Israeli heroism and Jewish submissive meekness." See her *Eichmann in Jerusalem: A Report on the Banality of Evil* (London: Penguin Books, 2006), 10.

123. Marx, "Prayer for the State of Israel," 56.

124. *ZC 1897*, [6].

125. *Jubilee*—speech by Alex Bein, "How the Basle Congress Was Convened," 47–50.

126. Amos Elon, *Theodor Herzl* (New York: Holt, Rinehart, and Winston, 1975), chapter 9 (187).

127. *Theodor Herzl: Briefe und Tagebücher*, 2:63–67 (June 3, 1895). Herzl applies the term to Baron Maurice de Hirsch after a disappointing interview with him.

128. *Jubilee*, 49—speech by Alex Bein, "How the Basle Congress Was Convened," 47–50; Vital, *Origins of Zionism*, chapter 11, esp. 299–308.

129. Vital, *Origins of Zionism*: on responses to the call for a Congress in West and East, 328–53; on the origins and experience of the Basel delegates, 359.

130. See Gottheil, "Zionism: The Kultur-Frage," *JE 1906*.

131. According to the agenda (Arbeits-Programm) in de Haas, *Theodor Herzl*, vol. 1, facsimile between pages 168 and 169, https://archive.org/stream/theodorherzlbiog01deha#page /168/mode/2up.

132. Zangwill confirms Herzl's command of the Congress: "In a Congress of impassioned rhetoricians he remains serene, moderate; his voice is for the more part subdued; in its most emotional abandonments there is a dry undertone, almost harsh. He quells disorder with a look, with a word, with a sharp touch of the bell" (*Dreamers of the Ghetto*, 434). Ironically, on the tenth anniversary of the Balfour Declaration (1927), the German-Jewish periodical *Menorah* commented that the Declaration was generally regarded as something incredible, by affirming what only a handful of Jews regarded as *Schwärmer* had proclaimed as the basis for solving the Jewish question (i.e., the international recognition of the Jewish claim to Palestine). E.G. Fried, "Die Balfour-Deklaration zum 2. November," *Menorah* (Nov. 1927): 11.646, http://sammlungen.ub.uni-frankfurt.de/cm/periodical/titleinfo/2920853.

133. *ZC 1897*, [5]. While Herzl denied the Jews' desire or need for the sympathy of non-Jews, Max Nordau, speaking immediately after, was to argue almost the opposite: the failure of popular sympathy among non-Jews had precluded the efficacy of legal emancipation, resulting in the anti-Semitic backlash to which the Zionist Congress was a response (12–13).

134. Herzl repeats his use of the term "feierlich" ("solemn"): "Bei dieser feierlichen Gelegenheit . . . sei unser Bekenntnis feierlich wiederholt." Did he have the Shema, the Jewish confession of faith, repeated on this occasion? It is out of character, though he did wish to imbue the Congress with a quasi-religious atmosphere. Epstein affirms Herzl's judgment that the compulsory formal dress contributed to the solemnity (*Dream of Zion*, 58).

135. While opposed to a Zionism dependent on philanthropy, Herzl emphasized the movement's friendly orientation toward non-Jews, hence his use of "menschenfreundlich" (*ZC 1897*, [8]).

136. *ZC 1897*, [191], mentions dignity and moderation. *Die Welt*, Sept. 3 1897, 18, adds this sentence, not found in the official transcript: "Wir haben unsere Fahne nicht in die Tasche gesteckt, und dennoch keine schädliche Exaltationen uns zu Schulden kommen lassen."

137. *Die Welt*, Sept. 3, 1897, 2–3.

138. *Die Welt*, Sept. 3, 1897, 1.

139. *JC/Cowen*, 12.

140. *JC/Cowen*, 12, 18; Epstein, *Dream of Zion*, 60; Heid, "Der schönste Mann."

141. *Die Welt*, Sept. 3, 1897, 5, 9; *JC/Cowen*, 18; Epstein, *Dream of Zion*, 70, 79; Jacob de Haas, *Theodor Herzl*, 1:174.

142. *Theodor Herzl: Briefe und Tagebücher*, 2:539 (Sept. 2, 1897).

143. *ZC 1897*, [20–21].

144. Jer 31:15 (RSV).

145. Jacob de Haas, *Theodor Herzl*, 1:168–70.

146. Lippe refers in his speech to "unsere Frommen" (*ZC 1897*, [2]). In a previous work, I rendered this "the pious among us"; but because *Hasid* is Hebrew for "pious," and because Lippe was a *maskil* from Galicia, where there was raging conflict between Haskalah and Hasidism, I believe that "unsere Frommen" means, simply, the Hasidim. Cf. Michael J. Reimer, "'The good Dr. Lippe' and Herzl in Basel, 1897: A translation and analysis of the Zionist Congress's opening speech," *Journal of Israeli History* 34:1 (2015): 1–21.

147. *JC/Cowen*, 39.

148. Getzel Kressel, "Schach, Fabius," *EJ* 2nd ed., 18:98.

149. For this reason, I find unconvincing Eyal Chowers's assertion that Zionism displayed "skepticism toward any language-based construction of the world (as exemplified by its distrustful attitude toward international law and agreements)." See his *Political Philosophy of Zionism*, 14. As for foreign policy, Israel actively sought agreements with major powers in order to enhance its position both regionally and internationally. On the motivations, see Tzahor, "David Ben Gurion's Attitude Toward the Diaspora," 16; and Sachar, *History of Israel*, 424–26, 458–63, 470–71, 482–85, 567–71. On United States-Israel relations, see John J. Mearsheimer and Stephen M. Walt, *The Israel Lobby and U.S. Foreign Policy* (New York: Farrar, Straus, and Giroux, 2007).

150. Philpott, Daniel, "Sovereignty," *The Stanford Encyclopedia of Philosophy* (Summer 2016 Edition), Edward N. Zalta, ed., http://plato.stanford.edu/archives/sum2016/entries/sovereignty.

151. Amos Oz, among others, made the comparison: see Roger Cohen, "What Will Israel Become?" *New York Times*, Dec. 20, 2014.

152. The Hebrew term for "disaster" and referring to the mass murder of Jews in World War II; the term is increasingly preferred to "Holocaust."

153. Laqueur, "Zionism and its Liberal Critics," 182.

154. Tzahor, "David Ben Gurion's Attitude," 16. Ben Gurion's use of this argument was disingenuous; Yehuda Bauer also ridicules this argument in his *Rethinking the Holocaust* (New Haven: Yale University Press, 2001), 259.

155. Reprinted in Hertzberg, *Zionist Idea*, 561.

156. Elon, *The Israelis*, 204. Gershon Shafir—like Elon, a critic of Israeli relations with the Palestinians—makes the same point, that there was no "realistic alternative course to the pursuit of nationhood and sovereignty" (*Land, Labor and Origins*, xii).

157. Gottheil, "Zionism," *Jewish Encyclopedia (1906)*.

158. Hertzberg, *Zionist Idea*, 266.

159. Cited in Laurence J. Silberstein, *The Postzionism Debates: Knowledge and Power in Israeli Culture* (New York: Routledge, 1999), 51.

160. Lavinia Cohn-Sherbok and Dan Cohn-Sherbok, *Judaism: A Short Introduction* (Oxford: OneWorld, 1997), 51 (emphasis added).

161. Marc Ellis, *Beyond Innocence and Redemption: Confronting the Holocaust and Israeli Power* (San Francisco: Harper & Row, 1990), 2–3.

162. Michael L. Morgan, *Beyond Auschwitz: Post-Holocaust Theology in America* (Oxford: Oxford University Press, 2001), 169, 175–79, quoting 179.

163. A.B. Yehoshua, *Between Right and Right. Israel: Problem or Solution?* (Garden City, NY: Doubleday, 1981).

164. Shimoni, *Zionist Ideology*, chapter 8; see esp. 351, 361, 386–88. Shimoni recognizes history as relevant in the formation of the Jewish claim, but he concedes that any objective, historically based analysis of conflicting claims would favor the Arabs.

165. I owe this point to Professor Steve Glazer, Graceland University. The reductio ad absurdum of the alleged connection between Palestinian hostility to Israel and the Shoah is found in Prime Minister Netanyahu's assertion of a Palestinian hand behind Hitler's "Final Solution." See William Booth, "Netanyahu says Palestinian gave Hitler idea for Holocaust," *Washington Post*, Oct. 21, 2015.

166. Thus, David Engel, writing about Diaspora Jews' reaction to the condemnation of Zionism at the United Nations in 1975, speaks of the "essential role the Jewish state had come to play in their lives. Jews throughout the world understood international castigation of Zionism as directed against them, wherever they lived" (*Zionism*, 172). The quantitative evidence is drawn from

"A Portrait of Jewish Americans," Pew Research Center Report, Oct. 1, 2013, http://www.pewforum.org/2013/10/01/jewish-american-beliefs-attitudes-culture-survey/. (Jews in the United States constitute about 40 percent of the world's Jewish population, the single largest community of Jews outside Israel.) The Pew study suggested that nearly 70 percent of American Jews had an emotional attachment to Israel and that about 43 percent had visited Israel. Yet the same study indicated doubt about Israel's sincerity in seeking peace with the Palestinians among a majority of American Jews.

167. For a detailed comparison of Lippe and Herzl, see Reimer, "'The good Dr. Lippe' and Herzl in Basel."

168. Conforming here to the orthography of the Congress's published proceedings: *Judennot* in contemporary German. The word was probably chosen because Herzl had used it in his preface to *Judenstaat*, referring to it as the entirely real driving force behind his idea of creating a Jewish state, and proving that his plan was not a fantasy.

169. This schematic was too neat, and Ahad Ha'am's criticisms of the Congress make it plain that it overlooked the intensity of the cultural malaise affecting the *Ostjuden*. See Hertzberg, *Zionist Idea*, 262–69.

170. Mark Kupovetsky, "Population and Migration: Population and Migration before World War I," *YIVO Encyclopedia*.

171. An important reinterpretation of modern Jewish history is found in Lindemann, *Esau's Tears*.

172. Nordau may have been thinking of Gerson Bleichröder, Bismarck's banker and one of Germany's wealthiest men, and the Rothschilds (Lindemann, *Esau's Tears*, 115).

173. Acknowledging Lueger's political opportunism, Lindemann argues that the power and influence of Jewish liberals and capitalists in Vienna was also undeniable; see *Esau's Tears*, 337–47. See also Robert S.Wistrich, "Karl Lueger and the Ambiguities of Viennese Antisemitism," *Jewish Social Studies* 45 (1983): 251–62.

174. Lindemann summarizes reasons for the economic and professional advancement of Jews in Central Europe (*Esau's Tears*, 114–16). He also cites Werner Sombart, *Die Juden und das Wirtschaftsleben* (Leipzig: Duncker und Humblot, 1911), English trans., *The Jews and Modern Capitalism*, trans. M. Epstein (Kitchener, ON: Batoche Books, 2001).

175. *ZC 1897*, [100].

176. s.v. "Constitutive Rhetoric," James Jasinski, *Sourcebook on Rhetoric: Key Concepts in Contemporary Rhetorical Studies* (Thousand Oaks, CA: Sage Publications, 2001), 106–8.

177. On the problems this dichotomy poses, see Segel, "Das Judenvolk und die vier Weltgegenden," 319–30. Meybohm emphasizes the complexities inherent in this intra-Jewish dichotomy, as it was to a considerable extent an ideological construct. In her work, she juxtaposes stylized portraits of Herzl and Wolffsohn in Zionist historiography as representative of this dichotomy. Also, as argued here, she notes that this division, which everyone took for granted, actually undercut Zionist arguments for Jewish nationhood. See her *David Wolffsohn*, 57–69, esp. 64.

178. Fabius Schach, "Die russischen Juden in Deutschland," *Ost und West: illustrierte Monatschrift für modernes Judentum*, vol. 10–11, Oct.-Nov. 1905, 719–30, esp. 721, http:// sammlungen.ub.uni-frankfurt.de/cm/periodical/titleinfo/2583941.

179. Geoffrey Alderman, *Modern British Jewry* (Oxford: Oxford University Press, 1998), 120.

180. "The Hebrews from Russia: A Problem that Perplexes the American Jews," *New York Times*, July 16, 1882, 8. Rosenberg's comments regarding apprehensions about the mass of indigent immigrants from Europe are in *ZC 1897*, [80–81].

181. *ZC 1897*, [79].

182. On relations between Ashkenazic and Sephardic Jews in Palestine, and between Jews and non-Jews, see Michelle Campos, *Ottoman Brothers: Muslims, Christians, and Jews in Early Twentieth-Century Palestine* (Stanford: Stanford University Press, 2011). Campos shows that leading Zionists were indifferent or hostile to the Sephardim (206–7). An egregious example:

> [When] public criticism emerged in 1909 over the tensions between Ottomanism and Zionism.... the Zionist leader Max Nordau told Ottoman Jews who voiced criticism to stay out of internal Zionist affairs—in effect disenfranchising them from the very movement which sought to speak and act in their name. (207)

It is difficult to know the percentages of Sephardim and Ashkenazim in Ottoman Palestine. Sephardim predominated prior to Zionist settlement; but by 1914, the Ashkenazim appear to have outnumbered the Sephardim on account of immigration. This is based on the assumption that most immigrants taking Ottoman citizenship as well as non-citizen immigrants, were coming from the non-Ottoman lands of Eastern Europe. See Justin McCarthy, *The Population of Palestine: Population History and Statistics of the Late Ottoman Period and the Mandate* (New York: Columbia University Press, 1990), 13–24.

Michelle Campos's (*Ottoman Brothers*, 12–14) suggests that in 1900 there were about thirty thousand Ottoman Jews (mostly Sephardim) and thirty thousand foreign Jews (virtually all Ashkenazim), plus perhaps ten thousand Jews living in the Zionist agricultural colonies. Since the latter estimate pertains to the period before the Second Aliya (1904–1914), it seems the Ashkenazim had attained a numerical majority by 1914.

183. *ZC 1897*, [100], [106–7].

184. Frankel, "Parties and Ideologies: Hibat Tsiyon and the Bund," *YIVO Encyclopedia*.

185. Lindemann, *Esau's Tears*, 168–71, and esp. chapter 13, "Jews and Revolution (1917–1934)."

186. Although most Orthodox rabbis opposed Hasidism at first, they closed ranks with the Hasidim against the common threat of the Haskalah and modernism; s.v. "Hasidim," *JE 1906*.

187. s.v. "Haskalah," *JE 1906*.

188. There are two exceptions to the silence regarding Hasidism: Karl Lippe, who gave the first address, and Abraham Salz, the rapporteur for Galicia. Both hailed from Galicia; and both noted the influence of Hasidism, though they themselves were products of the Haskalah. The references are found in *ZC 1897*, [2] ("unsere Frommen") and [22] ("die Chassidim").

189. Lloyd P. Gartner, "Hasidism: History," *EJ*, 2nd ed., 8.397.

190. Thus as he began to conclude his address to the Congress: *ZC 1897*, [19].

191. Julius Berger, "Zionismus in Polen," *Der Jude: eine Monatsschrift* (1918), 5:296–97, http://sammlungen.ub.uni-frankfurt.de/cm/periodical/titleinfo/3102278.

192. *JC/Cowen* (40) complains of a lack of punctuality at the Congress.

193. *JC/Cowen*, 43.

194. Laqueur suggests that the question of Herzl's mandate was uppermost in the minds of his political contacts in Europe and the Ottoman Empire (*History of Zionism*, 98, 100).

195. Ger. "Staatsrabbiner." See Tamar Kaplan Appel, "Crown Rabbi," *YIVO Encyclopedia*.

196. Only the German text is given in this record of the proceedings.

197. Weizmann, *Trial and Error*, 63; Laqueur, *History of Zionism*, 107, 113.

198. The stenographic record betrays the impropriety of this "acclamation." Normally, when motions were adopted, the passive with *werden* was employed. Thus: "Der Antrag wird angenommen." In this one instance, *werden* is replaced with *erscheinen* (to seem or appear): "Der Antrag erscheint durch Acclamation

angenommen" (*ZC 1897*, [119]). And dissent did not disappear. The next speaker on the agenda, Max Bodenheimer, made a point of declaring himself in favor of *völkerrechtlich*, since this was the wording he himself had submitted to the committee that drafted the program (*ZC 1897*, [113], [122]).

199. Return, Restoration, and Redemption: *Rückkehr*, *Wiederherstellung*, and *Erlösung*. All of them are well attested within the rhetoric of this and other Congresses, but did not find their way into the Basel Program.

200. Paraphrasing Laqueur, *History of Zionism*, 106.

201. Most notably Ahad Ha'am: see Hertzberg, *Zionist Idea*, 262–69.

202. The estimations made by Max Bodenheimer and David Neumark, a Reform rabbi working in Bohemia, with respect to the representative character of the Congress, are completely contradictory. Bodenheimer alleges that the Congress can speak for all Jews: "Therefore, since at present we alone represent the Jewish people... based on a constituency of a substantial part of the Jewish people"; by contrast, Neumark says that "those of us here represent only a tiny fraction of Jewry" (*ZC 1897*, [122] and [136]). Reasons for Bodenheimer's confidence about the Congress's universal authority are derived from a legal-political theory propounded by Herzl in *Judenstaat*, discussed below. As for Bodenheimer's understanding of Zionism's goal, recall that he had designed the badge that declared the Jewish state as the sole solution to the Jewish question. See Vital, *Origins of Zionism*, 354.

203. Sachar, *History of Israel*, 46.

204. Vital, *Origins of Zionism*, 349, 360; Yehdua Slutsky, "Jacob Bernstein-Kogan (Cohen)," *EJ*, 2nd. ed., 3:486.

205. A later incarnation of this program is perhaps reflected in the fervent devotion to *Moledet* (Hebrew for "Homeland"). On Meron Benvenisti's critique of this "cult," see Silberstein, *Postzionism Debates*, 58–65.

206. The rift between political and practical Zionists existed among both *Westjuden* and *Ostjuden* (Vital, *Origins of Zionism*, 360). But the Russians, faced with more desperate circumstances, tended to favor the practical approach. Meybohm documents this division in German Zionism before Herzl, represented in frictions between Cologne and Berlin; see *David Wolffsohn*, 47–49.

207. It was a wishful scenario, but almost entirely wrong. The Zionists failed to get the Ottomans to authorize settlement in Palestine; the Jewish presence grew, but slowly, in the face of constant attrition; and the international agreement giving Jews the right to immigrate was a result of Zionist diplomacy, but it was only indirectly related to achievements of the new Yishuv. On the discussions leading to the Balfour Declaration, see Jonathan Schneer, *The Balfour*

Declaration: The Origins of the Arab-Israeli Conflict (Toronto, ON: Anchor Canada, 2012), chapter 24.

208. Shafir, *Land, Labor, and Origins*, 155–56, 245–46nn39–42.

209. Vital, *Origins of Zionism*, 359. Vital qualifies Kahn as merely "sympathetic" to Hovevei Zion, but this seems to be putting it too mildly. Harry Zohn describes Kahn as having a definite and early attachment to the movement; he was later Herzl's intermediary with the Rothschilds and Hirsch's Jewish Colonization Association. See Theodor Herzl, *Zionist Writings: Essays and Addresses*, Harry Zohn, trans., 2 vols. (New York: Herzl Press, 1973, 1975), 1:270n12.

210. *JC/Cowen*, 50–51. The text cited indicates that this denunciation took place during the morning debates, but it does not identify the speaker. There is a cryptic reference to a certain "Seff" who spoke in Russian (Hebrew is not mentioned) in the stenographic record, but our transcript places his remarks in the afternoon, not in the morning (see [168]).

211. This was particularly true of the discussion of Hebrew culture. Ahad Ha'am accused the Congress of neglecting the challenges facing Jews who had had a Jewish upbringing and education and were now confronting modern European culture (Hertzberg, *Zionist Idea*, 262–69). Gideon Shimoni argues that this "neglect" was deliberate, the result of Herzl's sensitivity to rabbis who saw Zionism as an assault on religious authority. See Shimoni, *Zionist Ideology*, 281–83.

212. The transcript contains a double error. It gives his name as "Glaser" rather than "Gaster"; and it makes him the chief of all Jewish congregations in Britain. The chief rabbi of the British Empire at this time was Hermann Adler, whose father had also held this office.

213. *JC/Cowen*, 57.

214. On the partially successful attempt by Rabbi Mohilewer to seize power over the organization of Hovevei Zion, see Shimoni, *Zionist Ideology*, 45.

215. Epstein, *Dream of Zion*, 88.

216. Two significant changes were made. The first concerned the nature and size of the associations qualified to send delegates to future Congresses—any association of Zionists (i.e., shekel-payers) was authorized to send delegates, one delegate per hundred members or fraction thereof. The second concerned the size of the General Council, or "Greater Actions Committee," the larger and more geographically representative administrative body, within which there existed a "Smaller Actions Committee" (i.e., the five-man Vienna Executive)—the General Council's membership was raised from fifteen to twenty-three to

allow for the representation of more regions. Most other articles were approved more or less as given in the draft.

217. Steiner pointed this out to the delegates; his remarks are in *ZC 1897* [157].

218. David Vital, *Zionism: The Formative Years* (Oxford: Clarendon Press, 1982), 13.

219. As may be inferred from data in N.M. Gelber and O.K. Rabinowicz, "Congress, Zionist," *Encyclopedia of Zionism and Israel*, 2:205–12; for more on changes after Herzl's death, see Vital, *Zionism: The Formative Years*, 416–25.

220. For the details of their clash, see *ZC 1897* [155].

221. Zangwill captures both the danger and decisiveness of the moment:

> [Herzl] quells disorder with a look, with a word, with a sharp touch of the bell. The cloven hoof of the Socialist peeps out from a little group. At once "The Congress shall be captured by no party!" And the Congress is in roars of satisfaction. (*Dreamers of the Ghetto*, 434)

222. See Ulrich von Alemann, "Die Enstehung und Entwicklung der deutschen Parteien," http://www.bpb.de/politik/grundfragen/parteien-in-deutschland/202312/entstehung-und-entwicklung-bis-1933, accessed May 30, 2017; a fuller discussion is in Bernd Faulenbach, *Geschichte der SPD: Von den Anfängen bis zur Gegenwart* (Munich: C.H. Beck, 2012), chapter 3; on the isolation and stigmatization of the party, see esp. 23–24, 32–33.

223. *ZC 1897*, [162] and [156]: the comments discussed here derive from Dr. Kornblüh [162] and Fabius Schach [156], respectively. While Herzl was no radical, he was not averse to playing on the Kaiser Wilhelm II's fear of the Social Democrats and his conviction that Jews were its driving force; he suggested to him that the success of Zionism in bringing Jews to Palestine would weaken the Social Democrats in Germany (Meybohm, *David Wolffsohn*, 297).

224. *JC/Cowen*, 52–54; Jess Olson, "The Late Zionism of Nathan Birnbaum," 270–71.

225. After summarizing Herzl's ideas, Zangwill notes the rivalry his leadership had provoked, in particular with Birnbaum:

> Not all his own ideas, these; some perhaps only half-consciously present to him, so that even in this very Congress the note of jealousy is heard, the claim of an earlier prophet insisted on fiercely. For a moment the dignified assembly becomes a prey to atavism, reproduces the sordid squabbles of the *Kahal*. As if every movement was not fed by subterranean fires, heralded by obscure rumblings, though 'tis only

the earthquake or the volcanic jet which leaps into history! (*Dreamers of the Ghetto*, 438.)

226. *Die Welt* noted that many in Basel were Birnbaum's students (Sept. 3, 1897, 11).

227. *ZC 1897*, [164]; Olson, "Late Zionism of Nathan Birnbaum," 271–74. It is telling that the second volume of David Vital's history of Zionism (*Zionism: The Formative Years*) nowhere mentions Birnbaum. On this episode within the Congress, see also Epstein, *Dream of Zion*, 89. Indeed, the denouement was so convoluted that the standard histories of Zionism have glossed over it. Birnbaum was first disqualified, then reinstated, as a member of the Vienna Executive. Herzl is usually treated as if he were the General Secretary of the Vienna Executive throughout the remaining years of his life, when in fact that position was first assigned to Birnbaum, who held it 1897–1899. Meanwhile, Herzl, disgusted with what he called the "Inaction Committee," proceeded to act without regard to the Vienna Executive. See also Pawel, *Labyrinth of Exile*, 343–45.

228. Olson, "The Late Zionism of Nathan Birnbaum," 256 (including n47), 257.

229. Olson, "The Late Zionism of Nathan Birnbaum," 257–68. On sources of Herzl's increasing wealth, see Pawel, *Labyrinth of Exile*, 125, 128, 153, 195–97.

230. For example, supreme authority vested in a regularly held assembly of delegates; a clearly articulated program approved by the assembly; the growth of a devoted and dues-paying mass membership; and—as Birnbaum's advocates pointed out—the need for employment of paid party officials and staff. Meybohm has also argued that the organizations underwent similar kinds of evolution in governance and leadership. See Meybohm, *David Wolffsohn*, 119–21, 160–61. In fact, both the ZO and SPD were characterized by a blend of democratic and authoritarian tendencies, but moved in the direction of greater democratization and bureaucratization. In terms of leadership, Meybohm makes an intriguing comparison between the successors to Herzl and Bebel (i.e., David Wolffsohn and Friedrich Ebert). However, as she points out, the SPD made a successful transition to a salaried political leadership, whereas the Zionists under Herzl and Wolffsohn failed to establish a financial base sufficient to do so. On the SPD's history, see also von Alemann, "Die Enstehung und Entwicklung der deutschen Parteien"; and Faulenbach, *Geschichte der SPD*, esp. 21–27. Perhaps most significant in this context was the fact that, their social class notwithstanding, many Jewish professionals and intellectuals were drawn to the SPD and it was therefore another political rival of Zionism.

231. Several delegates suggested increasing the size of the Actions Committee. Ironically, it was Farbstein, the leftist delegate, who proposed twenty-three—a number recalling the provincial Jewish councils (Sanhedrins) of antiquity (*Die Welt*, Sept. 3, 1897, 16). Before the changes, representation had been accorded as follows: Austria, including Galicia and Bukovina (2), Germany (1), Russia (2), Romania (1), England (1), France (1), United States (1), and Serbia and Bulgaria (1) (ten members besides the five-member Vienna Executive). After the changes: Austria without Galicia and Bukovina (1), Galicia (2), Bukovina (1), Germany (2), Russia (4), Romania (2), England (1), France (1), United States (1), Serbia and Bulgaria (1), Palestine (1), and Oriental Jewry (1) (eighteen members besides the five-member Vienna Executive). Although this was still not proportional to the actual Jewish populations of the respective countries, it was more equitable than the first draft.

232. Vital, *Zionism: The Formative Years*, 13, 47, 103–4, 413.

233. Walter Lehn, "The Jewish National Fund," 75–80. The title of the "Jewish National Fund" in Hebrew is "Keren Kayemeth LeIsrael." The Hebrew is better translated as "Fund for the Existence of Israel," suggesting the absolute necessity of acquiring Palestine's land to secure the material foundation of Israel's existence. I owe thanks to Prof. Glazer for drawing my attention to the nuances of meaning here.

234. Moritz Moses had specified that estates acquired through his scheme must not be sold to non-Jews (*ZC 1897*, [148]).

235. Schapira's presentation treats the entire question of land acquisition as one of finance only, of growing and managing a huge national fund, simply assuming the ready availability of land for sale in Palestine and an abundance of *Lebensraum*—in spite of Ahad Ha'am's warning some six years before that fertile land was hard to find, because nearly all of it was already under cultivation. While this was perhaps an exaggeration, it suggests nonetheless that concentrating on the financial dimension of land transfer without attending to its potential economic and social effects, in a situation where most Arabs' livelihoods were dependent on agriculture and Jews were a small proportion of the country's population, was a prescription for conflict. See Shafir, *Land, Labor, and Origins*, 200–202, 208. Dowty-Ahad Ha'am, "Truth," 161–62; and Dowty-Epstein, "Question."

236. Kaplan and Penslar, *Origins of Modern Israel*, "The Rothschild Administration," 24–26. The author of the document, Mordechai Ben Hillel Ha-Kohen, bemoans the indolence and irresponsibility of the farmers in the Rothschild colonies.

237. Shafir, *Land, Labor, and Origins*, chapter 3.

238. Neumann, *Land and Desire*, 163–64.

239. *The Diaries of Theodor Herzl*, trans. and ed. Marvin Lowenthal (New York: Dial Press, 1956), 224.

240. *ha-Protokol shel ha-Kongres ha-Tsiyoni ha-rishon be-Bazel, 1–3 be-Elul 657–29–31 be-Ogust 1897*, trans. Hayim Orlan (Jerusalem: R. Mas, 1997); *Premier Congrès Sioniste, Bâle 29–31 Août 1897*, Protocole officiel, trans. Michèle Mialane (Tunis: Workshop 19, 2013).

241. Margarita Pazi, "Authors of German Language in Israel," in *Insiders and Outsiders: Jewish and Gentile Culture in Germany and Austria*, ed. Dagmar C.G. Lorenz and Gabriele Weinberger (Detroit: Wayne State University Press, 1994), 124–26.

242. Michael Berkowitz, "The Debate about Hebrew, in German: the *Kulturfrage* in the Zionist Congresses, 1897–1914," in *Insiders and Outsiders*, ed. Lorenz and Weinberger, 113.

243. While highlighting lacunae this study fills, I do not wish to disparage the existing scholarship on Zionism, from which I have benefitted enormously, as evidenced in the annotations. Indeed, as a relative "outsider" to Jewish studies and Zionist history, I owe this observation to a bona fide "insider," Professor Michael Berkowitz, who has the authority to make it.

244. Thus, the speeches of Herzl and Nordau constitute less than 10 percent of the proceedings' text; and recent work on early Zionism has sought to correct the overemphasis on Herzl's role and overreliance on his oeuvre, as seen in Jess Olson's work on Nathan Birnbaum and Ivonne Meybohm's on David Wolffsohn. Among the reports submitted to the Congress that offer important data for historians of European Jewry, six are particularly substantive: the reports on Galicia, Britain, Romania, Austria, Bukovina, and Bulgaria. As for semantic obscurities in the text (*ZC 1897*), the following is a tiny sample: *Elaborat* [137]; *Motivenbericht* [130]; *Freilandcolonieen* [126]; *durch blaue Brille betrachten* [114]; and *volkstümlich-sittlich* [142].

245. *Proceedings of The Zionist Congress held at Basle, Switzerland, Aug. 29 to Sept. 1, 1897: The Proceedings in Full* (New York: Philip Cowen, 1897).

246. Multiple translations of these speeches are in circulation, and *JC/Cowen*'s are not the best. For instance, Hertzberg's anthology, *The Zionist Idea* (1959), has superior versions of the same two speeches (though his version of Nordau's speech is truncated). For Herzl, Hertzberg took over a translation found in Ludwig Lewisohn's 1955 biography of Herzl, *Theodor Herzl: A Portait for this Age* (Cleveland: World Publishing, 1955, 307–12), itself an emended version of Nellie Strauss's earlier work, *Congress Addresses of Theodor Herzl* (New York: Federation of American Zionists, 1917). The first text of Herzl's speech to

appear was in *Die Welt,* Sept. 3, 1897, 3–5 (in German); the *JC/Cowen* translation was not based on either this text nor on the stenographic record (1898).

Unfortunately, Lawrence Epstein, in his new book on the Congress, perpetuates the disproportionate attention devoted to the addresses of Herzl and Nordau and neglect of, in particular, the speeches delivered after Nordau on the first day. See his *Dream of Zion,* chapter 4.

247. In the case of Farbstein, the Anglo-Jewish aversion to socialism probably played a role in this neglect; see David Cesarani, *The Jewish Chronicle and Anglo-Jewry, 1841–1991* (Cambridge: Cambridge University Press, 1994), 55, 81.

248. Susan Bassnett, *Translation Studies,* 3rd ed. (London: Routledge, 2002); Edwin Gentzler, *Contemporary Translation Theories,* 2nd revised ed. (Clevedon, UK: Multilingual Matters, 2001).

249. To distinguish from a *contemporary* performative function, which it most certainly possessed. Herzl wanted the delegates to "perform" as though they were a national assembly, and the international press to treat them as such.

250. "Fifty Years of Zionism: address delivered by Dr. Chaim Weizmann at the Jubilee Celebration at Basle on August 31, 1947," *Jubilee,* 9–24, esp. 11. It is impossible to know to what extent this *Kongressdeutsch* has been corrected in transcribing the proceedings.

251. Thus, Jacob de Haas's address on English Jewry was given in English; see *ZC 1897,* [28–38].

252. See Jasinski, *Sourcebook on Rhetoric,* s.v. "Close Reading" (91–97) and "Intertextuality" (321–27).

253. Cited in Daniel Chandler, "Semiotics for Beginners: Intertextuality," http://visual-memory.co.uk/daniel/Documents/S4B/sem09.html, accessed 4 June 2017.

254. For Herzl's predecessors and contemporaries, the most accessible entry point remains Hertzberg, *Zionist Idea.* See also the corpus of Herzl's letters and diaries, compiled and annotated in *Theodor Herzl: Briefe und Tagebücher.* The website *Internetarchiv jüdischer Periodika* offers scores of Jewish German-language periodicals for the period 1806–1938.

255. The range of potential works to be consulted is immense, but standard reference works on Judaism and Zionism are: *Jewish Encyclopedia (1906)*; *EJ* (2nd. ed., 2007); *Encyclopedia of Zionism and Israel* (1971); Geoffrey Wigoder, ed., *New Encyclopedia of Zionism and Israel,* 2 vols. (Madison, NJ: Fairleigh Dickinson University Press, 1994).

256. Because of its date, the 1899 edition of *Muret-Sanders Encyclopaedic German-English and English-German Dictionary/Enzyklopädisches englisch-deutsches und deutsch-englisches Wörterbuch* has been of particular importance.

NOTES TO DAY ONE OF THE PROCEEDINGS, MORNING SESSION

1. Gen. 12:7, 13:15, 15:18, 17:8.

2. In arguing for a "natural" beginning to the redemption, Lippe echoes the works of Yehudah Alkalai of Bosnia (1798–1878) and Zvi Hirsch Kalischer of Posen (1796–1874), two rabbis who wrote decades before the beginnings of the Zionist movement. They sought, on the basis of traditional authorities, to galvanize Jews to undertake an immediate, self-organized return to the Holy Land. See Hertzberg, *Zionist Idea*, 102–15.

3. Ezra 1:1–4. "Negotiations" (Ger. "diplomatische Unterhandlungen") is a misnomer; the text records a royal edict. The famous Cyrus Cylinder (ca. 539 BCE) supports the plausibility of the repatriation policy presented in Ezra. As indicated above, the German text cited is *Zionisten-Congress in Basel (August 29, 30, and 31, 1897): Offizielles Protokoll* (Vienna: Verlag des Vereines "Erez-Israel," 1898), abbreviated *ZC 1897*.

4. Zech. 9:9. In traditional Jewish exegesis, the text depicts the arrival of the Messiah on his divine errand of peacemaking. Jews awaiting a miraculous redemption interpreted the verse to mean that the ingathering of Israel would follow the appearance of the Messiah; religious Zionists reversed the order. Christian interpretation sees in the verse a prophecy of Jesus's triumphal entry into Jerusalem one week before his crucifixion (Matt. 21:4–5).

5. Isa. 45:1, a remarkable passage in which the prophet designates Cyrus the Great the Lord's Messiah (anointed king). As noted above, Cyrus permitted the Jews' return to Jerusalem and authorized the rebuilding of the temple.

6. One of the most enduring themes in Zionism, echoing various passages in the Bible, the aspiration to turn the Holy Land, now allegedly a desolate waste, into a fruitful garden. It is among the most oft-cited arguments legitimizing the Jewish "return" to Palestine. For the same reason, it has been consistently disputed by advocates of Palestinian nationalism, who have documented extensive agriculture and arboriculture prior to the arrival of the Zionist settlers. See for example, Arafat's 1974 speech at the UN, https://en.wikisource.org/wiki/Yasser_Arafat%27s_1974_UN_General_Assembly_speech; see esp. para. 40.

An early Zionist source confirms the Palestinian position: Ahad Ha'am, writing in 1891, says: "From abroad, we are accustomed to believe that Eretz Israel is presently almost totally desolate, an uncultivated desert, and that anyone wishing to buy land there can come and buy all he wants. But in truth it is not so." See Dowty-Ahad Ha'am, "Truth," 154–81, quoting 161. See also Gad G. Gilbar, "The Growing Economic Involvement of Palestine with the West, 1865–1914," in *Palestine in the Late Ottoman Period: Political, Social, and*

Economic Transformation, ed. David Kushner (Leiden: Brill, 1986), 188–210.

7. Zerubbabel was of royal Davidic lineage and became governor of Jerusalem under the Persians, ca. 520 BCE (cf. Haggai 1:1.) Ezra and Nehemiah were responsible for instructing and reorganizing the restored Jewish community in Palestine in the fifth century BCE.

8. Assimilated Jews were those who entered the mainstream of European society and culture in the nineteenth century. Politically, they identified with the states in which they resided. An estimate of their numbers is impossible, but they were certainly a large element within Jewry, especially in Western Europe. Because they rejected the concept of Jewish nationhood, they were implacable enemies of Zionism. The Zionists in their turn attacked the assimilationists in their speeches and publications.

9. Judg. 7:3. The reference is to the warlord Gideon and his admonition to the fainthearted prior to his battle with the Midianites. The story depicts the the pre-monarchical period (before 1000 BCE).

10. Lam. 1:19. Lamentations is traditionally ascribed to the prophet Jeremiah.

11. Num. 14:4. Lippe sermonizes using a biblical contrast, recasting the characters as the Zionists and the assimilated Jews. The text concerns a division between the Israelites: those who remained loyal to Moses and to his vision of a future conquest of the Holy Land are, in this rendering, the Zionists; those who rebelled and wished to return to Egypt are equated with the assimilated Jews of modern Europe. The desire for Egypt is made the equivalent of a desire to remain in the Diaspora, for which the Zionist reproached assimilated Jews.

12. No verse of scripture corresponds to Lippe's declaration, but prayers for a return to Jerusalem are an integral part of the Orthodox liturgy.

13. The fulfillment of the Jews' mission in the Diaspora was a cardinal point of Reform Judaism, which emerged in the 1830s and 40s in Germany. Reform Jews understood Judaism in evolutionary and nonnational terms. Lippe may be alluding to such views.

14. Isa. 2:3. Lippe interprets a prophetic oracle that had an eschatological thrust. In Isaiah's vision, Zion becomes the Lord's seat of judgment, the center of the world, and the locus of the Gentiles' submission. Lippe seems to imply that the Zionist project will actually begin the fulfillment of this oracle.

15. For the foregoing, I have used a previous published work, with minor changes: "'The good Dr. Lippe' and Herzl in Basel, 1897: A translation and analysis of the Zionist Congress's opening speech," *Journal of Israeli History* 34.1 (2015): 1–21. It is reused here by permission of Taylor & Francis; *JIH*'s website is http://www.tandfonline.com/loi/fjih20.

16. *Schutzjudenthum* is the term Herzl uses here, which refers to the status of Jews in most parts of Europe prior to the emancipation of the nineteenth century. From medieval times, Jews were obligated to pay special taxes, or protection money ("Schutzgeld"), in return for which they were permitted to reside and work in a given location. This status could also be revoked. There is a difference between *ZC 1897* and the report of Herzl's speech in *Die Welt*, Sept. 3, 1897, where this revocability is made explicit (bracketed in the translation, italicized here): "Mit der Toleranz und dem Schutzjudenthum *auf Widerruf* haben wir nachgerade genug Erfahrungen gemacht." David Farbstein returns to this theme at the end of day one. He argues that, ironically, although assimilated Jews think they have gained equality, they are in fact still *Schutzjuden*, only now under the protectorate of the liberal bourgeoisie or one of the political parties [106–7].

17. The Ottoman government was not unaware of the aims of Zionist settlement in Palestine. See: Mandel, *Arabs and Zionism before World War I* (1976); Mandel, "Ottoman Policy and Restrictions on Jewish Settlement in Palestine" (1974); Mandel, "Ottoman Policy as regards Jewish Settlement in Palestine" (1975); Öke, "The Ottoman Empire, Zionism, and the Question of Palestine (1880–1908)."

18. It appears that Herzl made five journeys to Istanbul seeking to obtain a "charter" for Jewish settlement in Palestine in exchange for a "Jewish" loan to relieve Ottoman financial problems. Herzl visited for the first time in June 1896; but his most important visit was in May 1901, when he had a two-hour audience with Sultan Abdülhamit II. On no occasion did Ottoman officials confirm the feasibility of Herzl's plan, although it does appear that they sought to profit from suggesting to Herzl its potential acceptability. See Isaiah Friedman, *Germany, Turkey, and Zionism, 1897–1918* (Oxford: Clarendon, 1977), chapter 6.

19. This sentence is missing from the text of Herzl's speech as given in the Zionist organ, *Die Welt*, Sept. 3, 1897, 3–5. It is likewise missing from all English translations of the speech I have been able to consult—probably an indication that the translators relied on the text of *Die Welt* or another printed edition of the speech, rather than *ZC 1897*. In fact, the sentence is practically demanded by the sense of the preceding statement, which otherwise moves abruptly and inexplicably from an indignant denial of the charge of the Jews' lack of patriotism, to a discussion of how and which Jews will leave each region, and how their exodus will stabilize the political situation there.

20. Herzl appears here to call for the Congress to recite the *Shema Yisrael*, the Jewish confession of monotheism found in Deuteronomy 6:4. It is admittedly

out of character for the secular-minded Herzl to propose a liturgical act of this kind, but the German appears to indicate this: "Heute sei unser Bekenntniss feierlich wiederholt."

21. With few exceptions, I have followed the text of Nordau's speech as given in *ZC 1897*. In a couple of cases, I have revised the text by comparing it to that found in *Die Welt*, Sept. 3, 1897, 5–9. The reader is advised that there are numerous minor discrepancies between these two texts that have not been noted.

22. Reference here to the Pale of Settlement, those western provinces of the Russian Empire where the vast majority of Jews were permitted to live and work. Statutes regulating rights and restrictions pertaining to Jews were issued in 1804 and 1835; these laws prohibited most Jewish settlement outside the Pale and even in many cities inside, although individuals of substantial wealth or having special qualifications (as Nordau indicates) could reside in otherwise restricted areas. It has been estimated that the Russian Empire (including Russian-controlled Poland) was home to about 40 percent of world Jewry in the nineteenth century.

23. In the eighteenth century, Russia's merchants were divided into three guilds according to their declared capital. First-guild merchants were those possessing a minimum of ten thousand rubles; the minimum was raised to fifteen thousand rubles by the 1850s. Privileges attaching to membership in the first guild included the right to own and operate ships and factories, provide banking services, and conduct business abroad. See Liliya G. Nasyrova, "Legislative Measures of the Russian State Relating to Regulation of Entrepreneurial Activity Between the Mid-18th and Early 20th Centuries," *Terra Sebus: Acta Musei Sabesiensis*, Special Issue, 2014, 331–41, https://www.cclbsebes.ro/docs/Sebus_SI_2014/22_LGNasyrova.pdf; William L. Blackwell, *The Beginnings of Russian Industrialization* (Princeton: Princeton University Press, 1968), 102.

24. This statement, if taken literally, is misleading. While laws pertaining to the Pale of Settlement did restrict Jewish rights of residence, occupation, and movement, the total surface area of the provinces included in the Pale was immense (over one million square kilometers).

25. Nordau mentions Moroccan and Persian Jews, but he omits mention of Jews of the Ottoman Empire, including those living in Palestine. He does so perhaps in order to avoid a direct conflict with the preceding speakers (Lippe and Herzl), both of whom had made complimentary references to Sultan Abdülhamit II, and specifically to the favorable treatment which, they claim, Jews within the Empire enjoyed. In fact, however, Nordau subsumes these Jews

with those of Eastern Europe, North Africa, and Western Asia, who suffer from continual material want and intermittent physical violence.

26. Nordau echoes Herzl's attack on the limited imaginings of "practical people"; for which, see Herzl, *Judenstaat*, section titled "Allgemeiner Teil: Bedürfniss, Organ, Verkehr."

27. Deut. 8:3; cited by Jesus in Matt. 4:4.

28. Sancho Panza was squire to Don Quixote, in Cervantes's famous novel of the same name. His putative assignment as viceroy of Barataria, which he took to be an actual award for his service to Don Quixote, was in reality nothing more than a prank played upon him by some mischief-makers posing as noblemen. Nordau implies thereby that legal emancipation was analogous to a ruse, since Jews were offered theoretical rights, which were severely compromised in practice.

29. "Qui veut noyer son chien l'accuse de la rage." The quotation actually derives not from folk wisdom but from Molière (*Les femmes savantes*).

30. "Périssent les colonies plutôt qu'un principe!" Nordau quotes Antoine Barnave, who may have taken the words from Robespierre or other radicals, during a debate in the Constituent Assembly in May 1791. The debate concerned exclusion of nonwhites from assemblies in French overseas colonies; "pragmatists" insisted that exclusion was imperative for maintaining the colonies, while "radicals" insisted on equality without regard to race. The saying expresses the extent of their commitment to the egalitarian ideal, which was not however implemented. See "Barnave, Antoine-Pierre-Joseph-Marie," *Biographie Universelle*, F.-X. Feller, new ed. M. Pérennès (Paris, 1844), 2:74–75.

31. Correcting the text of *ZC 1897*, 15, which has "religiöse Weise" ("religious manner"), from the text in *Die Welt* (Sept. 3, 1897), 7, which has Nordau's obviously intended wording (i.e., "religiöse Weihe" ["religious sanction"]).

32. *Die Welt* (Sept. 3, 1897, 8), includes the bracketed sentence at this point, not found however in the text of *ZC 1897*: "Die Armuth zermürbt seinen Charakter und zerstört seinen Leib."

33. *ZC 1897* text has "Judah ben Halevus."

34. An allusion to an infamous anti-Semitic comment of Voltaire, in which he refers to a day when the Jews will have become a mortal danger to the human race: "Je ne serais point étonné que cette nation ne fût un jour funeste au genre humain." *Oeuvres complètes de Voltaire* (Paris: Chez Furne, 1837), *Lettres de Memmius á Ciceron (Lettre II)*, vi:72.

35. *ZC 1897*, 2, has "Oerter" and "Rappaport," stenographic errors which have been corrected to "Erter" and "Rapoport."

36. Public primary schools.

37. The *Gymnasium*, in the Austro-German system of education, is the most academically oriented secondary school, and it functions as the pathway to a university education in the arts and sciences.

38. A *Realschule* is a secondary school with a more practical and technical orientation than the *Gymnasium*, although language and liberal arts are also taught.

39. The hereditary Polish nobility.

40. Salz first deplores corruption "in den jüdischen Cultusgemeinden Galiziens" ("communities," plural), then suggests that the "Säuberungskampf" ("struggle for reform") must begin "in der Cultusgemeinde" ("community," singular). Hence my interpretative insertion, "individual," to qualify "community." The term could be translated as "congregation," but one must bear in mind that it was an officially recognized body in a given location representing all Jews vis-à-vis the state.

41. One hundred and forty thousand in the German text: an obvious error.

42. The quoted phrase appears thus in English, in the midst of the German text.

43. This appears to be a voluntary investment scheme workers in specific trades put money into, which provided financial benefits to its members. A reference to it is found in a short biography of Jacob Kuenzly, a Swiss immigrant to California, 1859. See online "Find a Grave: Mattie Gertrude Camk Kuenzly," https://www.findagrave.com/memorial/4454115, accessed Feb. 28, 2018.

44. At the time of the Zionist Congress, this office was held by Dr. Hermann Adler, who served in this position 1891–1911. He succeeded his father, Nathan Marcus Adler; the elder Adler had fallen ill and delegated his powers to his son beginning in 1879. The office still exists, now titled "Chief Rabbi of the United Hebrew Congregations of Great Britain and the Commonwealth." The term used in German is "Gemeinde," which I have elsewhere rendered as "community." But given that the official English nomenclature has "congregations," that term has been used here, albeit not with entire consistency.

45. Established by an Act of Parliament in 1870, the United Synagogue was a body of London synagogues, which created a joint financial administration in order to consolidate expenditure on communal services. Largely composed of Jews of English and German origin, it was markedly different, in both socioeconomic and cultural terms, from congregations established after the influx of Russian-Polish Jews began in the 1880s (s.v. "United Synagogue," *JE 1906*).

46. The "Federation of Synagogues" was established by sixteen Russian-Polish congregations in greater London in 1887, with the help of the Jewish philanthropist Samuel Montagu. They regarded most British Jews as alien and assimilated, and they wished to create a body separate from the United Synagogue. For the administrative history, see: University of Southhampton Special Collections, http://www.southampton.ac.uk/archives/cataloguedatabases/webguidemss248.page.

47. "The two great universities" are Oxford and Cambridge; the "better public school" referred to is a college within the structure of what came to be the University of London (i.e., "University College London"). The latter was established in 1828, and was distinguished by the fact that, unlike Oxford and Cambridge, it accepted students irrespective of race or religion. See Robert Anderson, *British Universities, Past and Present* (London: Continuum, 2006), 26–28.

48. Jews' College, a rabbinical seminary in London, was founded in 1855. It was reorganized and renamed in 1999, and is today known as "London School of Jewish Studies."

49. *JC/Cowen* (34) has a summary of de Haas's speech indicating that the numbers given in the following table are those of Jewish students receiving religious instruction in the different institutions named.

50. More commonly known as "London Board of Deputies" or "Board of Deputies of British Jews," it was established in the mid-eighteenth century to further the interests and promote the emancipation of Jews in Britain and its colonies. It gradually evolved from an organization of London Jews to one representing provincial Jewish congregations as well. The London Board was headed by the pious philanthropist, Sir Moses Montefiore, 1835–1885. S.v. "Board of Deputies of British Jews," *EJ*, 2nd ed.

51. The Board of Delegates is to be distinguished from the Board of Deputies, although the president of the latter was also president of the former. The Board of Delegates was a council representing the Russian-Polish "Federation of Synagogues," or, as de Haas calls them here, the "Federation of Smaller Synagogues," set up in 1887, as noted above.

52. A Yiddish term meaning "a tacit marital condition" (i.e., cohabitation not preceded by a public exchange of vows).

53. Also known as the Franco-Prussian War, July 19, 1870 to May 10, 1871. The war saw the capture of Emperor Napoleon III and the replacement of the Second Empire by the Third Republic.

54. The decree of October 24, 1870, known as the Decree of Crémieux, naturalized the Jews en masse. In fact, this was the last in a series of laws

distinguishing Algerian Jews from their Muslim neighbors and assimilating them to the ranks of the immigrant European population. See s.v. "Algeria," *JE 1906*.

55. Under the reign of Napoleon III (1852–1870), Algeria had been under the authority of a military governor. The military regime in Algeria retarded the expansion of *colon* control over Algerian lands; the downfall of Napoleon III's government precipitated the overthrow of military government in Algeria and the triumph of *colon* power, realized now through a civilian administration. See John Ruedy, *Modern Algeria: The Origins and Development of a Nation*, 2nd ed. (Bloomington: Indiana University Press, 2005), chapters 3 and 4.

56. The 1890s witnessed a wave of anti-Semitic activism in Algeria, including riots which began in Mostagenem in 1897, spread to many other towns, and continued intermittently until the end of 1899. See s.v. "Algeria," *JE 1906*.

57. The original text has "neutralisieren," an obvious typographical error.

58. Correction to original text, which has "Tleman."

59. Pineles's precise words are "gesicherte Heimstätte"; the term "legally" is implied but not stated. His formulation anticipates the Zionist program adopted on the second day of the Congress, after much debate, which ultimately referred to a "die Schaffung einer öffentlich-rechtlich gesicherten Heimstätte in Palästina" (the creation of a homeland in Palestine, secured by public law).

60. The Treaty of Paris, 1856, marked the end of the Crimean War, which had pitted Russia against the Ottoman Empire, the latter power supported by Britain and France. Russia's defeat in the war led to the termination of its protectorate over Moldavia and Wallachia, areas still formally under Ottoman suzerainty and referred to in diplomatic parlance as "the Principalities." The 1856 treaty and subsequent agreements concerning the governance of the Principalities gave greater autonomy and somewhat greater unity to these, the core territories of what was to become the country of Romania.

61. The Treaty of Berlin, 1878, settled questions of Balkan politics after the Russo-Ottoman War of 1877–1878. Serbia, Montenegro, and Romania were recognized as fully independent states; Bulgaria was an autonomous territory tributary to the Ottoman Empire. The treaty stipulated that religious equality was to be observed in all of the above lands; there was to be no discrimination against Jews, in particular. Article 44 applied to Romania and stated that

> difference in religious beliefs and confessions shall not be brought against any one as a ground for exclusion or unfitness as regards the enjoyment of civil and political rights, admission to public offices, functions, and honors, or the exercise of various professions and industries

in any place whatever. Freedom in outward observance of all creeds will be assured to all subjects of the Romanian state, as well as to strangers, and no obstacle will be raised either to the ecclesiastical organization of different bodies, or to their intercourse with their spiritual heads.

S.v. "Berlin Congress," *JE 1906*. Articles with the same formulae applied to Serbia and Bulgaria, as Pineles notes. But, whereas Serbia and Bulgaria actually implemented emancipation, the Romanian government disenfranchised many of its Jews by declaring them aliens, who could be naturalized only by a special act of the legislature.

NOTES TO DAY ONE, AFTERNOON SESSION

1. Lev. 18:7.

2. The original text has "christkatholisch," a reference to so-called Old Catholics; i.e., German, Swiss, and Austrian Catholics who broke from Rome over the doctrine of papal infallibility declared in 1870. They subsequently vernacularized the mass and dropped the requirement of clerical celibacy. Georg von Schönerer, mentioned in the previous paragraph, was among the pan-German nationalists who encouraged Roman Catholics to join the Old Catholics, presumably because continued loyalty to Rome was seen as infringing upon one's commitment to the racially and linguistically defined nation.

3. Referring to Minister-President Count Badeni's April 1897 ordinance, making knowledge of both Czech and German a requirement of the civil service in Bohemia. Since Czechs learned German in school but few German speakers knew Czech, the law was regarded by the German-speaking population as discriminatory. As a result, rioting broke out in Vienna, Prague, and elsewhere, leading to Badeni's fall from power in November 1897. The entire episode augured the future fracturing of Austria-Hungary along ethnolinguistic lines. See Robert Bideleux and Ian Jeffries, *A History of Eastern Europe: Crisis and Change* (London: Routledge, 1998), 351.

4. "Cleansed of Jews," similar to the contemporary usage, "ethnic cleansing."

5. A reference to the failed January 1863 Polish uprising against Russian rule, in which some Jews cooperated with the Polish nationalists.

6. The Leitha River was the boundary between Austria proper and the Kingdom of Hungary; hence "the Paradise beyond the Leitha" ("das transleithanische Paradies") is simply a facetious reference to Hungary.

7. Jews attained civil equality in Hungary 1867; laws passed in 1895 and after put Judaism on a par with Christianity as a religion. See Géza Komoróczy, "Israeliten/Juden in ihrer Gemeinde. Juden in der ungarischen Gesellschaft der Nachkriegszeit, 1945–2002," in *Jüdische Gemeinden. Kontinuitäten und Brüche* (Berlin/Vienna: Philo, 2002), 63.

8. An evocation of the German translation of *Hamlet*. The famous line in English, "Something is rotten in the state of Denmark," is rendered "Etwas ist faul im Staate Dänemarks" (*Hamlet*, 1.4.90).

9. The images here—serpent, paradise, sword, tree of knowledge—are obviously borrowed (but reused in a curious fashion) from the story of the temptation and fall in Gen. 3. The point seems to be that Jews must give up a false paradise to gain a true one (i.e., Zion).

10. A mythical city of gold in South America, sought after by early European explorers of the continent—hence, the designation of a utopia, a Shangri-La.

11. Ger. "Curiensystem." The electoral system was complex and included "classes" of large landowners, urbanites, rural communities, merchants and artisans, etc.

12. Ger. "Stimmvieh," an expression taken over from a rare but lexicographically attested expression, "voting cattle," found in nineteenth-century American English.

13. The allusion here is to a remark by Bismarck, first made in 1876 (and later reiterated, in a slightly modified form it appears, in 1888). Renouncing German involvement in Balkan disputes, Bismarck declared: "Der ganze Balkan ist mir nicht die gesunden Knochen eines einzigen pommerschen Musketiers wert": "The whole of the Balkans is not worth the [healthy] bones of a single Pomeranian musketeer." The more famous rendering of this statement has "grenadier" instead of "musketeer."

14. "Schaagspropheten"—probably derived from the Yiddish, *shegetz*, for "impure Gentile." The term is, to my knowledge, otherwise unattested.

15. "Żyd," Polish for "Jew."

16. In *Judenstaat*, Herzl makes repeated reference to the Jews' "overproduction of middle-class intelligentsias" using these terms—"unsere Ueberproduction an mittleren Intelligenzen." He cites this as the immediate cause (*causa proxima*) of the rise of a new anti-Semitism in Europe (section titled "Gründe des Antisemitismus"). The phrase occurs three times in *Judenstaat*; but the standard translation of the first occurrence is, misleadingly, "excessive production of mediocre intellectuals" (Hertzberg, *Zionist Idea*, 219). "Mediocre" has a derisive connotation not necessarily found in the German "mittler"; and the

groups Herzl has in mind are mostly not "intellectuals" as the term is used in English—he means officers, professors, officials, jurists, and physicians (see his "Schlusswort," where the standard translation refers, correctly, to "middle class" rather than "mediocre"—see also Hertzberg, *Zionist Idea*, 225).

17. I Macc. 2:51.

18. Belkovsky's strictures against Bulgarian anti-Semitism in 1897 stand in contrast to Bulgarian behavior during World War II, when king, clergy, and common people cooperated in protecting the country's Jewish minority from deportation and slaughter. See Michael Bar-Zohar, *Beyond Hitler's Grasp: the Heroic Rescue of Bulgaria's Jews* (Holbrook, MA: Adams Media, 1998).

19. Referring to Konstantin Jireček, whose *Geschichte der Bulgaren* (1876) attracted the attention of the European public because it appeared at the same time as the Bulgarian struggle to throw off Ottoman rule.

20. Ger. "ihres Catechismus den Juden gegenüber . . . ."

21. (1) Petko Stoichev Karavelov (1843–1903): leading liberal politician of Bulgaria after its establishment as an autonomous principality in 1878. As prime minister, 1884–1886, he "unified" Bulgaria with the adjoining territory of Eastern Rumelia, leading to war with Serbia in 1885, from which Bulgaria emerged victorious. (2) Dragan Tsankov (1828–1911): liberal politician and Bulgarian prime minister, 1880, 1883–1884. Tsankov was known for his governmental reforms, which included seeking to limit the power of the Bulgarian Orthodox Church, on account of his support for the Bulgarian Greek Catholics. He also favored a pro-Russian foreign policy. (3) Stefan Nikolov Stambolov (1854–1895): Bulgarian nationalist and politician. After the Ottoman defeat in the Russo-Ottoman War (1877–1878), he helped to organize the new Bulgarian principality. Stambolov's seven-year premiership, 1887–1894, was marked by rapid economic and cultural development, as suggested by Belkovsky's comments. (*ZC 1897* consistently refers to "Stambuloff," with the associated adjectival form "stambulistisch," rather than "Stambolov." The latter spelling of this political leader's name is currently attested while the former is not. Hence the discrepancy between the spelling of his name in German text and English translation.) (4) Vasil Radoslavov (1854–1929): his "Radoslav Liberal Party" emerged in 1887, when he was prime minister for the first time. He was known for a pro-Austrian, pro-German policy; he led Bulgaria as prime minister throughout World War I, aligning it with the Central Powers.

On the personalities, parties, and policies of modern Bulgarian politics, see Charles Jelavich and Barbara Jelavich, *The Establishment of the Balkan National States, 1804–1920* (Seattle: University of Washington Press, 1977), chs. 9 and 11, 192–96, 288–90, 310–11; for a contemporary survey of Jewish life, see *JE 1906*, s.v. "Bulgaria." A recent scholarly study is Marco Dogo, "Loyalty Sorely Tried: The Jews and the Bulgarian State (1878–1935)," in *The Jews and the Nation-States of Southeastern Europe from the 19th Century to the Great Depression*, ed. Tullia Catalan and Marco Dogo (Newcastle upon Tyne, UK: Cambridge Scholars Publishing, 2016), 73–103.

22. Meaning "Banner" or "Flag."

23. Referring to Jews who fought for Bulgaria in the 1885 Serbo-Bulgarian War, since this was the first time Jews were conscripted.

24. *Svetlina* means "Light." The other title in *ZC 1897*, given as *Seplasoije*, corresponds to no known Bulgarian word. The title, as corrected here in the English text, *Suglasie*, means "Concord," and it was in fact a newspaper related to the Tsankovists (personal communication from Associate Professor Dr. Lyumir Georgiev, Head of Manuscript, Documentary, and Heritage Division, Bulgarian National Library, Nov. 5, 2015).

25. I have not been able to determine the meaning of this title.

26. Konstantin Stoilov (1853–1901), Bulgarian lawyer and politician. Stoilov was a conservative who served twice as prime minister, most notably 1894–1899. Ironically, in the light of Belkovsky's remarks, Stoilov's government was known for its defense of Jewish rights. Stoilov had won a court case for Jews accused of ritual murder in 1893. "Thus Stoilov became the political point of reference for the Bulgarian Jews." See Dogo, "Loyalty Sorely Tried," 89.

27. Nikola Mitakov was the founder of a newspaper in 1893, at first titled *Bulgaria za Bulgarite* ("Bulgaria for the Bulgarians"), then retitled, as Belkovsky notes, *Bulgaria bez Evrei* ("Bulgaria without Jews"). While repeating old anti-Semitic accusations such as the blood libel, it focuses its attack on alleged Jewish and Armenian attempts to dominate the Bulgarian economy. See Veselina Kulenska, "The Antisemitic Press in Bulgaria at the End of the 19th Century," *Quest: Issues in Contemporary Jewish History*, issue 3 (July 2012), http://www.quest-cdecjournal.it/focus.php?issue=3&id=296.

28. Ger. "sind judenrein oder besser, judenrein geworden."

29. Literally "right of the first night," it refers to a theoretical right of a social superior (king, feudal lord, tribal chieftain, etc.) to sleep with a bride belonging to a socially subordinate group, prior to her union with her husband. The extreme application here (presumably rare) implies that that any Gentile Bulgarian has the right to violate any Jewish woman.

30. Referring to Dr. Alexander Mintz's report on Austria-Hungary [46–56].

31. Although an idiom, which perhaps came naturally in describing deep emotion, it is also probably not coincidental that here, as in other places, a Congress speaker employs a locution previously used by Herzl. In this case it

is found in his Congress address, where he says: "Das moderne, gebildete... Judenthum bekam einen Stich mitten in's Herz" (*ZC 1897*, 5).

32. Perhaps alluding to pioneering nineteenth-century studies of crowd psychology. This same thesis is basic to Reinhold Niebuhr's *Moral Man and Immoral Society: A Study in Ethics and Politics* (New York: Charles Scribner's Sons, 1932).

33. The self-designation of the Hungarians; or an ethno-linguistic term to refer to the same.

34. Tisza-Eszlár was a Hungarian village where, in 1882, the mysterious disappearance of a young peasant girl a few days before Passover led to an outcry against Jews allegedly responsible for her death—the blood libel. Subsequent investigations were protracted and marked by gross manipulation of witnesses and evidence. Although the accused were acquitted by July 1883, the case demonstrated that, despite Hungary's liberal regime, old prejudices against Jews were deeply rooted, especially in rural areas. See *JE 1906*, s.v. "Tisza-Eszlar Affair."

35. Ger. "Heimstätte." In most other places, including the Basel Program, this has been rendered "homeland"; but Rosenberg refers above to the ancient homeland (Heimatland), and that is clearly not the sense here.

36. Established in 1893 and existing until the present. Its major concerns during the 1890s included assisting in immigrant settlement, providing vocational training for girls and women, offering Jewish education in areas without synagogues, and advocacy of general social reforms, such as the abolition of child labor. See http://www.ncjw.org/content_85.cfm?navID=27.

37. A generally accepted translation of the three terms would be "nation," "tribe," and "people"; Birnbaum is probably thinking of the Latin *natio*, *gens*, and *populus*. For background, see Hans-Werner Goetz, "Die 'Deutschen Stämme' als Forschungsproblem," in Heinrich Beck et al., eds., *Zur Geschichte "der Gleichung germanisch-deutsch"* (Berlin: Walter de Gruyter, 2004), 229–53, esp. 231.

38. Ger. "Jargonjuden."

39. "den eigentlichen orientalischen Juden." So we have two kinds of oriental Jews; i.e., the Jews of Eastern Europe and the "really" oriental Jews of the Middle East and North Africa. It appears to leave out the Sephardim long settled in but not originally native to Eastern lands; but it is probable that the Sephardim, who are seldom referred to in the Congress, are subsumed under the rubric "oriental" (Birnbaum's orientalism is treated at greater length in the introduction).

40. A theme treated similarly by Nordau: see above [16–17].

41. "Cultursteuer" in the original, a typographical error for "Cultussteuer."

42. Ger. "Gemeinwesen," which could be translated more literally by the antique-sounding "commonwealth."

43. Alluding to Exodus 16:3: "Would that we had died by the hand of the Lord in the land of Egypt, when we sat by the fleshpots and ate bread to the full..." The passage refers to an episode in the wanderings of the people of Israel when, afflicted with hunger, they "murmured against" Moses and yearned for a return to a comfortable slavery in Egypt. Lippe alluded to the same passage in his opening address; see reference on [4].

44. Birnbaum refers here to the several Balkan states which gained autonomy or independence in the latter part of the nineteenth century: Montenegro, Serbia, Romania, and Bulgaria.

45. Philhellenism was a factor in deciding Britain, France, and Russia to intervene in 1827 on behalf of the Greek revolution.

46. The most important Christian edifice in Jerusalem, the Church of the Holy Sepulchre, contains within its precincts, according to tradition, both Golgotha, the site of Jesus's crucifixion, and the tomb (sepulchre) where Jesus was buried, and from which, according to the canonical gospels, he was miraculously resurrected on Easter.

47. Alluding to Hegel's *Vorlesungen über die Philosophie der Geschichte* (12/11):

> Hier haben wir es mit Völkern zu tun, welche wußten, was sie waren und wollten. Der Boden angeschauter oder anschaubarer Wirklichkeit gibt einen festeren Grund als der der Vergänglichkeit, auf dem jene Sagen und Dichtungen gewachsen sind, welche nicht mehr das Historische von Völkern, die zu fester Individualität gediehen sind. [Here we are dealing with peoples who knew what they were and sought. The ground of perceived or perceptible reality supplies a firmer basis than that of the past upon which those sagas and poems have arisen, which no longer constitute the historical for peoples who have developed a definite individual identity.]

The most scholarly of the addresses offered at the Congress, Farbstein's speech seeks to establish Zionism as a movement generated by a self-conscious, empirically minded people, undeceived by unhistorical illusions, peoples such as are exalted by Hegel.

48. Ger. "Junker."

49. "Everything is made within the household."

50. Ger. "als Fremde... in fremden Ländern." The passage evokes Exodus 2:22, where Moses calls himself a "stranger in a strange land" (AV).

51. Ger. "Wucherjude" (i.e., a Shylock, a heartless moneylender).

52. According to Farbstein, Mendelssohn was not yet an "ordentlicher Schutzjude." The statement appears to be in error, however. According to other sources, Mendelssohn received extraordinary protection (i.e., he was an "ausserordentlicher Schutzjude") as early as 1763.

53. *ZC 1897* lacks a comma to distinguish between Abraham Markus (spelling corrected from "Marcus") and Veitel Ephraim; "Itzing" corrected here and in the glossary to "Itzig."

54. Peasant alcoholism and other social evils in rural Eastern Europe were commonly blamed on Jewish tavernkeepers. See "Tavernkeeping," *YIVO Encyclopedia*.

55. Voltaire penned a work titled *Des Juifs* in 1756, which was later incorporated into his more famous *Dictionnaire Philosophique* of 1764. To the former work, Isaac de Pinto, a rich Portuguese Jew in the Netherlands, replied in in his *Apologie pour la nation juive: Réflexions critiques sur le premier chapitre du VIIe tome des oeuvres de M. Voltaire* (Amsterdam, 1762), trans. Philip Lafanu, "Critical Reflexions" in Antoine Guénée, ed., *Letters of Certain Jews to Monsieur Voltaire* (Philadelphia, 1795), 19–36. The episode is documented and analyzed in Adam Sutcliffe, "Can a Jew be a Philosophe? Isaac de Pinto, Voltaire, and Jewish Participation in the European Enlightenment," *Jewish Social Studies* 6:3 (2000), 31–51.

56. Farbstein refers to Émile Arton (Aron), a French financier of Jewish origins who bribed members of the Chamber of Deputies in order to win approval for floating a loan to rescue the Panama Canal. The company went bust in 1889 and the scandal, which was enormous, broke in 1892. See William I. Brustein, *Roots of Hate: Anti-Semitism in Europe before the Holocaust* (Cambridge: Cambridge University Press, 2003), 193–94; an older account is found in *JE 1906*, s.v. "Arton, Léopold Émile (formerly Aaron)."

57. Ger. "Die Juden Westeuropas." Since postulate number 2 deals otherwise entirely with *Die Juden Osteuropas*, I assume this is an error made by the speaker or the transcriber.

58. Jews granted privileges by the sovereign or aristocracy.

59. Edmond de Rothschild.

60. Probably referring to Baron Maurice de Hirsch's Jewish Colonization Association (JCA), founded in 1891 to assist Jews in material need to emigrate and establish themselves in new lands. The JCA began its aid to Jewish colonists in Palestine in 1896; in 1899, it took ownership of the farms previously owned and managed by Edmond de Rothschild.

61. Quoting a famous poem, "Georg Herwegh," by Heinrich Heine. Herwegh was a famous poet but also a dedicated revolutionary. Farbstein is perhaps suggesting that the time has come to cross over from the "poetry" of utopian idealism to the "prose" of political struggle.

62. Borrowing language Marx's *Communist Manifesto*, from the peroration in part 4.

NOTES TO DAY TWO OF THE PROCEEDINGS, MORNING SESSION

1. The petition concludes with words echoing those of Herzl's opening speech: "Wir wollen den Grundstein legen zu dem Haus, das dereinst die jüdische Nation beherbergen wird" ([4]). The critical role of Galician Jewry at the Congress and for Zionism is signalled by the selection of this petition for public reading; recall also that the first of the regional reports concerned Galician Jewry, by Abraham Salz ([21–28]).

2. It appears that this original Hebrew text forms the basis of the translation of Mohilewer's letter in Hertzberg's *Zionist Idea* (398–405), since Hertzberg's translation departs substantially from the German rendering given orally at the Congress and recorded in the present stenographic protocol. The many minor differences between Hertzberg and the translation given here will be ignored, but some important differences are noted and the pages in Hertzberg indicated. For the significance of Mohilewer to the early Zionist movement, the reader is referred to Hertzberg's brief but incisive comments introducing the Mohilewer letter (399–400).

3. Kaminka's free rendering using Herzl's language: Mohilewer does not in fact refer here to the "Jewish question" at all. Rather, as part of his prayer, he asks that the Zionists find favor as "they stand and plead for Thy people and Thy land" (Hertzberg, *Zionist Idea*, 401).

4. Hertzberg (*Zionist Idea*, 402) renders this sentence: "We are pledged, in particular, that the total conduct of the meeting will be in a manner acceptable to the Hovevei Zion and to their distinguished government." The German translation omits mention of Hovevei Zion and says only that the Congress will take into account "den russischen Zionisten und deren politischen Verhältnissen."

5. Mohilewer expressed himself much more forcefully here: "I feel certain that this expression of good faith will be observed to the full; if, nevertheless, opinions are expressed which are not in accordance with the above pledge, they will find no response" (Hertzberg, *Zionist Idea*, 402).

6. The implication being, perhaps, that the Russians, as the pioneers of the Zionist movement, have already proven themselves sacrificially committed to the cause, whereas parvenus like Herzl have yet to show the same degree of devotion.

7. "Sons of Zion" (Hertzberg, *Zionist Idea*, 402); here and elsewhere the term "Zionist" is given either by this expression or by "Lovers of Zion." One is reminded here of Ahad Ha'am's criticism of the First Zionist Congress on precisely this point, setting Hebrew *Hibbat Zion* in opposition to German *Zionismus*.

8. Hertzberg, *Zionist Idea*, 402: "Were it not for fear of the police, they would devour us alive." The image of enemies who "devour" the Jews derives from Ps. 124:3.

9. Kaminka turns a hopeful affirmation into a stiff warning. Hertzberg's text runs: "If all factions will really understand this thought, this covenant of brothers will surely stand" (*Zionist Idea*, 402).

10. As given in *ZC 1897*, "Ischub Erez Israel" (i.e., the settlement of the Land of Israel). Hertzberg (*Zionist Idea*, 402) renders this "the resettlement of our country."

11. "Hibbat Zion" in the original; Kaminka Germanizes it as "Liebe zu Zion."

12. "The basis of Hibbat Zion is the Torah, as it has been handed down to us from generation to generation, with neither supplement nor subtraction" (Hertzberg, *Zionist Idea*, 403). Kaminka abbreviates this statement and refers only to "die überkommene jüdische Lehre."

13. Alluding to the vocation of the prophet Jeremiah, but with a twist, since Jeremiah was called to both destroy and rebuild: "See, I have set you this day over nations and over kingdoms, to pluck up and to break down, to destroy and to overthrow, to build and to plant" (Jer. 1:10).

14. "We must, therefore, carefully avoid injuring the 'Halukah' funds in Jerusalem in any way" (Hertzberg, *Zionist Idea*, 403).

15. Hertzberg's text adds that this brochure or pamphlet should be distributed, in particular, "among our eminent sons in all countries of the Diaspora" (*Zionist Idea*, 403).

16. The Hertzberg translation of this phrase renders it "this first Congress of Lovers of Zion"; Kaminka terms it simply "die erste zionistische Versammlung."

17. The Hertzberg text draws here on a biblical metaphor, suggesting that in the age to come, as in the halcyon days of Solomon, every man will dwell "under his vine and under his fig tree" (I Kgs 4:25). See *Zionist Idea*, 404.

18. "Zutritt denen, die auf dich vertrauen." This does not correspond at all to the Hertzberg text (*Zionist Idea*, 404), which has "courage to those that await thee."

19. The phraseology here recalls several biblical passages (e.g., Ps. 107:42, Ps. 68:2, and Dan. 7:26).

20. Zech. 8:7-8. The German rendering of the Hebrew given here emphasizes the singular unity of the people of Israel ("dass sie ... nur ein Volk seien").

21. Herzl seems to have found retrospective enjoyment in recalling that he had "pulverized" Mandelkern ("zermalmte den Mandelkern"). See *Theodor Herzl: Briefe und Tagebücher*, 2:541 (Sept. 3, 1897). I owe the point to Lawrence Epstein, who catches the play on words: Mandelkern's name means "almond." See Epstein, *Dream of Zion*, 82.

22. The official proceedings contain nothing about the content of this letter. However, *JC/Cowen* says the following:

> A letter was also read addressed by M. Zadoc Kahn, Grand Rabbin of France, to Dr. Herzl. Having had occasion to forward a letter from Dr. Braun in the United States, the Grand Rabbin wrote that he profited by the opportunity to state that he would not fail to follow with much interest the deliberations of the Congress at Basle. Whatever might be the opinion as to the utility and opportuneness of the Congress, he would not deny that it merited every attention. Differences of opinion were inevitable. But he prayed with all his might that God might guide and inspire all the leaders of the movement and that the debates and the resolutions which would be arrived at would tend to the benefit of Judaism and of their coreligionists throughout the world. (41–42)

23. The last phrase here is an attempt to translate "Gewerbetreibende." As part of the Basel Program, it has been translated many times, in quite different ways. *JC/Cowen* renders it "industrialists and men following professions" (42). Laqueur, in his *History of Zionism*, translates "those pursuing other trades" (106). Sachar, in *A History of Israel*, makes it "artisans" (46).

24. The term in the original is a compound adjective, "völkerrechtlich."

25. Herzl uses the term "öffentlich-rechtlich" (usually hyphenated). According to Friedman, *Germany, Turkey, and Zionism* (95), this term had the flexibility Herzl wanted. To the Ottomans it could mean simply Ottoman law, while to the European governments it could mean international law and a justification for their intervention. But, as argued in the introduction, the Ottomans were not taken in by this sleight of hand, as Friedman also notes (95–96).

26. The query was prompted by the fact that Dr. Moritz Kornblüh, an attorney of Freiland, Austria, attended the Congress with his wife, Wilhelmina.

27. Ger. "völkerrechtlich gesicherte Heimstätte." Motzkin has retrojected his preferred wording of the Basel Program into Pinsker's mouth. However,

Pinsker's pamphlet does begin with reference to relations between peoples on the basis of *Völkerrecht* (international law); see *Autoemanzipation*, 6.

28. Bodenheimer's discourse here draws on the Hegelian valorization of the state as the highest form of human community, and on Fichte's idealization of the nation-state.

29. Herzl, anticipating precisely this objection, had strenuously denied that the Zionist project was utopian (*Judenstaat*, section titled "Vorrede"). Bodenheimer is alluding to Herzl and his critics.

30. Bodenheimer replies here to the leader in *Allgemeine Zeitung des Judenthums*, June 11, 1897, in which two rabbis, Dr. S. Maybaum of Berlin and Dr. H. Vogelstein of Stettin, asked the Zionists who had given them a "mandate" to hold a Congress.

31. Bodenheimer claims a mandate for the Congress in terms that echo Herzl's *Judenstaat* (the section titled "Society of Jews und Judenstaat: Negotiorum gestio"). Herzl had argued that a *gestor*—an agent of the people who protects their interests in an emergency—cannot wait for an electoral mandate in such a situation but must act to protect them, and that such action has legal legitimacy.

32. A reference to Sultan Bayezid II's order to Ottoman authorities to accept and assist Jews who had been expelled from Spain in 1492.

33. Echoing here the syndrome highlighted by Nordau in his keynote address.

34. Allusion to Raimondo Montecuccoli (1609–1680), an Italian commander in service of the Hapsburgs. Montecuccoli asserted that to make war you need three things: money, money, and money. See Richard Bassett, *For God and Kaiser: The Imperial Austrian Army, 1618–1918* (New Haven, CT: Yale University Press, 2015), 36.

35. As discussed in the introduction, Bodenheimer's (actually Schapira's) proposal was realized in the establishment of the Keren Kayemeth LeIsrael/Jewish National Fund (KKL/JNF), established in 1901. According to its charter, KKL/JNF lands became the inalienable property of the Jewish people, and they could be leased and worked only by Jews. It was, next to the government, the biggest single owner of land in Palestine by 1948, although Jewish-owned land still made up only a small fraction of the overall surface area of Palestine.

36. As a result of a currency reform in the Austro-Hungarian Empire, the krone replaced the gulden/florin in 1892. In 1897, it was valued at about one twenty-fourth of the British pound sterling and was roughly equal to the French franc. See Heinz Handler, "Two Centuries of Currency Policy in Austria" (September 1, 2016), Oesterreichische Nationalbank, *Monetary Policy & The*

Economy, Q3/2016, 61–76, https://ssrn.com/abstract=2849381; on currency equivalents, see http://www.historicalstatistics.org/Currencyconverter.html, accessed January 22, 2017.

37. An agricultural *Freilandcolonie* called "Eden" was set up in Germany in 1893. The basic principle of its organization was that the land was owned by the association, while leaseholders were free to manage and produce on their plots as they wished (interestingly, the individual plots were termed *Heimstätte*), within the limits of the association's rules (it was a vegetarian community), http://www.eden-eg.de/bodenrechtjackisch.htm, accessed June 23, 2014.

38. Such a bank was incorporated in London in 1899 under the title Jewish Colonial Trust; its Palestine subsidiary, the Anglo-Palestine Company, subsequently Anglo-Palestine Bank, was set up in 1902.

39. Academic associations for Jews already existed in Berlin, Vienna, and elsewhere, from the 1880s, but Jewish athletic associations, or "Turnvereine," were new. The Zionists capitalized on a growing popular interest in sports. Since Jews were often excluded from such clubs, they formed their own. These clubs were an important means of recruiting youth into the movement. See Marsha L. Rosenblit, *The Jews of Vienna, 1867–1914: Assimilation and Identity* (Albany: SUNY Press, 1983), 165; Daniel Wildmann, *Der veränderbare Körper: Jüdische Turner, Männlichkeit, und das Wiedergewinn von Geschichte in Deutschland um 1900* (Tübingen: Mohr Siebeck, 2009).

40. The legendary oath taken at the Rütli, now usually dated to 1291 (if indeed historical), was foundational to the struggle of the Swiss confederation for freedom. It features in Schiller's enduringly popular drama, *Wilhelm Tell* (1804), and was the subject of a famous painting by Henry Fuseli. Recall that the Congress was meeting on Swiss soil. See Anthony D. Smith, "Fuseli (Fussli), Henry (1741–1825)," in *Encyclopaedia of Nationalism*, ed. Athena S. Leoussi, (New Brunswick: Transaction Publishers, 2001), 101.

NOTES TO DAY TWO, AFTERNOON SESSION

1. Blumenfeld is requesting the equivalent of the "legislative history" of the program, which is here termed "die Motive" (relevant explanatory materials). This would presumably reveal the intent of the program's authors in selecting certain keywords within the program.

2. Point 2 in the Congress's printed agenda concerned the Zionist Program, and Point 3 was the Zionist Organization.

3. There were three subheadings under Point 3, "The Zionist Organization": a) Centralization of Zionist activities, b) National Fund, and c) Agitation.

4. Ger. "Faustrecht." The concept refers to the enforcement of justice without reference to the authority of the state, as occurred especially in premodern times; alluded to by Hellmuth Karasek, "Die Rückkehr des Faustrechts," *Hamburger Abendblatt*, 17.01.15.

5. Hovevei Zion is characterized as a "statutenfreier Verband," an association without bylaws, in contrast to the parliamentary structure of the Basel Congress.

6. I have generally translated "Volk" as "people" but here as "nation," in order to bring out Bernstein-Kohan's desire to see the normalizing of the Jewish condition: "as a nation among nations" translates "als Volk unter den Völkern." For Bernstein-Kohan, as for most other secular Zionists, the Jews are to feel themselves part of an international community qua nation; the dichotomy "the nation"/ "the nations," which in the Bible signals an overarching qualitative distinction between Jews and Gentiles, disappears.

7. Probably a reference to the expanding power of the French and Russians in the Levant, and of Catholic and Orthodox establishments in Palestine. The French had intervened militarily in Lebanon's internal strife in 1860, and they offered protection and aid to Catholics throughout the Levant; meanwhile, Russia acquired considerable property in various parts of Palestine after 1856. See Arnold Blumberg, *Zion before Zionism, 1838–1880* (Syracuse, NY: Syracuse University Press, 1985), 102–7.

8. The opposed factions described here soon came to be identified as "practical" and "political" Zionists.

9. Ger. "Palästinafreunde" (here and elsewhere in this passage).

10. The section which follows, in which Bernstein-Kohan argues the need for a carefully prepared and dedicated vanguard of Jews to lead the way in Palestine, the coordination of land purchasing, thorough study of Palestine's agriculture, autonomy of the new settlements, etc., is based on observations and criticisms made in Dowty-Ahad Ha'am, "Truth," 161–78.

11. "ein großer Theil der jetzigen jüdischen Generation hat alle Fähigkeit zu einem jüdisch-selbständigen und volkstümlich-sittlichen Leben verloren." The latter adjectival phrase, "volkstümlich-sittlich," corresponds to the terms used with regard to the famous Kulturkampf of the 1870s in Germany, as found in an article in the *National Zeitung*, February 25, 1872; see Michael B. Gross, "Kulturkampf and Unification: German Liberalism and the War against the Jesuits," *Central European History* 30:4 (1997): 545–66, citation on

545. Gross renders "eine volkstümliche Sittlichkeit" as "a morality arising from the people;" it is contrasted here to a moral order imposed from the outside (i.e., by Rome or its clergy). Martin Buber, following the lead of Ahad Ha'am, speaks of the same desideratum in a Jewish context when he writes of the need for a national movement to educate its children in "the great spiritual values whose source is the primordial national spirit," once again conjuring a "self-determined" morality that arises from the national community. The text is cited and discussed in Ehud Luz, *Parallels Meet: Religion and Nationalism in the Early Zionist Movement (1882–1904)*, trans. Lenn J. Schramm (Philadelphia: Jewish Publication Society, 1988), ix.

12. The benevolent colonization societies referred to are the societies affiliated to Hibbat Zion.

13. Original text has "aus gewissen Gründen," a stenographic error for "aus Gewissengründen" ("for reasons of conscience").

NOTES TO DAY THREE OF THE PROCEEDINGS, MORNING SESSION

1. As noted above, no "Reverend Glaser" existed; the reference is to a "Rev. Dr. Gaster," head of the Sephardic congregations in Britain. See *JC/Cowen*, 50. Gaster is also referred to in Jacob de Haas's report on British Jewry [30]; and he is also listed (and his correct title given) among those who sent letters of sympathy to the Congress [197].

2. As was noted in the introduction, some Russian delegates did not wish to be registered in the list of Congress attendees. See Vital, *Origins of Zionism*, 356–57.

3. The significance of this article is highlighted by Epstein, *Dream of Zion*, 88. Epstein takes the article as not only an affirmation of democracy within the Zionist movement but a preempting of any attempt to put the new movement under the authority of preexisting associations or the leadership of Hovevei Zion.

4. "Actionscomité." As elaborated below, the Executive Committee of the Zionist movement was a so-called Actions Committee that actually comprised two overlapping sections. First, there was the Grosses Actionscomité [Greater Actions Committee (GAC)], which was supposed to consist of twenty-three members (not all positions were filled at all times). This group is also referred to sometimes as the Zionist General Council. Within this council there was an Inner Actions Committee [Engeres Actionscomité (EAC)], which was the central Executive of the movement, made up of five men residing permanently in Vienna. The former was nominated and elected by the territorial committees;

the latter was elected directly by the Congress. In practice, the Vienna Executive (or EAC) became, because of the difficulties of travel and communication, not to mention Herzl's own autocratic tendencies, the functional Executive of the entire Zionist Organization. See Vital, *Zionism: The Formative Years*, 13–14.

5. The text has "Executivcomité." The term is different but still denotes the "Actionscomité." There is often confusion in the use of these terms, and whether the GAC or EAC is being referred to has to be decided primarily by context rather than nomenclature.

6. Schapira's statement sounds contradictory, but it is also possible that something ("nicht"?) has dropped out of the record. Or he may be renouncing a general debate on organization so that discussion and voting on the details may proceed; or he may be renouncing debate on the Zionist organization in order to arrive more speedily at a "special debate" on the national fund.

7. Since the proceedings indicate the wording of the paragraph in question actually reads "jeder Zionist," a retrojective alteration in the text on [151] may have occurred. Unless he was mistaken, Schach saw or heard a draft which read "Jeder" without qualification.

8. Schauer is never mentioned as participating in the present discussion. So the comment here is enigmatic. It appears to refer to the comment of Steiner on [157], although Steiner indicates there that the question of the participation of individual non-delegates was *not* to be raised since it was self-evident.

9. Here the reference is to the twenty-three-member Grosses Actionscomité (GAC). Jewish immigration to Bukovina increased rapidly in the latter half of the nineteenth century, and a large Jewish bourgeoisie emerged; Jews were the source of nearly half the tax revenues collected from this region. S.v. "Bucovina," *YIVO Encyclopedia*.

10. Schalit's motion appears to come out of the blue, and the record of the proceedings may be defective at this point. The ensuing discussion is also hard to follow. However, the motion and debate on it reflect two crucial issues in the early history of Zionism. First, there was the obvious tension between a bourgeois leadership and a substantial leftist faction within the movement, which took the German Social Democratic Party's organization as its inspiration and model, as Schalit's subsequent remarks reveal. Second, Herzl's feigned incomprehension of Schalit's proposal was in reality a manifestation of fierce interpersonal strife between himself and Nathan Birnbaum, his forerunner in the leadership of Austro-German Zionism. Although Birnbaum is not named, Herzl's diaries show that he interpreted the proposal as a brusque attempt to wrest leadership from him and give it to Birnbaum, with a stipend as General Secretary

to boot. Herzl conflates the ideological and interpersonal issues in his treatment of the incident, since he castigates Birnbaum for deserting Zionism for socialism. The episode is analyzed from Birnbaum's standpoint by Olson, "The Late Zionism of Nathan Birnbaum," 270–72; for Herzl's views, see Epstein, *Dream of Zion*, 81, 89.

11. The sense is that there would be an unwillingness of Executive Committee members to serve if the General Secretary were to be imposed on them, as suggested by Herzl's diary entry on this incident; see the analysis of Olson, "The Late Zionism of Nathan Birnbaum," 270–71.

12. Reading "abwesend" rather than "anwesend" (the text must be in error here).

NOTES TO DAY THREE, AFTERNOON SESSION

1. Schnirer's report begins in the third person, but switches back and forth between a third-person summary and a first-person, presumably verbatim transcript.

2. The passage referred to is actually Ps. 132:14.

3. The reference is to a line ascribed to Cato the Elder, *Ceterum censeo Carthaginem esse delendam* (Furthermore, I think that Carthage must be destroyed). The phrase has come to mean a formula concluding a speech that is unrelated to the content of the address, but which elicits the assent of the hearers by invoking an opinion they all share.

4. The reference is to Isa. 59:20. JPS Tanakh translates: "He [God] shall come as Redeemer to Zion." A rendering closer to Kaminka's is found in the nineteenth-century translation of the Tanakh: "Aber für Zion kommt er als Erlöser." See *Die vier und zwanzig Bücher der Heiligen Schrift nach dem masoretischen Texte*, ed. Leopold Zunz (Berlin, 1848).

5. Kaminka refers here to the first point of the program adopted on the second day of the Congress, which commits Zionism to the "effective promotion of settling Palestine with Jewish agriculturalists, craftsmen, and those pursuing other trades and professions" [114].

6. The same point is made by Pinsker in the first lines of his *Autoemanzipation*: "A moment of quiet has ensued, after the lamentations for the bloody acts of violence, and both agitator and sufferer can pause to catch their breath. Meanwhile, the Jewish refugees are—with the very same money that had been collected for their emigration—being 'repatriated'!"

7. Ger. "Zionsfreunde," literally "Friends of Zion."

8. Translating "Um ein gemeinsames Vorgehen zu ermöglichen," not "Vergehen"; this is an obvious stenographical or typographical error in the original text.

9. Ger. "Zionsfreunde."

10. Deut. 8:7-8.

11. The first reference may be to Beer in Transjordan (Num. 21:16); the second may also have been situated in southern Transjordan, but it may be confused here with ancient Bostra (now Busra al-Sham) because of the mention of Roman-era construction.

12. Ger. "Nationaljudenthum."

13. Ger. "erster Vorsteher." The reference seems to be to a lay official who, as the head of a lay council, managed the affairs of the synagogue congregation. In some contexts, such an official is known as the synagogue president.

14. Abdülhamit II ascended the throne August 31, 1876. So it was exactly twenty-one (not twenty-three) years since his accession.

15. Löwe is obviously responding here to Herzl's disparaging remarks about previous projects of colonization ([7]).

16. Julius Lippert, Austrian historian, author of many works, including *Kulturgeschichte der Menschheit in ihrem organischen Aufbau*, 2 vols., 1886–1887.

17. "Deutscher Schulverein." See glossary.

18. Ger. "Jargon." Throughout this speech, there is no reference to Yiddish as such.

19. Rosenheck's claim that the Jews are recognized by the Austrian state as a national group like other national groups, contradicts Mintz's statement that the Jews are recognized as a confessional body only: "It goes without saying that, according to the law, we are nothing other than a confession: the law disregards our national character" [47].

20. "Hochschule (nicht Universität)." I have used "college" to translate "Hochschule" (which is emphatically not a "high school"), although the German and United States systems of education are not easily compared.

21. Isa. 2:3. NB Karl Lippe cited the same verse to close his speech, the first address to be given at the Congress ([4]).

NOTES TO DAY THREE, EVENING SESSION

1. "S. Massel" is Joseph Ezekiel Massel, a Zionist activist of Lithuanian origin who settled in Manchester. His son, Symon Massel (S. Massel), was

ten years old when the Congress took place. (He was later an editor of *Zionist Banner*, 1910–1914.)

2. It was this effect of Zionism that was highlighted by Solomon Schechter, founding father of Conservative Judaism in the United States. "Foremost of all, Zionism has succeeded in bringing back into the fold many men and women, both here and in Europe, who otherwise would have been lost to Judaism" (Hertzberg, *Zionist Idea*, 511).

3. I have inserted "not" (hence brackets); its equivalent, "nicht," is missing from *ZC 1897*, 191. However, the transcript of Herzl's closing remarks published in *Die Welt*, September 3, 1897, 18, has "nicht." Without it, we must suppose that Herzl was not only contradicting himself but wished to draw attention to that fact!

4. Sentence is given in *Die Welt*, September 3, 1897, 18, but not found in *ZC 1897*, 191.

5. 2 Sam. 3:38.

6. Rabbi Arthur Cohn, a few moments before, had also emphasized the impact of Nordau's speech; Mandelstamm's comment offers further evidence that this speech was the Congress's *tour de force*.

GLOSSARY

ABDÜLHAMIT II, SULTAN (R. 1876–1909). Thirty-fourth sultan of the Ottoman dynasty and the last to exercise effective authority over the apparatus of state. Herzl obtained an audience with the Sultan in May 1901 but never succeeded in convincing him to issue a charter for Jewish colonization in Palestine. The Sultan was suspicious of Ashkenazic Jewish immigration to Palestine, fearing the creation of a nationality problem such as had occurred in the Balkans. From 1882 the Ottoman government attempted to restrict the flow of immigrants and their purchases of land. Restrictions were tightened after the 1897 Congress, although Jews could always enter Palestine legally as pilgrims; and European Jews were under the protection of the states in which they were citizens.

ACHI'ASAF [ACHIASSAF] (EST. 1893). Modern Hebrew publishing house in Warsaw. Founded by Avraham Leib Shalkovich and others, Achi'asaf published four journals, an annual review, and a variety of books. Ahad Ha'am edited its leading journal and was a major influence on its publishing agenda, which promoted modern Jewish nationalism.

ADLER, HERMANN (1839–1911). Ashkenazic chief rabbi of the British Empire, 1891–1911. Born in Germany, he received an education combining elements of rabbinic studies and modern curricula, studying in London, Prague, and Leipzig. He took over many duties of the chief rabbinate from his father, Nathan Marcus Adler, when the latter fell ill in 1879. From 1891 he was president of Jews' College, London; he held many other positions of leadership within British Jewry. Like many Orthodox rabbis, he opposed Zionism as a preempting of the divine will for the Jews, which was to remain in Diaspora until the advent of the Messiah.

AHAD HA'AM ("ONE OF THE PEOPLE," PEN NAME OF ASHER ZVI GINZBERG) (1856–1927). Russian-Jewish rabbi, journalist, businessman, and activist in Hibbat Zion. Born into a Hasidic household and educated in the traditional

Hebrew curriculum, he pursued private studies that led him to adopt a skeptical attitude toward religion. He began his career as a writer in 1889 and had a significant influence on modern Hebrew style. As a leader in Hibbat Zion, he criticized the failings of its early settlers in Palestine, as well as the inefficiency of the movement's administration. Nevertheless, he defended Hibbat Zion against its detractors, especially Theodor Herzl, insisting that, for all its faults, it addressed the desperate need for a national-cultural aggiornamento among the Jews of the East. He worked in London, 1907–1921, and mentored Chaim Weizmann, whose personal diplomacy led to the issuing of the Balfour Declaration. Ahad Ha'am moved to Tel Aviv in 1921; he died there in 1927.

ALLIANCE ISRAÉLITE UNIVERSELLE (EST. 1860). The first international philanthropic organization founded by and for Jews, its stated purpose was to work for the "emancipation and moral progress of the Jews" worldwide. Based in Paris and led by French Jews, its work was at first concentrated in Eastern Europe, North Africa, and the Middle East. To ensure support from Jews regardless of religious or political tendency, the AIU refused to take a position on intra-Jewish issues. It established schools in many countries, including Palestine, and campaigned for the civil rights of Jews wherever these were limited by law or violated in practice.

ANGLO-JEWISH ASSOCIATION (EST. 1871). The AJA was organized at a time when the work of the older Alliance Israélite Universelle was jeopardized by a break in relations between French and German Jews on account of the Franco-Prussian War. Like its older, sister institution in Paris, it sought to improve the lives of disadvantaged Jews by supporting education and schemes of colonization, and to protest against religious persecution of Jews, especially in Romania and Russia.

AUTOEMANCIPATION (1882). Landmark Zionist pamphlet, authored by Leon Pinsker. Pinsker's work responded to the pogroms of 1881 by arguing that Jewish hopes for assimilation in Europe and Russia were vain; legal emancipation had not altered this fact. The Jews remained strangers in their homelands and thus ever the objects of xenophobia. What was required was self-emancipation; i.e., Jews uniting to liberate themselves and establish their own territorial state, in order to become equals within the society of nations.

BADENI, KASIMIR FELIX, COUNT (1846–1909). Polish aristocrat and minister-president (prime minister) of Austria, 1895–1897. Badeni was from Galicia, where he had served as provincial governor. His brief term as minister-president featured outbreaks of violence, ostensibly provoked by a language policy in Bohemia that favored the Czech over the German population. Georg von Schönerer, the pan-German politician, led opposition to Badeni's government; riots took place in Vienna, Prague, and elsewhere. Emperor Franz Josef sacked Badeni to quell the unrest, and the language policy was repealed. Badeni had also resisted the election of the anti-Semitic Karl Lueger as mayor of Vienna; Lueger's accession was finally sanctioned in April 1897, prior to Badeni's dismissal.

BADER, GERSHOM (1868–1953). Galician-Jewish journalist, author, and Zionist activist. As a journalist, Bader contributed to periodicals in a variety of languages (Hebrew, Polish, and German) but is best remembered for championing Yiddish. He was especially active in promoting Zionism after moving to Lemberg/Lvov, and attended the First Zionist Congress as a delegate from Austrian-ruled Galicia. In 1912, he moved to New York and became prominent in the American Yiddish press.

BAHAR, JACQUES (1858–19?). French-Jewish sociologist, journalist, practical Zionist, and rapporteur on Algerian Jewry at the First Congress. Bahar was born in Marseille. An associate of Bernard Lazare, he adopted radical socialist views, and was an outspoken advocate for Dreyfus. He lived in Algeria for several years prior to the First Zionist Congress. He took part in the first two Zionist Congresses; at the Second Congress he was part of a loosely organized leftist faction. Although a member of the Zionist General Council (Grosses Actionscomité), he protested against the narrowly political orientation of Herzl's Zionism. Like Lazare, he also objected to the bourgeois character of the Zionist leadership and resigned his position in 1899.

BAKSHEESH [TURKISH/ARABIC: BAQSHISH, BA'SHISH]. A tip or gratuity for services rendered; or, as it was and is often used when dealing with officials, a bribe or kickback paid for circumventing legal regulations or expediting business.

BAMBUS, WILLY (1862–1904). German-Jewish activist for Hibbat Zion, practical Zionism, and Jewish charitable work. Born and educated in Berlin, Bambus was a leader in Esra, the first Hovevei Zion society in Germany. While supporting the idea of a general congress of Zionists, he had tense relations with Herzl because he (Bambus) advocated continued colonization, seeking to make it more viable by setting up outlets for the sale of Palestine products. He opposed assimilation and sought to awaken German Jews to their obligations toward their suffering brethren in the East. For the latter purpose, he took a leading role in the Hilfsverein der deutschen Juden (Charitable Society of German Jews), which offered aid to Jews displaced by pogroms, poverty, and natural disasters.

BE'ER TUVIA (EST. 1896). Jewish agricultural colony (*moshava*) near the southern Mediterranean coast of Palestine. The site of Be'er Tuvia had been occupied by another Jewish farming community, Qastina (est. 1887). The former had been settled by Jews of Bessarabia with funding from Baron Edmond de Rothschild. However, the colony failed due to shortages of water, conflicts with Arab neighbors, and quarrels with Rothschild. The area was resettled as Be'er Tuvia, with financing from Hovevei Zion of Odessa.

BELKOVSKY, GREGOR (1865–1948). Russian-Jewish political economist, member of Hibbat Zion, and rapporteur on Bulgarian Jewry at the First Congress. Born and educated in Odessa, Belkovsky became active in Hibbat Zion there. Moving to Bulgaria in 1893, he taught political economy and legal history in Sofia, but remained in close contact with Odessa. Embracing Herzl's leadership from 1896, Belkovsky became his liaison and advocate with the Odessa Committee and assisted him in organizing the 1897 Congress. Belkovsky was a Russian member of the Zionist General Council (Grosses Actionscomité) from 1899, having returned to Russia in 1897. He immigrated to Palestine in 1924, residing in Tel Aviv until his death in 1948.

BEN ISRAEL, MENASSEH (1604–1657). Sephardic rabbi, printer, and author of numerous apologetic works on the Tanakh and Judaism. From a family of Portuguese Jews, Ben Israel settled in Amsterdam, where, in addition to his duties as a rabbi, he began work as a printer. He established Amsterdam's first Hebrew printing press in 1626. It appears that, for political and religious reasons, he sought a legally sanctioned readmission of Jews to England, where they had already begun to settle. He travelled to England in 1655 and corresponded with Cromwell concerning this issue. He died in the Netherlands in 1657.

BEN-YEHUDA, ELIEZER (1858–1922). Lithuanian-Jewish journalist and Hebrew lexicographer. Born into a Hasidic family, Ben-Yehuda studied both traditional Jewish and secular subjects in a variety of venues, including the Sorbonne. Impressed by the linguistic nationalisms of Greece, Italy, and Bulgaria, Ben-Yehuda believed that a revived Jewish nationalism was possible but depended on the vernacularization of Hebrew. He moved to Jerusalem in 1881 and championed Hebrew as a way of uniting Jews from different lands and of differing religio-ideological tendencies. He promoted the use of Hebrew within the homes and schools of the Yishuv, compiled the first modern Hebrew dictionary, and established a committee to coin new words and standardize usage that evolved into today's Academy of the Hebrew Language.

BERNSTEIN-KOHAN [-KOGAN, -COHEN, KOHAN-BERNSTEIN], JACOB (1859–1929). Russian-Jewish physician, a leading figure in Hibbat Zion and Congress-Zionism. Born in Kishinev, Bernstein-Kohan studied medicine in St. Petersburg. An early member of Hibbat Zion, he attended the First Zionist Congress and was the only Russian delegate to deliver a prepared report; he was also elected to the Zionist General Council (Grosses Actionscomité). He was among the leaders of the so-called Democratic Fraction at the Zionist Congress of 1901, which opposed Herzl's autocratic manner and his devaluation of the practical and cultural dimensions of Zionism. He worked for a few years as a physician in Palestine, beginning in 1907; but he clashed with conservative settlers in Petah Tikvah and returned to Russia.

BIERER, RUBEN [REUBEN] (1835–1931). Galician-Jewish physician and activist in Hibbat Zion and Congress-Zionism. Born in Lemberg/Lvov, he was active in regional politics, seeking to combat Polish dominance and assert the interests of the large Jewish community. He went to Vienna to study medicine. While there, he helped establish Kadimah, a Jewish-nationalist student society that supplied Herzl with some of his first recruits. Bierer worked in Sofia in the 1890s, during which time he established Bulgaria's first Zionist associations. He returned to Galicia around 1900 and continued his activism there.

BILU (EST. 1882). Hebrew acronym based on Isaiah 2:5 ("O House of Jacob, come, let us go"), the name of a Russian-Jewish Zionist organization that encouraged Jews to immigrate to Palestine, work the land, and achieve political independence. The organization arose under the leadership of Israel Belkind and a group of Jewish students in Kharkov, in reaction to the pogroms of 1881. The group grew in number but divided internally over various issues. In the end, only a handful of "Biluim" ever reached Palestine; they experienced severe difficulties and many left. Those who remained found work at Mikveh Israel and Rishon LeZion; in 1884, some Biluim founded Gedera, their own agricultural community. Although their immediate achievements were meager, they are enshrined in Zionist historiography as impatient pioneers committed to a national renaissance in Palestine through a "return" to agriculture.

BIRKENSTEIN, HEINRICH (1858–1932). German-Jewish businessman and Zionist. An obscure figure, Birkenstein lived and worked in Frankfurt am Main. He attended the First Zionist Congress, where his most substantive contribution was to deplore the lack of knowledge of economics in Germany and to propose a committee on political economy as a component of the new Zionist Organization.

BIRNBAUM, NATHAN (1864–1937). Austrian-Jewish intellectual, rapporteur on the cultural basis of Zionism at the First Congress. Birnbaum rejected both assimilation and religious practice in his youth, believing instead in the distinctiveness of Jewish national identity. At the University of Vienna, he helped found Kadimah, a Jewish-nationalist fraternity, in 1883; he went on to coin the term *Zionismus* to designate the movement to revive Jewish nationhood. Though elected to serve as General Secretary of the Zionist bureau in Vienna, Birnbaum had difficult relations with Herzl. His thinking continued to evolve; he turned from Zionism and began to support cultural-national autonomy for Jews in the Diaspora, including advocacy of Yiddish as the national language. Some years later he embraced Orthodox Judaism and became a leader in the anti-Zionist Agudat Israel.

BLUMENFELD, EMIL (1854–1918). Austrian-Jewish attorney and Zionist. Born in Galicia, Blumenfeld took a doctorate in law at the University of Vienna. He was a member of the Jewish-nationalist fraternity, Kadimah, led by Nathan Birnbaum; he attended the First Zionist Congress and took part in several debates. He practiced law in Jaroslaw (now in Poland), where he remained until his death in 1918.

B'NAI B'RITH (EST. 1843). American-based international Jewish service organization. B'nai Brith ("Sons of the Covenant") originated among American Jews as a philanthropic fraternal lodge. As such, its members worked to ameliorate the living conditions of poor Jews, support the academic and cultural development of Jewish youth, fight anti-Semitic persecution and discrimination both in the United States and abroad, and take part in humanitarian relief. Although non-Zionist until the 1930s, it offered some aid to the new Yishuv in Palestine before that time; in the 1930s it also supported the purchase of land by the Jewish National Fund. It is now an advocate for Israel in the international arena and works to foster Israel-Diaspora relations.

BODENHEIMER, MAX (1865–1940). German-Jewish lawyer in Cologne, key figure in setting up the Zionist Organization, and director of the Jewish National Fund, 1907–1914. Bodenheimer helped to found Hovevei Zion in Cologne in 1893, and published a pamphlet urging settlement in Palestine as the solution for suffering Russian Jews. Bodenheimer responded warmly to Herzl's *Judenstaat* and played crucial roles in the First Congress, as a member of the committee that drafted the Basel Program and as rapporteur on the structure of the Zionist Organization. He remained an active Zionist, settling in Jerusalem in 1935.

BROCINER, JOSEF (1846–1918). Romanian-Jewish merchant, activist in defense of Jewish rights, leader among Romania's Hovevei Zion. Born and educated in Jassy, Brociner settled in Galatz, where he became a prominent merchant and Freemason. Active throughout his life in the defense of Romanian Jews (who were not emancipated until 1923), he was president of the local committee of the Alliance Israélite Universelle, of a group seeking to found colonies of Romanian Jews in Palestine, and of the Union of Jewish Congregations in Romania, established at his urging in 1901. He proposed to Herzl the founding of a Zionist association in Romania.

BROMBERG, SIGMUND [BROMBERG-BYTKOWSKI, ZYGMUNT] (1866–1923). Author, teacher, translator, and Zionist activist. Born in Stryj, educated in law at the University of Vienna, Bromberg wrote and spoke to audiences in Austria-Hungary to promote Jewish national pride from the 1880s onward. He was active primarily in Galicia, where he helped to organize Palestine's first settlement of Jews from that region. He attended the First Zionist Congress as a representative from Tarnów in Galicia. He is remembered chiefly as a playwright and translator, with facility in German, French, and Polish.

CAMBON, JULES (1845–1935). French civil servant and diplomat. Educated as a lawyer, he served in the Franco-Prussian War, then entered the civil service in 1871. He was appointed governor-general of Algeria in 1891 and served in that capacity until 1897, when he was appointed France's ambassador to the United States. In Algerian historiography, he is generally regarded as a liberal and reform-minded governor, who sought to curb *colon* abuses but fell afoul of the powerful *colon* political network in Paris.

CARVAJAL, ANTONIO (1590–1659). A wealthy Portuguese-Jewish merchant who arrived in London around 1635. In the period of Cromwell's Protectorate, in 1655, he was "endenizened" (i.e., granted many of the rights of an English subject). He was the first Jew to be so favored by the English government since the expulsion of 1290.

CHASCHMAL, AKIWA [HASHMAL, AKIVE] (B. CA. 1842). Romanian-Jewish intellectual. Born in Bucharest, Chashmal became an exponent of the Haskalah (Jewish Enlightenment) in his native city. He was an agent for several of the most prominent Hebrew-language journals published outside Romania, and his home was a center of religious and philosophical discussion.

COBDEN, RICHARD (1804–1865). British parliamentarian, free-trade ideologue, and anti-imperialist. Cobden led the Anti-Corn Law League, a pressure group that succeeded in convincing Parliament in 1846 to end tariffs on the importation of grain, reducing the cost of bread and undercutting profits of the still dominant class of landlords. While advocating laissez-faire economics, he was also a critic of military expenditure and imperial expansion, including British rule over South Asia.

COHN, ARTHUR (1862–1926). Orthodox rabbi of Basel. Cohn took his doctorate from the Orthodox rabbinical seminary in Berlin and served as rabbi of the Orthodox congregation of Basel from 1885. Persuaded to address the First Congress, he expressed Orthodox reservations toward secular Zionism; he attended several subsequent Congresses, but by 1911 he had turned against Zionism and helped to establish the anti-Zionist Agudat Israel.

CONGRESS POLAND. Also known as Russian Poland, it was the large swathe of Poland-Lithuania which was de jure autonomous but was de facto under the authority of the Russian Tsars. It was referred to as "Congress Poland" because its status was settled at the Congress of Vienna, 1815. The legal fiction of Polish autonomy ended in 1867, when the territory was incorporated into the Russian Empire.

Crémieux, Isaac Adolphe (1796–1880). French-Jewish lawyer and politician, president of the Alliance Israélite Universelle (AIU), French minister of justice (1870). Crémieux defended Jewish rights in some notable legal cases in the 1820s; in 1840 he travelled to Damascus to seek the release of Jews falsely accused in the so-called Damascus Affair. In 1864, he assumed presidency of the AIU. In 1869 he returned to politics as an elected member of the Legislative Assembly and became minister of justice in the Government of National Defense set up during the Franco-Prussian War. In 1870, he issued the Décret Crémieux, granting French citizenship to all Algerian Jews. Jewish support for republicanism contributed to its victory in postwar French politics.

Crown Rabbi. Also known as *kazyonny ravvin* ("official rabbi"), a crown rabbi was an educated Jew appointed by the Russian government to keep records and execute administrative tasks within a Jewish community; he was therefore required to know Russian, German, or Polish, in addition to Yiddish and Hebrew. Established in the nineteenth century, the crown rabbinate was an institution created by the Tsars to monitor their vast Jewish population, inculcate loyalty to the state, and promote certain reforms, but its rabbis were often regarded as lacking in proper religious training and never displaced "spiritual rabbis" as the primary authorities in Jewish communities.

Cuza, Alexandru Ioan, Prince (1820–1873). First prince of a unified but not yet independent Romania, which he ruled as "Domnitor," 1859–1866. Cuza was born to an aristocratic landowning family in Moldavia, received a modern European education, and served as an officer in the Moldavian army. He took part in the 1848 uprising that swept through both Moldavia and Wallachia (and most of Europe). His popularity was confirmed in elections in 1859, which made him prince of both provinces, enabling him to implement a de facto unification, albeit under Ottoman suzerainty until 1878. His liberal program included measures of land reform, universal manhood suffrage, and the extension of public education. However, the reform of land tenure alienated the landowning elite and he was overthrown in a coup d'état in 1866.

Cyrus the Great (r. ca. 559–530 BCE). Persian ruler, founder of the Achaemenid Empire. Cyrus expanded the Persian Empire to include lands from the Balkans to India. He is remembered for toleration toward the diverse religions within his realms, in particular his authorizing Jewish exiles in Babylon to return to Jerusalem and rebuild the temple.

DAVIDSOHN, ELIAHU [DAVIDZON, ELYOHU] (1873–1923). Russian-Jewish radical intellectual and journalist. Davidsohn was born to a wealthy family of Vilna, educated at a Russian high school, then studied economics at the University of Berlin. He joined the Russisch-jüdischer wissenschaftlicher Verein (Russian-Jewish Academic Society) in Berlin; at first he was ideologically close to the socialist-Zionist ideas of Nahman Syrkin, but he also sought to promote Yiddish culture through articles for David Pinski's *Tsayt-gayst*. He attended the First Zionist Congress, but his political and social thought soon evolved away from Zionism; he rejected Jewish nationhood and propagated revolutionary-socialist and Darwinist ideas.

DECKERT, JOSEPH (1843–1901). Founder and parish priest of the Church of St. Josef-Weinhaus (est. 1889) in Vienna. Deckert was notorious for his anti-Semitic speeches and writings, in which he argued that the Jews were the greatest danger to Vienna and Christianity since the Turks in the seventeenth century.

DERISHAT ZION (SEEKING ZION) (1862). Hebrew text by R. Zvi Hirsch Kalischer. In this pre-Zionist work, Kalischer advocated a "natural beginning of the redemption," basing his argument on classical Jewish sources. The implication was that the traditional eschatology must be altered and that Jews must begin settling in Palestine before the advent of the Messiah. Kalischer's work prepared the way for some Orthodox Jews to embrace Zionism, in spite of its secular leadership and political orientation.

DEUTSCHER SCHULVEREIN (GERMAN SCHOOL SOCIETY) (EST. 1880). A voluntary association for the promotion of German-language education in the Austro-Hungarian Empire.

DUNANT, HENRI (1828–1910). Swiss businessman, founder of the Red Cross, and Christian Zionist. Born in Geneva to a devout Calvinist family, Dunant himself evinced a sincere religious commitment as a youth. He went into banking and business, founding enterprises in colonial Algeria. Shocked at the lack of services for wounded soldiers at the battle of Solferino (1859), he founded an organization for the relief of the wounded, which evolved into the International Committee of the Red Cross (est. 1863). Like many conservative Protestants of the nineteenth century, he believed in the necessity of a Jewish restoration to the Holy Land; Dunant launched an abortive company for Jewish colonization (1867), and hoped that Napoleon III of France would sponsor a revived Jewish polity. He did not attend the First Zionist Congress, but he wrote to Herzl of his enthusiasm for Zionism; Herzl mentioned him as among the foremost Christian Zionists.

EBNER, MAYER (1872–1955). Lawyer, journalist, and Jewish political leader in Bukovina and Romania. Ebner hailed from Czernowitz, capital of the Austrian province of Bukovina. Raised in an assimilated household, anti-Semitic outrages convinced him of the Jews' need to assert their national rights. In 1891, he founded Hasmonaea, a Jewish-nationalist student society, then joined the Zionist movement. He attended the First Congress, where he reported on conditions in Bukovina, and was present at many subsequent Congresses. Exiled to Siberia after Russian forces captured Czernowitz in World War I, he returned home in 1917. He became a champion of Jewish civil rights in Romania when Bukovina was annexed by that country in 1918. He immigrated to Palestine in 1940.

EDICT OF TOLERANCE (1782). Law granting Jews in Habsburg domains wider educational and economic opportunities. Issued by Emperor Joseph II of Austria as part of a broader program of "enlightened" reforms, it removed the requirement that Jews wear identifying bands on their clothing, abolished the humiliating "body tax," opened schools and universities to Jewish children, and offered Jews the possibility of entering occupations in agriculture, industry, and trade. While a significant step toward equality for Jews, the underlying aim was to direct Jewish energies toward "productive" work, making them of greater benefit to the state.

EHRENPREIS, MARCUS (1869–1951). Rabbi, author, and prominent figure in the renaissance of Hebrew language and literature. Ehrenpreis was born in Galicia but studied Jewish history in Berlin. He served as a rabbi in Croatia, Bulgaria, and Sweden. He assisted in preparations for the First Congress, acting as a cultural consultant for Herzl, which included translating the invitation to the Congress into Hebrew. At the Congress he was elected one of four assessors. He also gave an address on Hebrew culture late on the third day of the Congress.

From 1908 Ehrenpreis withdrew from Zionism and promoted instead a kind of "spiritual nationalism," affirming assimilation and the ongoing mission of Jews in the Diaspora.

EIN ZEITIM (EST. 1891). Jewish agricultural colony (*moshava*) near Safed, in the upper Galilee. The Hebrew "Spring of Olives" corresponds to the name of a nearby Arab village with the same meaning, "'Ayn Zaytun." It had a long history of Jewish habitation, but in its modern incarnation was settled by Hovevei Zion of Minsk. The land was acquired by Baron Edmond de Rothschild, who funded development of its viticulture and tree crops.

'EKRON (EST. 1883). Jewish agricultural colony (*moshava*) in the plain south of Jaffa. Rabbi Samuel Mohilewer, a leader of Hovevei Zion, persuaded Baron Edmond de Rothschild to fund the settlement, made up of a small group of experienced farmers from the village of Pavlova in Russia. With funding came Rothschild administration; as in other colonies, there was friction between administrators and settlers. Rothschild visited the colony in 1887 and named it in memory of his mother, Betty/Batya, hence 'Ekron was also known as Mazkeret Batya. Mohilewer's remains were brought to the city, which has a museum devoted to him.

EMANCIPATION. THE granting of legal and economic rights to Jews, equal to those of non-Jewish citizens. Since the Theodosian Code (438), the rights of Jews had been restricted by law in most Christian polities. These restrictions evolved to include, e.g., residential segregation of the Jews in ghettoes, a prohibition on the ownership of land, the barring of Jews from schools and universities, ineligibility for public office, and restrictions on the kinds of trades Jews could enter. Emancipation meant the formal abolition of these constraints, which began in France at the time of the French Revolution (1791) and continued during the nineteenth and twentieth centuries. Full emancipation was enacted in different countries at different times (e.g., Austria-Hungary in 1867, Italy 1870, Germany 1871, Russia 1917).

EPHRAIM, [NATHAN] VEITEL [HEINE] (1703–1775). German-Jewish court jeweler, mint operator, and commodity merchant in eighteenth-century Berlin. Like Daniel Itzig, and in cooperation with him, Ephraim was an agent of Frederick the Great, helping to finance the Seven Years War (1756–1763). He built up his family's fortune through sales and delivery of various goods, including salt, grain, and silver. The proceeds were invested in manufacturing and in the purchase of numerous landed estates. Like Abraham Markus before him, he and Itzig were granted legal rights and privileges equal to those of Christian bankers.

ERETZ YISRAEL [EREZ ISRAEL]. Land of Israel (Heb.). There is no single, unambiguous delimitation, in the Torah or elsewhere, of the Holy Land. "Eretz Yisrael" is generally to be equated with the similarly vague, albeit less elastic designation, "Palestine." (Although it is sometimes alleged that Jews used only, or almost exclusively, the former, biblical designation for the Holy Land, records of the Zionist Congresses and other documents prove otherwise.)

ERTER, ISAAC [YITZHAK] (1792–1851). Galician-Jewish physician and Hebrew journalist. Among the pioneers of the Haskalah (Jewish Enlightenment) in Galicia, Erter taught in Lemberg/Lvov before embarking on a career as a physician, taking his degree in medicine from the University of Budapest. He edited a journal promoting modern culture and became famous for his Hebrew satires. In his early life he received help from Nachman Krochmal and Solomon J.L. Rapoport, other important figures of the Galician Haskalah.

ESRA (EST. 1884). First German society of Hovevei Zion. Organized in Berlin, Esra undertook to support Jewish settlement in Palestine by helping immigrants, funding colonies, and promoting the sale of Palestine products (e.g. at the Berlin Exhibition of Trade and Industry, 1896). Among its leading members were Willy Bambus and Heinrich Loewe, who travelled to encourage the establishment of branches in other German cities. While continuing its activities into World War I, it gradually lost its raison d'être after the rise of Congress-Zionism.

FARBSTEIN, DAVID (1868–1953). Zionist activist, rapporteur on the economic basis of Zionism at the First Congress, and Swiss Jewish politician. Farbstein was born in Warsaw and educated at Berlin, Zürich, and Bern. In Berlin, he came under the influence of Nachman Syrkin, who sought to reconcile socialist theory with Jewish nationalism. Farbstein settled in Switzerland, worked as a lawyer and politician, and became the first Jew elected to the Swiss parliament in 1922. He advised Herzl regarding the venue of the First Congress and assisted in its organization; he went on to assist in the organization of the Jewish National Fund. However, he abandoned Zionism after Herzl's death.

FLÜRSCHEIM, MICHAEL (1844–1912). German-Jewish manufacturer and social reformer. Son of a Jewish merchant family, Flürscheim became a wealthy industrialist. As a factory owner, he undertook the amelioration of social conditions for workers; he became convinced of the need for sweeping economic and social reforms, including the nationalization of land (with compensation), after which it would be subject to renewable leases for its users. He travelled widely, campaigning for implementation of his reforms in Germany, Switzerland, and New Zealand.

FREDERICK THE GREAT [FREDERICK II] (R. 1740–1786). King of Prussia, famed as an "Enlightened Despot." Frederick established Prussia as one of Europe's great powers by acquiring Silesia and part of Poland, and by centralizing the state administration. Partial to French culture and a friend of Voltaire, he was an essayist in his own right who promoted humane and tolerant governance, which did not go as far, however, as establishing the legal equality of all subjects or their representation through a participatory process.

GAMBETTA, LÉON (1838–1882). French republican politician who assumed extraordinary powers during and after the Franco-Prussian War (1870) and after the war midwifed the establishment of the Third Republic (1875). During the war, Gambetta took the initiative to form a Government of National Defense; he became, as minister of war and interior, the most powerful man in France. He was elected to the new National Assembly in 1871 and exploited divisions among French monarchists to bring about the installation of a republican system.

GASTER, MOSES (1856–1939). Romanian-Jewish scholar and Zionist. Born in Bucharest, Gaster was educated there as well as in Leipzig and Breslau. An outstanding linguist, he began his university career in Romania but took a position in Slavonic literature at Oxford after being expelled from his homeland in 1885. As the *hakham* (Sephardic rabbi) of the Bevis Marks Synagogue in London in 1887, he was the acknowledged leader of Britain's Sephardic Jews. Besides his scholarly pursuits, he supported Zionism from its beginnings in Romania and took part as a vice president at the Second, Third, and Fourth Congresses. Gaster hosted discussions between the Foreign Office and the Zionists at his home in London, and the first draft of the Balfour Declaration was composed there.

GEDERA (EST. 1884). Jewish agricultural colony (*moshava*) in Palestine, established by Biluim. The land of the new colony, located considerably to the south of Jaffa, was purchased from the French consul with funds from Hovevei Zion. The Biluim of Gedera persevered in spite of many difficulties but also remained dependent on Russian Hovevei Zion. This led to controversy when the latter received complaints about the irreligious behavior of the Biluim, who were brought under a measure of rabbinic discipline. The colony was notorious for its bad relations with Arab neighbors.

GINZBERG, ASHER. See Ahad Ha'am.

GOITEIN, JACOB L. (1867–1939). Hungarian-Jewish businessman and Zionist. Goitein was born in Hőgyész, Hungary, to a distinguished family of rabbis. He relocated to Frankfurt am Main where he entered business. He attended the First Zionist Congress and emigrated to Palestine in 1934. (His nephew, Shelomo Dov Goitien, was a Zionist activist in Frankfurt and Berlin, later a world-renowned scholar of medieval Jewry in the Islamic world; S.D. Goitein had emigrated previously, in 1923.)

GOLUS EDOM. "The exile of Edom" (Yid.). Golus (Heb. Galut) refers to the exile of the Jews from Palestine. Edom is a rabbinic cipher for Rome, so the Golus Edom refers to the exile resulting from the Roman destruction of Jerusalem and the Second Temple in 70 CE. Also referred to as the "third exile," the first was the (now disputed) sojourn of the Israelites in Egypt during the second millennium BCE, while the second was the Babylonian exile which began in the sixth century BCE.

GORDON, DAVID (1831–1886). Lithuanian-Jewish teacher, journalist, and activist in Hibbat Zion. Born near Vilna and given a traditional education there, he also pursued secular studies on his own. He moved to England in the 1850s, where he taught Hebrew and German; he moved to German-ruled Poland in 1858 and began his career as assistant editor and later editor-in-chief of the Hebrew weekly, *HaMaggid*. In the pages of this journal he advocated Jewish colonization of Palestine with a view to restoring Jewish nationhood; he thus played a leading role in the emergence of Hibbat Zion. He attended its founding conference at Kattowitz/Katowice in 1884.

GRACCHUS, GAIUS (154–121 BCE). Roman tribune, famous for his populist rhetoric and policies. His reforms included protections against judicial abuses, changes in land tenure, increased spending on infrastructure, and the importation of an abundant supply of grain to keep the price of bread low. Riots in 121 BCE led the Senate to organize an armed challenge to Gracchus's supporters and to the latter's suicide.

GREGORIG, JOSEF (1846–1909). Manufacturer of undergarments and populist politician in Vienna. Gregorig was educated at Vienna's School of Commerce and set up as a small independent manufacturer. He became a follower of the anti-Semitic politician and later mayor of Vienna, Karl Lueger. Gregorig drew big crowds at his electoral rallies in Vienna's popular districts, and was elected to the municipal council, the Lower Austrian Assembly, and the Imperial Parliament. He was a member of Lueger's Christian Socialist Party; when the Christian Socialists dropped him, he founded his own Bund der Antisemiten (League of Anti-Semites).

GROSS, WILHELM (1855–1928). Hungarian-Jewish commercial agent, with offices in Jaffa and Jerusalem. Gross was an Austro-Hungarian subject but moved to Palestine sometime in or before 1896. He established a thriving import firm in Jaffa, obtaining a variety of goods from Europe, mostly from Austria-Hungary, for Jews residing in the new colonies. Gross was a vital source of data for Adam Rosenberg in his report on Palestine at the 1897 Congress, which Gross also attended. Gross offered his support to Herzl immediately after the publication of the latter's *Judenstaat*, and he supplied Herzl with lodging and other forms of assistance during his visit to Palestine in 1898.

GUDENUS, LEOPOLD, COUNT (1843–1913). Austrian nobleman, diplomat, and politician. Educated by Jesuits in Belgium, Gudenus served as an Austrian diplomat in Rome, Paris, and St. Petersburg. He was a representative of the great landowning class in the Lower Austrian Assembly and in the Imperial Parliament in the 1880s and 90s. He subsequently occupied a series of positions at the Habsburg court, including chief treasurer. As speaker of the assembly in 1897, Gudenus was dependent on the anti-Semitic Christian Socialists to maintain his own authority, which he used to obstruct motions of minority factions, including the German nationalists and liberals.

HAAS, JACOB DE (1872–1937). Anglo-Jewish Zionist journalist and organizer. His family was of Dutch origin, but he was born and educated in London, where he became the editor of London's *Jewish World*. He became a supporter of political Zionism after Herzl's visit to London in 1896. At the First Congress he acted as the English secretary, as well as delivering a report on British Jewry. He served in effect as Herzl's personal agent, first in Britain and later in the United States where he settled in 1902. He was made secretary of the Federation of American Zionists; Louis D. Brandeis, the Supreme Court Justice, embraced Zionism due to de Haas's influence. Brandeis and de Haas continued to cooperate to advance the Zionist cause in the United States.

HADERA (EST.1891). Jewish agricultural colony (*moshava*) near the Mediterranean coast between Jaffa and Haifa. The low, marshy lands where Hadera was founded were purchased by Lithuanian Hovevei Zion from a Maronite of Haifa; the area was settled by Lithuanian Jews. The principal threat to the colony's viability was malaria; Baron Edmond de Rothschild financed draining the marshes and planting eucalyptus trees in order to combat the disease. After the improvement of the environment, Hadera became a major citrus-growing area.

HALEVI, JUDAH (1075–1141). Hispano-Jewish poet, physician, and philosopher. Halevi was probably born in Toledo shortly before the city fell to the Reconquista. He removed thence to Muslim Spain, later to Egypt and Syria, dying, according to tradition, in Crusader-dominated Palestine. He is best known for his many works of Hebrew poetry, which he composed on both secular and sacred subjects. Some of his religious verse has entered the synagogue liturgy.

HALUKKA. Alms collected in the Diaspora for the support of Jews living in Palestine, especially those who had settled there in order to devote themselves to the study of Torah. Zionism distinguished itself from this traditional charitable institution by advocating the economic independence of Jews settling in Palestine and, therefore, the legitimacy of their pursuit of secular livelihoods.

HAMELITZ (THE ADVOCATE) (EST. 1860). Hebrew-language journal, published in Russia 1860–1904. As a forum for public debate among Jews, *HaMelitz* was perhaps the most important Hebrew-language periodical in Russia during the second half of the nineteenth century. Its founder, Alexander Zederbaum, promoted ideas of the Haskalah (Jewish Enlightenment), and advocated Jewish-nationalism and the colonization schemes of Hovevei Zion. The journal gave extensive coverage to the Zionist Congresses.

Har-Tuv ['Artuf] (est. 1895). Jewish agricultural colony (*moshava*) in the hills west of Jerusalem. Har-Tuv in Hebrew means "Mount Goodness," but the name actually derives from ʿArtuf, a preexisting Arab village. Land from ʿArtuf had been purchased in the 1870s and eventually passed into the hands of Bulgarian Hovevei Zion, who established a small agricultural colony there. It received little outside assistance and its survival was uncertain. Har-Tuv was the only colony of Sephardic Jews to be founded during the First Aliya.

Hasmonaea (est. 1891). Jewish-national student society in Czernowitz, established by Mayer Ebner and several colleagues. The society was modelled on Kadimah, launched by Jewish students in Vienna in 1883. The name derives from the Hasmoneans (also known as the Maccabees), the family that led the Jewish revolt against the Seleucids in 167 BCE; under Hasmonean leadership, Jews established an independent state in Palestine, 165–63 BCE.

Hechler, William (1845–1931). Protestant clergyman, Christian Zionist, friend and supporter of Herzl. Hechler was born to an Anglo-German family; Hechler's father had relocated from Germany to England and became an Anglican missionary in India. Influenced by his father's religious devotion and philo-Semitism, Hechler became convinced that the Jews' restoration to Palestine was a necessary condition for the apocalyptic return of Jesus Christ. He was an immediate enthusiast for Herzl's Zionism, believing it to be the fulfillment of biblical prophecy. As chaplain of Britain's embassy in Vienna, Hechler put Herzl in touch with Germany's elite, including the Grand Duke of Baden and Kaiser Wilhelm II. Hechler attended several Zionist Congresses and advocated Christian aid to Zionism to his wide circle of contacts in Germany and Britain.

Heine, Heinrich (1797–1856). German-Jewish poet and journalist. Born in Düsseldorf, educated in Berlin and Göttingen, Heine was baptized a Christian in his late twenties, ostensibly in order to qualify for a position in the Prussian civil service. Instead he turned to writing, and his poetry, newspaper articles, and essays made him a literary star of the Romantic era. Despite his baptism, Heine retained a Jewish sensibility, and valued, as he understood them, both the Hebraic and the Hellenic poles of European civilization. However, his satire and criticism alienated persons across the political spectrum, and he lived much of his life in France, where he both married and died.

HERBST, KARL (1865–1919). Bulgarian government official, Zionist organizer and publicist. Herbst was born in Bukovina to a German-speaking Jewish family that subsequently moved to Edirne/Adrianople. Herbst moved again later to Sofia (in autonomous Bulgaria), where he entered government service. He helped to translate Herzl's *Judenstaat* into Bulgarian, founded a Zionist journal for Bulgaria, and attended the First and Fourth Zionist Congresses.

HERTZKA, THEODOR (1845–1924). Hungarian-Jewish economist, journalist, and social reformer. Like Herzl, Hertzka was from a Hungarian-Jewish family and educated in Vienna, and like Herzl, he worked for a time for *Die Neue Freie Presse*. Hertzka was interested in economic and social reforms; while sensitive to the issue of anti-Semitism, his solution was to promote interethnic and intersectarian cooperation, and reforms that would balance individual initiative and social justice. His depiction of a modern, pan-European colonial commune in Africa is depicted in his utopian novel, *Freiland*. While Herzl dismissed attempts to implement the vision of *Freiland* as a joke, his own utopian novel, *Altneuland*, in which he envisions a future Jewish state in Palestine, shows *Freiland*'s influence.

HERZL, THEODOR (1860–1904). Austrian-Jewish journalist, founding father of political Zionism. Born in Budapest, educated in Vienna, Herzl took a degree in law but made his living as a journalist, playwright, and essayist. He embraced Zionism as a result of encounters with resurgent anti-Semitism in Vienna and Paris. He published *Der Judenstaat* (English trans., *The Jewish State*) in 1896; in 1897 he convened the Zionist Congress, and organized and led the Zionist Organization. Herzl presided at the first six Congresses (1897–1903). He traveled widely to promote Zionism and in search of governments and statesmen who might help the Zionists obtain a charter for settlement in Palestine. He obtained an audience with the Ottoman Sultan in May 1901 but failed to get from him the charter he was seeking. Herzl exhausted his family's resources and sacrificed his own health in his unceasing labors for Zionism.

HESS, MOSES (1812–1875). German-Jewish philosopher, socialist, and proto-Zionist publicist. Born in Bonn, Hess received some elements of a Jewish education but was more profoundly influenced by Hegel; he collaborated for a short time with Karl Marx and Friedrich Engels. He broke with Marxian socialism and moved to Paris, where he returned to his Jewish roots. His major work, *Rom und Jerusalem* (Rome and Jerusalem), argues for the inevitability of anti-Semitism and the necessity of a restored Jewish nationhood. Like Mazzini, Hess believed in a modern ethnonationalism that contributes to universal brotherhood.

HILLEL THE ELDER (FL. 30 BCE–10 CE). Rabbinic sage, interpreter of Jewish scripture and law. According to tradition, Hillel was born in Babylonia but immigrated to Palestine, where he became the foremost teacher of Torah. He founded a school of biblical and legal interpretation that became predominant within Judaism after the destruction of Jerusalem in 70 CE. In traditions about his conduct, Hillel's mildness in interpreting the law, humility in personal relations, and counsel to avoid conflict, are often contrasted to the stringency, abrasiveness, and belligerence of Shammai, the other leading rabbi of the same generation.

HIRSCH-GEREUTH, CLARA, BARONESS DE (1833–1899). Clara de Hirsch, wife of Baron Maurice de Hirsch. Born in Antwerp, she received a liberal education and assisted her father in business, legislative work, and philanthropy. Her maternal uncle was for many years head of the Alliance Israélite Universelle. She married Maurice in 1855; they lived in Munich, Brussels, and Paris. She had a decisive influence on her husband's help for Jews in difficult circumstances. He left her as sole administrator of his estate upon his death in 1896. Her generosity was legendary; in the three years after her husband's death she dispensed about fifteen million dollars in charity.

HOVEVEI ZION/HIBBAT ZION, "LOVERS OF ZION"/ "LOVE OF ZION" (HEB.). A loose network of groups that arose in Jewish communities in various parts of Russia and Romania in the 1880s, in reaction to persecution in those countries; similar groups took shape in Jewish communities elsewhere in Europe. The groups' raison d'être was to support immigration to Palestine and the founding of self-supporting settlements, in the hope of reviving Jewish nationhood. Groups from Russia predominated in this proto-Zionist activism; a conference in Kattowitz/Katowice in 1884 made Leon Pinsker chairman of a central committee located in Odessa. Divisions in leadership, lack of funds, and the constraints of operating under Russian surveillance, weakened the movement.

Nevertheless, the eventual adhesion of most Hovevei Zion to Herzl's Congress-Zionism was crucial to the latter's success.

IBN GABIROL, SOLOMON (CA. 1021–1058). Hispano-Jewish philosopher and poet. Born in Málaga, he lived for a time in Saragossa and died in Valencia. He is best known for his Neoplatonist work, composed in Arabic but known in its Latin translation, *Fons Vitae*, in which he argued for the universality of matter and form. The work had little impact on Jewish thought but exercised a powerful influence on medieval Christian scholasticism.

ITZIG, DANIEL (1723–1799). Jewish banker and industrialist in eighteenth-century Berlin, head of the city's Jewish community. As an agent of the Prussian monarchs, especially Frederick the Great, Itzig made a fortune in the Seven Years War (1756–1763). For his services to the crown, he and his family were awarded a patent of naturalization in 1791, granting them full legal equality with Christian subjects, the first Jews of Prussia to receive such recognition. While an observant Jew, he encouraged the liberal education of his fifteen children, both sons and daughters; he also helped to underwrite Jewish intellectuals, including Moses Mendelssohn, who prepared the way for the Haskalah (Jewish Enlightenment).

JASINOWSKI, ISRAEL (1842–1917). Russian-Jewish organizer of Hovevei Zion's founding conference at Kattowitz/Katowice, then a member of Hovevei Zion's central committee. Born and educated in Russia, he attained prominence as a lawyer and Zionist leader in Warsaw. He attended the first seven Zionist Congresses; he joined the Territorialist faction when the Zionist movement split over the so-called Uganda Scheme in 1903. He left the Zionist movement in his later years.

JEWISH COLONIZATION ASSOCIATION (EST. 1891) [ABBREVIATED J.C.A./ I.C.A.]. Association established and endowed by the Jewish philanthropist Baron Maurice de Hirsch for the purpose of settling impoverished Jews, primarily from Russia, in agricultural colonies in the Americas. From 1896 it began work in Palestine, and in 1899 received title to colonies owned by Baron Edmond de Rothschild. It was reorganized under the name Palestine Jewish Colonization Association (commonly referred to as PICA) in 1924. Unlike colonies established on lands purchased by the Jewish National Fund, PICA did not adhere to a policy of excluding Arab labor.

JOSEPH OF AUSTRIA [JOSEPH II] (R. 1765–1790). Habsburg emperor, famed as an "Enlightened Despot." Joseph was Holy Roman Emperor but co-regent with his mother, Empress Maria Theresa, 1765–1780; then, after her death in 1780, sole Emperor and ruler of Habsburg domains, 1780-1790. He pursued agrarian reforms, relaxed censorship, and sought to broaden and secularize education, although many of his innovations lapsed under his successors. His most notable achievements with respect to religious liberty were the Patent of Toleration, 1781, granting freedom of worship to several categories of non-Catholic Christians, and the Edict of Tolerance, 1782, removing certain taxes and disabilities that had applied only to Jews.

JOSEPHUS, FLAVIUS (CA. 37–100). Jewish historian and apologist. Governor of Galilee at the time of the Jewish revolt against Rome (66), Josephus surrendered to Roman forces and became an advisor to the future emperors Vespasian and Titus. Many Jews regard him as a traitor on account of his defection to the Romans, although his apologetic works defend the nobility of Judaism against its detractors and his histories are essential sources for the study of the ancient Near East, including the origins of Christianity.

JUNKERS. The old landed nobility of northeastern Germany, particularly of Prussia, whose members dominated the central government and officer corps first of Prussia, then of a unified Germany, from the eighteenth century until the country's defeat in World War II.

KAHN, ZADOK (1839–1905). Last Grand Rabbi of France, head of French Hovevei Zion. His father was a peddler in Alsace, but his maternal grandfather was a rabbi. Kahn was educated at a yeshiva in Strasbourg, then at the rabbinical college in Metz. He became Grand Rabbi of Paris in 1868 and of France in 1889 (after his death the position was eliminated). As an advisor to Baron Edmond de Rothschild, he drew the Baron's attention to the needs of Russian Jews seeking to settle in Palestine and arranged for the Baron to meet Samuel Mohilewer, among others. Herzl had several meetings with Kahn and corresponded with him about potential projects; Kahn addressed a sympathetic letter to the First Congress but never made a public endorsement of Zionism.

KALISCHER, ZVI HIRSCH (1795–1874). Rabbi, proto-Zionist publicist and organizer. Born in Posen, he had a traditional education and became rabbi of Toruń/Thorn. He joined a Palestine colonization society in 1860 and published his *Derishat Zion* (Seeking Zion) in 1862. A defender of Orthodox Judaism against Reform, he nonetheless argued, on the basis of sacred literature, for a "natural beginning of the redemption," meaning Jewish settlement in Palestine before the advent of the Messiah. He travelled widely to agitate for his ideas, and influenced the Alliance Israélite Universelle to found an agricultural school in Jaffa, 1870.

KAMINKA, ARMAND (AHARON) (1866–1950). Rabbi, religious scholar, lecturer, and rapporteur on the history of modern Jewish colonization in Palestine at the First Congress. Kaminka was born in the Russian Empire but studied in Berlin and Paris. He served as rabbi in several cities, including Prague. He taught Jewish religion and philosophy at the University of Vienna and published scholarly works on the Bible and Talmud. Kaminka was among Herzl's liaisons with Russia's Hovevei Zion but later broke with Herzl because of Kaminka's more "practical" orientation. At the First Congress, he made a German translation of Rabbi Mohilewer's Hebrew letter for the participants, besides offering a report on conditions in the Palestine Jewish colonies.

KATTOWITZ CONFERENCE (1884). Kattowitz/Katowice, a city in Prussian-controlled Silesia before 1921, today in Poland. Kattowitz hosted the organizing conference of the Hovevei Zion/Hibbat Zion movement in November 1884. Most participants were from Jewish communities in Russia since there were few groups elsewhere. Thirty-two delegates attended. The conference discussed the agricultural settlement in Palestine and formed a central committee. Leon Pinsker, author of *Autoemancipation* (1882), was elected chairman of the central committee which was based in Odessa (hence often known as the Odessa Committee).

KARAITES. A sect within Judaism that arose in the ninth century CE; it rejected the oral Torah and rabbinic elaborations of the Hebrew Bible. It was regarded as a heresy by mainstream Judaism because of its repudiation of the Talmud's authority. The sect still exists, but whereas its adherents were comparatively numerous in the past, they are today a tiny minority within world Jewry.

KEHILLA. HEBREW term for "congregation." The meaning varies according to historical epoch and geographical context; the evident meaning, as used at the Congress, is that of an organized local congregation or community, responsible for the care of its members.

KIMCHI, DAVID (1160–1235). Medieval Jewish exegete. Kimchi was born and died in France (Narbonne). He came from a distinguished line of scholars but outshone his predecessors in the depth and breadth of his scholarship. His work encompassed Hebrew grammar and lexicography, but he is best remembered for commentaries on various sections of the Bible, including Genesis, the Prophets, and the Psalms. Despite the attacks on Christianity contained in these commentaries, they were translated into Latin and became standard references for Christians as well as Jews.

KINNOT. DIRGES chanted on the fast of Tisha B'Av, the day commemorating the destruction of the first and second temples of Jerusalem. It corresponded to August 8, 1897, and so had been commemorated just three weeks before the First Zionist Congress. The peroration in Nordau's address to the Congress evokes this well-known Jewish ceremony of mourning, anticipating the sorrowful response of the delegates when hearing the depressing details of Jewish life in an age of renewed anti-Semitism.

KOKESCH, OSER (1859–1905). Galician attorney, Zionist activist and leader. Born in Brody, Kokesch took his doctorate in law at the University of Vienna. As a student, he was an early adherent of Kadima, the Zionist fraternity, and of Admath Jeschurun, an association for Jewish settlement in Palestine. He worked closely with Herzl on preparations for the First Congress, where he was elected a member of the five-man Vienna Executive (Engeres Actionscomité). He was treasurer of the Zionist Organization's Vienna office; he contributed to the founding of both the Jewish Colonial Trust (the Zionist bank) and the Jewish National Fund. He remained a member of the Zionist Executive until his death.

KORKIS, AVRAHAM (1865–1922). Austrian civil servant, writer and editor, Zionist activist and ideologist. Born and raised in Galicia, Korkis studied law at the University of Lemberg. He was employed as a clerk in the office for commerce and industry in Galicia. He was active in Zionism as a student and went on to lead a coalition of Jewish-nationalist and Zionist organizations in Galicia in the 1890s. He helped to found and edit the influential Jewish-nationalist journal of Galicia, *Przyszłość* (Pol., "The Future"), and collected and published data on the social and economic conditions of the Jews in Galicia. He attended the First Zionist Congress and was elected a member of the Zionist General Council (Grosses Actionscomité) for Galicia.

KORNBLÜH, MORITZ (FL. 1875–1930). Austrian-Jewish attorney. An obscure figure in early Zionism, he appears to have received his schooling in Teschen in Silesia; presumably, he took his doctorate in law in Vienna and worked for a time as a lawyer in Freiland, Austria. He and his wife, Wilhelmina, attended the First Zionist Congress. His two notable interventions were to ask concerning the right of women to vote and to declare that any Jew serious about his religion must be a Social Democrat.

KORNFELD, SIEGMUND [SIGMUND] (1859–1927). Czech-Jewish psychiatrist and Zionist. Born in Bohemia as the son of a merchant, Kornfeld studied medicine in Prague and Vienna. He had an extensive clinical practice, lectured at the University of Vienna, and authored works on psychology and philosophy. He took part in the First Zionist Congress and was elected to the Zionist General Council (Grosses Actionscomité) as a representative for Austria.

KROCHMAL, NACHMAN (1785–1840). Galician-Jewish philosopher and historian. Krochmal devoted himself to the intensive study of both classical Hebrew philosophical texts and contemporary German philosophy, being strongly influenced by Hegel. He taught the famous rabbi and scholar, Solomon J.L. Rapoport, who became rabbi of Prague in 1840. Krochmal presented a profound philosophical study of Jewish history in his magnum opus, *Moreh Nevukhey HaZeman* (A Guide for the Perplexed of the Time), the title of which evokes a famous work of Maimonides.

LANDAU, SAUL RAPHAEL (1870–1943). Polish-Jewish lawyer, journalist, and advisor to Herzl. Born in Galicia, Landau completed his doctorate in law in Vienna. Active in the Jewish-nationalist cause, he contributed numerous articles to German and Polish periodicals. He joined Herzl after the publication of *Judenstaat*, suggesting the establishment of a Zionist journal in 1897 (*Die Welt*), which he edited for a brief time. Among the drafters of the Basel Program, he fell out with Herzl in 1898, founding a separate Zionist organization for Jewish workers, whose needs became his main concern. He evolved ideologically away from Zionism to the support of Jewish nationalism in the Diaspora.

LAZARE, BERNARD (1865–1903). French-Jewish journalist and activist. Born and raised in Nîmes, Lazare moved to Paris where he attained notoriety as a poet and journalist. He authored an influential study of the history of anti-Semitism (1894) and led the public battle to vindicate Alfred Dreyfus. He likewise exposed the persecution of Jews in Romania and Armenians in Ottoman Turkey. He was elected a member of the Zionist General Council (Grosses Actionscomité) for France at the First Congress; in fact, he attended only the Second Congress, where his appearance, as the champion of Dreyfus, was a sensation. However, he soon became disillusioned by the bourgeois character of the Zionist leadership. He broke with the movement because its mode of organizing and financing Jewish settlement violated his anarchist principles, and on account of its complaisance toward Sultan Abülhamit II, in spite of the latter's brutal repression of the Armenians.

LEVANDA, LEV OSIPOVICH (1835–1888). Russian-Jewish educationist, journalist, and fiction writer. Born in Minsk, he was educated there and in Vilna, in both traditional and secular subjects. Levanda worked as a consultant on curricula in Jewish schools. He wrote for a variety of Jewish newspapers, and his fiction depicts changes in Jewish society in mid-nineteenth century Russia. His ideological orientation shifted from assimilationist toward Jewish-nationalist and Zionist.

LIPPE, KARPEL [KARL] (1830–1915). Romanian-Jewish physician and Zionist activist, leader among Romanian's Hovevei Zion. Born in Galicia, he settled in Jassy, Romania, where he practiced medicine. Lippe did not support Herzl's notion of an independent Jewish state; rather, he argued that Jews ought to settle in Palestine and seek autonomy within the multinational Ottoman Empire. Nonetheless, as the senior Zionist attending the Congress, and as a notable figure among Hovevei Zion, he was accorded the privilege of opening the Basel Congress as its honorary president.

LIPPERT, JULIUS (1839–1909). Austrian educationist, historian, and politician. Born in Bohemia, Lippert studied law, history, philosophy, and German philology at the Karls-Universität in Prague. He became a teacher and administrator in the existing Austrian secondary-school system, but also sought to develop more popularly accessible forms of education during his forays into Austrian politics. His anticlerical orientation led him into occasional conflict with the Austrian authorities. His most famous and influential work was a two-volume history of human civilizations, *Kulturgeschichte der Menschheit in ihrem organischen Aufbau* (The History of Human civilization in its Organic Development)

(1886). A leftist and Darwinist, Lippert presented world history as the movement toward more liberal and progressive social forms.

LOEWE [LÖWE], HEINRICH (1869–1951). German-Jewish librarian, scholar, and Zionist organizer. Born near Magdeburg in Germany, he studied oriental languages and history in Berlin. He helped Leo Motzkin and others in forming an association for Russian students with a Jewish-nationalist orientation in Berlin (Russisch-jüdischer wissenschaftlicher Verein, or Russian-Jewish Academic Society); he likewise joined Willy Bambus in launching Germany's first Zionist association in 1892. Loewe visited Palestine in 1895 and 1897, and he represented the new Yishuv at the First Congress. Loewe was a librarian at the University of Berlin until his dismissal by the Nazi regime. He emigrated to Palestine in 1933 and became the head of the Tel Aviv municipal library. He is also remembered for his scholarship on Jewish folklore.

LUBLINSKI, SAMUEL (1868–1910). German-Jewish author, literary historian, self-styled philosopher of religion, and, for several years, a prominent Zionist. Born in East Prussia, Lublinski entered the book trade for a time, before devoting himself to writing, in Berlin and Weimar. He wrote many plays, but he is remembered for a weighty study of the history of German literature. While in Berlin, he joined the Zionists, attended the First Congress, and wrote for *Die Welt* (including the lead article about the Congress which appeared on 3 September 1897). But he gave up Zionism because, as he put it, his identification with German culture was too deep.

LUEGER, KARL (1844–1910). Christian-Socialist, anti-Semitic Austrian politician, and mayor of Vienna, 1897–1910. Of humble origins, Lueger studied law and, as an attorney, established a reputation as a defender of the common people. He entered politics in the 1870s; embracing anti-Semitism for opportunistic reasons, he founded the Christian Socialist Party in 1893. The new party appealed to Vienna's Catholic petite bourgeoisie on account of its anti-capitalist and anti-Semitic program. Although his party won a substantial majority in Vienna's local elections in 1895, the Hapsburgs resisted appointing him mayor until 1897. His legacy, including major social and infrastructural improvements in Vienna, was vitiated by his vocal anti-Semitism, which influenced the young Adolf Hitler during his Vienna years.

MAIMONIDES [MOSHE BEN MAIMON] (1138–1204). Hispano-Jewish philosopher, scientist, legal scholar, and physician. Born in Spain, Maimonides migrated from there due to the increasing intolerance of the al-Muwahhidun (Almohades), first to Morocco, then to Palestine, and finally to Egypt. Known by his acronym, Rambam, he was among the greatest of medieval polymaths. Within Judaism, he is known foremost for his codification of Jewish law and his thirteen articles of faith, often regarded as the finest summary of Jewish belief. His use of Aristotelian logic in defense of theism exercised a profound influence on both Jewish and non-Jewish philosophers, including Thomas Aquinas.

MALZ, DAVID (1862–1939). Galician-Jewish jurist, Zionist writer and orator. Malz was born in Lemberg/Lvov and educated in law. He was active in Zionist associations from 1882. He worked closely with Adolf Stand, wrote and spoke on behalf of the Zionist cause throughout Galicia (his works include an influential play in Polish), attended the First and Second Zionist Congresses, and was a member of the Zionist General Council (Grosses Actionscomité) representing Galicia. He died in Soviet-controlled Poland late in 1939.

MANDELKERN, SOLOMON (1846–1902). Russian-Jewish philologist, poet, teacher, and translator. Born in Volhynia, he received a traditional education, was influenced by Hasidism, and became a rabbi; changing course, he pursued scientific studies at universities in St. Petersburg, Jena, and Leipzig (where he finally settled). He was active in Hibbat Zion and attended the First Zionist Congress. He is remembered principally for his poetry; translation of various works into Hebrew, German, and Russian; and works of scholarship, above all his Hebrew-Latin concordance of the Bible.

MANDELSTAMM, MAX (1839–1912). Lithuanian-Jewish ophthalmologist, activist in Hibbat Zion and Zionism. Mandelstamm studied medicine in Russia and Germany, becoming a lecturer in ophthalmology at Kiev University. He responded to the 1881 pogroms by supporting emigration from Russia and helped to found Hibbat Zion. He joined Herzl's new Zionist movement and was elected to the Zionist General Council (Grosses Actionscomité); later, adopting a position known as Territorialism, he gave priority to the urgent need for a land, that need not be Palestine, to receive indigent Jewish immigrants.

MANTEUFFEL, BARON MAXIM [CARL EDUARD ZOEGE VON] (1864–1950). Austrian nobleman and Christian Zionist. Manteuffel had an estate in Tyrol where he trained young Jews from poor families in viticulture to prepare them for settlement in Palestine. He visited Palestine in 1897 in order to observe conditions in the new Yishuv. When Herzl learned of Manteuffel's plans, he asked him to conduct a clandestine inquiry into alleged abuses in the administration of Jewish colonies taken over by Baron Edmond de Rothschild. Manteuffel declined the request; but he did take part in the First Zionist Congress, where Herzl, in his closing address, noted his devotion to the cause, along with several other "Christian Zionists."

MARKUS [MARCUS], ABRAHAM (FL. 1761). German-Jewish banker and entrepreneur during the reign of Frederick the Great. Little is known about him, but on February 4, 1761, he became the first Jew to receive from Frederick the Great legal rights and privileges equal to those of Christian bankers, which applied as well to his heirs; he was also permitted to purchase a house in Berlin and to bequeath it to his children. In March of the same year, Veitel Ephraim and Daniel Itzig were accorded the same rights.

MARMOREK, OSCAR (1863–1909). Austrian-Jewish architect and one of Herzl's close collaborators. Marmorek was born in Galicia but educated in Vienna and Paris. He designed several important secular buildings in Austria, as well as some synagogues. Cofounder of the Zionist newspaper, *Die Welt*, he was a member of the Zionist Executive in Vienna, 1897–1905.

MARRANOS. Also known as *conversos*, Marranos were Jews of medieval Spain and Portugal who converted to Christianity, many if not most under duress (including threats of expulsion or execution), but who allegedly maintained a clandestine loyalty to Judaism. The name is of uncertain origin. In his address to the First Congress, Nordau makes them the archetype of the Jew who lives a duplicitous life in order to escape persecution, although he regards latter-day Marranos as more culpable than their predecessors.

MASSEL, JOSEPH (1850–1912). Lithuanian-Jewish printer, translator, and Zionist activist. Born in the Vilna governorate of the Russian Empire, Massel had a traditional education and remained an observant Jew. He emigrated to England in 1882 and set up as a printer in Manchester; he published his own translations of great English poetry into Hebrew. His publishing agenda also included works advocating the revival of Hebrew as a national language and support for Jewish settlement in Palestine. He attended the First Zionist Congress, where he proposed the melding of the scattered Hovevei Zion groups into the new Zionist Organization. Massel offered hospitality to Chaim Weizmann when he arrived in Manchester in 1904.

MAZKERET BATYA. See ʿEkron.

MENDELSSOHN, MOSES (1729–1786). German-Jewish philosopher and educator, public advocate of Jewish modernism and assimilation, forerunner of the Haskalah (Jewish Enlightenment). Mendelssohn was born in Dessau but moved to Berlin in his youth. Though self-educated, he so impressed Berlin society by his brilliance that he was accepted into the social and intellectual elite and offered protected status by Frederick the Great. Influenced by Maimonides, he adopted a rationalist position with respect to truth, arguing that the core of Judaism was not its doctrine of God, which was accessible to reason, but its special, revealed legislation. He translated the Torah into German and promoted the idea that Jews could assimilate to the general culture without being disloyal to their faith.

MENELAUS (R. 171–161 BCE). Hellenizing high priest under the Seleucids. Menelaus was a leading figure among the party of Hellenizing Jews, who sought to make Jerusalem into a Greek polis. He bribed the Seleucid king, Antiochus IV Epiphanes, to obtain the office of high priest, although he lacked the pedigree necessary to occupy that office. He redoubled his disgrace by cooperating with Antiochus in desecrating the Jerusalem temple and plundering its treasury, sealing his reputation as a traitor to his people.

METULLA (EST. 1896). Jewish agricultural colony (*moshava*) in the upper Galilee. Metulla derives from the Arabic "Matallah" (i.e., a place with a view). Matallah was the name of the Druze village where the new moshava was set up; an agent of Baron Edmond de Rothschild effected purchase of lands long cultivated by Druze peasants from an absentee landowner. The result was years of conflict with the former Druze tenants, who finally settled for compensation from the Jewish Colonization Association, after the latter assumed responsibilities for the Rothschild colonies in 1899. The colony was made up of families with agricultural experience elsewhere in Palestine, but, besides strife with the Druze, it struggled to survive because of isolation, internal quarrels, and defective methods of cultivation.

MEISELS, DOV BER (1798–1870). Rabbi of Kraków and then of Warsaw, and an outspoken advocate of Polish national independence and Jewish cooperation with other Poles. Meisels derived from a distinguished Jewish family of Kraków. He became chief rabbi of Kraków in 1832 and of Warsaw in 1856. He was politically active in both cities, using his religious influence and considerable wealth to support the 1830 Polish revolt against Russian rule, Polish demonstrations in 1861, and the big uprising of January 1863, and urging fellow Jews to act in concert with the Polish nationalists. He was twice expelled by the Russians, but he was permitted to return to Poland, where he died in 1870.

MEYER [KREMENETZKY], JOHANN (1850–1934). Electrical engineer, entrepreneur, Zionist leader and founding director of the Jewish National Fund. Born in Odessa, Kremenetzky took his engineering degree in Berlin. In 1880 he moved to Vienna, where he was successful in building up a large firm manufacturing electric light bulbs. He was an early supporter of Herzl, attended the First Congress, and was elected a member of the Vienna Executive (Engeres Actionscomité); he remained on the Executive, 1897–1905. He worked closely with Herzl and his house became the first archive of Herzl's literary estate. His most salient contribution to Zionism was his draft for the organization of the Jewish National Fund and his service to that body, 1901–1907. He founded several industrial enterprises in Palestine after World War I.

MIKVEH ISRAEL (EST. 1870). "The Hope of Israel," an agricultural training school established by Charles Netter in Jaffa on behalf of the Alliance Israélite Universelle. The school was envisioned as a means of helping Persian Jews move to Palestine and become self-supporting. Although little came of this venture, the school was important in helping Russian immigrants of the First Aliyah, especially members of the Bilu movement; it has continued to function and has trained generations of Jewish farmers and agricultural researchers.

MINTZ, ALEXANDER (FL. 1877–1910). Viennese Jewish lawyer and rapporteur on Austrian Jewry at the first Congress. Mintz began his practice in 1897 and was granted the honorific *Justizrat* in 1910. He served for many years in the legal department of Austria's *Allgemeine Depositenbank*. He served on the program committee of the First Congress and was elected to the five-man Vienna Executive; he participated in the 1898 and 1901 Congresses but he turned against Zionism sometime thereafter.

MISHMAR HAYARDEN (EST. 1890). Jewish agricultural colony (*moshava*) in the upper Galilee. Named "Guardian of the Jordan" because of its location along the river north of Lake Tiberias, the community was established on lands previously purchased by an American Jew. The new settlement first received assistance from Hovevei Zion; it was later taken over by the Jewish Colonization Association.

MITZRAYIM. EGYPT (HEB.). Like the Arabic for Egypt, "Misr," the Hebrew derives from an ancient designation that has, apparently, a dual form. Various etymologies have been suggested; perhaps "The Two Egypts," in reference to the union of the upper and lower Nile basins.

MONTEFIORE, MOSES (1784–1885). Anglo-Jewish businessman and philanthropist. Montefiore was born in Livorno when his parents were there on business, but the family was already established in England and Moses was educated and apprenticed there. He was enormously successful as a stockbroker for Nathan Mayer Rothschild, whose sister he had married. Retiring from the stock exchange in the 1820s, he devoted the remainder of his long life to humanitarian causes, especially the improvement of the conditions of Jews in lands where they had not yet attained emancipation. As a pious Jew, Montefiore believed in the traditional eschatology, yet he visited Palestine seven times, endowing various charitable institutions but also seeking to make the Jews of that country more self-sufficient. He is thus often regarded as a forerunner of Zionism, although he did not envision the creation of a Jewish state by means of popular mobilization and diplomacy.

MOTZA (EST. 1894). Jewish agricultural colony (*moshava*) just west of Jerusalem. The land where Motza was established was purchased by two Ottoman Jews from the Arabs of Qalunya (Kolonia) in 1859. In 1893, the Jerusalem Lodge of B'nai B'rith acquired the land and decided to build a farming settlement there. Motza was to be a model colony, an alternative to the Rothschild dependencies. A leading member of Motza was Samuel Broza, a Russian Jew whose vineyards Herzl toured during his trip to Palestine in 1898.

MOSES, MORITZ (1848–1903). Jewish merchant of Kattowitz and a major figure in Hovevei Zion. Active from his youth in promoting Jewish settlement in Palestine, Moses was one of the few present at both the Hovevei Zion conference in Kattowitz/Katowice in 1884 and the 1897 Congress in Basel.

He attended four Congresses in all. At the First Congress, he presented a fantastic scheme to raise billions of francs from various sources, in order to fund Palestine colonization.

MOHILEWER, SAMUEL [SHMUEL] (1824–1898). Orthodox rabbi and a founding father of religious Zionism. Born into a rabbinical family in the Vilna governorate, Mohilewer ministered in various Jewish communities before becoming rabbi of Bialystok in 1883. While staunchly Orthodox, he was well acquainted with secular thought and knew Russian, Polish, and German. He advocated a conciliatory approach to the *maskilim* (Jews influenced by Enlightenment culture) and the cooperation of Orthodox Jews with the Zionist leadership, thereby contributing to the formation of a religious faction within the early Zionist movement known as "Mizrachi" (from Merkaz Ruhani, "spiritual center"). He was among the founders of Hibbat Zion, acting as honorary president at its founding conference in Kattowitz in 1884. He sought to persuade Jewish philanthropists, including Edmond de Rothschild (whom he met in September 1882), to help Jews fleeing Russia in order to settle in Palestine.

MOTZKIN, LEO (1867–1933). Leading Russian-Jewish Zionist. Born near Kiev to a wealthy family, Motzkin pursued his advanced studies in Berlin, where he helped to establish an academic association for Russian Jews with a nationalist orientation (Russisch-jüdischer wissenschaftlicher Verein, or Russian-Jewish Academic Society). While the students were naturally sympathetic to Hibbat Zion, Motzkin adopted Herzl's political Zionism and helped in organizing the First Congress. At the Congress, Motzkin spoke in favor of a program that called for international recognition of a Jewish right to Palestine. He visited Palestine at Herzl's request and delivered a controversial report on the severe defects of the Palestine colonies at the Second Congress. He remained prominent within the Zionist leadership throughout his life, presiding at the Seventeenth and Eighteenth Congresses. He published an influential report on the condition of Jews in Russia in 1910, and he lobbied for the protection of Jewish minority rights at the Paris Peace Conference in 1919.

NAQUET, ALFRED JOSEPH (1834–1916). French-Jewish chemist and left-wing politician. Naquet taught in Paris and Palermo before turning to politics. Taking part in the overthrow of the monarchy in 1870, he became a staunch leftist in the Third Republic's Chamber of Deputies. He is chiefly remembered for his successful agitation in favor of a divorce law, enacted in 1886. He was accused but acquitted of corruption in the Panama Canal scandal of the 1890s.

NETTER, CHARLES (1826–1882). French-Jewish businessman and philanthropist. Born in Strasbourg, Netter had business interests that took him to Moscow, London, and Paris. He settled in Paris around 1851, where he took part in founding the Alliance Israélite Universelle, serving as its treasurer. AIU was generally opposed to Jewish immigration to Palestine, but Netter convinced the organization to assist Oriental Jews to resettle there in agricultural colonies. To this end he established Mikveh Israel (the Hope of Israel), an agricultural school located in Jaffa, after obtaining an Ottoman firman in 1870; he was its principal 1870–1873. Disappointed in the results of his project, he at first opposed further settlement in Palestine, especially of Russian Jews in 1881, preferring rather to send them to the United States. But during another visit to Palestine in 1882 he encountered some of the new immigrants and changed his outlook. He died at Mikveh Israel in the same year.

NEUMARK, DAVID (1866–1924). Reform rabbi, philosopher, and Zionist. Neumark was born in Galicia and studied at the rabbinical college in Berlin. He served as rabbi in Austrian-ruled Bohemia before taking up teaching positions, first in Berlin, then in Cincinnati. As a scholar, he produced historical and philosophical works explicating the evolution of Judaism, rejecting the immutability of scripture and law. Unlike most Reform rabbis, he embraced Zionism, but argued that it must be based on Jewish spiritual and moral values.

NICHOLAS I, TSAR (R. 1825–55). As Tsar of Russia, Nicholas was the epitome of Romanov autocracy. His reign was profoundly reactionary, as evidenced by new measures restricting the Jews' rights of residence within the country and involvement in public life, which reflected the Tsar's phobia about their commercial power and invidious influence on the Russian population. He combined his love of the army and aversion to the Jews by conscripting Jewish youths for military service. Harsh methods of impressment were employed, and the new policy was clearly aimed at forcing the conversion and assimilation of Jewish conscripts.

NORDAU, MAX (1849–1923). Austrian-Jewish physician, author, and the most celebrated orator of the Zionist Congresses. Born in Budapest, educated in Vienna, Nordau took a degree in medicine. After moving to Paris, he became famous for works of social and cultural criticism. He met Herzl in 1892 and supported him in his turn toward political Zionism. Nordau's addresses at the Congresses surveyed the condition of world Jewry. He was first vice president of the First Congress, and presided at Congresses held after Herzl's death, 1905–1911.

ODESSA COMMITTEE (1884–1917). Executive committee of Russian Hibbat Zion. Chaired by Leon Pinsker from its founding until his death in 1891, the Odessa Committee sought to coordinate the activities of the autonomous societies affiliated to Hibbat Zion. It was weakened by the rabbis' distrust of its secularist leadership, meager income, and lack of government sanction for its activities until 1890. In that year, it was formally licensed as the Society for the Support of Jewish Agriculturalists and Artisans in Palestine and Syria; in 1891, it established an office in Jaffa to direct its activities in Palestine. Although continuing to operate until the Bolshevik Revolution, when it was dissolved, it was increasingly overshadowed by Congress-Zionism.

OSMAN BEY, MAJOR (1836–1901). Anti-Semitic publicist, author of a book alleging a Jewish conspiracy aiming at world conquest. Details of his life are disputed; his given name was Frederick Millingen, but he also went under the name of Major Vladimir Andrejevich. He spent time in Istanbul, where he became an Ottoman officer (hence the title by which he is most widely known). His most important publication, under the English title *The Conquest of the World by the Jews*, seems to have appeared first in German in 1873, after which it was translated into other European languages.

PALE OF SETTLEMENT. First demarcated by the Catherine the Great in 1791 and of fluctuating boundaries, this was a region of the Russian Empire, consisting mainly of its western provinces, where Jews were legally permitted to reside. Jews were barred from residence outside the Pale unless they belonged to certain categories (such as merchants in possession of a certain capital), or could obtain special permission from the Tsar's government. Conditions in the Pale varied, but poverty was widespread. Throughout the nineteenth century and until its abolition in 1917, Russia's Pale and Congress Poland (also under Russian control) had, together, the biggest concentration of Jewish communities in the world.

PARIS COMMITTEE (EST. 1894). Although the Odessa Committee had acted as the executive of Russian Hovevei Zion, activists both inside and outside Russia agitated for an international executive based in Western Europe. In January 1894, representatives of Hovevei Zion from Russia, Germany, Austria, England, the United States, and France, met to establish a central committee to coordinate activities and finances of the disparate national groupings, since this was impossible for the Odessa Committee to do. The Paris Committee was thus formed. Although it gave support to some Palestine colonies (e.g., Be'er Tuvia/Qastina and Mishmar HaYarden), it was crippled by Baron Edmond de Rothschild's refusal to recognize its authority, as well as the withdrawal of the British.

PETAH TIKVA (EST. 1878). First modern Jewish-owned agricultural colony (*moshava*) in Palestine, located east of Jaffa, known as "mother of the moshavot." The settlement, whose name means "Door of Hope" (derived from Hos. 2:15), was originally established by Orthodox Jews living in Jerusalem; although the 1878 settlement was abandoned, it was refounded in 1882, when it was reinforced by Russian immigrants of the First Aliya and received support from Hovevei Zion. It came under Rothschild administration in 1887. Like other moshavot set up in the 1880s and 90s, it represented a breakthrough in reorienting Jewish settlement beyond Palestine's "holy cities," opening up possibilities of agricultural settlement and aiming at economic self-sufficiency.

PHILO (FL. 10 BCE–45 CE). Hellenistic Jewish philosopher. A native of Alexandria, his work reflects the deep influence of Greek philosophical and mystical thought on Diaspora Jewry. In particular, Philo is famous for his use of the allegorical method of interpreting scripture, in order to harmonize Jewish doctrine with Platonism. He defended Judaism against pagan detractors, and led an embassy of Alexandrian Jews to Rome to petition the Emperor, Caligula, to restore their traditional rights and privileges.

PINELES, SAMUEL (1843–1928). Romanian-Jewish businessman, rapporteur on Romanian Jewry at the first Congress. Pineles was a leader among Hovevei Zion of Romania and was secretary of the Romanian office of the Alliance Israélite Universelle. Of Galician origin, his family relocated to Galatz in Romania, where he went into business. He was instrumental in founding the Romanian colonies in Palestine, Zikhron Ya'akov and Rosh Pina. He participated in the preparatory meetings of the First Zionist Congress, was elected third vice president of the Congress, and became a member of the Zionist General Council (Grosses Actionscomité). He attended the first ten Zionist Congresses and was also among the founders of the Jewish Colonial Trust, the Zionist bank.

PINSKER, LEON (1821–1891). Russian-Jewish physician, author, and foremost leader of Russian Hovevei Zion. Born in Russian Poland, educated in Odessa and Moscow, Pinsker took a degree in medicine and was honored for his service in the Crimean War (1853–1856). At first an outspoken advocate of assimilation, Pinsker's optimism about the Jews' future in Europe and Russia was shattered by the pogroms of 1881. In the following year he reacted by penning *Autoemancipation*, a pamphlet which argued that anti-Semitism, as a psychopathology, was ineradicable, and that Jews must recover their dignity and self-respect through "self-emancipation" (i.e., organizing to acquire a territory and establish a Jewish nation-state). Although at first indifferent to the location of the state, he was recruited to lead Hovevei Zion, a loose-knit coalition of Russian groups seeking to sponsor new, self-supporting Jewish colonies in Palestine. Pinsker's reversal in thinking, as well as his Zionist ideas and plans, are strikingly similar to those of Herzl, whose *Judenstaat* was to appear fifteen years later.

QASTINA. SEE Be'er Tuvia.

RAPOPORT, SOLOMON JUDAH LOEB (1790–1867). Galician rabbi and scholar of Jewish history. Rapoport was influenced by Nachman Krochmal, who was his teacher for a time. He authored several critical studies of famous Jewish scholars, thereby contributing to the new scientific study of Jewish history, *Wissenschaft des Judentums*. He became rabbi of Prague in 1840, where he remained until his death.

REHOVOT (EST. 1890). Jewish agricultural colony (*moshava*) in the coastal plain south of Jaffa. The name of the colony derives from Gen. 26:22 and denotes "wide expanses" (although the biblical site was far from present-day Rehovot). The colony was established by Warsaw's Hovevei Zion on land of an Arab village, Khirbet Duran, purchased from Arab landowners. The colonists sought to remain independent of Rothschild's tutelage, although they did receive assistance (e.g., in the form of subsidized purchases of their grape harvest).

RISHON LEZION (EST. 1882). Second modern Jewish-owned agricultural colony (*moshava*) in Palestine, located south of Jaffa. The name, meaning "first to Zion," derives from Isa. 41:27. The settlers lacked a reliable water supply and experience in farming; the colony would have perished had it not been for Baron Edmond de Rothschild, whose dispatch of funds and advisors allowed the colony to survive, and eventually to become an important center of viticulture and wine production. However, the settlers chafed under Rothschild's administration, and there were open clashes in 1883 and 1887.

ROHLING, AUGUST (1839–1931). Catholic theologian and author of anti-Semitic and anti-Protestant works. Born in Westphalia, Rohling was educated at Münster and Paris, and taught in Münster, Milwaukee (Wisconsin), and finally Prague. He published a critique of the Talmud, *Der Talmudjude* (The Talmudic Jew) (1871), which became a source of anti-Semitic propaganda in the late nineteenth century. Interestingly, he hailed Zionism as the solution to the Jewish question.

ROKEAH, ELIEZER [LAZAR] (1854–1914). Hebrew and Yiddish journalist, early advocate of modern Jewish settlement in Palestine. Previously resident in Safed, he arrived in Romania around 1880 in order to urge Romanian Jews to emigrate to Palestine. He encouraged Dr. Karpel Lippe to assume leadership in this proto-Zionist cause, and he remained active as a journalist in Romania and Galicia, publishing a variety of Yiddish and Hebrew periodicals under such titles as *Der Emigrant* (The Emigrant), *Die Hoffnung* (The Hope), and *Talpiyyot* (Turrets).

RÓNAY [RÓNAI], JÁNOS (1849–1919). Hungarian-Jewish lawyer, Zionist activist, rapporteur on the situation of Hungarian Jewry at the First Congress. Rónay authored *Kosmopolitismus és Nationalismus különös tekintettel a zsidóság jelenkori állására* (Cosmopolitanism and Nationalism with Special Consideration of the Jewish Situation in Our Time, 1875) and *Zion und Ungarn* (Zion and Hungary, 1897). In close contact with Herzl, he was one of seven Hungarian Jews to attend the 1897 Congress, and he became the first president of the Hungarian Zionist Organization.

ROSENBERG, ADAM (1858–1928). German-American Jewish lawyer, Zionist, and rapporteur on American Jewry and conditions in Palestine at the First Congress. Born in Philadelphia, he was raised in an Orthodox home in

Hamburg but returned to the United States. Though trained as a lawyer, his main interest was in Jewish causes, most especially Shavei Zion ("Returners to Zion"), similar to Hovevei Zion. Rosenberg sought to unite all such groups; he sojourned in Palestine for varying periods, 1891–1897. He attended only the First Zionist Congress; while remaining an activist, he was subsequently alienated from the Zionist Organization's leadership.

ROSENHECK, SALOMON (1862–1934). Austrian-Jewish physician and Zionist. Born in Galicia, Rosenheck took a degree in medicine and attained the position of *Stadtarzt* (government-appointed physician) in Kolomea (Kolomyia, now in Ukraine), where he was also head of the local Jewish community. He was honorary president of numerous Zionist associations. He attended the First Zionist Congress, where he asked the Congress to support legal recognition of Yiddish within Austrian Galicia.

ROSH PINA (EST. 1882). A Jewish agricultural colony (*moshava*) in the northeastern Galilee. Rosh Pina was settled by Romanian Jews of Hovevei Zion. Like many other early colonies, it failed to become self-supporting and came under Rothschild's administration in 1883. The name of the settlement, commonly translated "cornerstone," derives from the Hebrew of Ps. 118:22.

ROTHSCHILD, BARON EDMOND DE (1845–1934). Banker, philanthropist, patron of Jewish settlement in Palestine. Born in France, the son of James-Mayer de Rothschild, Edmond had a lifelong interest in Jewish causes. He was especially concerned with aiding Russian Jews who sought to settle in Palestine after the pogroms of 1881. Although never formally a member of Hovevei Zion, he rescued numerous settlements founded by the latter from financial ruin; several of these were brought under his own paternalistic administration. His meeting with Herzl on July 18, 1896 was unproductive; Rothschild opposed Herzl's political ambitions because he believed it would endanger the new Yishuv by provoking the Ottoman government. He continued to support the new Yishuv throughout his life, donating immense sums for settlement, cultural institutions, and building infrastructure in Palestine. His contributions earned him the title "Father of the Yishuv"; he was also referred to as "The Well-Known Benefactor."

RUBENSTEIN, SOLOMON B. (1867–1916). Russian-Jewish merchant in London, Zionist activist. Rubenstein was born and educated in Russia; he emigrated to

England in 1893. A successful timber merchant, he visited the Jewish agricultural colonies in Palestine, sought to promote the revival of Hebrew, and took a leading role, alongside Chaim Weizmann, in the English Zionist Federation. He attended the First Congress in Basel.

RUELF [RÜLF], ISAAC (1831–1902). Rabbi, journalist, activist on behalf of Russian Jewry, and pioneer Zionist. Rülf descended from a poor German-Jewish family but was ordained a rabbi, took his doctorate in 1865, and became rabbi of Memel in East Prussia, close to the border with Russian-ruled Lithuania. His efforts to raise funds to relieve the suffering of Jews in Russia and reports on their desperate conditions, were instrumental in making German Jews aware of the situation in the East. He was moved by Pinsker's *Autoemancipation*; his own response to the pogroms of 1881 was to author *Arukhat Bat 'Ammi* (The Healing of the Daughter of My People), a text that reinforced Pinsker's ideas but also extended them, projecting a Hebrew-speaking Jewish state in Palestine. He was active in Hibbat Zion, then became a supporter of Herzl and the Zionist Congresses, and forcefully criticized Germany's anti-Zionist rabbis, the so-called *Protestrabbiner*.

SALZ, ABRAHAM (1864–1941). Zionist leader in Galicia, rapporteur on the situation of Jews in Galicia at the First Congress. Born in Tarnów, he studied law in Vienna. In 1893, he was elected president of a committee formed by the Zionist societies of Galicia. He was second vice president of the First Congress, and participated in every Congress held before World War I. After the war he remained active in the Zionist cause in his native Galicia, which became part of a reconstituted Poland.

SCHACH, FABIUS (1868–1942). Lithuanian-Jewish teacher and journalist, early advocate of Zionism in Germany. Born in Russia-ruled Lithuania, schooled in rabbinics, he went on to study at Riga and Berlin. In the latter location he met Max Bodenheimer, who invited him to teach Hebrew in Cologne. With Bodenheimer and David Wolffsohn, he became a leader in the German Zionist Federation and attended the First Congress. He clashed with Herzl over the wording of the Basel Program, which he argued should include explicit reference to obtaining international recognition of a Jewish right to Palestine. Ironically, he subsequently defected from and opposed Zionism, although he continued to write about Jewish problems. He died in the Shoah, at Theresienstadt, in 1942.

SCHADCHEN. The matchmaker of a traditional Jewish community.

SCHAFFER, SABBATAI SHEFTL (1862–1933). Orthodox rabbi of Baltimore, one of the founders of American Zionism. Schaffer was born in Russian-ruled Latvia and took advanced degrees in Leipzig and Berlin. He emigrated to the United States in 1893 to become rabbi of the Orthodox congregation Shearith Israel in Baltimore. He helped establish the Baltimore Zion Association in 1895 and represented it to the First Zionist Congress. He was a leader in the Federation of American Zionists from 1898, and also attended the Fifth Zionist Congress in 1901.

SCHÄFFLE, ALBERT (1831–1903). German sociologist, journalist, political economist. Educated in Tübingen, Schäffle started out as a journalist in Stuttgart, but entered German and Austrian politics; he was for a brief time minister of commerce in the Austrian government, 1871. After leaving politics, he composed a four-volume study, *Bau und Leben des sozialen Körpers* (Construction and Life of the Social Body) (1875–1878). The work sought to synthesize the natural and social sciences. It attempted to explain the social-psychological foundations of the state, justify state intervention in the economy, and encourage cooperation between bourgeoisie and proletariat.

SCHALIT, ISIDOR (1871–1954). Austrian-Jewish dentist, a leading figure within early Congress-Zionism, and secretary of the Zionist Executive in Vienna. Born in Galicia, Schalit grew up in Vienna and took a degree in medicine at the University of Vienna. Joining the group of Jewish-nationalist students, Kadimah, he and his colleagues were among Herzl's earliest recruits to political Zionism. For a short time he edited the Zionist organ, *Die Welt*; he also worked closely with Herzl in making detailed arrangements for the First Congress in Basel. Schalit attended most subsequent Congresses, down to 1951. He ran unsuccessfully for the Austrian parliament in 1907 and fought for the national-minority rights of Jews in Austrian Galicia and Bukovina; he emigrated to Palestine in 1938.

SCHAPIRA, HERMANN (1840–1898). Lithuanian-Jewish professor of mathematics, among the early leaders of Hibbat Zion and Congress-Zionism. Schapira received a traditional education and became a rabbi, but then turned his attention to scientific studies, which he pursued in Kovno/Kaunas and Berlin. Penury forced him to interrupt his studies in order to go into business in Odessa, where he was among the founders of Odessa's Hovevei Zion. He returned to his studies, obtaining a professorship of mathematics at Heidelberg, but continued to agitate for Zionism, now among German Jews. At the First Congress, he proposed the establishment of two institutions that would prove crucial for the spread of Zionism, i.e., a national fund for the purchase of land on behalf of the entire Jewish people (est. 1901), and a Hebrew university in Palestine (est. 1918).

SCHAUER, RUDOLF (1869–1930). German-Jewish lawyer, Zionist, rapporteur at the First Congress. Schauer offered only a brief comment about the situation of Jews in Germany at the First Congress. In May 1898, he was a member of a preparatory committee, along with David Wolffsohn and Max Bodenheimer (both of Cologne), for establishing the Jewish Colonial Trust, the Zionist bank. When it was incorporated in 1899, he became one of its first three governors.

SCHNEIDER, ERNST (1850–1913). Austrian master mechanic and anti-Semitic politician. Schneider studied at several schools and institutes in Austria; after his apprenticeship, he attained renown as a maker of precision scientific instruments. Active in Vienna's brotherhood of mechanics, he entered politics in 1880, representing Vienna's small tradesmen and adopting an anti-Semitic position. As an advocate for the interests of tradesmen he was among the early adherents of the Christian Socialist Party led by Karl Lueger. Schneider was an elected member of the Imperial Parliament, 1891–1907; his political decline was occasioned by accusations of ballot manipulation, along with blatant attacks on Austria's Jews.

SCHNIRER, MOSES [MORITZ] T. (1861–1941). Zionist activist in Vienna. Born in Bucharest, he studied medicine in Vienna. He became a Zionist as a student, helped found the Jewish fraternity Kadimah, then played an important role in preparing the First Congress (where he acted as one of four assessors). At the Congress itself he helped draft the constitution of the Zionist Organization and gave an address in which he criticized corruption in the Palestine colonies. A staunch adherent of political Zionism, he accompanied Herzl in his visit to Palestine in 1898, where they met Kaiser Wilhelm II in an unsuccessful attempt to win him over to the Zionist cause.

SCHÖNERER, GEORG VON (1842–1921). Austrian landowner and pan-German anti-Semitic politician. Schönerer studied in Germany and Hungary and entered imperial politics in the 1870s. From 1879, he was the leading figure in Austria's populist and racialist pan-German movement, which pitted him against the Hapsburg monarchy, the Catholic Church, and liberal political parties. A force to be reckoned with in Austrian politics, he opposed Prime Minister Count Badeni's language policy in Bohemia, which favored the Czech population over the German; the struggle ended in Badeni's dismissal. Schönerer's influence waned after 1907. He is remembered chiefly as having influenced the young Adolf Hitler, who was in Vienna 1907–1913.

SHECHITA. THE slaughtering of animals according to Jewish ritual law.

SOKOLOW, NAHUM (1859–1936). Polish-Jewish journalist and Zionist activist. Born in Russian Poland, Sokolow was trained in traditional Jewish disciplines but educated himself in modern languages and secular subjects. He wrote for the Hebrew journal *HaTzefira* (The Dawn) and later became the journal's editor. The journal's eminence and longevity (1862–1931) explain why Sokolow has been dubbed the father of modern Hebrew journalism. Sokolow was cautious in his support for Hibbat Zion and for Herzl as well; but after Sokolow's attendance at the First Zionist Congress, he became an enthusiast for Herzl's program and went on to assume leading roles in the Zionist Organization, promoting Zionism in the United States, pressing for a British endorsement of Zionism (a prelude to the Balfour Declaration), then chairing the Zionist delegation to the Paris Peace Conference in 1919.

SPEISER, PAUL (1846–1935). Swiss jurist and politician. Born in Basel, Speiser studied law in Switzerland and Germany. He returned to Basel where he taught commercial and tax law at the university, held positions in the civil court system, and became active in politics at the local and national levels, eventually becoming the president of the Swiss Nationalrat (National Council) in 1907–1908. At the time of the First Zionist Congress in Basel, Speiser presided over the cantonal government and attended part of the proceedings.

SPIERS, DAYAN BERNARD (1835–1901). A prominent London Jew who served on the London Bet Din (rabbinical court). Spiers had a significant influence on Samuel Montagu (1832–1911), the famous banker, politician, and philanthropist active in a variety of Jewish causes.

SPINOZA, BARUCH (1632–1677). Dutch-Jewish philosopher. Born in the Netherlands but of Sephardic parentage, Spinoza achieved posthumous fame as one of the greatest of early modern rationalists, comparable to Descartes. He pronounced on a wide array of subjects, including politics, ethics, biblical criticism, theology, psychology, etc. His radical monism and unorthodox views of God, scripture, and the relationship between religion and the state, earned him the opprobrium of most of his Jewish and Christian contemporaries.

STAND, ADOLF (1870–1919). Galician-Jewish journalist and editor, Zionist orator and organizer. Stand was born in Lemberg/Lvov and studied law at the university there. He was active in fighting assimilation and promoting Zionism from the 1880s. He wrote and edited journals in Polish and was renowned for his oratory. He joined Herzl's new movement, participating in the 1897 Congress and later becoming a member of the Zionist General Council (Grosses Actionscomité), but his support of practical Zionism put him at odds with Herzl. Entering Austrian politics, he represented Brody as a Jewish nationalist in parliament, 1907–1911; he fled Galicia in 1914 in the face of the Russian advance, residing in Vienna for the remainder of his life.

STEINER [YORK-STEINER], HEINRICH (1859–1934). Publisher, author, and Zionist leader. Born in Slovakia, Steiner settled in Vienna, where he became a journalist, editor, and publisher. Herzl's *Judenstaat* converted him to Zionism. He was present at the meeting in March 1897 where the decision was taken to hold a Zionist Congress; he also helped Herzl launch the Zionist organ, *Die Welt*. At Basel in 1897, he presented the constitution of the Zionist organization on the third day of the Congress. He was a strict political Zionist, rejecting any diversion from the course set by Herzl; in his writing, he insisted that, regardless of language and cultural orientation, the Jews constituted a distinct nation. He settled in Palestine in 1933.

STURDZA, DMITRIE (1833–1914). Romanian statesman. Sturdza was a scion of a powerful Moldavian family that had held high office under Ottoman rule. Educated in Romania and Germany, he acted as secretary to Prince Cuza, who effectively united the Danubian principalities in 1859. Disillusioned with Cuza, he supported his removal by a coup in 1866; he subsequently held a variety of ministerial posts, including the premiership. A rigid Romanian nationalist, he sought to restrict the rights of non-Romanian "aliens," including Jews.

TANNAIM (CA. 10–220 CE). Jewish scholars of the oral Torah during the period leading up to the compilation of the Mishnah at the beginning of the third century CE. By tradition, the period begins with the generation of Hillel and Shammai and ends with that of Judah HaNasi. The religious thought and practice of the Tannaim were foundational for rabbinic Judaism.

TEMKIN [TIOMKIN], VLADIMIR (1861–1927). Russian-Jewish engineer, activist in Hibbat Zion and Congress-Zionism. Born in Yelizavetgrad, educated in St. Petersburg, he was director of Hibbat Zion's Jaffa office in 1891. He attended the 1897 Congress, where he served as the Russian-language secretary. He became a member of the Zionist General Council (Grosses Actionscomité) in 1898. With other Russian Zionists, he opposed Herzl's projected settlement of Jews in East Africa (as a temporary refuge from anti-Semitic outrages in Russia). After the Bolshevik Revolution in 1917, he settled in Paris and took a leading role in the Revisionist Zionist movement.

USSISHKIN [USSISCHKIN], MENACHEM (1863–1942). Russian-Jewish Zionist, advocate of "practical" Zionism (i.e., immediate and ongoing colonization), in contrast to Herzl's "political" orientation. Ussishkin was born in Dubrovno, studied engineering in Moscow, and worked in Yekaterinoslav and Odessa. He was elected secretary of Moscow's Hovevei Zion in 1885 and travelled to Palestine with Ahad Ha'am in 1891. Hebrew secretary for the First Zionist Congress, he served as president of the board of the Jewish National Fund, 1921–1942. He settled in Jerusalem in 1919.

VOLTAIRE [FRANÇOIS MARIE AROUET] (1694–1778). French philosopher, dramatist, and historian. Arguably the most influential intellectual of the eighteenth century, Voltaire was the epitome of the European Enlightenment in virtue of his advocacy of freedom of speech and thought, and, most famously, his hostility to religious intolerance. A Deist himself, he believed in the possibility of progress through scientific endeavor and the rational reform of social institutions. His literary works satirized the folly and inhumanity of his contemporaries; his voluminous correspondence with other leading intellectuals, including heads of state, ensured that his ideas were disseminated throughout Europe. Notwithstanding his championing of toleration, Voltaire's works abound with anti-Semitic aspersions; e.g., that Jews are racially alien to Europe and degenerate in character.

WADI CHANIN (EST. 1883). Jewish agricultural colony (*moshava*) along the Jaffa-Jerusalem road, now the town of Ness Ziona. The Arabic name of the area was Wadi Hanayn; it had been acquired by a German Templer in 1878, hence the Germanization of the name to "Chanin." Various hardships caused the German to leave Palestine; he subsequently exchanged his Palestine land for land owned by Reuben Lehrer in Odessa. Lehrer and family settled in Palestine in 1883, and other Russian Jews soon enlarged the community. Michael Halperin established an adjacent settlement under the name Ness Ziona in 1891, and with the merging of the two communities the name of the latter prevailed.

WELLENHOF, PAUL HOFMAN VON (1858–1944). Austrian teacher, literary scholar, and politician. Wellenhof derived from the nobility of Styria, but came to prominence as a German-nationalist deputy in the lower house of the Imperial Parliament, 1901–1907 and 1911–1918. In the aftermath of World War I, he was a member of the provisional national assembly that established the First Republic.

WERNER, SIEGMUND (1867–1928). Austrian-Jewish physician and dentist, writer and editor, and assistant to Theodor Herzl. Born and educated in Vienna, Werner graduated in medicine in 1896. An active Zionist in his student days, he became Herzl's loyal aide from 1896. He edited the Zionist organ *Die Welt*, 1897–1899 and 1903–1905, attended the Congresses, and was at Herzl's side at the time of his death in 1904. Moving to Moravia, he took up dentistry; he worked in the military medical corps for Austria-Hungary in World War I.

WISSOTZKY, KALONYMUS-ZE'EV (1824–1904) (Forename given as "K.W." in text of proceedings). Lithuanian-Jewish businessman, philanthropist, and activist in Hibbat Zion. Wissotzky was born and educated in Russian-ruled Lithuania; he moved to Moscow in 1858, where he established a successful tea company (Ahad Ha'am was for a time the company agent). He contributed to a variety of Jewish causes, including Hebrew literature and Palestine colonization. He attended the Kattowitz/Katowice conference and visited Palestine in 1885. His report on his visit was used by Hibbat Zion to determine its policy toward the various colonies; during the same visit he set up a coordinating committee for the movement in Jaffa.

WOLFFSOHN, DAVID (1856–1914). Zionist businessman and Herzl's successor as president of the Zionist Organization. Born in Lithuania, Wolffsohn studied under the distinguished scholar, R. Isaac Rülf, later a leader among Hovevei Zion. He relocated to Cologne in 1888 where he prospered as a timber merchant; he helped to found a group of Hovevei Zion there. He was convinced of Herzl's program when he read *Judenstaat* and met him in 1896, becoming Herzl's companion and offering significant financial support for his activities. He advised Herzl on matters of Jewish traditions and religious observances (about which Herzl knew little). He was one of four assessors at the First Congress. Wolffsohn was the first president of the Jewish Colonial Trust, the Zionist bank, and, because of his extremely close association with Herzl, was elected his successor as president of the Zionist Organization, 1905–1911.

YESUD HAMA'ALA (EST. 1883). Jewish agricultural colony (*moshava*) in the upper Galilee, near what was once Lake Hula. The name derives from Ezra 7:9, a reference to Ezra's decision to go up to Jerusalem from Babylon. The colony's lands were purchased from a Jew who had acquired rights of partnership with local Bedouin in the 1870s. The land was settled by Jews from Congress Poland, who struggled however to survive, on account of malaria, occasional attacks by Bedouin, and defective methods of farming. The colony was saved from collapse by Baron Edmond de Rothschild's intervention and oversight, beginning in 1887.

ZEDERBAUM, ALEXANDER (1816–1893). Russian-Jewish journalist, publisher, and activist in Hibbat Zion. Born in Russian Poland, Zederbaum moved to Odessa in 1840, where he lived for three decades before moving to St. Petersburg. While in Odessa, he launched what became Russia's most influential Hebrew weekly, *HaMelitz* (The Advocate), in 1860. The journal had a liberal-modernist orientation and promoted a Jewish-nationalist agenda. It publicized the work of Hovevei Zion in the 1880s; Zederbaum himself attended the Kattowitz/Katowice conference in 1884, and pressed the Russian government to grant legal recognition to the Odessa Committee or, as it was officially styled, The Society for the Support of Jewish Agriculturalists and Artisans in Palestine and Syria (the central committee of Russia's Hovevei Zion).

ZIKHRON YA'AKOV (EST. 1882). An early settlement of Romanian Jews on the central coast of Palestine, sponsored by Hovevei Zion. It came under Baron Edmond de Rothschild's administration in 1883, at which time it was renamed for the latter's father James (Jacob) de Rothschild.

ZION. Hill on the eastern side of ancient Jerusalem on which the temple was located and hence the holiest site in Judaism. The western wall of the temple enclosure, the so-called Wailing Wall, dates from the days of Herod the Great (first century BCE) and has remained throughout the centuries an active place of prayer for Jews. The elevated enclosure itself, under Muslim jurisdiction since the sixth century, is known to Muslims as al-Haram al-Sharif (the Noble Sanctuary); the Dome of the Rock and al-Aqsa Mosque are situated within its precincts. (Visitors to what is today called Mount Zion in Jerusalem are in a misnamed location.)

ZION (est. 1892). Name of a Vienna-based coalition of Hovevei Zion groups in Austria, also known as Verband der österreichischen Vereine für Colonisation Palästinas und Syriens (Union of Austrian Societies for the Colonization of Palestine and Syria). Founded under the leadership of Nathan Birnbaum, Moses Schnirer, Saul Landau, and others, the association sought to raise funds for Palestine colonization; the members of the Vienna chapter of Zion were among the first to support Herzl's call for a political program.

ZION CENTRAL COMMITTEE. See Paris Committee.

BIBLIOGRAPHY

The American Jewish Yearbook 5660. Edited by Cyrus Adler. Philadelphia: Jewish Publication Society, 1899. http://www.ajcarchives.org/AJC_DATA/Files/1899_1900_2_Formatter.pdf.

Alderman, Geoffrey. *Modern British Jewry.* Oxford: Oxford University Press, 1998.

Alemann, Ulrich von. "Die Enstehung und Entwicklung der deutschen Parteien." Accessed Feb. 26, 2018. http://www.bpb.de/politik/grundfragen/parteien-in-deutschland/ 202312/entstehung-und-entwicklung-bis-1933.

Allgemeine Zeitung des Judenthums (Leipzig and Berlin).

Anderson, Robert. *British Universities, Past and Present.* London: Continuum, 2006.

Arafat, Yasser. "Yasser Arafat's 1974 UN General Assembly speech." UN General Assembly, New York, 29th Session, 2282nd Plenary Mtg, Agenda Item 108, Official Records, A/PV.2282 and Corr. 1, November 13, 1974. https://en.wikisource.org/wiki/Yasser_Arafat%27s_1974_UN_General_Assembly_speech.

Arendt, Hannah. *Eichmann in Jerusalem: A Report on the Banality of Evil.* London: Penguin Books, 2006.

Aschheim, Steven E. *Brothers and Strangers: The East European Jew in German and German-Jewish Consciousness, 1800–1923.* Madison: University of Wisconsin Press, 1999.

Avineri, Shlomo. *The Making of Modern Zionism: The Intellectual Origins of the Jewish State.* New York: Basic Books, 1981.

Bar-Zohar, Michael. *Beyond Hitler's Grasp: the Heroic Rescue of Bulgaria's Jews.* Holbrook, MA: Adams Media, 1998.

Bassett, Richard. *For God and Kaiser: The Imperial Austrian Army, 1618–1918.* New Haven, CT: Yale University Press, 2015.

Bassnett, Susan. *Translation Studies.* 3rd ed. London: Routledge, 2002.

Bauer, Yehuda. *Rethinking the Holocaust.* New Haven, CT: Yale University Press, 2001.

Berkowitz, Michael. "The Debate about Hebrew, in German: the *Kulturfrage* in the Zionist Congresses, 1897–1914." In *Insiders and Outsiders: Jewish and German Culture in Germany and Austria*. Edited by Dagmar C.G. Lorenz, and Gabriele Weinberger, 109–15. Detroit: Wayne State University Press, 1994.

———. "Die Schaffung einer jüdischen Öffentlichkeit: Theodor Herzl und der Baseler Kongress von 1897." In *Europäische Öffentlichkeit: transnationale Kommunikation seit dem 18. Jahrhundert*. Edited by Jörge Requate and Martin Schulze Wessel, 79–91. Frankfurt: Campus Verlag, 2002.

———. *Zionist Culture and West European Jewry before the First World War*. Cambridge: Cambridge University Press, 1993.

Bideleux, Robert, and Ian Jeffries. *A History of Eastern Europe: Crisis and Change*. London: Routledge, 1998.

Blackwell, William L. *The Beginnings of Russian Industrialization*. Princeton: Princeton University Press, 1968.

Blumberg, Arnold. *Zion before Zionism, 1838–1880*. Syracuse, NY: Syracuse University Press, 1985.

Booth, William. "Netanyahu says Palestinian gave Hitler idea for the Holocaust," *Washington Post*, Oct. 21, 2015. https://www.washingtonpost.com/news/worldviews/wp/2015/10/21/netanyahu-says-palestinian-gave-hitler-idea-for-the-holocaust/.

Borochov, Ber. *The National Question and the Class Struggle*. First published 1903. Translated by Poale Zion. https://en.wikisource.org/wiki/The_National_Question_and_the_Class_Struggle.

Brustein, William I. *Roots of Hate: Anti-Semitism in Europe before the Holocaust*. Cambridge: Cambridge University Press, 2003.

Cahnman, Werner J. "Munich and the First Zionist Congress." *Historia Judaica* 3 (1941): 7–23.

Campos, Michelle. "Between 'Beloved Ottomania' and 'The Land of Israel': the Struggle over Ottomanism and Zionism among Palestine's Sephardi Jews, 1908–1913." *International Journal of Middle East Studies* 37 (2005): 461–83.

———. *Ottoman Brothers: Muslims, Christians, and Jews in Early Twentieth-Century Palestine*. Stanford: Stanford University Press, 2011.

Cesarani, David. *The Jewish Chronicle and Anglo-Jewry, 1841–1991*. Cambridge: Cambridge University Press, 1994.

Chandler, Daniel. "Semiotics for Beginners: Intertextuality." Accessed Feb. 26, 2018. http://visual-memory.co.uk/daniel/Documents/S4B/sem09.html.

Chowers, Eyal. *The Political Philosophy of Zionism: Trading Jewish Words for a Hebraic Land.* Cambridge: Cambridge University Press, 2013.
Cohen, Roger. "What Will Israel Become?" *New York Times*, Dec. 20, 2014. https://www.nytimes.com/2014/12/21/opinion/sunday/roger-cohen-what-will-israel-become.html?_r=0.
Cohn, Henry J. "Theodor Herzl's Conversion to Zionism." *Jewish Social Studies* 32:2 (1970): 101–10.
Cohn-Sherbok, Lavinia, and Dan Cohn-Sherbok. *Judaism: A Short Introduction.* Oxford: OneWorld, 1997.
De Haas, Jacob. *Theodor Herzl: A Biographical Study.* 2 vols. Chicago: Leonard, 1927.
Dogo, Marco. "Loyalty Sorely Tried: The Jews and the Bulgarian State (1878–1935)." In *The Jews and the Nation-States of Southeastern Europe from the 19th Century to the Great Depression.* Edited by Tullia Catalan and Marco Dogo, 73–103. Newcastle upon Tyne, UK: Cambridge Scholars Publishing, 2016.
Dowty, Alan. "'A Question That Outweighs All Others': Yitzhak Epstein and Zionist Recognition of the Arab Issue." *Israel Studies* 6:1 (2001): 34–54.
———. "Much Ado about Little: Ahad Ha'am's 'Truth from Eretz Yisrael,' Zionism, and the Arabs." *Israel Studies* 5:2 (2000): 154–81.
Ellis, Marc H. *Beyond Innocence and Redemption: Confronting the Holocaust and Israeli Power.* San Francisco: Harper & Row, 1990.
Elon, Amos. *The Israelis: Founders and Sons.* New York: Penguin, 1983.
———. *Theodor Herzl.* New York: Holt, Rinehart, and Winston, 1975.
Engel, David. *Zionism.* Harlow, UK: Pearson-Longman, 2009.
Epstein, Lawrence J. *The Dream of Zion: The Story of the First Zionist Congress.* Lanham, MD: Rowman and Littlefield, 2016.
Evans, Richard J. *The Coming of the Third Reich.* New York: Penguin Books, 2005.
Faulenbach, Bernd. *Geschichte der SPD: Von den Anfängen bis zur Gegenwart.* Munich: C.H. Beck, 2012.
Feller, F.-X. *Biographie Universelle.* M. Pérennès. New ed. Paris, 1844.
Fried, E.G. "Die Balfour-Deklaration zum 2. November," *Menorah* 11 (Nov. 1927): 644–646. http://sammlungen.ub.uni-frankfurt.de/cm/periodical/titleinfo/2920853.
Friedman, Isaiah. *Germany, Turkey, and Zionism, 1897–1918.* Oxford: Clarendon, 1977.

Fukuyama, Francis. *The End of History and the Last Man.* New York: Avon Books, 1992.

Gentzler, Edwin. *Contemporary Translation Theories.* 2nd revised ed. Clevedon, UK: Multilingual Matters, 2001.

Gilbar, Gad G. "The Growing Economic Involvement of Palestine with the West, 1865–1914." In *Palestine in the Late Ottoman Period: Political, Social, and Economic Transformation.* Edited by David Kushner, 188–210. Leiden: Brill, 1986.

Goetz, Hans-Werner. "Die 'Deutschen Stämme' als Forschungsproblem." In *Zur Geschichte der Gleichung "germanisch-deutsch."* Edited by Heinrich Beck et al., 229–53. Berlin: Walter de Gruyter, 2004.

Gross, Michael B. "Kulturkampf and Unification: German Liberalism and the War against the Jesuits." *Central European History* 30:4 (1997): 545–66.

Handler, Heinz. "Two Centuries of Currency Policy in Austria" (Sept. 1, 2016). Oesterreichische Nationalbank, *Monetary Policy & The Economy* Q3 (2016): 61–76.

Hegel, G.W.F. *Vorlesungen über die Philosophie der Geschichte.* First published 1837. http://gutenberg.spiegel.de/buch/vorlesungen-uber-die-philosophie-der-geschichte-1657/1.

Heid, Ludger, "Der schönste Mann." *Zeit Online*, Aug. 29, 1997. http://www.zeit.de/1997/36/Der_schoenste_Mann.

Hertzberg, Arthur. *The Zionist Idea: A Historical Analysis and Reader.* First published 1959. Philadelphia: Jewish Publication Society, 1997.

Herzl, Theodor. *The Congress Addresses of Theodor Herzl.* Translated by Nellie Strauss. New York: Federation of American Zionists, 1917.

———. *The Diaries of Theodor Herzl.* Translated and edited by Marvin Lowenthal. New York: Dial Press, 1956.

———. *The Jews' State, A Critical English Translation.* Translated and introduced by Henk Overberg. Lanham, MD: Rowman and Littlefield, 2012.

———. *Der Judenstaat: Versuch einer moderner Lösung der Judenfrage.* Vienna: M. Breitenstein, 1896. https://www.gutenberg.org/files/28865/28865-h/28865-h.htm.

———. *Theodor Herzl: Briefe und Tagebücher.* Edited by Alex Bein et al. 7 vols. Berlin: Propyläen Verlag, 1983–1996.

———. *Zionist Writings: Essays and Addresses.* Translated by Harry Zohn. 2 vols. New York: Herzl Press, 1973, 1975.

Hobbes, Thomas. *Leviathan.* First published 1651. Edited by Michael Oakeshott. New York: Touchstone, 1962.

Hyman, Paula E. "Jews and Judaism." In *Europe 1789–1914: Encyclopedia of the Age of Industry and Empire*. Edited by John Merriman and Jay Winter. 5 vols. Detroit: Charles Scribner's Sons, 2006.

Jasinski, James. *Sourcebook on Rhetoric: Key Concepts in Contemporary Rhetorical Studies*. Thousand Oaks, CA: Sage Publications, 2001.

Jelavich, Charles, and Barbara Jelavich. *The Establishment of the Balkan National States, 1804–1920*. Seattle: University of Washington Press, 1977.

Jewish Encyclopedia. Edited by Isidore Singer et al. 12 vols. New York: Funk and Wagnalls, 1901–1906. http://www.jewishencyclopedia.com/.

The Jubilee of the First Zionist Congress, 1897–1947. Jerusalem: Executive of the Zionist Organization, 1947.

Der Jude: eine Monatsschrift (Berlin).

Kaplan, Eran, and Derek Penslar, eds. *The Origins of Israel, 1882–1948: A Documentary History*. Madison: University of Wisconsin Press, 2011.

Karpat, Kemal. *Ottoman Population, 1830–1914: Demographic and Social Characteristics*. Madison: University of Wisconsin Press, 1985.

Katz, Ethan B., Lisa Moses Leff, and Maud S. Mandel, eds. *Colonialism and the Jews*. Bloomington: Indiana University Press, 2017.

Komoróczy, Géza. "Israeliten/Juden in ihrer Gemeinde. Juden in der ungarischen Gesellschaft der Nachkriegszeit, 1945–2002." In *Jüdische Gemeinden. Kontinuitäten und Brüche*. Edited by Eleonore Lappin, 63–101. Berlin/Vienna: Philo, 2002.

Kornberg, Jacques. *Theodor Herzl: From Assimilation to Zionism*. Bloomington: Indiana University Press, 1993.

Kulenska, Veselina. "The Antisemitic Press in Bulgaria at the End of the 19th Century." *Quest: Issues in Contemporary Jewish History*, issue 3 (July 2012). http://www.quest-cdecjournal.it/focus.php?issue=3&id=296.

Kury, Patrick. "Jüdische Lebenswelten in einer Zeit raschen Wandels. Ostjuden, Zionistenkongresse, Überfremdungsängste um 1900." In *Acht Jahrhunderte Juden in Basel: 200 Jahre Israelitische Gemeinde, Basel*. Edited by Heiko Haumann, 140–51. Basel: Schwabe Verlag, 2005.

Kushner, David, ed. *Palestine in the Late Ottoman Period: Political, Social, and Economic Transformation*. Leiden: Brill, 1986.

Laqueur, Walter. *A History of Zionism*. New York: Schocken Books, 1978.

———. "Zionism and its Liberal Critics, 1896–1948." *Journal of Contemporary History* 6:4 (1971):161–82.

Lehn, Walter. "The Jewish National Fund." *Journal of Palestine Studies* 3:4 (1974): 74–96.

Lentin, Ronit. *Israel and the Daughters of the Shoah: Reoccupying the Territories of Silence.* New York: Berghahn Books, 2000.
Leoussi, Athena, ed. *Encyclopaedia of Nationalism.* New Brunswick: Transaction Publishers, 2001.
Lewisohn, Ludwig. *Theodor Herzl: A Portrait for this Age.* Cleveland: World Publishing, 1955.
Lindemann, Albert S. *Esau's Tears: Modern Anti-Semitism and the Rise of the Jews.* Cambridge: Cambridge University Press, 1997.
Lockman, Zachary. *Comrades and Enemies: Arab and Jewish Workers in Palestine, 1906–1948.* Berkeley: University of California Press, 1996.
Lorenz, Dagmar C. G., and Gabriele Weinberger. *Insiders and Outsiders: Jewish and Gentile Culture in Germany and Austria.* Detroit, MI: Wayne State University Press, 1994.
Luz, Ehud. *Parallels Meet: Religion and Nationalism in the Early Zionist Movement (1882–1904).* Translated by Lenn J. Schramm. Philadelphia: Jewish Publication Society, 1988.
Mandel, Neville J. *The Arabs and Zionism before World War I.* Berkeley: University of California Press, 1976.
———. "Ottoman Policy and Restrictions on Jewish Settlement in Palestine: 1881–1908—Part I," *Middle Eastern Studies* 10:3 (1974): 312–32.
———. "Ottoman Practice as regards Jewish Settlement in Palestine: 1881–1908," *Middle Eastern Studies* 11:1 (1975): 33–46.
Marr, Wilhelm. *Der Sieg des Judenthums über das Germanenthum, vom nicht confessionellen Standpunkt aus betrachtet.* Bern: Rudolph Costenoble, 1879.
Marx, Rabbi Dalia. "The Prayer for the State of Israel: Universalism and Particularism." In *All the World: Universalism, Particularism, and the High Holy Days.* Edited by Rabbi Lawrence A. Hoffman, 49–76. Woodstock, VT: Jewish Lights Publishing, 2014.
McCarthy, Justin. *The Population of Palestine: Population History and Statistics of the Late Ottoman Period and the Mandate.* New York: Columbia University Press, 1990.
Mearsheimer, John J., and Stephen M. Walt. *The Israel Lobby and U.S. Foreign Policy.* New York: Farrar, Straus, and Giroux, 2007.
Menorah: jüdisches Familienblatt für Wissenschaft, Kunst und Literatur (Vienna).
Meybohm, Ivonne. *David Wolffsohn: Aufsteiger, Grenzgänger, Mediator— Eine biographische Annäherung an die Geschichte der frühen Zionistischen Organisation (1897–1914).* Göttingen: Vandenhoek & Ruprecht, 2013.

Morgan, Michael L. *Beyond Auschwitz: Post-Holocaust Theology in America.* Oxford: Oxford University Press, 2001.
Muret-Sanders Encyclopaedic English-German and German-English Dictionary/ Enzyklopädisches englisch-deutsches und deutsch-englisches Wörterbuch. 2 vols. Berlin: Langenscheidtsche Verlagbuchhandlung, 1899.
Nasyrova, Liliya G. "Legislative Measures of the Russian State Relating to Regulation of Entrepreneurial Activity between the Mid-18th and Early 20th Centuries." *Terra Sebus: Acta Musei Sabesiensis.* Special Issue, 2014, 331–41. https://www.cclbsebes.ro/docs /Sebus_SI_2014/22_LGNasyrova.pdf.
Neumann, Boaz. *Land and Desire in Early Zionism.* Translated by Haim Watzman. Waltham, MA: Brandeis University Press, 2011.
Niebuhr, Reinhold. *Moral Man and Immoral Society: A Study in Ethics and Politics.* New York: Charles Scribner's Sons, 1932.
Öke, Mim Kemal. "The Ottoman Empire, Zionism, and the Question of Palestine (1880–1908)." *International Journal of Middle East Studies* 14 (1982): 329–41.
Olson, Jess. "The Late Zionism of Nathan Birnbaum: The Herzl Controversy Reconsidered." *AJS [Association for Jewish Studies] Review* 31:2 (2007): 241–76.
———. *Nathan Birnbaum and Jewish Modernity: Architect of Zionism, Yiddishism, and Orthodoxy.* Stanford: Stanford University Press, 2013.
Orlan, Haiyim. "The Participants in the First Zionist Congress." *Herzl Year Book (1965),* 133–52. New York: Herzl Press, 1965.
Ost und West: illustrierte Monatschrift für modernes Judentum (Berlin).
Patai, Raphael, ed. *Encyclopedia of Zionism and Israel.* 2 vols. New York: Herzl Press, 1971.
Pawel, Ernst. *The Labyrinth of Exile: A Life of Theodor Herzl.* New York: Farrar, Straus, and Giroux, 1989.
Pazi, Margarita. "Authors of German Language in Israel." In *Insiders and Outsiders: Jewish and German Culture in Germany and Austria.* Edited by C. Dagmar, G. Lorenz, and Gabriele Weinberger, 124–31. Detroit: Wayne State University Press, 1994.
Penslar, Derek J. "Herzl and the Palestinian Arabs: Myth and Counter-Myth." *Journal of Israeli History* 24:1 (2005): 65–77.
———. *Israel in History: The Jewish State in Comparative Perspective.* London: Routledge, 2007.

———. "What We Talk About When We Talk About Colonialism: A Response to Joshua Cole and Elizabeth Thompson." In *Colonialism and the Jews*. Edited by Ethan B. Katz, Lisa Moses Leff, and Maud S. Mandel, 327–40. Bloomington: Indiana University Press, 2017.

Pinsker, Leon. *Autoemanzipation*. First published 1882. 6th ed. Berlin: Jüdischer Verlag, 1933. http://ldn-knigi.lib.ru/JUDAICA/LPinskA.htm.

Piterberg, Gabriel. *The Returns of Zion: Myths, Politics, and Scholarship in Israel*. London: Verso, 2008.

"A Portrait of Jewish Americans." Pew Research Center Report, Oct. 1, 2013. http://www.pewforum.org/2013/10/01/jewish-american-beliefs-attitudes-culture-survey/.

Premier Congrès Sioniste, Bâle 29–31 Août 1897, Protocole officiel. Translated by Michèle Mialane. Tunis: Workshop 19, 2013.

The Proceedings of the Zionist Congress held at Basle, Switzerland, August 29, 30, and 31, 1897. Reprinted from *The Jewish Chronicle*. London: Philip Cowen, 1897.

ha-Protokol shel ha-Kongres ha-Tsiyoni ha-rishon be-Bazel, 1–3 be-Elul 657–29–31 be-Ogust 1897. Translated by Hayim Orlan. Jerusalem: R. Mas, 1997.

Raphael, D.D. *Hobbes: Morals and Politics*. London: Routledge, 1977.

Reimer, Michael J. "'The Good Dr. Lippe' and Herzl in Basel, 1897: A Translation and Analysis of the Zionist Congress's Opening Speech." *Journal of Israeli History* 34:1 (2015): 1–21.

Rodinson, Maxime. *Cult, Ghetto, and State: The Persistence of the Jewish Question*. Translated by Jon Rothschild. London: Al Saqi Books, 1983. https://rosswolfe.files.wordpress.com/2016/04/maxime-rodinson-cult-ghetto-and-state-the-persistence-of-the-jewish-question.pdf.

———. *Israel: A Colonial-Settler State?* Translated by David Thorstad. New York: Monad Press, 1973.

Rosenblit, Marsha L. *The Jews of Vienna, 1867–1914: Assimilation and Identity*. Albany: State University of New York Press, 1983.

Ruedy, John. *Modern Algeria: The Origins and Development of a Nation*. 2nd ed. Bloomington: Indiana University Press, 2005.

Sachar, Howard M. *A History of Israel: From the Rise of Zionism to Our Time*. New York: Knopf, 1979.

Said, Edward. *Orientalism*. New York: Vintage Books, 1979.

———. *The Question of Palestine*. New York: Times Books, 1979.

Schneer, Jonathan. *The Balfour Declaration: The Origins of the Arab-Israeli Conflict*. Toronto: Anchor Canada, 2012.

Segel, Binjamin W. "Das Judenvolk und die vier Weltgegenden." *Ost und West*, vol. 8/9 (Aug.–Sept. 1916): 319–30. http://sammlungen.ub.uni-frankfurt.de/cm/periodical/pageview/2608330.

Shafir, Gershon. *Land, Labor, and the Origins of the Israeli-Palestinian Conflict, 1882–1914*. Cambridge: Cambridge University Press, 1989.

Shavit, Yaacov. *Jabotinsky and the Revisionist Movement, 1925–1948*. Abingdon: Frank Cass, 1988.

Shimoni, Gideon. *The Zionist Ideology*. Hanover, NH: Brandeis University Press, 1995.

Silberstein, Laurence J. *The Postzionism Debates: Knowledge and Power in Israeli Culture*. New York: Routledge, 1999.

Sombart, Werner. *The Jews and Modern Capitalism*. Translated by M. Epstein. Kitchener, ON: Batoche Books, 2001. http://classiques.uqac.ca/classiques/sombart_werner/Jews_and_modern_capitalism/sombart_jews_capitalism.pdf.

The Stanford Encyclopedia of Philosophy (Summer 2016 Edition). Edited by Edward N. Zalta. http://plato.stanford.edu/archives/sum2016/entries/sovereignty.

Sutcliffe, Adam. "Can a Jew be a Philosophe? Isaac de Pinto, Voltaire, and Jewish Participation in the European Enlightenment." *Jewish Social Studies* 6:3 (2000): 31–51.

Thompson, Elizabeth F. "Moving Zionism to Asia: Texts and Tactics of Colonial Settlement, 1917–1921." In *Colonialism and the Jews*. Edited by Ethan B. Katz, Lisa Moses Leff, and Maud S. Mandel, 317–26. Bloomington: Indiana University Press, 2017.

Tzahor, Zeev. "David Ben Gurion's Attitude toward the Diaspora." *Judaism* 32:1 (1983): 9–22.

Vital, David. *The Origins of Zionism*. Oxford: Clarendon, 1975.

———. *Zionism: The Formative Years*. Oxford: Clarendon, 1982.

Voltaire. *Oeuvres complètes de Voltaire*. Paris: Chez Furne, 1837.

Weizmann, Chaim. *Trial and Error: The Autobiography of Chaim Weizmann*. London: Hamish Hamilton, 1949.

Die Welt (Vienna).

Wigoder, Geoffrey, ed. *New Encyclopedia of Zionism and Israel*. 2 vols. Madison, NJ: Fairleigh Dickinson University Press, 1994.

Wildmann, Daniel. *Der veränderbare Körper: Jüdische Turner, Männlichkeit, und das Wiedergewinn von Geschichte in Deutschland um 1900*. Tübingen: Mohr Siebeck, 2009.

Wistrich, Robert S. "Karl Lueger and the Ambiguities of Viennese Antisemitism." *Jewish Social Studies* 45:3/4 (1983): 251–62.
Wolfe, Patrick. "Settler colonialism and the elimination of the native." *Journal of Genocide Research* 8:4 (2006): 387–409.
Yehoshua, A.B. *Between Right and Right. Israel: Problem or Solution?* Garden City, NY: Doubleday, 1981.
YIVO Encyclopedia of Jews in Eastern Europe. Edited by Gershon D. Hundert. 2 vols. New Haven: Yale University Press, 2008. http://www.yivoinstitute.org/publications/index.php?tid=109&aid=269, http://www.yivoencyclopedia.org.
Zangwill, Israel. *Dreamers of the Ghetto.* New York: Harper and Brothers, 1898.
Die Zeit/Zeit Online (Hamburg). www.zeit.de.
Zertal, Idith. *Israel's Holocaust and the Politics of Nationhood.* Translated by Chaya Galai. Cambridge: Cambridge University Press, 2005.
Zionisten-Congress in Basel (29, 30, und 31. August 1897): Offizielles Protokoll. Vienna: Verlag des Vereines "Erez-Israel," 1898.
Zunz, Leopold, ed. *Die vier und zwanzig Bücher der Heiligen Schrift nach dem masoretischen Texte.* Berlin, 1848.

INDEX

Note: Page numbers in italics indicate figures; those with a *t* indicate tables.

Abdülhamit II, Ottoman Sultan, 63, 292, 372n14; Herzl's negotiations with, 16, 95, 350n18; Lippe on, 90–91
Actions Committee (*Actionscomité*), 254–56, 266, 270, 345n231, 369n4, 370n5
Adler, Hermann, 342n212, 353n44
Adler, Nathan Marcus, 353n44
Ahad Ha'am (Asher Zvi Ginzberg), 11, 28, 29, 364n7; on Eretz Israel, 7, 73, 348n6; on Jewish education, 63; on modernism, 46–47; on Palestinian settlements, 345n235
Ahawath Zion Society, 203
Ahlwardt, Hermann, 13
Alexander II, Russian Tsar, 10
Algeria, 355nn55–56; anti-Semitism in, 355n56; Arabs of, 130–31, 354n54; Christians of, 130–31; Jews of, 55, 129–32, 354n54
Aliya: First, 6–8, 10–11, 324n14; Second, 74, 75
Alkalai, Yehudah, 348n2
Alliance Israélite Universelle (AIU), 3, 64, 280, 297; Anglo-Jewish Association and, 123–24; Bodenheimer on, 217; Bulgarian schools of, 165
Anglo-Jewish Association (AJA), 123–24
anti-Semitism, 50, 141; anti-Zionism as, 48; Birnbaum on, 177–79; Farbstein on, 52, 197–98; Herzl on, 12–13, 93, 96; Nordau on, 50–51, 97–108, 335n133; Pinsker on, 9–10, 324n21; of Voltaire, 194, 352n34, 362n55. *See also individual countries*
Arabs, 11, 24, 28–33, 45, 48, 130–31, 285. *See also* Palestine
'Arafat, Yasir, 348n6
Arendt, Hannah, 334n122
Argentina, 94
Armenians, 135, 148, 359n27
Arton, Émile, 195, 362n56
Aschheim, Stephen, 26
Ashkenazic Jews, 323n11; in Bulgaria, 55, 165; in Palestine, 339n182; in United Kingdom, 119
assimilated Jews, 172–73; anti-Zionism of, 55–57, 349n8; Birnbaum on, 176–78; Bodenheimer on, 217–18; in Bukovina, 150; Farbstein on, 200; in Galicia, 110–11; Herzl on, 96; Lippe on, 91; Nordau on, 97–98, 104–6; organizations of, 216–19, 223; Pinsker on, 8–9; in United Kingdom, 53
Austrian Jews, 52, 68, 99, 137–46, 157; legal rights of, 138, 139, 142, 144, 372n19; population of, 20; poverty among, 143–44; Zionism among, 145
Avineri, Shlomo, 9

Badeni, Kasimir Felix, Count, 139, 356n3

Bader, Gershom, 225
Bahar, Jacques, 55, 129–32, 259, 273, 301
Balfour Declaration (1917), 28, 33, 45
Bambus, Willy, 72–74, 76, 289–92
Bar-Kochba, 34–35
Barnave, Antoine, 352n30
Bar-On, Mordechai, 47
Basel Program, 31, 44; draft of, 58; Nordau on, 31, 333n104; religious references in, 61
Bayezid II, Ottoman Sultan, 366n32
Be'er Tuvia colony, 282t
Bein, Alex, 36–37
Belkovsky, Gregor, 55, 153–69, 273, 358n18
Ben Gurion, David, 34–36, 334n120; on Diaspora Jewry, 35–36; tribute to First Zionist Congress of, 34–35
Ben Israel, Menasseh, 118
Bentinck, Count, 305
Berkowitz, Michael, 325n34, 346n243
Berlin, Treaty of (1878), 134, 153, 355n61
Bernstein-Kohan (Kohan-Bernstein), Jacob, 62–63, 238–46, 273
Bierer, Ruben, 223
Bilu (organization), 282t
Birkenstein, Heinrich, 229, 268, 270
Birnbaum, Nathan, 14, 28–30, 53–54, 66, 271–72; anti-Zionist views of, 24, 26; Herzl and, 70–71, 344n227, 370n10; on Jewish state, 32, 174–85; orientalism of, 24–25, 53–54, 332n101; on *Ostjuden/Westjuden*, 24–26, 53–54, 174–81, 329n73; Zangwill on, 343n225
Bismarck, Otto von, 338n172, 357n13
Bleichröder, Gerson, 338n172

blood libel, 134, 147, 160, 359n27, 360n34
Blumenfeld, Emil, 214, 215, 227–28, 261–63, 265
B'nai B'rith, 64, 217, 223
Bodenheimer, Max, 43, 208, 215–26, 263, 265, 273–77; Basel Program of, 31; on bylaws, 231, 234; day three address of, 255–56; day two address of, 61–62, 64; as Jewish National Fund chairman, 72; on Jewish state, 32, 326n45; Neumark and, 341n202; on voting rights, 69
Bohemia, 143–46, 356n3
Borochov, Ber, 26, 28, 30, 330n79
British Jews, 54, 171; charitable programs of, 121–24; country of origin of, 118–19, 119t, 124–25; de Haas on, 53–55, 102, 117–29, 238; history of, 117–18; marriage customs of, 125; population of, 118t; schools of, 120–21, 121t; socioeconomic status of, 57, 126–28; Zionism and, 128–29. *See also* United Kingdom
Brociner, Josef, 223
Bromberg, Sigmund, 256, 261, 266–70
Buber, Martin, 28–30, 369n11
Bukovinan Jews, 55, 133, 145–52, 266, 370n9
Bulgaria, 51; anti-Semitism in, 156–69, 358n18; Austria and, 157; economy of, 160–62; political parties of, 155–58, 358n21; Romania and, 133, 155, 355n61; Serbian war with, 358n21, 359n23
Bulgarian Jews, 55, 99, 153–69, 238; conscription of, 156, 359n23; legal rights of, 167–69; Macedonian merchants and, 162; population of, 158, 167; poverty

among, 162–66; schools of, 164–66

Cambon, Jules, 131
Campos, Michelle, 339n182
Canada, 28, 331n88
Carvajal, Antonio, 118
Cato the Elder, 371n3
Cervantes, Miguel de, 100, 352n28
Chashmal, Akiwa, 89
Chowers, Eyal, 336n149
Christian Socialists, 52, 116, 170
Christian Zionists, 23, 76, 305, 329n68
Cohn, Arthur, 22, 40, 67, 76, 303–5
Cohn-Sherbok, Lavinia, 47, 48
colonialism, 23–31, 331n84; Epstein on, 330n82, 332m92; Jabotinsky on, 332n101; Meybohm on, 330n74; Piterberg on, 331n85
Congress-Zionism, 2, 10, 12; Ben Gurion on, 35; Hasidism and, 57; responsibilities of, 66–67. *See also* Zionist Congresses
Cossacks, 132
Cowen, Philip, 78
Crémieux, Isaac Adolphe, 129–30
Crimean War (1853–1856), 355n60
Crown Rabbis, 203
currency exchange rates, 68, 151, 254, 366n36
Cuza, Alexandru Ioan, Prince, 133
Cyrus the Great, Persian King, 90, 348nn3–5

Davidsohn, Eliahu, 274
de Haas, Jacob, 42, 53, 55, 238; address of, 117–29, 118t, 119t, 121t; as Congress secretary, 97
de Pinto, Isaac, 362n55
Deckert, Joseph, 140
Diaspora Jewry, 75, 219; Ben Gurion on, 35–36; Mohilewer on, 42
Dreyfus, Alfred, 13

Drumont, Édouard, 13
Dunant, Henri, 305, 329n68

Eastern Rumelia, 156, 358n21
Ebner, Mayer, 55, 146–52, 266, 273
Ehrenpreis, Marcus, 17, 225, 258, 264, 294–98; address by, 74–76; Basel Program of, 31; as Congress assessor, 97
'Ekron colony, 282t
Eliot, George (Mary Ann Evans), 6, 323n13
Elon, Amos, 37, 46
Engel, David, 4, 337n166
Ephraim, Veitel, 192
Epstein, Lawrence J., 335n134, 369n3
Epstein, Yitzhak, 332n92, 347m246
Eretz Yisrael, 90; Ahad Ha'am on, 7, 73, 348n6; Hertzberg on, 364n10; Mohilewer on, 205
Erter, Isaac, 110
Esra Society (Berlin), 244, 282.283t

Fackenheim, Emil, 47
Farbstein, David, 97, 233, 260, 269; on Actions Committee, 266, 345n231; day one speeches of, 52–53, 55, 57, 186–201; on *Schutzjuden*, 192, 200, 350n16, 362n52; on voting rights, 69; on Zionism, 200–201, 361n47
Faustrecht, 368n4
Feiwel, Berthold, 38–39
Fichte, Johann Gottlieb, 366n28
Flürscheim, Michael, 223
Franco-Prussian War (1870–71), 129, 354n53
Frederick the Great, Prussian King, 192
Freilandcolonieen, 223, 367n37
French Jews, 59, 129–30
French Revolution, 101–2, 352n30
Fukuyama, Francis, 321n2

Fuseli, Henry, 367n40

Gabe, Peter, 158–59
Galicia, 51, 113; Bukovina and, 148; Poland and, 146
Galician Jews, 225, 247, 298, 363n1; Mintz on, 141–45; Nordau on, 50, 99, 100; population of, 113, 115; in Romania, 133; Salz on, 110–17, 363n1; schools of, 111
Gambetta, Léon, 129–30
Gaster, Moses, 67, 120, 253, 342n212
Gedera colony, 281, 282t
German Jews, 21–23, 37, 53; religious schools of, 153; Russian Jews and, 54; Schauer on, 153; Socialist Democrats and, 69–71, 343nn222–23, 344n230, 370n10
Glazer, Steve, 323n11
Goitein, Jacob L., 237
Golus Edom ("exile of Edom"), 89–90; Bernstein-Kohan on, 239–42, 246; Birnbaum on, 181, 183; Mohilewer on, 206–7
Gordon, Aaron David, 29–30
Gottheil, Richard, 6, 46
Gracchus, Gaius, 189
Greece, 133–34, 166, 185, 361n45
Gregorig, Josef, 140
Gross, Wilhelm, 289–90
Gudenus, Leopold, Count, 141
Gypsies (Roma), 135

Haas, Jacob de. *See* de Haas, Jacob
Hadera colony, 283t
Halevi, Judah, 108
Halukka, 206, 279, 280, 289, 364n14
Har-Tuv colony, 282t
Hasidism, 56–57; in Galicia, 110–11; Lippe on, 42; Palestine settlement by, 90
Haskalah movement, 56–57, 336n146, 340n186

Hasmonaea (organization), 152
Hebrew language and literature, 80; revival of, 74–75, 176, 225–26, 229, 294–98
Hechler, Wiliam, 305
Hegel, G.W.F., 321n2, 361n47, 366n28
Heimstätte (homeland), 31–32, 43, 61, 72, 360n35
Heine, Heinrich, 108, 220, 363n61
Herbst, Karl, 258–59, 262, 268
Hertzberg, Arthur, 4, 6, 34, 363n2, 363n4, 364n10
Hertzka, Theodor, 223
Herwegh, Georg, 363n61
Herzl, Theodor, 12–17, 36–48, *39*, 64; Abdülhamit II and, 16, 95, 350n18; on Actions Committee, 271; on anti-Semitism, 12–13, 93, 96; Birnbaum and, 70–71, 344n227, 370n10; "clericalism" of, 59, 67; closing address by, 304–6; on *Geldjuden*, 37; Hovevei Zion and, 12, 38, 323n13; on Jewish state, 32, 35, 59, 62; Klausner on, 16–17; Lippe and, 50; as moderator, 59; opening address by, 92–97; on Palestinian "homeland," 31, 43; photograph of, *18*; Pinsker and, 12, 14, 16, 35; on Social Democrats, 69–70; Vital on, 326n49; Weizmann on, 16; *Der Judenstaat*, 12–13, 16, 29, 37, 44, 59, 62
Herzog, Isaac, 36
Hess, Moses, 187
Hibbat Zion. *See* Hovevei Zion
Hildesheimer, Hirsch, 3, 21, 42
Hillel (Jewish scholar), 108
Hirsch, Maurice, Baron of, 282, 362n60
Hirsch-Gereuth, Clara, Baroness of, 123

Hobbes, Thomas, 1–2, 45, 48, 68, 76; Fukuyama on, 321n2; Herzl and, 321n3
Holocaust, 35–36, 45–48, 57
Hovevei Zion (Hibbat Zion), 14, 63–64, 67–68, 128–29, 368n5; Bernstein-Kohan on, 239–43; First Aliya and, 10–12; Hasidism and, 57; Hertzberg on, 363n4; Herzl and, 12, 38, 323n13; Mohilewer on, 61, 205–7, 342n214, 364n12; Paris Committee of, 73–74; Torah and, 205–6, 364n12; Zionism versus, 60–61, 364n7
Hungarian Jews, 53–54; Mintz on, 147; Nordau on, 99; Rónay on, 170–71

Ibn Gabirol, Solomon Ben Yehuda, 108
Inner Actions Committee, 369n4
International Red Cross, 305, 329n68
internationalism, 176–78, 218
Irish Jews, 117–29, 118t, 119t
Isaiah, 90, 348n5, 349n14, 371n4, 372n21
Itzig, Daniel, 192

Jabotinsky, Vladimir, 28–30, 45–46, 332n101
Jaffa, Palestine, 7, 289, 296
Jasinowski, Israel, 89, 273
Jeremiah, 42, 92, 364n13
Jewish Colonial Trust, 14
Jewish Colonization Association (JCA), 206, 283t, 287, 289; British support of, 123–24; establishment of, 362n60
Jewish National Bank, 224
Jewish National Fund (JNF), 14, 72, 273–77, 366n35
Jireček, Konstantin, 358n19

Joseph II, Austrian Emperor, 192
Josephus, Flavius, 226
Judennoth ("Jewish distress"), 50, 53, 338n168
judenrein, 143, 167, 356n4
jüdische Nationalversammlung (Jewish national assembly), 62
Jung Israel (organization), 73
Junkers, 200

Kadimah fraternity, 13–14, 72
Kahn, Zadok, 59, 208–9, 365n22
Kalischer, Zvi Hirsch, 3, 187, 280, 348n2
Kaminka, Armand, 72–74, 204–7, 279–80, 292
Kaplansky, Shlomo, 329n70
Karaites (Jewish sect), 98
Karavelov, Petko Stoichev, 155–56, 358n21
Kattowitz Conference (1884), 10, 14, 19, 89, 281
Keren Kayemeth LeIsrael (KKL). *See* Jewish National Fund
Kimchi, David, 279–80
Kinnot, 109
Klausner, Joseph, 16–17, 331n88
Kohan-Bernstein (Bernstein-Kohan), Jacob, 62–63, 238–46, 273
Kokesch, O., 271
Kook, Abraham Isaac, 322n8
Korkis, Avraham, 273
Kornblüh, Moritz, 211, 237, 258, 267, 343n223, 365n26
Kornfeld, Siegmund, 273
Krochmal, Nachman, 110
Kuenzly, Jacob, 353n43

Ladino language, 165
Landau, Samuel Hayyim, 322n8
Landau, Saul Raphael, 173–74, 211, 258, 268, 270
Laqueur, Walter, 22, 340n194

Lazar, Bernard, 273
League of Nations, 45
Lebanon, 286, 368n7
Levanda, Lev Osipovich, 187
Likud Party, 29
Lindemann, Albert S., 338nn173–74
Lippe, Karpel, 78; on Hasidim, 42; Herzl and, 50; on Jerusalem, 26; Löwe on, 74; opening address by, 18–19, 23, 89–92; on Zionism, 31, 89–92
Lippert, Julius, 296, 372n16
Lithuania, 194
Locker, Berl, 28, 30
Löwe, Heinrich, 72–74, 229, 237, 272, 289, 292–94
Lublinski, Samuel, 39–40, 260–61
Lueger, Karl, 13, 52, 137, 139–40

Machtwille (will to political power), 62, 64
Maimonides, Moses, 108, 191
Malz, David, 271, 272
Mandel, Neville J., 334n115
Mandelkern, Solomon, 43, 208
Mandelstamm, Max, 273, 305–6
Markus, Abraham, 192, 292
Marmorek, Oscar, 40–41, 109, 211, 228–29, 233–34, 270
Marranos, 106
marriage customs, 125–26, 177
Marx, Karl, 52
Massel, Joseph Ezekiel, 303, 372n1
Maxim, Baron of, 305
medieval Jews, 103, 107, 189–94, 279–80
Meisels, Dov Ber, 146
Mendelssohn, Moses, 192, 362n52
Menelaus, 226
Messiah, 3, 42, 348nn4–5; Lippe on, 90; Mohilewer on, 207; Nordau on, 105
Metula colony, 283t

Meybohm, Ivonne, 321n4, 330n74, 339n177
Meyer (Kremenetzky), Johann, 271
Mikveh Israel, 280, 287–88
Minkov, Mina G., 160
Mintz, Alexander, 97, 214, 290; on Austrian Jews, 99, 137–47, 372n19; on Galician Jews, 141–45
Mishmar HaYarden, 283t, 287
Mitakov, Nikola, 159–60, 359n27
Mitchell, John, 305
Mizrachim, 20, 55
Mohilewer, Samuel, 42, 56, 59, 273, 322n8; on Hibbat Zion, 61, 205–7, 342n214, 364n12; as Zionist General Council member, 67
Moldavia, 132–33, 355n60
Molière (Jean-Baptiste Poquelin), 352n29
Montagu, Samuel, 354n46
Montecuccoli, Raimondo, 366n34
Montefiore, Moses, 280, 281
Montenegro, 355n61
Moravia, 143–46
Moroccan Jews, 99–100, 132, 351n25
"Mosaic confession," 178
Moses, Moritz, 89, 222–23, 246–51, 250–51t
Motza colony, 282t
Motzkin, Leo, 43–44, 60–61, 211–16, 236, 257, 277
Munich, 21–23, 37
mutual profit associations, 117, 126

Napoleon III, French Emperor, 354n53, 355n55
Naquet, Alfred, 194
National Council of Jewish Women (US), 172–73
nationalism, 14, 36, 44–51, 75; Birnbaum on, 32, 174–85; colonialism and, 23–31; Herzl

on, 32, 35, 59, 62; Mintz on, 139, 143, 146; Motzkin on, 211–14; socialism and, 56, 139, 198n
Netter, Charles, 280
Neumark, David, 227, 260, 294, 341n202
Nicholas I, Russian Tsar, 132
Niebuhr, Reinhold, 360n32
Nordau, Max, 40–43, 60, 97, 214, 215; address by, 50–52, 57, 97–109; on anti-Semitism, 50–51, 97–108, 335n133; on Basel Program, 31, 333n104; Kahn's letter read by, 208–9; photograph of, *41*; Schauer on, 153

Odessa (Ukraine), 196, 244, 246
öffentlich-rechtlich (public-legal), 44, 214, 355n59, 365n25
Orientalism, 29, 329n74, 360n39; of Birnbaum, 24–25, 53–54, 332n101
Orlan, Haiyam, 19–20, 20t
Osman Bey, Major, 160
Ostjuden, 10, 37; "enthusiasm" of, 40; German bias against, 22; "oriental" Jews and, 360n39; Zionist General Council on, 71–72
Ostjuden/Westjuden, 4, 53–56, 322n11; Birnbaum on, 24–26, 53–54, 174–81, 329n73; Farbstein on, 193–200; at First Zionist Congress, 20, 64; Glazer on, 323n11; Nordau on, 50, 53, 100–108; Yiddish and, 75
Ottoman Empire, 25; Bernstein-Kohan on, 241–44; Jewish state in, 31–33, 44, 50, 63, 209–10, 213; Jews expelled from Spain in, 219, 366n32; Jews of, 20, 33–34, 55, 219, 328n60, 351n25; Russian wars with, 355n60, 355n61, 358n21

Overberg, Henk, 325n35

Pale of Settlement, 51, 195–97, 351n22. *See also* Russian Jews
Palestine, 45, 224, 330n79; Arabs of, 11, 24, 28–33, 29, 33, 45, 48, 130–31, 285; Ashkenazim in, 339n182; Bernstein-Kohan on, 240–46; Birnbaum on, 183–85; cultural significance of, 23–24; early Jewish settlements in, 6–8, 42, 73, 94, 282–83t; Moritz Moses on, 246–51, 250–51t; Ottoman government and, 11, 16, 31–33, 44, 50, 63; Sephardim in, 55, 339n182
Panama Canal, 362n56
Paris, Treaty of (1856), 133, 355n60
patrie, 31–32, 43
Penslar, Derek J., 332n93
Persian Jews, 99–100, 351n25
Petah Tikva, 281, 282t
Philo Judaeus, 108
Pineles, Samuel, 89, 97, 132–36, 273
Pines, Yehiel Michael, 322n8
Pinsker, Leon, 281; on anti-Semitism, 9–10, 324n21; Herzl and, 12, 14, 16, 35; *Autoemancipation*, 8–12, 16, 43–44, 212, 281, 371n6
Pinto, Isaac de, 362n55
Poalei Zion (Workers of Zion), 26, 329n70
Polish Jews, 8, 146, 171; medieval, 193–94; poverty among, 198; in United Kingdom, 124–25, 354n46, 354n51; in United States, 171–72
prison system, British, 126

Rabinowitz, Mordechai, 40
Rachmanut, 122
Radoslav, Vasil, 158, 358n21
Rapoport, Solomon Judah Loeb, 110

Rappaport, Arnold de Porada, 112, 115
rechtlich (legal), 61; *öffentlich* and, 43, 214–15, 355n59, 365n25; *völkerrechtlich* and, 43–44, 60–61, 211–15, 341n198, 365n27
Red Cross organization, 305, 329n68
redemption (*Erlösung*), 50, 348n2
Rehovot colony, 282t
Rishon LeZion, 282t
Rodinson, Maxime, 33, 329n72
Rohling, August, 160
Rokeah, Lazar, 89
Roma (Gypsies), 135
Roman Catholic Church, 13, 106, 151–52, 219, 356n2
Romania, 133, 155, 355n61
Romanian Jews, 8, 247, 308; Lippe on, 89–92; Nordau on, 50, 98–99; occupations of, 133; in Palestine, 6, 89; Pineles on, 132–36; population of, 132; poverty among, 135; schools of, 133, 135; in United Kingdom, 124–25; Zionism among, 89, 132, 135–36
Rónay, János, 54, 170–71
Rosenberg, Adam, 54, 56, 72–74, 171–73, 285–90
Rosenheck, Salomon, 235–37, 298–99, 372n19
Rosh Pina colony, 89, 283t
Rothschild, Edmond de, 10–11, *11*, 282, 362n60; Bernstein-Kohan on, 245; colonies' administration by, 72–73, 282–83t; Herzl and, 37, 42, 43; Mandelkern on, 208; Mohilewer on, 206
Rousseau, Jean-Jacques, 101
Rubinstein, Solomon B., 42, 136
Rülf, Isaak, 59, 67, 207, 273, 326n45
Rumelia, Eastern, 156, 358n21
Russia, 33; Crimean War and, 355n60; international organizations prohibited in, 68; Ottoman wars with, 355n61, 358n21; pogroms in, 6, 8–10, 32, 158–59
Russian Jews, 8–9, 50–51, 247, 351n23; emigration by, 54; Farbstein on, 195–97; German Jews and, 54; Herzl on, 95; Hovevei Zion and, 37–38; military service required of, 132; Nordau on, 98; population of, 20; poverty among, 197–98; in United Kingdom, 124, 354n46, 354n51; in United States, 171–73. *See also* Pale of Settlement
Russian-Jewish Committee (UK), 124
Ruthenia, 116

Said, Edward, 323n13, 329n74
Salisbury, Lord, 124
Salz, Abraham, 97, 99, 110–17, 273, 363n1
Schach, Fabius, 43–44, 209–10, 215, 230–31, 260, 268, 343n223
Schaffer, Sabbatai Sheftl, 227, 230
Schalit, Isidor, 18, 266–67, 370n10
Schapira, Hermann, 63, 222–23, 257, 264, 274–76, 296, 299–301
Schauer, Rudolf, 53, 97, 153
Schechter, Solomon, 373n2
Schiller, Friedrich von, 367n40
Schneider, Ernst, 140
Schnirer, M.T., 72–74, 232, 258, 261, 263, 269–71, 277–78
Schönerer, Georg von, 138, 139, 149, 356n2
Schutzjuden ("protected Jews"), 45, 55, 94; Farbstein on, 192, 200, 350n16, 362n52
Segel, Binyamin W., 323n11
Sephardic Jews, 20, 55, 106, 219; of Bulgaria, 161–62, 165–66; of Great Britain, 117–20; as

"oriental" Jews, 360n39; of Palestine, 33–34, 339n182
Serbia, 20t, 55, 134, 254, 355n61; Bulgarian war with, 358n21, 359n23
Shafir, Gershon, 27, 63–64, 337n156
Shavit, Yaacov, 332n101
Shimoni, Gideon, 29, 48, 337n167, 342n211
Shoah. *See* Holocaust
slavery, 129, 188–89
Smolenskin, Peretz, 16
Social Democratic Party (SPD), 228, 269; in Austria, 139, 142; in Germany, 69–71, 343nn222–23, 344n230, 370n10
socialism, 12–13, 177, 180; Christian, 52, 116, 170; nationalism and, 56, 139, 198n
socialist Zionism, 26, 29–30, 198n
Speiser, Paul, 305
Spiers, Dayan Bernard, 120
Spinoza, Baruch, 108, 187
Stambolov, Stefan Nikolov, 157–59, 358n21
Stand, Adolf, 273–74
Steiner, Heinrich, 67, 236, 253–55, 259, 261–63, 267–68, 271
Sturdza, Dmitrie, 134
Switzerland, 20–23, 67, 226, 367n40
Syria, 189, 224, 281–82
Syrkin, Nachman, 198n, 325nn37–38

Talmud, 187–88, 191, 279
Talmud-Torah schools, 120, 121t
Tarnów (Galicia) massacre, 112
Temkin, Vladimir, 97, 233
Tisza-Eszlár affair, 170
Tolerance, Edict of (1782), 192
Torah, 48, 61; Hibbat Zion and, 205–6, 364n12; Simchat, 249
Tsankov, Dragan, 156, 358n21

United Kingdom, 45, 53; Balfour Declaration of, 33; immigration policies of, 124; prison system of, 126. *See also* British Jews
United Nations, 45, 337n166
United States, 53, 54, 56, 171–73
United Synagogue (London), 119, 353n45, 354n46
Ussishkin, M., 97
usury, 126, 159, 191–92, 194

Vital David, 20–21, 326n49, 344n227
völkerrechtlich (international-legal), 43–44, 60–61, 211–15, 341n198, 365n27
Voltaire (François-Marie Arouet), 194, 352n34, 362n55

Wadi Chanin colony, 282t
Wallachia, 132, 133, 355n60
Weizmann, Chaim, 16, 59, 79, 326n44
Wellenhof, Hoffman von, 142
Werner, Siegmund, 173
Westjuden. See *Ostjuden/Westjuden*
Wilhelm II, German Kaiser, 70, 343n223
Wissotzky, K.W., 281
Wolffsohn, David, 43; on Actions Committee, 266; on bylaws, 229, 232, 236, 237; as Congress assessor, 97

Yehoshua, A.B., 48
Yesud HaMa'ala colony, 281, 283t
Yiddish, 25, 75, 79, 225, 298; Birnbaum on, 175–76; Nordau on, 104
York-Steiner, Heinrich. *See* Steiner, Heinrich

Zangwill, Israel, 331n88, 335n132, 343n221, 343n225

Zechariah, 90, 348n4
Zederbaum, Alexander, 281
Zikhron Ya'akov colony, 89, 283t
Zion (Austrian organization), 244
Zion Central Committee, 287–88
Zionism, 44–48, 59; Bernstein-Kohan on, 239–40; Birnbaum on, 174–85; as colonialism, 23–31; cultural, 29, 74–75; definitions of, 47, 380; Farbstein on, 200–201; goals of, 31–36, 43–44, 48, 209, 215; Hovevei Zion versus, 60–61, 364n7; Jewish objections to, 21–23; Judaism as, 47; "latent," 75; Lippe on, 31, 89–92; as modernism, 38, 47, 54; political versus practical, 63, 75, 341n206; Revisionist, 29, 30; socialist, 26, 29–30, 198n
Zionist Congresses, 16–17, *19*; Arab objections to, 33; Bernstein-Kohan on, 240; general plan for, 62; labor committees of, 173. *See also* Congress-Zionism
Zionist flag, 32
Zionist General Council, 66, 67, 71–72, 369n4
Zionist Organization, 17, 58; Bodenheimer on, 216–19; debate on, 227–38; decentralization of, 68; periodical of, 14, *15*; SPD and, 344n230, 344n231
"Zionist Party," 260